GRAMMAR OF THE SINDHI LANGUAGE

GRAMMAR OF THE SINDHI LANGUAGE

COMPARED
WITH THE SANSKRIT-PRAKRIT AND THE COGNATE INDIAN VERNACULARS

DR. ERNEST TRUMPP

GYAN

Published by

Gyan Publishing House
5, Ansari Road
Daryaganj, New Delhi-110002
Phone: 011-47034999, 9811692060
E-mail: books@gyanbooks.com

Distribution Network
gyanbooks.com
India, USA, Canada, UK, Australia, France

ISBN : 978-81-212-4401-5 (PB)
First Published, 1872

2nd Impression 2020

Printed at: Gyan Press, Delhi.

Grammar of the Sindhi Language
Author: Dr. Ernest Trumpp

GRAMMAR

OF THE

SINDHI LANGUAGE.

COMPARED

WITH THE SANSKRIT-PRAKRIT AND THE COGNATE INDIAN VERNACULARS,

BY

DR. ERNEST TRUMPP.

PRINTED BY ORDER OF HER MAJESTY'S GOVERNMENT FOR INDIA.

TRÜBNER AND CO., 60, PATERNOSTER ROW, LONDON.

F. A. BROCKHAUS, LEIPZIG.

1872.

DEDICATED

TO

SIR BARTLE FRERE, K. C. B.

AS A TOKEN

OF HIGHEST REGARD AND ESTEEM

BY HIS OBEDIENT HUMBLE SERVANT

E. TRUMPP.

PREFACE.

The Grammar, which is now offered to the learned Public, has been compiled already years ago, but as there were no means of printing it, it was laid aside hopelessly. That it has finally been rescued from oblivion is owing to the enlightened patronage of Her Majesty's Government for India, which liberally granted the printing expenses.

I am afraid, that I have given rather too much than too little by endeavouring to render the Grammar as complete as possible; I trust, however, that this object may have been attained to some extent at least.

A beginner will do well, after he has acquainted himself with the Sindhī system of sounds, to commence at once with the declensions and to turn bye and bye to the formation of themes after he has got a fair insight into the fabric of the language. The *Introduction* is intended for those only, who wish to penetrate more deeply into the origin and nature of the Sindhī.

The quotations, which I have added, I hope may prove useful to introduce the beginner into the study of the Sindhī literature; most of the quotations are taken from my edition of the Shāha jō Risālō[1]), but many others also from manuscripts in my possession, which I collected during my former stay in Sindh. What we need now most is a critically sifted edition of the popular Sindhī tales and songs, which are very numerous and from which a good collection might be made. The next desideratum is an enlarged Sindhī Dictionary, as the late Capt. Geo. Stack's Dictionary, which is very good as far as it goes, is not sufficient for reading older or more difficult pieces. We may fairly expect, that these deficiencies will soon be remedied by Mr. Peile, the present energetic and enlightened Director of Public Instruction in the Bombay Presidency, for which the thanks of the learned Public will be due to him.

The Sindhī is by no means an easy language, it is on the contrary beset with more intricacies and difficulties than any of its Prākrit sisters. But on the other hand it amply repays to the philologist the labours he bestows on it; for the Sindhī has preserved a great many forms, for which we look in vain in the

---

1) Published with the title:

Sindhī Literature. The Dīvān of Abd-ul-Latīf, known by the name of: Shāha jō Risālō, 739 pages. Printed by F. A. Brockhaus, Leipzig, 1866.

In the quotations Sh. stands as an abbreviation for it.

cognate idioms. For the purpose of intercomparing the modern Ārian dialects the Sindhī is therefore invaluable. For this reason we have pointed out, in the form of *annotations*, the relation of the Sindhī with the Sanskrit-Prākrit on the one hand and with the modern cognate idioms on the other hand, to give some impulse to a comparative study of the North-Indian Vernaculars, which as yet has been totally neglected.

The Sindhī Grammar of the late Capt. Stack is an accurate and meritorious work, but as all first attempts (for the Sindhī Grammar of Wathen does not deserve the name) incomplete and destitute of a Syntax. I sincerely wish, that the deficiencies of his work, from the emendation and enlargement of which he was prevented by an untimely death, may have been made up by the Grammar now offered to the Public.

The English reader will no doubt meet in this Grammar with many an expression, which he will consider as erroneous or ill-chosen. For all such and similar mistakes I must beg his pardon, which the kind reader surely will not withhold, when he is told, that the idiom, into which I endeavoured to clothe my thoughts, is not my mother-tongue.

Whilst this Grammar was passing through the press, I had gone to India for the purpose of translating the Sikh Granth. In order not to delay too long the printing of it, I could only see and correct a proof-sheet once. The unavoidable consequence was, that owing to the letters of this Grammar being loaded with so many dots and distinguishing marks, a number of misprints has crept in, which the student is requested to correct first after the affixed list of misprints.

REUTLINGEN, 4th June, 1872.

E. TRUMPP.

CONTENTS.

Page.

INTRODUCTION. On the relation of the Sindhī to the Sanskrit and Prākrit . . . . I–L

The Sindhī Alphabet. §. 1. 1–6

I. The Sindhī consonantal system. §. 2. 7–21

II. The Sindhī vowel system. §. 4. 21–28

Other orthographie signs. §. 5. 28–30

Section I. The Formation of Themes in Sindhī.

Chapter I. The termination of Sindhī nouns. §. 6. 31–44

Chapter II. Primary themes. §. 7. 45

I. Formation of abstract nouns. §. 8. 46–51

II. Formation of appellatives and attributives. §. 9. 51–57

Chapter III. Secondary themes. §. 10.

I. Formation of abstract nouns 57–62

II. Formation of appellatives, attributives and possessives 63–77

Chapter IV. Formation of diminutives. §. 11. 77–80

Chapter V. Compound nouns. §. 12. 80–88

Chapter VI. Gender of nouns. §. 13. 88–98

Chapter VII. Formation of the Feminine from masc. bases. §. 14. 98–103

Page.

Section II. The Inflexion of Nouns.

Chapter VIII. I. Formation of the Plural. §. 15. 104–111
II. Formation of cases; case-affixes. §. 16. 111–122
III. The Formative. §. 17. 122–128
Survey of the Sindhī declensional process.
Declension of the Genitive affix جو and سَنْدو. §. 18 128–130
I. Declension 130–134
II. Declension 134–136
III. Declension 136–137
IV. Declension 138
V. Declension 139
VI. Declension 140–142
VII. Declension 142–144
Chapter IX. Adjectives. §. 19.
Position of adjectives 145–148
Formation of gender. §. 20 148–152
Adjectives ending in 'u' 152
Adjectives ending in ō 153
Adjectives ending in ū, ā 154
Adjectives ending in ī, e 155
Comparison of Adjectives. §. 21 156–157
Chapter X. Numeral adjectives. §. 22.
I. Cardinal numbers 157–169
Inflexion of cardinal numbers. §. 23 . . 169–173
II. Ordinal numbers. §. 24 174–176
Inflexion of the ordinals. §. 25 176–178
III. Arithmetical figures. §. 26 178–179
IV. Collective numbers. §. 27 180–181
V. Proportional numbers. §. 28 182–183
VI. Reduplicative numbers. §. 29 184
VII. Fractional numbers. §. 30 184–188
Chapter XI. Pronouns.
I. Pronouns of the I and II Person. §. 31 188–194
II. Demonstrative pronouns. §. 32 194–202
III. The relative pronoun. §. 33 202–204

Page.
IV. The correlative pronoun. §. 34 . . . . . 204—206
V. Interrogative pronouns. §. 35 . . . . 206—209
VI. Indefinite pronouns. §. 36 . . . . 210—215
VII. The reciprocal pronoun. §. 37 . . . . 215—217
VIII. Pronominal adjectives. §. 38 . . . . 218—224
IX. Pronominal suffixes. §. 39 225
I. Pronominal suffixes attached to nouns. §. 40 . . . . 227—242
II. Pronominal suffixes attached to postpositions and adverbs. §. 41. 242—249

Section III. The Verb.

Chapter XII. Formation of the verbal themes. §. 42. . . . . 250—260
The Imperative. §. 43 . . . . 260—268
The participle present. §. 44 . . . . . . 268—271
The participle past. §. 45 . . . . 271—279
The participle of the Future passive. §. 46. 279—280
Indeclinable past participles. §. 47 . . . 280—284

Chapter XIII. Formation of the tenses and persons. §. 48.
I. Simple tenses 284
1) The Potential. . . . . 285—287
2) The Aorist . . . . 288—291
3) The Future . . . . 291—293
II. Compound tenses.
1) The compound Potential 293
2) The present tense . . . . 293—295
3) The habitual Aorist 295
4) The Imperfect 295
5) The Perfect 296
6) The Pluperfect 296
7) The compound future tenses 297

Chapter XIV. The auxiliary Verbs.
A) The auxiliary verb هُوݨ. §. 49 . . . . . 297—304
B) The auxiliary verb تهِيݨ. §. 50 . . . . 305—312

Chapter XV. Inflexion of the regular verb.
A) Inflexion of the neuter verb. §. 51 . . . 312—322

Page.

B) Inflexion of the transitive Verb. §. 52.
1) Active Voice . . . . 322—330
2) Passive Voice . . . . 330—338
Chapter XVI. Compound Verbs. §. 53. . . . . 338—344
Chapter XVII. The Verb with the pronominal suffixes. §. 54.
1) The pronominal suffixes attached to the auxiliary verbs هُون and تِهِمَّن. §. 55. 346—360
2) The pronominal suffixes attached to the regular verb. §. 56 . . . . 360—379

Section IV. Adverbs, Postpositions, Conjunctions and Interjections.

Chapter XVIII. Adverbs. §. 57. . . . . 380—398
Chapter XIX. Postpositions. §. 58. . . . . . . 398—409
Chapter XX. Conjunctions. §. 59. . . . . . . 410—417
Chapter XXI. Interjections. §. 60. . . . . . . 418—424

SYNTAX.

I. THE ANALYTICAL PART.

Section I. The Noun.

Chapter I. On the absence of the article. §. 61. 425—428
Chapter II. On the gender of Nouns. §. 62 . 428—431
Chapter III. Number. §. 63. . . . . 431—435
Chapter IV. Cases of the Noun.
I. The Nominative. §. 64 . . . . 435—438
II. The Vocative. §. 65 . . . . 438—441
III. The Instrumental. §. 66 . . . . 441—443
IV. The Genitive. §. 67 . . . . 443—452
V. The Dative. §. 68 . . . . 452—455
VI. The Accusative. §. 69 . . . . 455—459
VII. The Locative. §. 70 . . . . 459—463
VIII. The Ablative. §. 71 . . . . 463—466
Chapter V. Pronouns.
I. Personal Pronouns. §. 72 . . . . 466—469

Page.

II. Demonstrative pronouns. §. 73 . . . . . 470—472
III. The relative and correlative pronoun. §. 74. 472—476
IV. The interrogative pronouns. §. 75 . . . . 476—477
V. The indefinite pronouns. §. 76 . . . . . 477—478
VI. The reflexive pronoun. §. 77 . . . . . 478—481

Section II. The Verb.

Chapter VI. The Infinitive. §. 78. . . . . . . 481—483
Chapter VII. The Gerundive. §. 79. . . . . . 483—484
Chapter VIII. The Participles. §. 80. . . . . . 484—491
Chapter IX. The tenses of the verb.
I. The Present. §. 83 . . . . 491—494
II. The Imperfect. §. 84 494
III. The Aorist. §. 85.
1) The simple Aorist 495
2) The habitual Aorist . . . . 496—497
IV. The Perfect. §. 86 . . . . 497—498
V. The Pluperfect. §. 87 . . . . 498—499
VI. The Future and Future past. §. 88 . . . 500—501
Chapter X. The Moods.
I. The Indicative. §. 89 501
II. The Potential. §. 90 . . . . 502—504
III. The Imperative. §. 91 . . . . 505—506

II. THE SYNTHETICAL PART.

Section III. The simple Sentence.

Chapter XI. Subject and Predicate. §. 61. . . 507—508
Chapter XII. Concord of the Subject and Predicate. §. 93. 509
Chapter XIII. Enlargement of the sentence by a near and remote object. §. 94. . . 510—513
Chapter XIV. Enlargement of the sentence by a nearer definition of the verb as predicate. §. 95. . . . . 513—514
Chapter XV. Omission of the verb as predicate. §. 96. 515

Page.

Section IV. The compound Sentence.

Chapter XVI. I. Coordination of sentences. §. 97. 516–517
Chapter XVII. Contraction of coordinate sentences into one; concord of two and more subjects and predicates. §. 98. 517–519
Chapter XVIII. II. Subordination of sentences. §. 99.
1) Subordination of a sentence by subjunctive particles. §. 100 520–525
2) Subordination of a sentence by the relative and relative adverbs. §. 101. 525–526
3) Subordination of a sentence by an interrogative pronoun or particle. §. 102 . . . 526
Chapter XIX. Abbreviation of subordinate sentences. §. 103. 527
Chapter XX. On the indirect oration. §. 104. 528

Appendix I. On the Sindhī Calendar. 529–533
Appendix II. Survey of the different Sindhī-Arabic Alphabets. 534–535

INTRODUCTION.

THE RELATIONSHIP OF THE SINDHI TO THE SANSKRIT AND PRAKRIT.

The Sindhī is a pure Sanskritical language, more free from foreign elements than any other of the North Indian vernaculars. The old Prākrit grammarians may have had their good reason, to designate the Apabhransha dialect, from which the modern Sindhī is immediately derived, as the lowest of all the Prākrit dialects; but if we compare now the Sindhī with its sister-tongues, we must assign to it, in a grammatical point of view, the first place among them. It is much more closely related to the old Prākrit, than the Marāṭhī, Hindī, Panjābī and Bangālī of our days, and it has preserved an exuberance of grammatical forms, for which all its sisters may well envy it. For, while all the modern vernaculars of India [1]) are already in a state of complete decomposition, the old venerable mother-tongue being hardly recognisable in her degenerate daughters, the Sindhī has, on the contrary, preserved most important fragments of it and erected for itself a grammatical structure, which surpasses in beauty of execution and internal harmony by far the loose and levelling construction of its sisters.

The Sindhī has remained steady in the first stage of decomposition after the old Prākrit, wheras all the

1) In speaking of the modern vernaculars of India we exclude troughout the Drāvidian idioms of the South, which belong to quite a different stock of languages.

other cognate dialects have sunk some degrees deeper; we shall see in the course of our introductory remarks, that the rules, which the Prākrit grammarian Kramadīshvara has laid down in reference to the Apabhransha, are still recognisable in the present Sindhī, which by no means can be stated of the other dialects. The Sindhī has thus become an independant language, which, though sharing a common origin with its sister-tongues, is very materially differing from them.

The Sindhī, which is spoken within the boundaries of Sindh proper, is divided into three dialects, which grammatically differ very little from each other, but offer considerable discrepancies in point of pronunciation. The dialect of lower Sindh, comprising the Indus-Delta and the sea-coast, is called लाड़ी lāṛī, from लाड़ु lāṛu[1]), by which lower Sindh is designated. The dialect, which is spoken north of Haiderābad, is called सिराइकी sirāikī, from सिरो sirō, by which Upper Sindh is designated; the dialect in vogue in the Thar, or desert of Sindh, is called थरेली tharēli, from थरु tharu, the desert.

The dialect of Lāṛ, though employed in most Sindhī compositions, is not the purest; the vowels are frequently contracted and the consonants too much softened down by assimilation. The northern or Sirāiki dialect has remained far more original and has preserved the purity of pronunciation with more tenaciousness, than the southern one. With reference to this superiority of the northern dialect to the southern the Sindhīs like to quote the proverb:

लाड़ जो पढ़्यो सिरे जो ढग़ो

lāṛa jŏ paṛhyō sirē jŏ ḍhagō.

The learned man of Lār is an ox in Upper Sindh.

---

1) लाड़ु is not a proper noun, but an appellation, signifying: „sloping ground;" the same is the case with सिरो sirō, which signifies the upper country.

The dialect of the Thar is vigorous but uncouth and already intermingled with the Māṛvāṛī; it is spoken by the Shikārīs, Ḍheḍhs (ढेढ carrier) and other outcast tribes. As far as I know, there are no literary compositions extant in this dialect.

The object of these introductory remarks is to show the relative position, which the Sindhī holds to the Sanskrit and Prākrit; and in order to elucidate this subject, we shall lay down the rules and principles, by which the present Sindhī vowel and consonantal system has been derived from the Sanskrit by the medium of the Prākrit. Thus, we hope, a solid basis also will be gained for intercomparing the Sindhī with its other sister-tongues. By this process alone, which will enable us, to assign to the Ārian stock, what has been taken from it, though much altered now in shape and outward appearance by dint of contraction and assimilation, we shall on the other hand be able to trace out a certain residuum of vocables, which we must allot to an old aboriginal language, of which neither name nor extent is now known to us, but which, in all probability, was of the Tātār stock of languages and spread throughout the length and breadth of India before the irruption of the Ārian race, as all the other vernaculars contain a similar non-Ārian residuum of words, which have been already designated as "provincial" by the old Prākrit grammarians.

The following investigation is destined for such as may be competent, by their previous studies, to penetrate more deeply into the real nature of the modern idioms of India, and for them, I trust, these outlines may prove useful and at the same time incentive, to follow up more deeply the intricate path, which I have pointed out.

I. THE SINDHI VOWEL SYSTEM.[1])

§. 1.

We consider first the single vowels, their change, substitution, contraction or elision in Sindhī.

1) ऋ (ṛ) and its permutations.

The Sindhī, like the old Prākrit, has cut off ऋ from its system of sounds; for it is either treated as a vowel, in which case it is changed to i, a etc., or as a consonant, in which latter case it coincides with र (r).

At the beginning of a word ऋ, if standing by itself, is changed to रि (ri), just as in Prākrit, e. g. Sindhī रिछु ričhu, bear, Prāk. रिछ, Sansk. ऋक्ष.

But if ऋ be joined to a consonant, the following rules hold good:

a) ṛ is usually dissolved into i, as: ड़िसणु disaṇu, to see, Sansk. दृश् (but Prāk. दक्ख), Hindī देखना; विछूं vičhū̃, scorpion, Prāk. विच्छुओ (or विश्चुओ), Sansk. वृश्चिक; किओ kiō, done, Prāk. किद, Sansk. कृत; गिण्हणु giṇhaṇu; to take, Sansk. गृह्ण, Prāk. गेण्ह.

b) ṛ is dissolved into u, if the consonant, to which it is joined, happens to be a labial, as: ॿुढो ƃuḍhō, old, Prākrit on the other hand वड्ढ, Sansk. वृद्ध; मुओ muō, dead, Prāk. मुदो or already मुओ (by elision of द), Sansk. मृत. In such instances, as सुणणु suṇaṇu, to

1) In order to facilitate the intercomparison of the Sindhī with the Sanskrit and Prākrit we have used in these introductory remarks a modified Sanskrit alphabet, the particulars of which see further on under the Sindhī alphabets. The romanized transcription, which we have added-every-where, is in accordance with the Standard Alphabet by Prof. Dr. Lepsius, 2ᵈ edition.

hear, Prāk. सुण्, the original root-vowel (Sansk. श्रु) has been preserved.

c) In most instances though ṛ is dissolved into ar, irrespective of the consonant to which it may be joined, as:

मरणु maraṇu, to die, Prāk. मर्, Sansk. मृ.
भरणु bharaṇu, to fill, Prāk. भर्, Sansk. भृ.
धरणु dharaṇu, to place, Prāk. धर्, Sansk. धृ.
सरणु saraṇu, to move, Prāk. सर्, Sansk. सृ.

In such like instances the Sindhī, as well as all the other cognate dialects, is quite in accordance with Prākrit usage, the Sanskrit verbal noun being taken as the base of the infinitive in the modern idioms. In other instances though the Sindhī is not so liberal in dissolving ṛ, as the Prākrit; it has managed, on the contrary, in many cases to preserve ṛ by changing it to ir or transposing the same, as: मिर्दंगु mirdangu (or: मिर्धंगु mirdhangu) a tabor, Prāk. मुइंगो, Sansk. मृदङ्ग; विर्खु virkhu, taurus (planet), Sansk. वृष; हिर्धों hirdhō[1]), heart, Prāk. हिअअं, Sansk. हृदयम्, but the more Prākritical form हिंओ hĩō, is also in use in Sindhī.

In a few cases ṛ has been preserved by being changed to simple r (subscribed), in conjunction with a dental t, d, or a cerebral ṭ, ḍ; as: ज़ाट्रो jāṭrō, son-in-law, Prāk. जामाउओ, Sansk. जामातृक; in this form म has been elided, which is rather of rare occurrence, and the dental has passed into a cerebral, the affix क being dropped altogether; similarly माट्रे māṭrē, and its derivatives, as: माट्रेजो māṭrējō, माट्रेतो māṭrētō etc., corresponding to the Prākrit form माउओ, Sansk. मातृक.

---

1) The aspiration of ध is caused by the following r, which very frequently aspirates a preceding consonant, as we shall have often occasion to notice.

2) The Diphthongs ऐ ai and औ au.

Properly speaking there are no diphthongs in Sindhī, as little as in Prākrit; ai is generally pronounced loosely as a-i, and au as a-u. The Sindhī, however, is somewhat tighter in its pronunciation and not quite so effeminate as the Prākrit, so that it will depend more or less on the option of the speaker, if he will contract ai or au into a real diphthong, or pronounce them separately as two distinct vowels. From the manner of writing, no safe conclusion can be drawn, as a fixed system of orthography is still a desideratum. It may however be laid down as a general rule, that the Sindhī ignores diphthongs and pronounces them as two distinct vowels.

a) The diphthong ai.

α) In such words, as are borrowed from the Arabic or Persian, the original diphthong is generally retained, and written and pronounced accordingly, as: सैरु sairu, journey; Arab. سَيْر; पैदा paidā, created, Pers. پَيْدا; likewise in such nouns, as have been taken from the Hindūstānī, as: पैसो paisō, a pice. On the rest it is quite optional, to write and pronounce for instance सैन saina or सइन sa-ina, hint; the Hindūs prefer the loose Prākrit pronunciation (a-i, a-u), the Muhammedans more the Arabic or Persian method (ai, au).

β) But generally the diphthong ai is contracted into ē in Sindhī, which is always long, and never anceps, as in Prākrit; e. g. वेरु vēru, enmity, prāk. वइरं (Lassen quotes also a form वेरं), Sansk. वैरं; वेज़ु vēju, physician, Prāk. वेज्ज, Sansk. वैद्य; सेंधोलूणु sēndhōlūṇu, rocksalt (literally, Sindh-salt), from the Sansk. सैंधव, Sindhī, and लवण salt (Prāk. लोण).

In a similar manner also अय ay, which in Sindhī is treated in the same way as ai, is frequently contracted into ē, as: नेणु nēṇu, eye, Prāk. णअणं, Sansk. नयनं; सेजा sējā, bed, Prāk. सेज्जा, Sansk. शय्या.

γ) The original diphthong ai may also be contracted to ī, as: धीर्जु dhīrju, firmness, Sansk. धैर्य्यं, Prāk. धीर. This Sindhī form is so far a proof for the correctness of the Prākrit rule, as धीर्जु can only be derived from धैर्य्य, and not from धीर itself; similarly Hindī धीर्ज.

b) The diphthong au.

The same, that has been remarked on the diphthong ai, may also be stated of the diphthong au; it may be optionally pronounced as a diphthong, but is more commonly separated into its component vowels.

α) This diphthong is generally preserved in words borrowed from the Arabic or Persian, as: दौरु dauru, a period, arab. دَوْر; औरत aurata, woman, Arab. عَوْرَت; also in pure Sindhī words it is used and written, as: औखो aukhō, difficult; भौंरु bhaũru, a large black bee, Sansk. भमर; लौंगु laũgu, a clove, Sansk. लवङ्ग. In such pure Sindhī words though the diphthong may also, after the analogy of the Prākrit, be separated into a-u, as: वउड़णु va-uṛaṇu, to seek, or: वौड़णु vauṛaṇu; भउणणु bha-uṇaṇu, to wander about, or: भौणणु bhauṇaṇu.

At the end of a word no diphthong is admissible, and it must always be pronounced अउ a-u, for the sake of inflexion, as: सउ sa-u, hundred (Prāk. सअ) जउ ja-u, barley, Pers. جَو, Sansk. यव; चउ ca-u, say, imperative of चवणु, to say.

β) But very frequently this diphthong is contracted to ō, as: गोरो gōrō, fair, Sansk. गौर; जोभनु jōbhanu, time of youth, Prāk. जोव्वणं, Sansk. यौवनम्; मोड़ु mōṛu, a crest, Prāk. मउडं (Sansk. मुकुट); भोणो bhōṇō, or भउणो bha-uṇō, a vagabond. The same rule also is occasionally applied to Arabic or Persian words, as: कोम kōma, a clan, or: कौम kauma, Arab. قَوْم.

γ) The diphthong au may also be contracted to ū, as: सूरिहाई sūrihāī, heroism, Prāk. सोरिअं Sansk. शौर्य; लुणु lūṇu, salt, Prāk. लोण, Sansk. लवणं (अव being treated like au).

§. 2.

3) The vowels a, ā; i, ī; u, ū; ē; ō.

Having considered the diphthongs ai and au in their relative position to the Sanskrit and Prākrit, we submit now the common Sindhī vowels to a nearer examination.

a) The vowels a, ā.

The short vowel अ a, is more tenaciously kept fast in Sindhī, than in the Prākrit, and the Sindhī very frequently recurs directly again to the original Sanskrit, as: पको pakō, cooked, Sansk. पक्क, but Prāk. पिक्क; अंगारु angāru, coal, Sansk. अङ्गार, but Prāk. इङ्गालो; सुपनो supanō, dream, Sansk. स्वप्न, but Prāk. सिविण; वलि vale, a creeper, Sansk. वल्ली, but Prāk. वेल्लि. But there is no lack of examples on the other hand, in which original a has been likewise shortened to i, as: खिमा khimā, patience, Prāk. खमा, Sansk. क्षमा; मिञ miṅa, marrow, Sansk. मज्जा.

In this way a has been shortened to i in all those forms, which are already alleged by the Prākrit grammarian Kramadīshvara in the Apabhransha dialect (compare: Lassen, Instit. Linguae Prāk. p. 454) as: जिंअ-तिंअ jīa-tīa (Apabhransha: जिध-तिध, instead of जध-तध); जिति-तिति jite-tite, where-there (Apabhransha: जेत्थु-तेत्थु[1]), from यत्र-तत्र); किति kite, where? (Apa-

1) e is in Prākrit before a double consonant = ĕ = ĭ.

bhransha: केत्यु, from an original form कत्तु, instead of क्वच, thence the common Sansk. form कुत्र). The Sindhī adverb इंअ īa or ईंअ īa, thus, corresponds to the Prāk. इअ, and is regularly derived from the Sansk. adverb इत्थम् (not from इति, which Lassen has already doubted) with the elision of h (īa = iha).

Short a is occasionally, but rarely, changed to u, as: राउरु rā-uru, tax, Sansk. राजकर (but not in the examples quoted by Lassen §. 173, 3).

Long ā is in Sindhī frequently preserved in such forms, where in Prākrit it has been already shortened (owing to the contraction or assimilation of the following compound consonant): as: बैराग़ी bairāgī, a religious ascetic, Prāk. बेरग्ग, Sansk. बैराग्य; मारिख mārikha, way, Prāk. मग्ग, Sansk. मार्ग; जाट्रा jāṭrā, pilgrimage, Prāk. जत्ता, Sansk. यात्रा; वाघु, vāghu, tiger, Prāk. वग्घु, Sansk. व्याघ्र. Long ā has been shortened in कोड्डरि kō-ḍare, spade, Sansk. कुदाल.

Long ā is weakened to ĭ in the following adverbs, after the analogy of the Prākrit, as: जड्डिहिं-तड्डिहिं ja-ḍehẽ-taḍehẽ, when-then; कड्डिहिं kaḍehẽ, when? which are derived from the Sansk. adverbs: यदा-तदा, कदा.

Long ā as a feminine termination of Prākrit nouns is in Sindhī occasionally permuted for ī or even ĭ (e), as: वाई vā-ī, speeck, Prāk. वाआ, Sansk. वाच्; धुरि dhure, origin, Prāk. धुरा, Sansk. धुर्. The only example of final आ of a masc. theme being changed to i is राइ rā-e, prince, Prāk. राआ, Sansk. राजा nom.

In a certain number of words, ending in the Sansk. crude state in तृ (but nom. sing. ता), final ā has been changed in Sindhī (as now and then already in Prākrit) to u, as: पिउ, father, Prāk. पिआ (by elision of त), Sansk. nom. पिता; भाउ bhāu, brother, Prāk. भाआ, Sansk. भ्राता; and by the same levelling process: माउ

māu, mother, Prāk. माआ, Sansk. माता; राउ rāu, prince (besides राइ); पंधु pandhu, journey, Sansk. पन्था m.

As regards the vowel changes in the midst of a word, the Sindhī adheres on the average to Prākrit usage, as: पथरु patharu, bed, Prāk. पत्थर, Sansk. प्रस्तार, Hindī बिस्तर्), different from the else identical word पथरु stone, Prāk. पत्थर, Sansk. प्रस्तर (Hindī पत्थर्); मया mayā, compassion, Sansk. माया (Hindī likewise मया); देवली dēvalī, temple (in Sindhī with the fem. termination ī), Prāk. देउल्ल, Sansk. देवालय (Hindī likewise देवल्).

b) The vowels i, ī.

Short i is in Sindhī pronounced like short ĕ, when preceded or followed by ह h, and regularly so, when ending a word, as: इहड़ो ĕharō, such a one, मिहिति mĕhĕtĕ, a mosque; ग़ालि gāle, word. Short i corresponds therefore often to the Prākrit ए ē, which is considered short, when followed by a compound consonant, whereas ए ē is in Sindhī always long; e. g. Prāk. गेण्ह, Sindhī ग़िण्ह (ग़िण्हणु), to take; निंड्र nindra, sleep, Prāk. णेद्द or णिद्द, Sansk. निद्रा; चिन्हु činhu, sign, Prāk. चेन्ध or चिन्ध, Sansk. चिह्नं.

It is a curious phenomenon in Sindhī, that occasionally a short i is interpolated in a syllable, which the effeminate pronunciation finds too harsh for the ear. This is particularly the case, when a syllable closes with a double n or n followed by another consonant (especially a liquida). The consequence of this effeminate pronunciation is, that the n thus separated by the interpolation of i, becomes nasalized, as: संइन sāina, sign, hint, instead of सन्न, from संज्ञा; संइसारु sāisāru, world, instead of संसारु; मंइजल māijala, a day's journey, instead of मंजल (مَنْزِل), and is frequently no longer heard at all, especially in the mouth of the Muhammedans, who write: مئِزل ma-izala, سئِسارُ sa-isāru etc.

Lengthened is ĭ in कीं kĩ, what, Prākrit already की, from the Sanskrit किम्; further in शींहु sĩhu, lion, Prāk. सीह, Sansk. सिंह; but not in ज़िभ jibha, tongue, Prāk. जीहा, Sansk. जिह्वा.

Long ī is kept fast by the Sindhī in many instances, where in Prākrit it has been shortened to ĭ, in consequence of the assimilation of consonants, as: तीर्थु tīrthu, a holy bathing-place, Prāk. तित्थ, Sansk. तीर्थ.

Long ī is rarely shortened to ĭ, and this only, when ending a noun, as: नारि nāre, a woman, Prāk. et Sansk. नारी.

Long ī passes into ē in those instances, which have been already marked out by the old Prākrit grammarians, as Prākrit केरिस, एरिस etc., Sansk. कीदृश, ईदृश etc. The corresponding Sindhī forms are: केहरो, kēharō, what? (by transposition of ह, instead of केरहो); केरु kēru, who, (by elision of ह, instead of केर्हु kērhu; in the Apabhransha dialect r on the other hand has been dropped, as: केही). The Prākrit form एरिस (Apabhransha एही) has not been taken up by the Sindhī, but other forms have been created from the pronominal bases की, जो, तो, इहो, उहो, by adding to them the diminutive affix ड़ो ṛō, as: किहड़ो kĕhaṛō, of what kind; जिहड़ो-तिहड़ो jĕharō — tĕharō, of which kind — of such a kind; इहड़ो ĕharō, of this kind, उहड़ो uharō, of that kind.

c) The vowels u, ū.

On the whole the Sindhī has taken up those changes, which these vowels have been made subject to in Prākrit;

but in some special cases it has remained more original, than the Prākrit, as: पुरुसु purusu, man, Prāk. पुरिसो, Sansk. पुरुष; मुखिरी, mukhirī, a bud, Prāk. मउलं, Sansk. मुकुलं.

U is changed to a in: ग़रो gārō, heavy, Prāk. गरुअ, Sansk. गुरु; ड्बलु ḍabalu, weak (Prāk. still दुब्बल), Sansk. दुर्बल; or it may be dropped altogether, as: परि pare, on, upon, Prāk. उवरि, Sansk. उपरि.

U is changed to ō only in the following instances, as: मोती mōtī, pearl, Prāk. मोत्त (mŏtta) Sansk. मुक्त; पोथी pōthī, book, Prāk. पोत्थुओ, Sansk. पुस्तक; कोड़रि kōḍare, a spade, Sansk. कुदाल.

Long ū is preserved more tenaciously in Sindhī, than in Prākrit, e. g. नूरो nūro, a hollow ring on the ankle, Prāk. णेउरं Sansk. नूपुर. — In such cases, where original u has been depressed to ŏ in Prākrit, the original vowel generally reappears in Sindhī, as: उखिरि ukhirī, a mortar, Prāk. ओक्खलं, Sansk. उलखल; पुठि puṭhe, power, Prāk. पोट्ठि, Sansk. पुष्टि, which is, though identical in form, not to be confounded with पुठि puṭhe, the back, Sansk. पृष्ट, Hindī पीठ.

d) The vowels ē and ō.

In Sindhī, as well as in Prākrit, ē and ō are no longer looked upon as Guṇa-vowels, but as simple sounds. In Sindhī ē and ō are always long, never anceps, as in Prākrit; for the short Prākritical ĕ short i is substituted in Sindhī, as: हिकु hiku, one, Prāk. एक्क; and for the short Prākritical ŏ short u, as stated already.

Both vowels keep their place very steadfastly and frequently reappear in such cases, where they have been already shortened in Prākrit, owing to the assimilation of consonants, as: प्रेमु prēmu, love, Prāk. पेम्म (pĕmma); जोभनु jōbhanu, time of youth, Prāk. जोव्वणं (jŏvvaṇam); जोगु jōgu, fit, Prāk. जोग्ग, Sansk. योग्य.

Quite exceptional is the shortening of ō to u in लुहरु luharu, blacksmith, instead of: लोहकारु (Sansk. लोहकार), where ā has been likewise shortened to ă; and the change of ē to ī in पीज़ु pīju, draught, Sansk. पेय; खीं khī̃, wellfare, Sansk. क्षेम; नींहु nī̃hu, love, Prāk. णेहो, Sansk. स्नेह; मींहु mī̃hu, rain, Prāk. मेहो, Sansk. मेघ.

When ending a noun ē and ō are frequently shortened to ĕ and ŭ respectively, especially in poëtry; but these changes being peculiar to Sindhī, we shall consider them hereafter separately. The peculiarity of the Apabhransha dialect, as noted by the grammarian Kramadīshvara, is fully borne out by the modern Sindhī; it uses likewise in the locative singular ĕ (i) instead of ē, as परडेहि paraḍēhe, in a foreign country, घरि gharĕ, in a house etc. In the same way, as the Apabhransha, the Sindhī also changes to a great extent the Prākrit termination ō to u, as: कमु kamu, business, Prāk. कम्मो etc. The same may also be said of the ablative sing. termination आदो (= ā — ō with elision of द) which is commonly shortened to ādu in the Apabhransha dialect, and in Sindhī further to ā-u: as घराउ gharā-u, from a house. This old Sindhī ablative termination is now-a-days generally contracted to अंउं āū̃ (ā being likewise shortened to ă, and to avoid the hiatus, both vowels being nasalized) but ā-u is still very frequently used in poëtry.

§. 3.

The elision, contraction and insertion of vowels.

These three points, so important in the old Prākrit, we may, as far as the Sindhī is concerned, sum up under the following brief remarks:

a) An elision of vowels takes far more rarely place in Sindhī, than in the Prākrit, because the consonants do not so easily give way; there is however no lack of instances, in which the Sindhī accedes to Prākrit usage, as: **दुआरो** duārō, temple (different from **दुआरु** door, Sansk. **द्वार**), Sansk. **देवालय**, where ē has been elided; **सिआरो** siārō, the cold season, Prāk. **सीआरो**, Sansk. **शीतकाल**; **कुंभरु** kumbharu, potter, Sansk. **कुंभकार**; **पखाल** pakhāla, a pair of leather-bags, Sansk. **पयःखल्ल**; **रिणु** riṇu, the desert (the Riṇ), Sansk. **इरिणं**; **धिअ** dhia, daughter (prākrit already **धीआ**, see Lassen p. 172, note); **बि** bi, also, Prāk. **वि**, Sansk. **अपि**.

b) As regards the contraction of vowels, the Sindhī coincides more fully with the Prākrit, though in some instances I have noticed a deviation from Prākrit analogy, as: **चोथों** čōṭhō̃, the fourth, Prāk. **चउत्थ**, Sansk. **चतुर्थ**; **मोरु** moru, peacock, Prāk. **मोर**, Sansk. **मयुर**; **लूणु** lūṇu, salt, Prāk. **लोण**, Sansk. **लवण**; **सोनु** sōnu, gold, Sansk. **सुवर्ण**.

c) With reference to the insertion of vowels the Sindhī agrees on the whole with the Prākrit.

α) An original compound consonant is separated by the insertion of a vowel, to render its pronunciation more easy for a Sindhī organ. The insertion of a respective vowel depends on the sequence of vowels or the varga of the consonant, which is to be separated from the preceding one, though this rule is by no means strictly adhered to.

a is inserted in cases like the following: सराह sarāha, praise, Prāk. सलाहा, Sansk. श्लाघा; सलोकु salōku, a šlōka, Prāk. सिलोक्क, Sansk. श्लोक.

i is inserted, as: इस्त्री istrī, woman, Prāk. इत्थी, Sansk. स्त्री; वरिहु varĕhu, year, Prāk. वरिसो, Sansk. वर्ष; मिलणु milaṇu, to be obtained, Prāk. मिलाण, Sansk. root म्लै.

u is inserted, as: सुपनो supanō, dream, Prāk. सिविण, Sansk. स्वप्न; सुमरणु sumaraṇu, to remember, Prāk. सुमर्, Sansk. स्मर् (root स्मृ).

β) On the other hand the Sindhī very frequently has gone a step farther and dispensed with the insertion of a vowel by pushing the root-vowel between the compound consonant and dropping the final consonant, as: सेणु sēṇu, friend, Prāk. सणेह, Sansk. स्नेह; or more commonly it drops simply one of the compound consonants, as: नुहु nuhu, daughter-in-law, Prāk. सोण्ह, Sansk. स्नुषा; सघणु saghaṇu, to be able, Prāk. सक्कणोमि, Sansk. सक्नोमि.

§. 4.

Sandhi, Hiatus and Euphony.

The Sindhī, as well as the Prākrit, dispenses totally with the rules of Sandhī, and vowels may therefore meet, without being subject to the laws of euphony. To separate however in some measure concurring vowels, the Sindhī very liberally employs the use of Anusvāra, whereby a certain nasalizing pronunciation has been imparted to the language, which is in some measure disagreeable to our ear; e. g. आंऊं ā̃ū̃, I; सुखांऊं sukhā̃ū̃, nom. plur. of सुखा, vows; खांइणु khā̃iṇu, to burn; गंऊं gā̃ū̃, cow etc. The Anusvāra is further inserted, to facilitate the lengthened pronunciation of a vowel, as: मींहु mĩhu, rain, Sansk. मेध; this is particularly the case, when a noun ends in a long vowel, as प्रीं prī̃, friend, भूं bhū̃, earth etc.

On the other hand there are also examples to be met with, where original Anusvāra has been dropped in Sindhī, as: मासु māsu, or माहु māhu, meat, Sansk. मांस.

II. THE SINDHI CONSONANTAL SYSTEM.

§. 5.

In comparing the Sindhī letters (see below the Sindhī alphabets) with the Prākrit alphabet, we see at the first glance, that the Sindhī has retained the letters श š, ङ ṅ, ञ ń and न n, as single letters, which have disappeared already from the Prākrit alphabet, except when preceding a consonant of their respective vargas.

श š, is in Sindhī by no means a palatal sibilant, as in Sanskrit, but a simple dental sound, equally unknown in Sanskrit and Prākrit, which has become naturalized in all the modern idioms (with the exception of the Gujarātī), and which corresponds to our common dental sh. It is derived from various sources:

a) from the Sanskrit palatal sibilant श, as: शब्दु šabdu, word, Sansk. शब्द; शरीरु šarīru, body (besides सरीरु sarīru), Sansk. शरीर; शुक्रु šukru, friday, Sansk. शुक्र.

b) from the Sanskrit dental sibilant स s, as: शींहु šĩhu, lion, Sansk. सिंह; शाहू šāhū, rich (by the Musalmāns generally pronounced साऊ sā-ū) Sansk. साधु; the s of Persian words is also now and then changed to š, as: शीख šīkha, a spit, Pers. سيخ.

c) from the Sanskrit cerebral sibilant ष ṣ, as: कशणु kašaṇu, to pull, Sansk. कृष (Hindī कसना); किश्णु kišṇu,

Krishṇa, Sansk. कृष्ण; विशु višu, world (besides विसु) Sansk. विषय.

The letter ش of Arabic and Persian words is always rendered by श, as: शहरु šaharu, town, Pers. شَهَر; शाहु šāhu, king, Pers. شاه.

This is a very remarkable deviation from the principles of the Prākrit, where the letter श has been changed to स, and further to ह.

In Sindhī the use of the letter श is confined to a limited number of indigenous vocables (those, which have been borrowed from foreign sources, not being taken into account), but that it is still to be considered more or less exceptional, may be concluded from the circumstance, that the Prākrit rules concerning its permutations (श = स = ह) are still in full force in Sindhī, as: सुणणु suṇaṇu, to hear, Prāk. सुणामि, Sansk. शृणोमि; फासी phāsī, or फाही phāhī, a noose, Sansk. पाश; देसु dēsu, country, Sansk. देश; ड॒ह ḍaha, ten, Prāk. दह, Sansk. दश.

The same law holds good with reference to the cerebral ष ṣ, which like श, passes into स or ह, as: नुहु nuhu, daughter-in-law, Sansk. स्नुषा; विसु visu, world, Sansk. विषय; वेसु vēsu, disguise, Sansk. वेष.

श and ष are in Sindhī also frequently changed to छ čh, as: किछ॒ड़ी kičhaṛī, rise and pulse boiled together (Hindī खिचड़ी), Sansk. कृशरा; छंछरु čhančharu, Saturday, Sansk. शनिश्चर; छ čha, or छह čhaha, six, Prāk. छा, Sansk. षट्. This permutation seems in Sindhī to be so deeply rooted, that even the ش of Arabic and Persian words is occasionally changed to छ, as: छाल čhāla (besides शाल), would to God, Arab. شاءالله; छाबसि čhābase, bravo! Pers. شَابَاش; पाछाहु pāčhāhu, king, Pers. پَادشاه.

The cerebral ष is occasionally written in Sindhī, but only by Brāhmans, and even with them its use depends on their relative knowledge of Sanskrit. We may therefore as well leave out this letter from the consonantal system of the Sindhī, as its actual pronunciation is completely ignored. In Capt. Stack's Sindhī Dictionary some words are given with the cerebral ष, such as: विषई vișai, voluptuary, डुष्टु ḍușțu, bad, कष्टु kașțu, wretchedness etc., but the letter itself as well as those words are only known to the Brāhmans.

The guttural ङ ṅ, as well as the palatal ञ ń, keep their place in Sindhī as single letters, e. g. अङु aṅu, body (Hindī अंग् or आंग्), Sansk. अङ्ग; मङणु maṅaṇu, to ask (Hindī मांग्ना), Sansk. मार्गण (r. मृग्); मञणु mańaṇu, to heed (Hindī मान्ना), Sansk. मानन. In the kindred dialects both these nasals are only used in conjunction with a letter of their varga, and never as single consonants (the Panjābī alone being excepted).

The cerebral ण ṇ has not supplanted the dental न in Sindhī, as in Prākrit, but both are sharply kept asunder; ण ṇ is also used as a single consonant, in the same way as ङ ṅ and ञ ń, and is of very frequent occurrence, in which respect the Panjābī alone agrees with the Sindhī, the other dialects using ण ṇ only before letters of the cerebral class, with the exception of the Hindūstānī, which is destitute of a cerebral nasal.

§. 6.

1) Single consonants at the beginning of a word.

At the beginning of a word the following consonants occur in Sindhī:

1) Gutturals: क k, ख kh; ग g, घ gh; — ह h; — — ग़ ḡ.
2) Palatals: च č, छ čh; ज ǰ, झ ǰh; — य y; — श š, ज़ j̄.
3) Cerebrals: ट ț, ठ țh; ड ḍ, ढ ḍh; — ड़ ṛ; — — ड॒ ḍ̄.
4) Dentals: त t, थ th; द d, ध dh; न n; र r; ल l; स s; —
5) Labials: प p, फ ph; ब b, भ bh; म m; व v; — — ब़ b̄.

This scheme deviates from that of the Prākrit in some essential points, which we have partly already noticed.

Peculiar to the Sindhī is the cerebral ड़ ṛ, beginning a word, which is not found in any of the other dialects. It is, however, also in Sindhī confined to the two interjections ड़े ṛē and ड़ी ṛī; the former is used in calling out to a man, the latter in calling out to a woman. There can be no doubt, that we have in both forms the Sansk. interjectional adverb अरे (which form is also used in Sindhī) which has been vindicated by Dr. Caldwell (Comparative Grammar of the Drāvidian languages, p. 440) to the Drāvidian idioms of the south, and the original signification of which is: o slave! The correctness of Dr. Caldwell's statement is borne out by the Sindhī, in which besides ड़े and ड़ी, also अड़े and अड़ी is used, corresponding to the Drāvidian aḍā.

All those consonants, as arrayed above, hold their place at the beginning of a word, when standing single; but when a noun happens to be compounded, then the first consonant of the second noun is no longer considered initial, and may therefore be elided, as: सिआरो siārō, the cold season, Prākrit already मीआरो, Sansk. शीत—काल.

1) क k is not subject to aspiration, as in some examples of the Prākrit, e. g. खुज्ज, Sansk. कुब्ज, Sindhī कुॿो kuḇō, hump-backed; neither is k changed to च at the beginning of a word, but frequently at the end (being an affix) and in the case of the genitive affix जो even to the media ज j.

The k of Arabic-Persian words on the other hand is now and then aspirated or even changed to خ χ, as: کھُتَابُ khutābu, school, or خُتَابُ χutābu, from the Arabic کُتّاب; سُکھَانُ sukhānu, a rudder, Arab. سُکّان.

2) ग g is aspirated in the single instance of घरु gharu, a house, Prāk. घर (instead of गहे), Sansk. गृह.

3) त t is very frequently changed to the corresponding cerebral ट ṭ. The tendency of the dentals, to surrender their place to the corresponding cerebrals, has so much got the upper hand in Sindhī, that its consonantal system differs therein quite materially and significantly from the old Prākrit; e. g. ट्रामो ṭrāmō, copper, Prāk. तांब, Sansk. ताम्र (Hindī तांबा); ट्रे ṭrē, three, Prāk. तिण्णि, Sansk. त्रीणि (Hindī तीन्); the same may also be stated of the aspirate थ th, as: ठाणु ṭhāṇu, stable, Prāk. थाण, Sansk. स्थान.

The cerebral ट (ठ) with its media ड (ढ) comprises the most non-Ārian elements of the language; nearly ¾ of the words, which commence with a cerebral, are taken from some aboriginal, non-Ārian idiom, which in recent times has been termed "Scythian"[1]), but which we would prefer to call Tātār. This seams to be a very strong proof, that the cerebrals have been borrowed from some idiom anterior to the introduction of the Arian family of languages; the Sanskrit uses the cerebrals very sparingly, but in Prākrit, which is already considerably tinged with so-called "provincial" (i. e. non-Ārian) elements, they struggle already hard to supplant the dentals.

4) द d, as well as its tenuis त t, is very frequently changed to the corresponding cerebral ड ḍ, and, as even ḍ did not seem hard enough at the beginning of a word, it was changed in most cases to the peculiar Sindhī ॾ ḍ̤ (the pronunciation of which see under the Sindhī alphabets), as: ॾोली ḍ̤ōlī, a kind of sedan chair, Prākrit already डोला, Sansk. दोला; ॾंडु ḍ̤anḍu, a stick, Prāk.

---

1) This term, though used by Dr. Caldwell and Mr. Ed. Norris, we find too vague; Tātār is more specific, as we understand by this term a certain family of languages.

डगड, Sansk. दगड; ड्डिअणु ḍianu, to give, Prāk. देमि, Sansk. root दा; ड्डिसणु ḍisaṇu, to see, Prāk. दक्ख Sansk. दृश्. But if r be joined to the cerebral media, the simple cerebral (ड) must be used, as ड्ड ḍ is already by its own nature a double cerebral, e. g. ड्राखा ḍrākha, grape, Sansk. द्राक्षा (Hindī दाख). The simple cerebral ड ḍ is very seldom to be met with at the beginning of a word, and must be carefully distinguished from ड्ड ḍ, as: डिठो ḍiṭhō, obstinate, but ड्डिठो ḍiṭhō, seen, participle past of ड्डिसणु to see.

द d, is changed to its aspirate ध dh in the single instance of धिअ dhia, daughter, after the precedent of the Prākrit धीदा or धीआ.

5) Initial प is aspirated in some instances, as: फासी phāsī or फाही phāhī, a noose, Sansk. पाश (Hindī फांसी); now and then it passes also to the semi-vowel व (by the medium of ब b) as: वाझो vājhō, a Hindū schoolmaster, Sansk. उपाध्याय (initial u having first been dropped).

6) The semi-vowel य y has become now very scarce in Sindhī at the beginning of a word, as: यभणु yabhaṇu, coire; यटो yaṭō, stout; यारंहं yārāhā̃, eleven. After the analogy of the Prākrit initial य is generally changed to ज, as: जो jō, who, Sansk. यो; जसु jasu, fame, Sansk. यश.

In words, borrowed from the Arabic or Persian, y is always preserved, as: यारु yāru, friend, Pers. يار etc.

The only instance, where initial य has been changed to ल l in Sindhī is लठि laṭhe, a walking-stick; the same is the case in Prākrit, लट्ठि, Sansk. यष्टि.

§. 7.

2) Single consonants in the midst of a word.

According to a common Prākrit rule the following consonants:

क k, ग g; च č, ज j; त t, द d; प p, ब b,

when standing single in the midst of a word, may either be retained or elided. This rule we find corroborated by the Sindhī, but not without some essential restrictions, the consonants being on the whole more frequently retained than elided, as the effeminacy of pronunciation has not yet reached that degree of indistinctness in Sindhī, which so peculiarly characterizes the Prākrit. We shall therefore find, that in many instances the Sindhī has followed the already beaten track, but has more frequently preserved the old harder form, or chosen its own way of elision and contraction. The semi-vowels are but rarely totally elided in Sindhī; they either keep their place or are dissolved into their corresponding vowels.

Examples of elision: सुई suī, needle, Prāk. सूई, Sansk. सूची. किओ kiō, done, Prak. किदो, Sansk. कृत; राउ rāu, prince, Prāk. राआ, Sansk. राजा; चउमासो ča-umāsō, the rainy season, Sansk. चतुर्मास; सरउ sara-u, autumn, Prāk. सरदो, Sansk. शरद्; पिउ piu, father, Prāk. पिआ, Sansk. पिता.

This process of elision is extended even to foreign words, as: नाखुओं nākhuō̃, a ship-master, Pers. ناخدا.

But more frequently the consonants keep their place, as: सागरु sāgaru, the sea, Prāk. साअरो, Sansk. सागर; नगरु nagaru, town, Prāk. णअरो, Sansk. नगर; वचनु vačanu, promise, Prāk. वअणं, Sansk. वचनं.

It is quite characteristical, that the Prākrit does not elide the cerebrals, for which it shows already such a predilection, but, wherever possible, it changes the dentals into cerebrals, to guard them thus against elision. This process we find in full operation in the modern dialects, which have sprung from the Prākrit; the common dentals have become too weak for the mouth of the people, a circumstance, which receives a particular light from the manner, in which the modern Indians write and pronounce European words; every dental is without mercy changed by them into a cerebral, which proves at least so much, that the cerebrals are more familiar to them, than the dentals.

Let us now briefly glance over the exceptions, which have been noted down by the Prākrit grammarians.

1) According to the rule, laid down at the head of this paragraph, the letters क k, ग g, च č, ज j are, when not elided, retained. The exceptions from this rule in Prākrit are not borne out by the Sindhī, and seem therefore to have been more of a local character. The only exception, which is corroborated by the modern idioms, is the Prākrit form बहिणी, sister, Sansk. भगिणी, which must be explained by an original form बघिणी, from which बहिणी has sprung; Hindī बहिन् and Sindhī, by transposition of the aspiration, भेणु bhēṇu.

क k, may pass into its corresponding media ग, as: भग़तु bhağatu, a worshipper, Sansk. भक्त; सग़ति sağate, strength, Sansk. शक्ति. On the contrary there is a transition of ग to क (and by the influence of following r to kh) in खड़ kẖaḍa, a pit, Prāk. गड्ड, Sansk. गर्त.

2) The cerebral ट ṭ and its aspirate ठ ṭh, frequently pass into their corresponding media, as: कंढी kanḍhī, a necklace (besides कंठी), Sansk. कण्ठीय. This is fully borne out by the modern dialects, especially the Sindhī, which goes already a step further in this downward course, and changes ड ḍ to ड़ ṛ, and ढ ḍh to ढ़ ṛh; e. g. बड़ु baṛu, the Indian fig-tree, Sansk. वट; ट्रोड़णु ṭrōṛaṇu, to break, Sansk. त्रोटन; पढ़णु paṛhaṇu, to

read, Sansk. पठ्; पीढ़ी pīṛhī, throne, Sansk. पीठी; लुढ़णु luṛhaṇu, to roll down, Sansk. लुठ्.

To this permutation also the original Sanskritical ड ḍ is subject in many instances, as: जुड़णु juṛaṇu, to be joined, Sansk. जुड्; पीड़णु pīṛaṇu, to press, Sansk. पीड्; जड़ु jaṛu, inanimate body, Sansk. जड. In a similar manner also the Sansk. ढ ḍh may be changed to ढ़ ṛh, as: मूढ़ु mūṛhu, ignorant, Sansk. मूढ.

But by far the greatest number of words, in which ṛ or ṛh is to be found, is of non-Ārian origin.

3) त very often passes into its media द, as: खांदि khānde, patience, Sansk. क्षान्ति. The Sansk. participial termination अन्त (अत्) is always changed in Sindhī to अंदो andō, as: हलंदो halandō, going, कंदो doing. त is even changed to an aspirated cerebral, but only in such cases, where the aspiration has been caused by an elided r, as: वठु vaṭhu, taking, Sansk. वृत्ति. त is preserved in many instances, where in Prākrit it has passed into the media द, as रुति rute, season, Prāk. उदुज, Sansk. ऋतु. In words borrowed from the Arabic (or Persian) त is occasionally aspirated, as: हिम्मथ himmatha, Arab. هِمَّت; साअथ sāatha, hour, Arab. سَاعَت.

4) प only rarely passes into its media ब, as बि bi, also, Sansk. अपि; रज्बूतु rajbūtu, a Rajput, Sansk. राजपुत्र; Prāk. उबरि upon, but Sindhī परि.

On the other hand there is a transition of the media to the tenuis in the abstract affix प, पो, पणु etc. (Hindī बन्), from the Sansk. affix त्व, त्वन (v = b = p), as: ड॒ाहप ḍāhapa, wisdom.

Final प is now and then changed to u (p = b = v = u), as: ताउ tāu, heat, Sansk. ताप, Hindī ताव tāō.

5) The substitution of ल in lieu of ड has been preserved in the case of: तलाउ talāu, a tank, Prāk.

तलाञ्चं, Sansk. तडाग. In other examples however the course, taken by the Prākrit, has again been abandoned, and a new one struck out; e. g. the Prākrit डालिम, pomegranate, sprung from the Sanskrit दाडिम (by the substitution of ल for ड) becomes in Sindhī ड्राढूं ḍāṛhū̃ (Hindī दाड़िम्), the initial dental द being first changed to ड ḍ and then hardened to ड्र ḍ, and ड ḍ passing into ड़ ṛ with an additional aspiration (which is rather unusual).

The modern idioms deviate in this respect from the Prākrit, that they change ड ḍ to ड़ ṛ, instead of substituting ल for ड; but therein also lies a hint, how the substitution of ल for ड has been possible. The change must have been effected by the medium of ड़ ṛ (not of र, as Lassen supposes), which approaches ल very closely in sound. This explains sufficiently such like cases as: पीलो pīlō, yellow, Sansk. पीत; the change must have passed through the following stages, as: पीत = पीद = पीड = पीड़ = पील.

6) The substitution of र r for द in those numerals, which are compounded with दश, has been retained in Sindhī, as well as in the cognate dialects, e. g. Prāk. एञ्चारह, Sindhī यारंहं yārāhā̃, eleven; Prāk. बारह, Sindhī ब़ारंहं b̤ārāhā̃, twelve; Prāk. तेरह, Sindhī तेरंहं tērāhā̃, thirteen; द however must be standing by itself, for Prāk. चउद्दह, Sindhī चोड़ंहं čōḍāhā̃, fourteen.

§. 8.

3) Single Aspirates in the midst of a word.

On the average the aspirates are in Sindhī more frequently preserved, than elided, though the Prākrit laws, concerning their elision, are also in force.

a) The letters ख kh, घ gh, थ th, ध dh, भ bh may be elided in this wise, that only the spiritus ह

remains. This phenomenon is so far of great importance, as the Prākrit seems to indicate thereby, that it considers the aspirates as compound consonants, like gh, bh etc., the base of which is dropped and the spiritus ह alone retained. The aversion of the Prākrit against the aspirates seems to point to a Tātār under-ground current in the mouth of the common people, the Drāvidian languages of the south being destitute of aspirates. Against this tendency of clearing away the aspirates the modern idioms react far more strongly than the old Prākrit, their pronunciation proving in this respect much tighter, than that of their immediate common mother-tongue.

Examples of elision: मुंहुं mūhū, face, Prāk. मुहं, Sansk. मुख; but मुखु mukhu is also in use in Sindhī; मींहु mīhu, rain, Prāk. मेहो, Sansk. मेघ; in Sindhī also मेघु; सही sahī, friend, Prāk. सही, Sansk. सखि; कहणु kahaṇu, to say, Prāk. कह, Sansk. कथ्; लहणु lahaṇu, to obtain, Prāk. लह्, Sansk. लभ्.

In some instances the Sindhī advances beyond the Prākrit by dropping ह, which has been severed from its base, as; साऊ sāū, upright, Prāk. साहु, Sansk. साधु.

b) But more commonly the aspirates in question are retained, as: सुखु sukhu, pleasure, Prāk. सुखं; अधीरो adhīrō, hasty, Prāk. अधीरो; सुघड़ु sugharu, shrewd, Sansk. सुघट.

c) The aspirates छ čh, झ ǰh, ठ ṭh, ढ ḍh, फ ph are retained unaltered; e. g. इछा ičhā, wish, Sansk. इच्छा; अछो ačhō, white, Sansk. अच्छ; कंठी kanṭhī, a kind of necklace, Sansk. कण्ठीय; ढूंढणु ḍhūnḍhaṇu, to seek, Sansk. ढूंढण; सफलु saphalu, fruitful, Sansk. सफल.

d) The aspirate ठ ṭh may also pass into its corresponding media, as: सुंढि sunḍhe, ginger, Sansk. शुण्ठी, Hindī सोंठ्; कंढी kanḍhī, a kind of necklace (besides कंठी); गंढि gaṇḍhe, a bundle, Prāk. गण्ठि, Sansk. ग्रन्थि.

The cases of a media passing into its corresponding tenuis are very rare, as: सुठो suṭhō, pure, Sansk. शुद्ध, Hindī again सुध्.

e) The aspirated dental थ th passes in some instances into its corresponding media ध, as: पंधु pandhu, journey, Sansk. पन्था m. The aspirated dentals may also be exchanged for their corresponding cerebrals, as: बुढो buḍhō, old, Prāk. वड्ढ, Sansk. वृद्ध; मूढु mūḍhu, a fool, Prāk. मुद्ध, Sansk. मुग्ध.

The transition of an aspirated dental to its corresponding non-aspirate is very rare, as मदु madu, liquor, Sansk. मधु (Hindī मद् and मधु).

§. 9.

4) Single nasals.

The dental न n, is now and then changed to the palatal ञ ń, as: थञु thańu, woman's milk, Sansk. स्तन, Hindī थन् (udder). न is changed to the cerebral ण ṇ in धेणु dhēṇu, a milk-cow, Sansk. धेनु. In the case of लिमु limu, a nimb-tree, न has been exchanged for ल, Sansk. निम्बु, Hindī नीम् and लीम्.

The palatal ञ ń is in some instances substituted for ज्ज jj (= Sindhī ज़ ǰ), as मिञु mińu, marrow, Sansk. मज्जा; but besides मिञु the form मिज़ miǰa, is also in use. Similarly ञ ń may supplant ण्ण ṇṇ, as: पुञी puńī, virtuous, Prāk. पुण्ण, Sansk. पुण्य; सुञो suńō, empty, Prāk. सुण्ण, Sansk. शून्य. It only rarely happens, that a cerebral ṇ is changed to a dental one, as: पुनो (= punnō) accomplished, participle past of पुज़णु, Sansk. पूर्ण.

A single म m in the midst of a word is now and

then elided, as: सांई sāī̃, lord, Sansk. स्वामी (= स्वामिन्); but the form सामी sāmī has likewise been preserved.

म m is further elided in the affixes मन् (= इमन्) and मय, as: अछाणि ačhāṇe, whiteness, from अछो ačhō, white; लोहांओं lōhā̃ō̃, made of iron; further in the affix मत्, as: भर्यतु bharyatu, a carrier of burden, from भरी, a load. These forms we shall explain further on in the formation of themes.

§. 10.

5) The semi-vowels य y, and व v.

1) In Prākrit य y has lost its hold in the midst of a word; it is either dissolved into the vowel i, or changed to ज j, or dropped altogether. In Sindhī on the contrary य may keep its place in the midst of a word; it is even frequently inserted, to avoid a hiatus, as: आयो āyō, come, भर्यो bharyō, filled, though these forms may also be written and pronounced: आइओ ā-i-ō, bhar-i-ō, which is frequently done in poëtry, to gain a syllable. The cases, where य has been dropped altogether in Sindhī, are rare, as: वाउ vā-u, wind, Prāk. already वाऊ, Sansk. वायु; य is frequently contracted, as: नेणु nēṇu, eye, Prāk. णअणं, Sansk. नयनं; at the end of a word the elision of य is more common, as: विशु višu, world, Sansk. विषय. After the precedent of the Prākrit य is exchanged for ज in cases like the following: सेज sēja, bed, Prāk. सेज्जा, Sansk. शय्या; पीज़ु pīju, draught, Sansk. पेयं etc.

य as a sign of the passive verb is in Sindhī, as already in Prākrit, always changed to ज j, a method, by which the Sindhī has gained a regular passive voice, whereas all the kindred dialects are compelled to make up the passive by compositions; e. g. ड्डिसिजणु ḍisijaṇu, to be seen, active ड्डिसणु ḍisaṇu, to see, Hindī देखा जाना etc.

2) व v is, after the analogy of य, either preserved or dissolved into u; but if the laws of euphony require it, it is again reinstated between two vowels, and very rarely dropped altogether; e. g. जीउ jĭu, life, formative जीव jīva (instead of जीअ jīa), Prāk. जीअं, Sansk. जीव; देवी dēvī, goddess; on the other hand देउ dēu, a demon, formative देव dēva; पवनु pavanu, wind, Prāk. पउणु, Sansk. पवन. It is also now and then totally elided; as: जिअणु jiaṇu, to live; ड्डींहु ḍĩhu, day, Prāk. दिअहो, Sansk. दिवस, especially when compounded with another consonant, as we shall see hereafter. It may also be contracted, as: पूणु pūṇu, to fall, instead of पवणु; चूणु čūṇu, to say, instead of चवणु. In the prefix अव it may also be contracted to औ au, as: औसारु ausāru or अवसारु avasāru, want of rain; औतारु autāru or अवतारु avatāru, an Avatār.

A euphonic insertion of व takes place in the word छांव čhāva shade, to keep the two vowels ā-a asunder; in Prākrit already, for similar reasons, ह has been inserted, छाहा (comp. Varar. II, 18), Sansk. छाया.

§. 11.

6) The liquidae र r and ल l; the sibilant स s and the spiritus ह h.

1) र r and ल l are not elided in Sindhī, but keep their respective places; ल is frequently exchanged for र in Sindhī, as: केलो kēlō or केरो kērō, name of a flower; बुर्बुली burbulī, a nightingale, from the Persian بُلْبُل; सिआरु siāru, a jackal, Hindī सिआल, Sansk. शृगाल;

डुबि़रो ḍubirō, weak, instead of: डुबि़लो ḍubilō, which is also in use, Sansk. दुर्बल; सराह sarāha, praise, Prāk. सलाहा, Sansk. श्लाघा. The only example, in which र has been changed to ज = ज़ is पुज़णु pujaṇu, to be accomplished (Hindī likewise पूज्ना) from the Sansk. पूरण.

2) The sibilant स (be it original or a derivative from श and ष) either keeps its place or is changed to ह, as: देसु dēsu, country, more generally: ड्रेहु ḍēhu, Sansk. देश; मासु māsu, flesh, or माहु māhu, Sansk. मांसं.

In the case of हंजु hanju or हंझु hanjhu, a wild goose, original स has been exchanged for ज or श (in Hindī हंस् or हांस्), Sansk. हंस. Similarly हंज hanja or हंझ् hanjha, tear, Sansk. अश्रु, Prāk. अंसु (initial h being in Sindhī of a euphonic nature in this case); in the same way the Sindhī demonstrative pronoun इझो ijhō seems to have sprung from एस = एष, and उझो ujhō from the remote demonstrative base u, and sō (= sa).

3) ह h remains unaltered in Sindhī; in some instances however it is dropped for euphony's sake, as: सरहो sarahō, joyful, Sansk. सहर्स (= सहरसो = सहरहो = सरहो) साऊ sā-ū or साहू sāhū, the same as: साधु or साधू honest.

Remark. The final consonants, their respective changes and permutations we may here as well pass over, as the modern Indian vernaculars have already so much receded from the old Prākrit, that partly quite new formations have been introduced, which preclude any nearer comparison with the Prākrit. The particular changes or elisions, to which the final consonants are subject in Sindhī, we shall supply in their proper places.

§. 12.

7) Compound consonants.

For a thorough insight into the nature of the North Indian vernaculars this point is of the greatest importance; for thus only we can trace out the changes, which the Sanskrit has undergone in the mouth of the common people, if we follow up the laws, according to which the Sanskrit sounds have been decomposed into the Prākrit and its modern daughters, or weakened at least to such a degree, that they are now scarcely recognisable. We can perceive a principle pervading this process of decomposition similar to that, by which out of the old Latin the modern Romanic tongues have been derived, and the mutual congruity is often surprising.

We meet here again with the same principle, which we have seen operating in the decomposition of the vowels and the single consonants. The effeminacy of pronunciation, which absorbs every hard and rough sound, and which consequently rather bears up with vowels, though they may form a displeasing hiatus, than with consonants, which are elided wherever possible, can in a far less degree endure compound consonants. All means are therefore employed, either to smooth them down or to assimilate them, in order to adjust them for a Prākrit mouth, a consonant compounded of letters of different vargas being incompatible with Prākrit rules of euphony. It is understood, that in such an idiom a conjunction of three letters is quite out of question; the utmost which the Prākrit can endure, is the same letter doubled, as क्क kk, त्त tt etc.; र and ह alone cannot be doubled.

Another means, to do away with a compound consonant, is to dissolve the same into its component parts by the insertion of a vowel, a method, to which recourse is had very frequently in Prākrit and the modern vernaculars.

But even such a doubled consonant is as yet thought too hard; we perceive therefore already a tendency, as well in the old Prākrit as in its daughters, to clear away the doubling of a consonant by prolonging the preceding vowel, to restore thereby again the quantity of the syllable, as: आगि़ āge, fire, Prāk. अग्गि, Sansk. अग्नि, Hindī आग्; Hindī भीत् wall, Sindhī भिति, Sansk. भित्ति.

§. 13.

A) Assimilation of the first four consonants of the five vargas.

These are the following:

क k, ख kh; ग g, घ gh.
च č, छ čh; ज j, झ jh.
ट ṭ, ठ ṭh; ड ḍ, ढ ḍh.
त t, थ th; द d, ध dh.
प p, फ ph; ब b, भ bh.

The ground-law of the Prākrit is this: when two consonants form a compound, the former must give way to the latter, by being assimilated to the same; thereby originates the only conjunction of consonants, which is suffered in Prākrit, the doubling of the same consonant. In the dental class this doubling of a consonant does not prevent it from passing over into the cerebral class; in the other vargas the transition of a so doubled consonant to another varga is rare, as the consonant gains more strength by being doubled. The only example of such a transition to another varga is सर्वगु़ sarvagū, omniscient, Prāk. सर्वज्ज, Sansk. सर्वज्ञ, where the doubled palatal has been changed into a double guttural (ग़ = ग्ग), a transition, which is natural enough in a single consonant, but which is very seldom to be met with in a doubled consonant. सघणु saghaṇu, to be able, Prāk. सक्कणोमि, Sansk. शक्नोमि

(Hindī सक्ना), and perhaps a few others, which may have escaped my notice.

On the whole the Sindhī, as well as the kindred dialects, agrees with this ground-law of the Prākrit[1]), without making it an immutable rule of its proceedings: for it may also assimilate the following consonant to the preceding. In many instances the Sindhī is more original, than the Prākrit, by preserving such like conjunctions of consonants, as are usual in Sanskrit.

Examples of assimilation.

सुतो sutō, asleep, Prāk. सुत्तो, Sansk. सुप्त; उपनो upanō, created, Prāk. उप्पण्ण, Sansk. उत्पन्न; भतु bhatu, boiled rice, Prāk. भत्त, Sansk. भक्त (Hindī भात्, by prolonging the preceding vowel); लधो ladhō, received, Prāk. लद्ध, Sansk. लब्ध. But on the other hand: कुबो kuḇō, hump-backed, Prāk. खुज्जो, Sansk. कुब्ज.

But an original compound consonant may also be preserved unaltered in Sindhī, as: शब्दु šabdu, word, Prāk. सद्द, Sansk. शब्द; मुक्तो, mukto, free, Prāk. मुत्त, Sansk. मुक्त.

It depends however more or less on the option of the speaker, if he will pronounce a compound consonant as such, or separate the same by the insertion of a vowel, as: शब्दु šabdu, or शबिदु šabidu, the inserted i being pronounced so rapidly, that it is scarcely perceptible. The Musalmāns therefore, when writing with Arabic letters, never place the sign ǰazm (ـْـ) above a consonant, destitute of a vowel, but always add the kasr, which is nearly equal to ǰazm, it being scarcely heard at all in

1) It must be stated here, that according to the common method of writing the Sindhī, a double consonant is not expressed generally, but only in such instances, where two words, written else in the same way, are to be distinguished, as اُنَ una, by him, and اُنَّ unna, wool.

pronunciation. The next vowel, thus inserted, is usually i (kasr), but a or u may also be employed, according to euphony or the sequence of vowels, as: भग़तु bhağatu, a worshipper, Sansk. भक्त; सग़ति sağate, power, Sansk. शक्ति (Hindī सकत् f.).

§. 14.

B) Assimilation of the nasals.

a) A nasal, preceding a consonant, generally keeps its place as: अंतु antu, end, Sansk. अन्त. A preceding nasal may be dropped altogether, if the preceding vowel happen to be a long one, as: मासु māsu, flesh, Sansk. मांसं; गाड़ो gāḍō, a cart, Sansk. गन्त्री (Hindī गाड़ी), the doubled consonant being cleared away in the latter instance by the prolongation of the preceding vowel.

The compound न्म nm is severed by the insertion of a vowel, as: जनमु janamu, birth, Sansk. जन्म.

b) In a compound consonant the following nasal is assimilated to the preceding consonant, as: आग़ि āğe, fire, Prāk. अग्गि, Sansk. अग्नि; लग़ो lağō, applied, Prāk. लग्ग, Sansk. लग्न; भग़ो bhağō, broken, Sansk. भग्न.

The compound consonant however may also remain unaltered, or be taken asunder by the insertion of a vowel, as: रत्नु ratnu or रतनु ratanu, jewel; सुज़ाणु sujānu, wise, Prāk. सुज्ज, Sansk. सुज्ञ; सुपनो supanō, dream, Sansk. स्वप्न.

The nasal may also be pushed forward, to escape being assimilated: as: नंगो nangō, naked, Prāk. नग्गो, Sansk. नग्न.

On the reverse a following nasal may also assimilate a preceding consonant, as: सइन sa-ina, hint, Sansk. संज्ञा; राणी rāṇī, queen, Sansk. राज्ञी. The nasal may also assimilate a preceding consonant in such a wise, that it draws the same over at the same time to its own varga. The only example of such an assimilation (if it be not to be explained in some other way) is the reflexive pronoun पाणु pāṇa, self, Prāk. अपाण, Sansk. आत्मा; in Hindī we have the form आप्, which has sprung from अप्प, instead of अत्त (= आत्मा); compare on this head: Lassen §. 67.

c) The nasals may assimilate a preceding or following semi-vowel, as: पुञी puñī, virtuous, Prāk. पुराण, Sansk. पुण्य; सुञो suñō, empty, Prāk. सुराण, Sansk. शून्य; उन्न unna, wool, Sansk. ऊर्ण; चउमासो ča-umāsō, the rainy season, Sansk. चतुर्मास.

On the other hand notice पूरो pūrō, full, Sansk. पूर्ण; चूरु čūru, pulverized, Sansk. चूर्ण, where the semi-vowel r has assimilated the nasal, r being stronger in sound, than n.

म्र mr in the Sanskrit आम्र āmra, is changed in Sindhī to mb, as: अंबु ambu, mangoe, Prāk. अम्ब (Hindī आम्); but in the case of the Sindhī word ट्रामो ṭrāmo, copper, Sansk. ताम्र, Prāk. तम्ब (Hindī तांबा or तामा) the semi-vowel r has been pushed forward to t = ṭ, as r may easily hold its place in conjunction with a dental or cerebral.

म्ब mb is assimilated to mm, as: निमु nimu (= nimmu) a lime-tree, Sansk. निम्ब; म्ल ml is taken asunder, after the analogy of the Prākrit, as: मिलणु milaṇu, to be obtained, Prāk. मिलाण, Sansk. म्लै, Hindī likewise मिलना.

§. 15.

C) Assimilation of the semi-vowels.

a) The semi-vowel य y.

α) If the semi-vowel य happen to be joined to a preceding consonant, it is assimilated to the same, as:

3*

जोगु jōgu, fit, Prāk. जोग्ग, Sansk. योग्य, Hindī जोग्; वाघु vāghu, a tiger, Sansk. व्याघ्र; वइसु va-isu, a Vaishya, Sansk. वैश्य (Hindī बैस्). It may, however, also hold its place, as: वाक्यु vākyu, a sentence, Sansk. वाक्य, though this is very rarely the case.

β) य, when compounded with a preceding र, is elided, as: तुरी turī, a small trumpet, Prāk. तुरं, Sansk. तूर्य; धीर dhīra, firmness, Prāk. धीरं, Sansk. धैर्य; आरु āru, sense of honor, Sansk. आर्य, Hindī अरिज्. But य may also be preserved by being changed to ज, as: धीर्जु dhīrju, the same as: धीर; सूरिजु sūriju, the sun, Prāk. सूरो or सुज्जो, Sansk. सूर्य; अचुर्जु ačurju, wonderful, Prāk. अच्छरिअं, Sansk. आश्चर्य.

γ) य joined to a preceding dental is either simply dropped, as: नितु nitu, always, Prāk. निच्च, Sansk. नित्य; आड़ितु āḍitu, the sun, Sansk. आदित्य, or it may also, though rarely, be preserved, as: मठ्यां maṭhyā̃, falsely, Prāk. मिच्छा, Sansk. मिथ्या. But the more usual way is that य, being first assimilated to a preceding dental, draws the same over to its own (i. e. palatal) class, so that त्य is changed to च्च, थ्य to च्छ, द्य to ज्ज and ध्य to ज्झ (for which double consonants, as remarked already, the simple bases are only written in Sindhī); e. g. विज़ा vijā, science (ज़ = ज्ज), Prāk. विज्जा, Sansk. विद्या; अज़ु aju, to-day, Sansk. अद्य (Hindī आज्); खाज़ु khāju, food, Sansk. खाद्यं; मंझु, manjhu, the midst, Prāk. मज्झो, Sansk. मध्य; बझणु bajhaṇu, to be bound, Sansk. बध्य्; वाझो vājhō, a Hindū schoolmaster, Sansk. उपाध्याय; हचा hačā, murder, Sansk. हत्या.

δ) य joined to a preceding ह is changed to झ jh, as: गुझो gujhō, concealed, Prāk. गुज्झाओ, Sansk. गुह्यक.

ε) य is assimilated to a preceding ल, but final ल, instead of being doubled in consequence thereof, is aspirated, e. g. कल्ह kalha, yesterday, Prāk. कल्ल, Sansk. कल्यं (Hindī कल्); मुल्हु mulhu, price, Sansk. मूल्य; in the midst of a word य is simply assimilated to ल (the doubling not being expressed in Sindhī), as: पलङ्गु palangu, a bedstead, Sansk. पर्यङ्क (r being exchanged for l); पलाणु palāṇu, a pack-saddle, Prāk. पल्लाण, Sansk. पर्याण.

b) The semi-vowel र r.

α) र is assimilated to a preceding or following consonant, as: अगु agu, the front, Prāk. अग्गो, Sansk. अग्र; गूजरी gūjarī, name of a Rāgiṇī, Sansk. गुर्ज्जरी; गजणु gajaṇu, to thunder, Sansk. गर्जन (but Hindī गरज्ना); कमु kamu (= kammu), business, Prāk. कम्मो, Sansk. कर्मन् (Hindī काम्); मुंढी mundhī, head, Sansk. मूर्द्धन्; सपु sapu, snake; Sansk. सर्प; सिघो sighō, quick, Sansk. शीघ्र (Hindī शीघर्); चकी čakī, a mill, Sansk. चक्र; निभागु nibhāgu, misfortune, Sansk. र्निभाग.

On the other hand र, preceding or following a consonant, may just as easily hold its place, without being assimilated, as: चर्चो čarčō, silly talk, Sansk. चर्चा; प्री prī, friend, Sansk. प्रिय; पर्भु parbhu, a festival, Sansk. पर्व (व = ब, and ब aspirated by the influence of र); गर्बु garbu, pride, Sansk. गर्व; शुक्रु šukru, Friday, Sansk. शुक्र; सुर्गु surgu, heaven, Sansk. स्वर्ग; धर्मु dharmu, religion, Prāk. धम्म, Sansk. धर्म.

Very frequently such a compound is again dissolved into its constituent parts by the insertion of a vowel, as: पिरी pirī, friend, or प्री prī; पिरिभाति piribhāte, break of day, Sansk. प्रभात; or r is transposed for euphony's sake, as: पर्तापु partāpu, splendour, Sansk. प्रताप; पर्तु partu, leaf (of a book), Sansk. पत्र; ड्रिघो ḍrighō, long, Prāk. दिग्घ, Sansk. दीर्घ; किर्ति kirte, trade, किर्तु kirtu, action, Sansk. कृांत and कृत; ट्रकु ṭraku, a spinning wheel, Sansk. तर्कु.

It very rarely happens, that r is totally elided in a compound, as: वाघु vāghu, tiger, Sansk. व्याघ्र; राति rāte, night, Sansk. रात्रि (Prāk. रत्ती by ejection of ā); भाउ bhāu, brother, Sansk. भ्राता. The ejection of r in these and such like examples is caused by the preceding long vowel, which precludes the possibility of assimilating the compound consonant, or by the consonant, with which r forms a conjunction, being initial. In such cases, as रत्ती, the Prākrit has preferred to drop the long vowel, in order to make room for assimilation.

β) When compounded with a preceding dental, r is in most cases assimilated to the same in Prākrit, though it may also keep its place; in Sindhī on the other hand r is, when following a dental, mostly preserved, and the assimilation takes place only in the dialect of Lāṛ (Lower Sindh), whereas in the dialect of the Upper country (Sirō) the original compound is preserved, the dental only being commonly changed to a cerebral (or even to an aspirated cerebral, by the influence of r); e. g. पुट्रु puṭru, son, Prāk. पुत्त, Sansk. पुत्र (in Lāṛ: पुट्टु puṭṭu, according to the analogy of the Prākrit); मिट्रु miṭru, friend, Prāk. मित्त, Sansk. मित्र (in Lāṛ: मिट्टु miṭṭu); चंड्रु čanḍru, the moon, Prāk. चन्द, Sansk. चन्द्र; खेट्रु khēṭru, a field, Sansk. क्षेत्र; मंट्रु manṭru (or with transiton to the media) मंड्रु manḍru, an incantation, Sansk. मन्त्र; ट्रे ṭrē, three, Sansk. त्रि; ड्ढ्रु ḍaḍhru, or ड्ढु ḍaḍhu, a cutaneous disease, Sansk. दद्रु; ढ्रापणु ḍhrāpaṇu, to be satiated, Sansk तर्पण (by transition of the tenuis into the media). In those adverbs, which are compounded with the adverbial affix त्र, त्र is, after the precedent of the Prākrit, changed in Sindhī to थ, as: किथे kithē, where; जिथे jithē, in which place; तिथे tithe, in that place etc.

R, when preceding a dental, may likewise be assimilated to the same, as: कतणु kataṇu, to spin, Sansk. कर्त्तन; कतर katara, scissors, Sansk. कर्त्तरी; वटि vaṭĕ, a wig, Sansk. वर्त्तिका; खड़ khaḍa, a pit, Prāk. गड्डो, Sansk. गर्त. On the other hand the compound may also be retained unaltered, as: अर्धांगु ardhāngu, palsey, Sansk. अर्धाङ्ग; अर्थु arthu, object, Sansk. अर्थ; तीर्थु tīrthu, a holy bathing-place, Sansk. तीर्थ; or the compound may again be dissolved by the insertion of a vowel, as: मूरति mūrate, image, Sansk. मूर्ति; कीरति kīrate, glory, Sansk. कीर्ति, Prāk. कित्ति; तीरथु tīrathu = तीर्थु.

γ) र्व rv is either assimilated, as: सभु sabhu, all, Sansk. सर्व, Hindī सब् (the aspiration of b being caused in Sindhī by the influence of elided r); or the compound may be retained unaltered, as, सर्वसग॒ति sarvasag̱ate, omnipotent; or the compound may be dissolved again by the insertion of a vowel, as: पूरबु pūrabu, the east, Sansk. पूर्व.

δ) In the compound श्र šr the semi-vowel r may either be assimilated, as, सुओ suō, heard, Prāk. सुदो (= सुतो), Sansk. श्रुत; ससु sasu, mother-in-law, Sansk. श्वश्रू; or, the compound may be retained, as: श्री šrī, prosperity; or more commonly, the compound is dissolved by the insertion of a vowel, as सिराधु sirādhu, funeral obsequies, Sansk. श्राद्ध (Hindī श्राद्ध). The Sanskrit अश्रु, tear, Prāk. already अंसु (instead of आसु) has become in Hindī आसूं; the Sindhī form is हंज hanja or हंझ hanjha (with initial euphonic h), s being changed in this instance to ज or झ; Panjābī likewise anjhu.

The same holds good with reference to the compound

स्र sr, as: सहसु sahasu, thousand, Prāk. सहस्स, Sansk. सहस्र.

The compound र्श rś and र्ष rṣ are assimilated in Sindhī as well as in Prākrit, as: वसणु to rain, Sansk. वर्ष; पासो pāsō, side, Sansk. पार्श्व (Hindī पास्); सिसी sisī, head and neck, Sansk. शीर्ष (Hindī सीस्); or they are preserved (of course with transition of श and ष to स), as: दर्सनु darsanu, interview, Sansk. दर्शन; तर्सणु tarsaṇu, to wait, Sansk. तर्षण; the compound र्ष rṣ may also be dissolved into रस, and this again into रह, as: सरहो sarahō, happy, Sansk. सहर्ष (compare §. 11, end).

c) The semi-vowel ल l.

α) ल forming a compound with another consonant at the beginning of a word, is severed from the same by the insertion of a vowel, as: सराह sarāha, praise, Prāk. सलाहा, Sansk. श्लाघा (r = l in Sindhī); किलेसु kilēsụ, fatigue, Sansk. क्लेश (Hindī कलेस्); सलोकु salōku, a Slōka, Sansk. श्लोक.

β) In the midst of a word ल is assimilated to any consonant, save य, र and व, as: बकरु bakaru, vegetables, Prāk. वक्कल, Sansk. वल्कल; or it is severed again from the compound by the insertion of a vowel, as: लुक, hot wind, Prāk. उक्का, Sansk. उल्का, the initial vowel u being thrown back to serve in place of an inserted vowel.

d) The semi-vowel व v.

α) व, joined to a preceding consonant at the beginning of a word, is either dissolved into u, as: सुर्गु surğu, heaven, Sansk. स्वर्ग; दुआरु duāru, door, Prāk. दुआरो, Sansk. द्वार; सुआउ suāu, taste, Sansk. स्वाद; or it is totally elided (i. e. assimilated to the preceding consonant) as: जलणु jalaṇu, to burn, Sansk. ज्वलन; सर्गु sarğu (besides सुर्गु), heaven, Sansk. स्वर्ग; साईं sāī̃, lord, or सामी sāmī, Prāk. सामि, Sansk. स्वामिन्; सहुरो sahurō, father-in-law, Sansk. श्वशुर; ससु sasu, mother-in-law, Sansk. श्वश्रु. व v may also be severed from the compound by the insertion of a vowel (a or u), as: सवाड़ु savāḍu, taste, flavour (besides सुआउ), Sansk. स्वाद; दुवारु duvāru, door (besides दुआरु). व very rarely assimilates a preceding consonant, as: ॿ b̄a, two, Sansk. द्व (= vva = bba = b̄).

β) व v being joined to a preceding consonant in the midst of a word, is assimilated to the same, as: पको pakō (= pakkō) cooked, Prāk. पिक्क, Sansk. पक्व; सतु satu, strength, Prāk. सत्त, Sansk. सत्व.

In the abstract affix त्व, त्वन, the dental on the other hand is assimilated to the semi-vowel व, which latter is first changed to the labial ब, and then to the corresponding tenuis प, so that we have in Sindhī the forms प pa, पो pō, पणु paṇu or पणो paṇō, as: ॿान्हप b̄ānhapa, ॿान्हपो b̄ānhapō etc., slavery, from ॿान्हो b̄ānhō, a slave.

The regular form of assimilation however is also in use, but only in a few examples; त्व is in this way assimilated to त्त tt = ट्ट ṭṭ, and the double consonant again cleared away by the prolongation of the preceding vowel, as: छोकिराटु čhōkirāṭu, time of youth, from छोकरु čhōkaru, a boy.

The semi-vowel may also be dissolved into u, as: परमेसुरु paramēsuru, supreme lord = God, Prāk. already परमेसुर, Sansk. परमेश्वर; or it may be retained, as: दानेस्वरी dānēsvarī, liberal, besides: दानेसुरी dānēsurī.

§. 16.

D) Assimilation of the sibilants.

a) The palatal sibilant श š.

α) श š, when preceded by च č and छ čh, is assimilated to them, as: अचुर्जु ačurju, wonderful, Prāk.

अच्छरिअ, Sansk. आश्चर्य (long ā being shortened in Prākrit and Sindhī, and in compensation thereof the following consonant doubled, to restore again the quantity of the syllable); शनिचरु šaničaru, Saturday, Sansk. शनैश्चर (Hindī सनीचर्).

β) The compound च्च čč (which however is rendered in Sindhī, as all double consonants, by its simple base) arising from the assimilation of श्च, is, after the analogy of the Prākrit, frequently aspirated in Sindhī, on account of the inherent tendency of the sibilant towards aspiration (स = ह), as: विछूं vičhū̃, scorpion, Prāk. निच्छुओ, Sansk. वृश्चिक; पछुताउ, pačhutāu, repentance, Sansk. पश्चात्ताप, final प being changed (by b = v) in Sindhī to u.

γ) श followed by म, assimilates the same, as: रसी rasī (= rassī), a rope, Prāk. रस्सि, Sansk. रश्मि, but not necessarily; for: कश्मीरु kašmīru, Kashmīr.

b) The cerebral sibilant ष ṣ.

α) The compound ष्क ṣk (of ष्ख I have hitherto not met any instances) is assimilated in Sindhī to क (= क्क), and not to क्ख kkh, as in Prākrit; e. g. ड़ुकालु ḍukālu, famine, Sansk. दुष्काल; निकमी nikamī, useless, Sansk. निष्कर्म; सुको sukō, dry, Sansk. शुष्क (Hindī, as in Prākrit, सूका).

β) The compounds ष्ट ṣṭ and ष्ठ ṣṭh, are assimilated in Sindhī to ṭṭh, as: ड़िठो ḍiṭhō, seen, Prāk. दिट्ठ, Sansk. दृष्ट; गोठु gōṭhu, a village, Prāk. गोट्ठी, Sansk. गोष्ठी; निठरु niṭharu, obstinate, Prāk. निट्ठुर, Sansk. निष्ठुर; मिठो miṭhō, sweet, Sansk. मिष्ट.

The compound is also retained unaltered, as: ड़ुष्टु ḍuṣṭu, bad; but this is only done by Brāhmans, who understand Sanskrit; the common people ignore it completely.

The cerebral ठ, which has sprung from ष्ट or ष्ठ by assimilation, may also pass into its corresponding media ढ ḍh, and this again to ढ़ ṛh, e. g. कोढ़ु kōṛhu, leprosy, Sansk. कुष्ठ (the preceding vowel u having been lengthened in Sindhī to ō, to clear away the double consonant ṭṭh or ḍḍh).

γ) The compounds ष्प ṣ̌p, ष्फ ṣ̌ph are assimilated to फ in Sindhī, as: ॿाफ ḇapha, steam, Prāk. वप्फो, Sansk. वाष्प (Hindī बाफ़्, and even with aspiration of ब: भाफ़्).

In compound words ष्प is simply assimilated to प p (= pp) as: निपुट्रो niputrō, without a son, Sansk. निष्पुत्र.

δ) In the compounds ष्म ṣ̌m and ष्ण ṣ̌ṇ, ष is in Prākrit exchanged for h and placed after म and ण respectively; in Sindhī the original compound may be preserved, as: विष्णु viṣ̌ṇu, Prāk. विण्हु; विष्णवहू viṣ̌ṇavahū, a worshipper of Vishṇu; by the Musalmāns however words of this kind are simply written وِشْنُ, وِشْنوَهُو, Hindūstānī likewise وِشْنُ, as cerebral ṣ̌ is ignored by the common people.

ε) The compound ष्य ṣ̌y (and ष्व ṣ̌v) is in Prākrit assimilated to स्स ss, but in Sindhī to ख kh (= kkh) as: सिखु sikhu, a disciple = Sikh, Sansk. शिष्य.

c) The dental-sibilant स s.

α) The compound स्क sk is assimilated in Prākrit to ख kh, in Sindhī however to क k, as: कंधु kandhu, shoulder, Prāk. खंधो (खंदो), Sansk. स्कन्द (Hindī कंध्).

β) The compounds स्त st and स्थ sth are assimilated to थ (= tth) and त्स ts to छ č̌h (= čč̌h), as: थञु thañu, woman's milk, Sansk. स्तन; थिओ thiō, become, Sansk. स्थित; थंभु thambhu, post (Prākrit on the other hand

खम्भो), Sansk. स्तम्भ; वथु vathu, thing, Sansk. वस्तु; हथु hathu, hand, Prāk. हत्थो, Sansk. हस्त (Hindī हाथ्); थाणो thaṇō, place, Sansk. स्थान; अथ atha, is, Prāk. अत्थि, Sansk. अस्ति; वछि vače, a buffalo calf, Prāk. वच्छो, Sansk. वत्स.

The compound स्त st however may also, instead of being assimilated, be dissolved into its constituent parts by the insertion of a vowel, and when the compound happens to be initial, by prefixing a vowel, as: अस्तुति astute, praise, Prāk. थुई, Sansk. स्तुति; इस्तिरी istirī, woman, Sansk. स्त्री.

γ) स्प sp is assimilated to प (= pp), स्फ sph to फ (= pph), प्स ps to प (= pp) respectively as: फुटणु phuṭaṇu, to be broken, Sansk. स्फुट्; फुड़्ती phuṛtī, activity, Sansk. स्फूर्त्ति; लपी lapī, a dish of coarse wheaten flour, Sansk. लप्सिका; but प्स may also remain unassimilated, as: लप्सी.

In compound words स्प sp may be preserved, as: विस्पति, vispate, Thursday, Sansk. वृहस्पति; or the compound, especially at the beginning of a word, may be dissolved into its constituent parts, as: पारसु pārasu, the philosopher's stone, Sansk. स्पर्श (मणि), Hindī likewise पारस्.

δ) The compound स्न sn, when beginning a word, is either dissolved into its consistuent parts by the insertion of a vowel, as: सनानु sanānu, bathing, Sansk. स्नान; सनेहो sanēhō, a message of love, Sansk. स्नेह; or the preceding स is cast off altogether, as: नींहु nĩhu, love, Sansk. स्नेह (Hindī नेह्), Prāk. also णेहो; नुहु nuhu, daughter-in-law, Prāk. णोग्हा, Sansk. स्नुषा.

ε) The compound स्म sm is assimilated to स s (= ss) as: विसाई visāī, stupor, Sansk. विस्मय; or dissolved again by the insertion of a vowel, as: सुमरणु sumaraṇu, to remember, Sansk. स्मृ; विसामणु visāmaṇu, to be stunned, Sansk. विस्मि (विस्मय, Prāk. विम्हओ); or s is changed to h and placed after म (similarly to ष्म), as Prākrit म्ह = स्म, in the pronominal forms तुम्हे, अस्मे (cf. Lassen p. 331, 4; p. 329, 5), In Sindhī the म of the conjunct म्ह is also changed to v, as तव्हीं tavhī̃, you, instead of तुम्हीं tumhī̃.

ζ) The compound स्य sy is assimilated to स s (= ss) and thence farther to ह h, as: मुंहिं mũhī, तुंहिं tũhī etc., which must have sprung from an original form मस्य, तुस्य etc., Prāk. already मह, तुह (thence also the other Prākrit forms मज्झ, तुज्झ = मह्य, तुह्य = मस्य, तुस्य); तांहिं tãhē, of that (nom. sing. सो sō) Prāk. तस्स, Sansk. तस्य.

d) The compound क्ष kṣ.

This compound letter is assimilated in Sindhī:

α) To ख kh (= kkh), as: अखि akhe, eye, Sansk. अक्षि; खीरु khīru, milk, Sansk. क्षीर; खारो khārō, brackish, Sansk. क्षार; खेतु khetu, field, Sansk. क्षेत्र; खिमा khimā, patience, Sansk. क्षमा; खीं khī̃, wellfare, Sansk. क्षेम; रखणु rakhaṇu, to keep, Sansk. रक्षण; खांदि khande, patience, Sansk. क्षान्ति.

All these instances are against Prākrit usage, according to which क्ष ought to have been assimilated to छ čh, though ख is also admissible in Prākrit, and prove distinctly, that the Sindhī has followed its own course, independently of the Prākrit.

β) क्ष is also assimilated to छ čh, after the precedent of the Prākrit, as: रिछु ričhu, a bear, Sansk. ऋक्ष; छुरी čhurī, a knife, Sansk. क्षुरी; छिनणु čhinaṇu, to pluck, Sansk. क्षिण्; लछणु lačhaṇu, sign, Sansk. लक्षण but लखणु lakhaṇu is also in use in Sindhī.

According to Prākrit rule every consonant (the nasal n excepted), which is joined to क्ष, must be dropped;

but the Sindhī so far deviates from the Prākrit, that it separates any such consonant by the insertion of a vowel, as: Prāk. लच्छी, but Sindhī लछिमी lačhimī, the wife of Vishṇu, Hindī likewise लछमी, Sansk. लक्ष्मी. On the other hand the Sindhī assimilates the nasal in the compound क्ष्ण kšṇ to ख (kh = kš), whereas the Prākrit changes the same to ण्ह, as: Sindhī तिखो tikhō (= tikkhō), quick, Prāk. तिण्ह, Sansk. तीक्ष्ण.

A change of ख kh (= kš) to the spiritus ह h is found in Hindī, after the analogy of the Prākrit, as: Hindī दाहिना right (opposed to left), instead of the more common दक्खिणा, but not in Sindhī, which simply clears away the doubling of the letter in Prākrit by the prolongation of the preceding vowel, as: ड़ाखिणो ḍākhiṇō, right, southerm.

§. 17.

F) The spiritus ह h.

The spiritus ह cannot be assimilated to any other consonant. If therefore ह be joined to any other consonant, the compound is again separated into its component parts in the following way:

a) In the compounds ह्न hn, ह्म hm, ह is put after the nasal, a euphonic transposition, which is already common in Prākrit, as: ब़ाहि ƀāhe, fire (instead of ब़ांहि ƀãhe), Prāk. वण्ही, Sansk. वह्नि; चिन्हु činhu, mark, Sansk. चिह्न; the hardened Prāk. form चिन्ध or चेन्ध is not used in Sindhī.

The compound म्ह (instead of ह्म hm) is in Sindhī, on account of the preponderance of the labial, already exchanged for म्भ mbh, as: ब़ांभणु ƀāmbhaṇu, a Brāhman, Prāk. वम्हण, Sansk. ब्राह्मण.

b) ह्य hy is assimilated to झ jh (by transposition: hy = yh = jh), as: ग़ुझो ġujhō, concealed, Prāk. गुज्झाओ, Sansk. गुह्यक.

c) ह्व hv is assimilated to भ in Sindhī (hv = vh = bh), whereas in Prākrit the following semi-vowel is simply elided, as: ज़िभ jībha, tongue, Prāk. जीहा, Sansk. जिह्वा, (Hindī जीभ्).

§. 18.

E) Assimilation of three conjunct consonants.

In Sindhī, as well as in Prākrit, a compound, consisting of three consonants, can only then be tolerated, if the first consonant happen to be a nasal: as: चंड्रु čanḍru, moon, मंट्रु manṭru, incantation.

As regards the assimilation of three conjunct consonants the preceding rules come into operation. If no assimilation takes place, the one or the other of the consonants thus joined together, is severed from the rest by the insertion of a vowel, as: शास्तिरी šastirī, a Shāstrī, learned in the Shāstras (a usūal title of a Brāhman), from the Sansk. शास्त्र. In reference to the assimilation itself the following rules are to be observed.

a) If one of the consonants happen to be a semi-vowel, it is dropped, and the assimilation of the remaining two consonants is effected according to the usual method, as: मराठी marāṭhī, a Marāṭhī man (or. adj.), Sansk. महाराष्ट्र; अग्यों agyō̃, the foremost, Sansk. अग्र्य; पासो pāsō, side, Prāk. पास, Sansk. पार्श्व.

The semi-vowel य alone, when preceded by a dental, forms an exception to this rule, this compound being changed to the corresponding palatal (see §. 15, γ), as: संझो sanjhō, evening, Prāk. संज्झा, Sansk. सन्ध्य.

b) When of three conjunct consonants the two former or the two latter can be assimilated, preference is given to the stronger assimilation, as: मछु mačhu, fish, Prāk. मच्छो, Sansk. मत्स्य; in this instance त्स ts is assimilated to छ (ččh), the assimilation of it being stronger than that of स्य to स्स.

§. 19.

G) Elision of a double consonant.

The doubling of a consonant renders the same so much stronger, that even a long vowel, preceding it, must give way and is weakened to its corresponding short one. On the other hand a double consonant, as noticed already, may again be rendered simple; but in this case the preceding vowel, to make up for the quantity of the syllable, must be prolonged, as: राति rāte, night, Prāk. रत्ती, Sansk. रात्रि; कमु kamu (= kammu), business, Prāk. कम्मो, Hindī on the other hand काम्.

It is quite against the genius of the language, to elide totally a double consonant; notwithstanding this some few examples of this kind are to be met with in Sindhī, as: ड॒आरि ḍuāre, illness, ड॒आरी, adj. ḍuārī, ill, Prāk. दुब्बल, Sansk. दुर्बल; मिअो miō, friend (corroborated already by the Prākrit, which however preserves also the original from मित्तो). In these and such like examples the process cannot have been such, that a double consonant is elided at once, but it must first have been reduced to its simple base by the prolongation of the preceding vowel, as: मीतो mītō, instead, of मित्तो; from this base has sprung again, according to the usual laws of elision, the form मीअो mīō, in which, against the ordinary process, long ī has been shortened to ĭ, मिअो.

In the forms ड॒आरि and ड॒आरी, original double b must have been changed to vv (both letters, b and v, being already identical in Prākrit) previous to its elision; but it is quite an extraordinary phenomenon, that the following vowel has been lengthened instead of the preceding one.

Far more easily may one of the compound consonants be elided, when preceded by a long vowel, which renders the assimilation impossible, especially if one of the compound consonants be a semi-vowel, as: वाघु vāghu, a tiger, Sansk. व्याघ्र; राणी rāṇī, queen, Sansk. राज्ञी. Thus even two semi-vowels may disappear, as: पासो pāsō, side, Sansk. पार्श्व.

§. 20.

H) A double consonant at the beginning of a word.

A compound consonant at the beginning of a word is subject to the same laws of assimilation, as in the midst (or end) of a word. But as a double consonant would not be utterable at the beginning of a word, one of the assimilated, i. e. doubled consonants is simply cast off, so that only the simple base of the consonant remains, as: जलणु jalaṇu, to burn, instead of: ज्जलणु jjalaṇu, Sansk. ज्वलन; वाघु vāghu, tiger, instead, of व्वाघु vvāghu; कंधुं kandhu, shoulder, instead of क्कंधुं kkandhu. But if a word be compounded, the common laws of assimilation are applied (to the second), as: ड॒ब॒लु ḍub̤alu, weak, Prāk. दुब्बल.

Those compounds, which are not susceptible of assimilation, are dissolved into their component parts by the insertion of a vowel, as: किलेसु kilēsu, weariness, Prāk. किलेस, Sansk. क्लेश; सुमरणु sumaraṇu, to remember, Prāk. सुमर्, Sansk. स्मर् (स्मृ); or the first letter of the compound is cast off, which is particularly the case, if this happen to be a sibilant, as: नींहु nīhu, love, Prāk. सणेह saṇēha, Sansk. स्नेह; but if the sibilant be followed by a semi-vowel, the latter, as the weaker, is dropped, as: साहु sāhu, breath, Sansk.

ग्वास; सालो sālō, wife's brother, Prāk. सालो sālō, Sansk. श्याल.

त्र tr and द्र dr, which in Sindhī are commonly changed to the corresponding cerebrals, keep their place as well at the beginning as in the midst (or end) of a word, as: ट्रे ṭrē, three; ड्राख ḍrākha, grape, but Hindī दाख्, Sansk. द्राक्षा.

THE SINDHI ALPHABET.

§. 1.

Up to the present time various alphabets have been in use in Sindh, the Muhammadan portion of the community using the Arabic characters, loaded with many dots, to express the sounds peculiar to the Sindhī, and the Hindū population employing different alphabets of their own, which vary very much, according to the locality, in which they are used, though all of them are originally derived from an old Sanskrit alphabet. These latter alphabets, which are known in Sindh by the name of the Banyā̃ characters, are utterly unfit for literary purposes, as they have become greatly mutilated in the course of time and are very deficient in the vowel and consonant system, so that the Hindū merchants themselves, after a lapse of time, are hardly able to reproduce with accuracy what they have entered in their ledgers. No alphabet suits the Sindhī better, than the Sanskrit alphabet, the Sindhī being a genuine daughter of Sanskrit and Prākrit. But appropriate as the Sanskrit characters are to the Sindhī sounds, they will under the present state of society in Sindh be hardly in their right place, religious prejudices preventing the great majority of the population from using them in their writings. Sindh has been the first Indian country, which has succumbed to the fury of the Moslim invaders, and Hinduism and the culture of Sanskrit literature has been so completely swept away from its borders, that it is now, as has been stated, "a country without castes and Brahmins."

The Muhammadans of Sindh, as soon as they tried to employ their native idiom for literary purposes, detected, that the Arabic system, which had been forced upon them as a necessary consequence of the Islām, was deficient in many sounds, and they endeavoured to make up for this deficiency by dotting the nearest corresponding Arabic letters. The manner, in which they have done this, has not been very satisfactory. They were not led by any system and therefore the emendation, they attempted at, stopped half-way.

In the guttural class the Arabic base ک (k) was indiscriminately used to express the sounds k, kh; g, gh, g̃; the aspiration (kh, gh) was left unnoticed, and for the media g not even the corresponding Persian letter (گ) was supplied; the guttural ṅ was expressed by the compound نک (nk).

In the palatal class the aspirate čh was happily distinguished by an additional dot (= ڇ), and jh marked likewise ڄ; also the peculiar Sindhī j̄ (dy) was not forgotten and marked by ڃ; the palatal ń (ny) was again expressed by the compound نج, so that in this class all sounds were provided with distinguishing marks.

In the cerebral class, which is completely wanting in the Arabic system, the bases of the dentals were retained and the dots distributed in such a way, as to distinguish them from the corresponding dentals, viz.: ٽ = ṭ; ٺ = ṭh; ڊ = ḍ, ڍ = ḍh, ڏ = ḓ, a method, which is not without ingenuity; but the cerebral ṛ and the cerebral ṇ were again completely forgotten (i. e. they were expressed by the corresponding dentals ر r and ن n) and left to the knowledge of the reader.

The dental class did not offer many difficulties; only the aspirates had to be provided with diacritical marks, which was done in the following way: ٿ = th, ڌ = dh.

The same was the case with the labial class, where the aspirates only were to be pointed out by peculiar marks; but here their skill seems to have left them. In order to express ph, refuge was taken to the peculiar Arabic and Persian letter ف (f), which was provided with two additional dots = ڦ, bh having been expressed already by ڀ; the peculiar Sindhī b̄ was dexterously rendered by ٻ.

The Sindhīs had in this undertaking apparently the Sanskrit alphabet before their eyes, where the aspirates are written and treated as one sound. Accordingly they tried to express the aspiration of a letter by additional dots, which overloaded the few Arabic bases with diacritical signs.

The necessity further, to provide marks for the cerebral class, compelled them, to distribute afresh the dots for the dental aspirates, so that the eye finds only with difficulty a resting-place in the confuse mass and position of diacritical marks, as: ٽ = ṭ, ٿ = t; ٺ = ṭh; ٿ = th.

This attempt to adapt the Arabic characters to the sounds of a Prākrit language is very interesting, though the method applied has followed a wrong track and has not been extended to all the sounds of the language. The way, in which this has been done in Hindūstānī, is far more correct, in fact, the only course, which can be taken in adapting the Arabic letters to an Indian language. The Arabic system knows no aspirates, and consequently the aspiration must be expressed by an additional ھ h, if the original character of the Arabic alphabet is to be preserved in any way; else a quodlibet will be made out of it, which may be designated by any name but Arabic.

It was therefore soon found, when European scholars began to pay attention to the Sindhī, that the common Sindhī characters would not do for scientific purposes. New characters were in consequence composed by a Bombay civilian and unfortunately introduced into the government schools of Sindh, without being first submitted to the examination of competent scholars.

This new system, instead of striking at the root of the previous confusion, merely endeavoured to make up some deficiencies of the old, while retaining all its errors, so that it cannot even boast of the compactness of the old system.

The alterations and emendations were the following:

In the guttural class, where the old system was most deficient, as we have seen, the Persian letter گ g has been justly taken in, and from the Hindūstānī, the aspirate گھ gh, of which we fully approve. We should now reasonably expect to find the compound کھ kh corresponding to گھ gh; but to our utter surprise we find the old error repeated, and 'kh' again rendered by the simple base ک k. So it has happened, that all the prints published in this character are disfigured by the letter ڪ, which is now used throughout as the simple base for k, whereas it is well known, that ڪ is only used at the beginning of a word, when connected with a following letter and in the midst of a word only, when unconnected with the preceding and connected with the following letter, and that it is in no way differing, as regards its pronunciation, from ک; as a final letter the shape of ڪ has never been seen before.

The guttural ṅ, which in the old system was consequently rendered by نک (nk), has been expressed in the new system by ڱ, which is quite inappropriate; for the base is not 'g', but 'n', pronounced with the guttural organ, and in the Arabic consonantal system it can only be rendered by a compound letter (نگ ng). The peculiar Sindhī g̱ is marked ڳ; we have only to point out the inapplicability of two dots beneath گ, and the frequent confusions, to which it will give rise.

In the palatal class we meet with the same inconsequence; the aspirate čh has been taken over from the old system (ڇ), whereas for ǰh the Hindūstānī compound جھ has been borrowed. In the other letters of this class only the dots have been differently distributed; ǰ̄ (in the old system marked ڃ) has been expressed by ڄ, and the palatal ń by ڃ, which is less to the point than the old ڿ, which was as correct as it could be rendered.

In the cerebral class only the dots have been differently arranged as: ṭ = ٽ (old system ٺ), ṭh = ٺ (old system ٽ); ḍ = ڊ (old system the same), ḍh = ڍ (old system the same), ḍ̄ = ڏ (old system ڌ); the cerebral ṛ, which had not been marked at all in the old system, has been borrowed from the Hindūstānī (ڙ), and the cerebral 'ṇ' is marked by the antiquated method of placing a ط above it (ڻ), which is highly inconvenient in writing, and has therefore been justly discarded in Hindūstānī, where formerly the cerebrals used to be marked by the same letter.

In the dental class the old system has been retained unaltered.

In the labial class the base ف was retained for ph, with additional dots (= ڦ; old system ڤ); bh was rendered by ڀ, as in the old system.

We fully allow, that the old Sindhī system of writing did not answer its purposes, quite abstracted from its deficiency; but instead of emendating the old system by a different distribution of dots and inserting a few Hindūstānī letters, we consider it far more advisable, to adopt the whole Hindūstānī consonantal system, and to mark those sounds, which are peculiar to the Sindhī, by convenient dots.

The Sindhī language is restricted to the comparatively small province of Sindh; we cannot therefore see any reason, why the Hindūstānī alphabet, which is known throughout the length and breadth of India, and which is a compact system in itself, should not be preferred to such a motley composition?

The number of the Indian alphabets should not be augmented, but rather, wherever possible, be restricted, as they only serve as barriers to mutual intercourse. If therefore the old system of writing proves unfit for literary purposes, we consider it for the best, to substitute one universally known, instead of emendating imperfectly a local alphabet, which has no chance to spread beyond its narrow borders.

As under the present circumstances it is not likely, that the Hindū portion of the community will adopt the Hindūstānī alphabet, owing to religious scruples on their side, we have chosen for them the Hindī characters, with some slight deviations from the system employed by Capt. Stack, which were imperatively necessary, and which will be noticed further on. We may say the same of the Hindī alphabet, what has been remarked on the Hindūstānī; it is well known throughout India, and the common vehicle of literature amongst the whole Hindū population. An emendation of the old Banyã characters would have been far more useless, than that of the Arabic system current amongst the Moslims.

§. 2.

I. The Sindhī consonantal system.[1])

	SINDHI.						ARABIC LETTERS.
Gutturals:	ک; کھ क; ख k; kh	گ; گھ ग; घ g; gh	ڱ ङ ṅ	ھ ह h	... ...	ڳ ग़ ḡ	ع ح خ غ ق . . . . . ʿ ḣ χ γ q
Palatals:	چ; چھ च; छ č; čh	ج; جھ ज; झ ǰ; ǰh	ڃ ञ ń	ي य y	ش श š	ڄ ज़ ǰ̄	
Cerebrals:	ٽ; ٽھ ट; ठ ṭ; ṭh	ڐ; ڐھ ड; ढ ḍ; ḍh	ڻ ण ṇ	ڙ; ڙھ ड़; ढ़ ṛ; ṛh	... ...	ڏ ड़ ḍ̄	
Linguals:	. .	. .	. .	. .	. .	. .	ض ظ ص ط t̲ s̲ δ̲ z̲
Dentals:	ت; تھ त; थ t; th	د; دھ द; ध d; dh	ن न n	ر; ل र; ल r; l	س स s	... ...	ث ذ ز (ژ Pers.) . . . . ϑ δ z (ž)
Labials:	پ; پھ प; फ p; ph	ب; بھ ब; भ b; bh	م म m	و व v	... ...	ٻ ब़ b̄	ف . f

We subjoin here the common alphabetical order of the Arabic-Sindhī Alphabet:

---

1) In the Romanized transcription we have followed the Standard Alphabet, by Prof Lepsius (2[d] edition).

Unconnected.	Final.	Med.	Initial.	Name.	Pronunciation.
ا	ـا	ـا	ا	اَلِف	ʼ
ب	ـب	ـبـ	بـ	بي	b
ٻ	ـٻ	ـٻـ	ٻـ	ٻَه	b̄
پ	ـپ	ـپـ	پـ	پي	p
ت	ـت	ـتـ	تـ	تي	t
ٿ	ـٿ	ـٿـ	ٿـ	ٿَه	ṭ
ث	ـث	ـثـ	ثـ	ثي	ϑ
ج	ـج	ـجـ	جـ	جِيم	ǰ
ڄ	ـڄ	ـڄـ	ڄـ	ڄَه	j̄
چ	ـچ	ـچـ	چـ	چي	č
ح	ـح	ـحـ	حـ	حي	h̆
خ	ـخ	ـخـ	خـ	خي	χ
د	ـد	ـد	د	دَال	d
ڐ	ـڐ	ـڐ	ڐ	ڐَه	ḍ
ڏ	ـڏ	ـڏ	ڏ	ڏَه	ḍ̄
ذ	ـذ	ـذ	ذ	ذَال	δ
ر	ـر	ـر	ر	ري	r
ڙ	ـڙ	ـڙ	ڙ	ڙَه	ṛ
ز	ـز	ـز	ز	زي	z
ژ	ـژ	ـژ	ژ	ژي	ž

Unconnected.	Final.	Med.	Initial.	Name.	Pronunciation.
س	ـس	ـسـ	سـ	سِين	s
ش	ـش	ـشـ	شـ	شِين	š
ص	ـص	ـصـ	صـ	صَاد	s̱
ض	ـض	ـضـ	ضـ	ضَاد	ẕ
ط	ـط	ـطـ	طـ	طوِي	ṯ
ظ	ـظ	ـظـ	ظـ	ظوِي	δ̱
ع	ـع	ـعـ	عـ	عَيْن	ʿ
غ	ـغ	ـغـ	غـ	غَيْن	γ
ف	ـف	ـفـ	فـ	فِي	f
ق	ـق	ـقـ	قـ	قَاف	q
ڪ	ـڪ, ـك	ـڪـ	ڪـ کـ	ڪَاف	k
گ	ـگ	ـگـ	گـ	گَاف	g
ڳ	ـڳ	ـڳـ	ڳـ	ڳَاف	ḡ
ل	ـل	ـلـ	لـ	لَام	l
م	ـم	ـمـ, ـمـ	مـ	مِيم	m
ن	ـن	ـنـ	نـ	نُون	n
ڻ	ـڻ	ـڻـ	ڻـ	ڻَه	ṇ
و	ـو	ـو	و	وَاو	v
ه	ـه, ـھ	ـهـ, ـھـ	هـ	هِي	h
ي	ـي	ـيـ	يـ	يِي	y

The (purely) Arabic letters are also used as numeral values, in recording (by brief sentences, in which the sum of all the letters must be added together) historical events.

ا	1	ح	8	س	60	ت	400
ب	2	ط	9	ع	70	ث	500
ج	3	ي	10	ف	80	خ	600
د	4	ك	20	ص	90	ذ	700
ه	5	ل	30	ق	100	ض	800
و	6	م	40	ر	200	ظ	900
ز	7	ن	50	ش	300	غ	1000

This method of computation is called abǰad, from the first four letters, which are pronounced as a group. The following technical groups are:

هَوَز, حَطِي, كَلْمَن, سَعْفَص, قَرْشَت, ثَخَذ, ضَظَغ.

The Arabs have borrowed this whole system from the Hebrews and have therefore also followed the order of the Hebrew alphabet; the first nine letters represent the units 1 — 9; the nine following the tens, the nine following the hundreds and the last غ a thousand.

The order of the Hebrew alphabet goes only as far as ت (400); from thence the Arabs have gone their own way, by using those letters, which are peculiar to their own language.

1) The Gutturals.

The gutturals k, g are pronounced in the common manner; their aspirates, kh, gh, as all other aspirates, form, according to the Sanskrit system, one sound, and must therefore be pronounced by a strong breathing of the respective simple base. Peculiar to the Sindhī is the guttural ṅ, which is throughout used as an independent sound (like the english ng in "sing"), and never precedes the letters of its own varga or class, in which case Anusvāra or simple n is employed (see Introduction §. 5). In the Hindī alphabet it is expressed by ङ, it being an original Sanskrit sound, but the Arabic system, which knows only one dental n (ن), offers great difficulties in this as in other respects. In Hindūstānī an independent guttural ṅ is not to be met with; we have therefore been compelled to circumscribe it by the compound نگ ng, which comes nearest to it, following therein the track of the old Sindhī alphabet. But one difficulty still will remain, that the guttural simple ṅ can thus not be distinguished from the guttural ṅ preceding a letter of its own varga, as: اَنگُ (अङु) aṇu, body, and اَنگُ (अंगु, or more properly: अङ्गु) angu (aṅgu) a limb. In the alphabet, now in use, an attempt has been made, as has been adverted to, to obviate this difficulty (viz.: ڱ = ṅ), but we cannot agree, that the problem has been solved satisfactorily, a false base having been chosen for the guttural nasal. Practically the difficulty will be easily surmounted by any careful student, as there are only a few nouns in the language, in which simple guttural ṅ is found.

We subjoin here an alphabetical list of all those words, in which the simple (unconnected) guttural nasal is to be found:

اَنگُ m. aṅu, body; اَنگارو m. aṅārō, Tuesday. اَنگاري f. aṅārī, a disease of the gums etc. اَنگاريو m. aṅāryō, a bruise in the sole of the foot; اَنگرُ n. aṅaru, coal; اَنگُرُ m. aṅuru, a finger's breadth. آنگرِ f. āṅure, a finger; toe; اَنگَڻُ m. aṅaṇu, courtyard; آنگُوٺهو m. āṅūthō, the thumb; آنگُوٺِهي f. āṅūṭhī, a thumb-ring. ڀهَانگو m. bhāṅō, share, and its derivatives, as: ڀهَانگائِتو adj. bhāṅāitō, in shares; ڀهَانگيرو m. bhāṅērō, a sharer. ڦهينگَڻو m. phēṅaṇō, the orbicular excrement of camels (ڦهينگِڻِي f. phēṅiṇī, the orbicular excrement of sheep etc.). جَانگُورو m. ǰāṅūrō, the wild Beru fruit; جَانگُورِي f. ǰāṅūrī, the wild Beru tree; چَنگو adj. čaṅō, good, and its derivatives. دهِنگائِي m. dhiṅāī, a manufacturer of saltpetre; ڏانگوَرَڻُ v. a. ḍāṅōraṇu, to flog; ڏُنگِٽو adj. ḍuṅiṭō, stout; ڏُنگِرِي f. ḍuṅirī, a stick to beat clothes with (in washing); ڏهُنگِڻو m. ḍhuṅiṇō, name of a fish. رَنگُ m. raṅu, colour; رَنگَڻُ v. a. raṅaṇu, to dye, and its derivatives; رَنگو m. raṅō, a carpenter's chalk-string. سَانگاهَ f. sāṅāha, or: سَانگهَ f. sāṅaha, care, and its derivatives (as: سَانگاهِتو adj. sāṅāhitō, careful, سَانگاهُو adj. sāṅāhū, ditto); سَانگاهَڻُ v. n. sāṅāhaṇu, to be careful. سَنگُ m. saṅu, connexion by marriage, and its derivatives; سِنگُ m. siṅu, born, and its derivatives; سِنگارِي f. siṅārī, name of a fish (or: سِيگارِي sīṅārī); سَنگرُ m. saṅaru, the seed-pod of the thorn-tree; سَنگَڻُ v. a. saṅaṇu, to point out; سِينگَ f. sīṅa, bow. ڳَانگو m. ḡāṅō, or ڳانگِي f. ḡāṅī, name of a fruit and shrub (Grewia betuloefolia). لَنگُ m. laṅu, lameness (لَنگو adj. laṅō, lame); لِنگُ m. liṅu, limb; لِنگَ f. liṅa, a trip in carrying; لِنکو m. linō, time, turn (besides: لِنگا f. linā, ditto). مَنک f. mana, a betrothed girl; مُنک m. munu, a grain of mung; مَنگَر m. manaru, fire; مُنگِرو m. munirō, a mallet (used by washermen); مَنگَڻُ v. a. mananu, to ask, to beg, and its derivatives; مونکو adj. mōno, having the colour of mung; نِنگنو adj. & adv. ninunō, entirely, wholly. وَانگَڻُ m. vānanu, the egg-plant, and its derivatives; هِنگ f. hinu, Assafoetida; هِنگِرو m. hinirō, name of a fruit of an aquatic plant.

Another letter peculiar to the Sindhī is گ, ग़, g̱; it is not found in Hindī or Hindūstānī, nor in any of the cognate dialects, and we have therefore been compelled to provide it with a mark of its own. After the precedent of the Paṣṭō we have added a hook below the under parallel line, which marks off this letter strongly enough, without giving rise to any confusion or misconception. The pronunciation of g̱ is quite peculiar; it is that of the letter g uttered with a certain stress in prolonging and somewhat strengthening the contact of the closed organ, as if one tried to double the sound in the beginning of a word, as gga. The pronunciation is so far quite in accordance with the origin of this and the other three letters, peculiar to the Sindhī, though they are now treated to all intents and purposes as simple letters; e. g. اَگُ āg̱u, the front, Prāk. अग्ग, Sansk. अग्र (compare Introduction §. 15, *b*); لَگو lag̱ō, applied, Prāk. लग्ग, Sansk. लग्न (see Introduction §. 14); بهَگو bhag̱ō, broken, Prāk. भग्ग, Sansk. भग्न. In other instances, where an original doubling of g cannot be proved etymologically, the use of this harsh g̱ must be explained by the influence of the following letters, as: گوٿهُ g̱ōṭhu, a village, Prāk. गोट्ठ, Sansk. गोष्ठ; in this, as in similar cases, the weight of the double ṭṭh, which in Sindhī has been reduced to its simple base by the prolongation of the preceding vowel, seems to have been thrown forward on g. Such an influence is especially exercised by a following r, as: ڳَرو g̅arō, heavy, Prāk. गरुअ, Sansk. गुरु.

Both letters, g and g̅, must be carefully distinguished in pronunciation, as the signification of a word varies considerably according to the use of one or the other letter, as: گَرو garō, mangy, but ڳَرو g̅arō, heavy etc.

2) The palatals.

The palatals ج ǰ and چ č, and their respective aspirates جهه ǰh, and چهه čh, are pronounced in the common Indian way as simple sounds, and are grammatically treated as such, though they are, according to their present pronunciation, compound sounds. Originally they cannot have been pronounced, as they are at present, for else the grammatical rules of Pāṇini would be incomprehensible. In our days ج is pronounced as english j, and چ as english ch, that is to say, as dž and tš respectively; how these sounds, if they are to be treated as simple ones, should be aspirated or doubled by any human organ, is past our conception. The old pronunciation of these letters[1]) must have gone through great variations, till they have become the compound sounds of the modern Indian idioms.[2]) In the Roman transcription they have therefore not been marked by the palatal stroke (‿), but by the same sign, with

---

1) See Standard alphabet, p. 93.

2) The pronunciation of the Marāṭhī च and ज as ts and dz respectively before the vowels a, ā, u, ū, ai, ō, does not fall under this head, as this is owing to Drāvidian influences and only occurs in words of non-Arian origin.

which the sibilant sh (= š) is provided, to point out their modern pronunciation.

The Sindhī has preserved the palatal nasal ń (ञ) as an independent sound, which never precedes the letters of its own varga, for which purpose anusvāra (and in Hindūstānī writing simple ن) is used. The Hindūstānī being destitute of a palatal nasal, we had to provide a new character. Following the analogy of the old Sindhī alphabet we chose for it the compound ڄ, which comes nearest to it, for the palatal ń of the Sindhī is properly a compound sound, and is pronounced ny. The proper circumscription by ني would not do for this reason, that the palatal ń is still considered by the Sindhī as a simple sound and rendered in Sanskrit writing by ञ; it ought therefore to be pointed out, as near as possible, as such, for which purpose the compound ڄ answers much better, than ني, which latter would give rise to many misconceptions. In the Romanized transcription it has simply been furnished with the palatal line = ń.

The sign chosen for it in the alphabet at present in use viz.: ڃ, is not to the purpose, as the base is not ج, but the nasal ن, with a subsounding y.

The sibilant ش, श š, which we have inserted in our scheme in the palatal row, is no longer a palatal sound at all, but a pure dental sh = š. The original pronunciation of श is more than doubtful; now-a-days it is in no way differing from our common sh, and might therefore be as well classed under the dentals. The Arabic-Persian ش is always rendered in Sanskrit writing by श; but it is also found in pure Sindhī words, as: شِينْهُ šīhu, lion etc. compare; Introduction §. 5.

Peculiar to the Sindhī is ڄ, ॼ, ǰ. It is now treated as a simple sound, but it has in most cases, as etymology proves, sprung from a double ǰǰ (= ज्ज), and is still pronounced as a compound sound = dy; e. g.: اَڄُ āju (= adyu), to-day, Prāk. अज्ज, Sansk. अद्य (on the assimilating process see Introd. §. 15.); وِڄا vijā, science, Prāk. विज्जा, Sansk. विद्या; وِڄُ vēju, physician, Prāk. वेज्ज, Sansk. वैद्य. In other nouns though an original doubling of ڄ cannot be traced etymologically, as: ڄَٽُ jaṭu, a Jat, Hindī जट; and ڄ is in such instances frequently exchanged for ج, as: ڄاٽِري jāṭrī, or: جاٽِري jāṭrī, a pilgrim, Sansk. यात्री).

3) The Cerebrals.

The cerebrals ٽ ṭ and ڊ ḍ, and their respective aspirates, ٺ ṭh and ڍ ḍh are common to all the North-Indian vernaculars; they are pronounced by turning the tip of the tongue towards the roof of the mouth whilst sounding the dental bases, t, d, etc. respectively.

The Sindhī has likewise preserved an independent cerebral ڻ, ण, ṇ, which is not bound to the letters of its own varga as: وَڻُ vaṇu, a tree (Sansk. वनं) ٿَڻُ thaṇu, the teat of an animal, Hindī थन्, Sansk. स्तन. It is pronounced very hard and resembles much the compound nṛ (in Paṣ̌tō it is therefore very frequently rendered by nṛ).

In Sindhī it exchanges therefore occasionally its place with the cerebral ṛ, as: ماڻهون māṇhū̃, man, or: ماڙهون māṛhū̃. The cerebral ڊ ḍ, which in Prākrit already frequently supplants the dental d, has in Sindhī given birth to two other cerebral sounds, viz.: ڏ, ड ḍ, and ڙ, ड़ ṛ, and this again aspirated, ڙه, ढ़ ṛh.

ڏ, ड ḍ is pronounced in a similar way as g̈; the cerebral ḍ (ڊ) is uttered with a certain stress in prolonging and somewhat strengthening the contact of the closed organ, as if a double ḍ was to be pronounced.

Originally it is, as g̃, a double ḍ, as may be still proved in most cases by etymology; e. g.: وڏو vaḍ̄ō, great, Prāk. वड्ड, Sansk. वड्र; چوڏهون čōḍ̄ahō̃, the fourteenth, Prāk. चोद्दहो. But the Sindhī, which is very fond of hard cerebral sounds, often employs this letter ḍ̄, where no original doubling of the cerebral has taken place, especially at the beginning of words, where the full stress of the voice can be laid upon it, as: ڏولي ḍ̄ōlī, a kind of sedan chair, Prāk. डोला, Sansk. दोला (compare Introd. §. 6. 4). The simple cerebral ڊ has been thus nearly totally supplanted at the beginning of a noun by ḍ̄, and ḍ is only found in a few nouns, to distinguish them from others written else quite alike, as: ڊِٺهو ḍiṭhō, obstinate, but ڏِٺهو ḍ̄iṭhō, seen.

It has therefore been a great mistake of Capt. Stack, that he has not distinguished ड ḍ from ड़ ḍ̄, and marked both sounds by the same diacritical dot (= ड़), though he has been aware of their different pronunciation. A Sindhī will never confound ڏ ḍ̄ with ڊ ḍ; they are in his mouth thoroughly distinct from each other and have been differently marked already in the old Sindhī alphabet (viz.: ḍ = ٻ, and ḍ̄ = ڏ). We were therefore compelled in this respect to deviate from Capt. Stack's Sanskrit alphabet, retaining for the simple cerebral ḍ the original Sanskrit letter ड, and marking the sound of ḍ̄ by a line beneath ड (= ड॒), the dot beneath ड being reserved for some other sound, which we shall presently notice.

The cerebral ڙ, ड़ ṛ, and its aspirate ڙه, ढ़ ṛh have sprung from the cerebral ڊ ḍ and ڊه ḍh respectively (see Introduction §. 7, 2), as: گُڙ g̃uṛu, molasses, Sansk. गुड; ڏِڙهتا ḍ̄riṛhatā (ड्रिढ़ता) firmness, Sansk. दृढता. We have noticed already (l. c.), that by far the greatest number of words, in which ṛ or ṛh is to be found, is taken from some aboriginal tongue, which is now lost, and wich must have had a great predilection for cerebral sounds (as the Drāvidian idioms of the south) and to the influence of which the preponderance of the cerebrals in the north Indian vernaculars must be ascribed.

The two peculiar letters ट़ (ṭr) and ड़ (ḍr), which Capt. Stack in his Sindhī Grammar has advocated for the Sindhī under the cerebral class, are found, on nearer investigation to be compound sounds (see Introduction, §. 15.) and may therefore be safely discarded from the alphabet, as they ought to be written ट्र ṭr and ड्र ḍr respectively, as: पुट्रु puṭru, son, Prāk. पुत्त, Sansk. पुत्र; ड्राख ḍrākha, grape, Sansk. द्राक्षा. A subscribed r is also found in some nouns with the aspirate ढ ḍh, as: ढ्रापणु ḍhrāpaṇu, to be satiated, and its derivatives, as: ढ्राइणु ḍhrāiṇu, to satiate; ढ्राउ ḍhrāu, satiety, all of which are sprung from the Sansk. root तृप् (तर्पण); ड्ढ्रु ḍaḍhru (also written: ड्ढु ḍaḍhu), a cutaneous disease, Sansk. दद्रु, Hindī दाद् (compare Introduction §. 15. *b.* β).

We have not inserted the cerebral ṣ ष in the Sindhī alphabet, though in Capt. Stack's Sindhī Dictionary a few words are written with ष. This letter is completely ignored by the common people and left unnoticed in the old Sindhī alphabet; only a Brāhman now and then uses it, to show his knowledge of Sanskrit (compare Introduction §. 5).

4) The dentals.

The dental row offers nothing particular; र r, which is considered a cerebral in Sanskrit, has become a pure dental in the modern idioms.

5) The labials.

It is to be noted, that ڦ, फ ph, is to be pronounced as the aspirate of پ, प p, and never as f, which is of Arabic or Persian origin, wherever found.

Peculiar to the Sindhī is the letter ٻ, ॿ b̄; it is pronounced in the same way as ḡ and ḏ, being originally a double b, as: ٻَ b̄a, two, Sansk. द्व (= vva = bba; see Introduction §. 15. *d.* α); ڪُٻو kub̄ō, hump-backed (see Introd. §. 13); ڏُٻَلُ ḏab̄alu, weak, Prāk. दुब्बल, Sansk. दुर्बल. In other nouns however an original doubling of b cannot be traced out, and the language seems to use ب b and ٻ b̄ quite arbitrarily, as: بَابو bābō, father, but, ٻَابو bab̄ō, father's brother, both nouns being derived from the Turkish بَابَا father.

The nasal of this class is m; but when preceding a letter of its own varga it is supplanted by simple n (or anusvāra), as in all the other rows; e. g.: اَنْبُ (अंबु) ambu, a mango; ڪُنْڀَارُ (कुंभारु) kumbhāru, a potter.

§. 3.

On the purely Arabic letters.

The Sindhī, as well as the Hindūstānī, has, in consequence of the forced introduction of the Islām, been considerably mixed up with Arabic elements, and though the vulgar pay no attention to the particular pronunciation of the genuine Arabic sounds, the original Arabic orthography has been generally adhered to.

Under the guttural class we find the letters: ع, ح, خ, غ, ق, the Roman transcription of which we have conformed to the Standard alphabet, though these letters are somewhat differently pronounced in Sindhī. ع, which is in Arabic treated as a consonant, is generally ignored and only its accompanying vowel articulated, as: عَقُلُ ʿaqulu, intelligence, is sounded: akulu. In the midst of a word ع is either passed unnoticed (i. e. only the respective vowel is uttered) as: نِعمَت niamata (properly:

niꜥamata) or ع with its accompanying vowel is pronounced as a long syllable, as: نَعْلْبَنْدُ a ferrier, is sounded like: nālbandu (properly: naꜥlbandu) and by ignorant people also written accordingly; or the ع with its respective vowel is dropped altogether; as: طَعَامُ food (taꜥāmu) is commonly pronounced: tāmu. The same is the case at the end of a word, where ع with its vowel is contracted by the vulgar to a long syllable, as: جَمَعَ receipt-account (jamaꜥa) is pronounced like jamā, and mostly written accordingly; only the Mullās, who pretend to a knowledge of Arabic, affect the deep guttural articulation of the Arabic. In Sanskrit writing ع is therefore simply rendered according to its accompanying vowel, and not dinstinguished by any particular mark or dot.

The deep Arabic ح ȟ is treated in the same way and pronounced as simple h, as: حَالُ ȟālu, state, is sounded: hālu. The Arabic and Persian خ χ is commonly pronounced by the vulgar (especially the Hindūs, who are quite unable to articulate χ) as kh, as: شِيخَ šīχa, a spit, is sounded: šīkha (Pers. سِيخ).

The Arabic or Persian غ γ is pronounced in Sindhī as simple g, and very frequently exchanged for گ in writing, as: بَاغُ bāγu, garden, is sounded as: bāgu; غَمُ γamu, grief, as: gamu etc.

The deep guttural ق q of the Arabic is articulated in Sindhī like simple k, as: قومَ qōma, a tribe, clan (Arabic قَوْم), is pronounced like: kōma; قَوْلُ qaulu, word, like: kaulu etc. The Hindūs ignore all these foreign letters in their writings and render them by the nearest Sanskrit consonants, as has been adverted to.

The lingual letters, which are peculiar to the Arabic, are not distinguished in Sindhī pronunciation from the corresponding dentals; ط ṯ is sounded like common t, and ص s̱ like z; ظ δ and ض ẕ likewise as z. The Hindūs on the other hand pronounce ظ and ض like ǰ, and render these letters promiscuously according to their actual pronunciation, which is frequently done by the Musalmāns likewise, especially the unlearned.

The Arabic letters, which figure under the dental row, viz.: ث ϑ, ذ δ, and ز z (the two latter of which are also common to the Persian) are pronounced in Sindh (and India generally) as follows: ث like s, ذ and ز like z, whereas the Hindūs pronounce these two latter consonants like ǰ and render them also accordingly by ज़, which is not unfrequently done by the Moslims also.

The Arabic and Persian ف f is sounded by the Muhammadans as f, but by the Hindūs as ph, and rendered in their writings by फ़

§. 4.

II. The Sindhī vowel system.

We next subjoin a tabular survey of the Sindhī vowel system.

1) Simple vowels:

اَ,	آ	اِ	اِي	اُ	اُو
अ,	आ	इ	ई	उ	ऊ
a,	ā	i (e)	ī	u	ū

اي	او
ए	ओ
ē	ō

2) Diphthongs:

اَيْ	اَوْ
ऐ	औ
ai	au

3) Nasalized vowels.

اَن	آن	اِن	اِين	اُن	اُون
अं	आं	इं	ईं	उं	ऊं
ã	ā̃	ĩ	ī̃	ũ,	ū̃
		اِين	اون		
		एं	ओं		
		ẽ	õ		
		اَيْن	اَوْن		
		ऐं	औं		
		aĩ	aũ		

1) Simple vowels.[1]) The Sindhī uses all the vowels, common to the Sanskrit and Prākrit; but it is to be noted, that i, when preceded or followed by h, or when closing a word, has the sound of short e (see Introduction §. 2. *b*). Ē and ō are in Sindhī, as already in Prākrit, simple (and not Guṇa) vowels (see Introduction §. 2. *d*), and consequently always long (and not anceps, as in Prākrit).

As the Arabic is destitute of the sounds ē and ō, a great difficulty arises in Sindhī as well as in Hindūstānī, how to distinguish ī from ē, and ū from ō. The Indian grammarians have therefore invented the term of يائی مَجْهُول yā-e majhūl, or the unknown ي for the sound ē, and وَاوِ مَجْهُول vave majhūl, or the unknown و, for the sound ō; but at the same time no practical measures were taken, to mark off ē and ō by any diacritical sign, and the reader was left to help himself,

1) As we shall further on employ only the Hindūstānī characters, we cannot enter here more minutely on the Sanskrit vowel system, and we refer therefore the student for nearer information to any Sanskrit grammar. We shall only make use of the Sanskrit characters in the course of this grammar, as occasion may call for.

as best he could. But as the distinction of ī from ē and ū from ō is somewhat difficult for a beginner, especially a European, and for the right understanding of the language very important, we have contrived to distinguish ē from ī by a perpendicular line, as: کي kē, some, کِي kī, somewhat; and ō from ū by placing the sign ـٓ above و, as: توٓن tō̃, from-on; تُون tū̃, thou. In prints, destined for the use of natives, these distinctions may be dispensed with as more or less superfluous; but in prints, intended for the use of Europeans I have no doubt they will prove very serviceable and clear away many a stumbling block.

In Arabic writing the short vowels a, i, u are not expressed in the body of the consonants, but by mere marks, placed above or beneath the consonant, after which they are to be sounded; if the consonant happen to be an aspirate, the vowel mark is placed on the accessory ھ. The mark for a is ـَ, and is called فَتْحَه fatḥah (in Persian زَبَر zabar); the mark for i is ـِ, and is called كَسْرَه kasrah (in Persian زِير zīr, pronounced in India: zēr); the mark for u is ـُ, and is called ضَمَّه ẕammah (in Persian پيش pīš, pronounced in India: pēš) e. g. فَنَ fana, فِنِ fini, فُنُ funu. But if a noun commence with a short vowel, ا (alif) must serve as base for the these vowels, the vowels themselves being considered only as auxiliary signs for the consonants, as: اَنَ ana, اِنِ ini, اُنُ unu. In Arabic initial ا is in these cases always provided with hamzah, as: أَنَ, إِنِ, أُنُ, but in Hindūstānī it is dispensed with, to which practice we shall also adhere in Sindhī.

The three long vowels: ā, ī, ū are expressed in the body of the consonants by the letters ا, ي, و, with the addition of the respective vowel points; in this case

ا, ي, و are called سَاكِن sākin, or quiescent, because they are not moved by a vowel of their own; e. g.: هَارِي hārī, a peasant; مَارُو mārū, a beater; مُوڙِي mūṛī, capital (in trade) چِيڪَاٽ čīkāṭu, creaking. The same holds good with reference to the vowels ē and ō, which are not (originally) distinguished in writing from ī and ū, as: چهيرو čhērō, whetting.[1])

Long a, when initial, is expressed by ا and the sign ~ placed above it, as: آدَرُ ādaru, courtesy. This sign is called مَدَّهْ maddah, i. e. extension, and is properly an alif placed above horizontally. Long i and u, when initial, must be preceded by alif, to support the respective vowel point, as ي and و themselves are quiescent; e. g.: اِيهو īhō, this very person; اُوهو ūhō, that very person. The same is the case with ē and ō, as: ايڏو ēḍō, so large, اوڏو ōḍō, near.

ي and و, when quiescent, should be provided with the sign jazm (ـْ), to indicate thereby, that they are not moved by a vowel of their own, as: اِيْهو, اُوْهو, پِيْرُ pīru; but this practice is generally neglected in Hindūstānī, as superfluous. If on the other hand ي and و be moved by a vowel put above or beneath them, they are no longer quiescent, but regular consonants, as: يَارُ yāru, friend; نِيَانُ niyāṇu, a tank; وَڻُ vaṇu, tree; نِوَائِي nivāi, want of wind; وَاوَ vāva, formative of وَاءُ vāu, wind.

---

1) In some Arabic nouns final ى (generally without dots) is used with the power of alif, as: عِيسَى ʿīsā, Jesus; ذِكرَى ḏikrā remembrance. Note also the antiquated writing صَلوت ẕalāt, prayer, تَوْرِيت taurāt, the Thōrah (pentateuch), which is falsely pronounced in India: taurēt.

2) The diphthongs ai and au.

The diphthongs ai and au are expressed in Arabic by a preceding fatĥah and a following quiescent ي or و, which should be provided in this case with jazm, to prevent mistakes, as: اَيْٽرُ aiṭru, spinning wheel; بَيْراڳِي bairāgī, an ascetic; اَوْٺهو auṭhō, impure; چَوْڌَارِي čaudhārī, round about. At the end of a noun no diphthong is admissible in Sindhī; compare Introduction, §. 1, 2.

3) The nasalized vowels or Anusvāra.

We have noticed already, that the simple dental n (ن) is now used in Sindhī before the letters of any varga indiscriminately, which in Sanskrit writing is commonly expressed not by the dental न, but by the sign called Anusvāra (ं) e. g.: کَنگالُ (कंगालु) kangālu (properly: kaṅgālu) poor; گَنْجو (गंजो) ganjō, scald-headed; نَنْڍهو (नंढो) nanḍhō, small; رَنْدُ (रंदु) randu, path; ٻانبهَ (ॿांभ) bāmbha, hag.

But besides this full nasal the Sindhī also uses the proper Anusvāra, which only communicates to the respective vowel a nasalizing touch, very extensively, and as both, full n and the nasalizing touch, which is communicated to a vowel, are expressed in Sanskrit writing by Anusvāra, and in Hindūstānī by the dental n (ن), some confusion necessarily arises from this practice, to obviate which the following remarks should be carefully attended to.

α) Anusvāra (or ن) preceding another consonant must always be pronounced as a full nasal, if the vowel of the syllable be short, as: पंधु, پَنْڌهُ pandhu, journey; but if Anusvāra precede 'h' in a short syllable, it is always to be pronounced as such, i. e. only a slight nasalizing touch is thereby communicated to the vowel, as: जंहिं, جَنْهِن jāhē; मुंहु, مُنْھُ mũhu, mouth; in a few words, where full n precedes h, it must be rendered in Sanskrit writing by न, not by Anusvāra, as: चिन्हु činhu, a sign; थन्हणु thanhaṇu, to compress. In Hindūstānī writing no such distinction can be made, as there is only one (ن) at hand, which must serve as full nasal or Anusvāra, as the case may be; nothing is therefore left to the student, but to commit these few words to memory. We must repeat here, what has been remarked already, that the use of the Arabic characters offers great difficulties when applied to a Prākrit language of India.

b) Anusvāra preceding a consonant in a long syllable is to be pronounced as a full nasal, as: बांठि, بانٺھ bānṭhe, ravenousness; पींघ, پينگھ pīngha, a swing; कूंधु, ڪُوندھُ kūndhu, a young man; वेंदो, وِيندو vēndō, going; लोंबड़ु, لونبَڙُ lōmbaṛu, a male fox. But if the long vowels, provided with Anusvāra, be followed by h, s or v, they are to be pronounced with a nasalizing touch only, as: थांहर, ٿھانھر thā̃hara, steadiness; मांसु, مانْسُ mā̃su, meat, थांवरु, ٿھانْوَرُ thā̃varu, Friday; मींहु, مِينھُ mī̃hu, rain; मेंहि, مينھِ mē̃he, buffalo etc. Where full n precedes h in a long syllable, it must be rendered by न (in Hindūstānī writing a further distinction is impossible), as: ॿान्ही, ٻانھِي ḇānhī, a slave-girl, but: ॿांह, ٻانْھَ ḇā̃ha, arm.

c) At the end of a word Anusvāra always retains its proper nasalizing touch, be the final vowel short or long, as: प्रीं, پِرِين prī̃, friend; भूं, ڀھُون bhū̃, earth; मुंहिं mũhẽ (Formative of the I. pronoun sing.); also in compound words, as: भूंभूं, ڀھُون ڀھُون bhū̃ bhū̃, buzzing. This rule is based on the fact, that in Sindhī every word must needs end in a vowel (which however may be nasalized).

d) Anusvāra, placed between two vowels, be they short or long, always retains its proper nasalizing sound, as: अंइं, اَنئِن ãī, and; मांइणु, مَانئِڻُ mãiṇu, to measure; आंउं, آنئُون ãū, I; किआंउं, ڪِئَانئُون kiãū, it has been done by them (compare: Introduction §. 4).

The same holds good with reference to Anusvāra, following a diphthong (see: Introduction §. 1, 2), as: रौंशो, رَوْنشو raũšō, merriment (= rāušō); मैंठ, مَيْنٺهَ maĩṭha, madder (= māiṭha).

In the Romanized transcription, which we shall add throughout this grammar, the two different sounds of Anusvāra are rendered in this way, that the sound of full n is always expressed by n, whereas the nasalizing touch, which is communicated to a vowel by Anusvāra, is marked by the sign ~ placed above it, as: अंतु, اَنْتُ = antu; but आंउं, آنئُون = ãū.

We have already adverted to the great difficulties, under which the Hindūstānī labours to mark the original sound of Anusvāra, as it has only one n (and this the dental n) at its disposal. The difficulty is already great in Hindūstānī, and still greater in Sindhī, which is so much addicted to the use of nasalized vowels. In addition to what has been stated already, we beg to turn the attention of the student, as far as the Hindūstānī characters are concerned, to the following points:

Final ں has always the sound of Anusvāra proper (see under c) and need therefore not perplex the student, as: مَاڙهُون mãṛhũ, man; زالُون zālũ, women; اِئَان iã, from this place, تِئَان tiã, from that place.

Anusvāra, separating two short or long vowels (see under d) is rendered by ن, and can be recognized as such by its position; in this case, to obviate all misconceptions, we have furnished the second vowel with hamzah, to point out thereby, that the following vowel is not to be read together with the preceding, but that ن closes the first syllable, as: اِنئِ (इंअ) ī-a, thus; تِنئِ (तिंअ) tĩ-a, in that manner; گنُون (गंउ) gãũ, cow. If the second vowel chance to be a long one, ى (without dots) provided with hamzah must precede the same, to serve as basis for the vowel point (see further on under: Hamzah), as: سَانئِين sãĩ (सांई) lord; هِنئو (हिंओ) hĩō, mind; چِئَانئُون čiãũ, it has been said by them.

In such like instances, as exhibited under *a* and *b*, the Hindūstānī alphabet offers no means of distinguishing the full nasal from Anusvāra proper, as: ٻَانهِي ƀānhī, a slave-girl, ٻَانهَ ƀãha, arm, and these difficulties can only be overcome by practice. In the old Sindhī alphabet and in that now in use no notice whatever is taken of these and such like intricacies.

§. 5.

On the other orthographic signs.

1) The sign ٓ (مَدَّة maddah, prolongation) is placed on initial alif, to render it long, as: آتهَرُ ātharu, pack-saddle. In the midst and at the end of a word maddah is not placed on alif, if the preceding consonant be moved by fatĥah, in which case alif is called سَاكِن sākin, or quiescent, as: رَاجَا rā-jā, prince; مَالَا mā-lā, garland; but if the preceding consonant is provided with jazm (i. e. not moved by a vowel), alif must have the sign of maddah, as commencing a syllable, e. g.: قُرْآنُ qur-ānu, Qorān, not qu-rānu.

2) The sign ْ (جَزْم jazm, abscission), placed above

a consonant denotes, that the consonant thus marked is not moved by a vowel, as: وِيلْهو vel-hō, idle; مَرْڙُ mar̤-du, man; سَرْڳُ sar-gu, heaven. In old Sindhī writings the use of jazm is hardly to be met with, as they preferred to provide such a mute letter with kasrah, the sound of which was hardly heard in pronunciation, as: مَرِڙُ mar̤i-du, instead of مَرْڙُ mar̤-du, and served quite the purposes of jasm. We cannot adopt this system, as in many cases it will give rise to confusion and misconceptions.

3) The sign ـّـ (تَشْدِيد tašdīd) corroboration, placed above a consonant denotes, that the letter in question is to be doubled. In the old Sindhī writings the tašdīd is hardly ever to be met with, as they were in the habit to express even an originally double letter by its simple base, e. g.: ڪَمُ kamu, business, instead of ڪَمُّ kammu. It is now used only in such instances, where the doubling of a consonant is rendered necessary in order to distinguish two in other respects identical words, as: اُنَ una, by him, and اُنَّ unna, wool.

4) The sign ـٔـ (هَمْزَه hamzah, i. e. punction) is used in the midst and at the end of words as a vicarious base for ا; when two vowels, short or long, meet in a word, the second vowel must be supported by the base ی, furnished with hamzah, e. g.: پِئُ piu, father; جُئِ jue, the den of an animal; هِينئَرَ hīara, now; جُنئَ jūa, louse; قائِمُ qā-imu, standing; ڀهائُرَ bhāura, brothers; جِيئُ jī-u, life; ڪُئو kuō, rat; گهائُو ghā-ū, wounding; اَئِي a-ī, a goal etc.

A final short vowel, preceded by ā, ū, ō is usually supported by the sign hamzah alone, as: ڀهاءُ bhā-u, brother;

pō-e, after; هُوءِ hū-e, sound. But if و be radical in a word, hamzah with its accompanying vowel is placed upon ؤ, as: نَائُو nãu, fame, Formative نَاءْوَ nãva; گئُون gãũ, cow; ماڙهُئَ mārḥũa, Formative of: ماڙهون mārḥũ, man.

In the Formative Singular of such nouns, which end in ī, hamzah is dropped for brevity's sake, as: هَنڊِي handī, a pot, Formative: هَنْڊِيَ handia (instead of هَنْڊِئَ); but in nouns like سَائيِن sāĩ, lord, hamzah must be retained in the Formative, to prevent mistakes, as: سَائِئَ sãĩa.

Note. The sign ٱ (وَصْل vaṣl, conjunction) only occurs in Arabic phrases and constructions; it joins two words, the latter of which begins with alif, the accompanying vowel of which is dropped and the final vowel of the preceding word drawn over or rather joined to the following; e. g.: عَبْدُ ٱلْمَلِكِ ʒabdu-lmaliki (instead of: عَبْدُ أَلْمَلِكِ); قَالَ ٱسْمَعْ qāla-smaʒ (instead of: قَالَ إِسْمَعْ); بِسْمِ ٱللّٰهِ bismi-llāhi.

The use of the so-called Tanvīn (i. e. ـٌ اً, ـٍ, pronounced in Arabic 'un', 'an', 'in') in Sindhī is to be disproved of, as the Tanvīn is only a fanciful invention of the Arabian grammarians, and by no means fit to express the Sindhī nasalized short (and least the long) vowels.

SECTION I.

THE FORMATION OF THEMES IN SINDHI.

Chapter I.

The termination of Sindhi nouns.

§. 6.

In the formation of themes the relative position, which the Sindhī holds to the Sanskrit-Prākrit on the one side, and to its modern sister-tongues on the other side, is most clearly delineated.

The peculiarity of the Sindhī, and at the same time the great advantage, which is possesses over the kindred idioms consists therein, that every noun, substantive, adjective, pronoun, participle and infinitive ends in a vowel. By this vocalic termination the Sindhī has preserved a flexibility, and at the same time a sonorousness, of which the other modern vernaculars are completely destitute.

After what has been remarked on the nature of the diphthongs in Sindhī (see Introduction §. 1), it may be easily gathered, that no Sindhī noun can end in a diphthong. A Sindhī noun may therefore end in a, i (e), u; ā, ī, ū, ō; no noun ever ends in ē, and those, which seem to do so, are not in the Nominative, but in the inflected case. A final vowel may also be nasalized, as: مَاڙهُون māṛhū̃, man, چوٿهون čōthō̃, the fourth; پرِين prī̃, friend, which is especially the case, if a word terminate in a long vowel, but this constitutes, after what we have said on the nature of Anusvāra, no exception to the general rule.

In the formation of themes the Sindhī has in the main followed the course pointed out by the Prākrit, but it has created many new formations, independent and irrespective of the Prākrit. The levelling process of the modern idioms has already gained the ascendancy, and terminations, which the Prākrit, though seized already by the same tendency, has as yet kept asunder, have been thrown together into one class in Sindhī.

The Sindhī has lost the neuter, which has been already discarded in the Apabhransha dialect of the Prākrit, the immediate predecessor of the modern Sindhī. This, as it seems, has been the first step, to break the fetters of the old compact mother-tongue, and to initiate the levelling process of the present idiom.

Inasmuch as the Sindhī requires a vocalic termination for every noun, the distinction of the gender is not so perplexing as in the other dialects, which offer great difficulties in this point to the student. The terminations, which have been already fixed for the Prākrit, have been mostly retained in the Sindhī, with the exception of neuter nouns, which have been, for the most part, transferred to the masculine terminations, less to the feminine.

I. The termination u.

1) Masculine themes in u.

By far the greatest number of nouns end in Sindhī in **u**, and are, with a few exceptions, masculine. This short final u corresponds to the Prākrit termination **ओ** ō, which, according to the testimony of the old Prākrit grammarians, has been already shortened to u in the Apabhransha dialect.[1]) To this class belong in Sindhī:

---

1) In Marāṭhī final **अ** (= Sindhī u) has on the whole become already quiescent; the same is the case in Bangālī, except when final a is preceded by a double consonant, in which case it is heard. In Panjābī, Hindī and Hindūstānī final a has quite disappeared; for nouns like piu, father, māū, mother etc. are in Panjābī exceptional cases.

a) such nouns, as end in Prākrit in ō (= Sanskrit final अ), as: نَرُ naru, a man, Prāk. णरो, Sansk. नर; گهَرُ gharu, house, Prāk. घरो (Sansk. गृह); ڪَمُ kamu, business, Prāk. कम्मो, Sansk. कर्मन्. To this class belongs also a number of adjectives (though the majority of them has retained the termination ō), as: تَلُ talu, hidden; اَجَرُ ajaru, imperishable; اَچيتُ ačetu, careless. Most of the adjectives, borroved from the Arabic or Persian, assume this termination, as: تَمامُ tamāmu, whole; غَرِيبُ γarību, poor etc.

b) such nouns, as end originally in u, as: وَاءُ vāu, wind (Sansk. वायु n.; مَدُ madu, liquor, Sansk. मधु) n.

c) such nouns, as end in Sanskrit in tā (crude form tṛ), Prāk. ā (by elision of t), or which add in Prākrit the termination āro, as: پِءُ piu, father, Sansk. पिता, Prāk. पिअ; ڀهَاءُ bhāu, brother, Sansk. भ्राता, Prāk. already भादु (in Sindhī again with elision of d); ڀهَتارُ bhatāru, husband, Prāk. भत्तारो, Sansk. भर्त्ता (see Varar. V, 31).

2) Feminine themes in u.

These are, comparatively speaking, few in number; to this class belong such nouns, as end in Sanskrit in u, and are feminine as: وَٿهُ f. thing, Sansk. वस्तु; ڌهيڻُ dhēṇu, a milk-cow, Sansk. धेनु; or such, as have shortened ū to u, as: سَسُ sasu, mother-in-law, Sansk. श्वश्रू; وِڄُ, vijū, lightening, Prāk. विज्जू, Sansk. विद्युत्.

In a few themes original ā has been shortened to u, the Sindhī following herein the levelling process noticed under 1, *c* irrespective of gender, as: ماءُ māu, mother, Prāk. माआ, Sansk. माता; ڌيءُ dhiu, daughter, Prāk. already धीदा and धीआ, Sansk. दुहिता (see Varar. IV, 33; Lassen p. 172, note); نُنهُ nūhu, daughter-in-law (Sansk. स्नुषा); quite exceptional is ڀيڻُ bhēṇu, sister, Prāk. बहिणी (Hindūst. بہن), Sansk. भगिणी. A number of nouns ending in u, which are feminine, we shall enumerate when treating of the gender of nouns; their origin is in many cases unknown.

II. The termination o.

Besides the nouns ending in u, those ending in ō are the most numerous in Sindhī; they are all without exception masculine. The old Prākrit termination ओ (ō) has been split in Sindhī into two classes, in one of which ō has been shortened to u and in the other of which it has been retained unaltered.

A strict rule seems not to have been attended to in settling these two terminations, but usage alone seems to have decided for the one or the other; in many instances both terminations are promiscuously used. It is worthy of notice, that many nouns, which end in Sindhī in ō, have retained the corresponding termination ā (masc.) in Hindī and Hindūstānī and to a great extent also in Marāṭhī, Bangālī and Panjābī, and similarly those nouns, which terminate in Sindhī in u, have dropped the corresponding vocalic termination (i. e. अ, a) in the dialects quoted.

Examples: تَرو tarō, the sole of a shoe (Sansk. तलं n.) گلو galō, the throat (Sansk. गल m.), whereas on the other hand ڳَلُ g̈alu, cheek, corresponds to the Sansk. गल्ल m., لڙڪو luṛkō or لڙڪُ luṛku, a tear; سونارو sōnārō, goldsmith (Sansk. सुवर्णकार); on the other hand لُھَارُ luhāru, blacksmith (Sansk. लोहकार).

In some instances the language has made use of these two different terminations to derive words of somewhat different meanings from one and the same base, as: چُورو čūrō, powder, filings, and چُورُ čūru, adj. powdered (both from the Sansk. चूर्ण); مَتھو mathō, the head, and مَتھُ māthu, the top (both from the Sansk. मस्त n.).

We may however lay down some rules, by which the Sindhī seems to have been guided in retaining the original Prākrit termination ō:

1) Adjectives, derived directly from the Sanskrit-Prākrit, have on the whole retained the ending ō, as: چَنگو čaṅō, good (Sansk. चङ्ग); مِٺھو miṭhō, sweet (Sansk. मिष्ट); کھَارو khārō, bitter (but کھَارُ khāru, s. m. potash, both being derived from the Sansk. क्षार); رُکھو rukhō, hard (Sansk. रूक्ष). In many nouns though both terminations are allowed as: اَدھَرو adharō or: اَدھَرُ adharu, helpless; نِدھَرو nidharō or: نِدھَرُ nidharu, wretched; اَبھَرو abharō or: اَبھَرُ abharu, poor.

Adjectives derived by secondary affixes from other themes generally retain the termination ō, as: جَٽِکو jaṭikō, relating to a Jaṭ (جَٽُ); وَاڻِکو vāṇikō, belonging to a Vāṇyō (وَاڻِيو); رَسِيلو rasīlō, juicy (from رَسُ); کھَانڊِيرو khāndīrō, patient (from کھَانڊِ). Excepted are the affixes وَانُ (Prāk. वन्तो, Sansk. वत्), as: دَيَاوَانُ dayāvānu, compassionate; آلُ (आलु), as: دَيَالُ dayālu, the same as دَيَاوَانُ; آرُ (आरु), when forming substantives, as: ڍھَنَارُ dhanāru, herdsman, whereas the affix ārō generally forms adjectives, as: سَگھَارو saghārō, strong (from سَگھَ).

2) Verbal nouns, which are derived from the root of verbs by lengthening the root-vowel, take the termination ō, as:

گهاٽو ghāṭō, decrease, from گهٽڻ to decrease.

چاڙهو čārhō, increase, from چڙهڻ to rise.

The termination u however is also in use, especially with such themes, in which the root-vowel is not lengthened, as:

مرڪ marku, boasting, from مرڪڻ to boast.

جهٽ jhaṭu, snatching, from جهٽڻ to snatch.

3) Nouns of agency, which are derived from verbal roots by prolonging the root-vowel (if it be short) take likewise the termination ō, as:

واڍهو vāḍhō, carpenter, from وڍهڻ to cut.

ٽوٻو tōbō, diver, from ٽٻڻ to dive.

چيرو čīrō, sawyer, from چيرڻ to split.

4) Some nouns of foreign origin change (original) final ā or ah to ō in Sindhī, as: بابو bābō, father, Hindūst. (turkish) بابا; دروازو darvāzō, door, Pers. دروازه.

5) All participles present and past end in ō, as: هلندو halandō, going; هليو haliō, gone; ماريندو mārīndō, beating, ماريو māryō, beaten.

6) It is seldom the case, that an original final ā (fem.) has been changed to ō, and rendered thereby masculine, as: تارو tārō, star (Sansk. तारा fem.); Hindī likewise तारा masc. (Paṣ̌tō: ستوري stōrai m.); in Marāṭhī it is both masc. and fem.

Note. If we turn to the cognate dialects, we find, that the Gujarātī comes nearest to the Sindhī in this respect; for nearly all the nouns, which end in Sindhī in ō and u, have retained the termination ō. As the Gujarātī has preserved the neuter, it forms a regular neuter ending in उं ũ from masc. themes in ō, as: कुतरूं a dog (in general), but कुतरो a male dog. This neuter termination we consider identical with the Sindhī vocalic termination u, with the only difference, that Anusvāra, as the sign of the neuter, has been added.

In Marāṭhī, Hindī and Panjābī, final ō of the Sindhī and Gujarātī has been changed to ā. The Panjābī and Hindī (Hindūstānī) have lost the neuter, but the Marāṭhī, which has preserved it, forms from the masc. termination ā a regular neuter ending in ẽ (एं), which is in its origin nothing else but another masc. termination with the addition of final Anusvāra, just as in Gujarātī (compare on this point: Lassen, Instit. linguae Prāk. p. 429, 14); e. g.: केलें n. a plantain, Hindī: केला m., करणें, inf. (properly a neuter verbal noun, as in Sanskrit), Sindhī كَرَڻُ karaṇu (m.), Hindī करना karna (m.), Gujarātī: करणुं (n.), as in Marāṭhī.

In Bangalī the termination ā (= ō of the Sindhī) is only to be met with in a few nouns, as: gādhā, ass, ghōṛā, horse etc. (nouns like: pitā, kartā, do not come properly under this head, as they are Sansk. Nominatives); as a masc. termination of adjectives ā is unknown in Bangālī.

III. The termination ū (masc. and fem.).

Nouns ending in ū correspond generally to the Sanskrit-Prākrit termination u, which in Prākrit is lengthened in the Nom. Sing. to ū; those nouns, which end already in Sanskrit ū, retain this termination unaltered in Sindhī. Some feminine nouns, ending in ū, shorten their final ū again to u, adding at the same time one of the feminine terminations i (e) or a; e. g.: سَائُو sāū, upright (Prāk. साउ, Nom. Sing. साऊ, Sansk. साधु), Hindī साधू or साधु; تَارُون tārũ m. palate, Sansk. तालु n. (Hindī तालू); ٻهُون bhũ f. earth (or: ٻهُئِي bhuē), Sansk. भू; جُون jũ f. louse (or; جُئَ jũa), Sansk. यूक (with elision of final k in Sindhī); آبِرو ābirū, honor (or آبِروءِ ābirūe) Pers.

Under this head fall many appellatives and adjectives, ending in ū, āū and ākū, corresponding to the Sansk. affixes uka (उक) and āku (आकु), as: تارُو tārū, a swimmer (= tāruka), رَهاكُو rahākū or: رَهائُو rahāū, inhabitant, كهٽائُو khaṭāū, profitable (from كهَٽَ f. profit).

In some nouns ending in ū, a more complicated contraction has taken place, as: مَاڙهُون māṛhū̃, man, Prāk. माणुसो, Sansk. मानुष (ṇ of the Prākrit interchanging with ṛ, and स being exchanged for h); ڏاڙهُون ḍāṛhū̃, pome-granate, Sanskrit दाडिम, Hindūstānī دَاڑِم; ڪَڇهُون kačhū̃, tortoise, Sansk. कच्छप |(p = b = v = ū); وِڇهُون vičhū̃, scorpion, Prak. विच्छुओ, Sansk. वृश्चिक.

IV. The termination ā.

Nouns ending in ā correspond generally to the Sanskrit-Prākrit termination ā (आ) and are all feminine, as: چِنْتَا čintā, anxiety, Sansk. चिन्ता; هَچَا hačā, murder, Sansk. हत्या; جاٽرا jāṭrā, pilgrimage, Sansk. यात्रा; كهِمَا khimā, patience, Prāk. खमा, Sansk. क्षमा.

There exists a small number of masc. nouns, now ending in ā, which must not be confounded with the preceding fem. nouns, as they are of quite a different origin; they are derived from Sansk. themes ending (in their crude forms) in an (अन्) and ṛ (ऋ), and in the Nom. Sing. in ā, as: رَاجا rājā, prince; آتمَا ātmā, soul; كَرتَا kartā, the agent (in grammar). There are also a few foreign words, ending in ā, as: آشنَا āšnā, an acquaintance, Pers. آشنا.

A few adjectives end likewise in ā (or ā̃) as: ڏاتا ḍātā, liberal; تالاں tālā̃, exhausted etc.

V. The termination ă.

The vocalic ending ă is shortened from the preceding fem. termination ā, just as u has been shortened from ō. To this class belong in Sindhī:

1) such nouns, as end in Sanskrit and Prākrit in ā, as: جِبهَ jibha, tongue, Prāk. जीहा, Sansk. जिह्वा; نُنْهَ nūha (besides نُنْهُ) daughter-in-law, Sansk. स्नुषा; دهِئَ dhia (besides: دهِئُ), daughter, Prāk. धीदा or धीत्रा; سَئِنَ sa-ina, sign, Sansk. सञ्ज्ञा; مِنَجَ miṅa, marrow, Sansk. मज्जा. Further a great quantity of nouns, the formation of which is peculiar to the Sindhī, and which may be derived from every verbal root. This formation corresponds exactly to the Sanskrit affix अङ् (ā), which is added to the verbal root, to form fem. nouns, as Sanskrit: भिदा, breaking, from भिद् etc. In Sindhī the derivation of such nouns from verbs is quite general, and the language acquires thereby a great facility to form verbal nouns, as: چوکهَ čōkha, investigation, Infin. چوکهَڻُ (root: چوکهْ); ڪُڏَ guḍa, pounding, Inf. ڪُڏَڻُ (root: ڪُڏُ). The Sindhī always falls back on the Prākrit, especially in such nouns, as differ already from the Sanskrit, by dropping either a final consonant in Prākrit or affixing a new vocalic ending, as: آسِيسَ āsīsa, blessing, Prāk. आसिस, Sansk. आशिस्.

2) The feminines of such adjectives, as end in the masc. in u, as: ڪُبهَ kubha, fem. of ڪُبهُ kubhu, unfortunate; سُڄاڻَ sujāṇa, fem. of سُڄاڻُ, well-knowing.

Only a very small number of adjectives ends originally in ă, which remain unchanged in gender, number and case, as: جَالَ jāla, or جَارَ jāra, abundant; جَامَ jāma, much, many.

3) Many nouns fluctuate, as regards their termination, between a or i (e), as both short vowels form the common fem. terminations in Sindhī, e. g.: نَارَ nāra or نَارِ nāre, woman; آرَ āra or آرِ āre, affection; چھَنَ čhana or چھَنِ, čhane, a pond; رِيڙَ rīṛa or رِيڙِ rīṛe, quarrel. From the adjectives, ending in u, the feminine may be formed in final a or i (e), as: اَتورَ atōra, or: اَتورِ atōre, what cannot be weighed, masc. اَتورُ; چَرْيَٽَ čaryaṭa or چَرْيَٽِ čaryaṭe, mad, masc. چَرْيَٽُ.

This accounts easily enough for the phenomenon, that such nouns, as end in Prākrit in ī, have adopted in Sindhi the termination ă (simply exchanging one fem. termination for another), as: ڀيڻَ bhēṇa (besides: ڀيڻُ), sister, Prāk. बहिणी Sansk. भगिनी; ڌُرِ dhure, origin, Prāk. धुरा, Sansk. धुर्. But, though the respective fem. terminations are often exchanged, the original gender is commonly strictly adhered to in Sindhī, and the case is very rare, that an original masc. noun has been changed to a feminine, as: ٻاڦَ ɓapha, fem. steam, Sansk. वाष्प masc. (in Hindī it has become likewise a fem.).

Note. As regards the cognate dialects, the Bangālī has throughout preserved the original fem. termination ā; the Marāṭhī too has remained more faithful to the Prākrit, but it has already in many cases shortened ā to a, and then dropped it altogether (in pronunciation at least) as: जीभ jībh, tongue, वाट vāṭ, way etc. In the other dialects long final ā has either been preserved, or it has been thrown off altogether (after having first been changed to ă).

As in Sindhī every noun must needs end in a vowel, such fem. nouns, as are borrowed from the Hindūstānī, frequently adopt the fem. termination 'a' in Sindhī, as: Hindūst. زَمِين (f.)

earth, Sindhī زَمِينَ zamīna; Hindūst. مِلْک (f.) property, Sindhī مِلْکَ milka. In a few nouns the gender has been changed, as: Hindūst. کِتاب kitāb (fem.), Sindhī کِتابُ kitābu, masc.

VI. The termination ī. (masc. et fem.)

Themes in ī are in Sindhī of both genders; they are either masculine or feminine.

1) Masc. themes ending in ī.

The termination ī in masc. nouns corresponds:

a) To the Sansk. affix ī (= in), as: دهَرمِي dharmī, religious (Sansk. धर्मिन्), Nom. Sing. धर्मी; سوامِي svāmī, lord (Sansk. स्वामिन्); هَاتهِي hāthī, elephant (Sansk. हस्तिन्.

b) To the Sansk. affix ika (इक = क), by eliding k and lengthening i to ī; e. g.: هَارِي hārī, a peasant, Sansk. हालिक); اوٺهِي ōṭhī, a camel-rider (from اُٺهُ camel); ٺهيکِرِي ṭhēkirī, a seller of earthen ware (from ٺهيکِرُ, earthen ware).

c) To the Sansk. adjectival affix य y, by changing य to ī, as: پرِين prī̃, friend, Sansk. प्रिय; اَبهَاڳِي abhāgī, unfortunate, Sansk. अभाग्य.

d) To the Sansk. affix ईय īya, by eliding य, as: هِنْدِي Hindī, Indian; سِنْڌِي Sindhī, relating to Sindh. With this class coincide all the Persian and Arabic adjectives, formed by the so-called ياء نِسْبَتْ or y of relation, as: فَارْسِي fārsī, Persian; عَرَبِي ʿarabī, Arabic; زَخْمِي zaχmī, wounded.

e) To Sanskrit masc. crudes, ending in i, which generally have final i lengthened to ī in Sindhī, as: کَوِي kavī, poët, Sansk. कवि; کَلِيکَالُ kalī-kālu, the Kāli-period; in some nouns though original short i has been preserved, as: هَرِ hare, Vishṇu (Hindī: हरि and हरी); پَتِي pa-e, lord, master (= पति).

There remains a number of words in ī, which are masculine, the origin of which is unknown, as: ٻيلِي ƀēlī, servant; ٻَانڌهِي bāndhī, a log of wood floating in the river; مَانجهِي mānjhī, a brave man.

Note. The Bangālī and Marāṭhī agree with the Sindhī in this respect, as Bang. svāmī, Marāṭhī hattī etc. On the other hand both idioms have retained the masc. termination i, as Bang. pati, lord, Marāṭhī kavi, poët. In Panjābī, Hindī (Hindūst.) final i of masc. themes is occasionally preserved, but more generally dropped, as har = hari; kav = kavi; or lengthened to ī, as in Sindhī, as kalī = kal, kali.

2) Feminine themes ending in ī.

a) Feminine nouns, which end in Sanskrit and Prākrit in ī, remain unchanged in Sindhī, as: نَدِي nadī, river, Sansk. नदी; سَتِي satī, a virtuous woman, Sansk. सती; رَاڻِي rāṇī, queen, Sansk. राज्ञी.

The Prākrit termination आ (fem.) is occasionally changed to ī in Sindhī, as: وَائِي vāī, speech, Prāk. वाआ, Sansk. वाच् f.; in some nouns ī (Prāk.) is shortened to i (e), as: ڏِٺهِ ḍiṭhe, sight, Prāk. दिट्ठी, Sansk. दृष्टि. Neuter nouns, which end in Sansk. in ĭ, may accept in Sindhī the fem. termination ī, as: ڏهِي ḍahī, sour milk, Prāk. देहि, Sansk. दधि; مَاکِهِي mākhī, honey, Sansk. माक्षिकं, with elision of क.

b) The fem. termination ī corresponds to the Sanskrit-Prākrit affix ī, by which feminines are formed from masculine themes. In Sindhī this termination is used to derive feminines from masc. bases ending in ō and u, as: بهَلِي bhalī, fem. good, from the masc. base بهلو; گولِي gōlī, a slave-girl, from گولو a slave; بَانْبهَنِي bāmbhaṇī, the daughter or wife of a بَانْبهَنُ or Brāhman.

c) The fem. termination ī is frequently applied to express littleness, smallness, neatness, as: كَاتِي kātī, a small knife, from كَاتُ kātu, a large knife; مَاتِي māṭī, a small jar, from مَاتو māṭō, a large jar etc.

d) The fem. affix ī, which corresponds to the Sansk. abstract affix यं, derives abstract nouns from adjectives and substantives, as: چورِي čōrī, theft, from چورُ čōru, a thief; بهَلِي bhalī, goodness, from بهَلو bhalō, good; دوستِي dōstī, friendship, from دوستُ dōstu, friend.

VII. The termination i (ĕ) fem. (m.)

The ending 'i', which, with a few exceptions, denotes fem. nouns, corresponds to the Sanskrit-Prākrit termination ī; in others again is has been shortened from ī, in the same way, as final a from ā; e. g.: بُدهِ budhe, intelligence, Sansk. बुद्धि; مَتِ mate, opinion, Sansk. मति; نَارِ nāre, woman, Sansk. नारी.

The termination i (e) is generally used to derive feminines from adjectives and substantives ending in u, as: اَچيتِ ačēte, thoughtless, masc. اَچيتُ; سَدهَرِ sadhare, stout, masc. سَدهَرُ; گڏهِ gaḍahe, a jenny-ass, from گڏهُ a jack-ass; پَريتِ parīṭe, a washerwoman, from پَريتُ a washerman.

In some few nouns the original gender has been changed, as: آگِ āge, fire (fem.), Prāk. अग्गि (m.),

Sansk. **आग्नि** m.; دِيهہ dēhe (fem.), body, Sansk. **देह** (m. and n.); in the cognate dialects both are alike fem.

It is further to be observed, that in Sindhī final i (e) very frequently interchanges with final ǎ, both vowels constituting the regular fem. terminations, e. g.: آرِ āre or آرَ āra, fondness; گوڙِ gōṛe or گوڙَ gōṛa, thunder etc. Among these we must also reckon forms like ڌُرِ dhure, origin, Prāk. **धुरा**, short final a having been exchanged for i (e).

In Sindhī, as well as in the cognate dialects, some few masc. nouns have retained the original Sansk. termination ĭ, as: هَرِ hare, Vishṇu, وِرَسْپَتِ viraspate, the planet Jupiter (Thursday) پَئِي pa-e, lord, husband (= **पति**); in others again ĭ has been shortened from ī, as: کيهَرِ kēhare, lion, Sansk. **केशरिन्**, Hindī **केहर्** and **केहरी**; سَهائِي sahāe or سَهائِي sahāī, a helper.

To some nouns of foreign origin the termination i has also been added, as: خُدائِ χudāe, God (Pers. خُدا); سيٺهِ sēṭhe, a Hindī wholesale merchant (Hindūst. سيٹھ); خِضِرِ χiẕire, nom. prop. of a Pīr and fabulous prophet.

Some adjectives, mostly such, as have been borrowed from a foreign source, take also the termination ĭ (m. and fem.), as: خُشِ χuše, joyful (Pers. خوش); شادِ šāde, delighted (Pers. شاد); چَوْرَسِ čaurase, four-square, Sansk. **चतुरस्र**.

Chapter II.

Primary themes.

§. 7.

With reference to the formation of themes the Sindhī conforms on the whole to the system of the Prākrit, inasmuch as Prākrit themes are directly received into the Sindhī with such modifications, as are peculiar to the Sindhī; but besides this the Sindhī has set up new formations of themes, whereby the inherited stock of vocables, be they of Ārian or non-Ārian origin, is peculiarly remodelled. As regards the themes taken directly from the Prākrit, we must refer to the Sindhī system of sounds in our Introduction, which alone can give the necessary clue as to the origin or derivation of a theme from the Prākrit; in the following we shall only treat of those themes, which have been formed either by modifying the old inherited stock, or by new rules altogether, irrespective of the Prākrit. Nouns of Arabic or Persian origin we shall exclude from our present investigation, as they have nothing in common with the genuine Sindhī forms, but are intruders, without which the Sindhī may well exist; they partake so far of the general laws of the formation of themes, that a vocalic termination is affixed to them, according to their respective gender, to render them susceptible of inflexion.

Whe shall divide the Sindhī formation of themes after the precedent of the Sanskrit into two classes, viz: that of primary and secondary themes, that is, such themes, as are directly derived from verbal roots, and such, as are derived from primary nouns, by means of affixes.

§. 8.

I. Formation of abstract nouns.

1) Themes in ă, ĭ (ĕ); u, ō (ī fem.)

a) Themes in ă are formed from the simple root of the verb (which in Sindhī, as well as in Sanskrit, is always monosyllabical, derivative verbs excepted) by dropping the Infinitive (verbal) affix aṇu. In this way an abstract noun may be formed from every Infinitive of the language, exhibiting the abstract idea of the verb.

The affix ă corresponds to the Sansk. affix आ, which is added to the root of the verb (as: Sansk. पूजा, worship, from पूज् to worship) to form abstract nouns; in Sindhī final ā has been shortened to ă; see §. 6, V. e. g.:

جاڳَ jāga, wakefulness, Inf. جاڳَڻُ to be awake.

مَرْهَ marha, pardon, Inf. مَرْهَڻُ to pardon.

پِيڙَ pīṛa, pressure, Inf. پِيڙَڻُ to press.

سَگهَ sagha, strength, Inf. سَگهَڻُ to be strong.

In some roots 'a' is prolonged to ā and 'u' to ō, as:

جهاٽَ jhāṭa, snatching, Inf. جهَٽَڻُ to snatch.

ڀهولَ bhōla, error, Inf. ڀهُلَڻُ to err.

b) Themes in i (e) are formed in the same way as the preceding (i being only a variation of ă), with this difference, that the root-vowel must always be prolonged (viz: a = ā; u = ō; i = ē), e. g.:

گهاٽِ ghāṭe, descrease, Inf. گهَٽَڻُ to descrease.

گهومِ ghōme, vagrancy, Inf. گهُمَڻُ to wander about.

ويڙهِ vēṛhe, quarrel, Inf. وِڙهَڻُ to quarrel.

c) The termination 'u' corresponds to the Sansk. affix अ, which derives abstract nouns from verbal roots, with or without prolonging the root-vowel; the same is the case in Sindhī, where the root-vowel either remains unchanged, or is prolonged. E. g.:

مَرْکُ marku, boast, Inf. مَرْکَنُ to boast.

لَاهُ lāhu, descent, Inf. لَهَنُ to descent.

بهورُ bhōru, crumb, Inf. بهُرَنُ to crumble.

پهيرُ phēru, turn, Inf. پهِرَنُ to turn (v. n.).

d) Themes in ō are identical with those in u, both terminations interchanging very frequently (see §. 6, I. II.).

گهَاٽو ghaṭō, deficiency, Inf. گهَٽَنُ to decrease.

چَاڙهو čāṛhō, increase, Inf. چَڙهَنُ to rise.

جهَڳِڙو jhagiṛō, quarrel, Inf. جهَڳِڙَنُ to quarrel.

ڏيکهَارو ḍēkhārō, showing, Inf. ڏيکهَارَنُ to show.

The masc. termination ō is occasionally exchanged for the fem. termination ī, with some slight alteration of meaning, as:

چَاڙهِي čāṛhī, ascent, Inf. چَڙهَنُ to ascend.

ڏيکهَارِي ḍēkhārī, showing.

2) Themes in aṇu, aṇō, anī, aṇe.

a) Themes in aṇu coincide in Sindhī with the form of the Infinitive, which, according to the testimony of the old Prākrit grammarians, has already been the case in the Apabhransha dialect, the Infinitive of which terminated in अणं (compare: Lassen, Instit. ling. Prāk. p. 469, 5).

The old Sanskrit Infinitive in तुम् (the Latin supinum) has been lost in the modern vernaculars (the Gujarātī Infinitive, which ends in वुं, is properly a neuter Gerundive, and the Bangālī infinitive, which ends in tē, is a past participle, used as a verbal noun) and in its place the verbal noun in **अनं** is substituted, which in Marāṭhī has remained neuter (एं ē), but which in Sindhī and the other dialects has been classed under the masculine termination. The affix aṇu is added directly to the verbal root in Sindhī, and forms abstract nouns, corresponding to our Gerunds; as:

ڏِسَنُ ḍisaṇu, seeing, root: ڏِسْ.

هَلَنُ halaṇu, going, root: هَلْ.

مَرَنُ maraṇu, dying, root: مَرْ.

The naked verbal root, as pointed out, is in Sindhī nowhere to be met with, but always ends in the Imperative, where alone its crude form comes to light, in a vowel, which is either u (in intrans. verbs) or i (e) (in transitive verbs). According to the final vowel of the Imperative the junction vowel of the Infinitive or verbal noun varies in Sirō, as: مَارِنُ māriṇu (to beat), ليٽَنُ lēṭaṇu, to recline, but in Lāṛ no regard is had to this circumstance, and all Infinitives (irrespective of their transitive or intransitive signification) terminate in aṇu.

b) Themes in aṇō (which is originally only a variation of aṇu) express in Sindhī more a lasting action, occupation or state; e. g.:

ڏِئَڻو وَٿَهَڻو ḍiaṇō vaṭhaṇō, giving and taking (debt and and credit), besides: ڏِئَڻُ وَٿَهَڻُ, which is also in use.

ڀهِرِڻو bhariṇō (or bharaṇō) embroidering (literally: filling up).

مَنگِڻو māṅiṇō (or maṅaṇō) betrothal (literally: asking [for a bride]).

Note. It is remarkable, that all the other dialects, with the exception of the Bangālī and Gujarātī, have retained this termination of the Infinitive, as: Marāṭhī **करणें** (ē being originally identical with ō, see Lassen §. 144, 2), Hindī (Hindūst.) **करना**, Panǰābī: karnā.

c) More frequently than the termination aṇō, the feminine ending aṇī is used in Sindhī, serving at the same time to express smallness, neatness etc. of a state or action:

چَوَڻِي čavaṇī, saying, Inf. چَوَڻُ to say.

هَلَڻِي halaṇī, going, gait (comely), Inf. هَلَڻُ to go.

ڀَرِڻِي bhariṇī, embroidery, Inf. ڀَرَڻُ to fill.

وَڍَڻِي vaḍhaṇī, carpentering, Inf. وَڍَڻُ to cut.

Occasionally the termination aṇī is shortened to aṇi (aṇĕ), as:

ڳِهَڻِ ǧehaṇe, swallowing (besides: ڳِهَڻِي), Inf. ڳِهَڻُ to swallow.

The affix aṇī (or iṇī) joined to roots of causal verbs, signifies: expense for, wages for, as:

کَهَڻَائِي khaṇāṇī, expense for carrying or lifting up (porterage), Inf. کَهَڻَائِڻُ to cause to carry.

چَارَائِي čārāṇī, expense for grazing cattle, Inf. چَارَڻُ to cause to graze.

ڌُئَارِڻِي dhuāriṇī, expense for washing, Inf. ڌُئَارَڻُ to cause to wash.

3) Themes in ti.

This affix corresponds to the Sansk. affix ति, by which abstract nouns are derived from verbal roots, besides those, which are taken over directly from the Sanskrit. The junction vowel in Sindhī is ă, as:

کَهَپَتِ khapate, expense, Inf. کَهَپَڻُ to spend.

وَڻَتِ vaṇate, pleasure, Inf. وَڻَڻُ to please (act.).

آوَتِ جَاوَتِ āvate jāvate, income, expense (literally: coming, going); as Infinitives they are not used in Sindhī, but in Hindī.

چھَڏِتِ čhaḏate, remission, Inf. چھَڏَنُ to remit.

هَلَتِ halate, behaviour, Inf. هَلَنُ to go.

4) Themes in aṭu, āṭū (ā—ū), āṭī (fem.).

These affixes correspond to the Sansk. Uṇādi-affixes अतु, आतु which Bopp has justly referred to the Infinitive affix तु = तुम्. This is borne out by their signification, which in Sindhī nearly coincides with that of the Infinitive, as:

گھيرَٽُ ghēraṭu, surrounding, Inf. گھيرَنُ to surround.

چھِمْڪاٽُ čhimkāṭu, jingling, Inf. چھِمْڪَنُ to jingle.

بھُڻِڪاٽُ bhuṇikātu }
بھُڻِڪاءُ bhuṇikā-u } humming, Inf. بھُڻِڪَنُ to hum.

(by elision of ṭ.)

ڦيراٽِي phērāṭī, giddiness, Inf. ڦيرَنُ to cause to turn.

Note. A feminine may thus be derived nearly from all masc. bases.

5) Themes in aṭru (or: iṭru).

The Sindhī affix aṭru (or iṭru) corresponds to the Sansk. affix इत्र, and denotes an instrument, wherewith any thing is done or executed. In Lāṛ this affix is assimilated to aṭu (= aṭṭu) whereas in Sirō the original compound is preserved (only with transition of t into ṭ); the root-vowel is lengthened in some themes; e. g.:

واڄَٽرُ vājaṭru, a musical instrument, Inf. وڄَنُ to sound.

وهِٽرُ vahiṭru, a beast of burden, Inf. وهَنُ to labour.

6) Themes in ikō.

This affix corresponds to the Sansk. affix अक (the junction vowel 'a' having been changed to i in Sindhī), which in Sanskrit forms nouns of agency, but in Sindhī also abstract nouns; as:

ڏَڙِڪو ḍaṛikō, quarrelling, Inf. ڏَڙَڻُ to quarrel.

پِٽِڪو piṭikō, beating the forehead, Inf. پِٽَڻُ to strike one's head in grief.

§. 9.

II. Formation of appellatives and attributives.

7) Themes in ō.

This affix corresponds to the Sansk. affix अक (final क being commonly elided in Sindhī), and forms attributives from verbal roots, which imply habitual action or possession. The root-vowel, if it be short, must be prolonged, as in Sanskrit; e. g.:

واڍهو vāḍhō, carpenter, Inf. وَڍهَڻُ to cut.

چيرو čīrō, sawyer, Inf. چِيرَڻُ to split.

ٽوبو ṭōbō, diver, Inf. ٽُبَڻُ to dive.

گهورو ghōrō, seeker, Inf. گهورَڻُ to seek.

In some few instances the full Sansk. affix has been preserved, as:

گائِڪُ gāiku, singer, Inf. گائِڻُ to sing.

8) Themes in ū.

This affix corresponds to the Sansk. affix उक (final क beeing elided in Sindhī and u lengthened) and forms verbal adjectives or attributives, implying a habitual or characteristical action or state. The root-vowel, if short, is commonly prolonged before the accession of this affix; as:

وَادهُو vādhū, increasing, Inf. وَدهُڻُ to increase.

تارُو tārū, a swimmer, Inf. تَرَڻُ to swim.

ويڙهو vēṛhū, a quarrelsome person, Inf. وِڙهَڻُ to quarrel.

پھورو phōrū, a robber, Inf. پھُرَنُ to rob.

گھومُو ghōmū, a vagabond, Inf. گھُمَنُ to stroll about.

Without prolongation of the root-vowel:

رَهُو rahū, inhabitant, Inf. رَهَنُ to stay.

سَهُو sahū, patient, Inf. سَهَنُ to bear.

9) Themes in āku, ākū, āū.

This affix denotes the same idea of a habitual state or action, as the preceding. It corresponds to the Sansk. affix आकु which is added to the verbal root either unaltered, or with final 'u' lengthened, or with elision of क = ā-ū. In some instances the root-vowel is prolonged. E. g.:

رَهاکُو rahākū, } inhabitant, Inf. رَهَنُ to stay.
رَهائُو rahā-ū, }

پِئاکُ piāku, drinker, Inf. پِئَنُ to drink.

وِرچائُو virčāū, wearisome, Inf. وِرْچَنُ to be wearied.

ويکائُو vēkāū, for sale, Inf. وِکَنُ to be sold.

پيٽائُو pēṭāū, ill-wishing, Inf. پِٽَنُ to curse.

10) Themes in andō (and īndō).

This affix corresponds to the Sansk. affix अत्, Prāk. अन्तो (in Sindhī with change of the tenuis into the media), and forms in Sindhī, like as in Sanskrit and Prākrit, present participles. According to the final vowel of the Imperative the participle ends in andō (Imperative u) or īndō (imperative i); some participles are formed irregularly.

لَگَنْدو lagandō, applying, Imper. لَگُ, Inf. لَگَنُ to apply.

ڏِسَنْدو ḍisandō, seeing, Imper. ڏِسُ, Inf. ڏِسَنُ to see.

بھيلِينْدو bhēlīndō, trampling, Imper. بھيلِ, Inf. بھيلَنُ to trample.

تهيندو thīndō (irreg.), Imper. تهيءُ, Inf. تهِئَنُ to become.

Note. We advert to the fact, that all the other dialects have dropped the nasal in the Prāk. affix अन्तो; the Panǰābī has preserved it in a few forms, as: hundā, being, ǰāndā, going, but in the regular present participle the affix is always dā, with change of the tenuis into the media, just as in Sindhī. In Guǰarātī the present participle ends in tō, as: लखतो lakhtō, writing; in Hindī (Hindūst.) in tā, as: likhtā, hōtā, being etc. Hinduī tu, as: लिखतु likh-tu, writing. The Marāṭhī has formed two present participial affixes from the Sanskrit affix अत्; one in tā, corresponding to the Hindī form, as: लिहिता, writing, with which affix the terminations of the substantive verb अस्मि coalesce into the forms tō̃, tō̃s etc.; the other in at or īt. The Bangālī has discontinued the use of the present participle (with the exception of a few Sanskrit participles ending in at) and only employs the same in conjunction with the substantive verb āčhī, as: dēkhitēčhi, I am seeing; but dēkhitē is by no means to be confounded with the Infinitive, as it is commonly represented in Bangālī grammars, it is the Locative form of dēkhit, and signifies literally: I am in seeing (the Locative of the present participle is similarly used in Sindhī and Hindī).

11) Themes in āru, ārū, ārō.

These affixes correspond to the Sansk. affix आरु, and form in Sindhī verbal nouns, which imply a habitual action or occupation; their number is not very considerable; as:

گهورارو ghōrārō,
گهورارُو ghōrārū, } a pedlar, Inf. گهورَنُ to seek.

پُوڄارو pūǰārō, a worshipper, Inf. پُوڄَنُ to worship.

پينڃارو pīñārō, a cotton carder, Inf. پِنڃَنُ to card cotton.

پينارُ pēnāru, a beggar, Inf. پِنَنُ to beg.

12) Themes in ibō.

This affix corresponds to the Sansk. affix तव्य, incredible as this may appear. In Sindhī त has been elided and vv (= व्य) hardened to b (= bb). It forms now in Sindhī present participles passive, though its original use and signification has still been preserved in the formation of the future passive; as:

بُوساٽِبو būsāṭibō, being choked, Inf. بُوساٽَڻُ to choke.

ڎروهِبو ḍrōhibō, being cheated, Inf. ڎروهَڻُ to cheat.

جهلِبو jhalibō, being seized, Inf. جهلَڻُ to seize.

13) Themes in iṇō.

We have in Sindhī two themes in iṇō, which are quite of different origin and signification.

a) The affix iṇō, added to such verbs, as end in the Imperative in u, corresponds to the Sanskrit affix अन, which forms attributives and appellatives; in Sindhī the affix ana has been changed to iṇō; e. g.:

هَلِڻو haliṇō, going, Imper. هَلُ.

مُرڪِڻو murkiṇō, laughing, Imper. مُرڪُ.

چهرڪِڻو čhirkiṇō, shying, Imper. چهِرڪُ.

ڀُرِڻو bhuriṇō, crumbling, Imper. ڀُرُ.

پِنِڻو piniṇō, begging, Imper. پِنُ.

Some of these attributives are also used substantively, and as such they are also susceptible of the fem. termination, as:

چهِنڪِڻو čhiṇkiṇō, rattle, i. e. that which rattles.

ڦِرِڻو phiriṇō, spooling-wheel, i. e. that which turns round.

ڌهَنْوَڻِ dhāvaṇe, a pair of bellows, i. e. that which blows (the fire).

b) The other affix iṇō or aṇō corresponds to the

Sanskrit affix **अनीय**, by which the future passive participle is formed in Sanskrit. Thus in Sindhī a Gerundive may be derived from every transitive verb by means of this affix, as:

مَارِنو mariṇō, one who is to be beaten, Inf. مَارِنُ to beat.

ڏِئَنو ḍiaṇō, what is to be given, Inf. ڏِئَنُ to give.

دهُئَنو dhuaṇō, what is to be washed, Inf. دهُئَنُ to wash.

رَٿهَنو raṭhaṇō, what is to be taken, Inf. رَٿهَنُ to take.

In the same way a gerundive is derived form causal verbs, as:

وَرَائِنو varāiṇō, what ought to be returned, Inf. وَرَائِنُ to return (act).

دهُئَارِنو dhuāriṇō, what ought to be caused to wash, Inf. دهُئَارِنُ to cause to wash.

Note. In Hindī and Hindūstānī the Gerundive coincides with the Infinitive, with this difference, that the Gerundive is properly a masc. substantive, and therefore only a Gerund; very rarely the Infinitive is employed as a Gerundive proper (i. e. future passive participle), agreeing with its governing noun in gender, as in Sindhī. The Panjābī on the other hand quite agrees with the Sindhī in this respect, using the Infinitive as a regular Gerundive, agreeing with the governing noun in gender, number and case, like an adjective. The Marāṭhī forms the Gerundive by the affix **आवा (आवी, आवें)**, which corresponds to the Sansk. affix **तव्य**, Prāk. **तव्व**; in Marāṭhī **त** has been elided and in its place 'a' lengthened, as: **करावा** faciendus, **मोडावा** dirumpendus. In a similar way the Gerundive is formed in Gujarātī by the affix **अवो (= तव्व)** as: **लखवो** scribendus. In Bangālī occurs no proper formation of a Gerundive, but the Infinitive (in distinction from the verbal noun) is generally employed to express the idea of a Gerund, like in Hindī, as: amākē jāitē hai, mihi eundum est; but many original Gerundive forms are borrowed directly from the Sanskrit, as: kartavya etc., the affix anīya is also in use.

14) Themes in iō or yō.

The affix iō or yō is used to derive perfect participles; it corresponds to the Sanskrit affix त, Prākrit already द, and frequently altogether elided, for which reason y or i is inserted in Sindhī, to prevent the hiatus.

The perfect participle of transitive verbs always implies a passive signification, whereas that of intransitive verbs only expresses the idea of the Præterite.

In many instances the Sindhī has preserved the original Sanskrit-Prākrit forms of the perfect participles, modified according to the laws of elision and assimilation current in Sindhī.

پسيو pasyō (or پسِئو pasiō) seen, Inf. پَسَنُ to see.

جهليو jhalyō (or: جهلِئو jhaliō) seized, Inf. جهَلَنُ to seize.

موٽيو mōṭyō (or: موٽِئو mōṭiō), returned, Inf. موٽَنُ to return.

ڏِٺهو ḍiṭhō, seen; Sansk. दृष्ट, Prāk. दिट्ठो; Inf. ڏِسَنُ to see.

اُتو utō, said; Sansk. उक्त, Prāk. उत्तो; Inf. اُتَنُ to say.

Note. In reference to the formation of the perfect participles (the perfect participle active in वत् has completely disappeared from the grammar of the modern vernaculars) a great variation is to be noticed in the cognate dialects. The Panjābī, Gujarātī, Hindī and Hindūstānī quite agree in this point with the Sindhī, as Panjābī: ghalliā, sent, Inf. ghallṇā; Gujarātī: lakhyō, written; Hindī (Hindūst.): likhā (without insertion of euphonic i or y in the place of elided t or d), Inf. likhnā.

The Marāṭhī differs considerably in this respect from the idioms mentioned; it forms the perfect participle by affixing ला to the root of the verb (with the junction vowel a or i, according to the intransitive or transitive signification of a verb). The first traces of this affix must be sought already in Prākrit; the

Sansk. त has been changed in Prākrit to the corresponding media द, and this again to ड (ḍ); see Lassen: Instit. linguae Prāk., p. 363. We have seen already (Introd. §. 6, 4) that ड is frequently changed to ड़ ṛ in the modern idioms, and this is again exchanged for l; as: चालला gone, Inf. चालखें; मोडिला broken, Inf. मोडलें.

The Bangālī coincides in this point quite with the Hindī, as: dēkhā, seen (without insertion of euphonic i or y).

Chapter III.

Secondary themes.

§. 10.

Under this head we shall class all those themes, which are derived from other nouns by means of an affix. We shall pass again all those forms, which have been taken directly from the Sanskrit-Prākrit, and only treat of those formations, which are peculiar to the Sindhī.

I. Formation of abstract nouns.

Abstract nouns may be derived either from substantives or adjectives, the affixes which the Sindhī uses for this purpose, agree all, more or less, with the primitive Sanskrit-Prākrit affixes.

1) Themes in ī. (f.)

By the affix ī a very numerous class of abstract nouns is formed, which, after the analogy of the Persian, may be derived from any noun. The final vowel is always dropped before this affix, but in other respects the noun undergoes no change whatever.

The affix ī corresponds to the Sanskrit affix यं (n.); in Sindhī as well as in the other dialects the feminine form ī, which is already current in Sanskrit, has alone been retained; e. g.:

چورِي čōrī, theft, from چورُ čōru, thief.

مَنْدِي mandī, wickedness, from مَنْدو mandō, wicked.

كَمِي kamī, deficiency, from كَمِ kame, deficient.

2) Themes in āī. (f.)

The affix āī is only a variation of the preceding affix; final u (= ō) and ō are not dropped, as before the preceding affix, but changed to ā (as in the other dialects) to keep their place; e. g.:

نِرْمَلائِي nirmalāī, purity, from نِرْمَلُ nirmalu, pure.

كُوڙائِي kūṛāī, falsity, from كُوڙو kūṛō, false.

Both forms are therefore frequently used indifferently, as:

ڀَلِي bhalī, goodness, or: ڀَلائِي bhalāī, from ڀَلو bhalō, good.

3) Themes in tā and tāī. (f.)

The affix tā forms in Sindhī a very numerous class of abstract nouns from attributives and adjectives; the final vowel is always dropped and the union-vowel i inserted (except when the noun ends in i). The affix tā corresponds to the Sanskrit affix ता, which is used for the same purpose in Sanskrit. Besides the affix tā, the emphatic form with ī (tā-ī) is also in use; e. g.:

گهَٽِتا ghaṭita, } want, from گهَٽِ ghaṭe, deficient.
گهَٽِتائِي ghaṭitāī, }

جوڳِتا jōgitā, fitness, from جوڳُ jōgu, fit.

4) Themes in te; tī. (f.)

The affix te, which is else only used with primary formations, is in Sindhī also (though very rarely) found with secondary formations; the affix tī, which is also occasionally to be met with, is only a variation of te (i having been lengthened to ī); as:

سَنْوتِ sāvate, straightness, from سَنْئون sāõ, straight.

گهٽتِي ghaṭitī, deficiency, from گهٽ ghaṭe, deficient.

Note. The affix tī is also used in Hindūstānī, as: کَمْتِي deficiency, from کَمْ.

5) Themes in āṇe or āiṇe. (f.)

These affixes form a numerous class of abstract nouns from adjectives implying colour or some other inherent quality. They correspond to the Sanskrit affix इमन्, which forms abstract masc. nouns. In Prākrit the termination अन् may already be lengthened to आण (cf. Var. V, 47); in Sindhī म (m) has been elided, which is rather uncommon, and a feminine termination substituted for the masculine; the i of iman has been dropped = āṇe, whereas in the form āiṇe i has been inserted after ā, to render the 'a' more prominent. E. g.:

اَڇهاڻِ ačhāṇe, whiteness, from اَڇهو ačhō, white.

وِيڪِراڻِ vēkirāṇe, breadth, from وِيڪِرو vēkirō, broad.

وَڏاڻِ vaḍāṇe, greatness, from وَڏو vaḍō, great.

The affix āṇe (āiṇe) is very often exchanged for the affix āī (see 2.), and with many nouns both affixes are promiscuously used, as: ڪاراڻِ or ڪارائِي blackness.

Note. In Hindī and Hindūstānī the affix ma (= इमन्) is rarely used, and no longer as a masculine; e. g.: garimā, f., importance. In Gujurātī the affix āṇ is used (as neuter) e. g.: ऊंडाण depth, from ऊंडो deep; the Marāṭhī and Bangālī have preserved the original Sansk. termination mā (as masc.). In Panjābī, as in Gujarātī, the form āṇ (m.) is used, as: učāṇ, m., height, from učā, high.

6) Themes in pō, pā, pāī, pi; paṇu, paṇō; taṇu; āṭu.

These affixes form a very numerous class of abstract nouns from substantives and adjectives. We can see in this instance, how the Sindhī has menaged to derive from one and the same Sanskrit affix a whole series of abstract affixes, which at the first glance seem to have nothing in common.

The affixes pō, pa, pāī, pī are derived from the Sansk. abstract-affix त्व tva, which is assimilated to प्प (see Introd. §. 15, D, b.); from this the Sindhī has formed the various terminations pā, pa, pāī, pī.

From the self-same affix त्व, which has become त्तण in Prākrit (from an original त्वन), and which has been assimilated in the Apabhransha dialect to प्पण (see Lassen, p. 459, 9.) the Sindhī has derived the affixes paṇu or paṇō.

From the same source has also sprung the affix taṇu, but by a different process of assimilation, the semi-vowel v being assimilated to the preceding dental (cf. §. 15, D, b.).

Another form of assimilation is the affix āṭu (viz: tva = tta = ṭṭa = āṭa, the double consonant being cleared away by lengthening the preceding vowel), which is only rarely used.

The final vowels undergo various changes before the accession of the above mentioned affixes; final u is generally changed to 'a' or 'i', with the exception of the fem. nouns ending in 'u', which preserve 'u' (as radical) before all affixes; final ō is either weakened to 'a' or changed to ō; final ī is either shortened to 'i', or with a subsounding 'a' to 'ia', which is mostly the case before the heavy affixes paṇu, paṇō; final ū is shortened to 'u' with a subsounding 'a' (= ua) before the heavy affixes paṇu, paṇō; long ū though keeps now and then its place before them; before the lighter affixes pō, pa, pāī, pī final ū is shortened even to 'i' (for euphony's sake). Final short 'a' may be lengthened to ā, to distinguish the feminine themes from those ending in 'u'; but this depends on usage.

a) final u:

پَنْڍِتَپَنو paṇḍitapanō, m. The duty of a paṇḍit; from پَنْڍِتُ.

ڇهوڪِراٽُ čhōkirāṭu, m. The time of youth; from ڇهوڪرُ čhōkaru, a boy.

وَٺهپَ vaṭhupa; f. assistance; from وَٺهُ fem. laying hold of.

b) final ō:

نَنْڍهَپائِي nanḍhapāi, f. نَنْڍهَپَنُ nanḍhapaṇu, m. نَنْڍهيپو nanḍhēpō, m.	Time of youth; from نَنْڍهو nanḍhō, small.

c) final ī:

وَاهِپَ vāhipa, f. وَاهِپو vāhipō, m.	The duty of a وَاهِي m. or watchman.
ڪَاندهِئَپَ kāndhiapa, f. ڪَاندهِئَپَنُ kāndhiapaṇu, m.	The offixe of a ڪَاندهِي kāndhī, one who gives a shoulder in carrying a corpse.

مُکهِتَنُ mukhitaṇu, the duty of a مُکهِي mukhī or headsman.

d) final ū:

مَانْهِپو māṇhipō, مَانهُئَپَنو māṇhuapaṇo,	humanity, from مَانْهون māṇhū man.

مِرُونْپَنو mirūpaṇō, bestiality, from مِرُون mirū, wild beast.

e) final a:

رَنَاپَنُ ranāpaṇu, widowhood, from رَنَ rana, a widow.

زَالپَنُ zālapaṇu, womanhood, from زَالَ a woman.

Note. These abstract affixes are to be met with in all the cognate idioms. The Hindī and Hindūstānī use the affixes pan, panā and pā, corresponding to the Sindhī forms paṇu, paṇō and pō. The Gujarāthī: paṇ and paṇū (both neut.); the Marāṭhī: paṇ (n.) and paṇā (m.); the Panjābī: puṇā. The Bangālī comes nearest to the Sanskrit in this respect, having retained the original abstract affix tva unaltered.

7) Themes in kāru, kārō, kāra, kāre.

These themes fall under our consideration in this place not so much on account of their formation, as their signification, for we have here not to deal with an affix, but with an adjective, used to form compounds, and signifying: making, effecting. In Sindhī the original signification of कार has been already obliterated, and it is now used in the same way as an affix, to form a number of abstract nouns; e. g.:

لُچھِکارو lučhikārō, uneasiness, properly: that which makes لُچھہ lučha, or being tossed about.

وَݨکارُ vaṇakāru, } wood, forest; properly: that which
وَݨکارِ vaṇakāre, } produces trees (وَݨُ).

ٺهڍهِکارَ thadhekāra, cool temperature; properly: that which makes coolness (ٺهڍهِ).

8) Themes in kō and ō.

The affix kō serves originally to derive adjectives, and corresponds to the Sansk. affix इक; but in Sindhī it is sometimes used (as the preceding affix कार) to form abstract nouns; the affix ō is identical with kō, k having been elided. E. g.:

لُچھِکو lučhikō, uneasiness; the same as: لُچھِکارو.

دھوڙيو dhūṛyō, a duststorm; properly: that which makes sand (دھوڙِ).

§. 10.

II. Formation of apellatives, attributives and possessives.

9) Themes in ī.

This affix, which in Sindhī and the kindred idioms is so frequently employed, has sprung from three different sources:

a) The affix ī, corresponding to the Sanskrit affix इक.

This affix forms attributives and appellatives of various significations; the root-vowel is generally lengthened before the addition of this affix, i. e. 'a' becomes ā; 'i' : ē; 'u' : ō; e. g.:

اوٺِي ōṭhī, a camel-rider, from اُٺُ uṭhu, camel.

باڪِرِي bākirī, a seller of vegetables, from بَڪَرُ bakaru, vegetables.

ٺيڪِرِي ṭhēkirī, a seller of earthen-ware; from ٺيڪِرُ ṭhēkiru, earthen-ware.

b) The affix ī, corresponding to the Sansk. affix ईय, इय.

This affix denotes in all the modern vernaculars descent or relationship. Before its addition to a noun a final short vowel is dropped, long ū is shortened to 'u', and ō is changed to ā. In some instances final short 'u' (shortened from ō) is changed to ā (= ō) and thus preserved; e. g.:

سِنڌِي sindhī, of Sindh, from سِنڌُ f. sindhu, the country of Sindh.

هِنڊُئِي hinduī, relating to a Hindū, from هِنڊو, hindū, a Hindū.

لاڙِي lāṛī, لاڙائِي lāṛāī,	of Lāṛ, from لاڙُ m. laṛu, Lower Sindh.

سِرائِي sirāī, of Sirō, from سِرو sirō, Upper Sindh.

c) The affix ī, corresponding to the Sansk. affix इन्.
(Nom. Sing. ī.)

The Sindhī affix ī serves to form possessive nouns, like the Sansk. affix इन्; e. g.:

ڏانْهِي dāhī, complainant, from ڏانْهَ dāha, complaint.

روڳِي rōgī, sick, from روڳُ rōgu, sickness.

مالِي mālī, gardener, Sansk. मालिन्.

In such formations, as are peculiar to the Sindhī, a final short vowel may keep its place before the affix ī, as:

مَتَئِي mataī, tenacious of one's opinion or sect, from مَتِ make opinion or religion (final 'e' being exchanged for 'a', for euphony's sake).

10) Themes in āi.

The affix āī is only a variation of the affix ī (9, a), final 'u' and ō of such themes, as end in 'u' and ō being again changed before it to ā; nouns thus formed imply an occupation, habit or tendency, as:

باگائِي bāgāī, gardener, from باگُ bāgu, garden.

نيچائِي nēčāī, a maker of huqqah-snakes, from نيچو nēčō a huqqah-snake.

جهڳِڙائِي jhagiṛāī, a quarreller, from جهڳِڙو jhagiṛō, quarrel.

11) Themes in ū.

The affix ū, corresponding to the Sansk. affix उक, is added to substantives, by means of which, as in the primary formations, apellatives and adjectives are derived, denoting an habitual action or state. A final vowel is always dropped before the addition of this affix;

in some nouns the first vowel is lengthened at the same time; e. g.:

هَانُڃو hāńū, injurious, from هَانِ hāńe, injury.

وِيرُو vērū, revengeful, from وِيرُ vēru; enmity.

ڇهاپِرُو čhāpirū, a mountaineer, from ڇهپَرُ čhaparu, a range of hills.

بَاکهِرُو bākhirū, a man of Bakhar, from بَکهَرُ bakharu, a town of upper Sindh.

12) Themes in āū.

The affix āū is identical with the preceding, the only difference being that the final vowel of the theme is lengthened before the affix ū (fin. u = a = ā).

دهَرْمَائُو dharmāū, religious, from دهَرْمُ dharmu, religion.

شَرْمَائُو šarmāū, bashful, from, شَرْمُ šarmu, shame, modesty.

13) Themes in āõ.

The affix āõ is already so much corrupted, that its origin is scarcely recognisable; it corresponds to the Sanskrit affix मय, which forms adjectives, denoting "made of, consisting of." The labial m has been elided in this affix as well as in the abstract affix इमन्, and a has been lengthened in compensation thereof. The semi-vowel y has likewise disappeared, āõ = āyõ; the final Anusvāra is altogether euphonic and more or less optional; e. g.:

هَيڊْرَائُون haiḍrāõ, made of هَيڊْرَ haiḍra, turmeric.

جَانْبهَائُون jāmbhāõ, made of جَانْبهو jāmbhō, a kind of oil-seed.

لوهَائُون lōhāõ, made of لوهُ lōhu, iron.

14) Themes in ō.

This affix corresponds to the Sansk. affix अ; it

forms adjectives and attributives in the largest sense. The final short vowel of a noun is always dropped before this affix, and ū and ī are shortened. The root-vowel either remains unaltered or is lengthened, viz: 'a' to ā, ī to ē and 'u' to ō; as:

سَگهو saghō, strong, from سَگهَ sagha, strength.

وِنگو vingō, crooked, from وِنگُ vingu, a crook.

بهَکئُو bhakuō, stupid, from بهَکُو bhakū, a blockhead.

ويچو vēčō, mediator, from وِچُ viču, midst.

بَاروچو bārōčō, of a Beluch, from بَروچُ barōču, a Beluch.

اوٺهو ōthō, of a camel, from اُٺهُ uṭhu, camel.

گائو gāō, of a cow, from گَئُون gāũ, cow.

Iregular formations are:

مَاهيو māhyō, of a buffalo, from مينهِ mēhe, a buffalo.

سَيئون saiõ, hundredth (per cent), from سَوُ sau, hundred.

15) Themes in āru (aru), ārō; ālu.

These affixes correspond to the Sansk. affix आल (in Prākrit likewise आल cf. Var. IV, 26), which forms possessive nouns. In Sindhī r and l are interchanged, and in some nouns āru has been shortened to aru. The root-vowel commonly remains unaltered, but in some nouns 'u' is changed to ō (i. e. 'u' takes Guṇa); as:

ميهَارُ mēhāru, or } a buffalo keeper, from مينهِ mēhe,
ميهَرُ mēharu, } buffalo.

چوٽيَرُ čōṭyaru, having a چوٽِي čōṭī, bundle of hair on the crown of the head.

ڌهَنَارُ dhaṇāru, a herdsman, from ڌهَنُ dhaṇu, a herd of cattle.

اوٺهَارُ ōṭhāru, a camel-herd, from اُٺهُ uṭhu, camel.

جَوَالُ javālu, containing barley, from جَوُ jau, barley.

Some of these formations, with the affix ālu or ālō, are used in a substantive sense, their original possessive signification being more or less lost, as:

کهڙيالُ gharyālu, کهڙيالو gharyālō,	a Gong; literally: containing or expressing the hour (گهڙِي).

ڏِيالُ ḍiālu, candlestick; literally: having a light (ڏِيُو).

جهُڙالو jhurālō, cloudiness; literally: containing clouds (جهُڙُ).

16) Themes in īrō and īlō, or: ērō and ēlō.

These affixes correspond to the Sansk. ईर and ईल and form attributives, signifying: habit, quality or intensity; ērō and ēlo have sprung from the Prākrit affix illa (Var. IV, 25); e. g.:

کهانْڍهِيرو khāndhīrō, patient, from کهانْڍهِ khāndhe, patience.

هٺهِيلو haṭhīlō, obstinate, from هٺهُ haṭhu, obstinacy.

ڇهانوِيرو čhā̃vērō, ڇهانوِيلو čhā̃vēlō,	shadowy, from ڇهانْوَ čhā̃va, shade.

ٿهرِيلو tharēlō, of the Thar, having the custom of the Thar or desert.

چمِيلو čamēlō, leathern, from چَمُ čamu, leather.

17) Themes in iru.

This affix corresponds to the Sansk. affix र (with the union-vowel i) and forms attributives and appellatives as well as possessive nouns; a final vowel, short or long, is always dropped before the addition of this affix; e. g.:

سَنْڌهِرُ sandhiru, a house-breaker, from سَنْڌهِ sandhe, a hole in a wall.

جهاتِرُ jhātiru, a peeper, from جهاتِي jhātī, looking through a hole.

چهينْبهِرُ čhīmbhiru, a rebuker, from چهينْبهَ čhīmbha, rebuke.

جهَپِرُ jhapiru, one who snatches, from جهَپو jhapō, a snatch.

پيٽِرُ pēṭiru, a glutton, from پيٽُ pētu, belly.

وِهِرُ vihiru, poisonous, from وِهُ f. poison.

18) Themes in atu and ālū.

This affix has sprung from the Sanskrit affix मत् by elision of म; in some nouns 'a' has been lengthened, to compensate for the elision of m; it forms possessive nouns, just as in Sanskrit; e. g.:

بهرْيَتُ bharyatu, a porter, from بهَرِي bharī, a man's load.

پورهِيَتُ pōrhiatu, a labourer, from پورهِيو pōrhiō, labour.

ڏِڻيَاتُ ḍiaṇyātu, a debtor, from ڏِڻِي ḍiaṇī, a debt.

19) Themes in ētō (itō).

The Sindhī affix ētō corresponds to the Sansk. affix इत, denoting "to be provided with", to possess as one's own. The short i of the Sansk. affix has in Sindhī been produced to ē, on account of the accent; the final vowel is always dropped before this affix; e. g.:

پُٽريتو puṭrētō, having a son, from پُٽرُ paṭru, son.

ڌِهئيتو dhiētō, having a daughter, from ڌِهِيَ dhia, daughter.

جوئيتو jōētō, having a wife, from جوء jōe, wife.

بهائِتو bhāitō, having a brother, from بهاءُ bhāu, brother.

20) Themes in āitō.

This affix is identical with the preceding in derivation and signification, the only difference being that final ō, 'u' and 'a' are changed before it to ā, as:

وَارائِتو vārāitō, adj., at the right time, from وَارو vārō, time.

سَجھائِتو sajhāitō, adj., opportune, from سَجھُ sajhu, opportunity.

وَاٽائِتو vāṭāitō, having a road, from وَاٽَ vāṭa, a road.

21) Themes in ṛu and lu.

a) The affix ṛu corresponds to the Sansk. diminutive affix र, and is affixed to adjectives and participles present, with some slight variation of the original meaning; when added to adjectives the root-vowel is now and then lengthened. Final 'u' and ō are changed to 'a' before the addition of this affix; ī remains unaltered.

کھابَڙُ khābaṛu, left-handed, from کھَبو khabō, left.

سَاجَڙُ sājaṛu, right-handed, from سَاجو sājō, right.

کھَسَڙُ khasaṛu, sterile, from کھَسُ khasu, not fully developed.

ڪَاڇھِيڙو kāčhiṛō, of the province of Kač̌h, from ڪَاڇھِي, a Kāčhī.

لِکھَنْدَڙُ likhandaṛu, a writer, from لِکھَنْدو part. pres. writing.

b) The affix lu is identical with the affix ṛu (r [ṛ] = l) and turns preterite participles into simple adjectives; it is seldom found with adjectives, the signification of which it does not change materially.

وِئَلُ vialu, lost, from وِئو viō, gone, lost.

ڏِٺھَلُ ḍiṭhalu, seen, from ڏِٺھو ḍiṭhō, seen.

وِسُورِڙل visūṛalu, simple-minded, from وِسُورِڙو visūrō, simple-minded.

Similarly in Prākrit the affix r or l (dimin.) is added to nouns and adjectives, without essentially altering their signification (cf. Varar. IV, 26), as Sansk. विद्युत् lightening, Prāk. विज्जू or विज्जुली; पीत yellow, Prāk. पीअ or: पीअल.

The same affix ला we notice in the Marāṭhī, where it is added to preterite participles to turn them into real adjectives, as: चाललेला gone (from चालला); मोडिलेला broken (from मोडिला); the same holds good in Gujarātī, as: लखेलो, written (Adj.) (from लख्यो).

22) Themes in iṛyō.

The affix iṛyō is originally compounded of the diminutive affix ड़ (= ṛ) and the adjectival affix yō (य); it forms adjectives and attributives denoting inclination or hesitation; e. g.:

سَدهِڙيو sadhiṛyō, half-wishing; literally: being somewhat disposed to wish.

گهورِڙيو ghōriṛyō, a pedlar; i. e. one who is inclined to seek out.

پيرِڙيو pēriṛyō, a walker; literally: disposed to travel afoot.

پَرمَتِڙيو paramatiṛyō, easily persuaded; literally: disposed to take another's counsel.

23) Themes in āku and ākū.

These Uṇādi-affixes, which else only occur with primary themes, are in Sindhī also used (but very rarely) in secondary formations, as:

جهيڙاڪ jhēṛāku, } quarrelsome, from جهيڙو jhēṛō,
جهيڙاڪو jhēṛākū, } contention.

24) Themes in ikō.

This affix corresponds to the Sansk. affix क (in Sindhī with the addition of the union-vowel i) and forms adjectives, denoting relation, quality etc. A final vowel, short or long, is dropped before this affix; final ū alone is shortened to 'u' and takes the union-vowel 'a' instead of 'i'; e. g.:

واپارِڪو vāpārikō, mercantile, from واپارُ vāpāru, trade.

وانِڪو vāṇikō, relating to a وائيو vāṇyō or shopkeeper.

هارِڪو hārikō, relating to a هاري hārī or peasant.

مِروَڪو miruakō, brutal, from مِرُون mirū̃, a wild beast.

25) Themes in īčō or ēčō.

These affixes have sprung from the Sansk. affix इक, and form adjectives denoting descent or origin. In Sindhī 'i' has been lengthened to ī or even to ē, and the guttural k has been exchanged for the palatal č. The final vowel, short or long, is always cast off before these affixes; e. g.:

گوٺيچو gōṭhēčō, of the same village, from گوٺُ gō-ṭhu, village.

پاڙيچو pāṛēčō, of the same quarter, from پاڙو pārō, quarter.

پارِيچو pārēčō, of the opposite side, from پارِ adv., opposite.

ويڙهيچو vēṛhīčō, of the jungle, from ويڙهه vēṛhe, jungle.

26) Themes in ōkō.

This affix, which is added only to nouns or adverbs, denoting time, is identical with the affix क; the union-vowel ō is peculiar and not to be met with elsewhere; every final vowel, short or long, is dropped before it; e. g.:

وَرِهوکو varehōkō, yearly, from وَرِهُ varehu, year.

راتوکو rātōkō, nightly, from راتِ rāte, night.

هانوکو hānōkō, recent, from هاني hānē, now. adj.

کالهوکو kālhōkō, of yester (day or night), from کالهَ kālha, yesterday, adv.

پروکو parōkō, of last year, from پَر (fem.) last year.

A few other adjectives are formed by the same affix, with the further difference, that the root-vowel is lengthened, as:

چانڊروکو čānḍrōkō, moonlight, from چنڊُر čanḍru, moon.

27) Themes in āṇō (āṇu, iṇō), āṅikō.

This affix corresponds to the Sansk. affix इन, and forms adjectives denoting relation or descent. It is remarkable, that the original union-vowel 'i' has been dislodged in Sindhī and ā substituted in its place (compare with this such Latin forms, as: romānus, africānus). The adjectives, formed by the affix āṇō may moreover add the affix kō (with the union vowel 'i'), so that we thus have adjectives with a double affix, which do not materially differ from the simple forms in āṇō; e. g.:

چورانو cōrāṇō, } of a thief, from چورُ cōru, thief.
چورانِکو čōrānikō, }

لچانو lučāṇō, rascally, from لچو lučō, rascal.

ڌِيانو dhiāṇō, of a daughter, from ڌِيءَ dhia, daughter.

مِرئانو miruāṇō, of a wild beast, from مِرون mirū̃, wild beast.

ڀايانو bhāyāṇō, of a partner, from ڀائِي bhāī, partner.

In a few nouns a short root-vowel is lengthened, as:

چانڈرانو čānḍrāṇō,		
چانڈران čānḍrāṇu,	}	moonlight, from چنڈر čanḍru, moon.
چانڈرنو čānḍriṇō,		

28) Themes in ūṇō (ūṇikō).

a) This affix is identical with the preceding, but the union-vowel has been exchanged for ū; in signification there is no difference; e. g.:

سيٿھونو sēṭhūṇō, of a Sēṭh, from سيٿھ sēṭhe, a whole-sale merchant.

واتونو vātūṇō, oral, from وات vātu, mouth.

اڳونو agūṇō, preceding, from اڳ agu, front.

ڪالھونو kālhūṇō, of yester (— day or night), from ڪالھ kālha, yesterday.

To the affix ūṇō the affix kō (ikō) may be superadded, without altering the signification in any way, as: اڳونِڪو agūṇikō, the same as: اڳونو agūṇō.

b) There is another affix ūṇō, which is joined to numerals, identical in form with the preceding, but of different origin. It is derived from the Sansk. noun गुण (quality), with elision of g in Sindhī and prolongation of ū. In Panjābī both forms, guṇā and uṇā, are in use, so that there cannot remain any doubt about its derivation.[1]) It forms adjectives from numerals, signifying: having such a quality, or: manifold, as:

هيڪونو hēkūṇō, single (having a single quality), from هيڪ hēku, one.

پنجونو panjūṇō, quintuple, from پنج panja, five.

سَونو saūṇō, hundredfold, from سَو saū, hundred.

1) Compare also the Persian گانه, as: دوگانه twofold etc.

29) Themes in āṇī.

This affix, corresponding to the Sansk. affix आयनि, forms patronymics or nouns denoting descent; the short final 'i' of the Sansk. affix has been lengthened in Sindhī, as in other similar nouns. A final short vowel is dropped before this affix, likewise ō; final ī is changed to y (= i) and ū is shortened; e. g.:

مَحْمُودَانِي maȟmūdāṇī, son or descendant of مَحْمُودُ maȟmūdu.

آرِيَانِي āryāṇī, son of آرِي ārī.

آڏُئَانِي āḍuāṇī, son of آڏُو āḍū.

ٻَاگَانِي ٻāgāṇī, son of ٻَاگو ٻāgō.

30) Themes in īṇō.

This affix corresponds to the Sansk. affix ईन and forms adjectives denoting relation or descent; as:

سَنگِينو saṅīṇō, affianced, from سَنگُ saṅu, connexion by marriage.

وَسِينو vasīṇō, subjected, from وَسُ, power.

31) Themes in āṭhō.

This affix coincides with the Sansk. affix आट (with transition of ṭ into ṭh); it forms possessive nouns, as in Sanskrit; e. g.:

پَانيَاٺهو pāṇyāṭhō, damp (containing water), from پَانِي pāṇī, water.

چهَبَراٺهو čhaƀarāṭhō, containing چهَبَرُ čhaƀaru, a kind of grass.

32) Themes in āsō (āsū).

This affix, corresponding to the Sansk. affix श,

forms adjectives, denoting "to be full of", to be provided with"; as union-vowel ā has been inserted; as:

وارِيَاسو vāryāsō, sandy, from وارِي vārī, sand.

مَوَاسُ mavāsu, full of pride, from مَوُ mau, pride.

33) Themes in hāru or hārō.

This affix is in Sindhī and in the cognate dialects added to verbal nouns (i. e. the Infinitive); it forms a kind of participle, which is commonly used as a substantive noun. In Marāṭhī it forms the participle future, as it implies at the same time the notion of some future act or state; in Sindhī too it is now and then used in a future sense. It is to be noted though, that the Marāṭhī affix is not णार, as commonly shown in Marāṭhī grammars, but आर; a like mistake is generally to be met with in Gujarātī grammars, where it is stated to be नार. In Marāṭhī and Gujarātī the form of the affix is clearly enough आर, corresponding to the Sansk. adjective कार, making, doing, with elision of क. In Sindhī, Hindī and Panjābī it is hār, which form is to be explained in this way, that initial क has been originally aspirated by the following र (which is very frequently the case in Sindhī), and then elided, leaving h (see Introd. §. 8). In Sindhī the form hāru, hārō, is only added to the Infinitive, in other themes the original form kāru has been retained unaltered; e. g.:

سِرْجَڻهارُ sirjaṇahāru, the creator, Inf. سِرْجَڻُ to create.

لِکَهَڻهارُ likhaṇahāru, a writer, or one, who is about to write; Inf. لِکَهَڻُ to write.

34) Themes in kāru, karu.

The original adjective form kāru (in Sindhī also shortened karu) is also (but rarely) in use; it forms adjectives and attributives from substantives; as union-vowel ā is inserted:

جهيڙاڪارُ ǰhēṛākāru, } quarrelsome, causing quarrel,
جهيڙاڪرُ ǰhēṛākāru, } from جهيڙو ǰhēṛō, quarrel.

35) Themes in vānu.

The Sindhī has preserved in this affix the Nom. Sing. of the Sansk. affix वान् (= vān), and discarded the Prākrit form वन्तो; the same is the case in the cognate dialects, with the exception of the Gujarātī, which uses the termination वंत. It forms adjectives, implying possession; e. g.:

دَيَاوانُ dayāvānu, compassionate, from دَيَا dayā, compassion.

وِڄاوانُ viǰāvānu, learned, from وِڄا viǰā, learning.

سِيلَوانُ sīlavānu, virtuous, from سِيلُ sīlu, virtue.

36) Themes in vārō.

This is one of the most useful affixes of the modern vernaculars; it may be joined to any verbal noun or substantive, and denotes an owner or actor; this affix is most extensively used in Hindūstānī (vālā), where it is used as a substitute for different formations. It corresponds to the Sansk. affix वल, from which it has been derived by lengthening the root-vowel. It is to be observed, that وارو must be joined to the formative or oblique case of a noun.

گهَرَوارو gharavārō, owner of a house, from گهَرُ gharu, house.

گهَرنِوارو gharanevārō, owner of houses.

ڏِئَڻوارو ḍiaṇavārō, a giver, Inf. ڏِئَڻُ ḍiaṅu, to give.

وِچَوارو vičavārō, mediator, from وِچُ viču, midst.

ٻيڙِئَوارو ƀēṛiavārō, boatman, from ٻيڙِي ƀēṛī, boat.

37) Themes in yō.

The affix yō, corresponding to the Sansk. affix य, forms adjectives from substantives, as:

بهاڳيو bhāgyō, fortunate, from ڀاڳُ bhāgu, fortune; luck.

وِکوِکيو vikevikhyō, a grumbling person, from وِکوِک vikevike, grumbling.

جوئيو jōyo, effeminate, from جوء (زوء) jōe, wife.

Chapter IV.

Formation of Diminutives.

§. 11.

The Sindhī evinces a great facility in forming different kinds of Diminutives; it surpasses in this respect all the kindred dialects, being able to derive diminutives from any substantive, adjective or even participle.

The one method, to express the idea of a diminutive, is, to substitute the feminine termination for the masculine, the feminine expressing generally: smallness, littleness, nicety, as: ڪاتُ kātu, m. a large knife, ڪاتِي kātī, fem. a small knife (cf. §. 5, VI, 2, c).

An old diminutive formation has been preserved in a few straggling words, ending in ōṭru (ōṭrō) or ōṭu (ōṭō); the same formation is still current in the Paṣ̌tō (ōṭai, ūṭai), where diminutives are regularly derived by means of this affix. The origin of this diminutive affix is rather uncertain; e. g. Sindhī:

بَاهوٽِي bāhōṭī, a small fire, from بَاهِ bāhe, fire; جَاموٽرُ jāmōṭru, the headman of a village (literally: a little جَامُ jāmu or Jām, prince); ڏِيَاٽِي ḍiāṭī, a small light, from ڏِيُو ḍiō, an oil-light.

Besides these formations the Sindhī uses for the purpose of forming diminutives proper two affixes, which are originally identical; viz.: ēro (= rō, the union-vowel 'i' having been produced to ē, on account of the accent), which is added to adjectives only, and ṛō, which is promiscuously joined to adjectives and substantives. Both these affixes correspond to the Sanskrit diminutive affix र r, from which the Sindhī, after its own peculiar method, has menaged to form two separate diminutive affixes. The other diminutive affix of the Sanskrit, क k, is not in use in Sindhī, but is so in Hindī, Marāṭhī and Panjābī.

1) The affix ērō.

This deminutive affix is, as noted already, added to adjectives only and implies: somewhat more or less (as the case may be), rather, very; e. g.:

ڏِرگهيرو ḍrighērō, somewhat long, adj. ڏِرگهو ḍrighō, long.

ٿهوريرو thōrērō, rather little, adj. ٿهورو thōrō, little.

گهٽيرو ghaṭērō, rather deficient, adj. گهٽِ ghaṭe, deficient.

2) The termination ṛō, fem. ṛī.

This diminutive affix is joined to substantives and adjectives, even to such, as have already received the affix ērō; it denotes smallness, littleness, deficiency, tenderness or contempt. In order to point out more effectually the idea of the diminutive, the feminine termination ṛī may be chosen, instead of the masculine. The Sindhī poëts use the diminutives with great taste and delicacy, and know to give different shades to their pictures by their proper application. The final vowels undergo the following changes before the addition of the affix ṛō (ṛī):

1) Final u (m.) is changed to 'a' or 'i', with the exception of fem. nouns ending in 'u', wich remain unaltered.
2) In the same way final ō is changed to 'a' or 'i'.
3) Final 'a' remains unaltered.
4) Final 'i' remains unaltered or passes (for euphony's sake) into 'a'.
5) Final ī and ū are shortened with a subsounding 'a' (as union-vowel).

Final 'u'.

پَنْڌهَڙو pandhaṛō, a short journey, from پَنْڌهُ pandhu, journey.

هَٽِڙي haṭiṛī, a small shop, from هَٽُ haṭu, shop.

جِنْدُڙو jindurō, short life, from جِنْدُ jindu, life, fem.

وِڄُڙي viǰuṛī, a small flash of lightening, from وِڄُ viǰu, fem., lightening.

Final ō.

هِئڙو hīaṛō heart (endearing), from هِئُو hīō, heart.

ڀهولِڙو bhōliṛō, a small monkey, from ڀهولو bhōlō, monkey.

ٿهورِڙو thōriṛō, very little, from ٿهورو thōrō, little.
ٿهوريرِڙو thōrēriṛō, extremely little.

Final 'a'.

ڌهِئڙي dhiaṛī, a little daughter, from ڌهِيَ dhia, daughter.

Final 'i'.

اَکهِڙي akhiṛī, a small eye, from اَکهِ akhe, eye.

ڳالهَڙي g̈alhaṛī, a short word, from ڳالهِ g̈ālhe, word.

Final ī and ū.

مَنْدهِيَڙو mandhiaṛō, a small churning staff, from مَنْدهِي mandhī, a churning staff.

ڀهَتُئَڙي bhaṭuaṛī, a small scorpion, from ڀهَتُو bhaṭū, a scorpion.

Chapter V.

Compound nouns.

§. 12.

I. Nouns compounded with a preceding particle.

1) Nouns compounded with the negative particles a, aṇa, nā, nir, ni, ma.

All these negative particles are of Sanskrit origin and used in the same way and in the same sense, as in the Sanskrit. The negative particle 'a' is only used with adjectives, aṇa chiefly with participles and Gerundives, rarely with adjectives; nā with adjectives, and the shortened form na with Gerundives and participial adjectives; nir and ni (with assimilated r), only with adjectives (and abstracts, derived from adjectives). We have not mentioned expressly the negative particle dur (दुर्), which belongs to the same class, as it occurs in such formations only, as are borrowed directly from the Sanskrit and have already passed through the process of assimilation, usual in Sindhī, as: ڏُڪَالُ ḍukālu, famine, Sansk. दुष्काल (see Introd. §. 16, B). For the sake of a general survey we have summed up here all the negative prefixes, though the nouns compounded with them belong to the subsequent classes of compounds, as far as their composition is concerned.

Prefix a: اَچيتُ ačētu, thoughtless; thence.

اَچيتائِي acētāī, } thoughtlessness.
اَچيتِي ačētī, }

Prefix aṇa: اَنَتهِئڻو aṇathiaṇō, impossible.

اَنَپُڇهو aṇapučhō, unasked.
اَنويسَاهو aṇavēsāhō, unbelieving.
اَنويسَاهِي aṇavēsāhī, s. f., unbelief.

Prefix nā: نَاكَارو nākārō, useless.
نَاچَنْگو načaṅō, unwell.
نَاچَنْگَائِي načaṅāī, illness.

Prefix nă: نَتهِئڻو nathiaṇō, impossible.

نَتهِئڻِي nathiaṇī, impossibility.

نَكهَٽُو nakhaṭū, profitless.

Prefix ma: مَچهَڏُو mačhaḍū, not giving up.
مَكهَٽُو makhaṭū, profitless.

Prefix nir and ni: نِرْدَئِي nir-daī, unfeeling, Sansk. निर्दय.

نِرَاسُ nir-āsu, hopeless, Sansk. निराश.

نِدهَڻِكو ni-dhaṇikō, masterless (دهَڻِي).

نِپُٽرو ni-puṭrō, sonless (پُٽرُ).

2) Nouns compounded with the privative particles rē, without, and bē, without.

The privative particle rē, which is also used as a preposition, and as such always requires the Formative (oblique case), is derived from the Sanskrit preposition ऋते (Prākrit रित्ते = रिए, and contracted रे rē) without, excepted; bē is borrowed from the Persian and corresponds originally to the Sansk. prefix वि. These prefixes are in Arabic writing generally written separately and not joined to the noun, as:

rē: رِي كمو rē-kamō, useless.
رِي پَانيو rē-pāṇyō, waterless.
رِي چيو rē-čayō, untractable.

bē: بي سَگهو bē-saghō, powerless.
بي دِينو bē-dīnō, irreligious.
بي لَجو bē-lajō, shameless.

3) Nouns compounded with the particles of qualification su, well, ku, badly, and ava (au), away, from.

su: سُكَال sukālu, good time = cheapness.
سُچيت sučētu, attentive.
سُپرِين suprī, good friend = sweetheart.

ku: كُپَتِ kupate, dishonesty.
كُپَتيو kupatyō, dishonest.
كُنِيَاء kuniyāu, bad justice = oppression.

كُڏهنگو kuḍhangō, ill-bred.

ava (au): اَوگُن avaguṇu, اَوْگُن auguṇu, } vice.

اَوَتَرُ avataṛu, اَوْتَرُ autaṛu, } a bad landing place.

4) Nouns compounded with the possessive particle sa (shortened from the Sansk सह), implying "with", "provided with".

سَپهلو saphalō, fruitful.

سَبوجهو sabōǰhō, intelligent.

سَپُٽرو saputrō, having a son.

II. Nouns compounded with a substantive, adjective or numeral.

The Sindhī generally follows in the formation of its compound nouns the rules of the Sanskrit, though the compounds cannot be formed in Sindhī in the same unlimited number, as in Sanskrit, the want of case-inflexions offering an essential obstacle. No compound can be formed from more than two nouns, a noun compounded of three words is a linguistic impossibility in Sindhī, as in such a compound all idea of coordination or subordination would be completely lost. We shall consider the compounds current in Sindhī under the received Sanskrit appellations.

1) So-called Tatpuruṣa compounds, or conjunction of two nouns, of which the former stands in a case-relation with the latter.

These compounds are rarely used in common conversation, but more extensively in poëtical compositions. The former of the two nouns, which is dependent on the latter, must consequently be placed in the Formative, to express thereby its grammatical dependency. In reference to the method of writing these compounds there is no fixed rule; some of them, in which the idea of unity prevails so much, that they are considered as one word, are joined in writing accordingly; others again, in which the conjunction is more loose, are written separately; e. g.:

اُتَر واءُ utara-vāu, north-wind.

گهَر دهَڻي ghara-dhaṇī, master of the house.

مَتهي کهائو mathē-khāū, torturer, literally: eating one's head.

ڋيسَ نِڪَالوَ ḍēsa nikālō, banishment.

ڪَرَنِ ٽُرٽرو karane-ṭruṭrō; a lazy fellow; literally: broken of hands.

پَانَ بهَرُو pāṇa bharū, selfish; literally: filling oneself.

A peculiar kind of compound is formed by an adjective joined to a substantive, which by the addition of the affix vārō (see §. 10, 3, b) is turned again into a possessive noun; the adjective must in this case agree with its substantive in gender, number and case. Such compounds are, as far as their signification is concerned, Bahuvrīhis, but according to their composition Tatpuruṣas; for the latter reason we have inserted them in this place; as:

ٻِئي ڋيسَوَارو biē ḍēsavārō, a foreigner (a man of another country).

تِکِهي سُرْتِوَارو tikhia-surtevārō, a man of sharp understanding.

چَنگي پَهَوَارو čaṅē pahavārō, a man of good counsel.

More poëtical are compounds like:

وَڋِی دِلِ دَاتَا vaḍia dile dātā, a munificent giver (a giver of a great heart).

2) So-called Dvandvas, or aggregation of nouns.

In the sense of the Sanskrit Grammar there are no Dvandvas in Sindhī. Two nouns are frequently joined in Sindhī, expressing one common idea, but grammatically they are treated as two separate words. In Sindhī, as well as in the other cognate dialects, two nouns are frequently joined together, of which the latter is without a proper meaning, and only added to render the sound more full; these compounds are called alliterations.

وَتھُ پُڄُ vaṭhu puju, f., hurry; literally: taking (وَتھُ) arriving (پُڄُ).

چنگو بھلو čaṅō bhalō, very good; very well.

مَٽَ سَٽَ maṭa saṭa, exchange (مَٽَ and سَٽَ, both signifying exchange).

گھٽِ وَڌھِ ghaṭe vadhe, less or more.

جھُڙُ پھُڙُ jhuṛu phuṛu, rainy weather (جھُڙُ cloudiness; پھُڙُ drop).

اَڄُ صُبَھَنْ aju subaȟā, in a day or two; literally: to-day, to-morrow.

بَکَ شَکَ baka šaka, prattle; بَکَ talking, chatting, شَکَ being a meaningless alliteration.

But more frequently than by aggregation the Sindhī joins two nouns by inserting the Persian copula ō (frequently nasalized = ō̃); the final vowel of the preceding noun is dropped before it and both words are joined into one and written accordingly; in some instances though the final vowel of the preceding noun keeps its place before ō. These compounds are Dvandvas in a grammatical sense, only the latter noun being subject to the laws of inflexion.

راتوڏِينھُ rātōḍīhu, night and day.

هَنْڌھوهَنْڌھُ handhōhandhu, every place.

راتِٿوراتِ rate-ō-rāte, every night; night by night.

پَروپَرِ parōpare, kind by kind = every kind.

The conjunction may also be effected by the Persian copulative particle ā, in the same way as by ō; this ā too is very frequently nasalized in Sindhī = ā̃; the final vowel of the preceding word always disappears before ā or ā̃; as:

مُکهامُکهِي mukhāmukhī, meeting; literally: tête-à-tête.

مُکهاميلو mukhāmēlō, assembly; literally: face and meeting.

ويرانوير vērāvēra, adv., always; literally: time and time. (وير).

3) So-called Karmadhārayas, or descriptive compounds.

The Sindhī is now too simple, to admit of new compounds of this kind; the common rule is, as in the other dialects, that the adjective precedes its substantive and agrees with the same in gender, number and case. Some remnants however of original Karmadhāraya compounds have been preserved in Sindhī, and what is still more remarkable, the Sindhī has formed some similar compounds out of its own resources, in which the adjective is joined to the substantive in its original (else not occurring) crude state. It is to be noted, that all compounds of this description are written in one word; e. g.:

مَهاجَنُ mahājaṇu, a great merchant, Sansk. महाजन.

مَهارَاجُ mahārāju,
مَهراجُ maharāju, } a great prince.

وَڏکهائو vaḍakhāū, a glutton (great eater).

گهَڻگهُرو ghaṇaghurō, well-wishing.

مَٺهگهُرو maṭhaghurō, ill-wishing.

پَرمارْتهُ paramārthu, benevolence.

پَرلوکُ paralōku, the other world.

4) So-called Dvigus, or collective compounds.

This class of compounds, which is formed by a preceding numeral, is in frequent use in Sindhī; e. g.:

بِپَهَرِي bipaharī, midday; compounded of بِ bĭ, two and پَهَرِ, a watch of three hours.

بِهَڙ bihaṛe, a pair of water wheels.

چَوْمَاسو čaumāsō, a space of four months = the rainy season.

چَوْوَاٽو čauvāṭō, a place, where four roads meet; literally: having four roads.

پَنْجَسْنَانِي panjasnānī, washing of the five parts of the body (= head, two hands, two feet).

بَارَهَنْمَاسِي bārahãmāsī, a year = a twelvemonth.

5) The so-called Bahuvrīhis, or relative compounds.

This class of compounds, denoting posssession or relation, which again comprises all the four preceding classes, by changing them into adjectives, is still very numerous in Sindhī; for either original Bahuvrīhi compounds are borrowed directly from the Sanskrit, or new compounds are formed according to the same principles, which are laid down in Sanskrit. The final noun receives generally the adjectival affix ō (see §. 10; 14); in such compounds, as are taken directly from the Persian, the final noun may remain unchanged, its relative signification having been fixed already in Persian.

a) Bahuvrīhi formations from Tatpuruṣa compounds.

رَتَوَرَنو rata-varanō, having the colour of blood.

مَتهَمُهو matha-muhō, haughty; from مَتهُ top, and مُهُ (= مُنهُ) mouth.

پيٽَارْتهِي pēṭārthī, glutton; from پيٽُ pēṭu, belly, and اَرْتهِي arthī, having an object; having the belly for one's object.

b) Bahuvrīhi formations from Karmádhāraya compounds.

وَڏَواتو vaḍavātō, loquacious; literally: having a big mouth.

گهڻَبِجو ghaṇa-bijō, having much seed.

ٿورويرمو thōra-vēramō, having little delay = quick.

صافُدِلِ sāfu-dile, having a pure heart; Pers.

خُوشخِيالُ χuš-χiālu, joyful; Pers.

c) Bahuvrīhi formations from Dvigu compounds.

چَوْدَرو čaudarō, having four doors.

ٻِمَڻو ɓimaṇō, containing two maunds.

ٻارهَنْماهو ɓārahāmāhō, yearly = containing twelve months.

d) Bahūvrihi formations from such compounds, as are preceded by an adverb or prefix.

سَپُٽرو saputṛō, having a son.

سُچيت sučētu, attentive.

ڪُمَتيو kumatyō, dishonest.

Chapter VI.

Gender of nouns.

§. 13.

It has been stated already, that the Sindhī has lost the Neuter, most of the original neuter nouns having assumed a masculine, a less number the feminine termination. The gender of a Sindhī noun is easily recognizable, as every noun must end in a vowel; some terminations admit of no exceptions, others are common to both masculine and feminine nouns.

The termination ō is masculine without any exception; the termination ă is feminine without any exception; all the other terminations contain more or less exceptions.

1) The termination 'u'.

The termination 'u' is, according to its origin, generally masculine; but as original Sanskrit-Prākrit themes, ending in 'u' and being of the feminine gender, have been mixed up with it, a number of nouns have retained the feminine gender. In some of them an original feminine termination has been dropped and 'u' substituted in its place, whereas the gender of the noun has been preserved; in others again no reason can be detected, why they have been treated as feminines in Sindhī, the masculine gender having been retained in the cognate dialects; some few of them are of unknown origin, on which we cannot venture any conjecture.

As a general rule we may state, that, abstracted from the termination, all nouns are feminine, which imply a female being, as: مَاءُ māu, mother; ڌِيُءِ dhiu, daughter; نُنْهُ nūhu, daughter-in-law; سَسُ sasu, mother-in-law; ڀيڻُ bhēṇu, sister; ڌيڻُ dhēṇu, milk-cow; ڳَئُون gāū, cow; with some of them the feminine termination 'a' is also in use, as: ڌِيءَ dhia, نُنْهَ nūha, ڀيڻَ bhēṇa.

The following is a list of nouns ending in 'u', which are feminine:

اَڄُ aju, f., to-day; Sansk. अद्य, adv., Hindī आज्, adv.

اَنْسُ ansu, f., offspring; Sansk. अंश, m.; Hindī अंस्, m.

اَنگُ angu, or: اَنگھُ anghu, f., a rent, tear; origin unknown.

آنو ā̃u, f., slimy excrement, origin unknown.

ٻٻر bāburu, f., the acacia tree; Sansk. बव्बुर, m. Hindī बबूर, f.

بَرْکھ barkhu, f., shortened from بَرْکھت barkhata, blessing (Arab. بَرْکت; in Sindhī k has been aspirated by the influence of r) pronounced as a good omen in beginning to count = one.

ٻِنْدُ bindu, f., semen virile; Sansk. विन्दु, m., Hindī बिंद, m.

ڀَسُ bhasu, f., ashes; Sansk. भसन्, n.; Hindī भस्, m.

پَرُ paru, f., last year; Sansk. परुत्, adv.

پُوَنُو pūna-u, f., the day of the full moon; also پُونِي pūna-e; Sansk. पर्वन्, n.

تاکُ tāku, f., a leathern vessel; origin unknown.

تَنْدُ tandu, f., thread, wire; Sansk. तन्तु, m.; Hindī तांत, f.

ٿَرُ tharu, f., cream; origin unknown.

ٿَڃُ thańu, f., woman's milk; Sansk. स्तन, m.; Hindī थन, m.

ٽرکُ ṭraku, f., the spindle of a spinning wheel; Sansk. तर्कु; in Sindhī r has been pushed forward, to keep its place the more easily in conjunction with the cerebral; see Introd. §. 15, B, a.

ڄَرُ jaru, f., leech, afterbirth. Two words have been apparently melted into one. ڄَرُ leech, corresponds to the Hindūstānī زَلُو zalū (properly Persian), which has sprung from the Sanskrit जालुका; the final syllable kā has, as elsewhere, been cast off, but the original gender retained. ڄَرُ afterbirth, has been shortened from the Sansk. जरायु, m., Hindūstānī جير jĕr (Greek: γῆρας). In Hindūstānī the gender of جير seems to be doubtful, for Shakespear is silent about it; in Hindī it is considered masculine (Thompson, Hindī Dictionary).

جِنْدُ ǰindu, f., life; borrowed from the Panǰābī, where it is likewise fem.

جَوُ ǰa-u, f., sealing-wax; origin unknown.

جَوكهارُ ǰaukhāru, f., a salt, used in medicine; compounded of جَوُ barley, and كهارُ, which see.

جهِلُ ǰhilu, f., name of a plant (Indigofera pauciflora); origin unknown.

چُپُ čupu, f., or: چِپُ čipu, silence; taken from the Hindī, in which it is fem.

چِلُ čilu, f., name of a vegetable; origin unknown.

چَوُ ča-u, f., a jeweller's weight; origin unknown.

چهارُ čhāru, f., ashes; originally identical with كهارُ, Sansk. क्षार.

چهِلُ čhilu, f., bark, peel; Sansk. छल्लि or छल्ली; the original fem. termination i (ī) has been lost in this noun, but the gender retained; besides چهِلُ the form چهِلَ is also in use.

چيزُ čīzu, f., thing; tāken from the Hindūstānī (Persian) where it is fem.

دهاتُ dhātu, f., root; metal. Sansk. धातु, m.; Hindī धात् or धातु, m., but used as fem. in the sense of semen virile.

ڏڏهُ ḍaḍhu, f., ringworm; Sansk. दद्रु, m.; Hindī दाद्, m.

سَرُ sara-u, fem., autumn, Sansk. शरद्, fem., Hindī शरद्, fem.

سُگَنْدھُ sugandhu, f. (occasionally also masc.), perfume, Sansk. सुगन्ध, m., Hindī सुजन्ध्, m.

سِنْدھُ sindhu, f., the country of Sindh; the Indus; Sansk. सिन्धु, m.; Hindī सिन्ध् or सिन्धु, m.

کَٹُ kaṭu, f., rust (occasionally also m.); origin unknown.

کَسُ kasu, f., verdigris; origin unknown.

کَھارُ khāru, f., potash; Sansk. क्षार, m., n.; Hindī खार, m.

کَھڙُ khaṛu, f. (also masc.), oil-cake, Hindī खली, f., Sansk. खलं, n.

کَھنْڊُرُ khanḍru, f., sugar, Sansk. खराड, m.; Hindī खराड्, m.

گَرُ garu, f., the mange; Sansk. खर्जु, f.

ڳَرُ g̃aru, f., the pulp of any fruit; Sansk. गर्भ, m.

ڳَمُ g̃amu, f., name of a wild grass; origin unknown.

ڳَئُون gāū̃, f., cow; Sansk. गो, f.; Hindī गाइ, गो or गौ.

لِمُ limu, f. The nimb tree; the same as نِمُ, which see.

لَئُون lāū̃, f., devotion, love; Sansk. लय, m.; Hindī लय, f.

مَرُ maru, f., cerumen; Sansk. मलं, n.; Hindī मैल, f.

مَسُ masu, f., ink; Sansk. मसि, f.; Hindī मसि or मसी.

مِکھُ mikhu, } f., marrow; Sansk. मज्जा, Hindī मज्जा, f.
مِڃُ miñu, }

مَيْلُ mailu, f., dirt; see مَرُ, with which it is identical.

نِمُ nimu, f., the nimb tree; Sansk. निम्बूक, m.; Hindī नीम्बू or लीमू, m.

نَهَتهَرُ nahatharu, f., whitlow, from نَهُ nahu, nail and تهَرُ, which see.

وَتهُ vathu, f., thing; Sansk. वस्तु, n.; Hindī बस्तु, f.

وَٹهُ vaṭhu, f., seizure; Sansk. वृत्ति (election); the aspiration of ṭh has been effected by r.

وِجُ viju, f., lightening; Sansk. विद्युत्, f., Prāk. विज्जू, f.

وِرَءُ vira-u, f., allowance, ration; Sansk. वर्तन, n., stipulated pay.

وِسُ visu, } f., world; Sansk. विषय, m.; Hindī विषय्, m.
وِشُ višu, }

وَسَءُ vasa-u, f., a cultivated place; Sansk. root: वर्षित, provided with rain (and therefore cultivated).

وِکهُ vikhu, } f., poison; Sansk. विषं, n.; Hindī बिस्
وِهُ vihu, } or बिख्, m.

وَنْسُ vansu, f., lineage; Sansk. वंश, m.; Hindī बंस्, m.

هَنْجُ hanju, } f., a wild goose; Sansk. हंस, m.; Hindī
هَنْجهُ hanjhu, } हंस्, m. (see Introd. §. 11, 2.)

هِنْدُ hindu, f., India; originally an Arabic-Persian word, derived from the province nearest to the Persians, i. e. सिन्धु (by change of s into h); Hindūstānī: هِنْد, m.

هِنڱُ hiṅu, f., assa foetida; Sansk. हिङ्गु, m.; Hindī हिंग् or हींग् or हिङ्गु, m.

Under this head we must class all the imitative sounds, which end in 'u', and which are considered feminines, because their final 'u' is not subject to inflexion; the same may be stated of some Dvandvas, which consist properly of two Imperatives, ending in 'u', and which are likewise treated as feminines, being exempt from the laws of inflexion.

أَچُ وَنُجُ aču vańu, f., coming going (Imper.).

جھَنُو جھَنُو jhāu jhāu, f., grumbling (imitative sound).

چَو چَو ča-u, ča-u, f., } talking (Imper.).
چَو وَٹُ ča-u, vaṭu, f., }

ٹَنُو ٹَنُو ṭāu ṭāu, f., gabbling (imitative sound).

وَٿھُ پُجُ vaṭhu puǰu, f., hurry (Imper.).
etc. etc. etc.

2) The termination ū.

The termination ū is generally masculine; there are however some exceptions, the gender of which is regulated either by original Sanskrit usage, or by the practice of the cognate dialects. The imitative sounds, ending in ū or ũ, are all treated, on account of their inflexibility, as feminine. Such exceptions are:

آبِرو ābirū, f. (also: آبِروءِ ābirūe), honour; Hindūstānī آبْرو, f. (Pers.)

آنئُون ãũ, f., pride, egotism; identical with the I. personal pronoun of the Sing. J (Panǰābī: haũ, f.).

بھُو bhū, f., earth (also: بھُئِ bhue); Sansk. भू, f.

تَرُو tarū, f., a fine cord of camel's hair (root: تَرَنُ, to pass through).

جُون ǰũ, f., louse (also: جُئَ ǰua); Hindī जूं, f., Sansk. यूका, f.

چَمَجُون čamaǰũ, f., a kind of louse, adhering to the skin (چَمُ).

رُون رُون rũ rũ, f., imitative sound; the hum of a spinning wheel.

كُوكُو kū-kū, f., imitative sound, by which a dog is called.

گنٔو gāū, f., cow; the same as گنٔوں.

لُون lũ, f., small hair on the limbs (also: لُنئ lũa); Sansk. लोमन्, n.; Hindī लोम्, m.

وَهُو vahū, f., daughter-in-law; Sansk. वधू, Hindī बहू.

3) The termination ā.

The termination ā comprises, according to its origin, as we have seen, mostly feminine nouns; there are however a few masculine nouns, ending in ā, the gender of which is, in most cases, already fixed by the signification of the noun itself, or by the language, from which the noun in question is taken; such exceptions are:

راجا rājā, prince; Sansk. Nom. राजा, m.

لالا lālā, master; lord; Hindī लाला.

كرتا kartā, the agent (in grammar); Sansk. Nom. कर्ता.

آتما ātma, soul; Sansk. Nom. आत्मा, m.

مَاخُولِيا māχūlia, melancholy, Arab.; Hindūstānī, masc.

ڈيوَتا ḍēvatā, Deity; Hindī देवता, f.; Sanskrit देवता, f.

4) The termination ī.

The termination ī is, as stated already, divided between masculine and feminine nouns, yet so, that the feminine prevail considerably in number. All nouns denoting a male being (man or beast) are of course masculine, whereas nouns, denoting a female being, inanimate objects or abstract qualities are feminine; contrary to this general rule the following nouns are masculine:

آسِري āsirī, a large kind of tamarisk tree.

بَاندهِي bāndhī, a log of wood floating in the river.

بُنْدِي b̄undī, the muzzle of a gun-barrel.

بهَچِتِي bhačaṭī, name of a plant (Desmochaeta lappacea).

پَاکِي pākī, razor (by the Hindūs used as fem.)

پَاڻِي pāṇī, water.

پکهِي pakhī, bird.

تهُڏِي thuḍī, the lower stalk of a plant.

ٽِکِي ṭikī, a cake.

چهَٺهِي čhaṭhī, a religious ceremony, performed on the sixth day after childbirth.

ڏوگِي dōgī, a thick stick.

ڌَڙِي dhaṛī, a coloured edge to a cloth.

سُرْجَمُکهِي surǰamukhī, sunflower.

کُنْڏَلِي kunḍalī, horoscope.

گهَارِي ghārī, a stripe left unfinished.

گهِٽِي ghiṭī, a lane, alley.

لَاڙِي lāḍī, the ropes of a boat.

مُشْتَرِي muštarī, the planet Jupiter.

مُنْڏهِي munḍhī, head.

موتِي mōtī, pearl.

وَانگِي vāngī, a stick with ropes hanging from it, to carry water pots, etc.

5) The termination i (ĕ).

The termination 'i' (ĕ) is, with that of ă, the regular feminine ending in Sindhī. There are however a few masculine nouns, ending in 'i', which are mostly borrowed from foreign languages. As in conformity with the Sindhī laws of sound no word can end in a silent consonant, the quick and hardly perceptible sound 'i' (ĕ) has been added to some words, which end originally in a silent consonant, to render them susceptible of inflexion; to some foreign nouns too, which end in ā, the short vowel 'i' has been added, for euphony's sake, which however may interchange with 'u' in some cases.

اَحْمَدِ ahmade, Nom. prop.

خُدَاءِ χudāe, God (Pers.).

خِضِرِ χizire, Nom. prop. of a fabulous prophet.

راءِ rā-e (or: راءُ), prince; Hindī राइ.

سيٿِهِ sēṭhe, a Hindū wholesale merchant; Hindī.

قَيْصَرِ qaisare, Cæsar.

In some few instances original final ĕ of the Sanskrit has been preserved, without having been lengthened, as is usually the case in Sindhī, as:

پَئِي pa-e, lord (also: پَتِي patī); Sansk. पति.

وِرَسْپَتِ viraspate, the planet Jupiter; Sansk. बृहस्पति.

هَرِ hare, Viṣṇu; Sansk. हरि; Hindī हरि or हरी.

In others again original ī has been (contrary to the usual rule) shortened to ĭ, as:

ڪيهَرِ kēhare, lion, or: ڪيسَرِ kēsare, Sansk. केसरी.

ڪُوءِ kūe, street, besides: ڪُوئِي kūī, Pers.

سَهَاءِ sahāe, helper, besides: سَهَائِي sahāī.

Others again are to be taken as Bahuvrīhi compounds, in which final i (ĕ) may be preserved (see §. 12, 5. 6.), as:

صَافُدِلِ sāfudile, a sincere man = having a pure heart.

اَدهوَادهِ adhō-adhe, half-sharer = having half and half.

Chapter VII.

Formation of the Feminine from masculine bases.

§. 14.

The formation of the feminine from masc. nouns agrees in the main with Sanskrit and Prākrit usage. In some instances feminine derivatives have been taken directly from the Sanskrit or Prākrit, subject, of course, to the peculiar assimilating process of the Sindhī, as; رَاڻِي rāṇī, queen, Sansk. राज्ञी (see: Introd. §. 14, b.). Such like formations we shall pass by in the following remarks and only attend to the laws still current in Sindhī.

The Sindhī possesses in some cases separate words, to express the idea of the feminine, so that the process of deriving the feminine from the masc. base is superseded. These instances however are restricted to nouns, implying relationship, and the names of the commonest domestic animals, where the language has preferred to create separate words, instead of deriving them from the corresponding masc. base; as:

ڀيڻَ bhēṇa, sister;	ڀَاءُ bhāu, brother.
ڌِيَ dhia, or ڌِيُ dhiu, daughter;	پُٽرُ puṭru, son.
مَاءُ māu, mother;	پِيُ piu, father.
وَهُو vahū, daughter-in-law;	جَاٽرو jāṭrō, son-in-law.
ڏَاچِي ḍāčī, a female camel;	ڏَاگهو ḍāghō, a male camel.

گئُو ga-ū, cow; ڏانْڊُ ḍāndu, ox.

مينْھِ mēhe, a female buffalo; سانُ sānu, a male buffalo.

From other masc. bases the Sindhī forms regularly a feminine, as far as this is admissible; some nouns are only extant in the feminine, the masculine being out of place or having disappeared from the language.

1) Formation of the Feminine from masc. nouns in 'u'.

From substantives ending in 'u' the Sindhī forms the Feminine by changing 'u' into ī or ĭ (ĕ); with adjectives the termination 'i' (e) or 'a' may be optionally used. In the case of the substantives the use of the termination ī or 'i' (e) is more or less optional, but in some of them one or the other is preferred.

چھوڪِري čhōkarī,
چھوڪِرِ čhōkare, } girl, from چھوڪِرُ čhōkaru, boy.

گَڏھِ gaḍahe, jenny-ass, from گَڏھُ gaḍāhu, jack-ass.

پَرْٽِ parṭe, washerwoman, from پَرْٽُ parṭu, washerman.

ڌِيرَ dhīra or ڌِيرِ dhīre, firm, from ڌِيرُ dhīru, adj. m.

Besides this common formation of the feminine another method of forming the same by means of the affixes ṇī, ni, āṇī, āiṇi, is in use, which are however only added to nouns denoting human beings, castes, occupations etc. very rarely to names of animals or to adjectives.

All these affixes correspond to the Sansk. affix आनी (= न, see Bopp, Compar. Gram. §. 840), as: इन्द्राणी the wife of Indra etc. In Sindhī the original affix ānī (with change of the dental to the cerebral) has either been preserved, or ā (see Bopp sub loco) has again been cast out, and only ṇī (ṇe) added. All these affixes are joined to the feminine termination (i, seldom to ă), as:

جَٽِنِ jaṭiṇe, جَٽِنِي jaṭiṇī, جَٽيَانِي jaṭy-āṇī,	the wife of a جَٽُ Jaṭ.
گاهِنِ gāhiṇe, گاهِيَانِي gāhyāṇī,	a female singer; masc. not in use.

بَروچَانِي[1]) barōčāṇī, the wife (or female) of a بَروچُ or Beluch.

شِينْهَنِ sĩhaṇe, lioness, from شِينْهُ sĩhu, lion.

چهُوٽِنِ čhūṭiṇe, چهُوٽِنِي čhūṭiṇī, چهُوٽيَانِي čhūṭyāṇi,	swift, from چهُوٽُ čhūṭu, adj. m.

2) Formation of the Feminine from masculine nouns in ō.

From masc. nouns ending in ō the feminine is formed by changing ō into ī, as:

چهوِرِي čhōrī, a female orphan, from چهورو čhōrō, orphan, m.

گولِي gōlī, a slave-girl, from گولو gōlō, a slave m.

Besides this feminine termination the affixes ṇī, ṇi, āṇī, āiṇi are also in use with nouns denoting caste, trade or occupation, as:

لَنگهِنِ langhiṇe, لَنگهِنِي langhiṇī, لَنگهِيَانِي langhyāṇī, لَنگهِيَائِنِ langhyāiṇe,	the wife (or female) of a لَنگهو langhō or drummer (by caste).

1) After a Palatal short i is frequently cast out.

3) Formation of the Feminine from masculine nouns in ū.

Masc. nouns ending in ū form the feminine by the affixes ṇī or ṇi, with the union-vowel i, by which final ū is dislodged; final ū may also be shortened to 'u', which serves at the same time as union-vowel, e. g.:

هِنْدِنِي hindiṇī,
هِنْدِنِ hindiṇe, } the wife (or female) of a هِنْدو, Hindū.

or:

هِنْدُنِي hinduṇī
هِنْدُنِ hinduṇe }

The affixes āṇī or āiṇi are also in use, before the addition of which final ū is always shortened to 'u', as:

هِنْدُئانِي hindu-āṇī,
هِنْدُئائِنِ hindu-āiṇe, } a Hindū female.

4) Formation of the Feminine from masculine nouns in ī and ĭ.

From masc. nouns ending in ī and 'i' (e) the feminine is formed by means of the affixes ṇī, ṇi or āṇī; final ī is shortened to 'i', and serves thus as union-vowel; as:

كورِنِي kōriṇī,
كورِنِ kōriṇe,
كوريانِي kōryāṇī, } the wife (female) of a كورِي kōrī, weaver.

سيٺهِنِي sēṭhiṇī,
سيٺهِنِ sēṭhiṇe,
سيٺهِيانِي sēṭhyāṇī, } the wife (female) of a سيٺهِ sēṭhe, a Hindū wholesale merchant.

Note. The cognate dialects form the feminine from masc. nouns in the same way as the Sindhī, by changing either the masc. termination to the feminine, or by adding one of the above-mentioned fem. affixes.

The Hindī and Hindūstānī approach the Sindhī very closely in this respect; they form the feminine either by substituting the feminine termination ī, as: لَڑْکِي laṛkī, girl, from لَڑکا laṛkā, boy, براھمَنِي brāhmanī, the wife (or female) of a Brāhman, from براھمن brāhman; or by adding one of the affixes an, in, ānī, to the masc. base, as: سُنارَن sunāran (or sunārin), the wife of a سُنار sunār, goldsmith; شيرنِي šērnī, a lioness, from شير šēr, a lion; مِهْتَرانِي mehtarānī, the wife (daughter) of a mehtar, or sweeper.

The same law holds good in Gujarātī; either the feminine termination ī is substituted for the masculine, as: कुतरी a female dog, from कुतरो a male dog, or the feminine affixes एण, णी or आणी are added to the masc. base, as: वाघेण a tigress, from वाघ् tiger; ऊंट्णी, a female camel, from ऊंट a male camel; धणिआणी mistress, from धणी lord.

The formation of the feminine is quite analogous in the Panǰābī; for the masc. termination is either changed to the feminine, as: ghōṛī, a mare, from ghoṛā, a stallion, or the feminine affixes aṇ, ṇī, āṇī are added to the masc. base, as: uskaḷaṇ, a slanderous woman, from uskaḷī, a slanderous man; ū̃ṭṇī, a female camel, from ū̃ṭ, a male camel; mugalāṇī, the wife (or daughter) of a mugal.

The Marāṭhī forms the feminine from nouns in 'a' (quiescent) or ā by substituting the fem. termination ī, as: मुगली, girl, from मुगला boy; दासी, a slave-girl, from दास a slave; in nouns ending in 'a', the Sansk. fem. termination ā is occasionally to be met with, as: शूद्रा or शूद्री the wife of a शूद्र. Besides these two fem. terminations the affix īn or īṇ is to be found in nouns ending in 'a' (quiescent) or ī, as: वाघीण्, tigress, from वाघ, tiger, पापीण् a sinful woman, from पापी a sinner; धनीन् mistress, from धनी master.

The Bangālī stands nearest to the Sanskrit with regard to the formation of the feminine; it substitutes the fem. terminations ā or ī for those of the masculine, as: tanyā, daughter, from tanya, son; puttrī, daughter, from puttra, son. Adjectives or nouns of agency, ending in ka ('a' being quiescent) form their feminine always in kā, as: kārikā, doing, from kārak, m., gāyakā, a female singer, from gāyak, a male singer. Nouns in ī (= in) form their feminine by the affix nī, as: hattinī, a female elephant, from hattī, a male elephant; likewise patnī, mistress, from pati, master. Also the use of the affix āṇī or āṇi is strictly in accordance with Sanskrit practice, as: āčāryāṇī, the wife of an āčārya.

We find thus, that all the north-Indian vernaculars of Sanskrit origin fully agree in the formation of the feminine.

SECTION II.

THE INFLEXION OF NOUNS.

Chapter VIII.

I. Formation of the Plural.

§. 15.

The crude form of a Sindhī noun is always identical with its Nominative Singular, the Nominative Singular having no longer a case-sign in any of the modern Ārian tongues.

The Sindhī possesses no definite or indefinite article, as little as the Sanskrit or the Prākrit; if the one or the other is to be expressed for distinctness' sake, a demonstrative or indefinite pronoun (or the numeral "one") is placed before a noun. There is no longer a Dual in Sindhī, neither in Pāli nor Prākrit, nor in any of the modern Sanskritical tongues; we have therefore only to describe the formation of the Plural (Nominative), according to the respective terminations of nouns.

1) Nouns ending in ŭ.

Nouns ending in ŭ are, as we have stated already, for the greatest part masculine, a few of them only being feminine. According to their respective gender the Plural is formed, as follows:

a) Plural of masculine nouns ending in ŭ:

These nouns form their Plural by changing ŭ into ă, as: کھُوھُ khūhu, a well, Plur. کھُوھَ khūha, wells; وَرُ varu, husband, Plur. وَرَ vara. If final 'u' be preceded by short 'a', a euphonic v is inserted in the Plural, as: رَءُ ra-u, weed, Plur. رَوَ rava, weeds. But if final 'u' be preceded by any other vowel, but short 'a', the insertion of v is optional, as: گھاءُ ghāu, a wound, Plur. گھاوَ ghāva or: گھاءَ ghāa, wounds; ڏيو ḍēu, a god, Plur. ڏيوَ ḍēva or: ڏيءَ ḍēa, gods; but when a long vowel, preceding final ŭ, is nasalized, the insertion of v becomes necessary, as:

تھانءُ thā̃u, a dish, Plur. تھانوَ thā̃va, dishes.

The following two nouns form their Nom. Plural in an irregular way:

ڀاءُ bhāu, brother, Plur. ڀائرَ bhāura or: ڀائرُ bhāuru, brothers.

پئُ piu, father, Plur. پئرَ piura, fathers.

Both these Plurals point back to the Prākrit forms भाअरा (Nom. Sing. भाअरो) and पिअरा (Nom. Sing. पिअरो), and are therefore, properly speaking, not irregular (cf. Varar. V, 35).

Annotation. We have already noticed (§. 5, I.), that the Sindhī termination ŭ is shortened from the Prākrit ओ; in Prākrit nouns ending in ō form their Plural in ā, which has been shortened in Sindhī to ă.

The cognate idioms agree with the Sindhī in this respect. In Hindī and Hindūstānī, this class of nouns, having already dropped the terminating short vowel in the Singular, throw the same off in the Plural likewise, i. e. they remain unaltered in the Plural. The same is the case in Marāṭhī and Panǰābī; the Guǰarāṭī alone adds the Plural termination ō.

b) Plural of feminine nouns ending in ŭ.

These nouns form their Plural by changing final ŭ into ū̃, as:

وَٿُ vathu, a thing; Plur. وَٿُون vathū̃, things; وِڄُ viǰu, lightening; Plur. وِڄُون viǰū̃, lightenings.

The following nouns have, besides their regular Plural, also an irregular one, as:

بھيڻُ bhēṇu, sister (or: بھيڻَ bhēṇa); Plur. بھيڻُون bhēṇũ or: بھيڻَرُ bhēṇaru, بھيڻَرُون bhēṇarũ, sisters.

مَاءُ māu, mother; Plur. مَائُون māũ, or: مَائِرُ māiru, مَائِرُون māirũ, mothers.

ڌِيُءُ dhiu (or: ڌِيَءَ dhia), daughter; Plur. ڌِيُئُون dhiũ, or: ڌِيَئَرُ dhiaru, ڌِيَئَرُون dhiarũ, daughters.

نُهُ nuhu (or: نُهَ nuha), daughter-in-law; Plur. نُهُون nuhũ or: نُهَرُ nuharu, نُهَرُون nuharũ, daughters-in-law.

In the levelling process of decomposition these fem. nouns have adopted the same affix ara (or for euphony's sake: ira), as the irregular Plurals of masc. nouns, and as feminines they have lengthened the same also to arũ.

Annotation. In Pāli fem. nouns ending in 'u' remain either unchanged in the Plural, as: yāgu, sacrifice, Plur. yāgu, or ō (the Sansk. Plural affix अस्) is added to them (with inserted euphonic 'y') as: yaguyō; the latter is also the case in Prākrit, as: bahū, wife, Plur. bahūō, or the affix ō may be again shortened to 'u', as: bahūu. In Sindhī this Plural affix 'u' has been contracted with final 'u' (ū) into ū, and at the same time nasalized = ũ.

2) Nouns ending in ō (õ).

These form their Plural by changing final ō into ā, as: وَاڍھو vāḍhō, a carpenter, Plur. وَاڍھا; ٽوٻو tōbō, a diver, Plur. ٽوٻَا tōbā, divers. If final ō be nasalized, which is frequently the case, the nasal is also preserved in the Plural, as: چوٿھوں čōthō̃, the fourth, Plur. چوٿھَان čōthā̃.

If final ō be preceded by short 'a' (or nasalized: ā), a euphonic v is inserted between them in the Plural, as: تَئو taō, a pan; Plur. تَوَا tavā, pans; نَئون nāō̃, new; Plur. نَوَان nāvā̃; but if final ō be preceded by any other vowel, the insertion of v is optional, as: كُئُو kuō, mouse, Plur. كُئا kuā or: كُوا kuvā; ميئُو mēō, fisherman, Plur. ميئا mēā or: ميوا mēvā; گهائو ghā-ō, a fish-net, Plur. گهائا ghā-ā or: گهاوا ghāvā.

We have repeatedly adverted to the fact, that the Prākrit termination ō has in Sindhī either been shortened to 'u', or retained unaltered; the formation of the Plural of the latter description of nouns is quite in accordance with Prākrit usage (Sing. ō, Plur. ā).

Annotation. In the cognate idioms the masc. termination ā has been substituted instead of ō. In Hindī, Hindūstānī, Marāṭhī and Panǰābī masc. nouns ending in ā commonly change the same in the Plural to ē, a Plural termination, which is already in use in the inferior old Prākrit dialects (see: Lassen, Instit. Ling. Prāk. p. 430). The Gujarātī differs in this respect, as masc. nouns ending in ō add to the Plural termination ā the affix ō, as: čhōkarō, a boy, Plur. čhōkarā-ō; a similar formation of the Plural is already ascribed to the Māgadhī dialect of the Prākrit; cf. Lassen, p. 399.

3) Nouns ending in ū, ū̃.

Nouns ending in ū or, as it is more common, in ū̃, be they masc. or feminine, remain unchanged in the Plural, as: وِڇھُون vičhū̃, m., scorpion, Plur. وِڇھُون vičhū̃; گَئُو gaū, fem., cow, Plur. گَئُو gaū, cows.

In Pāli, masc. themes ending in 'u', lengthen the same in the Nom. Plural to ū, as bhikkhu, a beggar, Plur. bhikkhū; and such masc. themes, as end in ū in the Nom. Sing., remain unchanged in the Plural, as: abhibhū, a chief, Plur. abhibhū (contracted from abhibhuvō). In Prākrit masc. themes ending in 'u' lengthen their final vowel always in the Nominative Sing., to which in the Nom. Plural the affix ō (= अस्) is added, as: vāu, wind, Nom. Sing. vāū, Nom. Plur. vāūō, winds. This Plural affix ō may in Prāk. be again shortened to 'u', and in the modern dialects it is dropped altogether. In Sindhī ū is usually nasalized = ū̃.

Annotation. In Hindī, Hindūstānī, Marāṭhī and Panjābī masc. nouns ending in ū, remain unaltered in the Plural; but fem. nouns add in Hindūstānī the Plural termination ā̃, as ǰōrū, a wife, plural ǰōrūā̃, the Prākrit Plural affix ō being changed to ā, ā̃. The Guǰarātī keeps close to the Prākrit in forming the Plural of masc. nouns ending in ū, by adding the Plural affix ō, as: hindū, a Hindū, Plur. hindūō.

4) Nouns ending in ā (ā̃).

These are, as noticed already (§. 13, 3) for the most part feminine; they form their Plural hy adding the Plural affix ū̃, as:

هَچَا hačā, f., murder; Plur. هَچَائُن hačā-ū̃, murders.

The Plural of these nouns corresponds to the Prāk. Plural termination ā-ō or ā-u, ō (or shortened 'u') being added to final ā of the Singular (see Lassen p. 307). In Sindhī the Prāk. Plur. increment ō has been changed to ū, and at the same time nasalized.

Few nouns ending in ā are masculine; they remain unaltered in the Plural, as: لالا lālā, master, Plur. لالا lālā, masters.

The Prākrit Plural increment ō (ā-ō) has first been shortened to 'u', and then been dropped altogether in Sindhī.

Annotation. In Hindī and Hindūstānī fem. nouns ending in ā (ā̃) form their Plural by adding the increment ẽ, as balā, misfortune, Plur. balāẽ. This ē corresponds to the Prākrit affix ō, which in the inferior Prākṛit dialects is frequently changed to ē (cf. Lassen, p. 398, 408). Those masc. nouns, the final ā of which does not correspond to the Sindhī ō, remain likewise unaltered in the Plural. — In Panjābī fem. nouns ending in ā add either ī̃ or iā̃, the Plural increment ī̃ being a change from the Hindī ẽ, and iā̃ from the Prākrit affix ō, with euphonic 'i' or y. A few masc. nouns remain likewise unaltered in the Plural, as ātmā, soul; pitā, father etc. — The Guǰarātī entirely agrees with the Prākrit, adding simply ō to the fem. nouns in ā, as: mā, mother, Plur. mā-ō. — In Marāṭhī fem. nouns ending in ā do not undergo any change in the Plural, as: mātā, mother, Plur. mātā;

some masc. nouns, falling under this head, remain likewise unaltered in the Plural.

5) Nouns ending in ă.

These nouns being all feminine, form their Plural by changing final 'a' either to ū̃ (as in Lāṛ); or to ā̃ (as in Sirō); تَرَ tara, nostril, Plur. تَرُون tarū̃ or: تَرَان tarā̃, nostrils.

These nouns have been, as noted already, shortened from Sanskrit-Prākrit bases ending in ā; they either drop final 'a' before the Plural increment ā̃ (= Prāk. ō), or restore the original ā and drop the Plural increment ō = u, nasalising at the same time the final long vowel.

Annotation. This class of nouns is wantig in the cognate idioms, where final 'a' has become silent; e. g. Hindūstānī: jībh, f., tongue, Plural: jībh-ē̃, the Plural being made up by the increment ē̃ = Prāk. ō. — Panjābī: bā̃h, f., arm (Sindhi: بَانهَ bā̃ha), Plur. bā̃hā̃; Marāṭhī: jībh, f. Plur. similarly: jībhā. The Gujarātī is consequent in adding simply the Plural increment ō to fem. bases, ending in a quiescent consonant, as: sānjh, f., evening, Plur. sānjhō.

6) Nouns ending in ī (ī̃).

a) Masculine nouns ending in ī remain unaltered in the Plural:

بيلي bēlī, a servant, Plur. بيلي bēlī, servants; پرين prī̃, friend, Plur. پرين prī̃, friends.

In Prākrit masc. nouns ending in ī form their Plural by adding the increment ō, which has been shortened to 'u' and then cast off altogether in Sindhī.

b) Feminine nouns ending in ī add in the Plural the increment ū̃, shortening before this affix the preceding long ī, which may also, for euphony's sake, be changed to y; as: گولي gōlī, a slave-girl, Plur. گوليون gōliū̃, gōliyū̃, gōlyū̃; نِهَائِين nihāī̃ (or: nihā̃ī̃), a potter's kiln, Plur. نِهَايُون nihāyū̃.

Feminine nouns in ī add in Prākrit likewise the affix ō, which may be shortened to 'u'; in this case final 'u' has in Sindhī been lengthened to ū and nasalized at the same time, to distinguish the Plural of the feminine nouns from that of the masculine.

If final ī be preceded by any letter of the palatal class or by 'h', it is commonly dropped before the Plural affix ū̃, as: مَنجي manǰī, a stool, Plur. مَنجُون manǰū̃, stools; مَنجهي, f., manǰhī, a buffalo, Plur. مَنجهُون manǰhū̃, buffaloes.

Annotation. In Hindī and Hindūstānī fem. nouns follow the method of the Prākrit in forming their Plural, with the only difference, that the Prāk. Plural increment ō is changed to ā, and this again nasalized, as čhurī, knife, Plur. čhuriā̃. Masc. nouns in ī do not differ from their Singular. The Panǰābī quite accords with the Hindī, fem. nouns in ī adding the Plural termination ā̃, as dhī, daughter, Plur. dhīā̃, the masc. nouns in ī remaining unaltered in the Plural. The same may be remarked of the Marāṭhī. The Gujarātī stands nearest to the Prākrit in this respect, all nouns, be they masc. or feminine, adding simply the Plural affix ō.

7) Nouns ending in ĭ (ĕ).

a) Fem. nouns ending in 'i' (e) form their Plural by adding the Plural affix ū̃, as: رَاتِ rāte, night, Plur. رَاتِئُون rāteū̃, nights. — If 'i' be preceded by a palatal or h, it disappears before the Plural termination ū̃, as: مينهِ mẽhe, buffalo, Plur. مينهُون mẽhū̃, buffaloes.

جوءِ ǰōe, wife, forms its Plural either regularly, as: جويُون ǰōyū̃, or irregularly, as: جوئِرُ ǰōiru, جوهِرُ ǰōhiru, or جوئِرُون ǰōirū̃, wives.

b) Masc. nouns ending in 'i' (e) remain unchanged in the Plural, as: سيٺهِ seṭhe, a wholesale merchant, Plur. سيٺهِ sēṭhe.

Annotation. In Hindī and Hindūstānī, as stated already, final 'i' has been dropped, and such nouns, as end in Sindhī in 'a' or 'i', use there one common Plural increment, viz.: ẽ. In Gujarātī and Panjābī final 'i' has likewise disappeared in most cases, and ō and ã are respectively added as Plural terminations. In Marāṭhī fem. bases ending in 'i' remain either unchanged in the Plural or have final 'i' lengthened to ī. The lengthening of final 'i' in the Plural is more in accordance with Pāli and Prākrit usage (e. g. Pāli: ratti, night, Plur. rattī or rattiyō; Prāk. rattī-ō or: rattī-u). Masc. bases ending in 'i' remain similarly either unaltered in the Plural, or (according to some Panḍits) lengthen the same to ī (as in Pāli and Prākrit).

II. Formation of cases; case-affixes.

§. 16.

Properly speaking there is no longer a declension in Sindhī, nor in any of the modern languages of the Ārian stock; there are only a few remnants of the ancient Sanskrit, Pāli and Prākrit case-inflexions, all the other cases being made up by means of case-affixes or postpositions.[1]).

If we compare the modern Ārian dialects with the Pāli and Prākrit, we perceive at once the great deterioration, the modern idioms have undergone in this respect; for while the Pāli and Prākrit have as yet preserved all the cases of the Sanskrit, with the exception of the Dative, which has already become scarce in Pāli and has been discarded altogether in Prākrit, its functions being shifted to the Genitive, the modern idioms have lost nearly all power of inflexion and substituted in lieu of flexional increments regular adverbs, which we generally term postpositions. The same process we can notice in the modern Romanic tongues, where after the loss of the Latin declensional inflexions, prepositions have been substituted to make up for the lost cases.

---

1) In poëtry postpositions may also be placed before the noun, they govern, as the rhythm may require.

The great distinctive feature of the declensional process of the modern Ārian dialects, with the exception of the Bangālī, consists in the fact, that there are properly only two cases of a noun, the absolute or crude form, corresponding throughout to the Nom. Singular, and the Formative case, to which the various adverbs or postpositions are added, which serve to make up for the lost case-terminations. This latter case has been generally called the oblique case by European grammarians, but we prefer to call it the Formative (after the precedence of Dr. Caldwell).

The number of declensions, if they may be termed thus, depends therefore in Sindhī, as well as in the cognate idioms, on the various methods, in which the Formative is made up; for the case-signs remain the same, as well for the Singular as the Plural, since they are, as we shall presently see, originally either (Sanskrit) prepositions or adverbs.

We shall now first investigate the remnants of the ancient case-terminations in Sindhī and the adverbs or postpositions, which have been substituted for such cases, as have lost their original inflexions. In the arrangement of the cases we shall follow the common order, which has been instituted by the old Sanskrit grammarians, in order to facilitate the intercomparison.

1) The Nominative case of the Singular and plural we may pass over, since they have been noticed already.

2) The Accusative case of the Singular and Plural has been dropped in Sindhī, as well as in all the other kindred idioms. This has been already the case in the inferior Prākrit dialects, and is expressly mentioned of the Apabhranša, the mother of the modern Sindhī (see: Lassen p. 459).

We must keep this fact constantly before our eyes, that in Sindhī, as well as in its sister-tongues, there is no such thing (in a grammatical sense), as an Accusative case, the Accusative being now throughout identical with the Nominative. If we find therefore generally stated in European grammars, that the postposition کهي khē, or کو kō in Hindūstānī serves to denote also the Accusative case, we have, in the strictly grammatical sense of the word, to repudiate such an idea. Whe shall see under the Dative case, what the origin of that postposition is, and that will satisfactorily explain the syntactical peculiarities of the modern Indian tongues, which use such and similar postpositions, where we use either the Dative or the Accusative.

3) The Instrumentalis is not distinguished by any case-affix or postposition in Sindhī, but differs from the Nominative Sing. only by the change of the final vowel (where such a change is admissible). The Instrumentalis is in the Singular and Plural identical with the Formative (which see further on). From thence it would follow, that the Instrumentalis is originally the Genitive, which may be rendered very probable by the Instrumentalis of the Plural.

Annotation. The Hindī and Hindūstānī use as Instrumental case-affix nē. In Hinduī (see Garcin de Tassy, Rudiments de la langue Hindouī, 26, 99) we meet further the affixes nē, nẽ, ni and na, and in the Plural (a)n or nē, nẽ, ni, as in the Singular. In Panjābī we find the instrumental affix nai, or na, or only ī, or the Formative is promiscuously used for the Instrumentalis, just as in Sindhī. In Gujarātī we meet with ē as Instrumental affix. The Marāṭhī uses for the Instrumentalis Sing. the affix nē, and for the Plural nī. As to the origin of these various instrumental affixes there can hardly be a doubt. The Sansk. instrumental case-inflexion of the Singular nā, na (see Bopp, Comp. Gram. I, §. 158) has been used as a separate adverb in Hindūstānī and Panjābī (not in Marāṭhī, where it coalesces with the noun as a regular inflexion), or even been abbreviated to ī or ē (n being originally only a euphonic addition to the instrumental affix ā), as partly in Panjābī and in Gujarātī. In the Instrumentalis Plur. the Marāṭhī uses also (besides nī) the affix hī̃, corresponding to the Prāk. Plur. instrumental affix हिं or हि; see Lassen, p. 310. In Bangālī tē is used as instrumental affix, which is originally identical with the Ablative affix तो = तस्.

4) The Dative case has totally disappeared from the Prākrit and its functions have been assigned to the Genitive. We find therefore in the modern idioms the greatest discrepancy as to the method, in which the Dative case is provided for. In Sindhī the affix کھي khē is used, as well for the Singular as the Plural, being placed after the Formative Singular or Plural of a noun: as گھَرَ کھي ghara khē, to a house, گھَرَنِ کھي gharane khē, to houses. In poëtical language the postposition کَنِ kane or: کَنِ kaṇe is also used instead of کھي khē, which are apparently derived from the same source, as کھي, only by a different process of assimilation (cf. the Hindī: kan, kane, Hinduī कंह).

Annotation. The Bangālī uses as Dative affix kē, the Hindī and Hindūstānī kō (dialectically also pronounced 'kū' in the Dekhan), the Hinduī (according to Garcin de Tassy) also kõ, kaũ, kah, kãh, kahã and even hi.

Dr. Caldwell, in his Comparative Grammar of the Drāvidian languages has attempted to vindicate the Hindūstānī kō for the Drāvidian languages of the South; he says (p. 225): "In the vernaculars of northern India, which are deeply tinged with Scythian characteristics, we find a suffix, which appears to be not only similar to the Drāvidian, but the same. The Dative-Accusative in the Hindī and Hindūstānī is kō, or colloquially kū; in the language of Orissa ku, in Bangālī ki, in Sindhī khi, in Shingalese ghai; in the Uraon, a semi-Drāvidian Kole dialect, gai, in the language of the Bodos, a Bhūtan hill tribe, khō, in Tibetan gya. The evident existence of a connexion between these suffixes and the Drāvidian Dative case-sign ku, is very remarkable. Of all the analogies between the North-Indian dialects and the southern, this is the clearest and most important, and it cannot but be regarded as betokening either an original connexion between the northern and the southern races, prior to the Brahmanic irruption, or the origination of both races from one and the same primitive Scythian stock." If this case-sign kō or kū then be the clearest and most important analogy between the North-Indian vernaculars and the Drāvidian tongues, we shall see presently, that there will be no analogy whatever between them, though at the first sight the identity of both seems to be past any doubt. In the first instance the fact speaks already very strongly against such a supposition, that the Marāṭhī, which is the closest neighbour to the Drāvidian tongues, has repudiated the use of khē, kē or kō, and employed a Dative-affix, the origin of which we hope to fix past controversy. We shall further see, that the Gujarātī and Panjābī have also made up for the Dative case by postpositions, borrowed from the Sanskrit, without the slightest reference to the Drāvidian languages, and we may therefore reasonably expect the same fact from the remaining Arian dialects. It would certainly be wonderful, if those Arian dialects, which border immediately on the Drāvidian idioms, should have warded off any Drāvidian influence on their inflexional method, whereas those more to the north should have been "deeply tinged with Scythian characteristics." Fortunately we are able to show, that such an assumption is not only gratuitous, but irreconcilable with the origin of the above mentioned Dative-affixes.

We derive the Sindhī khē, the Bangālī kē, from the Sanskrit Locative कृते, 'for the sake of', 'on account of', 'as regards'. This will at once account for the aspiration of k in Sindhī; for this is not done by chance, but by a strict rule (see Introd. §. 1, e, note); in Bangālī r does not exercise such an influence on the aspiration of a preceding or following consonant, and therefore we have simply kē. The Sanskrit form कृते becomes in Prākrit first किते, then (by the regular elision of t) किए, and contracted kē, and in Sindhī, by reason of the elided r, khē. The Hindī and Hindūstānī form of this adverb kō we derive in the same way from the Sansk. कृतं which is used adverbially with the same signification as the Locative कृते. In Prākrit already, and still more so in the modern dialects, the neuter has been merged into the masculine; we have therefore first कितो, thence किओ, and contracted को, kō. We can thus satisfactorily account for the various forms: khē, kē or kō. That the proposed derivation of these adverbs does not rest on a mere fancy, is further proved by the Sindhī particle rē, 'without', which is derived in the same way from the Sansk. Locative ऋते, Prākrit रिते = रिए, and thence contracted rē (ria). It remains now for us to notice briefly the somewhat deviating forms of the Hinduī, as exhibited by Garcin de Tassy. In कों kō̃ and कौं kaũ a euphonic Anusvāra has been added, to which the modern tongues have taken a great fancy; kaũ is only a different pronunciation for kō̃, ō changing in Hinduī very commonly to au. The forms कह kah, or with euphonic Anusvāra कंह kãh or कहं kahã, present again another proof for the correctness of the proposed derivation of these adverbs. For we have in कह, कंह, कहं (Hindī also: kan, kanē, with a full nasal, and in consequence thereof with ejection of h) the same basis as in कों and कौं, only the assimilating process has been different. The vowel ऋ ṛ, when joined to a consonant, can, according to Prākrit usage, be resolved either into 'i' (as in किते) or into 'a' (as: कतं for कृतं) (see Varar. I, 27; Lassen p. 116, 2, a; Introd. §. 1); in consequence of the inherent r the following consonant is aspirated (as in Sindhī: kk = k), so that we get the form कथं; this aspirated थ th is again elided, so that h only remains (see Lassen p. 207; Introd. §. 8), and thus we have the forms कह, कहं. With the other alleged form हि hi, the matter stands different; we compare this Hinduī Dative affix with the Apabhranša Genitive affix हे, the Genitive, as noted already, supplying in Prākrit the place of the Dative (as to the analysis of this हे see Lassen p. 462 and 466).

The Marāṭhī uses two affixes to make up for the Dative, which are joined to the crude form by the so-called union-vowel, viz: स, s and ला lā. The first of these two, s, is identical with the Prāk. Genit.-Dative case termination स्स ss = Sansk. स्य sy, so that we have here the remnant of an ancient Sanskrit-Prākrit case-inflexion. The latter one, lā is more doubtful as to its origin. Lassen has already started a conjecture (see Instit. Ling. Prāk. p. 55, 99) as to the origin of this affix; he derives it from the Sansk. आल = आलय 'place habitation', signifying the place, where the action rests. We cannot endorse this derivation, as the Marāṭhī case-affix is not आल āla, but ला lā and we cannot see any reason, why initial long ā should have been transferred to the back of this particle. We would compare the Marāṭhī Dative affix lā with the Sindhī postposition lāe, 'on account of', 'for the sake of', 'for', Hindūstānī لِيئي līē, both of which are derived from the Sansk. root ला (रा) to give (Sindhī: لائِڻُ lāiṇu, to apply). This seems to me to be borne out by the modern Persian Dative-Accusative particle رَا rā, which as yet is very scantily used in the old Pārsī, and which, according to Spiegel's Pārsī grammar (p. 55) does not denote properly a Dative case, but originally signifies 'for the sake of', 'on account of'. The same particle we find also in the Paṣ̌tō, لَه lah, which corresponds to the modern Persian particle رَا. — In Bangālī we meet also (besides kē) especially in poētical language a Dative affix rē, which I do not hesitate to identify with the Marāṭhī ला and the Hindūstānī līē.

In Gujarātī the Dative-affix is nē, which we identify with the Sansk. preposition नि, Greek ἐν, Latin in. The Panǰābī uses as Dative affix nū, in which we likewise recognise the Sansk. preposition अनु, 'toward', 'to'.

5) The Ablative case is formed in Sindhī by the affix آن ā̃, which is always connected with the base itself and never written separately. The Sindhī shows itself thus fully conscious of the origin of this case-termination, which corresponds exactly to the Pāli-Prākrit Ablative case-termination ā, which originates from the Sanskrit ablative आत् by the elision of final t (see Lassen p. 352, 304); in Sindhī the final long vowel has again been nasalized, as in so many other instances. In the Singular final 'u', ō, 'a' are dropped before the affix ā̃, as: گهَران gharā̃, from a house, nom. گهَرُ gharu, a house; دَران darā̃, out of a defile, nom. دَرو darō; زَبانان zabānā̃, from the tongue, nom. زَبانَ zabāna, tongue. Those nouns, which end in the Singular in ī (ī̃) and ū (ū̃), shorten the same before the affix ā̃, as: نوڙِيان nōṛiā̃, from a rope, nom. نوڙِي nōṛī, a rope; مِرُوان miruā̃, from a wild beast, nom. مِرُوں mirū̃, a wild beast.

Nouns in 'i' (ĕ) generally retain their final vowel before the affix ā̃, but they may also drop it, as: پھُرِئَّان phureā̃, from (by) a robbery, nom. پھُرِ phure, a robbery; نِرْتَان nirtā̃, out of thought, with reflexion, nom. نِرْتِ nirte, thought. Nouns in ā either nasalize the same in the Ablative, or, more commonly, use the postposition کھَان khā̃ etc. In the Plural the Ablative affix ā̃ is joined to the full Formative in -ne, as: گھَرِنئَّان gharane-ā̃, from houses, مِرُوِنئَّان miruane-ā̃ (مِرُنِئَّان), from wild beasts etc.

Besides this common Ablative affix ā̃ we find in Sindhī also such forms, as: aũ (اَوْن), contracted: ō̃ (اوْن), and even ũ (اُون). In the more ancient idiom, as used by the Sindhī poēts, the Ablative Singular generally ends in ā-u. All these various Ablative affixes are derived from the Prākrit Ablative आदो (see Lassen p. 302, 304, 599), which becomes (by the elision of d) āō, or shortened: āu.

The Sindhī uses also the postposition کھَان[1]) khā̃, کھَوْن khaũ, کھوْن khō, to express the idea of the Ablative; all these and other postpositions require the Formative of a noun. Other postpositions, which are used to make up for the Ablative, see under the list of postpositions.

Annotation. Nearest to the Sindhī comes the Marāṭhī in this respect, which uses as Ablative-case terminations the affixes

---

1) The postposition کھَان khā̃ etc. is derived form the same source, as کھِي, with the only difference, that the Ablative termination ā̃, aũ etc. has been added. The same is to be said of the Ablative postposition کنَان kanā̃, derived from کنِ, by the same process.

ūn and hūn, occasionally also tūn. In Bangālī and Panǰābī we find the Ablative affix tē (though in Panǰābī a regular Ablative termination ō̃ is also to be met with), which has sprung from the Prākrit Ablative termination तो tō; similar to it is the Guǰarātī Ablative affix thī, which has been aspirated. In Hindī we find also thī, but most in use is sē, apparently identical with the Prākrit Genitive termination है (see Lassen p. 462).

6) The Sanskrit Genitive-case termination स्य, in Pāli and Prākrit स्स ss, has been lost in all the modern tongues, with the exception of the Bangālī, where ss has been hardened to r. All the other dialects have taken to a new way of forming the Genitive, of which we find already some traces in the old Vedic language: the noun, which ought to be placed in the Genitive case, is changed into an adjective by an adjective affix, and thence follows, as a matter of course, that this so-called Genitive, which is really and truly an adjective, must agree in gender, number and case with its governing noun as all other adjectives.

The Sindhī employs for this purpose the affix جو ǰō (fem. جي ǰī), corresponding to the common adjective affix kō (= Sansk. क), with transition of the tenuis (č = k) in tothe media (ǰ), very likely to establish thereby some distinction between these two originally identical affixes. In Sindhī this adjective affix جو ǰō is always written separately, whereas the common adjective affix kō is joined to the base, as in Sanskrit (see §. 10, 24); it follows always the Formative Sing. or Plur. of a noun, as: گهَرَ جو دهَڻِي ghara ǰō dhaṇi, the master of the house, گهَرَنِ جو دهَڻِي gharane ǰō dhaṇī, the master of the houses; مُرْسَ جِي جوءِ mursa ǰī ǰōe, the wife of the man; مُرْسَنِ جُون جوئِيُون mursane ǰū̃ ǰōyū̃, the wives of the men. In poëtry سَنْدو sandō, 'belonging to', is used quite in the same way, as جو, as:

پرِيَان سَنْڊي پَار ڏي priyā̃ sandē pāra ḍē, towards the direction of the friends.

Annotation. The Marāṭhī uses as Genitive case-affix चा, with transition of the guttural क into the corresponding palatal, as in Sindhī, yet without changing the tenuis into the media. The Hindī and Hindūstānī have preserved the original Sanskrit adjective affix क, without changing it into the palatal kā; in Hinduī we meet also with the affix ko and kau. The Panjābī and Gujarātī seem to make an exception from what we have just stated. In Panjābī the Genitive case-affix is dā, in which we recognise the Prāk. Ablative affix दो dō (= तस्), turned into a Genitive affix. This Panjābī Genitive case-affix will clear up the Paṣ̌tō Genitive prefix ډ da, being identical with it in origin. The Gujarātī employs as Genitive case-affix nō, which is another adjective affix, corresponding in signification with क and used in Sindhī (see §. 10, 27), to form adjectives in the same way, as kō (on the origin of this affix nō see Bopp's Comp. Gram. III, §. 839).

7) The original Sanskrit Locative termination 'i' has been preserved in Sindhī, though the Locative can now only be distinguished in masc. bases ending in 'u', as: هَنْڌهِ handhe, in a place, nom. هَنْڌهُ handhu; مَٿهِ mathe, on the top, nom. مَٿهُ mathu, the top. In nouns, ending in any other vowel, but 'u' (masc.), the Locative must be expressed, for perspicuity's sake, by an adverb or postposition, requiring the Formative of a noun, as: ڪوٺِيءَ مِين kōṭhia mẽ or: ڪوٺِيءَ مَنجهِ kōṭhia manjhe, in a room. In poëtry the Formative of any noun is commonly used also as Locative, without a postposition.

Annotation. In Marāṭhī the Locative affix 'i' has been lengthened to ī and at the same time nasalized = ī̃. Besides this we meet also with the Locative termination आंत्, which is originally the Sansk. Ablative, used as a Locative. In Bangālī the Locative ends in ē (i), as in Sindhī, or is expressed by the affix tē. In Panjābī the Locative is generally expressed by adverbial postpositions, though the Locative itself has not been altogether lost; we find there the affix ĩ, as in Marāṭhī, or ē, which are always joined to the base of a noun. In Gujarātī the Locative is either expressed by the affix ē, or by the help of postpositions. In Hindī and Hindūstānī the Locative, as a distinctive case, has been quite lost and must always be expressed by postpositions. Still some vestiges of it are lingering in the so-called participles absolute, as: hōtē, or with the emphatic hī, hōtēhī, in being. Some other idiomatic phrases, as: اُس دِن us din, on that day etc. point also to an original Locative.

8) The Vocative is expressed in Sindhī by prefixing one of the interjectional particles: ē, hē, hō or yā, and, when speaking to an inferior, ṛē (fem. ṛī) or arē.[1]) The final vowel of a noun in the Vocative either undergoes a change or remains unaltered. In the Vocative Singular masc. nouns ending in 'u' change the same to 'a', as: اِي مِيهَارَ ē mēhāra, o buffalo-keeper! nom. مِيهَارُ mēhāru; those ending in ō change the same to ā, as: اِي سُومِرَا ē sūmirā, o Sūmirō! those ending in ū, ī, 'i' remain unaltered, as: اِي پُنهُون ē Punhū̃, o Punhū̃! In the Vocative Plural nouns ending in 'u' (m.) have the termination ō or ā, as: اِي يَارو ē yārō or: يَارَا yāra, o friends! (nom. sing. يَارُ); those ending in ō terminate in the Vocative Plur. in ā, ō and au, as: اِي مَنْگتَا ē mangatā, o beggars! or: مَنْگتو mangatō, مَنْگتَوْ mangatau (مَنْگتَوُ mangata-u), Nom. Sing. مَنْگتو mangatō; those ending in ū (ū̃) terminate in ō or ā, before which affixes the preceding ū (ū̃) most be shortened, as: اِي وَاٽَاهُئَا ē vāṭahuā or اِي وَاٽَاهُئو ē vāṭāhuō, o travellers! Nom. Sing. وَاٽَاهُو vāṭāhū; those ending in ī terminate in the Plural

1) About the origin of ṛē, ṛī, arē, see Dr. Caldwell's Compar. Grammar of the Drāvidian languages p. 440.

in ā, ō and au (a-u), shortening at the same time the final ī of the base, as: اِي ڪيچِئا ē kēčiā, اِي ڪيچِئو ē kēčiō, or: اِي ڪيچِئؤ ē kēčiau, o Kēčīs! Nom. Sing. ڪيچِي kēčī, an inhabitant of Kēč (in Beluchistān); occasionally 'ah' is added in the Vocative Singular, as: حامِيَه ḥamiah, o protector! and in the Vocative Plural final ā is even lengthened to 'āhu' for the sake of the rhyme, as: پِرياهُ priyāhu, o friends! those ending in 'i' (e), add in the Vocative Plural simply the affix ō or ā: اِي سيٺهِئو ē sēṭheō, or: اِي سيٺهِئا ē sēṭheā, o wholesale-merchants! Nom. Sing. سيٺهِ sēṭhe.

F e m i n i n e nouns ending in 'u', 'a', ā, ī, 'i' (e) in the Nom. Singular, remain u n a l t e r e d in the Vocative Sing.; in the P l u r a l the Vocative is likewise identical with the Nominative. The few fem. nouns, which end irregularly in the Nom. Plural in 'u', as: ڀيڻَرُ bhēṇaru, sisters etc., retain likewise their final 'u' in the Vocative Plural, as: اِي ڀيڻَرُ ē bhēṇaru, o sisters! when ending in ū̃, they drop in the Vocative final Anusvāra, as: اِي ڌِيئَرُو ē dhiarū, o daughters! Nom. Plur. ڌِيئَرُون dhiarū̃.

The Vocative may also be used without any interjectional prefix, as: مَاڙهُئا māṛhuā, o men!

§. 17.

III. The Formative.

The F o r m a t i v e or oblique case, though in Sindhī throughout identical with the Instrumentalis, is by itself no case, but represents merely the euphonic change of the final vowel of a noun previous to the accession of any flexional particle or postposition, by means of which the various cases are made up. The changes, which the final vowel of a noun undergoes before the accession of any adverbial postposition, are on the whole the same as those before any other affix. In Sindhī the postpositions do not coalesce with the noun itself, the language still being conscious of the fact, that it has to deal with original adverbs. We have hinted already, that the Formative is originally the Genitive; it would be rather difficult, to prove this in reference to the Formative of the Singular, but that the Formative of the Plural originally represents the Genitive Plural, is borne out by the Prākrit and the kindred modern idioms. In Prākrit the Genitive Plural ends in **आण, ईण, ऊण,** in the Apabhranša dialect **अहं, इहं, उहं**, thence the Sindhī Formative Plural ā̃, ẽ, or -ne.

Though the Formative be, in all likelihood, the Genitive of the Prākrit, the adjectival affix جو has been added to it, to turn it into an adjective, the modern idioms once having taken this course to supply the Genitive. From thence it was only a consequent step, to use the ancient Genitive as the base, to which all the other declensional postpositions were added, i. e. the Genitive was turned into the Formative.

1) The Formative of nouns ending in 'u' (masc. and fem.)

a) Masculine nouns ending in 'u' change final 'u' in the Formative Sing. to 'a', as: دَاسُ dāsu, a slave, Form. دَاسَ dāsa; دَاسَ جو dāsa jō, دَاسَ کهي dāsa khē etc. If final 'u' be preceded by a short 'a', the insertion of euphonic v becomes necessary, as: رَءُ ra-u, a weed, Form. رَوَ rava; the same is the case, when final 'u' is preceded by a long nasalized ā, as: ٿهانءُ thā̃u, a dish, Form. ٿهانوَ thā̃va. But if final 'u' be preceded by any other vowel, the insertion of euphonic v is optional, as: وَاءُ vāu, wind, Format. وَاوَ vava or وَاءَ vāa; ڏيو ḍēu, a demon, Format. ڏيوَ ḍēva or ڏيو ḍēa; when final 'u' however is preceded by short or long 'i', no euphonic insertion is required, as: ڏِنو ḍīu, a mound, Format. ڏِنو ḍīa; وِيئُ vīu, a meadow, Format. وِيئَ vīa; جِيئُ jīu, life, Format. جِيئَ jīa.

The following nouns ending in 'u' retain their final 'u' unaltered in the Formative Singular:

پِئُ piu, father; Format. پِئُ, as: پِئُ جو piu jō etc.
بهَاءُ bhāu, brother, Format. بهَاءُ, as: بهَاءُ کهي bhāu khē etc.

but پِيئُ pīu, sweetheart, بهَاءُ bhāu, price, are regular.

The Formative Plural ends either in ã, ẽ or -ne, as: Nom. Sing. پهُلُ phulu, a flower; Nom. Plur. پهُلَ phula; Format. Plur. پهُلان phul-ã, پهُلين phul-ẽ, or: پهُلَنِ phula-ne. The Formative in ã and ẽ is generally used without a following postposition, and that in -ne more with a following postposition, as being more sonorus; but in poëtry the one or other form is used as required by the metre.

Those nouns, which form their Plural irregularly, as: بهَاءُ bhāu, brother, Nom. Plur. بهَائُرَ bhāura or: بهَائُرُ bhāuru; پِئُ piu, father, Nom. Plur. پِئُرَ piura, derive their Formative Plural either from the Nominative Singular or the Nominative Plural, as: بهَائُنِ bhāune or: بهَائُرَنِ bhāurane; پِئُنِ piune or, پِئُرَنِ piurane; the contracted form of the Formative (i. e: ã, ẽ) is never used with them.

b) Feminine nouns ending in 'u' remain unaltered in the Formative Sing., as: مَاءُ māu, mother, Format. مَاءُ, مَاءُ جو māu jō; in the Formative Plural the long ū of the Nom. Plur. is shortened before the Format. termination -ne, as: وِجُ viju, lightening, Nom. Plur. وِجُون vijū, Format. Plur. viju-ne.

Those fem. nouns, which have, besides their regular Plural, also an irregular one, derive their Formative Plur. from either form, as: بهينُ bhēṇu, sister, Nom. Plur. بهينُون bhēṇū or: بهينَرُ bhēṇaru (بهينَرُون bhēṇarū); Format. Plur. بهينُنِ bhēṇune or: بهينَرُنِ bhēṇarune.

2) The Formative of nouns ending in ō (ō̃).

Nouns ending in ō change the same in the Formative Sing. to ē, as: مَتهو mathō, head, Format. مَتهي mathē. If final ō be preceded by 'a' or ā, a euphonic v may be inserted, as: دَئو daō, the glare of the sun, Format. دَئي daē or: دَوي davē; نَائو nāō, felt, Format. نَائي nāe or: نَاوي nāvē; if ō be preceded by any other vowel, no insertion of euphonic v takes place, as: ڏِئو ḍiō, lamp, Format. ڏِئي ḍiē; چُوئو čūō, perfumed oil, Format. چُوئي čuē. If a noun end in a nasalized ō (= ō̃), the Anusvāra is retained in the Formative, as; نَائون nāō̃, the ninth, Format. نَائين nāē̃.

If ō be preceded by y, it is commonly dropped in the Formative, as:

پورهِيو pōrhyō (or pōrhiō), labour, Form. پورهي pōrhē.

رُوپَيو rūpayō, rupee, Format. رُوپَئي rūpaē.

The Formative Plural ends either in ā̃, ē̃, the termination of the Nomin. Plural (ā) being dropped before them, or in -ne, final ā of the Nom. Plural being shortened to 'a' before it; as: كُلهو kulhō, the shoulder, Nom. Plur. كُلهَا kulhā, Form. Plur. كُلهَان kulhā̃, كُلهين kulhē̃, or: كُلهَنِ kulhane; كوئو kūō, rat, Nom. Plur. كُوئا kūā, Format. Plur. كُوئان kūā̃, كُوئين kūē̃, or: كُوئَنِ kūane.

3) The Formative of nouns ending in ū (ū̃).

Nouns ending in ū change the same in the Formative Singular to ua, as: وَاگهُو vāghū, crocodile, Format. وَاگهُوَ vāghua. If final ū be nasalized (= ū̃), the Anusvāra is commonly retained in the Formative, as: وِڇهُون vičhū̃, scorpion, Format. وِڇهُنوَ vičhūa.

The Formative Plural ends either in u-ā̃, u-ē̃, or u-ne, ua-ne, long ū and ū̃ being shortened before the terminations of the Formative, as: رَهُو rahū, a resident, Nom. plur. رَهُو rahū, residents, Format. Plur. رَهُوَان rahuā̃ (or: رَهُئَان), رَهُئِين rahuē̃, رَهُنِ rahune, رَهُئَنِ rahuane; مِرُون mirū̃, a wild beast, Nom. Plur. مِرُون mirū̃, wild beast, Format. Plur. مِرُئَان miruā̃, مِرُئِين miruē̃, مِرُنِ mirune, مِرُئَنِ miruane.

4) The Formative of nouns ending in ā (ā̃).

Nouns ending in ā remain unaltered in the Formative Sing., as, آگيَا, f., āgyā, command, Format. آگيَا āgyā; رَاجَا rājā (m.), king, Format. رَاجَا rājā; in the Formative Plur. they end (according to the termination of the Nomin. Plural: ā-ũ) in u-ne, as: آگيائُنِ agyāune; also رَاجَائُنِ rājāune, masc.

5) The Formative of nouns ending in 'a'.

Nouns ending in 'a' remain unchanged in the Formative Sing., as: كَامَ kāma, a beam, Format. كَامَ kāma; in the Formative Plur. they terminate (according to their Nom. Plural) either in ã (ẽ) or u-ne, as: كَامَان kāmã, كَامِين kāmẽ, كَامُنِ kāmune.

6) The Formative of nouns ending in ī (ī̃).

a) Masc. nouns ending in ī change the same in the Formative Sing. to i-a, as: مَالِي mālī, a gardener, Formative مَالِيَ mālia. Those nouns, which have final ī nasalized (= ī̃), retain the Anusvāra in the Formative, as: پرِين prī̃, friend, Format. پرِئَ prīa. The Formative Plural ends either in i-ã (yã), i-ẽ (yẽ), or in i-ne, ia-ne (yane), iu-ne (yune), as: مَالِيَان maliã, مَالِئِين māliẽ; مَالِنِ māline, مَالِئَنِ māliane (مَالْيَنِ), مَالِئُنِ maliune (مَالْيُنِ).

b) Feminine nouns ending in ī change the same likewise in the Formative Sing. to i-a, as: ٹوپِي ṭōpī, a hat, Format. ٹوپِيَ ṭōpia; the Formative Plural also quite agrees with that of the masc. nouns, as: ٹوپِيَان ṭōpiã, ٹوپِئِين ṭōpiẽ, ٹوپِنِ ṭōpine, ٹوپِئَنِ ṭōpiane, ٹوپِئُنِ ṭōpiune. Such fem. nouns, as have dropped final ī in the Nom. Plural (cf. §. 15, 6), drop the same also in the contracted form of the Formative Plur., as: مَنجِي manjī, a stool, Nom. Plur. مَنجُون manjũ, Format. Plur.

مَنجَان manǰā̃, مَنجين manǰẽ; but: مَنجِنّ manǰiane, مَنجُنِ manǰiune are also in use. Some other nouns also, in which final ī is not preceded by a palatal, drop 'i' in the contracted form of the Formative Plural, as: كوڙين kōṛẽ, in scores, from كوڙي kōṛī, a score.

7) The Formative of nouns ending in 'i' (e).

Nouns ending in 'i' (fem. and masc.) remain unaltered in the Format. Sing., as: بهتِ, f., bhite, a wall, Format. بهتِ bhite; كيهَرِ kēhare (m.), a lion, Format. كيهَرِ kēhare. In the Formative Plural of fem. nouns the same terminations are employed as with fem. nouns ending in ī, as: بهتِيَان bhitiā̃, بهتِئين bhitiẽ, بهتِنِ bhitine, بهتِنّ bhitiane, بهتِنُ bhitiune. In the Formative Plural final 'i' is frequently dropped altogether, especially in poëtry, but only in the contracted form of the Formative, as: بهَتين bhatẽ, in (different) ways, from بهَتِ bhate, habit, manner.

The Formative Plural of masc. nouns ends in -ne, the contracted form ā̃, ẽ hardly ever being in use with them, as: كيهَرِنِ kēharine.

جوء ǰōe, wife, which forms its Plural either regularly جوئيون ǰōyu, or irregularly: جوئِرُ ǰōiru, جوهِرُ ǰōhiru, has in the Format. Plur. either جوئِنِ ǰōyune or: جوهِرِنِ ǰōhirine.

§. 18.

We let now follow, for the sake of perspicuity, a survey of the Sindhī declensional process. As the Genitive affix جو ǰō is originally an adjective affix, by means of which the noun is turned into an adjective, dependent on the governing noun in gender, number and case, we premise the inflexion of جو, which, according to its terminations ǰō and ǰī, is inflected after the manner of nouns ending in ō and ī (fem.). As stated already, جو always requires the Formative of a noun, as all postpositions.

SINGULAR.

	Masculine.	*Feminine.*
Nom.	جو ǰō.	جِي ǰī.
Form.	جي ǰē.	جي ǰē; جِی ǰia.
Vocat.	جا ǰā.	جِي ǰī.

PLURAL.

Nom.	جا ǰā.	جُون ǰū̃; جِئُون ǰiū̃.
Form.	جي ǰē; جَنِ ǰane.	جي ǰē; جِنِ ǰine; جُنِ ǰune; (جِئَنِ ǰiane; جِئُنِ ǰiune.)
Vocat.	جا ǰā.	جُون ǰū̃; جِئُون ǰiū̃.

In poëtry the diminutive form جَڙو ǰaṛō, جَڙِي ǰaṛī is occasionally used instead of جو, as:

كالهَ قَرِيبَنِ لَڏِئو اَڄُ تُنْهِن جَڙِي وارَ

Yesterday (thy) relatives have departed (this life); to-day it is thy turn. Golden Alphabet II, 4.

In the same way as جو ǰō the adjective سَنْدو sandō (belonging to, own) is very frequently used in poëtry, and inflected regularly, as:

SINGULAR.

	Masculine.	*Feminine.*
Nom.	سَنْدو sandō.	سَنْدِي sandī.
Form.	سَنْدي sandē.	سَنْدِی sandia.
Vocat.	سَنْدا sandā.	سَنْدِي sandī.

PLURAL.

	Masculine.	*Feminine.*
Nom.	سَنْڌا sandā.	سَنْڌِيُون sandiū̃.
Form.	سَنْڌَنِ sandane, سَنْڌين sandẽ.	سَنْڌِنِ sandine; سَنْڌِيَنِ sandiane; سَنْڌِيُنِ sandiune.
Vocat.	سَنْڌا sandā.	سَنْڌِيُون sandiū̃.

I. DECLENSION.

Nouns in u (masc. and fem.)

a) Masc. nouns in 'u'.

SINGULAR.

Nom. ڏيهُ ḍēh-u, a country.
Format. } Instrum. } ڏيهَ ḍēh-a.
Gen. ڏيهَ جو ḍēh-a jō etc.
Dative. ڏيهَ کهي ḍēh-a khē.
Accusat. ڏيهُ ḍēh-u (ڏيهَ کهي).
Locat. ڏيهِ ḍēh-e, or: ڏيهَ مين ḍēha mẽ etc.
Ablat. ڏيهان ḍēh-ā̃; ڏيهوُن ḍēh-ō̃; ڏيهُون ḍēh-ū̃.
ڏيهَوْن ḍēh-aū̃; ڏيهاءُ ḍēh-āu or: ڏيهَ کهان ḍēha khā̃ etc.
Vocat. اِي ڏيهَ ē ḍēh-a; ڏيهَ ḍēh-a.

PLURAL.

Nom. ڏيهَ ḍēh-a, countries.
Format. } Instrum. } ڏيهان ḍēh-ā̃; ڏيهين ḍēh-ẽ; ڏيهَنِ ḍēha-ne.
Gen. ڏيهَنِ جو ḍēhane jō etc.
Dative. ڏيهَنِ کهي ḍēhane khē.

Accus. ڏيھَ ḍēh-a (ڏيھَنِ کھِي).

Locat. ڏيھَنِ مين ḍēhane mẽ etc. (ڏيھين ḍēh-ẽ).

Ablat. ڏيھَنِيَّان ḍēhane-ā̃ etc.; ڏيھَنِ کھَان ḍēhane khā̃ etc.

Vocat. ڏيھو ḍēh-ō; ڏيھَا ḍēh-ā.

An irregular noun.

SINGULAR.

Nom. پِئُ pi-u, father.
Format. } پِئُ pi-u.
Instrum. }
Genit. پِئُ جو piu jō etc.
Dative. پِئُ کھِي piu khē.
Accus. پِئُ pi-u (پِئُ کھِي).
Ablat. پِئُ کھَان piu khā̃ etc.
Vocat. پِئُ pi-u.

PLURAL.

Nom. پِئُرَ piu-ra, fathers.
Format. } پِئُنِ piu-ne; پِئُرَنِ piura-ne.
Instrum. }
Dative. پِئُنِ کھِي piune khē; پِئُرَنِ کھِي piurane khē.
Accus. پِئُرَ piura (پِئُنِ کھِي; پِئُرَنِ کھِي).
Ablat. پِئُنِيَّان piune-ā̃; پِئُرَنِيَّان piurane-ā̃ etc.
پِئُنِ کھَان piune khā̃; پِئُرَنِ کھَان piurane khā̃ etc.
Vocat. پِئُرو piur-ō.

---

1) In poëtry an additional vowel may be joined to the final ā of the Vocative, for the sake of the metre, as: وَڻَاءُ vaṇāu, oh ye trees, instead of وَڻَا vaṇā; وَڻَاھَ vaṇaha, وَڻَاءَ vaṇāa. Sh. Majōurī, III, 6. 7. 8.

پھرِي پَنْھَن جي بھَانِ پَسَان مُلکُ مَلِيرَ جو

Having returned to my own cowpen, may I see the country of Malīr. Sh. Um. Mār. I, 13.

وِسَارِجِ مَ وَرَ کھِي پَنْجِ مُنْدھَ مَرِي

Forget not (thy) husband; o woman (rather) die! Sh. Um. Mār. II, 6.

کَارِي مُنْھِ قِيَامَ ڏِينْھِ آنئُون تھِئَّان مَنجھَان عَاصِنِ

May I be of a black face (literally: in a black face) on the day of the resurrection from amongst the sinners. Maj. 731.

پَرَڏِيھَان پَنْدھُ کَرِي هَلِي آيو هِتِ

Having made a journey from a foreign country he has come hither. Sh. Sōr. I, 2.

پھَٽِئَّا پير نَقِيرِ جَا سِيرُون تھِئَّا سِي

Wounded were those feet of the poor woman from the journey (سِيرُ). Sh. Ābirī VI, 6.

ڏُزْڏُ ڏِيوَانو ڏھَارِيو چَرِيو لَاهِ چِتَاء

The thief, the mad man, the stranger, the fool take out of thy mind. Maj. 291.

آءُ اوْرَاھُون سُپِرِين پَرِي وَنجُ مَ پِيئَ

Come near, o sweetheart, do not go away, my friend! Sh. Ābirī X, 3.

سُدِھ سَنْدِي سَجَّنِين جي کو ڏِيمِ اِينئَ

If one give me thus intelligence of my friends. Maj. 733.

دوسَ دوسَتِئَّان ڏُورِ کَرِي تھو ڏَيَا ڏِيکھَارِي

Having separated the friends from the friends he shows compassion. Sh. Sōr. I, Epil.

اُٿهو ويڄا مَ وِهو وَنڄو ڏَرَب کهَڻي

Stand up, ye physicians, do not sit down, go off with your medicines! Sh. Jam. Kal. I, Epil.

b) Feminine nouns in 'u'.

SINGULAR.

Nom. وِڄُ vij-u, lightening.
Format. } Instrum. } وِڄُ vij-u.
Genit. وِڄُ جو viju jō etc.
Dative. وِڄُ کهي viju khē.
Accus. وِڄُ vij-u (وِڄُ کهي).
Ablat. وِڄُ کهان viju khā̃ etc.
Vocat. وِڄُ vij-u.

PLURAL.

Nom. وِڄُون vij-ū̃.
Format. } Instrum. } وِڄُنِ viju-ne.
Genit. وِڄُنِ جو vijune jō etc.
Dative. وِڄُنِ کهي vijune khē.
Accus. وِڄُون vij-ū̃ (وِڄُنِ کهي).
Ablat. وِڄُنئان viju-ne-ā̃ etc.; وِڄُنِ کهان vijune khā̃ etc.
Vocat. وِڄُون vij-ū̃.

An irregular noun.

SINGULAR.

Nom. مَاءُ mā-u, mother.
Format. مَاءُ mā-u.
Vocat. مَاءُ mā-u.

PLURAL.

Nom. مَائُون mā-ũ; مَائِرُ mā-i-ru; مَائِرُون mā-i-rũ, mothers.

Format. مَائُنِ māu-ne; مَائِرُنِ māiru-ne.

Vocat. مَائُون mā-ũ, مَائِرُ mā-i-ru.

لَنُون سِين اُتهِي لَڏِ کِي نَہ رَسَانِي کيچَ کهي

Having risen with love depart; nothing (else) will bring thee to Kēč. Sh. Maʒδ. II, 10.

پِرِين وَنجُ مَہ پَرَڏِيهَڙِي موٽِي چُئِيسِ مَاءُ

O friend, do not go to a foreign country, said to him again his mother. Maj. 83.

هوتُ هَلَنْدِنِ کهَٽِيو اَنگهُنِ چَاڙهِي اَنگُ

The sweetheart has been won by those, who set off, placing rent upon rents (i. e. in their clothes). Sh. Ābirī, VII, 7.

بهينَرُ آئُون بهورِي مُون سَنگُ سُنجَانِي نَہ کِيٿو

O sisters, I am simple-minded; by me unknowingly a marriage has been contracted. Sh. Ābirī V, 16.

II. DECLENSION.

Nouns in ō (õ).

SINGULAR.

Nom. مِيڙَاکو mēṛāk-ō, crowd.

Format. } مِيڙَاکِي mēṛāk-ē.
Instrum. }

Genit. مِيڙَاکِي جو mēṛāk-ē jō etc.

Dative. مِيڙَاکِي کهي mēṛākē khē.

Accus. مِيڙَاکو mēṛāk-ō (مِيڙَاکِي کهي).

Ablat. ميڙاڪان mēṛāk-ā̃ etc.; ميڙاڪي ڪهان mēṛākē khā̃.

Vocat. ميڙاڪا mēṛāk-ā.

PLURAL.

Nom. ميڙاڪا mēṛāk-ā, crowds.

Format. }
Instrum. } ميڙاڪان mērāk-ā̃; ميڙاڪين mēṛāk-ẽ; ميڙاڪنِ mē-rāka-ne.

Genit. ميڙاڪنِ جو mēṛākane jō.

Dative. ميڙاڪنِ کهي mēṛākane khē.

Accus. ميڙاڪا mēṛāk-ā (ميڙاڪنِ کهي).

Ablat. ميڙاڪنِان mēṛākane-ā̃ etc.; ميڙاڪنِ ڪهان mēṛā-kane khā̃ etc.

Vocat. ميڙاڪا mēṛāk-ā; ميڙاڪَوُ mēṛāk-au; ميڙاڪو mēṛāk-ō.

تهانوُ ڀَري گهڻ موتين ڀاڳي ڏِنائين

Having filled the dish with many pearls she gave it to the lucky one (ڀاڳيو). Māǰ. 714.

هاٿِي جي هِينئو وِهي تہ ٻہِ گهڻو مُلهُ گهوڙان

The elephant, though he walk slowly, is yet of greater price than a horse. Sh. Šhī̃ha Kēḍ. I, 2.

اُٿِيءُ ديوانا دُورِ ٿِيءُ هاڻي هِتِ مَ وِيهُ

Get up, o mad one! be off! do not sit now here! Maj. 249.

سِڙهَہ سَنوان لاڄو نَنوان مُهانا سَنڌنَ مِيرَ

The sails are straight, the ropes are new, their chiefs are the Muhāṇōs (fishermen). Sh. Sur. I, 12.

كُتهَلِ كَجَاوَنِ مِين جَاڙهي هوَتَ هَلَايو

Having lifted the killed one (fem.) into the paniers (كَجَائوَ), the friend has driven off. Sh. Ābirī X, Epil.

كُلهَنِئّان كوَرِينِ عَاشِقَ عَبْدُ ٱلّطِيفُ چَوِي

The lovers scoop out (their head) from the shoulders, says ʿAbd-ul-Laṯīf. Sh. Kal. I, 7:

تَرِي تُنَ پِتّاسِ پَاسَنِئُون پَانِي وَهي

In the bottom she (i. e. the boat) has got holes; from the sides water flows in. Sh. Sūr. III, 6.

III. DECLENSION.

Nouns in ū (ũ).

SINGULAR.

Nom. رَهَاكُو rahāk-ū, an inhabitant.

Format.
Instrum. } رَهَاكُوَّ rahāk-ua.

Ablat. رَهَاكُوَّان rahāku-ã; رَهَاكُوَّ كهَان rahākua khã etc.

Vocat. رَهَاكُو rahāk-ū.

PLURAL.

Nom. رَهَاكُو rahāk-u, inhabitants.

Format.
Instrum. } رَهَاكُئّان rahāku-ã; رَهَاكُئِين rahāku-ẽ;

رَهَاكُئّنِ rahākua-ne or: رَهَاكُنِ rahāku-ne.

Ablat. رَهَاكُنِئّان rahakune-ã etc.; رَهَاكُنِ كهَان rahākune khã etc.

Vocat. رَهَاكُئو rahaku-ō; رَهَاكُئّا rahāku-ā.

دَارُوَّ جَا دَانَا ڏِنَمِ هوَتَ هَتهَنِ سَان

Grains of medicine have been given by me to the sweetheart with (my) hands. Sh. Kōhiārī IV, 9.

پَهُچَائِجِ پُنْهُنءَ کهي هِيءَ پِيَادِڙِي پَاندهِي

Cause to come to Punhū this foot-traveller (fem.). Sh. Kōh. IV, Epil.

ڈهولِيَا مَارُو مُون سين پَرْچَنِ شَالَ پَنْوُهَارَ

O darling Mārū, would that the Paũhārs would be reconciled with me! Sh. Um. Mār. I, Epil.

سَچُ جيهِي سؤنَ مُنْهِ نَ پيئي مَاڙهُئِين

Truth like gold has not fallen into the mouth of of the people. Sh. Jam. Kal. VIII, 7.

مِرُنّان مؤرَان پکهنَان وَائِيَ بِيَ مَ بهُلُ

By wild beasts, by ants, by birds, by (any) other speach be not misled. Sh. Kal. I, 16.

مِينڍهَا دهُئِي نَ مَارُئِي مَحَلِين مَارُنّان دهَارَ

Māruī does not wash the braids in the palaces, away from the Mārūs. Sh. Um. Mār. III, 5.

جَنِ ڳَئُنِ ڳَاڙو نَ ڏِنو تَنِ پُرِ کِيُون پَارِيُون

By those cows, by which not a drop was given, the pots have been filled. Haz. Sār. V, 47.

مَتَان رَهو مَاڙهُنّا نَنْگَرَ جي آدهَارَ

Do not remain, o people under the protection of Nangar (i. e. Taṭṭha)! Verses of the Māmuīs.

Note. It is a poëtical license, if a noun is not inflected in the Formative for the sake of the rhyme, as:

اُوچو تُون آکَاسَ تي آن بهوَنو مَتهي بهُون

High above the sky art thou, I am a wanderer upon earth (بهُون instead of بهُنءَ). Sh. Sōr. I, 3.

IV. DECLENSION.

Nouns in ā (ā̃).

a) feminine.

SINGULAR.

Nom. هَچَا hač-ā, murder.

Format.
Instrum. } هَچَا hač-ā.

Ablat. (هَچَان hač-ā̃); هَچَا كهَان hačā khā̃ etc.

Vocat. هَچَا hač-ā.

PLURAL.

Nom. هَچَائُون hačā-ū̃, murders.

Format.
Instrum. } هَچَائُنِ hačāu-ne.

Ablat. هَچَائُنِئَان hačāune-ā̃.

Vocat. هَچَائُون hačā-ū̃.

b) masculine.

SINGULAR.

Nom. رَاجَا rāǰ-ā (رَاجِا rāǰā), a king.

Format.
Instrum. } رَاجَا rāǰ-ā.

Ablat. رَاجَا كهَان rāǰā khā̃ etc.

Vocat. رَاجَا rāǰ-ā.

PLURAL.

Nom. رَاجَا rāǰ-ā, kings.

Format.
Instrum. } رَاجَائُنِ rāǰāu-ne.

Ablat. رَاجَائُنِئَان rāǰāune-ā̃; رَاجَائُنِ كهَان rāǰāune khā̃ etc.

Vocat. رَاجَائو rāǰā-ō.

كَانهِي وَاتَ جِيجَا تَنِ جَتَنِ سَان

There is no way with those Jats, o aunt! Sh. Hus. VI, Epil.

سو تَان توئِي سَانُ جَنْهِن لَئِ جَفَائُون كَرِين

That one is with thyself, on whose account thou causest thyself troubles. Sh. Ābirī III, 5.

V. DECLENSION.

Nouns in ă.

SINGULAR.

Nom. سَدهَ sadh-a, wish.
Format. } Instrum. } سَدهَ sadh-a.
Ablat. سَدهَان sadh-ã; سَدهَ كهَان sadha khã etc.
Vocat. سَدهَ sadh-a.

PLURAL.

Nom. سَدهَان sadh-ã; سَدهُون sadh-ũ, wishes.
Format. } Instrum. } سَدهَان sadh-ã; سَدهِين sadh-ẽ; سَدهُنِ sadhu-ne.
Ablat. سَدهُنِئَان sadhune-ã; سَدهُنِ كهَان sadhune khã etc.
Vocat. سَدهَان sadh-ã; سَدهُون sadh-ũ.

سَاهَرَ جِى صَلَاحَ بَارِ لَنْگهَايَسِ بَاجهَ سَان

By the counsel of Sāhaṛu (the buffalo-keeper) I have been made to pass the whirlpool with the mercy (of God). Sh. Suh. II, 2.

وَحدَتَان كَثْرَت تهِي كَثْرَت وَحدَت كُلُّ

From the unity multiplicity has sprung; multiplicity is all unity. Sh. Kal. I, 15.

وِهُ مَ مُنْدهَ بهَنْبهورَ مِين هُنَ پُجَنْدِئَنْ هَانِ

Sit not, o lady! in Bhambhōru, thou wilt now come up to him. Sh. Hus. VIII, 3.

لُکھُون لَگَنِ کوسِیُون ڏاڏھا تَپَنِ ڏِينھَ

Hot winds blow, oppressively hot are the days. Sh. Dēsī III, Epil.

آگَرَ اوطاقُنِ مِينِ کھَٽھُورِيُون کھَٽُنِ

In the men's sitting rooms is aloe-wood, on the couches musk. Sh. Mūm. Rāṇō II, 3.

VI. DECLENSION.

Nouns in ī (ī̃).

a) Masculine nouns.

SINGULAR.

Nom. سَاڻِي sāṇ-ī, companion.
Format. } Instrum. } سَاڻِيَ sāṇ-ia.

Ablat. سَاڻِئَان sāṇi-ā̃; سَاڻِيَ کھَان sāṇia khā̃ etc.

Vocat. سَاڻِي sāṇ-ī (سَاڻِيَه sāṇi-ah).

PLURAL.

Nom. سَاڻِي sāṇ-ī, companions.
Format. } Instrum. } سَاڻِئَان sāṇi-ā̃ (سَاڻِيَان sāṇiy-ā̃); سَاڻِئِين saṇi-ē̃;
سَاڻْيَنِ saṇya-ne (سَاڻِئَنِ saṇia-ne); سَاڻْنُنِ sāṇyu-ne (سَاڻِئُنِ sāṇiu-ne); سَاڻِنِ sāṇi-ne.

Ablat. سَاڻْيَنِئَان sāṇyane-ā̃ etc.

Vocat. سَاڻِئَا sāṇi-ā; سَاڻِئو sāṇi-ō.

پيرين ھيٺھِ پِرِيَنِ جي آنٹُون وِچھَايَان وَارَ

Under the feet of (my) friend I spread out my hair. Maj. 231.

تَڏِهِن قَاضِيَ چيو قَيْسَ کهي مَنَان لَاهين مَرَم

Then said the Qāẕī to Qaisu: dropp bashfulness from (thy) mind. Maǰ. 183.

کَنَا نَارِنِ حَامِيَه هَانِ ٻَچَائِج هِيئُ

From the women, o protector! deliver now this man. Sh. Sōr. I, 9.

پيرين آنسُون نَ پُڄِنِي ڏيهُ پرِيَان جو ڏُورِ

On (my) feet I cannot arrive; the country of (my) friends is far off. Sh. Khambh. I, Epil.

کَامُون ڇِهِجَاهُ گهَڻيُون گهُرْجَنِو اوٺهَا

Cut off wands, many are necessary for you, o ye camelmen! Sh. Ābirī XI, 7.

حَالُ مُنْهِن جو هِهَڙو پَسو تهَا پرِيَاهُ

My condition is such, as ye see, o friends! Maǰ. 441.

b) Feminine nouns.

SINGULAR.

Nom. گولِي gōl-ī, a slave-girl.

Format. } Instrum. } گولِيَ gōl-ia.

Ablat. گولِيَّان gōli-ā̃; گولِيَ کهَان gōlia khā̃.

Vocat. گولِي gōl-ī.

PLURAL.

Nom. گولِيُون gōliy-ū̃ (گولِئُّون gōli-ū̃; گوليُون gōly-ū̃).

Format. } Instrum. } گولِيَّان gōli-ā̃; گولِئِين gōli-ē̃; گولِيَّنِ gōlia-ne (gō-lya-ne); گولِئُّنِ gōliu-ne; گولِنِ gōli-ne.

Ablat. گولِيَّنِيَّان gōliane-ā̃ etc.

Vocat. گولِئُّون gōli-ū̃.

تَڏِهِن ٻَائِيَ چِيو ٻَانهِيَ کهِي تہ اُتهِي اُٺهہ پَلَانِ

Then said the lady to her slave-girl: having risen saddle the camel! Maj. 738.

ڏُکهِي ڏُکهہ وِسَارِ سيجَ ڀهِڃِي ڪَرِ سَسُئِي

O afflicted one, forget (thy) grief; break in pieces (thy) bed, o Sacuī! Sh. Maꝫδ. VI, 6.

گوڙيُون گولَاڙَنِ جُون چَپُٽِيَ سَانُ چُنْڊِينْدِي

The kernels of the golāṛōs (coccinea indica) will I pick with a snap of the fingers. Sh. Um. Mār. II, Epil.

ٻُکِي ڏِينْدَا ٻَاجهہ جِي نِهَارِي نَاڙُون

They (i. e. the physicians) give a pill of mercy, having seen the pulses (نَاڙِي). Sh. Jam. Kal. II, 18.

رَانِنِ وَرِي رُوهہ گونْدَرَ لَتهَا گولِئِين

To the queens pleasure has returned; the griefs of the slave-girls have been taken off. Sh. Dēsī, Čhōṭ. 3.

سَرْتِيُون سَاهُ سَنْدوِمِ تهِئُو حَوَالِي هوتَ جِي

O companions, my soul has been confided to the protection of my sweetheart. Sh. Dēsī VII, 11.

VII. DECLENSION.

Nouns ending in ĕ (i).

SINGULAR.

Nom.	گالهِہ gālh-e, story (fem.).
Format. / Instrum.	گالهِہ gālh-e.
Ablat.	گالهِيَّان gālhe-ā̃; گالْهوُن gālh-ō̃ etc.
Vocat.	گالهِہ gālh-e.

PLURAL.

Nom. ڳالھِئُون gālhe-ū̃, stories.
Format.
Instrum. } ڳالھِئان gālhe-ā̃; ڳالھِئين gālhi-ē̃; ڳالھِئَنِ gāl-hea-ne; ڳالھِئُنِ gālheu-ne; ڳالھِنِ gālhi-ne.

Ablat. ڳالھِنِئان gālhine-ā̃ etc.

Vocat. ڳالھِئُون gālhe-ū̃.

مِيَان مُون کھِي مِهِتِ جِي کو ڏيکھارِي وَاٽَ

O friend, may some one show me the way to the mosque! Maj. 131.

کاکِئان وَنجُ مَ کِيڏَهِين رَاڻَا تو نَ رِهَاءِ

From Kāke do not go anywhere! it is not right for thee, o Rāṇō! Sh. Mūm. Rāṇ. I, Epil.

تَان مَڃِ مُحَمَّدُ کارَنِي نِرتِوُن مَنْجهَان نِينْهَ

Acknowledge then Muhammad, the intercessor, out of thought and love (نِرْتِ). Sh. Kal. I, 2.

آيَلِ اُنِ نَ وِسَهَان هَنْجھُون جِي هَارِينِ
اَنِئُو آبُ اَکھِنِ مِين تهَا ڏِهَ کھِي ڏيکھَارِينِ

O mother, I do not trust them, who shed tears,
Having brought water into their eyes they show a sandhill. Sh. Jam. Kal. I, 20.

مِينْھُون پَانَ مُرَادِيُون تهَدهَا چَرَنِ تهَرَ
سَارِي آچِئُو سَامُھِيُون ڏِئَنِ کھِيرَ سَجَرَ

The self-willed buffaloes graze the cool deserts,
Having come in front of the cow-house they give fresh milk. Sh. Sār. IV, 14.

دِيگِين دوُگ كَرّهَنِ جِتِ كُبِين كَنِكو نَ لَهِي

In the caldrons the limbs boil, where in the eddies a grain does not sink. Sh. Kal. II, 27.

جِلْدَ سُونْهَارَا سَبهِين پَرِين بِئَّا مُصْحَفَا موچَارَا

Volumes beautiful in all ways, and other elegant books. Maǰ. 141.

مَتِئُون موّتَنَ سَنْدِيُون كَاكِيُون كِي نَ ڏِئوم

O sisters, give me by no means counsels to return! Sh. Dēsī VII, 6.

b) Masculine nouns.

SINGULAR.

Nom. كِيهَرِ kēhar-e, lion.

Format. } Instrum. } كِيهَرِ kēhar-e.

Ablat. كِيهَرِئَّان kēhare-ā̃ etc.

Vocat. كِيهَرِ kēhar-e.

PLURAL.

Nom. كِيهَرِ kēhar-e, lions.

Format. } Instrum. } كِيهَرِئَّان kēhare-ā̃; كِيهَرِئِين kēhari-ē̃; كِيهَرِنِ kē-hari-ne.

Ablat. كِهَرِنَّان kēharine-ā̃ etc.

Vocat. كِهَرِئو kēhare-ō.

اِيئَ كَيْسَرِ جِي كَارِ جِنئَ هَاتهِيَ كهِي هَتهُ هَنِي

This in the business of the lion, that he strikes his hand into the elephant. Sh. Šīha Kēḍ. 7.

Chapter IX.

Adjectives.

§. 19.

The Sindhī adjectives and participles have the same terminations as the substantives and may therefore be classed under the same heads as the substantives.

The general rule, that the adjective must agree with its substantive in gender, number and case, holds good in Sindhī likewise.

In reference to the gender no exception takes place; but if an adjective or participle be referred to two preceding substantives, the one of which is masculine, the other feminine, the adjective or participle follows in the Plural masculine, as:

نَرُ ۽ مَادِي سِرْجِيَا اَتهَسِ

He created them male and female. Gen. I, 27.

With regard to the number the following exception takes place. When an adjective precedes a noun in the inflected case of the Plural, it may remain in the inflected case of the Singular, as:

كُوڙِي نَبِيُنِ كهي to false prophets, or: كُوڙَنِ نَبِيُنِ كهي

The same is the case, when an adjective precedes a noun in the Vocative Plural, the adjective being then commonly put in the Vocative Singular, as: اِي سِنْڌِهِي مَاڙهُئَا o Sindhī men! instead of: اِي سِنْڌِهِئَا مَاڙهُئَا.

But it does not fall under this head, when an adjective or participle is referred to a preceding substantive followed by the postposition كهي khē; for in this case there exists no grammatical connexion between the adjective and substantive, but the adjective is used absolutely as:

اُنْهَنِ بِنْهِي بهَائُنِ کهِي سَمُنْڊَرَ مِين جَارُ وِجهَنْدَوَ ڏِٺهائِيِن

He saw those two brothers throwing their net into the sea. Matth. IV, 18.

ڏُونگَرَنِ کهِي اُونچو بهَانْيِمِ

I thought the hills high.

As to the case it may be observed, that adjectives, which end in ī and ū may remain uninflected, when immediately followed by a substantive in the Formative, as:

مَـ ڪِجِ پَنْدهَڙو وِيرو مَاڻهُنِ سَاتهَ مِين

Do not make a journey in the caravan of vindictive men!

بِنْهِي کهِي بَهُون پَرِين وِچَارَنِ وِرُوهَ

To both the helpless there was in many ways pleasant conversation. Maj. 198.

An adjective, following a substantive, may be put in the Ablative case, whereas the preceding substantive is only put in the Formative, as:

جو ڏِيهَ ڏَاڏَائَان آئِيو ڏِنم تَنْهِن طَعْنو

He who has come from the grand-father's country, has given me a reproach. Sh. Um. Mār. II, 2.

When an adjective precedes or follows a noun in the contracted form of the Formative Plural, it assumes the same form, as:

ٻُچهڙِين مَاڻهُئِين کهِي چهڏِي هَلُ

Wicked men forsake.

گهورِيَان گهڻين[1] بهَتِئِين سَنْدِي بَاجهَ بِئَنِ

I seek in many ways the mercy of others. Sh. Jam. Kal. V, Epil. I.

---

1) گهڻين is contracted instead of گهڻِئِين.

ڪَانڊِين ٿَانڊِين ٻَاٻُرِين پَچَان مَرُ پِيئِي

By the burning coals of the thorn and babul tree I am indeed roasted! Sh. Jam. Kal. III, 3.

Adjectives precede, as a rule, their substantives, as:

مَاڙهُون پَنْهَن جِي نَنْڍِهِيَ اَکِهَ سَان جَڳَتُرُ تهو ڏِسِي

Man sees with his small eye the world.

چَنگو سُرَهو سُڳَنْڌو ٻوڙُ مَنْجِهِس پِٿو آهِي

Good, fragrant, sweet-smelling food was contained therein.

An adjective may also follow its substantive, especially when the adjective contains more syllables than its substantive, as:

تَارَا مُنْڍهَ جِي ڏِينْهَ کهَان اَنْجَا تَائِين پَنْهَن جَنِ سَنْڌهَنِ
ٿهِيَلَنِ کهَان ڦهيرُ نَه ڪَرِي ٻُورِي ڦهيرِي مين آهِنِ.

The stars from the day of beginning are, without having deviated from their fixed intervals, in full turning.

Two and more adjectives very frequently follow their substantive as:

دوسَ مِٺهَا دِلِدَارَ عَالَمُ سَبهُه آبَادُ ڪَرِين

O sweet and charming friend, make the whole earth blooming! Sh. Sār. IV, 12.

خُدَاء جَانُو ڏَاهِي اِهَڙَا ڀهيدَ پَنْهَن جِي ڪَلَامَ مَنجهِ
وِچُورِيَا آهِنِ

By the knowing and wise God such secrets have been explained in his word.

To adjectives, as well as to substantives, very frequently an emphatic ī accedes in all cases, signifying 'very', 'quite', 'truly', without altering in any way the termination of the adjective (the feminine Singular of adjectives ending in ō alone being excepted; see §. 20, 2), as: اوچتوئي ōčitōī, quite accidental; غَرِيبِئِي γarībeī (Sing. fem.) very humble.

اَگِئِينئِي پَنْڌَهَ جوَ سَاتهِي کَرِ سَانْبَاهُ

O companion, make preparation of the very instant journey! Golden Alph. I, 1.

§. 20.

Formation of gender.

With reference to the derivation of the feminine from masculine nouns the general rules, which have been laid down in Chapter VII, §. 14, are equally applicable to adjectives. Some minor points, in which adjectives differ in this respect from substantives of the same termination, will be noticed under the following heads.

1) Adjectives ending in 'u'.

These change the masc. termination 'u' either to 'e' (i) or to 'a', as:

نِڌهَرُ nidharu, helpless, fem. نِڌهَرِ nidhare or: نِڌهَرَ nidhara.

اُدهَرَ نِڌهَرَ ابهَرِي اَسُونْهِين آنهِيَان

Forlorn, helpless, wretched, unacquainted I am! Sh. Ābiri VIII, 1.

Some adjectives of Sindhī origin, but more so those borrowed from the Arabic or Persian, remain without any change of gender, number and case, as: سَرْسُ sarsu, plentiful (s.); گَڏُ gaḍu, mixed (s.); سَهِجُ sahiju, easy (s.); عَبَثُ ʒabaϑu, vain (a.); تَمَامُ tamāmu, whole (a.); خُوبُ χūbu, good (p.); دُرسُ dursu, right (corrupted from دُرُسْتُ (p.)); مَاتُ mātu, done for (p.); پَشِيمَانُ pašimānu, ashamed (p.); حَيْرَانُ ħairānu, bewildered (a.); هَلَاكُ halāku, killed (a.); صَافُ sāfu, clean (a.); مَعْلِمُ maʒlimu, known (corrupted from مَعْلُومُ (a.)), etc. etc.

مَرَنَان اَڳِي جِي مُئَا سِي مَرِي تِهِنَّ نَہ مَاتُ

Those who have died before dying, they are not done for when dead. Sh. Maʒδūrī IV, 7.

جو وِيڄَنِ جِي وَاتِ دَارُوَّ تَنْهِن دُرْسُ کِيَا

By the medicine, which is in the mouth of the physicians, they have been made whole. Sh. Jam. Kal. II, 17.

وَوڙِئو جَنِ وَرَنِ سِين پُونْڍِيُون تِتِ پَشِيمَانُ

Those who have looked about with men, will there be put to shame. Maj. 266.

2) Adjectives ending in ō (ō̃).

These change the masc. termination to ī (ī̃); as: کُوڙو kūṛō, false, fem. کُوڙِي kūṛī; نَئون nāō̃, new, fem. نَئِين nāī̃.

When an adjective or participle ends in yō (or iō), being preceded by a consonant, the y (i) is dropped before the fem. termination ī, as: ڏُکهيو ḍukhyō or: ڏُکهِئو ḍukhiō, pained, fem. ڏُکهِي ḍukhī; کِئو kiō, done, fem. کِي kī; but پِئو piō, fallen (Part. perf. from پَوَنُ) makes its feminine پيئِي pēī, not pī. When yō however is preceded by a vowel, the feminine is formed regularly in yī, as: چَيو čayō, said (Part. perf. from چَوَنُ), fem. چَيِي čayī; كَيو kayō, made (another form of the part. perf. of كَرَنُ), fem. كَيِي kayī; آيو āyō, come (part. perf. from اَچَنُ), fem. آيِي āyī; but the y may just as well be dropped in such like forms, as: čaī, kaī, āī etc.

When the emphatic ī accedes to the feminine Singular, then the masc. termination ō is changed to yāī in the Nominative, as: مُنو munō, blunt, with the emphatic ī in the feminine: مُنيَائِي munyāī; but the other cases of the feminine are quite regular, and hardly ever found with an emphatic ī.

پَسو لَجَ لَطِيفُ چَٹِي كِيڈِي كهِي كَكهَنِ

Look, says Laṯif, what credit (is given) to pieces of straw! Sh. Suh. VIII, 1.

جي پَسِي مُنهُ مِهَارَ تَہ سِگهِيَائِي سَجِي تهِٹِي

If she sees the face of the buffalo-keeper, she becomes quickly well. Sh. Suh. Čhōṭ. 5.

3) Adjectives ending in ū (ū̃).

These do not change their termination in the feminine, as: سَهُو sahū, masc. and fem., patient; وِيڙهُو vēṛhū, masc. and fem., quarrelsome.

4) Adjectives ending in ā (ā̃).

These are comparatively few in number and admit of no change of gender, as: ڏَاتَا ḍātā, masc. and fem., liberal; تَالَان tālā̃, masc. and fem., worried. The greater number of them is indeclinable, as: صَفَا safā, pure (a.); فَنَا fanā, extinct (a.); ڦهَان phā̃, tired; جُدَا judā, separate (p.).

5) Adjectives ending in ă.

They admit of no change of gender and are all indeclinable[1]), as: وَدهِيکَ vadhīka, excessive; سُنجَ suńa, empty, barren; دهَارَ dhāra, separate, or compounded: دهَارودهَارَ dhārōdhāra; جَالَ ǰāla or جَارَ ǰāra, much; جَامَ ǰāma, much.

جِيئُ سَبهکَنْهنِ جِيئَ سِين دَرْسَن دهَارودهَارَ

(His i. e. God's) life is with the life of every one; but the aspect is quite different. Sh. Kal. I, 24.

سِرَ جُدَا دهَڙَ دهَارَ دوُکَ جَنْهِين جَا دِيکِ مِين

Whose heads (are) asunder, the trunks separated, the limbs in the caldron. Sh. Kal. II, 24.

6) Adjectives ending in ī (ĭ).

These remain unchanged in the feminine, as: بَارِي bārī, carrying a burden, masc. and fem.; سَوَادِي savādī, savoury, masc. and fem.; some are only used in the feminine.

7) Adjectives ending in e (i).

They do not differ in the feminine, like those ending in ī; as: چَوْرَسِ čaurase, masc. and fem., square. Most of them are indeclinable, chiefly those of foreign origin, e. g.: سُدهِ sudhe, pure; ڏدهِ ḍadhe, wrong; مُکهِ mukhe,

1) Stack exhibits in his Sindhī Grammar the paradigma سَکهَرَ sakhara and inflects it in the Formative Plural; but in his Dictionary he gives سَکهَرُ sakharu, which is the proper termination. I have never met with an adjective ending in 'a', inflected in any way, for the cardinal numbers پَنْجَ panǰa five etc. can hardly be classed under this head.

supreme; خُوشِ χuše (p.), pleasant (generally pronounced short and partly also written خُشِ); شَادِ šāde (p.), joyful; بَرَابَرِ barābare (p.), abreast, right; بَجَاء bajāe (p.), performed.

The feminine affixes ṇī, ṇe, āṇī (yāṇī), āiṇe (yāiṇe) are occasionally used with adjectives ending in u, ō, ū, ī, if some inherent quality, habit or occupation of living beings is to be marked out (the details see Chapter VII, §. 14), as: غَرِيبِنِ چهوکَرِ γarībiṇe čhōkare, a girl (habitually) humble; سَادهُنِي رَنَ sādhuṇī rana, a (thoroughly) virtuous widow; هوڎِيَانِي ڎاچِي hōḍiyāṇī ḍāčī, an obstinate (female) camel.

We subjoin here a survey of the inflexion of adjectives.

1) Adjectives ending in 'u'.

SINGULAR.

	Masculine.	Feminine.
Nom.	اَچيتُ ačētu, thoughtless.	اَچيتَ ačēta; اَچيتِ ačēte.
Format.	اَچيتَ ačēta.	اَچيتَ ačēta; اَچيتِ ačēte.
Vocat.	اَچيتَ ačēta.	اَچيتَ ačēta; اَچيتِ ačēte.

PLURAL.

	Masculine.	Feminine.	
Nom.	اَچيتَ ačēta.	اَچيتُون ačētū;	اَچيتِيُون acētiū.
Format.	اَچيتين ačētē, etc. اَچيتَنِ ačētane.	اَچيتُنِ ačētune; etc.	اَچيتِنِ ačētine. etc.
Vocat.	اَچيتو ačētō.	اَچيتُون ačētū;	اَچيتِيُون ačētiū.

2) Adjectives ending in ō.

SINGULAR.

	Masculine.	*Feminine.*
Nom.	رُکھو rukhō, dry.	رُکھِي rukhī.
Format.	رُکھي rukhē.	رُکھِيَ rukhia.
Vocat.	رُکھا rukhā.	رُکھِي rukhī.

PLURAL.

Nom.	رُکھا rukhā.	رُکھِيُون rukhiyũ (rukhiũ).
Format.	رُکھين rukhẽ etc.	رُکھِنِ rukhine etc.
	رُکھَنِ rukhane.	
Vocat.	رُکھا rukhā; رُکھَؤ rukha-u; رُکھو rukhō.	رُکھِيُون rukhiyũ.

SINGULAR.

Nom.	آگِئون ag̅iō̃, prior.	آگِين ag̅ī̃.
Format.	آگِئين ag̅iẽ.	آگِنِئَ ag̅īa.
Vocat.	آگِئان ag̅iã.	آگِين ag̅ī̃.

PLURAL.

Nom.	آگِئان ag̅iã.	آگِيُون ag̅iyũ (ag̅iũ).
Format.	آگِئين ag̅iẽ etc.	آگِنِ ag̅ine etc.
	آگِئَنِ agiane.	
Vocat.	آگِئان ag̅iã;	آگِيُون ag̅iyū (ag̅iũ).
	آگِئَؤ ag̅iau;	
	آگِئو ag̅iō.	

3) Adjectives ending in ū.

SINGULAR.

	Masculine.	*Feminine.*
Nom.	سَهُو sahū, patient.	سَهُو sahū.
Format.	سَهُوَ sahua.	سَهُوَ sahua.
Vocat.	سَهُو sahū.	سَهُو sahū.

PLURAL.

Nom.	سَهُو sahū.	سَهُو sahū.
Format.	سَهُئِين sahuẽ etc.	سَهُئِين sahuẽ etc.
	سَهُوَنِ sahuane.	سَهُوَنِ sahuane.
	سَهُنِ sahune.	سَهُنِ sahune.
Vocat.	سَهُئو sahuō.	سَهُئو sahuō.
	سَهُوَا sahuā.	سَهُوَا sahuā.

4) Adjectives ending in ā.

SINGULAR.

Nom.	ڏَاتَا ḍātā, liberal.	ڏَاتَا ḍātā.
Format.	ڏَاتَا ḍātā.	ڏَاتَا ḍātā.
Vocat.	ڏَاتَا ḍatā.	ڏَاتَا ḍātā.

PLURAL.

Nom.	ڏَاتَا ḍātā.	ڏَاتَائُون ḍātāū̃.
Format.	ڏَاتَائُنِ ḍātāune.	ڏَاتَائُنِ ḍātāune.
Vocat.	ڏَاتَائو ḍātāō.	ڏَاتَائُون ḍātāū̃.

5) Adjectives ending in ī.

SINGULAR.

	Masculine.	*Feminine.*
Nom.	ڎُکهِي ḍukhī, afflicted.	ڎُکهِي ḍukhī.
Format.	ڎُکهِیَ ḍukhia.	ڎُکهِیَ ḍukhia.
Vocat.	ڎُکهِي ḍukhī.	ڎُکهِي ḍukhī.

PLURAL.

Nom.	ڎُکهِي ḍukhī.	ڎُکهِيُون ḍukhiyū (ḍukhiū̃).
Format.	ڎُکهِئِين ḍukhiẽ etc.	ڎُکهِئِين ḍukhiẽ etc.
	ڎُکهِنِ ḍukhine etc.	ڎُکهِنِ ḍukhine etc.
Vocat.	ڎُکهِيًا ḍukhiā̃.	ڎُکهِيُون ḍukhiyū̃.
	ڎُکهِئُو ḍukhiō.	

6) Adjectives ending in e (i).

SINGULAR.

Nom.	هِکَمُتهِ hikamuṭhe, unanimous.	هِکَمُتهِ hikamuṭhe.
Format.	هِکَمُتهِ hikamuṭhe.	هِکَمُتهِ hikamuṭhe.
Vocat.	هِکَمُتهِ hikamuṭhe.	هِکَمُتهِ hikamuṭhe.

PLURAL.

Nom.	هِکَمُتهِ hikamuṭhe.	هِکَمُتهِئُون hikamuṭhiū̃.
Format.	هِکَمُتهِئِين hikamuṭhiẽ etc.	هِکَمُتهِئِين hikamuṭhiẽ etc.
	هِکَمُتهِنِ hikamuṭhine etc.	هِکَمُتهِنِ hikamuṭhine etc.
Vocat.	هِکَمُتهِئُو hikamuṭhiō.	هِکَمُتهِئُون hikamuṭhiū̃.

§. 21.

Comparison of adjectives.

The Sindhī, as well as the cognate idioms, has lost the power to form a Comparative and Superlative degree after the manner of the Sanskrit (and Persian) by means of adjective affixes, and it is very remarkable, that the Semitic way of making up for the degrees of comparison has been adopted. In order to express the idea of the Comparative, the object or objects, with which another is to be compared, is put in the Ablative, or, which is the same, the postpositions کَهَان khã, کهوَن khõ, کهُون khũ, مَان mã, مَنجهَان manjhã and similar ones (see the Postpositions) are employed, the adjective itself remaining in the Positive. In order to express the idea of the Superlative, the pronominal adjective all is placed before the Ablative. By the Ablative the difference or distance, which exists between the objects compared, is pointed out.

مِٺهَائِيَان مِٺهو گهَڻو ڪَڙو نَاهِ ڪَلَامُ

Much sweeter than sweetness, (and) not bitter is the word. Sh. Kal. III, 10.

سَوَ سِسِنِيَّان اَگِرو سَنْدو دوسَان دَمُ

More valuable than a hundred heads is the breath of the friend (Plur.). Sh. Kal. II, 30.

سَاهَ رَڳنِئُون اوڊِڙو وَاحِدَ جو وِصَالُ

Nearer than the breath and the veins is the union of the one (God). Maj. 5.

پِيَارِي پِرِيهِن کهون ڪَرِي جَا تو مَنِجِي جوءِ

The wife, whom thou hast respected, having loved her more than thy Lord (Plur.). Mēnghō 8.

جي بھانئين تہ پرنئَ مِڙان تہ ڏوھَنئُون گُنُ بھانئِ

If thou likest to meet (thy) friend, then esteem virtue more than vices. Sh. Jam. Kal. VIII, 22.

جيکوکو ھِنَنِ حُکُمَنِ مؤن ھِکِڙِي سَبھَ کھان نَنْڍھِي کھي بھَنجي ۽ ماڻھُنِ کھي اِئين سيکھارِي سو آسْمانَ جي پاتِشاھِيَ مِين سَبھَ کھان نَنْڍھو چئِبو

Whosoever break one of these least commandments and teach the people thus, he will be called the least in the kingdom of heaven. Matth. V, 19.

Chapter X.

Numeral adjectives.

§. 22.

The Sindhī possesses a great variety of numeral adjectives.

I. The CARDINAL NUMBERS are:

١ ھِڪُ hiku; ھيڪُ hēku; ايڪُ ēku; ھِڪِڙو hikirō; ھيڪِڙو hēkirō, one.

٢ ٻہ ba, two.

٣ ٽرِي ṭrē, three.

۴ چارِ čāre, four.

٥ پَنْجَ panja, five.

٦ ڇھَ čha, or: ڇھَھَ čhaha, six.

٧ سَتَ sata, seven.

٨ اَٺھَ aṭha, eight.

٩ نَنْوَن nāvā, nine.

١٠ ڏَهَہ ḍaha, ten.

١١ يارَهَن yārahā̃; اِڪارَهَن ikārahā̃; ڪارَهَن kārahā̃, eleven.

١٢ ٻارَهَن b̄ārahā̃, twelve.

١٣ تيرَهَن tērahā̃, thirteen.

١٤ چوڏَهَن čōḍahā̃, fourteen.

١٥ پَنْدرَهَن pandrahā̃; پَنْڌران pandhrā̃, fifteen.

١٦ سورَهَن sōrahā̃, sixteen.

١٧ سَترَهَن satrahā̃, seventeen.

١٨ اَڙَهَن aṛahā̃, eighteen.

١٩ اُڻيهَہ uṇīha, اُڻويهَہ uṇivīha, nineteen.

٢٠ وِيهَہ vīha, twenty.

Annotation. The Sindhī numerals are all derived from the Sanskrit by the medium of the Prākrit. — Sansk. एक, one, Prāk. एक्क; in Sindhī a euphonic h has been preposed, as: hiku (= hikku). When commencing to count the Hindūs use to say instead of hiku: بَرْڪهُہ barkhu, and the Musalmāns: بَرْڪهَت barkhata, invoking thereby a blessing. — Sansk. द्वि, two, Prāk. दो; in Sindhī the crude form dva has been assimilated to vva and thence to b̄a (= bba). Besides ٻَ b̄a we meet also occasionally the form ڏُون ḍū̃, which has sprung from the Prākrit दोण्णि. — Sansk. त्रि, three, Sindhī ٽري ṭrē, whereas the Prāk. form तिण्णि has given rise to the Hindūstānī تِين. Sansk. चतुर्, four, Prāk. चत्तारि; in Sindhī the conjunct tt has again been elided = čāre. — Sansk. पञ्चन्, Prāk. पञ्च; in Sindhī (and Panǰābī) the tenuis č has been changed into the media ǰ (but in Hindūstānī and Marāṭhī again pānč). — Sansk. षष्, six; Prāk. छ, as in Sindhī. — Sansk. सप्तन्, seven, Prāk. सत्त; Sindhī: sata (= satta); Panǰābī: satt; but in Hindūstānī and Marāṭhī: sāt, the conjunct tt being dissolved by lengthening the preceding vowel. — Sansk. अष्टन्, Prāk. अट्ठ; Sindhī:

aṭha (= aṭṭha); Panjābī: aṭṭh; but Hindūst. and Marāṭhī: āṭh. Sansk. नवन्, nine, Prāk. णव; Sindhī: nāvā̃; Panjābī: nō̃; Hindūst.: nau; Marāṭhī: nava. — Sansk. दशन्, ten, Prāk. दस; Sindhī: ḏaha; Marāṭhī: dahā; Hindūstānī and Panjābī: das.

In Sanskrit the first nine numbers are prefixed to दशन्, ten, to form the following nine numerals; but in Prākrit and consequently in Sindhī (as well as in the cognate dialects) they undergo already so great changes, that the way, in which they have been compounded, is at the first sight scarcely recognisable. The Prākrit form दस is in these compounds first changed to दह and thence to रह, as: Prākrit एआरह = Sansk. एकादशन् eleven; Sindhī: yārahā̃, with elision of k, or without elision of k: ikārahā̃ or kārahā̃ (initial 'i' being dropped). — Prāk. बारह = Sansk. द्वादशन्, twelve; Sindhī: bārahā̃. — Prākrit तेरह = Sansk. त्रयोदशन् thirteen; Sindhī: tērahā̃. — Prākrit चउद्दह = Sansk. चतुर्दशन्, fourteen; Sindhī: čōḏahā̃. An exception forms the Sindhī: pandrahā̃ or pandhrā̃, fifteen, the Prākrit form of which is पण्णरह = Sansk. पञ्चदशन्, the conjunct nč, which in Prākrit has been assimilated to the cerebral ṇṇ, having been changed in Sindhī to nd before the liquida r. Prākrit सोलह(?) = Sansk. षोडशन् (Var. II, 23?), sixteen; Sindhī: sōrahā̃; Hindūstānī: sōlah. Prākrit सत्तरह(?) = Sansk. सप्तदशन्, seventeen; Sindhī: satrahā̃; Hindūstānī: satrah. — Prākrit अट्ठरह = Sansk. अष्टादशन्, eighteen; Sindhī: aṛahā̃, the Prākrit cerebral conjunct ṭṭh being changed in Sindhī to ṛ (see Introd. §. 7, 2) and assimilating the following dental r, by throwing out the long ā; Panjābī: aṭhārā̃; Hindūstānī: aṭhārah; Marāṭhī (with elision of medial ā): aṭharā. — Sansk. ऊनविंशति (Prākrit form unknown), one less than twenty (Latin: un-de-viginti); Sindhī: uṇīha or uṇivīha; the Sanskrit विंशति twenty, becomes in Prākrit वीसई; thence Sindhī: vīha; in compound numerals the v is generally elided, when preceded by a consonant, as: uṇīha or uṇivīha; Panjābī: unnī; Hindūstānī: unīs; Marāṭhī: ēkuṇīs.

٢١ ایڪيھہ ēkīha, twenty one.

٢٢ ٻاويھہ ƀāvīha, twenty two.

۲۳ ٽريويھ ṭrēvīha, twenty three.

۲۴ چوويھ čōvīha, twenty four.

۲۵ پَنْجويھ panjvīha, twenty five, or: پَنْجيھ panjīha.

۲۶ ڇهَويھ čhavīha, twenty six.

۲۷ سَتَاويھ satāvīha, twenty seven.

۲۸ اَٺهَاويھ aṭhāvīha, twenty eight.

۲۹ اُنَٽريھ unaṭrīha, twenty nine.

۳۰ ٽريھ ṭrīha, thirty.

Some of the units are lengthened in these compounds, as: ٻا bā, سَتا satā, اَٺها aṭhā, but apparently not after a fixed rule. — چارِ čāre, four, is, when compounded with another numeral, contracted to čō, after a different process of assimilation, चतुर् being first dissolved into ča-ur, and thence into čō, by assimilating the semi-vowel r with the following v. The same is the case in Panjābī, Hindūstānī and Marāṭhī.

ٽريھ ṭrīha, thirty, is derived from the Prākrit तीसआ, Sansk. त्रिंशत्, the Sanskrit termination शत् being changed in Prākrit to सद् and thence to सआ or सा, and consequently in Sindhī to ha. — چاليھ čālīha, fourty, Sansk. चत्वारिंशत्, the conjunct tt in the Prākrit form (very likely चत्तारिसा?) being elided in Sindhī and r changed to l, in Panjābī and Marāṭhī even to ḷ, as: čāḷī, čāḷīs; Hindūstānī: čālīs. The remaining tens follow the common rules of assimilation, as: Sindhī پَنجاھ panjāha, fifty, Sansk. पञ्चाशत्, Prāk. पणासा, the Sindhī keeping closer to the Sanskrit in this word, than the Prākrit; Panjābī likewise: panjāh; Hindūstānī: pačās, but Marāṭhī: pannās. — سَٺهِ saṭhe, sixty, Sansk.

षष्टि. — سَتَرِ satare, seventy, makes an exception, final t (Sansk. सप्तति) having been changed to r; the same is the case in Panjābī (sattar), Hindūstānī (sattar) and in Marāṭhī (sattar). — أسِي asī, eighty, Sansk. अशीति; Panjābī and Hindūstānī assī, but Marāṭhī aisī. — نَوي navē, ninety (in Lāṛ also نوء nōe), Sansk. नवति; Panjābī likewise: navvē; Hindūstānī navē, but Marāṭhī navvad.

٣١ ايكَترِيهَ ēkaṭrīha, thirty one.
٣٢ ٻَترِيهَ ɓaṭrīha, thirty two.
٣٣ ٽريترِيهَ ṭrēṭrīha, thirty three.
٣٤ چوترِيهَ čōṭrīha, thirty four.
٣٥ پَنْجَترِيهَ panjaṭrīha, thirty five.
٣٦ ڇهَترِيهَ čhaṭrīha, thirty six.
٣٧ سَتَترِيهَ sataṭrīha, thirty seven.
٣٨ اَٺهَترِيهَ aṭhaṭrīha, thirty eight.
٣٩ اُڻيتاليهَ uṇētālīha, thirty nine.
٤٠ چَاليهَ čālīha, fourty.

When چَاليهَ is preceded by the units (amongst which must also be numbered uṇ, one less), it is changed to تَاليهَ tālīha; but in this case the units require the conjunctive vowel ē, to facilitate the pronunciation. This change of č to t is not yet to be found in the older Prākrit, but seems to belong to a later period of the language. Lassen only mentions (§. 33, 4), that t is occasionally changed to ṭ and č, thence we may conclude, that vice versa č also was liable to be changed to t. The same is the case in the Panjābī (iktāḷī) and Hindūstānī (iktālīs), but not in Marāṭhī (ēkēčālis).

۴۱ اِيكيتَالِيهَ ēkētālīha, forty one.

۴۲ بَائِيتَالِيهَ bāētālīha, forty two.

۴۳ ٽريتَالِيهَ ṭrētālīha, forty three.

۴۴ چوئِيتَالِيهَ čōētālīha, forty four.

۴۵ پَنْجِيتَالِيهَ panjētālīha, forty five.

۴۶ ڇهَائِيتَالِيهَ čhāētālīha, forty six.

۴۷ سَتِيتَالِيهَ satētālīha, forty seven.

۴۸ اَٺهيتَالِيهَ aṭhētālīha, forty eight.

۴۹ اُڻِوَنْجَاهَ uṇivanjāha, forty nine.

۵۰ پَنْجَاهَ panjāha, fifty.

پَنْجَاهَ panjāha (pronounced also: پَنْجَاهُ panjāhu), when preceded by the units, is, for euphony's sake, changed to وَنْجَاهَ vanjāha the tenuis p being softened to the media b, and thence to v. The same change takes place in the kindred idioms.

۵۱ اِيكوَنْجَاهَ ēkvanjāha, fifty one.

۵۲ بَاوَنْجَاهَ bāvanjāha, fifty two.

۵۳ ٽريوَنْجَاهَ trēvanjāha, fifty four.

۵۴ چووَنْجَاهَ čōvanjāha, fifty three.

۵۵ پَنْجوَنْجَاهَ panjvanjāha, fifty five.

۵۶ ڇهَاوَنْجَاهَ čhavanjāha, fifty six.

۵۷ سَتْوَنْجَاهَ satvanjāha, fifty seven.

۵۸ اَٺهوَنْجَاهَ aṭhvanjāha, fifty eight.

۵۹ اُڻهَٺهِ uṇahaṭhe, fifty nine.

۶۰ سَٺهِ saṭhe, sixty.

سَٺهِ saṭhe and سَتَرِ satare, when preceded by the

units, are changed, for euphony's sake, to haṭhe and hatare, initial (and now medial) s being softened to h. The same is the case in Panǰābī, but in Hindūstānī and Marāṭhī the s of sāṭh is retained, whereas that of sattar is softened to h.

۶۱ ايڪَهَٺهِ ēkahaṭhe, sixty one.
۶۲ ٻَاهَٺهِ ɓāhaṭhe, sixty two.
۶۳ ٽِريهَٺهِ ṭrēhaṭhe, sixty three.
۶۴ چوَهَٺهِ čōhaṭhe, sixty four.
۲۵ پَنْجَهَٺهِ panǰahaṭhe, sixty five.
۶۶ ڇَهَاهَٺهِ čhāhaṭhe, sixty six.
۶۷ سَتَهَٺهِ satahaṭhe, sixty seven.
۶۸ اَٺَهَٺهِ aṭhahaṭhe, sixty eight.

۶۹ اُڻَهَتَرِ uṇahatare, sixty nine.
۷۰ سَتَرِ satare, seventy.

۷۱ ايڪَهَتَرِ ēkahatare, seventy one.
۷۲ ٻَاهَتَرِ ɓāhatare, seventy two.
۷۳ ٽِريهَتَرِ ṭrēhatare, seventy three.
۷۴ چوَهَتَرِ čōhatare, seventy four.
۷۵ پَنْجَهَتَرِ panǰahatare, seventy five.
۷۶ ڇَهَاهَتَرِ čhāhatare, seventy six.
۷۷ سَتَهَتَرِ satahatare, seventy seven.
۷۸ اَٺَهَتَرِ aṭhahatare, seventy eight.
۷۹ اُڻَاسِي uṇāsī, seventy nine.
۸۰ اَسِي asī, eighty.

The units preceding اَسِي asī and نَوي navē, are joined to them by the conjunctive vowel ā; the same is the case in the cognate dialects.

٨١ ايکاسِي ēkāsī, eighty one.
٨٢ ٻِئاسِي b̄iāsī, eighty two.
٨٣ ٽرِئاسِي ṭriāsī, eighty three.
٧۴ چوراسِي čōrāsī, eighty four.
٨٥ پنجاسِي panǰāsī, eighty five.
٨٦ ڇهَاسِي čhahāsī, eighty six.
٨٧ سَتَاسِي satāsī, eighty seven.
٨٨ اَٺهاسِي aṭhāsī, eighty eight.

٨٩ اُڻانوِي uṇānavē, eighty nine.
٩٠ نَوِي navē, ninety.

٩١ ايکانَوِي ēkānavē, ninety one.
٩٢ ٻِئانَوِي b̄iānavē, ninety two.
٩٣ ٽرِئانَوِي ṭriānavē, ninety three.
٩۴ چورانَوِي čōrānavē, ninety four.
٩٥ پنْجانَوِي panǰānavē, ninety five.
٩٦ ڇهَانَوِي čhahānavē, ninety six.
٩٧ سَتانَوِي satānavē, ninety seven.
٩٨ اَٺهانَوِي aṭhānavē, ninety eight.

٩٩ { نَوانَوِي navānavē, نَدهَانَوِي nadhānavē*), وَدهَانَوِي vadhānavē, } ninety nine.

١٠٠ سَوُ sau, hundred.

---

*) We cannot offer a satisfactory explanation of these two curious forms. The corresponding Hindust. numeral is: ninānavē, the Panǰābī naṛinavē. We can understand, how the Panǰābī naṛ (nan = naṇ = naṛ) could be changed in Sindhī to naḍ or naḍh; but we cannot well perceive, that ḍ or ḍh should have been exchanged for a dental d or

Annotation. سَو sau is derived from the Sansk. शत, Prāk. सअ; Panjābī sau or sai; Hindūstānī likewise sau or sai; Marāṭhī (in compounds) šẽ; Gujarātī sō.

The numbers above one hundred are commonly formed as in English by placing the lesser number after hundred, as:

١٠١ هِکُ سَوُّ هِکُ hiku sau hiku, one hundred (and) one.

١٠٢ هکُ سَوُّ ٻَہ hiku sau ḇa, „ „ „ two.

But there are two other ways of making up these numbers; the one is to place before sau the lesser number in an adjective form, as اِيکو سَو ēkō sau, literally: one hundred having or possessing one; or to put after the numeral adjective the noun utar (originally an adjective) which is contracted with the termination of the preceding numeral into ōtar, as: اِيکوتَرْسَو ēkōtarsau, one above one hundred. This utar (Sansk. उत्तर, adj., above) is used in a similar way in Marāṭhī.

١٠١ اِيکو سَو ēkō sau, or: اِيکوتَرْسَو ēkōtarsau,
one hundred (and) one.

١٠٢ ٻِڙو سَو ḇiṛō sau, or: ٻِروتَرْسَو ḇirōtarsau,
one hundred (and) two.

١٠٣ ٽِڙو سَو ṭriṛō sau, or: ٽِروتَرْسَو ṭrirōtarsau,
one hundred (and) three.

١٠٤ چوڙو سَو čōṛō sau, or: چوروتَرْسَو čōrōtarsau,
one hundred (and) four.

١٠٥ پَنْجو سَو panjō sau, or: پَنْجوتَرْسَو panjōtarsau,
one hundred (and) five.

---

dh, which would be a surprising phenomenon in a modern Prākrit idiom. In regard to vadhānavē it would be necessary to assume a change of n to v, of which we could not adduce another instance.

١٠٦ چهَهو سَوٗ čhahō sau, or: چهَهوتَرْسَوٗ čhahōtarsau, one hundred (and) six.

١٠٧ سَتيو سَوٗ satyō sau, or: سَتوتَرْسَوٗ satōtarsau, one hundred (and) seven.

١٠٨ اَٹهيو سَوٗ aṭhyō sau, or: اَٹهوتَرْسَوٗ aṭhotarsau, one hundred (and) eight.

١٠٩ نَڑو سَوٗ naṛō sau, or: نَڑوتَرْسَوٗ naṛōtarsau, one hundred (and) nine.

١١٠ ڎهو سَوٗ ḍahō sau, or: ڎهوتَرْسَوٗ ḍahōtarsau, one hundred (and) ten.

١١١ يَارَهو سَوٗ yārahō sau, or: يَارَهوتَرْسَوٗ yārahōtarsau, one hundred (and) eleven.

١١٢ ٻَارَهو سَوٗ ɓārahō sau, or: ٻَارَهوتَرْسَوٗ ɓārahōtarsau, one hundred (and) twelve.

١١٣ تيرَهو سَوٗ tērahō sau, or: تيرَهوتَرْسَوٗ tērahōtarsau, one hundred (and) thirteen.

١١٤ چوڎَهو سَوٗ čōḍahō sau, or: چوڎَهوتَرْسَوٗ čōḍahōtarsau, one hundred (and) fourteen.

١١٥ پَنْدرَهو سَوٗ pandrahō sau, or: پَنْدهروتَرْسَوٗ pandhrō-tarsau, one hundred (and) fifteen.

١١٦ سورَهو سَوٗ sōrahō sau, or: سورهوتَرْسَوٗ sōrhōtarsau, one hundred (and) sixteen.

١١٧ سَتْرَهو سَوٗ satrahō sau, or: سَتْرَهوتَرْسَوٗ satrahōtarsau, one hundred (and) seventeen.

١١٨ اَڑَهو سَوٗ aṛahō sau, or: اَڑَهوتَرْسَوٗ aṛahōtarsau, one hundred (and) eighteen.

١١٩ اُڻيهو سَوٗ uṇīhō sau, or: اُڻيهوتَرْسَوٗ uṇīhōtarsau, one hundred (and) nineteen.

١٢٠ وِيهو سَوٗ vīhō sau, or: وِيهوتَرْسَوٗ vīhōtarsau, one hundred (and) twenty.

١٢١ اِیکِیهوٗ سَوٗ ēkīhō sau, or: اِیکِیهوٗتَرْسَوٗ ēkīhōtarsau, one hundred (and) twenty one.

١٢٢ بَاوِیهوٗ سَوٗ bāvīhō sau, or: بَاوِیهوٗتَرْسَوٗ bāvīhōtarsau, one hundred (and) twenty two.

etc. etc.

١٣٠ ٹرِیهوٗ سَوٗ ṭrīhō sau, or: ٹرِیهوٗتَرْسَوٗ ṭrīhōtarsau, one hundred (and) thirty.

١٤٠ چَالِیهوٗ سَوٗ čālīhō sau, or: چَالِیهوٗتَرْسَوٗ čālīhōtarsau, one hundred (and) forty.

١٤١ اِیکیتَالِیهوٗ سَوٗ ēkētālīhō sau, or: اِیکیتَالِیهوٗتَرْسَوٗ ēkētā-līhōtarsau, one hundred (and) forty one.

etc. etc.

١٥٠ پَنْجَاهوٗ سَوٗ panǰāhō sau, or: پَنْجَاهوٗتَرْسَوٗ panǰāhōtarsau, one hundred (and) fifty.

١٦٠ سَٹهیوٗ سَوٗ saṭhyō sau, or: سَٹهیوٗتَرْسَوٗ saṭhyōtarsau, one hundred (and) sixty.

١٧٠ سَتَرِیوٗ سَوٗ sataryō sau, or: سَتَرِیوٗتَرْسَوٗ sataryōtarsau, one hundred (and) seventy.

١٨٠ اَسِیوٗ سَوٗ asyō sau, or: اَسِیوٗتَرْسَوٗ asyōtarsau, one hundred (and) eighty.

١٩٠ { نَوِیوٗ سَوٗ naviyō sau, or: نَوِیوٗتَرْسَوٗ naviyōtarsau,
نوٗیوٗ سَوٗ nōyō sau, or: نوٗیوٗتَرْسَوٗ nōyōtarsau, } one hundred (and) ninety.

When the numeral adjectives of the first series precede the Plural of سَوٗ sau, they must agree with their substantive in number, as:

٢٠١ (سَا or) اِیکَا بَہ سَوَ ēkā ba sava (or sā), literally: two hundreds having or possessing one.

٢٠٢ بِڑَا بَہ سَوَ biṛā ba sava, two hundred and two.

etc. etc. etc.

These numerals are not used in the Formative, as they are only employed in counting. The numerals of the second series remain unaltered, according to their original signification.

The hundreds are regularly made up by the Plural of سَوُ, as:

٢٠٠ (سَا or) ٻہ سَوَ ƀa sava (or sā) two hundred.

٣٠٠ ٽري سَوَ ṭrē sava, three hundred.

٤٠٠ چارِ سَوَ čāre sava, four hundred.

٥٠٠ پَنْجَ سَوَ panǰa sava, five hundred.

٦٠٠ چھہ سَوَ čha sava, six hundred.

٧٠٠ سَتَ سَوَ sata sava, seven hundred.

٨٠٠ اَٺهہ سَوَ aṭha sava, eight hundred.

٩٠٠ نَنْوَن سَوَ nāvā̃ sava, nine hundred.

١٠٠٠ { سَهَسُ sahásu (= sahassu), هَزارُ hazāru, } one thousand.

٢٠٠٠ { ٻہ سَهَسَ ƀa sahása, ٻہ هَزارَ ƀa hazāra, } two thousand.

١٠٠٠٠٠ لَکهہ lakhu, one hundred thousand.

٢٠٠٠٠٠ ٻہ لَکهہ ƀa lakha, two hundred thousand.

١٠٠٠٠٠٠ ڏَهہ لَکهہ ḍaha lakha, one million.

١٠٠٠٠٠٠٠ { کِروڙِ kirōṛe, کوڙُ kōṛu, } ten millions (one hundred lakhs).

٢٠٠٠٠٠٠٠ { ٻہ کِروڙِ ƀa kirōṛe, ٻہ کوڙَ ƀa kōṛa, } twenty millions.

١٠٠٠٠٠٠٠٠٠ اَرْبُ arbu, one thousand millions (one hundred karōṛs).

١٠٠٠٠٠٠٠٠٠٠٠ کهَرْبُ kharbu, one hundred thousand millions (one hundred arbs).

١٠٠٠٠٠٠٠٠٠٠٠٠٠٠ نِيلُ nīlu, ten billions (one hundred kharbs).

١٠٠٠٠٠٠٠٠٠٠٠٠٠٠٠ پَدَمُ padamu, one thousand billions (one hundred nīls).

Annotation. سَهَسُ sahásu is derived from the Sansk. सहस, Prāk. सहस्स. It is a regular substantive and inflected accordingly. هَزَارُ hazāru (s. m.) is of Persian origin. — لَکهُ lakhu, Sansk. लक्ष; Hindūst. lak (and lākh); Marāthī lākh; it is likewise treated as a substantive masc. — کِروڙ kirōṛe (Sansk. कोटि) is not inflected, whereas کوڙُ kōru is treated as a regular substantive. The following numerals, which belong more to the realm of fancy, are all substantives, as: اَرْبُ, Sansk. अर्बुद; کهَرْبُ, Sansk. खर्ब; نِيلُ, Sansk. ? پَدَمُ, Sansk. पद्म.

§. 23.

Inflexion of the cardinal numbers.

هِکُ hiku or هِکِڙو hikiṛō are regular adjectives and inflected according to their respective terminations (هِکُ m.; هِکَ fem. etc.); the other numerals have no change of gender, but are inflected in the Formative Plural, as:

بَ	ƀa, two;	Format. Plural:		بِنِ	ƀine.
ٽري	ṭrē, three;	„	„	ٽرِنِ	ṭrine.
چارِ	čāre, four;	„	„	چئِنِ	čaine.
پَنْجَ	panja, five;	„	„	پَنْجَنِ	panjane.
ڇهَ	čha, six;	„	„	ڇهَنِ	čhahane.
سَتَ	saha, seven;	„	„	سَتَنِ	satane.
اَٺهَ	aṭha, eight;	„	„	اَٺهَنِ	aṭhane.
نَوَن	nāvā, nine;	„	„	نَوَنِ	nāvane.
ڏهَ	ḍaha, ten;	„	„	ڏهَنِ	ḍahane.

The following numerals, from eleven-eighten, throw final Anusvāra off in the Formative Plural and drop the short a, preceding h, as;

يَارَهَنْ yārahā̃, eleven; Format. Plur. يَارْهَنِ yārhane.
بَارَهَنْ bārahā̃, twelve; „ „ بَارْهَنِ bārhane.
تيرَهَنْ tērahā̃, thirteen; „ „ تيرْهَنِ tērhane.
چوڏهَنْ čōḏaha, fourteen; „ „ چوڏهَنِ čōḏhane.
پَنْدرَهَنْ pandraha, پَنْدهرَان pandhrā̃, } fifteen; „ „ پَنْدهرَنِ pandhrane.
وِيهَ vīha, twenty; „ „ وِيهَنِ vīhane.

Those numerals, which end in ĕ (ĭ) and ē, are not capable of inflexion, as: سَٺهِ saṭhe, sixty; سَتَرِ satare, seventy; نَوي navē or نوء nōe, ninety; but اَسِي asī, eighty, makes the Format. Sing. اَسِيَ asia.

سَوُ sa-u, hundred; is inflected, as follows:

	SING.	PLUR.
Nom.	سَوُ sau;	سَوَ sava, or contracted سَا sā.
Format.	سَوَ sava;	سَوَنِ savane, سَانِ sāne, سَوين savẽ, سَئين saẽ.

The cardinal numbers, chiefly the decimal ones, are also used as collective numbers, and in this case they are inflected according to their respective terminations, e. g. ٽري ڏهون ṭrē ḍahū̃, three tens, Formative ٽرِنِ ڏهُنِ ṭrine ḍahune; چَارِ سَٺهون čāre sāṭheū̃, four sixties; نَوي navē forms the Plural نَوِيئُون navēū̃, Format. نَوِيئُنِ navēune. When used in a collective sense these numerals are mostly put in the Formative Plural ending in ẽ, as: وِيهين vīhẽ, in scores; سَوين savẽ, in hundreds, سَهَسِين sahásẽ, in thousands.

When a noun in the Formative Plural takes the termination ne or ẽ, the preceding numeral, like all other adjectives, must take the same too, or: ڏهَنِ ويرِنِ کهي to ten enemies, or: ڏهين ويرِئين کهي. ٻَ and ٽري do not admit of a Formative in ẽ, but make it ĩ, as: ٻين ḇĩ, ٽرين ṭrĩ; of چارِ there is a Formative as well in ĩ as in ẽ; چَئِين čaĩ or: چئين čaẽ; but the Formatives ḇĩ, ṭrĩ, čaĩ are also used with Formatives of nouns ending in ne.

The emphatic ī (hī) may also be affixed to the cardinal numbers to express completeness or intensity, as: ٻَئِي ḇaī or: ٻيئِي ḇēī, all two = both, Formative Plural: ٻِنْهِي ḇinhī or: ٻِنْهِين ḇinhĩ; or: ٻِنْهِنِ ḇinhine, ٻِنْهِنِي ḇinhinī. ٽريئِي ṭrēī, all three, Formative Plural: ٽِرِنْهِي ṭrinhī or: ٽِرِنْهِين ṭrinhĩ; or: ٽِرِنْهِنِ ṭrinhine, ٽِرِنْهِنِي ṭrinhinī. چارَئِي čāraī or: چاريئِي čārēī, all four, Formative Plural: چَئِنِي čainī. اَٺهَئِي aṭhaī, all eight, Formative Plural: اَٺهَنِي aṭhanī, etc.

The cardinal numbers, from two upwards generally require their substantive in the Plural; but they may also be constructed with the Singular, after the manner of the Persian. Sau, hazāru, sahásu, lakhu etc., being properly substantives, are either constructed with the Genitive Plural of the following substantive, or they have the same coordinated in the Plural. The numerals preceding a substantive may either be inflected according to the termination of the substantive or they may remain uninflected; when two or more numerals precede a substantive, the last only is inflected.

وِسَارِجِ مَ وِينَ جوُبهَنَ بَ ٽري ڏِينهَڙَا

Do not forget the words; in youth there are two, three short days. Sh. Jam. Kal. V, Epil.

بِين ٽرِين وَرِهَنِ جو خَرْچُ کهَڻِي وَڃَاءِ

Having taken provisions of two, three years, depart. Amulu Māṇiku, Stack's Gram. p. 147.

اَٺهَئِي پَهَر اَنِمرِي گهَڻو رُئِي سِين رَنْجَ

Being unwell she weeps much all the eight watches with grief. Maj. 562.

ڏَهَنِ وِيرِنِ وِچَ مِين آيو آهِي اِنْسَانُ

اِنْهِي ڏَهَنِي وِيرِنِ وِچَ مَان جو کهَٽِي جَنْگِ جُوَانُ

Man has come into the midst of ten enemies —
That young man, who wins the battle out of the midst of all these ten enemies etc. Sh. Barvō Sindhī, Čhōṭ. 18.

جَنْهِن جِي حُکُمَ مِين سَٺهِ اَسِي ٻَانْهِي آهِي تِنِ سَٺهِ

اَسِيئِي ٻَانْهِيَ کهِي گُلِيلِيُون هَٿهَنِ مِين آنهِينِ

Under whose command are sixty, eighty bond-maids; those sixty, eighty bond-maids have pellet-bows in their hands. Amulu Māṇiku, p. 141.

اُنْهِي مَحَلَّ سُفِيدَ دِيوَ وَٽِ سَوُ پَرِيُون بِہ نَچَنْدِيُون هُونْدِيُون

تَہ هُو چَونْدو جِي تُون هِنِ سَوُ پَرْيِنِ کهِي وِهَارِي مُون کهِي

نَچِيو تهِي ڏِيکهَارِين

In that very palace one hundred Fairies also will dance near the Dēv Sufēdu. Then he will say: if thou causest these hundred Fairies to sit down and showest me a dancing etc. Amulu Māṇiku, p. 144.

جِٹِّري تَنْهِن جُوانَ جي نَنْوَن سَا نَنْوَن گهَاءَ

In the body of that young man there are nine hundred and nine wounds. Sh. Kēḍ. VI, 7.

تَنْهِن سَان ڏَهَه سَا ڏَاتَارَ جَا چَڙهِيَا ڏُونْڊِين ٽِکهِين

With him ten hundred liberal persons mounted on swift boats. Ajāib, v. 253.

سَوين آهِنِ سَٿِنْسَارَ مِين ٻِيَا ڀِي ڏَاتَا ڏَلَ

Hundreds and also other multitudes of generous persons are in the world. Sh. Sōr. II, 3.

مَرْضَ تَان مُون کهِي تهِيَّا حَکِيمَنِ هَزَارَ

Thousands of physicians I have had for (my) disease. Sh. Ābirī I, Epil.

جي هُوَّنِي هوتَ هَزَارَ تَه ڀِه پَارِٽِ کو مَه پُنْهُنءَ سَان

If thou hast thousands of sweathearts, even then compare none with Punhū̃. Sh. Maꜫδ. V, 2.

اِيکَ قَصَرِ دَرَ لَکهَ سَهَسِين کَنِسِ ڪِنِکهِيُون

In one palace there are lakhs of doors, windows in thousands (belong) to it. Sh. Kal. I, 23.

جيڏَان قَاتِلَ کوڙَ اَکهِڙُون اوڏَانهِين کهَڻِين

Where there are ten millions of killers, in that direction lift up thy eyes. Sh. Jam. Kal. IV, 4.

پَلَنْگَ پَتهَرَنِيُون پَالکِيُون نَنْوَنْ لَکهَ نَاڻي نِيلَ

Of bedsteads, beddings, pālkis nine lakhs, nīls of hard cash. Sh. Sōr. II, 5.

§. 24.

II. ORDINAL NUMBERS.

پَهَريوں	paharyō̃,	the first.
پِهِريوں	peheryō̃,	
پِهِروں	peherō̃,	
ٻِئو	b̄iō,	the second.
ٻِيجو	b̄ījō,	
ٽِرِئو	ṭriō,	the third.
ٽِرِيجو	trījō,	
چوٿهوں	čōthō̃,	the fourth.
پَنْجوں	panǰō̃,	the fifth.
ڇَهوں	čhahō̃,	the sixth.
سَتوں	satō̃,	the seventh.
اَٺهوں	aṭhō̃,	the eighth.
نَائِئوں	nā̃ō̃,	the ninth.
نَووں	navō̃,	
ڏهوں	ḍahō̃,	the tenth.
يَارْهوں	yārhō̃,	the eleventh.
ڪَارْهوں	kārhō̃,	
ٻَارْهوں	b̄ārhō̃,	the twelfth.
تيرْهوں	tērhō̃,	the thirteenth.
چوڏْهوں	čōḍhō̃,	the fourteenth.
پَنْدَرَهوں	pandrahō̃,	the fifteenth.
پَنْدْهروں	pandhrō̃,	
سورْهوں	sōrhō̃,	the sixteenth.
سَتَرَهوں	satrahō̃,	the seventeenth.

اَڙهوڻ arhō̃, the eighteenth.

اُوڻيهوڻ ūṇīhō̃, the nineteenth.

وِيهوڻ vīhō̃, the twentieth.

ايڪيهوڻ ēkīhō̃, the twenty first.

ٻاوِيهوڻ ƀavīhō̃, the twenty second.

etc. etc.

ٽريهوڻ ṭrīhō̃, the thirtieth.

چاليهوڻ čālīhō̃, the fortieth.

پنجاهوڻ panǰāhō̃; the fiftieth.

سَٺهيوڻ saṭhyō, the sixtieth.

سَترِيوڻ sataryō̃, the seventieth.

اَسيوڻ asyō̃, the eightieth.

نوِيوڻ naviyō̃, } the ninetieth.
نوِيئوڻ navēō̃, }

سوِيوڻ saviyō, }
سَوئوڻ sau-ō̃, } the hundredth.
سَيئوڻ sai-ō̃, }

Of compound numbers only the last takes the form of the ordinal and is inflected, as:

هِڪُ سَوُ پهرِيوڻ hiku sau peheryō̃, the one hundred and first.

ٻه سوِيوڻ ƀa saviyō̃, the two hundredth.

ٻه سا ٻِئو ƀa sā ƀiō, the two hundred and second.

هزاروڻ hazārō̃, } the thousandth.
سَهَسوڻ sahásō̃, }

Annotation. The ordinals are regularly derived from the Prākrit; پِھرْيوْن peheryō̃, the first, though, has not followed the traces of the Prākrit (= पढम), but taken its own course of assimilation; Sansk. प्रथम, thence: pahama; the m of pahama has been changed in a rather unusual way to l (r), pahala, pahara, thence the Sindhī: paharyō̃ or peheryō̃. Hindūst. and Panjābī: pahilā, Marāṭhī likewise: pahilā. ٻِئو b̄iō, the second, points back to the Prākrit वीअ (shortened from विदिअ), and the other form ٻِجو b̄ijō, corresponds to the Prāk. दुइज्ज. ٽِرِئو ṭriō, the third, coincides with the Prākrit तीअ, with this difference, that original r has been preserved in Sindhī. چوٿھوْن čōthō̃, the fourth, Prākrit चउट्ठ; the original dental (th) has been preserved in Sindhī. The following ordinals are all regularly derived from the cardinals, by adding the affix ō̃ corresponding to the Sansk. affix तम, which has in Sindhī been changed to ō̃ by the elison of t (compare: Introd. §. 9). In Hindūstānī and Panjābī tama has been similarly changed to vā̃, in Marāṭhī to vā; the Gujarātī has preserved the affix mō, and the Bangālī even the whole affix tam.

§. 25.

Inflexion of the ordinals.

The ordinals are regularly inflected as adjectives according to their respective terminations:

SINGULAR.

	Masculine.	*Feminine.*
Nom.	پِھرْيوْن peheryō̃.	پِھرِين peherī̃.
Format.	پِھرْين peherē̃.	پِھرِئَ peherīa.
Vocat.	پِھرْيَان peheryā̃.	پِھرِين peherī̃.

PLURAL.

Nom.	پِھرْيَان peheryā̃.	پِھرْيُون peheryū̃.
Format.	پِھرْيِين peheryē̃.	پِھرْيِين peheryē̃ (peheriẽ).

Format.	پِهرْيَان peheryā̃.	پِهرْيَان peheryā̃.
	پِهرْيَنِ peheryane.	پِهرِنِ peherine.
		پِهرْيُنِ peheryune.
Vocat.	پِهرْيَان peheryā̃.	پِهرْيُون peheryū̃.
	پِهرِيو peheryō.	
	پِهرْيَو peheryau.	

پِهريۆن وِيرِي پَانْهَن جو آهِ نَحسُ نِجَسُ نَادَانُ

His first own enemy is the unlucky, wretched, ignorant man. Sh. Barvō Sindhī, Čhōṭ. 18.

كُوپَا كِلِي كوڎِيَا سَاهُو سِلِيدَارَ ·

هِكِڙَا بهَائُرَ بِئَّا بهَاتِرِيَا ٽِريَا جَانِي يَارَ

In the fort of Kūfā are happy the heroes clad in armour,
The first are the brothers, the second the nephews, the third the beloved friends. Sh. Kēḍ. III, 2.

ايكويِهِنءَ مَاهِ عَاشِق كهي وِٿو وِسِرِي پَانُ

مَخفِي ٿهِٿو مَحْبُوبَ سِين بَاوِيهِنءَ مَاهِ جُهَانُ

On the twenty first (date) self was forgotten to (= by) the lover;
Consciousness became hidden with the beloved on the twenty second. Maj. 518, 519.

كَارِهِين ڎِينهَ كَرَمُ وَرِٿو وِيرَاگِنِ جو

On the eleventh day the kindness of the Bērāgīs returned. Sh. Rāmak. II, 11.

The date of the year is not expressed by the ordinals, but by the cardinals:

مَاهَہ مُبَارِکَ رَمَضَانَ جِي سَتَاوِيهِنءَ سَارِي
قَدَرِ رَاتِ قِصّو پُنو ڏِينھہ اَنگارِي
اِکَارهَنّ سَا چهَتريهَہ هِجْرَت هو سَنّ
عَارِفَنِ جِي عِشْقَ جو فَاضِل جوڙِئو فَنّ

On the twenty seventh of the blessed month of Ramazān, according to calculation,
In the night of power the story was completed, on a Tuesday.
It was the year of the Hijrat eleven hundred thirty six (= A. D. 1724, 8th June).
By Fāzil was composed the science of the love of the wise ones (i. e. Sūfīs). Maǰ. 829.

§. 26.

III. ARITHMETICAL FIGURES.

The arithmetical figures or names of the numbers are expressed by adjectives, which are formed by adding the adjective affix ō to the cardinal numbers; some few have also, in order to distinguish the arithmetical figures from the ordinals, the affix kō.

اِيکو ēkō, هِکو hikō, containing the number 'one'; the number or figure 'one'.

ٻِکو bikō, the number 'two'.
ٽرِکو ṭrikō, " " 'three'.
چَوْنکو čaũkō, " " 'four'.
پَنْجو panjō, " " 'five'.
ڇهَکو čhakō, " " 'six'.
سَتو satō, " " 'seven'.
اَٺهو aṭhō, " " 'eight'.

نَانئُون	nā̃ō̃,	the number	'nine'.
ڏَهو	ḍahō,	„ „	'ten'.
يَارْهو	yārhō,	„ „	'eleven'.
ٻَارْهو	ḇārhō,	„ „	'twelve'.
تيرهو	tērhō,	„ „	'thirteen'.
چوڏهو	čōḏhō,	„ „	'fourteen'.
پَنْدَرَهو	pandrahō,	„ „	'fifteen'.
سوْرهو	sōrhō,	„ „	'sixteen'.
سَتَرَهو	satrahō,	„ „	'seventeen'.
اَڙهو	aṛhō,	„ „	'eighteen'.
اُوڻيهو	ūṇīhō,	„ „	'nineteen'.
وِيهو	vīhō,	„ „	'twenty'.
ايڪِيهو	ēkīhō,	„ „	'twenty one'.
etc.	etc.		
ٽريهو	ṭrīhō,	„ „	'thirty'.
چَالِيهو	čālīhō,	„ „	'forty'.
پَنْجَاهو	panǰāhō,	„ „	'fifty'.
سَٺهيو	saṭhyō,	„ „	'sixty'.
سَتَرْيو	sataryō,	„ „	'seventy'.
اَسيو	asyō,	„ „	'eighty'.
نَوِيو	naviyō,	„ „	'ninety'.
سَوِيو	saviyō,	„ „	'hundred'.

They are regularly inflected as adjectives ending in ō; ٻَہ ھِڪا two units; ٽِرِڪي کهَان پوءِ چَوْنڪو تهو لَڳي after the number three comes the number four.

§. 27.

IV. COLLECTIVE NUMBERS.

We have noticed already (§. 22), that the cardinal numbers may also be employed as collective numbers; but the Sindhī possesses also a peculiar kind of numerals, which express an aggregate sum; these are:

ڏَهاڪو ḍahākō, the sum of ten; about ten.

وِهارو vihārō, } the sum of twenty; about twenty.
وِيهارو vīhārō,

ٽِرهارو ṭrihārō, } the sum of thirty; about thirty.
ٽِريهارو ṭrīhārō,

چاليهارو čālhyārō, the sum of forty; about forty.

پَنْجاهِي panǰāhī, } the sum of fifty; about fifty.
پَنْجاهو panǰāhō,

سَاٺِيڪو sāṭhīkō, the sum of sixty, about sixty.

They are properly adjectives, formed by the affixes kō (§. 10, 24) and ārō, as: ڏَهاڪو ḍahākō, making ten; وِهارو virāhō, containing twenty. They may be constructed either as substantives with the noun in the Genitive, or as numeral adjectives, e. g.: ڏَهاڪو ڇوڪرن جو ten boys, literally: a decade of boys, or: ڏَهاڪو ڇوڪرَ.

To express more distinctly the indefiniteness of such a number, the adverb کهَنُ khanu (literally: piece, portion, Sansk. खण्ड) is added to them as well as to the cardinal numbers; e. g. وِهارو کهَنُ vihārō khanu, about twenty.

پَنْجَ هَزارَ کهَنُ مُرْسَ هُئا

They were about five thousand men. Matth. 14, 21.

چَوْنْکُ čaũku, چَوْنکِڙِي čaũkiṛī, the sum of four, کوڙِي kōṛī, a score, are only used substantively, the latter generally in the Formative Plural کوڙين kōṛẽ, in scores, as:

سَهسين شُکِرَانَا کوڙين بهالَ کَرِيمَ جَا

In thousands are the thanksgivings, in scores the favours of the kind one (i. e. God). Sh. Surāg̃ I, Epil. 1.

سَيْکِڙو saikiṛō, a hundred, is only used when speaking of interest, expressing our "per cent", as: بَہ سَا رُوپِيَا پَنْجين رُوپَئين سَيکِڙي اُدهَارْيَمِ I borrowed two hundred rupees at five rupees by the hundred (i. e. at five per cent). The percentage may also be expressed by an adjective (a so-called Bahuvrīhi, cf. §. 12, II, 5), compounded of the respective amount and the adjective ōtirō, 'having above', as:

ايکوتِرو سَوُ one hundred having one above it, i. e. one per cent;

بِروتِرو سَوُ two per cent.

ٽِرِوتِرو سَوُ three per cent.

etc. etc.

Of the same kind are the compound adjectives, such as: چَوْآنو (سَوُ) čauāno (sau), one hundred having four Annas, i. e. 4 Annas per cent; ٽِرِپَانيو (سَوُ) ṭripāṇyō (sau), one hundred having three quarters of a rupee, i. e. at three quarters of a rupee per cent, etc. When مِتِي mitī (interest) is used, سَوُ is omitted, as: ڏيڍهوتِرِي مِتِي, interest of one and a half.

§. 28.

V. PROPORTIONAL NUMBERS.

The numerals denoting 'fold', are:

هيڪونو	hēkūṇō,	single.
هيڪوٽو	hēkūṭō,	
ٻينو	b̄īṇō,	twofold.
ٻِٽو	b̄iṭō,	
ٽرينو	ṭrīṇō, threefold.	
چَئُونو	čaūṇō,	fourfold.
چَئْونو	čauṇō,	
پَنْجُونو	panjūṇō, fivefold.	
ڇهَُونو	čhahūṇō, sixfold.	
سَتُونو	satūṇō, sevenfold.	
اَٺُونو	aṭhūṇō, eightfold.	
نَئُونو	naūṇō, ninefold.	
ڏَهُونو	ḍahūṇō, tenfold.	
يَارْهُونو	yārhūṇō, elevenfold.	
ٻَارْهُونو	b̄ārhūṇō, twelvefold.	
تيرْهُونو	tērhūṇō, thirteenfold.	
چوڏهُونو	čōḍhūṇō, fourteenfold.	
پَنْدرهُونو	pandhrūṇō, fifteenfold.	
سورْهُونو	sōrhūṇō, sixteenfold.	
سَترْهُونو	satrahūṇō, seventeenfold.	
اَڙهُونو	aṛhūṇō, eighteenfold.	
اُڻِيهُونو	ūṇīhūṇō, nineteenfold.	
وِيهُونو	vīhūṇō, twentyfold.	

ايڪيهونو ēkīhūṇō, twenty-onefold.

ٽريهونو ṭrīhuṇō, fortyfold.

چاليهونو čālīhūṇō, fortyfold.

پنجاهونو panǰāhūṇō, fiftyfold.

سٺهيونو sathyūṇō, sixtyfold.

سترڀونو sataryūṇō, seventyfold.

اسيونو asyūṇō, eightyfold.

نويئونو navēūṇō, ninetyfold.

سئونو saūṇō, hundredfold.

In the same way the affix ūṇō (cf. §. 10, 28) is added to the fractional numbers, as:

اڌهونو adhūṇō, one half-fold.

سوائونو savāūṇō, one (or a certain sum) and a quarter-fold.

ڏيڍهونو ḏēḍhūṇō, one and a half-fold.

اڍهائونو aḍhāūṇō, two and a half-fold.

جڏهين آندو تڏهين پان کهان ٻينو دوزخ جو ٻار تها ڪريوس

When he has been brought over by you, then you make him twofold more a child of hell, than yourselves. Matth. 23, 15.

ٻيا ٻج چنگي دهرتي تي پيا سي ڦهريا ڪي سئونا ڪي سٺهيونا ڪي ٽريهونا

Other seeds fill upon good land; these brought forth fruit, some hundredfold, some sixtyfold, some thirtyfold. Matth. 13, 8.

§. 29.

VI. REDUPLICATIVE NUMBERS.

The numeral adverbs, denoting reduplication, are.

هيكارَ hēkāra, هيكرَ hēkara,	once.
ٻِهارَ bihāra, ٻِهرَ bihara,	twice.
ٽِرِهارَ ṭrihāra, ٽِرِهرَ ṭrihara,	thrice.
چوهارَ čōhāra, چوهرَ čōhara,	four times.

The further reduplicatives are commonly made up by the cardinals with the nouns وَارو vārō, ٻهيرو or لِنگو (liṅō).

Annotation. The affix هَارَ, or shortened هَرَ, has taken its origin from the Sansk. वार, Hindūstānī: bārah, Panǰābī: vārī; in Sindhī v has been elided and euphonic h inserted.

§. 30.

VII. FRACTIONAL NUMBERS.

The fractional numbers are of two kinds; they are either substantives or adjectives;

a) substantives are:

چوٿهِ čōthe, چوٿهائِي čōthāī, چوٿهو čōthō,	a quarter.

پاءُ pāu, a quarter; Plur. پاوَ pāva or پا pā.

ترِهائِي ṭrihāī, a third.

اَدهُ adhu, a half.

سَوائِي savāī, one and a quarter; a quarter more (than the whole).

ساڍهُ sāḍhu, one half more (than the specified sum).

ڏيڍهه ḍēḍhe, one and a half.

b) adjectives are:

پَوڻو pauṇō, } one quarter less (than the whole).
مُنو munō, }

اَدهُ adhu, } half.
آدهو ādhō, }

سَوا savā, one quarter more (than the whole).

ساڍها sāḍhā, one half more (than the whole).

ڏيڍهُ ḍēḍhu, one and a half.

اَڍائِي aḍhāī, two and a half.

Annotation. چوٿهه, چوٿائِي, چوٿو is derived from the Sansk. चतुर्थांश, Hindūstānī cauth, cauthāī; in the same way ترِهائِي is derived from the Sansk. तृतीयांश, Hindūstānī tihāī. پاءُ corresponds to the Sansk. पाद, Hindūstānī pāō; the adjective پَوڻو has sprung from the Sansk. adj. पादोन, Hindūst. paunā, Marāṭhī pāūṇ; the origin of مُنو is doubtful. اَدهُ is substantive and adjective at the same time, Sansk. अर्द्ध, Hindūst. ādhā. سَوائِي and the adjective سَوا are derived from the Sansk. सपाद, having a quarter, Hindūst. and Marāṭhī: savā; ساڍهُ and the adjective ساڍها (Plur. m.) from the Sansk. adjective सार्द्ध, having a half, with a half, Hindūstānī (Instrum.)

sāṛhē. ڏيڏهِ and the adjective ڏيڏهُ are apparently derived from an unusual Sansk. compound त्रि + अर्द्ध, having three halves, Hindūst. dēṛh, Panjābī ḍeḍh, Marāṭhī ḍīḍ. اَڏهائِي has drawn its origin from the Sansk. अर्द्धतृय, Hindūst. aṛhāī, Panjābī ḍhāī, Marāṭhī aḍīts.

In reference to the use of these fractional numbers it is to be observed, that مُنو is generally used with units, and پَونو with two, three etc., as: مُنو رُوپَيو, a rupee wanting a quarter = three quarters of a rupee; پَونا بہ رُوپَيا two rupees wanting a quarter = one rupee and three quarters; پَونو سَو one hundred wanting a quarter = 75. سَوا one quarter more, as: سَوا سيرُ one sēr and a quarter; سَوا ٽري سيرَ three sērs and a quarter.

سَوا is not inflected in the Singular, nor in the Nominative Plural, but it has a Formative Plural masc., viz.: سَوائِنِ savāine, سَوايَنِ savāyane or: سَوائين savāẽ, and fem. سَوائِنِ savāine or: سَوايُنِ savāyune; but generally it is not inflected at all, e.g.: سَوائِنِ چئِنِ مَڻَنِ سين with four maunds and a quarter or: سَوا چئين مَڻين سين. سَوا may also precede سَوُ, هَزَارُ etc., as: سَوا سَوُ one hundred and a quarter = 125; سَوا هَزَارُ one thousand and a quarter = 1250.

اَدهُ adhu, half, is a common adjective and used accordingly.

سَاڏها sāḍhā, adding one half, is only used with nouns of number subsequent to 'two', and therefore ever found in the Plural; its fem. is سَاڏهيُون sāḍhiyū̃.

تَڈِهِن سَاڈَهَا نَنْوَن سِيرَ سِنْڌُرَ تُرَاڙِي تورِي

Then she weighs with a balance nine sērs and a half of read lead. Maj. 320.

ڏيڍهُ ḍēḍhu, one and a half, is only used in the Singular and not compounded with other numbers, as: ڏيڍهُ آنو one Anna and a half; ڏيڍهُ رَتِي one ratī and a half.

اَڍهَائِي aḍhāī, two and a half, is only used in the Plural, without distinction of gender in the Nominative; in the Formative Plural it makes for the Masc. اَڍهَائِنِ aḍhāine, اَڍهَايَنِ aḍhāyane or: اَڍهَائِيِن aḍhāiẽ, and for the fem. اَڍهَائِنِ aḍhāine, اَڍهَايُنِ aḍhāyune, اَڍهَائِيِن aḍhāiẽ; اَڍهَائِي گَجَ two yards and a half; اَڍهَائِي توِيُون two Tōīs and a half; Formative: اَڍهَائِنِ گَجَنِ; اَڍهَايُنِ توِيُنِ etc.

From these fractional numbers another kind of adjectives has been derived, implying "consisting of, computed at such a rate, standing in such a relation", as:

پَاڻيو pāṇyō or پَاڻيَکُ pāṇyaku, only used in the compound: ترِپَاڻيو or: ترِپَاڻيَکُ, computed at at three quarters of a rupee.

پَائو pāō, compounded with cardinal numbers, as: ترِي پَائو, consisting of three quarters.

سَوَايو savāyō, computed at $1^1/_4$.

ڏيڍهو ḍēḍhō, consisting of $1^1/_2$.

ڏيڍهُئُون ḍēḍhuõ, standing in the $1^1/_2$ place.

اَڍهَايو aḍhāyō, consisting of $2^1/_2$.

اَڍهَائُون aḍhāõ, standing in the $2^1/_2$ place.

These are used as common adjectives and inflected and constructed accordingly.

The other fractional numbers may be made up by compositions, as:

اَدهُ پاءُ adhu pāu = $^1/_8$.

ڏيڍهُ پاءُ ḍēḍhu pāu = $^3/_8$.

ٻہ ٽرِهائي ƃa ṭrihāī = $^2/_3$.

پوڻا ٻہ pauṇā ƃa = $1^3/_4$.

etc. etc. etc.

Fractions with special application are:

پارُپو pārupō,
پائِلي pāilī,
پائِڻِ pāiṇe,
} a quarter of a rupee.

پائِڙي pāiṛī, the quarter of a گز (yard).

لارِي lārī, one third of a rupee.

اَدهيلِي adhēlī,
آدهِئو ādhiō,
} half a rupee piece.

اَدهِڙي adhiṛī, half a gaǰ, or half a ḍamiṛī (ڏمِڙِي).

Chapter XI.

Pronouns.

§. 31.

The personal pronoun is in Sindhī of two kinds: it is either used as an absolute pronoun or as a suffix, acceding to nouns, adverbs or verbs.

I. PERSONAL PRONOUNS.

The Sindhī has a personal pronoun only for the first and second person Singular and Plural, the third person is made up by means of demonstrative pronouns. A remnant of the old (now lost) personal pronoun of the third person has been preserved in the pronominal suffix of the third person, as we shall see hereafter.

1) The personal pronoun of the first person.

There are two forms in common use for the first person Singular, آئُون ā̃ū̃, and shortened آن ā̃; besides these مَان mā̃ or مُون mū̃ are also dialectically used in Sirō.

The great deterioration of the language is strikingly illustrated by the present forms of the absolute pronouns. The Prākrit form is **अहं** or **अहअं** (Sansk. **अहं**); but in the corrupted Apabhranša dialect, the mother of the modern Sindhī, we meet already the form **हउं**, from **हमु** (by elision of **म**), from which the Sindhī ā̃ū̃ has drawn its origin (Lassen, §. 183); the other form ā̃ has been simply contracted from **अहं**. The two other forms mā̃ and mū̃ are originally the Accusative, Sanskrit **मां** (Prākrit shortened **मं**), and are still used as the Formative Singular.

The Genitive مُنْهُن mū̃hū̃ or مُنْهِن mū̃hē̃, with the adjective affix جو jō, is to be referred to the Prākrit Genitive **मह** (Sansk. **मम**), Apabhranša **महु** (Lassen §. 183), the vowels being nasalized in Sindhī.

The Nominative Plural is اَسِين asī̃, Prākrit **अम्हे** (Sansk. root **अस्म**); in Sindhī m has been elided and final ē changed to ī (= ī̃); the Formative اَسَان asā̃ corresponds to the Prākrit Genitive Plural अम्हांण (Sansk. अस्माकं).

Annotation. In the cognate dialects the Accusative has similarly been used for the Nominative; Marāṭhī mī (inferior Prākrit dialect मइं, Lassen §. 183, 2), Formative ma (Prākrit Genitive मह); Hindūstānī maĩ, Formative mujhē or mujh (Prākrit Genitive मज्झ); Panjābī: maĩ, Formative maĩ; but Gujarātī: hū, Formative ma. In the Plural the Marāṭhī has in the Nominative āhmī, in the Formative āhmā̃; the Hindūstānī ham, Formative ham or hamō̃; the Panjābī asē̃, Formative asā; the Gujarātī hamē or hamō, Formative ham or hamō.

Inflexion of the first personal pronoun.

آنئُون ā̃ū̃ or آن ā̃, I.

SINGULAR.

Nom. آنئُون āū̃, آن ā̃; مَان mā̃, مُون mū̃;
Format. Instrum. } مُون mū̃, مَان mā̃; آن ā̃.
Genit. مُنْهُن جو mūhū̃ jō; مُنْهِن جو mūhē̃ jō; مُون جو mū̃ jō; آن جو ā̃ jō.
Dative. Accus. } مُون کهي mū̃ khē; مَان کهي mā̃ khē.
Ablat. مُونْهَان mū̃hā̃; مُون کهَان mū̃k hā̃ or مَان کهَان mā khā̃.

PLURAL.

Nom. اَسِين asī̃, we.
Format. Instrum. } اَسَان asā̃; اَسَانْهِن asā̃hē; اَسَانْهُون asā̃hū̃.
Genit. اَسَان جو asā̃ jō, اَسَانْهِن جو asā̃hē jō.
Dative. Accus. } اَسَان کهي asā̃ khē; اَسَانْهِن کهي asā̃hē khē.
Ablat. اَسَان کهَان asā̃ khā̃ etc.

آن جِي ڏِٺها هُونِ تَہ اَلْهَ ڪارَنِ ڳالهِ ڪَرِڄو

نيڻَ مُنْهن جا رُونِ رَاتوڏِينهان اُنِ کهي

If they have been seen by you, for God's sake tell (me). After them my eyes weep night and day. Sh. Hus. X, 22.

ڪِي نَہ ڇهَڏِينْدِيَسِ جَانِي آن جو قِيَامَتَا

By no means I shall give up my friend till the day of resurrection. Sh. Kēḍ. IV, Epil.

قَاضِي مُون کهي ڪِينئَ هَڻين مِيَان پِسِڻو مَرِيضُ

Kāẕī, why doest thou beat me, having seen me ill, o friend! Maj. 251.

مُونْهَانئِي اَڳِي هُونْدَ گهِرِيُون سَڀِهِ ڪهَڙَا ڪهَڻِي

Even before me all would have perhaps slided down (into the river) having taken their jars. Sh. Suh. I, 4.

آهِيسِ آرُ اَلّلهَ سين اَسان ڏَهُنْ اِيمَانُ

She in bashful before God and faithful towards us. Maj. 671.

اَسَانْهُون وَهي وِتِرو نِينْهُ سُپِيرِيَان سين

Our love flows excessively with our sweethearts. Maj. 675.

2) The personal pronoun of the second person.

The pronoun of the second person is تُون tũ, which points rather to the Sansk. त्वं, than to the Prāk. तुम; the Formative and Instrumentalis تو tō is derived from the Prāk. Instrum. तुए; the Genitive تُنْهُن tũhũ or تُنْهِن tũhẽ (with جو etc.) corresponds to the Apabhranša Genitive तुहं.

The Plural of this pronoun presents a great variety of forms, as: تَوْهِين tavhī̃, تَوِين tavī̃, تَهِين tahī̃, تَئِين taī̃; or: اَوْهِين avhī (avhē̃), اَوِين avē̃, اَهِين ahī̃, آئِين āī̃, اَنئِن āī.

The forms tavhī̃ etc. have been derived from the Prākrit Nom. Plural तुम्हे, tū having been changed to tav, and m elided. The forms avhī̃, ahī̃ etc. are very remarkable. As initial t is never elided, they cannot well be derived from tavhī̃ etc. It is therefore very probable, that these forms are to be referred to the Sansk. Plural युष्मे = Prāk. युम्हे, and with elision of initial y, umhē; in Sindhī 'u' has been changed to 'av' and m elided, as in tavhī̃.

The Formative تَوْهَان tavhā̃, اَوْهَان avhā̃ corresponds to the Prāk. Genitive Plural तुम्हाणं.

Annotation. The cognate dialects agree in all essential points with the Sindhī. Marāṭhī: tū̃, Formative tū or tūǰa (Prākrit तुह or तुज्झ; Nom. Plural tuhmī and Formative tuhmā̃. Hindūstānī: tū or taī; Genitive tē-rā (mē-rā), rā being used in this instance to form a pronominal adjective; the Formative tuǰh is properly the Prākrit Genitive तुज्झ, and the Instrumentalis tū coincides with the Sindhī tō. The Nomin. Plural tum is shortened from the Prākrit तुम्हे, and the forms tumhā (tumhā-rā), tumhō̃, tumh point back to the Prākrit Genitive Plural तुम्हाणं. Panǰābī: tū̃, Genitive tē-rā, Instrument. taī (Prākrit तइ), Formative taī (Prākrit Genitive ते). Nom. Plural: tusī̃, Formative: tusā. Gujarātī: tū, Genitive: tāhā-rō, Formative ta; Nom. Plural: tamē or tamō, Formative tam or tamō.

Inflexion of the second personal pronoun.

SINGULAR.

Nom. تُون tū̃, thou.
Format. } تو tō.
Instrum. }

Gen. تُنْهُن جو tũhũ ǰō (tũhē ǰō); تو جو tō ǰō.

Dative. / Accus. } تو کهي tō khē.

Ablat. توهَان tōhā̃; تو کهَان tō khā̃.

PLURAL.

Nom. تَوْهِين tavhī̃; تَوِين tavī̃; تَهِين tahī̃; تَئِين taī̃.
اَوْهِين avhī̃ (avhē̃); اَوِين avī̃; اَهِين ahī̃; آنئِين
ā̃ī̃; اَنئِن ā̃ī.

Format. / Instrum. } تَوْهَان tavhā̃, تَهَان tahā̃; اَوْهَان avhā̃; اَهَان ahā̃;
آن ā̃.

Gen. { تَوْهَان جو tavhā̃ ǰō etc.; اَوْهَان جو avhā̃ ǰō; تَوانْهِن جو tavā̃hē ǰō; اَوانْهِن جو avā̃hē ǰō } آهِن جو āhē ǰō.

Dative. / Accus. } تَوْهَان کهي tavhā̃ khē; اَوْهَان کهي avhā̃ khē.

Ablat. تَوْهَان کهَان tavhā̃ khā̃ etc.

The emphatic ī or hī, hī̃ is very frequently joined to this pronoun in all its forms.

تُونْهِين رَهِينْمِ رُوحَ مِين توهِي ڏانْهَ نِينَ

Even thou remainest in my heart; only towards thee my eyes (are directed). Maj. 211.

سَتْهَمِ سَاهيڙِنِ جَا طَعْنَا توهِي لَاء

Even for thy sake I have borne the tauntings of my companions. Sh. Mūm. Rāṇō I, Epil.

توهِي سَنْدو مِيهِنو بهَلِي کَرِي لَدهومِ

Even thy reproach has been welcomed by me. Maj. 341.

سَارِيَان گَا نَ سَرِيَر مِين طَاقَت توهَان دهَارَ

Separate from thee I cannot find any strength in my body. Sh. Suh. II, 4.

مِيَان مَنَعَ مُون کهي اَنڻِن گَا مَ کَريو

O friends, do not hinder me at all! Maj. 95.

چهَنِ چهڏِينْدِيَسِ کِي نَ کِي دوَسَ اَوَانهِن جو دَرُ

I shall not at all give up (your) shed nor your door, o friend! Sh. Barvō S. I, 16.

کَامِنِ آهِن جِي کُرَ جِي آڻِ وَڏَائِي آهِي

O handsome lady! the mark of your family is greatness. Sh. Um. Mār. II, 8.

پرِنئَ پُنجَاء آنڻون آوَان سِين اوَرِيَان

After my friend (is gone) I talk over with you my misfortunes. Sh. Hus. VI, 5.

II. DEMONSTRATIVE PRONOUNS.

§. 32.

1) The proximate demonstrative pronoun is هِي hī, هي hē or هِيُ hīu (also pronounced: هِءُ hiu); in Lāṛ initial h is commonly dropped, as: اِي ī, اي ē, اِيُ īu. The base of this pronoun is ī (cf. Bopp §. 360 sqq.); in the Formative another pronominal base is substituted, i-na, (Bopp §. 369; compare also the inflexion of इदम् 'this' in Sansk.).

Annotation. The Marāṭhī form of this demonstrative is hā, Formative: yā (Prākrit अअं = Sansk. अयम्); Hindūstānī: yeh, Formative: is (Sansk. अस्य); Plural: yē, Formative: in. Panǰābī: ih, Formative: is, Instrument.: in; Plural: ih, Formative: inā̃.

Inflexion of the proximate demonstrative.

هِي hī, this.

Nom. هِي hī; هي he; هِيءُ hīu or هِءُ hiu, masc., 'this'; 'he'.
هِي hī; هي hē; هِيءَ hīa or هِءَ hia, fem., 'this'; 'she'.

Format. / Instrum. } هِنَ hina or اِنَ ina, com.

Genit. هِنَ جو hina ǰō or اِنَ جو ina ǰō.

Dative. هِنَ کھي hina khē etc.

Accusat. { هِنَ کھي hina khē etc. / هِي hī etc.

Ablat. هِنَ کھان hina khā̃ etc.; هِنان hinā̃.

PLURAL.

Nom. هِي hī; هي hē, 'these'; 'they'; com.

Format. / Instrum. } هِنِ hine or اِنِ ine; هِنَنِ hinane or اِنَنِ inane.

Genit. هِنِ جو hine ǰō; هِنَنِ جو hinane ǰō.

Dative. هِنِ کھي hine khē; هِنَنِ کھي hinane khē.

Accus. { هِنِ کھي hine khē etc. / هِي hī; هي hē.

Ablat. هِنِ کھان hine khā̃ etc.

There is also an emphatic form of this pronoun: هيئِي hēī, this very one.

پُرَنُ پُنْھُنءَ پُٺِھ ميں اِيءَ سَعادَتَ سَنْديَامِ

To travel after Punhū̃, this is my happiness. Sh. Maɜδ. III, 1.

هِنَ پَاڻِيَ سين پَانْھِن جو مُورِ نَ مَنھو دھوءِ

With this water she does not wash at all her head. Sh. Suh. Čhōṭ. 3.

مَتهِي مُورانِئِين مَنَ مِين اِنَ کهي هُئِي

Nothing but wickedness has been in his heart. Maǰ. 244.

هَڏِهِين نَہ هُونْدو هِنَان پوء عَالَمَ مِين

Never it will be after this in the world. Sh. Khāhōṛ. III, 11.

جيکو هِنِ ننڍّهَنِ مَنجهَان هِڪِڙي کهي تهڌهي پَانِي

جو ڪٿورو پِيَارِي

Whoever shall give to drink unto one of these little ones a cup of cold water. Matth. 10, 42.

خُدَاء هِنَ[1]) پَهڻَنِ مَون اِبرَاهِيمَ لَاء پُٽرَ کَرِي تهو سَگهي

God can make sons for Abraham from these stones. Matth. 3, 9.

2) The emphatic proximate demonstrative is اهو ihō, 'this very'; 'this here'. It is properly a compound pronoun, consisting of the demonstrative base 'i', and 'hō' = Sansk. ह (इह), and therefore inflected according to both terminations.

SINGULAR.

Nom. اِهو ihō; اِيهو īhō; اِئو iō; اِيئو īō; masc.[2])
اِهَا ihā; اِيهَا īhā; اِئَا iā; اِيئَا īā; fem.

Format. / Instrum. } اِنْهي inhē; اِنْهِي inhī; اِنْهِيَ inhia; اِنِهَ ineha; com.

Genit. اِنْهي جو inhē ǰō etc.

Dative. اِنْهي کهي inhē khē etc.

1) It very rarely occurs, that the Singular of this pronoun is (after the manner of an adjective) joined to a noun in the Plural.

2) In poëtry the form اِيهُ ēhu also is to be met with.

Accus. { اِنْهي کهي inhē khē etc.
اِهو ihō; m.; اِهَا ihā, fem.

Ablat. اِنْهي کهَان inhē khā̃ etc.

PLURAL.

Nom. اِهي ihē, com.

Format. / Instrum. } اِنْهَنِ inhane; اِنْهِنِ inhine; اِنْهين inhē̃.

Genit. اِنْهَنِ جو inhane jō etc.

Dative. اِنْهَنِ کهي inhane khē etc.

Accus. { اِنْهَنِ کهي inhanē khē etc.
اِهي ihē, com.

Ablat. اِنْهَنِ کهَان inhane khā̃ etc.

The emphatic ī may also be added to this pronoun, to point the object out with still greater distinctness, as: اِهوئِي ihōī, this very same person, fem. اِهَائِي ihāī; Format. اِنْهيئِي inhēī; Plur. اِهيئِي ihēī; Format. اِنْهَنِي or commonly: اِنْهِين inhī̃.

اِهو سَائِنءَ جو سَبَبُ جو بُڏَا اُکَارِي بَارِ مَان

Even this is the cause of the Lord, that he draws forth the drowned ones from the eddy. Sh. Surāg. II, 16.

عَاشِقَ عَبْدُ ٱللَّطِيفُ چَوِي اِنْهِي پَهِ پِئَا

The lovers, says Abd-ul-Latīf, have fallen into this very reflection. Sh. Kal. I, 8.

اِهي کَمَ اِلَاهِي نَہ تَہ کُنَنِ مين کِيرَ کَهِري

Even these are the works of God; otherwise who wouldstep down into the whirlpools? Sh. Suh. VI, 13.

3) The demonstrative pronoun اِجهو ijhō, 'this one present' is only used in the Nom. Sing. and Plural. It is apparently compounded of the base 'i' and the Sansk. pronoun सः, s being now and then changed in Sindhī to j̈, and even to j̈h (see: Introduction §. 11, 2).

SINGULAR.

Nom. اِجهو ijhō; fem. اِجهَا ijhā.

PLURAL.

Nom. اِجهي ijhē, com.

اِجهي تهَا اَچَنِ كَاكِ كَكوَرِيَا كَاپَڙِي

They come here; the faqīrs have been made tawny by the Kāk (river). Sh. Mūm. Rāṇō II, 3.

4) The remote demonstrative pronoun is هُو hū or هو hō, in Lāṛ pronounced اُو ū or او ō. The base of this pronoun, hū, is not in use in Sanskrit, but in Prākrit a remnant of it has been preserved in the Genitive हे. Its theme must have been (according to Bopp, Comp. Gramm. §. 341) sva, from which 'hu' has been regularly formed. Its inflection quite agrees with that of هِي hī, only hu (u) being substituted instead of 'hi' in the Formative.

Annotation. The Marāṭhī does not know this pronominal base; it only uses tō, corresponding to the Sindhī sō. In Panj̈ābī we find uh, Instrum. un, and Formative us, Plur. uh, Formative unā̃. The Hindūstānī uses: woh, Formative us; Plural wē, Format. un (Hinduī: wah, Formative vā; Plur. wē, Formative: un). The Guj̈arātī, like the Marāthī, has only the theme tē.

SINGULAR.

Nom. هُو hū, هو hō, اُو ū, او ō, masc. }
هُو hū (هو hō), هُئَ hua; اُو ū, اُئَ ua, fem. } that; he, she.

Format. }
Instrum. } هُنَ huna, اُنَ una, com.

Dative. هُنَ کهي huna khē etc.

Accus. { هُنَ کهي huna khē etc.
{ هُو hū, هُئَ hua etc.

Ablat. هُنَان hunā̃, هُنَهَان hunahā̃, اُنَان unā̃; هُنَ کهَان huna khā̃.

PLURAL.

Nom. هُو hū; هو hō; هُوء hūe; اُوء ūe; هوء hōe, com.
Format. }
Instrum. } هُنَنِ hunane, اُنَنِ unane; هُنِ hune, اُنِ une. (emphatic: هُنِين hunī̃).

Dative. هُنَنِ کهي hunane khē; هُنِ کهي hune khē etc.

Accus. { هُنَنِ کهي hunane khē etc.
{ هُو hū; هو hō etc.

Ablat. هُنَنِ کهَان hunane khā̃ etc.

پَرڏيهَان پَنڌهُ کَرِي هَلِي آيو هُو

Having travelled from a foreign country he had come. Sh. Sōr. I, 3.

هُوء جَا پَائِنِ پيرَ مِين تَنْهِن آن جُتِيَ نَ جيهِي

I am not worthy of that shoe, which they put on (their) foot. Sh. Kōh. III, 8.

اُنَ دَرَ سِيئِي اَگهِيا جَنِ وِڃَايو وُجُودُ

At that door those are accepted, who have lost their existence. Sh. Surāg̃. I, Epil. 2.

هُوء مَحَلَّ هُوء مِهِتِئُون هُوء قَصَرَ قَاضِئَنِ

Those are the mansions, those the mosques, those the palaces of the Kāẕīs. Maj. 137.

كهُوهَا كَالهَہ كهَنِي اُنِ وِدهَا اوْتَر آسِرِي

Yesterday were raised by them the masts by the support of the north-wind. Sh. Surāg̃. III, 1.

5) The emphatic remote demonstrative is اُهو uhō, 'that very'; it is formed in the same way as اِهو ihō, only 'u' being substituted for 'i'.

SINGULAR.

Nom. اُهو uhō or اُئو uō, masc.
اُهَا uhā or اُئَا uā, fem.

Format. Instrum. } اُنْهي unhē; اُنْهِيَ nnhia; اُنِهَہ uniha, com.

Genit. اُنْهي جو unhē ǰō etc.

Dative. اُنْهي كهي unhē khē etc.

Accus. { اُنْهي كهي unhē khē etc.
اُهو uhō, m.; اُهَا uhā, fem.

Ablat. اُنْهي كهَان unhē khā̃.

PLURAL.

Nom. اُهي uhē, com.

Format. Instrum. } اُنْهَنِ unhane; اُنْهِنِ unhine; اُنْهِين unhē̃.

Genit. اُنْهَنِ جو unhane ǰō etc.

Dative. اُنْهَنِ كهي unhanē khē etc.

Accus. { اُنْهَنِ كهي unhane khē etc.
اُهي uhē, com.

Ablat. اُنْهَنِ كهَان unhane khā̃ etc.

The emphatic ī may also be added to this pronoun, اُهوئِي uhōī, 'that very same', fem. اُهَائِي uhāī,

Formative: اُنْهيئِي unhēī, اُنْهِي unhī or اُنَهِين unahī̃. Plural: اُهيئِي uhēī; Formative: اُنْهَنِي unhanī or اُنْهِين unhī̃.

اَڳِي تهِي سُڻِي اُنْهِي سَنْڌِي ڳالْهڙِي

The story of that very (person) was heard before. Sh. Khāhōṛī I, 11.

اُنْهِي گهَرَ مِين اَچِي اُنْهِي ٻَارَ کهِي ۽ اُنِهَ جِي مَاءُ مَرْيَمَ کهِي ڏِسِي هُنَ کهِي پيرين پَئِي پُوڄَائُون

Having come to that very house (and) having seen that very child and its mother Mary, they fell at his feet and worshipped (him). Matth. II, 11.

هِي چَنْڊُرُ اُهوئِي جوْ هُتِ پَسِي تهو پرِنءُ کهِي

This one sees the moon, and that one, who is there, (sees his) friend. Sh. Kambh. I, 3.

سَدَا اُهيئِي تو کهِي سَارِنِ
جِي نَـ کَڏِهِن مَنْجهِ ڳَامَ گُذَارِنِ

Even those remember thee always
Who never live in a town. Sh. Sārangu II, Epil.

اُنْهِين ڏَان اَحْمَدِ چَوِي آهِمِ سِکَ سَرْسُ

Even towards them, says Aĥmad, I have an immense longing. Umar Māruī X.[1]

6) The remote demonstrative pronoun اُجهو ujhō, that one present, is, like اِجهو ijhō, only used in the Nom. Singular and Plural. It is compounded of the base 'u' and the Sansk. pronoun सः (see: اِجهو).

---

1) A poëm, different from that contained in the Shāha jō Risāls.

SINGULAR.

Nom. اُجهو ujhō; fem. اُجها ujhā.

PLURAL.

Nom. اُجهي ujhē, com.

§. 33.

III. THE RELATIVE PRONOUN.

The relative pronoun in Sindhī is جو ǰō, 'who', 'what', Sansk. यो, Prāk. जो; the Formative Singular جَنْهِن ǰãhẽ corresponds to the Prākrit Genitive जस्स = जह, the vowels having been nasalized in Sindhī. The Nom. Plural is جي ǰē, as in Prākrit जे, and the Formative جِنِ ǰine or جَنِ ǰane points to the Prākrit Genitive Plur. जाण, ā having been shortened in Sindhī.

Annotation. The cognate dialects do not differ essentially from the Sindhī; Marāṭhī: Sing. ǰō, Plur. ǰē; Guǰarātī: Sing. ǰē, Plural ǰēō; Hindūst.: Sing. ǰō or ǰau; Formative ǰis; Plur. ǰō, Formative ǰin or ǰinh; Panǰābī: ǰō, Instrum. ǰin, Formative ǰis; Plur. ǰō, Format. ǰinā̃, Bangālī: ǰē or ǰine, Formative ǰā̃hā (Prāk. जास); Plur. ǰā̃hā-rā.

SINGULAR.

Nom. جو ǰō, masc.; جا ǰā, fem.

Format. }
Instrum. } جَنْهِن ǰãhẽ, com.

Genitive. جَنْهِن جو ǰãhẽ ǰō etc.

Dative. جَنْهِن کهي ǰãhẽ khē.

Accus. جَنْهِن کهي ǰãhẽ khē; جو ǰō; جا ǰā.

Ablat. جَنْهِن کهَان ǰãhẽ khā̃.

PLURAL.

Nom. جي ǰē, com.

Format. / Instrum. } جَنِ ǰane; جِنِ ǰine; جِنْهَنِ ǰinhane; جِنْهِنِ ǰinhine.
جِنَنِ ǰinane, جِنِنِ ǰinine.

Genit. جَنِ جو ǰane jō etc.

Dative. جَنِ کهي ǰane khē etc.

Accus. جَنِ کهي ǰane khē; جي ǰē.

Ablat. جَنِ کهَان ǰane khā̃ etc.

In poëtry the emphatic ī very frequently is added to the Formative Sing. and Plur. of this pronoun, as: Format. Sing. جَنْهِين ǰāhī̃; Format. plur. جَنِي ǰanī (also written جَنِين ǰanī̃), جَنْهِين janhī̃ (to be well distinguished from the Format. Sing.)

هو جَا پِکَ پُنْهُنءَ جِي چَتِيَان تَنْهِن چُوَاکو

That, which is the spittle of Punhū̃, of that will I lick a drop. Sh. Sah. II, Epil. 2.

جَنْهِن کهي سِکَ سَاهَڙَ جِي سَا گهِيڙُ نَہ پُڇهي گهَاتَ
جَنِ کهي عِشْقَ جِي اوْسَاتَ سِي وَاهُڙَ بهَائِنِ وِکهَڙِيُون

She, who has a longing for Sāhaṛu asks not for a slope in the ferry;
Those, who thirst after love, consider the brooks as small steps. Sh. Suh. III, 4.

جي سَنْجهيثِي سُتِيُون سِي مَرُ سُورَ سَهَنِ

Those who have fallen asleep on the evening, suffer pains indeed. Sh. Khāhōṛī III, Epil. 2.

وِينْدَا سِي اِيمَانَ سِين کَلِمو جَنِين وَاتِ

They will depart with faith, in whose mouth the creed is. Maj. 37.

آمَڙِ وَنجِي آنِ چرکهو آتَڻَ وِچِ مَان

کَتيُمِ جَنْهِين کَانِ سو کوهِيَارو کيچِ وِئو

O mother, go and bring me the spinning wheel from the courtyard.

The mountaineer, for whose sake I have spun, is gone to Kēč. Sh. Hus. III, 8.

پِکُون سي پِڳَنِ سِرَ جَنْهِين جَا سَٿِ مِين

Those drink draughts, whose heads are devoted. Sh. Jam. Kal. II, 25.

§. 34.

IV. THE CORRELATIVE PRONOUN.

The pronoun سو sō is nearly always used as the correlative of جو; it is seldom found isolated, in which case it retains its original signification 'that'. It corresponds to the Sansk. pronoun सः, Prāk. सो. The Formative Sing. تَنْهِن tāhē is derived from the Prāk. Genitive तस्स (Sansk. तस्य) = तह; the Nom. Plur. سي sē differs so far from the Sanskrit and Prākrit (ते), as having retained the base of the Singular; the Formative Plural تَنِ tane is to be referred to the Prāk. Genitive ताण, ā having been shortened, as in जाण.

Annotation. All the kindred idioms know this pronoun; Marāṭhī: tō, Plur. tē̃; Guǰarātī likewise: tē, Plur. tēō; Hindūst.: sō or taun, Formative tis; Nom. Plur. sō or taun, Formative tin, tinh or tinhō̃. Panǰābī: sō, Instrument. tin, Formative tis; Plur. sō, Formative tinā̃. Bangālī: sē, Formative tāhā, Plur. tāhā-rā.

SINGULAR.

Nom. سو sō; fem. سَا sā.

Format.
Instrum. } تَنْهِن tāhē.

Genit. تَنْهِن جو tāhē jō etc.

Dative. تَنْهِن کهي tāhē khē.

Accus. تَنْهِن کهي tāhē khē; سو sō; سَا sā.

Ablat. تَنْهان tāhā̃; تَنْهِن کهَان tāhē khā̃.

PLURAL.

Nom. سي sē; com.

Format.
Instrum. } تَنِ tane; تِنِ tine; تِنَنِ tinane, تِنِنِ tinine; تِنْهَنِ tinhane; تِنْهِنِ tinhine.

Genit. تَنِ جو tane jō etc.

Dative. تَنِ کهي tane khē etc.

Accus. تَنِ کهي tane khē; سي sē.

Ablat. تَنِّان taneā̃; تَنِ کهَان tane khā̃ etc.

The emphatic ī may also be joined to this pronoun, as: Nom. Sing. سوئِي sōī, fem. سَائِي sāī; Format. تَنْهِين tāhī. Nom. Plur. سِيئِي sēī, Format. تَنِي tanī or: تَنْهِين tanhī.

سو هِيئُ سو هُو سو اَجَلُ سو اَللّٰهُ

سو پِرِين سو پَسَاهُ سو وِيرِي سو وَاهَرُو

He is this, he is that; he is death, he is Allah.

He is friend, he is breath; he is enemy, he is helper. Sh. Kal. I, 19.

سُومِرَا سَاهِي تَنْهِن سَتِيَ وِجهُ مَ سَنْگهَرُون

O Sūmirō! do not confine in fetters that chaste woman! Sh. Um. Mār. III, 9.

تَنْهِين وِيلهَ كِثْوِمِ وَچَنُ وِيڙهِيچَنِ سِين

In that very time I have made an engagement with the inhabitants of the jungle. Sh. Um. Mār. I, 1.

جڏِهِن سُتِيُون جي پَتهَرِ پير ڊِگها کَرِي
تڏِهِن تَنْهِين کهِي سَاتهَ سُتِيِئِي چهَڏِئو

When they were fallen asleep, having stretched out their feet on the bed,
Then they were left behind by the caravan, whilst sleeping. Sh. Kōh. I, 8.

جَنْهِين سَنْدِي مُنْهَ مِين سَوِين سَهَسَ نَکَنِ
تَنِئَّان وَڍِهِئو هِيکَڙو تَ کِهَڙو تهورو تَنِ

In whose face there are hundred thousands of noses,
Cut off from those one, then what obligation is it to them? Sh. Mūm. VI, 22.

§. 35.

V. INTERROGATIVE PRONOUNS.

1) The interrogative pronoun کيرُ kēru, who?

This pronoun is only used absolutely. The Nominative base کيرُ kēru is derived from the Sanskrit कीदृश, Prāk. केरिस (see Introduction §. 2, 6); but the Formative Singular کَنْهِن kāhē, and the Format. Plural کَنِ kane point back to the Sansk. कः; Genitive Sing. कस्य, Prāk. कस्स = कह; Genitive Plural in Prākrit काण, the ā of which has been shortened in Sindhī.

Annotation. The cognate idioms fall back on the Sansk. base कः (i. e. on the Accus. Sing. कं), as Marāṭhī and Gujarātī: kōṇ; Hindūst.: kaun, Format. kis; Plural kaun, Format.

kin, kinh, kinhō̃; Panǰābī: kauṇ, Instrument. kin, Format. kis; Plural kauṇ, Formative kinā̃. Bangālī: kē, Formative kā̃hā; Plural kā̃hā-rā.

SINGULAR.

Nom. كيرُ kēru; fem. كيرَ kēra.
Format. / Instrum. } كَنْهِن kāhē̃, com.
Genit. كَنْهِن جو kāhē̃ ǰō etc.
Dative. كَنْهِن كهي kāhē̃ khē.
Accus. { كَنْهِن كهي kāhē̃ khē. / كيرُ kēru; كيرَ kēra.
Ablat. كَنْهِن كهَان kāhē̃ khā̃.

PLURAL.

Nom. كيرِ kēre, com.
Format. / Instrum. } كَنِ kane, كِنِ kine; كِنَنِ kinane, كِنِنِ kinine; كِنْهَنِ kinhane, كِنْهِنِ kinhine.
Dative. كَنِ كهي kane khē etc.
Accus. { كَنِ كهي kane khē etc. / كيرِ kēre.
Ablat. كَنِ كهَان khane khā̃ etc.

كيرُ آنْهِين كِتهَان هَلين كُجَاڙو نَالوهه

Who art thou? from whence proceedest thou? what is thy name? Maj. 167.

كيرَ بَانْبهَنِ كَنِ جِي كيرُ جَاڻي كيتَاسِ

Who is the brahman woman? whose (Genit. Plur.) is she? who knows her? Sh. Maǯδ. I, 14.

كيرِ هُنّا كيڏانْهه وِنّا كِهڙِي هُنّا جاتِ

Who have they been? wither are they gone? of what class have they been? Maj. 659.

2) The interogative pronoun چهَا čhā, what?

This pronoun is only used in a neuter sense and has no Plural. The Genitive چهَا جو čhā jō etc. signifies: of what sort, of what kind? With the postpositions کهي khē, کانِ kāne, کهَان khā̃, it signifies: what for? to what purpose? why? — It is derived from the Sansk. किम् what.

Annotation. The Hindūstānī uses kiā, the Panjābī kī and kiā, Format. kās; the Marāṭhī kāy (Formative kasā); Bangālī: ki, Format. kāha. Hinduī: kahā, Format. kāhē.

جي لُونَ جو سَوادُ وَنجي تَه چهَا سَان سَلُونو تهِئي

If the savour of the salt goes, whit what shall it be salted? Matth. 5, 13.

3) The interrogative pronoun کوهُ kōhu, what?

This pronoun is only used in a neuter sense, just as the preceding one, and is indeclinable. If signifies very frequently 'why', 'what for'. In poëtry it is occasionally shortened to کُهُ kuhu.

As to its derivation it is identical with چهَا (= kā, kahā), ā having been changed to ō in this instance. The same is also the case in Hinduī, where kaun, who? makes the Formative either in kā, kōhe or kāhe.

جِئّارِيَسِ سَنبهارَ کوهُ کَرِينْدُم گَڏِجي

I have been made alive by remembering (him); what will he do to me having met (me)? Sh. Suh. IV, 7.

سَدھِڙِيَا سَرِي جُون کُھ پَچَارُون کَنِ

Why do the vacillating ones talk of strong wine? Sh. Kal. II, 25.

4) The interrogative pronouns ڪيھو kēhō, ڪيھَرو kēhārō and ڪُجَاڙو kujāṛō, what? which?

These three interrogative pronouns may either be used absolutely or adjectively with a substantive. Instead of ڪيھو kēhō the form ڪيئو kēō is also used in Lāṛ; ڪيھَرو kēharo may also be written ڪِھَرو kĕharō or it may be contracted to ڪيرھو kērhō; about their derivation see Introd. §. 2, 6. They are inflected regularly. The Dative Sing. of ڪُجَاڙو, i. e. ڪُجَاڙِي ڪھي kujāṛē khē and the Ablative of the fem. Sing. ڪُجَاڙِيَان kujaṛeā̃ (frequently also written ڪُجَاڙِيَا) is generally used as an interrogative adverb, 'why?' 'what for?'

ڪيھِيَ پَرِ پَرِين ڏُکھِي ڏَاتَارَنِ رِي

In which wise wilt thou, o afflicted one! pass (thy time) without the bountiful? Sh. Jam. Kal. IV, 16.

تھِئو ڪُجَاڙو قَيْس ڪھي اَچِئو اِينئَ چَوَنِ

What has happened to Qais? having come they speak thus. Maj. 39.

ڪُجَاڙِي ڪھي تو ڪِئو ھِينئَ پَنْھَن جو حَالُ

Why has thy own state been made by thee thus? Maj. 655.

§. 36.

VI. INDEFINITE PRONOUNS.

1) The indefinite pronoun کوٗ kō, any one; some one.

The root of this indefinite pronoun is the same as that of the interrogative (Sansk. कोऽपि); the Formative Sing. and Plural is therefore identical in both pronouns.

SINGULAR.

Nom. کوٗ kō; fem. کا kā.
Format. } Instrum. } کَنْهِن kāhẽ, com.
Genit. کَنْهِن جوٗ kāhẽ jō etc.
Dative. کَنْهِن کهِي kāhẽ khē.
Accus. { کَنْهِن کهِي kāhẽ khē. / کوٗ kō; کا kā.
Ablat. کَنْهِن کهان kāhẽ khā̃.

PLURAL.

Nom. کِي kē, com.
Format. } Instrum. } کَنِ kane; کِنِ kine.
Genit. کَنِ جوٗ kane jō etc.
Dative. کَنِ کهِي kane khē.
Accus. { کَنِ کهِي kane khē. / کِي kē.
Ablat. کَنِ کهان kane khā̃.

کَمِ نَہ اِينْدُء کوٗ ٻِئوٗ پَنْهَن جِي پوٗکهِئِي رِي
کَنوٗ نَہ ڏِين تهوٗ کَنْهِن کهِي تُون مِيڙِئوٗ مَالُ دهَرِين

Nothing else will be of use to thee, except that, which thou hast sown thyself;
Not a grain givest thou to any one, accumulating thou hoardest up treasures. Mēnghō 10.

كِي چِمِكَنِ چِينَ تي كِي لَهَنِ سَمَرْقَنْدِنِ سَارَ

Some (lightenings) flash over China, some take notice of the Samarqandīs. Sh. Sār. IV, 12.

كَرِيَان بِي نَ كَنِ آهَرَ اُنَهِين آهِيَان

I do not other (work) for any, even his I am. Sh. Um. Mār. VII, 5.

The emphatic form of this pronoun is also in frequent use:

SINGULAR.

Nom. كَوئِي kōī, any one; fem. كَائِي kāī.
Format. كَنْهِين kāhī̃.

PLURAL.

Nom. كِيئِي kēī, or كَئِين kaī̃, كَنئِين kāī̃.
Format. كَنِي kanī or كَنْهِين kanhī̃.

دَرِ دوسَنِ چِي كَنئِين جو هُونْدا مُون جيهَا مُشْتَاقَ

Because there will be at the door of my friends some (= several) longing like me. Sh. Jam. Kal. VIII, Epil.

كَنْهِين كَنهِين مَانْهُئِين پِيئِي كَلَ كَائِي

To some, some men some (peculiar) knowledge has been allotted. Sh. Sōr. I, 17.

Instead of the emphatic form of this pronoun كو kō may also be repeated:

كوُ كوُ وِينُ كَلَالِ جوُ پِتِي سِرِ پِئُونَ

Some reproach of the liquor-seller (fem.) has fallen upon their gall-bag. Sh. Jam. Kal. IV, 18.

A neuter form of كوُ is كِي kī, something, a little; it is not inflected.

كَنوُ ڎُهِيلِي ڎَاكهِرِي كَمَنْڎَان كِي كَارِ

With hard labour scoop a little out the heart from the sugar-cane. Golden Alphab. VI, 8.

With a negation كوُ signifies: no one, nobody, and كِي kī: nothing; for emphasis' sake they are frequently reduplicated, in which case the negation is put between them, as: كوُ نَ كوُ kō na kō, nobody at all, كِي نَ كِي kī na kī, nothing at all.

هِنَ زَمَانِي مِين بهَلوُ سوُ بهَائِي
جنهِن وِيَاءُ نَ وَچهُ كوُ نَ پُٽرُ نَ پُهَائِي
نَ كِي هَرِّ نَ هَنْجَ كِي نَ كهَتهوُ نَ كهَاهِي
هِيٺهِ پُرَانِي مَٿهِي ڇهِنَلَ لَڄَ نَ لوءِ كَائِي

In this time that one is a good comrade
Who has no children, no buffalo calf, no son and no fortune;
Nothing in his bundle, nothing in his lap, no blanket, no sack,
A rope, at the bottom old and at the top broken, and no place whatever to live in. Golden Alphab. VII.

هِتوُنِئِين هَمْرَاهُ تهِينْدُءِ كُٽَنْبهَ مَنْجهوُن كوُ نَ كوُ

Not any one from thy family will be thy companion from hence. Mēnghō 3.

When كو is followed by the auxiliary verb آهي āhe (is) with a negation, a contraction takes places, as: كونهي kōnhē (instead of: كو نہ آهي) there is nobody (m.), كانهي kānhe (f.); كونهيكو kōnhēkō, there is nobody at all (m.), كانهيكا kanhēkā (f.); كِينهيكِي kīhēkī, there is nothing at all.

2) The compound indefinite pronoun جيكو jēkō, whoever.

The original form of this pronoun is جوكو jōkō, fem. جاكا jākā, which alone is in use in the Formative Sing. and Plural, in the Nominative Sing. and Plural however the form جيكو jēkō preponderates; it is composed of جي jē, if, and كو kō, literally: if any one. Instead of جيكو or جوكو the reduplicated relative جوجو jōjō (and as its correlative سوسو sōsō) is likewise in use; it is inflected in the same way as the single جو (or سو).

The neutral form of this pronoun, جيكِي jēkī, whatever, is not inflected.

SINGULAR.

Nom.	جيكو jēkō; fem. جيكا jēkā.
Format. / Instrum.	جَنْهِن كَنْهِن jãhē kãhē.
Genit.	جَنْهِن كَنْهِن جو jãhē kãhē jō etc.
Dative.	جَنْهِن كَنْهِن كهي jãhē kãhē khē.
Accus.	جَنْهِن كَنْهِن كهي jãhē kãhē khē. جيكو jēkō; جيكا jēkā.
Ablat.	جَنْهِن كَنْهِن كهَان jãhē kãhē khā̃.

PLURAL.

Nom. جيڪي jēkē.

Format. / Instrum. } جَنِ ڪَنِ ǰane kane; جِنِ ڪِنِ ǰine kine.

Genit. جَنِ ڪَنِ جو ǰane kane ǰō etc.

Dative. جَنِ ڪَنِ کهي ǰane kane khē.

Accus. { جَنِ ڪَنِ کهي ǰane kane khē.
{ جيڪي jēkē.

Ablat. جَنِ ڪَنِ کهان ǰane kane khā̃.

جيڪا هوئِسِ هِينئِي مين تَان سَا ڳَالِ سُڻِينِسِ

Whatever (word) be in his mind, hear that his word. Maǰ. 43.

جيڪِي جَپِينْدِين جَڳَدِيسَ کهي سو سَنْگِي تهِينْدُهه سَانُ

Whatever thou wilt pray to the Lord of the world, that will be thy companion (i. e. to the other world). Mēnghō 9.

Instead of جوڪو ǰōkō the poëts very frequently use ڪوجو, reverting the order of the two pronouns.

ڪَا جَا ڳَالهِ ڳرِي بِيجَلَ ٻُنْدَهَاء مُون

Whatever thing thou hast to say, o Bīǰalu, let me hear that! Sh. Sōr. II, 17.

جي جي وَنَ چَنگو پهَلُ نَ تهَا ڏِيَنِ سي ٻِي وَڍهي بَاهِ مِين تهَا وِجهجَنِ

Which trees soever give no good fruit, those are cut off and thrown into the fire. Matth. 7, 9.

There is also a reduplicated form of this pronoun: جيڪوڪو jēkōkō, but it is only used in the Nominative Sing. and Plural.

SINGULAR.

Nom. جيڪوڪو jēkōkō; fem. جيڪاڪا jēkākā.

PLURAL.

Nom. جيڪيڪي jēkēkē, com.

The neuter form of it is: جيڪيڪي jēkīkī.

جيڪوڪو پنهن جي ڀاء تي ٻي سبب تهو ڪاوڙجي سو عدالت جو ڏهاري تهيندو

Whosoever is angry with his brother without a cause, he will be guilty of judgement. Matth. 5, 2.

Annotation. Another compound of ڪو is هرڪو harkō, every one, whoever (Hindūstānī: harkōī); it is only used in the Singular and inflected regularly, as:

Nom. هرڪو harkō, fem. هرڪا harkā;

Format. هرڪنهن harkāhē, com.

§. 37.

VII. THE RECIPROCAL PRONOUN
پاڻ pāṇa, 'self'.

The reciprocal pronoun in Sindhī is پاڻ pāṇa, 'self', in person, in contradistinction to پاڻُ pāṇu, s. m., one's own person or personality. It is derived from the Sansk. आत्मा, soul, self, which becomes in Prākrit either अप्पा (Var. III, 48) or अप्पाण (Var. V, 45). From the latter Prākrit form appāṇa, the Sindhī پاڻ has sprung by dropping the first syllable 'ap'.

Annotation. The Marāṭhī reciprocal pronoun āpaṇ points likewise back to the Prākrit appāṇa, whereas the Hindūstānī āp (possessive: ap-nā) is to be traced back to the Prākrit form appā; similarly the Panjābī: āp, possessive āp-ṇā. In Gujarātī both Prākrit forms reappear: āp, and possessive: apaṇ-nō.

From the original signification of پَانَ pāṇa, 'soul' (like the Hebrew נֶפֶשׁ), its application may be easely explained. It refers in a sentence always to the chief-subject, be it distinctly expressed or only tacitly understood. In the Genitive (پَانْهَن جو pãhã ǰō etc.), which serves as a possessive pronoun, it may be translated by 'own'; but at the same time it points out with a peculiar nicety the subject, to which it must be referred, and may then be translated by the respective possessive pronoun, required by the subject.

SINGULAR and PLURAL.

Nom. پَانَ pāṇa, self; masc. and fem.
Format. }
Instrum. } پَانَ pāṇa.
Genit. پَانْهَن جو pãhã ǰō; پَنْهَن جو pãhã ǰō; پَان جو pã ǰō (in Lāṛ).
Dative. }
Accusat. } پَانَ کهي pāṇa khē.
Ablat. پَانَان paṇã; پَانَ کهَان pāṇa khã.

An adverbial form is پَانَهِين pāṇahī̃, of, from, by himself or themselves, in person; in a similar sense the Ablative پَانَان pāṇã is also used.

پَانَهِين سُنجَاڻي پَانُ پَانَ کَر پَانُ لهي

پَانَهِين پَسي پَانَ کهي پَانَهِين هِيئُ محْبُوبُ

By himself he knows his own person; his own person takes notice of himself;
By himself he sees himself; by himself he is beloved. Sh. Kal. I, 18.

پَانْهِن جو آهِين پَانَ آڏو محِيبَن کهي

Thou theyself art thy own (i. e. thy soul's friend);

thou (thyself art) in presence of (thy) friends. Sh. Ābirī V, 12.

پُوجَا كَرِ مَ پَانَ كهي جوڳي رَكهِج جوڳ

Do not worship thyself; o Jōgī, keep (thy) devotion! Sh. Rāmakalī VII, 20.

تُون پَنْهَن جي ڀاءُ كهي كِينئَ چَوَنْدِين تَ مُون كهي پَنْهَن جي اَكهِ مَون كَتَرُ كَڍهَنُ ڏي

How wilt thou say to thy brother: let me pull out the mote from thy eye? Matth. 7, 4.

In this last sentence the subject, to which the reciprocal pronoun is to be referred, must be found out from the context or the emphasis of the speaker.

دهُرِ dhure is not a reciprocal pronoun, as alleged by Capt. Geo. Stack; it is the Locative of دهُرُ dhuru, 'extremity', 'exact spot' (Panǰābī: dhur, adv.), used adverbially. The same is to be remarked of پِنْڊِ pinḍe, which is the Locative of پِنْڊُ pinḍu, s. m. 'body', and signifies: 'in person'. For this reason its Genitive is پِنْڊَ جو pinḍa jō etc.

پَرَ پُڇهُ پِنْڊُ پَانْهَن جو مَنْجهِس مُنْهُ پَايو

But ask thy own body (i. e. thyself), having turned thy face upon it. Golden Alphabet 43, 7.

'One another' is expressed in Sindhī in the following way:

هِينئَا هيكڙا ٻِئَنِ كهي سَدَائِين سَارِينِ

Their hearts always remember each other. Maj. 200.

§. 38.

VIII. PRONOMINAL ADJECTIVES.

Under this head we class only such adjectives, as participate more or less of the nature of pronouns and are somewhat irregular in their inflexion, and such, as are derived from pronominal themes. All other adjectives, which may, according to their position in a sentence, supply the place of the pronoun, we exclude from this list, such as: ڦُلاڻو fulāṇō, a certain person, هِڪِڙو hikiṛō, one, ٻِئو ƀiō, another, سَڄو sajō, whole, as they are treated and constructed as regular adjectives.

1) Indefinite pronominal adjectives.

We have to deal here with the pronominal adjectives سَڀُ sabhu, whole, all, every one; the emphatic form of which is سَڀوئِي sabhōī; with the compound سَڀُڪو sabhukō, every one, and مِڙيوئِي miṛyōī or مِڙوئِي miṛōī, all, whole, every one.

a) The pronominal adjective سَڀُ sabhu.

It is derived from the Sansk. सर्व, Prāk. सव्व; Hindūstānī: sab (Marāṭhī: sarv); in Sindhī b has been aspirated (as in Panjābī: sabh) on account of the elided r (see: Introd. §. 15, B. *c*.)

SINGULAR.

Nom.	سَڀُ sabhu; fem. سَڀَ sabha.
Format. / Instrum.	سَڀَ sabha, com.
Genit.	سَڀَ جو sabha jō etc.
Dative.	سَڀَ کهي sabha khē.

Accus. { سَبهَ کهي sabha khē.
سَبهُ sabhu; fem. سَبهَ sabha.

Ablat. سَبهَ کهَان sabha khā̃.

PLURAL.

Nom. سَبهِ sabhe, com.

Format. Instrum. } سَبهَنِ sabhane, سَبهِنِ sabhine; سَبهِنِنِ sabhinine; سَبهين sabhẽ.

Genit. سَبهَنِ جو sabhane jō etc.

Dative. سَبهَنِ کهي sabhane khē etc.

Accus. { سَبهَنِ کهي sabhane khē.
سَبهِ sabhe.

Ablat. سَبهَنِئَان sabhaneā̃ (سَبهِنَان sabhinā̃).
سَبهَنِ کهَان sabhane khā̃ etc.

In the Nom. Plur. we find occasionally سَبهي sabhē written, instead of سَبهِ sabhe. In the Formative Plural سَبهين sabhẽ may be used, instead of سَبهَنِ etc., when the noun immediately follows in the Formative (ẽ).

عُمَرِ سَبهَ عَبَثُ وَقْتَ وِنجَايَمِ پَانْهِن جَا

My whole life is useless; my time (pl.) has been lost by me. Sh. Surāg. V, Epil.

اَللّٰهَ اُنَ پِرنِئَ جَا سَبهي کَاجَ سَرَنِ

By Allah all the undertakings of that friend are carried out. Maj. 688.

وِيتهَا پَڑهَنِ پِرتِ سين نِتُ ترِمَايو نينَ

جِلْدَ سُونْهَارَا سَبهين پَرين بِنَّا مُصْحَفَ موچَارَا

Sitting they read with love, causing always their eyes to shed tears;

Volumes beautiful in all ways, and other elegant books. Maj. 140. 141.

سَائِنِيَ جو سَوْگَنْدُ جو سَاجَنُ سَبهِنَان سُنْهِنو

It is an oath of the Lord (i. e. by the Lord), that my friend is the most beautiful. Sh. Barvō Sindhī II, 6.

b) The pronominal adjective سَبْهوئِي sabhōī.

The inflection of سَبهوئِي, 'all', 'whole', 'every one', is somewhat irregular.

SINGULAR.

Nom. سَبهوئِي sabhōī; fem. سَبهَائِي sabhāī.

Format. / Instrum. } سَبهيئِي sabhēī; fem. سَبهَائِيَ sabhāia.
etc. etc.

PLURAL.

Nom. سَبهيئِي sabhēī, or: سَبهَئِي sabhaī, com.

Format. / Instrum. } سَبهِنِي sabhinī or: سَبهِنِين sabhinī̃.
etc. etc.

Ablat. سَبهِنَانئِي sabhinā̃ī or: سَبهِنِئَانئِي sabhineā̃ī.

آءُ پُنْهُون پيهِي وِئَّا سُور سَبهيئِي

Come in, o Punhū̃! all pains are gone! Sh. Dēsī II, Epil.

سَبهِنِي جِي سَيِّدُ چَوِي آهِي اُتِ اَمَانَ

The safety of all, says the Sayyid, is there. Sh. Ābirī V, 6.

توڏِيَ کهِي تَعْظِيمَ بِيُنِ سَبهِنَانئِي اَگرِي

To Tōḍī (Suhiṇī) belongs more honour than to all (others). Sh. Suh. III, 9.

c) The pronominal adjective سَبھُڪو sabhukō.

The compound pronominal adjective سَبھُڪو sabhukō is inflected as follows:

SINGULAR.

Nom. سَبھُڪو sabhukō; fem. سَبھَڪا sabhakā.

Format. سَبھَڪنھن sabhakāhẽ, com.

etc. etc. etc.

PLURAL.

Nom. سَبھَڪي sabhakē, com.

Format. سَبھَڪن sabhakane.

etc. etc. etc.

There is also a neuter form of this pronoun: سَبھُڪِي sabhukī. The emphatic form سَبھُڪوئِي sabhukōī is also used (see ڪوئِي).

سَانُوَنِ گھِري سَبھَڪا ھِيئَ سَرَھِي سِيَارِي

In Sāvaṇ (July—August) every one slips (into the river), this one (goes into it) merry in the cold season. Sh. Suh. III, 17.

اَچَان وِيلھَ سَبھَڪنھِين وَنجَان وَاجھَائِي

I come at every time, using shifts I go. Sh. Barvō Sindhī II, 7.

پِي پِيَالو عِشْق جو سَبھُڪِي سَمُجھوسُون

Having drunk a cup of love we understood every thing. Sh. Kal. II, Epil.

d) The pronominal adjective مِڙيوئِي miṛyōī.

The pronominal adjective مِڙيوئِي miṛyōī or مِڙوئِي miṛōī is inflected in the same manner as سَبھوئِي sabhōī.

SINGULAR.

Nom. مِڙيوئِي miṛyōī or: مِڙوئِي miṛōī; fem. مِڙيائِي miṛyāī.
Format. مِڙيئِي miṛyēī or: مِڙيئِي miṛēī; fem. مِڙيائِيَ miṛyāia.
etc. etc. etc.

PLURAL.

Nom. مِڙيئِي miṛyēī or مِڙيئِي miṛēī; مِڙئِي miṛaī (in Lāṛ); com.
Format. مِڙِنِي miṛinī; مِڙيَنِي miṛyanī.
etc. etc.
Ablat. مِڙِنئان miṛineā̃ or: مِڙِنِي کهَان miṛinī khā̃.

مِڙيوئِي چَنْگو وَنُ چَنْگو ڦهَلُ ڏهو ڏِئِي

Every good tree gives good fruit. Matth. 7, 17.

جِئَنُ نَاهِي جَڳَ مين ڏِينْهَ مِڙيئِي ٻُون

There is no living in the world; all the days (of life) are two. Sh. Kal. II, Epil.

مِڙِنئُون موکَل ڪالهَ کَنْدَا وِئا ڪاپَڙِي

The devotees, taking yesterday leave from all, went off. Sh. Rāmakalī VII, Epil.

The Locative Sing. masc. مِڙيئِي miṛēī, 'in all', 'throughout', 'altogether', is very frequently used, where we would employ the simple adjective all, whole; but it is to be noticed, that the Locative مِڙيئِي miṛēī always follows immediately the noun, on which the stress is thus to be laid.

لَڳو ڪوسو وَاءُ لوڪُ مِڙيئِي لَهَسِئو

A hot wind has set in; the world in all (i. e. the whole world) has been singed. Sh. Ābirī I, 11.

رَاتُو مِڙِيئِي رَتَ سَان ڪَارَنِ ڪَانڌهَ ڪَکوُر

The gravel-stone throughout (i. e. all) make red with blood for the sake of (thy) husband. Sh. Ābirī VIII, 8.

جَاجِڪَ تو مَتهاءِ مِلڪَ مِڙِيئِي گهورِيَان

O bard! upon thee (i. e. for thy sake) I sacrifice all (my) property. Sh. Sōr. IV, 10.

2) Correlative adjectives.

The Sindhī possesses a great facility to derive correlative adjectives from pronominal bases.

a) The pronominal adjectives, denoting 'quantity' are formed by affixing to the original Sanskrit-Prākrit bases or other bases formed alike, the adjectival termination rō, as: ڪيتِرو kētirō, how much? Sansk. कियत् Prāk. केत्तिअ. As similar phenomenon is to be noticed in the cognate idioms, as Hindūstānī: kittā and kitnā; Panjābī: kit-nā; Marāṭhī: kitī or with the affix k: kitīk; Gujarātī: kēt-lō; but Bangālī: kat.

b) The pronominal adjectives denoting 'size', are formed by affixing to the respective pronominal base the termination: ڏو ḍō, as: ڪيڏو kēḍō, how large? This termination is properly not an adjectival affix, but an adjective: وڏو vaḍō, 'great', the first syllable of which is dropped in this composition. This is clearly proved by the Marāṭhī, as: kē-vaḍhā, how great, and the Gujarātī: kē-vaṭō (but Panjābī: kē-ḍā, as in Sindhī).

All these pronominal adjectives admit again of a diminutive form, by adding the affix ṛō (see §. 11), as: ڪيڏِڙو kēḍiṛō, how small?

c) The pronominal adjectives denoting 'kind' are formed by adding to the pronominal bases kēha, jēha, tēha, ēha, hūa (ūha), the diminutive affix ṛō, in consequence of which the long vowel of the pronominal base is shortened to its corresponding short one, as: کِهَڙو kĕhaṛō, of what kind or manner?

The pronominal bases, from which these three kinds of adjectives are derived, are: ē or hē, this; ō (ū) and hō (hū), that; the relative ǰō (ǰē), the correlative sō (tē), and the interrogative kē.

We exhibit them in the following survey:

From the base:	Quantity.	Size.		Kind.
ē or hē	ايتِرو ētirō	ايڊو ēḍ̄ō	ايڊِڙو ēḍiṛō	اِهَڙو ĕhaṛō
	هيتِرو hētirō	هيڊو hēḍ̄ō	هيڊِڙو hēḍiṛō	هِئَڙو hiaṛō
	this much.	as large as this	as small as this	of this kind.
ō or hō	اوتِرو ōtirō	اوڊو ōḍ̄ō	اوڊِڙو ōḍiṛō	اُهَڙو uhaṛō
	هوتِرو hōtirō	هوڊو hōḍ̄ō	هوڊِڙو hōḍiṛō	هُئَڙو huaṛō
	that much	as large as that	as small as that	of that kind.
ǰō (ǰē) and sō (tē)	جيتِرو ǰētirō	جيڊو ǰēḍ̄ō	جيڊِڙو ǰēḍiṛō	جِهَڙو ǰĕhaṛō
	as much	as large	as small	of which kind.
	تيتِرو tētirō	تيڊو tēḍ̄ō	تيڊِڙو tēḍiṛō	تِهَڙو tĕhaṛō
	so much	so large	so small	of that kind.
kē	ڪيتِرو kētirō[1]	ڪيڊو kēḍ̄ō	ڪيڊِڙو kēḍiṛō	ڪِهَڙو kĕhaṛō
	how much	how large	how small	of what kind.

All these correlative adjectives are inflected regularly, according to their respective termination (masc. and fem.).

1) Not to be confounded with ڪيتِرو is the interrogative pronominal adjective ڪَنئُون kăō̃, which of more than two, Sansk. कतम; about its formation see Introd. §. 9.

§. 39.

IX. PRONOMINAL SUFFIXES,

attached to nouns and postpositions.

Instead of the inflected cases of the absolute personal and possessive pronouns the Sindhī uses very extensively the so-called suffixes or pronouns, which are affixed to nouns, postpositions (adverbs) and verbs. The use of these suffixes constitutes quite a peculiar feature of the Sindhī language and distinguishes it very a̠dva̠ntageously from all the kindred idioms of India, which are destitute of pronominal suffixes; but at the same time the construction of the sentences is very frequently thereby rendered so intricate, that it presents great embarrasments to a beginner. In this respect the Sindhī quite agrees with the Paṣ̌tō and the Persian, being the connecting link between the Indian and Iranian languages.

Here we shall describe the manner, in which the suffixes are attached to nouns and postpositions; the verbal suffixes will be treated in their proper place.

The pronominal suffixes, which are added to nouns and adverbs, are:

	Singular.	Plural.
I pers.	مِ me.	اُون ū̃ or هُون hū̃.
II pers.	ـه e.	وَ va.
III pers.	سِ se.	نِ ne or نَ na.

The suffix of the I pers. Sing. me corresponds to the Prākrit Genitive Sing. मे my; the Persian suffix is ـَم am, Paṣ̌tō me, as in Sindhī.

The suffix of the II pers. Sing. ĕ has sprung from the Sansk. Genitive Sing. ते, thy, t being elided in Sindhī according to Prākrit rule (see Introd. §. 7). In Persian final e (tē) has been dropped and t preserved (= at), whereas the Paṣ̊tō has retained the original form of this pronoun, only with transition of the tenuis into the media = د de.

The suffix of the III pers. Sing. se is to be referred to the Prākrit Genitive से (shortened from अस्य), literally: hujus. In Persian it has become ـَش, whereas in Paṣ̊tō s has been changed to h (Zend hē) and then altogether elided = يْ ē.

The suffix of the I pers. Plur. ũ or hũ accedes to postpositions only, no suffix of the I pers. Plur. being in use with nouns. It is a contraction from the Prāk. Genitive Plur. अम्हो, the first syllable being dropped in Sindhī. The Persian form is مَا mā, Paṣ̊tō مُو mū or اُم um.

The suffix of the II pers. Plur. وَ va is derived from the Sansk.-Prāk. Genitive Plur. वो; Persian on the other hand شُما (pointing to the Sansk. Genit. Plur. युष्माकम्) but Paṣ̊tō مُو mū (m = v).

The suffix of the III pers. Plur. ne or na has apparently sprung from an old pronominal base न na, which is already in Pāli substituted for सो, that; the Prāk. Genit. Plur. would be णोहिं (cf. Lassen p. 325; Var. VI, 4), shortened ne, or na from णाण.

These suffixes, according to their etymology, supply, when attached to nouns, the place of possessive pronouns; but when joined with postpositions or adverbs, they may stand in lieu of any inflected personal pronoun. The suffix however, which properly belongs to the noun, may also be attached to the verb, as will be explained under the verbal suffixes.

§. 40.

I. Pronominal suffixes attached to nouns.

When a suffix accedes to a noun, its final vowel undergoes in some instances a change. But it is to be noticed, that the suffixes are not used promiscuously with nouns, but for the most part only with those referring to man, far less with those referring to animals or to inanimate objects.

In the Nominative Singular:

1) Nouns ending in 'u' undergo no change before the suffixes.
2) Nouns ending in ō generally shorten the same to 'u'; but ō may also keep its place before the suffixes.
3) Masc. nouns ending in ī change the same for euphony's sake either to yu or to ya.
4) Fem. nouns ending in ī change the same either to ya or shorten it to 'i'.
5) Nouns ending in 'e' (i) remain unaltered before the suffixes.

In the Formative Singular the suffixes accede to the final vowel without any further change, with the exception of nouns ending in ō, the Formative Singular of which terminates before suffixes in ă, and not in ē.

In the Nominative Plural a final long vowel is shortened respectively and final nasal n dropped before the suffixes; but final ī of masc. nouns is changed to ya, as in the Nom. Sing.

In the Formative Plural the suffixes accede to the termination ne without any further change.

Nouns ending in ū (ũ) and ā are hardly ever found with suffixes; of nouns ending in 'a' there are some instances, but they are very rare, and only found in poëtry. On the whole the suffixes are for the most part attached to nouns ending in 'u' and ō, far less to those ending in ī (masc. and fem.) and 'e'.

The way, in which the suffixes are attached to nouns, may best be learnt from the following examples.

1) Nouns ending in u (masc.)

Nom. Sing. نيڻُ nēṇu, eye; Format. نيڻَ nēṇa.

Nominative.

Sing. {
I pers. نيڻُمِ néṇume, my eye.
II pers. نيڻُئِ néṇue, thy eye.
III pers. نيڻُسِ néṇuse, his eye.

Formative.

Sing. {
I pers. نيڻَمِ néṇame; نيڻَهِمِ néṇahime.
II pers. نيڻَئِ nénae; نيڻَهِ néṇahe.
III pers. نيڻَسِ néṇase; نيڻَهِنْسِ néṇahīse.

Nominative.

Plur. {
II pers. نيڻُوَ néṇuva, your eye.
III pers. نيڻُنِ néṇune, their eye.

Formative.

Plur. {
II pers. نيڻَوَ néṇava; نيڻَهِنْوَ néṇahīva.
III pers. نيڻَنِ néṇane; نيڻَهِنِ néṇahine.

Nom. Plur. نيڻَ nēṇa; Form. نيڻَنِ nēṇane.

		Nominative.	*Formative.*
Sing.	I pers.	نيڻَمِ néṇame, my eyes.	نيڻَنِمِ néṇanime.
	II pers.	نيڻَئِ néṇa-e, thy eyes.	نيڻَنِي néṇanī.
	III pers.	نيڻَسِ néṇase, his eyes.	نيڻَنِسِ nénanise.

	Nominative.	Formative.
Plur.	II pers. نيڻَو nēṇava, your eyes.	نيڻَنِو nēṇaniva.
	III pers. نيڻَن nēṇane, their eyes.	نيڻَنِن nēṇanine.

In the Formative Sing. there is instead of the suffix me, the form hime also in use, as: نيڻَهِم nēṇahime; and instead of se we find likewise the form hise, as: نيڻَهِس nēṇahise. In the Format. Plur. the suffix of the II pers. ĕ is generally contracted with the final e of the termination ne to ē (ẽ) or even ī, or hĕ is affixed, to avoid a hiatus, as: نيڻَني nēṇanē, نيڻَني nēṇanī or: نيڻَنهِ nēṇanehe.

In poëtry final 'u' is frequently lengthened again to ō before the suffixes; but final 'a' may also be likewise lengthened, if required by the metre, as: نيڻَانَ nēṇāna, instead of نيڻَنَ nēṇana.

Some nouns of this class, which do not change final 'u' in the Formative Singular, are somewhat irregular in attaching the suffixes. These are: پِئُ piu, father, ڀاءُ bhāu, brother, ماءُ māu, mother, ڌِيُ dhiu, daughter, نُهُ nuhu, daughter-in-law.

پِئُ piu, father.

SINGULAR.

Nomin. and Format.: پِئُ piu.

Sing.
- I pers. پِئُم piume; پِئَام piāme; پِنْهَم pinhame; پِنْهِم pinhime, my father.
- II pers. پِئُي piu-e; پِئَاءِ piāe; پِنْهي pinhē, thy father.
- III pers. پِئُس piuse; پِئَاس piāse; پِنْهَس pinhase, his father.

Plur. { II pers. پِئُوَ piuva; پِيَاوَ piāva; پِنْهَوَ piṇhava, your father.
III pers. پِئُنَ piuna; پِنْهُنِ piṇhune, their father. }

PLURAL.

Nomin. پِئُرَ piura; Format. پِئُرَنِ piurane or: پِئُنِ piune.

		Nominative.	*Formative.*
Sing.	I pers.	پِئُرَمِ piurame, my fathers;	پِئُرَنِمِ piuranime. پِئُنِمِ piunime.
	II pers.	پِئُرَئِ piura-e, thy fathers;	پِئُنِي piunī.
	III pers.	پِئُرَسِ piurase, his fathers;	پِئُنِسِ piunise.
Plur.	II pers.	پِئُرَوَ piurava, your fathers;	پِئُنِوَ piuniva.
	III pers.	پِئُرَنَ piurana, their fathers;	پِئُنِنِ piunine.

بهَاءُ bhāu, brother.

SINGULAR.

Nominative and Formative بهَاءُ bhāu.

Sing. { I pers. بهَائُمِ bhāume; بهَامِ bhāme; بهَانَمِ bhā-ṇame, بهَانِمِ bhāṇime, my brother.
II pers. بهَاءِ bhā-e; بهَانِي bhāṇē, thy brother.
III pers. بهَاسِ bhāse; بهَانُسِ bhāṇuse, his brother. }

Plur. { II pers. بهَائُوَ bhāuva, بهَانُوَ bhāṇuva, your brother.
III pers. بهَائُنَ bhāuna, their brother. }

PLURAL.

Nomin.: بهائُرَ bhāura; Format.: بهائُرَنِ bhāurane or: بهائُنِ bhāune.

Nominative.	*Formative.*
I pers. بهائُرَمِ bhāurame, my brothers.	بهائُرَنِمِ bhāuranime. بهائُنِمِ bhāunime.
etc.	etc.

ماءُ māu, mother.

SINGULAR.

Nominative and Formative: ماءُ māu.

Sing.
- I pers. مائُمِ māume; مَامِ māme; مَانْهِمِ māṇhime, my mother.
- II pers. مَاءِ māe; مَانِي maṇe, thy mother.
- III pers. مائُسِ māuse; مَاسِ māse; مَانُسِ māṇuse; مَانِسِ māṇise, his mother.

Plur.
- II pers. مَاوَ māva; مَانُوَ māṇuva, your mother.
- III pers. مَانِ māne; مَانُنِ māṇune, their mother.

PLURAL.

Nomin.: مائُرَ māura; Format.: مائُنِ māune.

Nominative.	*Formative.*
I pers. مائُرَمِ māurame, my mothers;	مائُنِمِ māunime.
etc.	etc.

دهِئُ dhiu, daughter.

SINGULAR.

Nomin. and Format. دهِئُ dhiu (دهِئَ dhia).

Sing. I pers. دهِئُمِ dhiume; دهِئَمِ dhiame; دهِينَمِ dhīṇame; دهِينِمِ dhīṇime, my daughter.

Sing. { II pers. دهِيَئِ dhiya-e; دهِيني dhīne, thy daughter.
III pers. دهِئُسِ dhiuse, دهِئَسِ dhiase; دهِينُسِ dhīnuse, his daughter.

PLURAL.

Nomin.: دهِئَرُ dhiaru; Format.: دهِئُنِ dhiune.

	Nominative.	*Formative.*
I pers.	دهِئَرُمِ dhiarume, my daughters.	دهِئُنِمِ dhiunime.
	etc.	etc.

نُهُ nuhu (or: نُهَ), daughter-in-law.

SINGULAR.

Nominative and Formative: نُهُ nuhu.

Sing. { I pers. نُهُمِ nuhume; نُهَمِ nuhame; نُهِنَمِ nuhiname; نُهِنِمِ nuhinime, my daughter-in-law.
II pers. نُهُئِ nuhu-e; نُهي nuhē; نُهِني nuhinē, thy daughter-in-law.
III pers. نُهُسِ nuhuse; نُهَسِ nuhase; نُهِنِسِ nuhinise, his daughter-in-law.

Plur. { II pers. نُهُوَ nuhuva, your daughter-in-law.
III pers. نُهُنِ nuhune; نُهَنِ nuhane, their daughter-in-law.

PLURAL.

Nomin.: نُهَرُ nuharu; Format.: نُهَنِ nuhane.

	Nominative.	*Formative.*
I pers.	نُهَرُمِ nuharume, my daughters-in-law.	نُهُنِمِ nuhunime.
	etc.	etc.

A noun with suffixes may be followed by postpositions; in this case the suffixes are added to the Formative of a noun.

مَاڙهُنِ چَيو مَائُسِ کهِي تَہ تُون پَانَ پُڇهِينْسِ

The people said to his mother: ask him thyself. Maj. 42.

اُهو پُٽرُء بَنِ پَوِي جو بهَائِمِ جو سِرُ وَڍهِي

May that thy son fall into the forest (i. e. away with that thy son), who will cut off my brother's head. Story of Rāe Diāču p. 1.

اَمَڙِ کهُهِ گهَروء مُونْهَان وَنجِي سَاتهَڙو

O mother, away with thy house (literally: to the well with thy house); away from me goes the little caravan. Sh. Hus. II, 7.

جهوَلَ نَہ جهَلِي سُنْهِنِي سَائِرَ سَتَ سَنْدِيَاسِ

جَنْهِن اِهَڙِي جَائِي عَاجِزَان سَا مَرُ مَرْکِي مَاسِ

پَسِين جِي پِمَّاسِ تَہ کِي عِشْقُ آنِئِين

By no perplexity was Suhiṇī kept back; in the stream was her devotion;

From which poor (woman) such a one was born, that her mother may well boast:

If thou seest her father, thou mayst also love him a little. Sh. Suh. III, 13.

مَاء ۽ بهَائُرَء بَاهَرِ بِيتهَا آهِينِ

Thy mother and thy brothers are standing outside. Matth. 12, 47.

مَانِسِ ۽ بهَائُرَنِسِ بَاهَرِ بِهِي سَائُسِ ڳالهَائِنُ گهُريو

His mother and his brothers, standing outside, wished to speak to him. Matth. 12, 46.

وِهَان جَان مَاٿهِہ کَرِي وِسَارِي وِيٺَانِ

تَان وَارِيَ جِينئَ وَنجِي هِنٿَون کِنِکِٿو کِيٺَانِ

When I sit in silence, having forgotten their abuses,
Then my heart goes like sand, moaning after them.
Maǰ. 679, 680.

اَجُ نَہ ڳَالهَائُونَ هُونِ ڏِينهَاڙِي ڀِجهِرِي

To-day there is no talk (ڳَالهَاءُ) of theirs; they are the whole day in the hut. Sh. Mūm. Rēṇō V, 12.

2) Nouns ending in ō.

Nouns ending in ō do not differ essentially from those in 'u', as regards the annexion of the suffixes; they generally shorten final ō to 'u', but they may also retain the same in the Nom. Sing., which is frequently the case in poëtry. The Formative Sing. always terminates in 'a', not in ē, when followed by suffixes. In the Nomin. Plural final ā may be likewise preserved before suffixes, instead of being shortened to 'a'.

مَتهو mathō, head.

SINGULAR.

Nom.: مَتهو mathō; Form.: مَتهي mathē = مَتهَہ matha.

		Nominative.	*Formative.*
Sing.	I pers.	مَتهُمِ mathume, my head;	مَتهَمِ[1]) mathame; مَتهَہِمِ mathahime.
	II pers.	مَتهُئِي[2]) mathu-e, thy head;	مَتهَئِي matha-e; مَتهَہِ mathahe.
	III pers.	مَتهُسِ mathuse, his head;	مَتهَسِ mathase; مَتهَہِنْسِ mathahīse.

1) In Sirō the people very commonly substitute 'i' instead of 'a' in the Formative Sing. as: مَتهِمِ mathime etc.

2) In poëtry the long vowels may be retained, as: مَتهوءِ ma-thō-e, مَتهَانِ mathā-na.

Plur.
- II pers. مَتهُو your head; مَتهَو mathava; مَتهَهِنْو mathahīva.
  mathuva,
- III pers. مَتهُنِ their head; مَتهَنِ mathane; مَتهَهَنِ mathahane.
  mathune,

PLURAL.

Nomin.: مَتهَا mathā; Format.: مَتهَنِ mathane.

		Nominative.	*Formative.*
Sing.	I pers.	مَتهَمِ mathame, my heads;	مَتهَنِمِ mathanime.
	II pers.	مَتهَيْ matha-e, thy heads;	مَتهَنِي mathanī; مَتهَنِهِ mathanihe.
	III pers.	مَتهَسِ mathase, his heads.	مَتهَنِسِ mathanise.
Plur.	II pers.	مَتهَو mathava, your heads.	مَتهَنِو mathaniva.
	III pers.	مَتهَنِ mathane, their heads.	مَتهَنِنِ mathanine.

کِیرُ آنهِین کِتهَان هَلِین کُنجَارُو نَالوِ

Who art thou, whence comest thou, what is thy name? Maj. 167.

جِتِي نَظَرُ نَاتهَ جو اُتِي اوتَارَانَ
اِهِي اُهُنجَاتَانَ لِکَا بهُنَنِ لوکَ مِین

Where the sight of the Lord is, there are their abodes.

These are their tokens: concealed they wander about in the world. Sh. Rāmak. II, 9.

3) Nouns ending in ī (masc.)

Nouns ending in ī (m.) generally change the same to ya, far less to yu, before the accession of the suffixes; in the Formative Sing. ē must always be changed to ya. The same is the case in the Nom. Plur., so that only the context can decide, whether a noun is put in the Nominative or Formative Sing. or in the Nominative Plural.

In poëtry a final short vowel may be lengthened before a suffix, as: دھَنیَاسِ dhaṇyāse, instead of: دھَنیَسِ dhaṇyase.

SINGULAR.

Nom.: دھَنِي dhaṇī, master; Form.: دھَنِیَ dhaṇya.

		Nominative.	*Formative.*
Sing.	I pers.	دھَنیَمِ dhaṇyame,	دھَنیَمِ dhaṇyame.
		دھَنیُمِ dhaṇyume, my master.	
	II pers.	دھَنیَئِ dhaṇya-e,	دھَنیَئِ dhaṇya-e.
		دھَنیُئِ dhaṇyu-e, thy master.	دھَنیَھِ dhaṇyahe.
	III pers.	دھَنیَسِ dhaṇyase,	دھَنیَسِ dhaṇyase.
		دھَنیُسِ dhaṇyuse, his master.	
Plur.	II pers.	دھَنیَوَ dhaṇyava,	دھَنیَوَ dhaṇyava.
		دھَنیُوَ dhaṇyuva, your master.	
	III pers.	دھَنیَنِ dhaṇyane,	دھَنیَنِ dhaṇyane,
		دھَنیُنِ dhaṇyune, their master.	

PLURAL.

Nom.: دهَنِي dhaṇī; Format.: دهَنِيُنِ dhaṇyune.

		Nominative.	*Formative.*
Sing.	I pers.	دهَنيَمِ dhaṇyame, my masters.	دهَنيُنِمِ dhaṇyunime.
	II pers.	دهَنيَئِ dhaṇya-e, thy masters.	دهَنيُنِي dhaṇyunī. دهَنيُنِهِ dhaṇyunehe.
	III pers.	دهَنيَسِ dhaṇyase, his masters.	دهَنيُنِسِ dhaṇyunise.
Plur.	II pers.	دهَنيَوَ dhaṇyava, your masters.	دهَنيُنِوَ dhaṇyuniva.
	III pers.	دهَنيَنِ dhaṇyane, their masters.	دهَنيُنِنِ dhaṇyunine.

وِيروِتَارَ وُجُودَ مِين پِريَمِ جِي پَچَارَ

There is constantly in my body the talk of my friend. Sh. Suh. IV, 7.

دهَنِيَمِ كَرِ مَه دهَارَ پَارَؤ تَنِ پِرِيَنِ كهَان

O my master, do not make apart (thy) quarter from those friends. Sh. Barvō III, 5.

جيدَان سَدهَرُ سُكهَنِيَاسِ تيدَان وَهِي وَهه سَامُهُون

Because her steersman is sturdy, therefore she floats facing the current. Sh. Surāg. III, 6.

4) Nouns ending in ī (fem.)

Nouns ending in ī (fem.) either shorten final ī to 'i' before the suffixes or change it to ya; the latter is always the case with adjectives and participles ending in ī. The termination of the Nomin. Plur. ū̃ is shortened to 'u' and the final nasal dropped before the suffixes.

SINGULAR.

Nom.: بَائِي bāī, lady; Format.: بَائِيٰ bā-ia.

		Nominative.	Formative.
Sing.	I pers.	بَائِمِ bāime,	بَايَمِ bāyame.
		بَايَمِ bāyame, my lady.	
	II pers.	بَايِي bāyē,	بَايِيٓ bāya-e.
		بَايِيٓ baya-e, thy lady.	
	III pers.	بَائِسِ bāise,	بَايَسِ bāyase.
		بَايَسِ bāyase, his lady.	
Plur.	II pers.	بَائِوَ bāiva,	بَايَوَ bāyava.
		بَايَوَ bāyava, your lady.	
	III pers.	بَائِنِ bāine,	بَايَنِ bāyane.
		بَايَنِ bāyane, their lady.	

PLURAL.

Nom.: بَايُون bāyū̃; Format.: بَايُنِ bāyune.

		Nominative.	Formative.
Sing.	I pers.	بَايُمِ bāyume, my ladies.	بَايُنِمِ bāyunime.
	II pers.	بَايُيِٓ bāyu-e, thy ladies.	بَايُنِي bāyunī.
	III pers.	بَايُسِ bāyuse, his ladies.	بَايُنِسِ bāyunise.
Plur.	II pers.	بَايُوَ bāyuva, your ladies.	بَايُنِوَ bāyuniva.
	III pers.	بَايُنِ bāyune, their ladies.	بَايُنِنِ bāyunine.

In poëtry final ī is occasionally not changed to ya, but simply to 'a', as:

جيکا پُچَنْدَمِ سَا

if there is any power of mine, it is that. Sh. Kēḍ. IV, 9.

پُپهِي puphī, a father's sister, has, besides the regular forms, also پُپهِنَمِ puphiṇame or: پُپهِنِمِ puphiṇime.

چوڏِهِنيءَ مَاهَ چَنْڊَرَ جِنيءَ پڳ مِين پَاگڙِيَاسِ

Like the moon on the fourteenth of the month was his turban in the plain. Sh. Kēḍ. V, 1.

کوتهِي کَنهِن نَه پُڇهِيَا اَنْدَرِ اَندوهِيَان

Not by any messenger have they been asked; inside is their grief. Sh. Rāmak. VI, 4.

5) Nouns ending in e (fem.)

Nouns ending in ĕ remain either unaltered before suffixes or change final ĕ (i) to ya, as well in the Nominative as in the Formative Singular.

SINGULAR.

Nom.: چهوکرِ čhōkare, girl; Format.: چهوکرِ.

		Nominative.	*Formative.*
Sing.	I pers.	چهوکَرِمِ čhōkarime, thy girl;	the same.
		چهوکَرْيَمِ čhōkaryame.	
	II pers.	چهوکَرِي čhōkarē, thy girl;	the same.
		چهوکَرْيئِ čhōkarya-e.	
		چهوکَرْيَهِ čhōkaryahe.	
	III pers.	چهوکَرِسِ čhōkarise, his girl;	the same.
		چهوکَرْيَسِ čhōkaryase.	

Plur.	II pers.	چھوکرِوَ čhōkariva, your girl; the same.
		چھوکَرْیَوَ čhōkaryava.
	III pers.	چھوکَرِنِ čhōkarine, their girl; the same.
		چھوکَرْیَنِ čhōkaryane.

PLURAL.

Nom.: چھوکَرْیُون čhōkaryū̃; Form.: چھوکَرِنِ čhōkarine.

		Nominative.	Formative.
Sing.	I pers.	چھوکَرْیُمِ čhōkaryume, my girls.	چھوکَرِنِمِ čhōkarinime
	II pers.	چھوکَرْیُیِ čhōkaryu-e, thy girls.	چھوکَرِنِي čhōkarinī
	III pers.	چھوکَرْیُسِ čhōkaryuse, his girls.	چھوکَرِنِسِ čhōkarinise.
Plur.	II pers.	چھوکَرْیُوَ čhōkaryuva, your girls.	چھوکَرِنِوَ čhōkariniva
	III pers.	چھوکَرْیُنِ čhōkaryune, their girls.	چھوکَرِنِنِ čhōkarinine.

The substantive noun جوٗء ǰōe or زوٗء zōe, wife, presents, when joined by suffixes, some irregularities, as:

SINGULAR.

		Nominative.	Formative.
Sing.	I pers.	جوٗئِمِ ǰōime, my wife.	The same.
		جوٗیَمِ ǰōyame;	
		جوٗنَمِ ǰōṇame; جوٗنْھَمِ ǰōṇhame;	
		جوٗنِمِ ǰōṇime; جوٗنْھِمِ ǰōṇhime;	

		Nominative.	*Formative.*
Sing.	II pers.	جوئي ǰōē, جويي ǰōye, thy wife. جويَئي ǰōya-e. جوڻي ǰōṇē, جوڻهي ǰōṇhē.	The same.
	III pers.	جوئِسِ ǰōise, جويَسِ ǰōyase, his wife. جوڻَسِ ǰōṇase; جوڻهَسِ ǰōṇhase.	The same.
Plur.	II pers.	جوئِوَ ǰōiva, جويَوَ ǰōyava, your wife. جوڻَوَ ǰōṇava, جوڻهَوَ ǰōṇhava.	The same.
	III pers.	جوئِنِ ǰōine, جويَنِ ǰōyane, their wife. جوڻَنِ ǰōṇane, جوڻهَنِ ǰōṇhane.	The same.

PLURAL.

	Nominative.	*Formative.*
I pers.	جويُمِ ǰōyume, my wifes.	جويُنِمِ ǰōyunime.
	etc.	etc.

جَڏهين هو عَدالَت جي گادِيءَ تي وِيٺهو تَڏهين جوڻَسِ

چوائي موڪِليُسِ

When he was seated on the judgement seat, his wife sent him word. Matth. 27, 19.

The other nouns, ending in ū, ā, 'a' are generally not used with suffixes, though occasionally one or another is found with a suffix; in this case final ū is changed to 'u' in the Nominative, and in the Formative to ua, whereas ā and 'a' keep their place before suffixes.

جي کا ڄمارانَ[1] سَا مَنجھِ ڪُونْڌَرَ ڪُڌِرِي

Whatever their lifetime is, it has been spent in sorrow. Sh. Rāmak. III, 4.

§. 41.

II. PRONOMINAL SUFFIXES attached to Postpositions and Adverbs.

The rules, according to which pronominal suffixes are attached to nouns, are also applicable in reference to postpositions and adverbs. Any pronominal suffix may be joined with a postposition, but with most of them only the suffix of the third person Singular and Plural is in use. It is however quite optional in Sindhī, either to subjoin a pronominal suffix to a postposition, or to put the absolute pronoun before it in the Formative, with or without the Genitive case-sign جي, as: وَٽِسِ vaṭise, with him, or: هُنَ وَٽِ huna vaṭe.

1) The postposition سَنْدو sandō.

سَنْدو sandō is originally not a postposition, but an adjective, and therefore declinable, as well as جو, the Genitive case-sign, for which it is very frequently substituted (see §. 18). It corresponds to the Panjābī sandā, being (Sansk. part. pres. सन्त = सन्) and signifies therefore: 'belonging to'. It is now used as a regular postposition, chiefly in connexion with suffixes, before such nouns, to which suffixes are not attached, either for the sake of the final vowel, or for perspicuity's sake, or, as in poëtry, for the sake of the metre.

1) Short 'a' may be lengthened to ā in poëtry for the sake of the rhyme.

SINGULAR.

Masc. سَنْدو sandō.

		Nom.: سَنْدو sandō.	Form.: سَنْدَ sanda.
Sing.	I pers.	سَنْدُمِ sandume, my.	سَنْدَمِ sandame.
	II pers.	سَنْدُهٔ sandu-e, thy.	سَنْدَهٔ sanda-e.
	III pers.	سَنْدُسِ sanduse, his.	سَنْدَسِ sandase.
Plur.	I pers.	سَنْدُون sandū̃, our.	سَنْدَئُون sanda-ū̃.
	II pers.	سَنْدُوَ sanduva, your.	سَنْدَوَ sandava.
	III pers.	سَنْدُنِ sandune, their.	سَنْدَنِ sandane.

PLURAL.

		Nom.: سَنْدَا sandā.	Form.: سَنْدَنِ sandane.
Sing.	I pers.	سَنْدَمِ sandame, my.	سَنْدَنِمِ sandanime.
	II pers.	سَنْدَهٔ sanda-e, thy.	سَنْدَنِي sandanī.
	III pers.	سَنْدَسِ sandase, his.	سَنْدَنِسِ sandanise.
Plur.	I pers.	سَنْدَئُون sanda-ū̃, our.	سَنْدِنِئُون sandineū̃.
	II pers.	سَنْدَوَ sandava, your.	سَنْدِنِوَ sandiniva.
	III pers.	سَنْدَنِ sandane, their.	سَنْدَنِنِ sandanine.

It has been stated already (see: nouns ending in ō, §. 40, 2) that ō and ā may also be preserved before the suffixes, as: سَنْدومِ sandōme, سَنْداسِ sandāse etc.

Fem.: سَنْدِي sandī.

SINGULAR.

		Nominative.	*Formative.*
Sing.	I pers.	سَنْدِيَمِ sandyame, my.	The same.
	II pers.	سَنْدِيَئِ sandya-e, thy.	„
	III pers.	سَنْدِيَسِ sandyase, his.	„
Plur.	I pers.	سَنْدِيَئُون sandyaũ, our.	„
	II pers.	سَنْدِيَوَ sandyava, your.	„
	III pers.	سَنْدِيَنِ sandyane, their.	„

PLURAL.

Sing.	I pers.	سَنْدِيُمِ sandyume, my.	سَنْدِيُنِمِ sandyunime.
	II pers.	سَنْدِيُئِ sandyu-e, thy.	سَنْدِيُنِي sandyunī.
	III pers.	سَنْدِيُسِ sandyuse, his.	سَنْدِيُنِسِ sandyunise.
Plur.	I pers.	(not in use).	(not in use).
	II pers.	سَنْدِيُوَ sandyuva, your.	سَنْدِيُنِوَ sandyuniva.
	III pers.	سَنْدِيُنِ sandyune, their.	سَنْدِيُنِنِ sandyunine.

The Plural of سَنْدَوْ is very little in use, سنْدو preceding a noun in the Plural generally in the Singular.

سوئِي سَاتِيهه مُنْهن جو سَاجَنُ جِتِ سَنْدوِمِ

Even that is my native country, where my sweetheart is. Maj. 86.

رَاجُ پَرْتو رَبَّ کهِي سُومَرَا سَنْدوِ

Thy government, o Sūmarō! has been reconciled to the Lord. Sh. Um. Māruī VI, Epil.

مَاڻھُون ڏِينْدَا مِيهَنَا جيڪي سِينَ سَنْدَاء

The people (and) whosoever are thy relatives, will give thee reproaches. Maj. 292.

زَالُنِ مَتهي ٻہ جوٽِيُون
مُڙسَنِ مَتهي وَارَ
هَتهين سوٽِيُون
مَتهين چوٽِيُون
اِهي سَنْدَنَ آچَارَ

The women have on the head two plaits,
The men have on the heads hair:
In the hands sticks,
On the heads plaits:
These are their habits. Verses of the Māmuīs.

جَنَّتَ سَنْدِيَنَ جُوء فَائِق هَلِيَا فِرْدوسَ ڏِي

The garden (of Eden) is their place; the noble ones have gone to Paradise. Sh. Kēḍ. IV, 5.

In poëtry سَنْدوَ is now and then used without suffixes, which must then be supplied from the context:

لَدهَائِي لَطِيفُ چوِي سَنْدَا ڏَانَ ڏِسَنِ

The worthy ones, says Laṯīf, see his gifts. Sh. Sōr. I, 14.

2) Postpositions ending in 'u'.

سَانُ sanu, with.

	SING.	PLUR.
I pers.	سَانُمِ sānume, with me.	سَانُھُون sānuhū̃, with us.
II pers.	سَانُئِي sanu-e, with thee.	سَانُوَ sānuva, with you.
III pers.	سَانُسِ sānuse, with him.	سَانُنِ sanune, with them.

In the same way the suffixes are attached to سِينُ sēṇu, with. In the third person Plural we meet often in poëtry the form سِينَانَ sēṇāna or سِينَانِ sēṇāne, instead of سِينُنِ sēṇune.

جَانِ جَانِ سَانُئِ سَاهُ تَانِ پَارِجِ کو مَ پُنْهُنءَ سَانِ

As long as there is a breath with thee, compare none with Punhū. Sh. Maꜩ. V, 5.

مُنْهِن جو سَاهُ وِئو سِينَانِ آيَلِ وِهَان کِينئَ بهَنْبهورَ مِين

My soul is gone with them, o mother! how shall I sit in Bhambōru? Sh. Hus. XI, Epil.

3) Postpositions ending in ĕ or ē (ẽ).

کَنِ kaṇe or کَنِ kane, near, with, to.

	SING.	PLUR.
I pers.	کَنِمِ kaṇime, to me.	کَنِئُون kaṇeū̃, to us.
II pers.	کَنِي kaṇē, to thee.	کَنِوَ kaṇiva, to you.
III pers.	کَنِسِ kaṇise, to him.	کَنِنِ kaṇine, to them.

About the derivation of کَنِ see §. 16, 4.

Other postpositions of this kind are: گَرِ ḡare, to; وَٽِ vaṭe, near, with; مَنجهِه manjhe, in; هيٺهِ hēṭhe, below etc. Before the suffix of the third person Sing. final i (e) is often lengthened to ī, as: وَٽِينْسِ vaṭīse, near him, and before the suffix of the third person Plur. to ī, as: مَنْجهِينَ manjhīna, in them.

اِيکَ قَصرِ دَرَ لَکهَ سَهَسِين کَنِسِ ڳِنکهِيُون

In one palace there are lakhs of doors, in thousands are to it windows. Sh. Kal. I, 23.

جيکَڏهِين اُنِنِ کَنئُون مَارِئُو تَڏهِين پُنُ کَهَٽِئُو اَساهِنْ جو آهِي

If we are beaten by them, even then it is our advantage. Sindhī Read. Book, p. 64.

کَا جَا ڳَالهِ ڳَرِي بِيجَلَ ٻُنْدهَاء مُون

Whatever be the matter with thee, o Bījalu, let me hear that. Sh. Sōr. II, 17.

ڳَرِنَ مَ ڳَرَهِيجِ رُوئِي ڪِجِ مَ پَڌهِرو

Do not unbosom thyself to them; weeping do not make it public. Sh. Ripa I, 8.

سَنْدَسِ چيلا وَٽِينْسِ آيا

His disciples came unto him. Matth. 5, 1.

Postpositions and adverbs ending in ē are treated differently; they either retain ē before the suffixes or they shorten it to ĕ (i); thus the postposition کهِي khē, the case-sign of the Dative or Accusative, retains its final ē before the suffixes, as: کهِيسِ khēse, to him (her, it), کهِينِ khēne or کهِينَ khēna, to them, whereas اُتِي utē, upon, shortens final ē to ĕ (i) as: اُتِسِ utise, upon him (her, it) or: اُتِهِسِ utehise; اُتِنِ utine, upon them or: اُتِهِنِ utehine. Others again vary, as: مَتهِي mathē, upon (properly the Locative of مَتهو mathō, the head), مَتهَئِي matha-e, upon thee (the Formative of مَتهو), but مَتهِسِ mathise, upon him (being properly the Locative of مَتهُ, the top).

چَوْمَاسوَ چَارِ مَاهَ مَتهَيِ وَسِنَّا مِينْهَ

During the rainy season, four months, rains have fallen upon thee. Maj. 646.

مَتهِسِ نَاهِ مَلَامُ جي كِي پُڇهين پُڇهُ سو

There is no reproach upon it; if thou wilt ask any thing, ask it. Sh. Khambh. I, 10.

To the postposition مين mẽ (in) the suffixes are attached in the following manner: مينْسِ mẽse, in him (her, it) or: مَينسِ maĩse (in Sirō); مَيْنُون maĩnũ, in us; مينِ mēne or مينَ mēna (in Sirō: مَيْنَ maina) in them.

4) Postpositions ending in ā, ã, āũ, õ.

Those, which terminate in ā, remain unaltered before a suffix, as: كِينَاء[1]) to thee, كِنَاسِ kēṇāse, to him, كينَانِ kēṇāne, to them. Similarly كهَان khã, from, as: كهَانْسِ khãse, from him, كهَانِ khane, from them (the final nasal being dropped before a following dental n); مَتهَان mathã, from upon (properly the Ablative of مَتهو mathō, the head), مَتهَانيِ mathãe, from upon thee, مَتهَانْسِ mathãse, from upon him; پُتهِنَّانْسِ puṭhiãse, from behind him, after him (properly the Ablat. of پُتهِ puṭhe, the back).

Before the suffix of the third person Plural a euphonic 'i' is occasionally inserted, especially in poëtry, as: مَنجهَانئِنِ manjhãine, instead of: مَنجهَانِ manjhāne, out of them.

Those ending in āũ, ãu, āu (termination of the Ablat. Sing.) remain likewise unchanged before suffixes, the final

1) This postposition or adverb is never found without suffixes.

nasal only being dropped before them, as: مَتهَانُسِ ma-thãuse, from upon it, مَتهَانوَ mathãuva, from upon you; کهَانُسِ khãuse, from it, کهَانُنِ khãune, from them.

Those ending in õ change it to ã before suffixes, as: پُٺَانسِ puãse, behind him (from پُٺون puõ).

تَڏهِن مَاءِ پُڇهي کهي مَجنِي کِهڙِي لَڳِي کِينَاهِ

Then the mother asked Majnõ: what (matter) has happened to thee? Maj. 44.

آتَنِ مُنْهُن جَا انگڙا کَهَل نَ پوي کِيتَانَ

My limbs melt, no languor befalls them. Sh. Khā-hōṛī, Epil. I.

آنئُون پَانَ مَتهَانئِ گهورِيَان اِينهِين چَيَانئِين

I sacrifice myself for thee; thus he spoke. Maj. 755.

سو سَبهوئِي حَالُ مَنجهَانئِنِ مَعْلُومُ تهِئِي

That whole state becomes known out of them. Sh. Kal. I, 17.

تَان سو عَيْنُ جو غَيْنُ جي مَتهَانسُ نُقْطو ڏُورِ کَرِين

Then that, which is γain, becomes ɛain, if thou remove from it the dot. Sh. Kal. I, 21.

هِيئُ سِرُ سَمَانو گهوتَ مَتهَانوَ گهورِيَان

This head is ready; o bridegroom, for you I sacrifice it. Sh. Kēḍ. IV, 8.

اِهَڙَا ڏِينهَ اِينْدَا جو گهوتُ کهَانئُنِ کهَسِبو

Such days will come, that the bridegroom will be taken from them. Matth. 9, 15.

SECTION III.

THE VERB.

The great deterioration, the modern Indian languages have undergone, is nowhere more apparent, than in their conjugational process. They have lost nearly all the Sanskrit tenses, especially those of the Past, which were too intricate for the conception of the vulgar, and have therefore been compelled to have recourse to compositions, in order to make up for the lost tenses. They differ very greatly as to the method, which they have followed in this respect, every one of them exhibiting some peculiar features, which are not to be met with in the other idioms.

Chapter XII.

Formation of the verbal themes, the Imperative and the Participles.

§. 42.

Formation of the verbal themes.

I. We have seen already (§. 7, 2) that the Infinitive of the Sindhī verbs, terminating in aṇu, corresponds to the verbal noun of the Sanskrit and Prākrit. The root of the Sindhī verb is therefore not to be sought in the Infinitive, but in the Imperative, which exhibits the crude form of the verb without an additional increment, except that of the final vowel, which is no part of the verbal root.

Properly speaking there is only one class of verbs in Sindhī, as all verbs, with a slight difference, are inflected alike. There are therefore no different conjugations, as in Sanskrit, but the same rules of inflection apply equally to all verbs.

In some tenses though there is a marked difference between neuter and active verbs, and we may therefore, for practical purposes, divide the Sindhī verbs into neuter and active ones.

1) The neuter or intransitive verb ends in the Infinitive in aṇu and in the Imperative in 'u', as:

هَلَڻُ hal-aṇu, to go, Imper. هَلُ hal-u, go.

وَرَڻُ var-aṇu, to return, „ وَرُ var-u, return.

But in derivative verbs, where the termination of the Infinitive is preceded by ā, the Infinitive ends, for euphony's sake, in iṇu, as:

ڪارائِڻُ kārā-iṇu, to be blackish, Imper. ڪاراءُ kārā-u.

When the verbal root ends in short 'a' or 'i', a euphonic v is inserted between it and the increment of the Infinitive, as:

پَوَڻُ pa-v-aṇu, to fall, Imper. پَءُ pa-u.

نِوَڻُ ni-v-aṇu, to bow, „ نِءُ ni-u.

2) The active or transitive verb ends in the Infinitive likewise in aṇu (in Sirō commonly in iṇu), and in the Imperative in 'e' (and partly in 'u'), as:

جهَلَڻُ jhal-aṇu, to seize, Imper. جهَلِ jhal-e.

ڦُرَڻُ phur-aṇu, to plunder, „ ڦُرِ phur-e.

But when the increment of the Infinitive is preceded by 'a', ā and ō, the Infinitive ends, for euphony's sake, in iṇu[1]), as:

مَئِڻُ ma-iṇu, to measure, Imper. مَءِ ma-e.

ڳالهائِڻُ gālhā-iṇu, to speak, „ ڳالهاءِ gālhā-e.

ڍوئِڻُ ḍhō-iṇu, to carry, „ ڍوءِ ḍhō-e.

---

1) Some Sindhīs, especially the Musalmāns, write and pronounce instead of āiṇu : ā-aṇu or contracted: āṇu.

If a verbal root (active or neuter) end in ī and ū, these vowels are respectively shortened before the increment of the Infinitive, as:

پِئَڻُ pi-aṇu, to drink, Imper. پِيءُ pī-u.

پُئَڻُ pu-aṇu, to string beads, „ پُوءُ pū-u.

In some instances radical ō is likewise shortened to 'u' in the Infinitive, as:

ڌُئَڻُ dhu-aṇu, to wash, Imper. ڌوءُ dhō-u.

رُئَڻُ ru-aṇu, to weep, „ رو rō.

A number of Sindhī verbs have a different form when used in a neuter or active sense, but it would be wrong to say, that such neuter verbs are changed into an active form; they recur to a different Sanskrit form, from which they are derived and must therefore be considered as independent verbs.

The most common of these are:

Neuter.		*Active.*
اُجهامَڻُ ujhāmaṇu, to be extinguished.		اُجائِڻُ ujhāiṇu.
اُڏامَڻُ uḍāmaṇu, to fly		اُڏائِڻُ uḍāiṇu.
ٻَجهَڻُ ƀajhaṇu, to be bound		ٻَڌهَڻُ ƀandhaṇu.
ٻُجهَڻُ bujhaṇu, to be heard		ٻُڌهَڻُ ƀundhaṇu.
ڀَڄَڻُ bhaǰaṇu, to be broken		ڀَڃَڻُ bhañaṇu.
ڀُڄَڻُ bhuǰaṇu, to be fried		ڀُڃَڻُ bhuñaṇu.
ڦاٽَڻُ phāṭaṇu, to be torn		ڦاڙَڻُ phāṛaṇu.
ڄاپَڻُ ǰāpaṇu, ڄَمَڻُ ǰamaṇu,	to be born	ڄَڻَڻُ ǰaṇaṇu.
ڇُهپَڻُ čhupaṇu, to be touched		ڇُهَڻُ čhuhaṇu.
ڇِڄَڻُ čhiǰaṇu, to be plucked		ڇِنَڻُ čhinaṇu.

Neuter.	*Active.*
دهوپڻ dhōpaṇu, to be washed . . .	دهوئڻ dhuaṇu.
ڏبهڻ ḍubhaṇu, to be milked. . . .	ڏهڻ ḍuhaṇu.
ڏجهڻ ḍajhaṇu, to be envious . . .	ڏهڻ ḍahaṇu.
ڎهراپڻ ḍhrāpaṇu, to be satiated. .	ڎهرئڻ (ڎهرائڻ). ḍhra-iṇu
رجهڻ rajhaṇu, to be boiled	رندهڻ randhaṇu.
رهڻ rahaṇu, to remain	رکهڻ rakhaṇu.
سڄڻ suj̄aṇu, to be heard.	سڻڻ suṇaṇu.
کسڻ kusaṇu, to be killed.	کهڻ kuhaṇu.
کهاڄڻ khāj̄aṇu, to be eaten	کهائڻ khāiṇu.
کهامڻ khamaṇu, to burn	کهانئڻ khā̃iṇu.
کهڄڻ khaj̄aṇu, to be raised	کهڻڻ khaṇaṇu.
گسڻ gasaṇu, to be abraded.	گهڻ gahaṇu.
لبڻ labaṇu, to be reaped	لڻڻ luṇaṇu.
لبهڻ labhaṇu, to be obtained . . .	لهڻ lahaṇu.
لوسڻ lūsaṇu, to be scorched	لوهڻ lūhaṇu.
ماپڻ māpaṇu, مامڻ mamaṇu, } to be contained. .	مائڻ māiṇu.
مسڻ musaṇu, to have ill luck . . .	مهڻ muhaṇu.
وسامڻ visāmaṇu, to be extinguished .	وسائڻ visāiṇu.
وکامڻ vikamaṇu, وکڻ vikaṇu, } to be sold	وکڻڻ vikiṇaṇu.
وهامڻ vehāmaṇu, to be passed. . .	وهائڻ vehāiṇu.
هپامڻ hapāmaṇu, to be lessened .	هپائڻ hapāiṇu.
يبهڻ yabhaṇu, to be copulated . .	يهڻ yahaṇu.

II. Almost from every neuter or active verb a Causal may be derived. Those causals, which have sprung from a neuter verb, are, as regards their signification, active, whereas those, which are derived from an active verb, are doubly active.

The Causal is derived by adding to the root of a verb the long vowel ā, to which the increment of the Infinitive accedes as usual; e. g.:

وِرْچَڻُ virčaṇu, v. n., to be tired; causal: وِرْچَائِڻُ vir-č-ā-iṇu, to cause to be tired or to tire.

ڏَسَڻُ ḍasaṇu, v. a., to show; causal: ڏَسَائِڻُ ḍasā-iṇu, to cause to show.

ڏھوئِڻُ ḍhōiṇu, v. a., to carry, causal: ڏھوئَائِڻُ ḍhō-ā-iṇu, to cause to carry.

But when the verb ends in radical 'a', euphonic v is inserted between the final root-vowel and the causal increment, as:

مَئِڻُ ma-iṇu, v. a., to measure; causal: مَوَائِڻُ ma-v-ā-iṇu, to cause to measure.

Exceptions to this rule:

a) When a verb ends in radical r, ṛ, ṛh, h, preceded by a short 'a', the causal increment may be inserted in the root itself, coalescing with the short radical 'a' to ā, as:

ٻَرَڻُ ɓaraṇu, v. n., to burn; caus.: ٻَارَڻُ ɓāraṇu, to kindle.

ڳَڙَڻُ gaṛaṇu, v. n., to drop; caus. ڳَارَڻُ gāṛaṇu, to cause to drop.

پَڙھَڻُ paṛhaṇu, v. a., to read; caus.: پَاڙھَڻُ pāṛhaṇu, to cause to read, to teach.

ڳَھَڻُ ğahaṇu, v. n., to work hard; caus.: ڳَاھَڻُ ğā-haṇu, to make work hard.

In a number of verbs, the final r (ṛ) of which is preceded by the vowel 'i', ā is inserted before the final radical and 'i' dropped, as:

سُدهِرَنُ sudhiraṇu, v. n., to be arranged; caus.: سُدهَارَنُ sudhāraṇu, to arrange.

وِسِرَنُ visiraṇu, v. n., to be forgotten; caus.; وِسَارَنُ visāraṇu, to forget.

کهِنڊِرَنُ kinḍiraṇu, v. n., to be spread; caus.: کهِنڊَارَنُ khinḍāraṇu, to spread.

اُجِڙَنُ ujiṛaṇu, v. n., to be waste; caus.: اُجَاڙَنُ ujāṛaṇu, to lay waste.

etc. etc.

But the regular mode of forming the causal is also in use, as:

اَڙَنُ aṛaṇu, v. n., to be caught; caus.: اَڙَائِنُ aṛā-iṇu, to entangle.

تَرَنُ taraṇu, v. a., to fry; caus.: تَرَائِنُ tarā-iṇu, to cause to fry.

پَڙهَنُ paṛhaṇu, v. a., to read; caus.: پَڙهَائِنُ parhā-iṇu, to cause to read.

سَنبَهَنُ sambahaṇu, v. n., to be ready; caus.: سَنبَهَائِنُ sambahā-iṇu, to get ready.

b) When final r or ṛ of a verbal root be preceded by the short vowels 'i' or 'u', the causal increment ā coalesces with them to ē and ō respectively, as:

پهِرَنُ phiraṇu, v. n., to turn; caus.: پهيرَنُ phēraṇu, to cause to turn.

کهِنڊِرَنُ khinḍiraṇu, v. n., to be spread; caus.: کهِنڊيرَنُ khinḍēraṇu, to spread (besides کهِنڊَارَنُ).

وِڇهُڙَنُ vičhuṛaṇu, v. n., to be separated; caus.: وِڇهوڙَنُ vičhōṛaṇu, to separate.

Those verbs, in which the root-vowel 'i' coalesces with the causal increment ā to ē, may add, besides the causal increment, ā to the end of the root, without altering the simple causal signification of the verb: as:

ڦِرَنُ phiraṇu, v. n., to turn; caus.: ڦيرَنُ phēraṇu or: ڦيرائِنُ phērā-iṇu.

Some verbs with radical 'u', form the causal in the common way, as:

ڪُڙَنُ kuṛaṇu, v. n., to be tired; caus.: ڪُڙائِنُ kuṛā-iṇu, to tire.

A few verbs change in the causal the final cerebral ṭ (ṭr) and ḍ to ṛ, as:

ٻُڏَنُ ḇuḍaṇu, v. n., to be drowned, caus.: ٻوڙَنُ ḇō-ṛaṇu, to drown.

ٽُرٽَرَنُ ṭruṭraṇu, v. n., to be broken, caus: ٽروڙَنُ ṭrō-ṛaṇu, to break.

c) If a verb end in radical 'i' or 'u', r is inserted after the causal increment ā, as:

ڏِيَنُ ḍi-aṇu, v. a., to give; caus.: ڏِيارَنُ ḍi-ā-r-aṇu, to cause to give.

چُوَنُ ču-aṇu, v. n., to leak; caus.: چُيارَنُ ču-ā-r-aṇu, to cause to leak.

The same is the case, when final h is preceded by 'i', as:

وِهَنُ veh-aṇu, v. n., to sit; caus.: وِهارَنُ veh-ā-r-aṇu, to cause to sit,

but if final h be preceded by 'u', the common rule holds good, as:

كُهَڻُ kuh-aṇu, v. a., to kill; caus.: كُهَائِڻُ kuhā-iṇu, to cause to kill.

On the reverse a euphonic r is inserted before the causal increment in such verbs, the final radical of which ends in ā, as:

گهَائِڻُ ghā-iṇu, v. a., to wound; caus. گهَارَائِڻُ ghā-r-ā-iṇu, to cause to wound.

There is a number of causal verbs, which cannot be brought under any of the foregoing rules; these are:

اُٿهَڻُ uthaṇu, v. n., to rise; caus.: اُٿهَارَڻُ uthāraṇu, to cause to rise.

ڈِڄَڻُ ḍrijaṇu, v. n., to be afraid; caus.: ڈِيڄَارَڻُ ḍrē-jāraṇu, to frighten.

سِکهَڻُ sikhaṇu, v. a., to learn; caus.: سِيکهَارَڻُ sēkhā-raṇu, to instruct.

سُمهَڻُ sumhaṇu, v. n., to fall asleep; caus.: سُمهَارَڻُ sumhāraṇu, to put to sleep.

وَڃَڻُ vańaṇu, v. n., to be lost; caus.: وِڃَائِڻُ vińāiṇu, to loose.

وِنْهجَڻُ vēhejaṇu, v. n., to bathe; caus.: وِنْهجَارَڻُ vē-hejāraṇu, to wash.

III. From most of the causal verbs a second causal may be derived, according to the rules laid down already, the first or simple causal being treated again as a theme by itself.

Simple caus.: وِرْچَائِڻُ virča-iṇu; double caus.: وِرْچَارَائِڻُ virč-ā-r-ā-iṇu, to cause (another) to weary.

Simple caus.: گَارَڻُ gāṛaṇu; double causal: گَاڙَائِڻُ gāṛ-ā-iṇu, to cause to shed (tears).

Simple caus.: وِچھوڙَڻُ vičhōṛaṇu; double caus.: وِچھوڙائِڻُ vičhōṛ-ā-iṇu, to cause to separate.

Simple caus.: ڦيرائِڻُ phēr-ā-iṇu; double caus.: ڦيرارائِڻُ phēr-ā-r-ā-iṇu, to cause (another) to cause to turn.

Simple caus.: گھارائِڻُ ghā-r-ā-iṇu; double caus.: گھارارائِڻُ ghā-r-ā-r-ā-iṇu, to cause (another) to cause to wound.

Annotation. The Prākrit forms the causal either by adding the increment ē (Sansk. ay) or āvē (Sansk. āpay = ābē = āvē, cf. Varar. VII, 26, 27). In the modern Indian idioms only the latter increment is in use, which has been shortened to ā in Sindhī, Hindūstānī and Bangālī, the syllable vē having been dropped. In Gujarātī the causal is formed by adding the increment āv (and vāḍ, when the verb ends in a vowel); in Panǰābī by means of the increment āā. In Marāṭhī āv is generally shortened to av.

The insertion of euphonic r in Sindhī (in Hindūstānī and Panǰābī l) has its precedent in the euphonic l, which is inserted in some Sanskrit causal themes.

The double causal is formed in Hindūstānī by inserting v before the simple causal increment ā; the same is the case in Panǰābī and Gujarātī.

IV. Almost from every neuter, active or causal verb a Passive may be derived by adding to the verbal root the increment جَڻُ jaṇu (j-aṇu). A few verbs, chiefly denominatives, are only found in the passive form, as: اُڪَنڍِجَڻُ ukanḍhijaṇu, to long for, اَنگِرِجَڻُ anguṛijāṇu, to be exchanged, ڏمِرجَڻُ ḍamirǰaṇu, to be angry etc. Any neuter verb may take the passive form, without changing its original signification.

The passive of neuter or intransitive verbs is mostly used impersonally (III pers. Sing.), whereas that of active and causal verbs is inflected through all persons.

The passive increment جَنُ jaṇu is joined to the verbal root, if it end in a consonant, with or without the conjunctive vowel 'i', as euphony may require it; but if the verbal root end in a vowel, the conjunctive vowel 'i' must always be employed, as:

پُورَنُ pūraṇu, v. a., to bury; pass.: پُورْجَنُ pūr-jaṇu, to be buried.

گهَٽَنُ ghaṭaṇu, v. n., to lessen; pass.: گهَٽِجَنُ ghaṭi-jaṇu, to lessen.

وِڃائِنُ viṅāinu, v. caus., to loose; pass.: وِڃائِجَنُ viṅā-i-jaṇu, to be lost.

Those verbs, which end in a radical 'a' and in the Imperative in 'u' (see §. 43), as: چَوَنُ ča-v-aṇu, Imper. چَوُ ča-u, to speak, drop before the increment of the passive the euphonic v of the Infinitive, as: چَئِجَنُ ča-i-jaṇu, to be spoken; پَوَنُ pa-v-aṇu, to fall, Imper. پَوُ, pass. پَئِجَنُ pa-i-jaṇu, to fall.

Those verbs, which shorten their final root-vowel (ī, ū, ō) before the increment of the Infinitive (§. 42, 2), retain their long vowel before the passive termination j-aṇu, as:

پِئَنُ pi-aṇu, v. a., to drink; Imper. پِيئُ pīu; pass. پِيجَنُ pī-jaṇu, to be drunk.

پُئَنُ pu-aṇu, v. a., to string beads; Imper. پُوءُ pū-u; pass. پُوئِجَنُ pū-ijaṇu, to be strung (as beads).

دهُئَنُ dhu-aṇu, v. a., to wash; Imper. دهوءُ dhō-u; pass. دهوئِجَنُ dhō-ijaṇu, to be washed.

Exceptions to these rules are:

ٿِئَنُ thi-aṇu, v. n., to become; Imper. ٿِيئُ thī-u; pass. ٿِجَنُ thi-jaṇu, to become.

كَرَڻُ karaṇu, v. a., to make; Imper. كَرِ kare (Prec. ڪِجِ kije); pass. ڪِجَڻُ ki-ǰaṇu, to be done.

Annotation. In Sanskrit the Passive is formed by adding y to the root of the verb; in Prāk. y is dissolved into īa or iǰǰa, and in the Apabhranša dialect ija or iǰǰa is employed for the formation of the Passive (Lassen, p. 467). The increment of the Passive is therefore in Sindhī ǰ, joined to the affix of the verbal noun or the Infinitive = ǰ-aṇu. The Sindhī (and to some extent the Panǰābī) is the only modern idiom of India, which has preserved a regular passive voice, all its sister languages being compelled to resort to compositions, in order to express a passive voice. The common way to form a passive voice in the kindred idioms is, to compound the past participle passive with the verb ǰānā, to go, as in Hindūstānī: مَیْن مَارَا جَاتَا هُون maĩ mārā ǰātā hū̃, I go being beaten = I am beaten. But the use of the passive voice, if it may be called so, is very limited in the cognate languages, and it is avoided wherever possible, which is greatly facilitated by a great number of verbs having a neuter or passive signification.

§. 43.

The Imperative.

The Imperative represents the root of a Sindhī verb, as stated already, and as the whole conjugational process depends a great deal upon it, its formation must be explained in the first place.

1) The Imperative of neuter and passive verbs always ends in 'u'[1]), as:

مَرَڻُ mar-aṇu, to die; Imper.: مَرُ mar-u.
اَچَڻُ ač-aṇu, to come; Imper.: اَچُ ač-u.

---

1) The only exception to this rule is:

ٻَابُوهَڻُ pābūhaṇu, v. n., to smile, which has in the Imperative, besides the regular ٻَابُوهُ pābūhu, also: ٻَابُوهِ pābūhe.

گَڍِجَڻُ gaḍ-ij-aṇu, to meet; Imper.: گَڍِجُ gaḍ-ij-u.

Those verbs, which insert a euphonic v in the Infinitive, drop it again in the Imperative, as:

نَوَڻُ na-v-aṇu, v. n., to bow, Imper.: نَوُ na-u.

If a final vowel has been shortened in the Infinitive, it is restored again in the Imperative, as:

ٿِيَڻُ thi-aṇu, v. n., to become, Imper. ٿِيءُ thī-u.

چُئَڻُ ču-anu, v. n., to leak, Imper. چُوءُ čū-u.

رُئَڻُ ru-aṇu, v. n., to weep, Imper. رو rō (= روءُ).

Similarly: وِهَڻُ veh-aṇu, v. n., to sit down; Imper. ويهُ vēh-u.

The following verbs form their Imperative both regularly and irregularly:

اَچَڻُ ač-aṇu, v. n., to come; Imper. اَچُ ač-u and آءُ ā-u[1]).

وَڃَڻُ vań-aṇu, v. n., to go; Imper. وَڃُ vań-u and وڃُون va-ū.

2) The Imperative of active and causal verbs ends in 'e', as:

پَالَڻُ pal-aṇu, v. a., to foster; Imper. پَالِ pāle.

گھَٽَائِڻُ ghaṭā-iṇu, v. caus., to lessen; Imper. گھَٽَاءِ ghaṭā-ē.

But there is a considerable number of active verbs, which end in the Imperative in 'u' and not in 'e'; some have both terminations. These are:

---

1) From an old root आ ā, which is no longer used in Sindhī, but in Hindūstānī (آنا ā-nā).

	Imperative.
اُپِنَڻُ upiṇaṇu, to sift	اُپِڻُ upiṇu.
آکھَڻُ ākhaṇu, to inform	آکھُ ākhu and آکھِ ākhe.
اُگھَڻُ ughaṇu, to wipe	اُگھُ ughu.
اَلَڻُ alaṇu, to deny	اَلُ alu.
ٻُجھَڻُ ɓujhaṇu, to understand. . .	ٻُجھُ ɓujhu.
ٻَنڌھَڻُ ɓandhaṇu, to bind. . . .	ٻَنڌھُ ɓandhu.
ٻُنڌھَڻُ ɓundhaṇu, to hear. . . .	ٻُنڌھُ ɓundhu.
ڀَڃَڻُ bhańaṇu, to break. . . .	ڀَڃُ bhańu.
ڀُڃَڻُ bhuńaṇu, to fry.	ڀُڃُ bhuńu.
پُڇھَڻُ pučhaṇu, to ask	پُڇھُ pučhu.
پُرْجھَڻُ purjhaṇu, to understand .	پُرْجھُ purjhu.
پَرُوڙَڻُ parūṛaṇu, to understand . .	پَرُوڙُ parūṛu.
پَڙھَڻُ paṛhaṇu, to read.	پَڙھُ paṛhu.
پَسَڻُ pasaṇu, to see.	پَسُ pasu.
پِنَڻُ pinaṇu, to beg	پِنُ pinu.
پُئَڻُ puaṇu, to string (beads). . .	پُوءِ pūu.
پِھَڻُ pihaṇu, پِيھَڻُ pīhaṇu, to grind	پِھُ pehu. پِيھُ pīhu.
پِئَڻُ piaṇu, to drink.	پِيئُ pīu.
ڄاڻَڻُ janaṇu, to know	ڄاڻُ jāṇu.
ڄَھَڻُ jahaṇu, to copulate	ڄَھُ jahu.
جھِڻِکَڻُ jhiṇikaṇu, to scold . . .	جھِڻِکُ jhiṇiku.
چُڀھَڻُ čubhaṇu, to prick	چُڀھُ čubhu.

	Imperative.
چَرَڻُ čaraṇu, to graze	چَرُ čaru.
چَکهَڻُ čakhaṇu, to taste	چَکهُ čakhu.
چُڳَڻُ čug̱aṇu, to peck up food . .	چُڳُ čug̱u.
چُگهَڻُ čughaṇu, to puncture. . .	چُگهُ čughu.
چُمَڻُ čumaṇu, to kiss	چُمُ čumu.
چُڻَڻُ čuṇaṇu, to crimple (cloth) .	چُڻُ čuṇu.
چَوَڻُ čavaṇu, to speak	چَؤُ čau.
چُهَڻُ čuhaṇu, to soak up	چُهُ čuhu.
چهِنَڻُ čhinaṇu, to pluck	چهِنُ čhiṇu.
چهُئَڻُ čhuaṇu, } to touch . . .	{ چهُوءُ čhū-u.
چهُهَڻُ čhuhaṇu, }	{ چهُهُ čhuhu.
دهائِڻُ dhāiṇu, to suck	دهاءُ dhāu.
دهُڻَڻُ dhuṇaṇu, to choose. . . .	دهُڻُ dhuṇu.
دهَنْوَڻُ dhāvaṇu, to blow (with bellows).	{ دهَنوُ dhā-u or { دهَنئِ dhā-e.
دهُوَڻُ dhuaṇu, to wash.	دهوءُ dhō-u.
ڏَرَڻُ ḍaraṇu, to eat up	ڏَرُ daru.
ڏِسَڻُ ḍisaṇu, to see	ڏِسُ ḍisu.
ڏَهَڻُ ḍahaṇu, to vex.	ڏَهُ ḍahu.
ڏُهَڻُ ḍuhaṇu, to milk	ڏُهُ ḍuhu.
رَکهَڻُ rakhaṇu, to keep.	رَکهُ rakhu.
سِبَڻُ sibaṇu, to sow.	سِبُ sibu.
سِکَڻُ sikaṇu, to long for	سِکُ siku.
سِکهَڻُ sikhaṇu, to learn	سِکهُ sikhu.
سَلَڻُ salaṇu, to divulge	سَلُ salu.
سَمُجهَڻُ samujhaṇu, to understand .	سَمُجهُ samujhu.

Infinitive	Meaning	*Imperative.*
سَنبهِرَڻُ sambhiraṇu,	to recollect .	سَنْبهِرُ sambhiru.
سُڃاڻَڻُ suñāṇaṇu,	to recognize . .	سُڃاڻُ suñāṇu.
سِڻِکَڻُ siṇikaṇu,	to blow the nose .	سِڻِکُ siṇiku.
سُڻِکَڻُ suṇikaṇu,		سُڻِکُ suṇiku.
سِنگهَڻُ singhaṇu,	to smell . . .	سِنگهُ singhu.
سُنگهَڻُ sunghaṇu,		سُنگهُ sunghu.
سُڻَڻُ suṇaṇu,	to hear	سُڻُ suṇu.
سَهَڻُ sahaṇu,	to endure	سَهُ sahu.
ڪَتَڻُ kataṇu,	to spin	ڪَتُ katu.
ڪَڍهَڻُ kaḍhaṇu,	to pull out . . .	ڪَڍهُ kaḍhu.
کهَائِڻُ khāiṇu,	to eat	کهَاءُ khā-u.
کهَٽَڻُ khaṭaṇu,	to earn	کهَٽُ khaṭu.
ڪَهَڻُ kahaṇu,	to say	ڪَهُ kahu.
ڪُهَڻُ kuhaṇu,	to kill	ڪُهُ kuhu.
کهَڻَڻُ khaṇaṇu,	to lift	کهَڻُ khaṇu.
کهَنْهَڻُ khāhaṇu,	to scratch . . .	کهَنْهُ khāhu.
کهيڏَڻُ khēḍaṇu,	to play	کهيڏُ khēḍu.
کهِئَڻُ khiaṇu,	to eat	کهِئُ khiu.
ڳِنهَڻُ ḡinhaṇu,	to take	ڳِنهُ ḡinhu.
گهُرَڻُ ghuraṇu,	to wish	گهُرُ ghuru.
گَهَڻُ gahaṇu,	to rub	گَهُ gahu.
ڳِهَڻُ ḡehaṇu,	to swallow	ڳِهُ ḡehu.
لَکهَڻُ lakhaṇu,	to ascertain . . .	لَکهُ lakhu.
لِکهَڻُ likhaṇu,	to write	لِکهُ likhu.

	Imperative.
لِنْبَڻُ limbaṇu, to plaster	لِنْبُ limbu.
لُڻَڻُ luṇaṇu, to reap	لُڻُ luṇu.
لَهَڻُ lahaṇu, to obtain	لَهُ lahu.
لَهَڻَڻُ lahaṇaṇu, to have to receive .	لَهَڻُ lahaṇu.
مُنجَڻُ munjaṇu, to send	مُنجُ munju.
مَڃَڻُ maṅaṇu, to heed	مَڃُ maṅu مَڃِ maṅe.
مَنگَڻُ maṅaṇu, to ask	مَنگُ maṅu.
مَڻَڻُ manaṇu, to shampoo	مَڻُ manu.
وَٺهَڻُ vaṭhaṇu, to take	وَٺهُ vaṭhu.
وِجهَڻُ vijhaṇu, to throw	وِجهُ vijhu.
وِڪڻَڻُ vikiṇaṇu, to sell	وِڪڻُ vikiṇu.
هَڻَڻُ haṇaṇu, to strike	هَڻُ haṇu.
يَهَڻُ[1]) yahaṇu, to copulate . . .	يَهُ yahu.

The following active verbs form their Imperative in an irregular way:

ڏِيَڻُ ḍianu, to give; Imper. ڏي ḍe (instead of: ڏِئُ ḍiu).

---

1) Capt. Stack in his Sindhī Grammar has adduced the following verbs also as active and ending in the Imperative in 'u':

ٻَڪَڻُ bakaṇu, to chatter,	سُنْهَڻُ sũhaṇu, } to suit, سُنْهَائِڻُ sũhā-iṇu, }
ڀُلَڻُ bhulaṇu, to forget,	
چَنبُڙَڻُ čamburaṇu, to stick close to,	وَچُڙَڻُ vačuraṇu, to stick to,
جهڪَڻُ jhakaṇu, to prate,	وِسَهَڻُ visahaṇu, to trust,
رُچَڻُ ručaṇu, to please,	وَڻَڻُ vaṇaṇu, to please;

but all these are properly intransitive verbs and therefore quite regular in their Imperative.

نِئَنُ nianu, to take away; Imper. نِي (instead of نِئُ niu).

Verbs which end in the Imperative Sing. in 'u', form the Plural in ō (or yō, with euphonic y, if the verb end in any other vowel but 'a' and ū), and those, which end in the Imperative Sing. in ĕ, form their Plural in yō or iō, as:

اَچُ aču, come,	Plur.	اَچو ač-ō.
دهوءُ dhō-u, wash,	„	دهويو dhō-yō.
پئُ pa-u, fall,	„	پَئو pa-ō.
ڍِي ḍē, give,	„	ڍِئو ḍiō.
جهَلِ jhal-ĕ, seize,	„	جهَليو jhal-yō or جهَلِيو jhal-iō.

An older form of the II. pers. Plur. is the termination hō, which is also in use, as; جهَلِهو jhal-ihō.

The other persons of the Imperative must be supplied from the Potential.

There is another from of the Imperative, ending in je[1]), which is added equally to the root of neuter and active verbs. This form of the Imperative is properly a Precative, implying exhortation, request or prayer, as:

موٽَنُ mōṭanu, to return; Imper. موٽُ mōṭu; Prec. موٽِجِ mōṭ-ije, please to return.

وِيٽَنُ vīṭanu, to scatter; Imper. وِيٽِ vīṭ-e; Prec. وِيٽِجِ vīṭ-ije, please to scatter.

If a verb end in 'i' or ī, the initial 'i' of ije is dropped, as:

---

1) In poëtry ije is now and then lengthened to ēje, as well in neuter as active verbs, ending in the Imperative in 'u' or 'e', as: كَريجِ kar-ēje, from كَرَنُ karaṇu, Imper. كَرِ kare. وَڃيجِ vaṅēje, from وَڃَنُ vaṅaṇu, to go, Imper. وَڃُ vaṅu.

کھٖئَنُ khiaṇu, v. a., to eat, Imper. کھِئُ khi-u; Prec. کھِجِ khi-je.

تھِئَنُ thiaṇu, v. n., to become; Imper. تھِيُ thī-u; Prec. تھِيجِ thī-je or: تھِجِ thi-je.

Quite irregular is کَرَنُ karaṇu, to do, in the Precative, as:

کَرَنُ karaṇu, Imper. کرِ kare, Prec. کِجِ ki-je or: کَجِ ka-je.

Neuter or such active verbs, as end in the Imperative in 'u', take frequently, especially in poëtry, the termination iju instead of ije, as:

سُنَنُ suṇaṇu, to hear; Imper. سُنُ suṇu; Prec. سُنِجُ suṇ-iju.

This termination is also now and then found in active verbs, ending in the Imperative in 'e', as:

بھَائِئِنُ bhā̃-iṇu, to think; Imper. بھَائِي bhā̃-e; Prec. بھَائِجُ bhā̃-iju.

The Plural of the Precative ends in ijō (or ējō, as the case may be), as:

پُورِجِ pūr-ije (پُورِيجِ pūr-ēje), shut up; Plur. پُورِجو pūr-ijō (پُورِيجو pūr-ējō).

Instead of ijō (ējō) the terminations ijā, ijāe (ijā̃-e), ijāhu (ijāu) ijāha are also in use, especially in a honorific sense, and are therefore also referred to a subject in the Nominative, as:

وَرِجُ var-iju, return;	Plur.	وَرِجَا	var-ijā.
وَڃِجُ vaṅ-iju, go;	„	وَڃِجَاءِ	vaṅ-ijā-e.
سُڻِجُ suṇ-iju, hear;	„	سُڻِجَاھَ	suṇ-ijāha.
پَڙھِجُ paṛh-iju, read;	„	پَڙھيجَاءُ	paṛh-ējā-u.

Annotation. In Prākrit the different (10) conjugations of the Sanskrit have already been discarded and only the first of them is in common use. The II pers. Sing. of the Imperative ends in Prākrit in 'a', which in Sindhī has been changed to 'u' and 'e' respectively; the II pers. Plur. ends in ha (Sansk. ध dha), and in Sindhī in ō, h being commonly dropped. — In the cognate idioms the final vowel of the II pers. Sing. of the Imperative has been dropped altogether; in the Plural the Imperative ends in ō, as in Sindhī, with the exception of the Marāṭhī, the Plural Imperative of which ends in ā, and the Bangālī, the Plural Imperative of which is identical with the Singular.

The Sindhī Precative is to be referred to the Prākrit increment ija or ijja, which is inserted between the root and the inflexional terminations in the Present, the definite Future and the Imperative (Varar. VII, 21). Lassen's conjecture (p. 357), that this increment has sprung from the Sanskrit Precative, is borne ont by the modern idioms. — The Gujarātī forms the Precative in the same way as the Sindhī by adding to the verbal root the increment aǰē (Plur. aǰō). — In Hindūstānī iyē is joined to the root of the verb for the III pers. Sing. (generally with āp etc.), it being considered more respectful to address a person in the III pers. Sing.; and iyō for the II or III pers. Plur.; ǰiē is only used, when the root ends in ī or ō. — In Panǰābī the increment ī̃ is added to the root for the II pers. Sing., and īō for the II pers. Plur. Similarly iō is joined to the root in Bangālī, as well for the II. pers. Sing. as Plur.

§. 44.

The participle present.

From the Imperative or the verbal root the Participle present is derived in the following way:

1) Neuter verbs ending in the Imperative in 'u', add to the root the affix andō (see §. 8, 11), as:

هَلَڻُ halaṇu, to go; Imper. هَلُ hal-u; Part. pres. هَلَنْدوُ hal-andō.

The same is the case with active verbs, the Imperative of which ends in 'u', as:

هَنَن hananu, to strike; Imper. هَن hanu; Part. pres. هَنَنْدو han-andō.

Some of these however use also the other form in īndō, as:

سُنَن sunanu, to hear; Imper. سُن sunu; Part. pers. سُنَنْدو sunandō or: سُنِيندو sunīndō.

Those verbs, which end in radical ā, and in the Imper. in 'u', form, for euphony's sake, their Participle present in īndō, and not in andō, as:

كهائِن khā-inu, v. a., to eat; Imper. كهاءُ khā-u; Part. pres. كهائِيندو khā-īndō.

ٻُڍّهائِن ḇuḍhā-inu, v. n., to become old; Imper. ٻُڍّهاءُ ḇuḍhā-u; Part. pres. ٻُڍّهائِيندو ḇuḍhā-īndō.

Those verbs, which shorten their final vowel in the Infinitive or insert a euphonic v (§. 42, 1. 2), do the same before the affix of the Participle present, as:

پَوَن pa-v-anu, to fall; Imper. پَوُ pa-u; Part. pres. پَوَنْدو pa-v-andō.

پِئَن pi-anu, to drink; Imper. پِيءُ pī-u; Part. pres. پِئَنْدو pi-andō.

دهُوَن dhu-anu, to wash; Imper. دهوءُ dhō-u; Part. pres. دهُوَنْدو dhu-andō.

In some verbs, with euphonic v inserted, a contraction takes place, as:

چَوَن ča-v-anu, to say; Imper. چَوُ ča-u; Part. pres. چَوَنْدو ča-v-andō or: چُونْدو čūndō.

هُوَن hu-anu, to be; Imper. هوءُ hō-u; Part. pres. هُونْدو hūndō (instead of هُئَنْدو hu-andō).

A similar contraction takes place in:

كهِئَنُ khi-aṇu, to eat; Imper. كهِئُ khi-u; Part. pres. كهِينْدو khīndō.

ڏِئَنُ ḍi-aṇu, to give; Imper. ڏي ḍē; Part. pres. ڏِينْدو ḍīndō.

نِئَنُ ni-aṇu, to take away; Imper. ني nē; Part. pres. نِينْدو nīndō.

The following verbs form their Participle present in an irregular way:

اَچَنُ aċ-aṇu, to come; Imper. اَچُ aċ-u; Part. pres. اِينْدو īndō.

وَڃَنُ vañaṇu, to go; Imper. وَڃُ vañu; Part. pres. وينْدو vēndō or وِينْدو vīndō.

2) Active and causal verbs form the Participle present by adding the affix īndō to the root, as:

ڀَرَنُ bharaṇu, v. a., to fill; Imper. ڀَرِ bhar-e; Part. pres. ڀَرِينْدو bhar-īndō.

ڳَنڍهَائِنُ ğanḍhā-iṇu, to cause to connect; Imper. ڳَنڍهَاءِ ğanḍhā-e; Part. pres. ڳَنڍهَائِيندو ğanḍhā-īndō.

The verb كَرَنُ karaṇu, to do, forms its Part. pres. both regularly and irregularly, كَرِيندو kar-īndō or: كَنْدو kandō, كِنْدو kindō.

3) The participle present of the Passive voice is formed by adding the affix ibō to the root of the passive theme (cf. §. 8, 13), as:

پَسَنُ pasaṇu, v. a., to see; pass. پَسِجَنُ pas-ijaṇu; Part. pres. پَسِبو pas-ibō.

چَوَنُ ča-v-aṇu, v. a., to say; pass. چَئِجَنُ ča-ijaṇu; Part. pres. چَئِبو ča-ibō.

دھوُئڻُ dhu-aṇu, v. a., to wash; pass. دھوِئجڻُ dhō-ijaṇu; Part. pres. دھوِئبو dhō-ibō.

پِئڻُ pi-aṇu, v. a., to drink; pass. پِيجڻُ pī-janu; Part. pres. پِيبو pī-bō.

تھِئڻُ thi-aṇu, v. n., to become; pass. تھِجڻُ thi-jaṇu; Part. pres. تھِبو thi-bō.

كَرَڻُ karaṇu, v. a., to do; pass. كِجڻُ ki-jaṇu; Part. pres. كِبو ki-bō (also: كَبو ka-bō).

The Participle present is also used in the sense of a Future, as will be seen under the future tense.

§. 45.

The Participle past.

From all Sindhī verbs, be they neuter, active (causal) or passive, a past participle may be derived by adding the affix iō or yō (the latter always, when the root ends in a vowel) to the root of the verb (see §. 8, 14). The past participle of neuter verbs implies simply a praeterite sense, whereas that of active (causal) verbs always denotes a praeterite passive signification.

جاڳَڻُ jāgaṇu, v. n., to be awake; p. p. جاڳِئو jāg-iō, having been awake.

كھَٽَڻُ khaṭaṇu, v. a., to gain; p. p. كھَٽيو khaṭ-yō, having been gained.

پَرْبھائِڻُ parbhāiṇu, v. caus., to quiet; p. p. پَرْبھايو parbhāyō, having been quieted.

پَرْكھِجڻُ parkhijaṇu, v. p., to be tested; p. p. پَرْكھِئو parkh-iō, having been tested.

Those verbs, which insert euphonic v in the Infinitive, drop it again before the affix of the past participle, as:

چَوَنُ ča-v-aṇu, to say; p. p. چَيو ča-yō.

نَوَنُ na-v-aṇu, to bow; p. p. نَيو na-yō.

If a verb end in 'i' or ī, the initial 'i' of the affix iō is dropped in the past participle; the same is commonly the case, when the root ends in one of the Palatals č, čh, ǰ, ǰh.

نِئَنُ ni-aṇu, to take away; p. p. نِئو ni-ō.

ٿِئَنُ thi-aṇu, to become; p. p. ٿِئو thi-ō.

جِئَنُ ǰi-aṇu, to live; p. p. جِيئو ǰī-ō.

ڪُڇهَنُ kučhaṇu, to speak; p. p. ڪُڇهو kučh-ō.

سوجهَنُ sōǰhaṇu, to investigate; p. p. سوجهو sōǰhō.

If final ō and ī has been shortened in the Infinitive, it is restored again (with a few exceptions) in the past participles, as:

ڌُئَنُ dhu-aṇu, to wash (Imper. ڌوءُ dhō-u); p. p. ڌويو dhō-yō.

جِئَنُ ǰi-aṇu, to live (Imper. جِيءُ ǰī-u); p. p. جِيئو ǰī-ō.

About the compound affixes ya-lu or ia-lu, ya-ṛō (ia-ṛō), which are attached to the past participle, in order to impart to it more the nature of an adjective, compare §. 9, 22.

A considerable number of verbs form their past participle in an irregular way, that is to say, they have retained the old Sanskrit-Prākrit form of the past participle, modified only according to the laws of transmutation of letters, as current in Prākrit and Sindhī. We subjoin here an alphabetical list of them.

اُبهَامَنُ ubhāmaṇu, v. n., to boil up; p. p. اُبهَانو ubhāṇō.

اُبهَنُ ubahaṇu, v. n., to stand; p. p. اُبِيٺهو ubīṭhō.

اُتَنُ utaṇu, v. a., to say; p. p. اُتو utō.

اُجَڻُ v. n., to be woven, } p. p. اُڻِئو uṇiō.
اُڻَڻُ v. a., to weave, }

اُجھامَڻُ ujhāmaṇu, to be extinguished; p. p. اُجھَانو ujhāṇō.

اَچَڻُ v. n., ačaṇu, to come; p. p. آيو āyō.

اُڏامَڻُ v. n., uḍāmaṇu, to fly; p. p. اُڏانو uḍāṇō.

اُکَرَڻُ v. a., ukaraṇu, to engrave; p. p. اُکَريو ukaryō or: اُکھَتو ukhatō.

اُگھَڻُ v. a., ughaṇu, to wipe out; p. p. اُگھَٺو ughaṭhō.

اَلَڻُ alaṇu, v. a., to deny; p. p. اَلتو altō.

اُلَھَڻُ ulahaṇu, v. n., to descend; p. p. اُلَٿو ulathō.

آڻَڻُ āṇaṇu, v. a.; to bring; p. p. آندو āndō.

ٻَجھَڻُ ٻajhaṇu, v. n., to be bound; } p. p. ٻَجھو ٻajhō or
ٻَندھَڻُ ٻandhaṇu, v. a., to bind; } ٻَڌو ٻadhō.

ٻُجھَڻُ ٻujhaṇu, v. n., to be heard; } p. p. ٻُڌو ٻudhō.
ٻُندھَڻُ ٻundhaṇu, v. a., to hear; }

ٻُڏَڻُ ٻuḍaṇu, v. n., to be drowned; p. p. ٻُڏو ٻuḍō.

ڀَڄَڻُ bhaǰaṇu, v. n., to run away; to be broken; } p. p. ڀَڳو bhaġō.
ڀَڃَڻُ bhańaṇu, v. a., to break; }

ڀِڄَڻُ bhiǰaṇu, v. n., to get wet; p. p. ڀِنو bhiṇō.

ڀُڄَڻُ bhuǰaṇu, v. n., to be fried; } p. p. ڀُڳو bhuġō.
ڀُڃَڻُ bhunaṇu, v. a., to fry; }

ڀُچَڻُ bhučaṇu, v. n., to be digested; p. p. ڀُتو bhutō.

ڀُڻَڻُ bhuṇaṇu, v. n., to wander about; p. p. ڀُنو bhuṇō.

ٻِهَڻُ bihaṇu, v. n., } to stand up; p. p. ٻِيٺو bīṭhō.
ٻِيهَڻُ bīhaṇu, v. n., }

پائِڻُ pāiṇu, v. a., to get; p. p. پاتو pātō.

پُڄَڻُ pujaṇu, v. n., to be finished; p. p. { پُنو punō, پُڄِتو pujitō.

پَچَڻُ pačaṇu, v. n., to be cooked; p. p. پَکو pakō.

پُرْجهَڻُ purjhaṇu, v. a., to understand, p. p. پُرْڌهو purdhō.

پَرْچَڻُ parčaṇu, v. n., to be reconciled; p. p. { پَرْتو partō, پَرْچو parčō.

پَرْنَڻُ parnaṇu, v. a., to entrust, p. p. پَرْتو partō.

پَوَڻُ pavaṇu, v. n., to fall; p. p. پِئو piō.

پُئَڻُ puaṇu, v. a., to string (as beads); p. p. پُوتو pūtō.

پهَاٽَڻُ phāṭaṇu, v. a., to tear; p. p. پهَاٽو phāṭō.

پهَاسَڻُ phāsaṇū, v. n., to be caught; p. p. پهَاتهو phāthō.

پهِٽَڻُ phiṭaṇu, v. n., to be injured; p. p. پهِٽو phiṭō.

پَهُچَڻُ pahučaṇu, v. n., to arrive; p. p. پَهُتو pahutō.

پهَسَڻُ phasaṇu, v. n., to be caught; p. p. پهَتهو phathō.

پهِسَڻُ phisaṇu, v. n., to burst; p. p. پهِتهو phithō.

پِهَڻُ pehaṇu, } v. n., to enter; p. p. پيٽهو pēṭhō.
پيهَڻُ pēhaṇu, }

پِيچَڻُ pīčaṇu, v. n., to be credited; p. p. پِيتو pītō.

پِيسَڻُ pīsaṇu, v. a., to grind; p. p. پِيٽهو pīṭhō.

پِئَڻُ piaṇu, v. a., to drink; p. p. پِيتو pītō.

پِيهَڻُ pīhaṇu, v. a., to grind; p. p. پِيٽهو pīṭhō.

تَپَڻُ tapaṇu, v. n., to be warm; p. p. تَتو tatō.

تُسَڻُ tusaṇu, v. n., to be gratified; p. p. { تُٽهو tuṭhō, ٽُٽهو ṭuṭhō.

ٿَکَڻُ thakaṇu, v. n., to be weary; p. p. ٿَکو thakō.

ترَاهَنُ ṭrāhaṇu, v. caus., to frighten; } p. p. ترَاٿهو ṭrāṭhō.
ترَهَنُ ṭrahaṇu, v. n., to be frightened; } p. p. ترَٿهو ṭraṭhō.

ڄَاپَنُ jāpaṇu, v. n., to be born; } p. p. ڄَائو jā-ō, ڄَايو
ڄَڻَنُ jaṇaṇu, v. a., to bring forth; } jāyō or ڄَڻِئو jaṇiō.

ڄَاڻَنُ jāṇaṇu, v. a., to know; p. p. ڄَاتو jātō.

جَبهَنُ ǰabhaṇu, v. n., to be copulated; } p. p. جَدهو ǰadhō.
جَهَنُ ǰahaṇu, v. a., to copulate; }

جُنبَنُ ǰumbaṇu, v. n., to be deeply engaged; p. p. جُتو ǰutō or جُنبِئو ǰumbiō.

جهَپَامَنُ ǰhapāmaṇu, v. n., to decrease; p. p. جهَپَانو ǰhapāṇō.

جهَلَنُ ǰhalaṇu, v. a., to seize; p. p. { جهَلتو ǰhaltō / جهَلِئو ǰhaliō.

چُڪَنُ čukaṇu, v. n., to be finished; p. p. چُڪو čukō.

ڇهُپَنُ čhupaṇu, v. n., to be touched; } p. p. ڇهُتو čhutō.
ڇهُهَنُ čhuhaṇu, v. a., to touch; }

ڇهُٽَنُ čhuṭaṇu, v. n., to get loose; p. p. ڇهُٽو čhuṭō.

ڇهِجَنُ čhiǰaṇu, v. n., to break; } p. p. ڇهِنو čhinō.
ڇهِنَنُ čhinaṇu, v. a., to break off; }

چُهَنُ čuhaṇu, v. a., to soak up; p. p. چُٿهو čuṭhō.

ڌهُڻَنُ dhuṇaṇu, v. a., to choose; p. p. ڌهُئو dhuō.

ڏُبهَنُ ḍubhaṇu, v. n., to be milked; } p. p. ڏُدهو ḍudhō.
ڏُهَنُ ḍuhaṇu, v. a., to milk; }

ڊرِجَنُ ḍriǰaṇu, v. n., to be afraid; p. p. ڊرِنو ḍrinō.

ڊرَهَنُ ḍrahaṇu, v. n., to tumble down; } p. p. ڊرَٿهو ḍraṭhō.
ڊرَاهَنُ ḍrāhaṇu, v. caus., to demolish; } p. p. ڊرَاٿهو ḍrāṭhō.

ڏِسَنُ ḍisaṇu, v. a., to see; p. p. ڏِٺهو ḍiṭhō.

ڏهراپڻُ ḍhrāpaṇu, v. n., to be satiated; } p. p. ڏهرائو ḍhrāō.
ڏهرائِڻُ ḍhrāiṇu, v. a., to satiate; }

ڏهڻُ ḍahaṇu, v. a., to torment; p. p. ڏڌهو ḍadho.

ڏِئڻُ ḍiaṇu, v. a., to give; p. p. ڏِنو ḍino.

رِجڻُ rijaṇu, v. n., to be watered; p. p. رِڌو ridō
رِجِئو rijiō.

رَجهڻُ rajhaṇu, v. n., to be boiled; } p. p. رَڌهو radhō.
رَندهڻُ randhaṇu, v. a., to cook; }

رُجهڻُ rujhaṇu, v. n., to be busy; p. p. رُڌهو rudhō.

رَچڻُ račaṇu, v. n., to be immersed; p. p. رَتو ratō.

رُسڻُ rusaṇu, v. n., to be sulky; p. p. رُٺهو ruṭhō.

رُنبهڻُ rumbhaṇu, } v. n., to be engaged; p. p. رُڌهو rudhō
رُبهڻُ rubhaṇu, } or رُنبهِئو rumbhiō.

رُوئڻُ ruaṇu, v. n., to weep; p. p. رُنو runō.

رِيجهڻُ rījhaṇu, v. n., to be pleased; p. p. رِيڌهو rīdhō.

سامائِجڻُ sāmāijaṇu, v. n., to arrive at the years of discretion; p. p. سامانو sāmāṇō or: ساماَيو sāmāyō.

سُڄڻُ suǰaṇu, v. n., to be swollen; p. p. سُونو sūṇō.

سُڄڻُ suǰaṇu, v. n., to be heard; } p. p. سُئو suō
سُڻڻُ suṇaṇu, v. a., to hear; } سُڻِئو suṇiō.

سِجهڻُ sijhaṇu, v. n., to be seethed; p. p. سِڌهو sidhō.

سُکڻُ sukaṇu, v. n., to be dry; p. p. سُکو sukō.

سَلڻُ salaṇu, v. a., to divulge; p. p. سَلتو salto
سَلِئو saliō.

سَمائِجڻُ samāijaṇu, v. n., to be contained; p. p. سمانو samāṇō.

سَمُجهَڻُ samujhaṇu, v. a., to understand; p. p. سَمُتو samutō or سَمُجهو samujhō.

سُمهَڻُ sumahaṇu, v. n., to go to sleep; p. p. سُتو sutō or سُمْهِئو sumhiō.

سَنْبهِرَڻُ sambhiraṇu, v. n., to be prepared; p. p. سَنْبهُورو sambhūrō, سَنْبهُوڻو sambhūṇō or: سَنْبهِرِئو sambhiriō.

ڪَرَڻُ karaṇu, v. a., to do; p. p. ڪِئو kiō, ڪَيو kayō; ڪِيتو kītō.

ڪُومَاٽِجَڻُ kūmāṭijaṇu,
ڪُومَائِجَڻُ kūmāijaṇu, } v. p., to wither; p. p. ڪُومَاڻو kumāṇō or ڪُومَايو kūmāyō.

کهَامَڻُ khāmaṇu, v. n., to be burnt; p. p. کهَاڻو khāṇō.

کهَپَڻُ khapaṇu, v. n., to be wearied; p. p. کهَتو khatō or کهَپِئو khapiō.

کهُپَڻُ khupaṇu, v. n., to be fixed; p. p. کهُتو khutō or کهُپِئو khupiō.

کهِسَڻُ khisaṇu, v. n., to be reduced; p. p. کهِٿو khithō.

کهُسَڻُ khusaṇu, v. n., to be plucked out; p. p. کهُٿو khuthō or کهُسِئو khusiō.

ڪُهَڻُ kuhanu, v. a., to kill;
ڪُسَڻُ kusaṇu, v. n., to be killed; } p. p. ڪُٺو kuṭhō.

کهَڻَڻُ khaṇaṇu, v. a., to lift up; p. p. کهَنيو khāyō or کهَڻِئو khaṇiō.

کهُهَڻُ khuhaṇu, v. n., to be tired; p. p. کهُٿو khuthō.

گپَڻُ gapaṇu, v. n., to stick (in mud); p. p. گَتو gatō.

ڳُتَڻُ ḡutaṇu, v. a., to plait together; p. p. ڳُتو ḡutō.

گَسَڻُ gasaṇu, v. n., to abrade;
گَهَڻُ gahaṇu, v. a., to rub; } p. p. گَٺو gaṭhō.

گُسَڻُ gusaṇu, v. n., to fail; p. p. { گُٺهو guthō, گُسِئو gusiō.

لَائِڻُ laiṇu, v. a., to apply; p. p. لَاتو lātō or لَايو lāyo.

لَاهَڻُ lāhaṇu, v. caus., to cause to descend; p. p. لَاٿهو lāthō.

لَبهَڻُ labhaṇu, v. n., to be obtained;
لَهَڻُ lahaṇu, v. a., to obtain; } p. p. لَڌهو ladhō.

لِڪَڻُ likaṇu, v. n., to be hidden; p. p. لِڪو likō or لِڪِئو likiō.

لِنْبَڻُ limbaṇu, v. a., to plaster; p. p. { لِتو litō, لِنْبِئو limbiō.

لُوسَڻُ lūsaṇu, v. n., to be scorched;
لُوهَڻُ lūhaṇu, v. a., to scorch; } p. p. لُوٺهو lūṭhō.

مَچَڻُ mačaṇu, v. n., to fatten; p. p. مَتو matō.

مُسَڻُ musaṇu, v. n., to be unlucky;
مُهَڻُ muhaṇu, v. a., to cause loss; } p. p. مُٺهو muṭhō.

مُنجهَڻُ munjhaṇu, v. n., to be perplexed; p. p. مُوڙهو muṛhō.

وَٺهَڻُ vaṭhaṇu, v. a., to take; p. p. وَرْتو vartō, وَرْدو vardō, وَٺِهتو vaṭhitō.

وِجهَڻُ vijhaṇu, v. a., to throw; p. p. وِڌهو vidhō.

وِرچَڻُ virčaṇu, v. n., to be wearied; p. p. وِرتو virtō.

وِسَامَڻُ visāmaṇu, v. n., to be extinguished; p. p. وِسَاڻو visāṇō.

وَسَڻُ vasaṇu, v. n., to fall (as rain), p. p. وَٺهو vaṭhō, اُٺهو uthō, وُٺهو vuṭhō.

وِڪَامَڻُ vikāmaṇu, v. n., to be sold; p. p. وِڪَاڻو vikāṇō.

وِڪِڻَڻُ vikiṇaṇu, v. a., to sell; p. p. وِڪِئو vikiō.

وَنَڃَڻُ vanaṇu, v. n., to go; p. p. وِئو viō.
وِنهِڄَڻُ vēhej̈aṇu, v. p., to bathe; p. p. وِهِتو vehetō.
وِهَڻُ vehaṇu, v. n., to sit; p. p. ويٺهو vēṭhō.

هَپامَڻُ hapāmaṇu, v. n., to lessen; p. p. هَپاڻو hapāṇō.
يَبهَڻُ yabhaṇu, v. n., to be copulated; } p. p. يَدهو yadhō.
يَهَڻُ yahaṇu, v. a., to copulate; }

§. 46.

The participle of the Future passive or the Gerundive [1]).

The participle of the Future passive or the Gerundive is formed by adding to the verbal root the affix iṇō (or aṇō, if the verb end in 'i' (ī) and optionally iṇō and aṇō, if the verb end in 'u' (ō)). The Gerundive can only be derived from active verbs; neuter verbs form also a similar participial noun by means of the affix iṇō, but it is not to be confounded with the Gerundive; see §. 9, 12.

The final vowel of a verbal root undergoes the same changes before the affix of the Gerundive, as before the affix of the Infinitive (§. 42), so that for practical purposes the rule may thus be given, that the termination of the Infinitive aṇu is simply changed to aṇō (iṇō), in order to form the participle of the Future passive. About the derivation of the affix iṇō see §. 8, 12.

وِجهَڻُ vijhaṇu, v. a., to throw; Gerund. وِجهِڻو vijhiṇō, what is to be thrown.

ڏِئَڻُ ḍiaṇu, v. a., to give; Gerund. ڏِئڻو ḍiaṇō, what is to be given.

---

1) A kind of participle of the Future active is formed by attaching the affix hāru to the Infinitive, as: هَلَڻهارُ halaṇa-hāru, one who is about to go; see §. 9, 33.

دھُوَڻُ dhuaṇu, v. a., to wash; Gerund. دھُوَڻو dhuaṇō or دھُئِڻو dhuiṇō, what is to be washed.

کھائِڻُ khāiṇu, v. a., to eat; Gerund. کھائِڻو khāiṇō, what is to be eaten.

§. 47.

Indeclinable past participles.

The Sindhī uses different past conjunctive or indeclinable participles.

1) The form most in use is that ending in ī (ō) or ē.

a) Neuter or such active verbs, as terminate in the Imperative in 'u', form the past conjunctive participle by joining to the verbal root the affix ī, as:

وَرَڻُ var-aṇu, v. n., to return; past part. conj. وَرِي var-ī, having returned.

سُڻَڻُ suṇaṇu, v. a., to hear; p. part. conj. سُڻِي suṇ-ī, having heard.

Those verbs, which end in a radical ī, coalesce with the affix of the past part. conj. to ī, as:

ٿِيَڻُ thiaṇu, to become; Imper. ٿِيءُ thīu; p. p. conj. ٿِي thī, having become.

Those verbs, which end in ū, shorten ū before the affix ī (as before the affix of the Infinitive), as:

پُوَڻُ pu-aṇu, to string (beads); Imper. پوءُ pū-u; p. p. conj. پُئِي pu-ī.

But those verbs, which shorten radical final ō to 'u' in the Infinitive, restore the same again in the past participle conjunctive, as:

رُوَڻُ ru-aṇu, to weep; Imper. رو rō; p. p. conj. روئِي rō-ī.

If in the Infinitive euphonic v has been inserted between the verbal root and the affix of the Infinitive, it is dropped again in the past part. conj., as:

چَوَنُ ča-v-aṇu, to speak; Imper. چَوُ ča-u; p. p. conj. چَئِي ča-ī, having spoken.

پَوَنُ pa-v-aṇu, to fall, forms either regularly: پَئِي pa-ī, or irregularly پيئِي pē-ī, having fallen.

The verb اَچَنُ ačaṇu, to come, makes in the p. p. conj. either regularly اَچِي ač-ī, or irregularly اَچي ač-ē. The verbs ڏِئَّنُ ḍiaṇu, to give (Imper. ڏي ḍē) and نِئَّنُ niaṇu, to take away (Imper. ني nē) make in the p. part. conj. ڏيئِي ḍē-ī and نيئِي nē-i or نَئِي na-ī.

Passive verbs, be they derived from neuter or active themes, form the p. part. conj. quite in the same way, as verbs of the active voice, by adding the increment ī (ō) to the passive base, as:

لوئِجَنُ lō-ij-aṇu, v. p. to be moistened; p. part. conj. لوئِجِي lō-ij-ī or لوئِجو lō-ij-ō, having been moistened.

b) Active and causal verbs, ending in the Imperative in 'e', form the past part. conj. by adding the affix ē to the root of the verb, as:

مَلَنُ malaṇu, v. a., to polish; p. p. conj. مَلي mal-ē, having polished.

لَڳائِنُ lagāiṇu, v. caus., to apply; p. p. conj. لَڳائي lagā-ē, having applied.

2) The second past participle conjunctive is formed by adding to the root of the verb, be it transitive or intransitive, the affix yō (or iō). This form is only used with a Present, Future or Imperative, and may therefore in most cases be translated by the present participle, as:

موٽَڻُ mōṭaṇu, v. n., to return; p. p. conj. موٽيو mōṭ-yō (mōṭ-iō).

سِتهَڻُ sithaṇu, v. a., to compress; p. p. conj. سِتهِئو sith-iō.

If the verb end in 'i' (ī), it coalesces with the affix iō, as:

ڏِئَڻُ ḍianu, to give; p. p, conj. ڏِئو ḍiō.

پِئَڻُ pi-aṇu, to dink (Imper. پِيئُ pīu); p. p. conj. پِئو piō.

Those verbs, which shorten original ō to 'u' in the Infinitive, restore the same again in the p. p. conj., as:

دهوئَڻُ dhu-aṇu, to wash (Imper. دهوءُ dhō-u); p. p. conj. دهويو dhō-yō.

روئَڻُ ru-aṇu, to weep (Imper. رو rō); p. p. conj. رويو rō-yō.

The verbs کهَڻَڻُ khaṇaṇu, to lift up, هَڻَڻُ haṇaṇu, to strike, کَرَڻُ karaṇu, to do, drop, as in the past participle, their final radical before the affix yō, as:

کهَڻَڻُ khaṇaṇu, p. p. conj. کهَنْيو khā̃-yō or: کهَيو kha-yō.

هَڻَڻُ haṇaṇu, p. p. conj. هَنْيو hā̃-yō or: هَيو ha-yō.

کَرَڻُ karaṇu, p. p. conj. کَيو ka-yō or: کِيو ki-yō (ki-ō).

3) The third past participle conjunctive is formed by adding to the root of transitive verbs, irrespectively of their termination in the Imperative, the affix ǰē (i-ǰē), and ǰī (i-ǰī) to the root of neuter verbs.

This form is generally used with the Present and Past tenses.

کهَڻَڻُ khaṇaṇu, v. a., to lift up (Imper. کهَڻُ khaṇu); p. p. conj. کهَڻِجي khaṇ-ijē.

وِرْچَڻُ virčaṇu, v. n., to be tired; p. p. conj. وِرْچِجي virč-ijī.

4) The fourth past participle conjunctive is formed

by putting كَرِي karē, the p. p. conj. of كَرَڻُ karaṇu, after the past partic. conj. ending in ī or ē. This compound form is used with the Present, the Future, the Past tenses and the Imperative, as:

وَرِي كَرِي varī karē, having returned; Inf. وَرَڻُ varaṇu.

مَلي كَرِي malē karē, having polished; Inf. مَلَڻُ malaṇu.

لوئِجِي كَرِي loij-ī karē, having been moistened; Inf. لوئِجَڻُ loij-aṇu.

Annotation. The indeclinable past participles are formed in Sanskrit either by the affix tvā or ya. In Prākrit tvā is changed to tūṇa and (by elision of t) to ūṇa, and ya becomes ia. In Sindhī the first form of the past participle conjunctive ending in ī (or ē) corresponds to the Prākrit affix ia. The second form of the p. p. conj., ending in yō, is identical with the first, and the same must be said of the third form ending in ǰī (or ǰē), the Sanskrit affix ya (Prākrit ia) having been changed in Sindhī to ǰa (= ǰē), as in the case of the Passive.

This is fully borne out by the kindred idioms. In Hindūstānī we find the following forms of the past part. conjunctive (Inf. mār-nā): mār, mār-ē, mār-kē, mār-karkē. In the first form mār the affix ia has apparently been dropped altogether, whereas in the second mar-ē the affix ia has been contracted to ē. The affix kē in mār-kē, corresponds to the Sindhī affix ǰē, ǰ having been changed to a guttural, with transition of the Media into a Tenuis. Mār-kar and mār-karkē are compound past participles conj. like the Sindhī form. Similarly we find in Panǰābī (Inf. ghall-nā, to send): ghall and ghall-kē.

The Guǰarāti uses two forms of the past part. conj., one ending in ī (used especially in compound verbs), as lakhī, having written, and the other in īnī, as lakhīnī. The first form is identical with the Sindhī affix ī, the latter, īnī, corresponds to the Prākrit affix uṇa, ī having been substituted for ū.

The Marāṭhī uses only one form of the past. part. conj., ending in ūn, as karūn, having done; this affix quite coincides with the Prākrit affix ūṇa. — The Bangālī uses either the affix yā (iyā), as dēkhiyā (dēk-ē or dēkh-ī also being employed), or the Locative of the past participle, dēkhitē, in the state of having seen.

Chapter XIII.

Formation of the Tenses and Persons.

§. 48.

In treating of the Tenses in Sindhī we must distinguish simple and compound Tenses.

I. Simple tenses.

In the Active and Passive Voice there are only three simple tenses, viz.: the Potential, the Aorist and the Future.

1) The Potential, which implies possibility, uncertainty or a wish, is formed by adding to the root of the verb the inflexional terminations. The absolute personal pronouns may also be put before the verb, where any stress is to be laid on the person, but they may also be omitted, where such is not the case, the respective person being sufficiently pointed out by the inflexional termination itself.

Neuter and such intransitive verbs, as end in the Imperative in 'u', and all passive verbs, receive the same personal terminations, whereas those transitive verbs, which end in the Imperative in 'e', differ from them in the I and partly in the II pers. Sing. and in all the persons of the Plural, by retaining their characteristic 'i' (e) before the inflexional terminations.

Personal terminations of the Potential.

Verbs ending in the Imperative in 'u'.			Verbs ending in the Imper. in 'e'.	
	Singular.	Plural.	Singular.	Plural.
I pers.	-ā̃	-ū̃	-yā̃, -iā̃	-yū̃, iū̃
II pers.	-ī̃, ẽ	-ō	-iẽ, yẽ; ī̃, ẽ	-yō, iō
III pers.	ē	-ane	-ē	-īne, ine

In reference to verbs, ending in the Imperative in 'u', it is to be observed:

a) A final long vowel is shortened before all the personal terminations in the same way, as before the affix of the Infinitive; e. g. رُئَڻُ ruaṇu, to weep, Imper. رو rō, Potential I pers. رُئان ru-ā̃, I may weep; پِئَڻُ piaṇu, to drink, Imper. پِيءُ pīu, Potential I pers. پِئان pi-ā̃, I may drink; پُئَڻُ pu-aṇu, to string (beads), Imper. پُوءُ pū-u, Potential I pers. پُئان pu-ā̃, I may string (beads). In poëtry an original long vowel may be restored again in the III pers. Sing., the personal termination ē being at the same time shortened to 'e', as: روءِ rō-e, he may weep, instead of رُئي ru-ē.

b) The euphonic v, which is inserted between the root of a verb ending in 'a', and the affix of the Infinitive, is commonly retained in the Singular and the III pers. of the Plural, but dropped commonly in the I and II pers. Plural, as: Inf. پَوَڻُ pa-v-aṇu, to fall, Potential, Sing. I pers. پَوان pa-v-ā̃, II pers. پَوِين pa-v-ẽ, III pers. پَوي pa-v-ē; III pers. Plur. پَوَنِ pa-v-ane; Plur. I pers. پَئُون pa-ū̃, II pers. پَئُو pa-ō. In the II and III pers.

Sing. however v may be also dropped, as چَئِين ča-ē̃, thou mayst say; چَئِي ča-ē[1]), he may say.

c) In the III pers. Plur. verbs, which end in 'u' (ū) or original ō) and 'a' (with euphonic v inserted) frequently contract the inflexional termination u-ane, a-v-ane, to ūne, as: رُونِ rūne, they may weep, instead of رُوَنِ ru-ane; پُونِ pūne, they may fall, instead of پَوَنِ pavane; چُونِ čūne, they may say, instead of چَوَنِ čavane.

A similar contraction takes place in the II pers. Sing. and in the III person Plur., if a verb end in 'i' (ī), as: ڏِين ḍī̃, thou mayst give, instead of ڏِئِين ḍi-ē̃; ڏِينِ dīne, they may give, instead of ڏِئَنِ ḍiane; نِين nī̃, thou mayst take away, نِينِ nīne, they may take away; پِينِ pīne, they make drink; کهِينِ khīne, they may eat; but the uncontracted form is equally in use.

d) Verbs, which end in a radical ā, and in the Imperative in 'u', insert in the I pers. Sing. and Plur. and in the II pers. Plur. a euphonic y before the flexional termination, as: ٻُڍّهَايَان ƃuḍhā-y-ā̃, I may become old, ٻُڍّهَايُون ƃuḍhā-y-ū̃, ٻُڍّهَايو ƃudhā-y-ō, we, you may become old. In the III pers. Plur. they end likewise, for euphony's sake, not in ane, but in ine, as: کهَائِنِ khā-ine, they may eat. An exception to this rule is کهَان khā̃, I may eat, instead of کهَايَان khā-y-ā̃.

In reference to verbs, ending in the Imperative in 'e', it is to be observed:

1) The characteristic 'i' (e) of the Imperative may be contracted with the inflexional termination of the

---

1) چَئِي ča-ē is even contracted to چِي čē, when used more in the sense of a particle, to quote the words of the speaker ('says he').

I and II pers. Sing. and the II and I pers. of the Plur. to yã, yẽ (yĩ), yũ, yō, or not, if the verb end in a consonant; but the contraction must take place, if the verb end in a vowel, as: چھَڏيَان čhaḏyã, or چھَڏِئّان, چھَڏيين čhaḏyẽ or چھَڏِئين čhaḏie etc.; but: بھَايَان bha-yã, بھَايين bhā-yẽ etc. from بھَائڻُ bhāiṇu, to think. In poëtry however the looser form is also in use, as: بھَائِئّان bhā-iã or بھَائِيَان bhā-iyã. In the II pers. Sing. the inflexional termination yẽ or yĩ may also be contracted to ẽ or ĩ, as: سَانڊھين sānḍhẽ or سَانڊِھين sānḍhĩ, thou mayst cherish.

In the III pers. Plural 'i' is generally lengthened to 'ī', and the initial 'a' of the inflexional termination āni dropped in order to distinguish the neuter and active verbs. But īne is again frequently pronounced and written ine, especially when the verb ends in a long ā, as: ڳالھَائِنِ gālha-ine, they may speak.

2) The verb ڪَرڻُ karaṇu, to do, forms the III pers. Plural either regularly in ڪَرِينِ karīne, or irregularly in ڪَنِ kane or ڪِنِ kine.

Annotation. The Sanskrit Potential has already quite disappeared in Prākrit. But, abstracted from this significant circumstance, there can be no doubt, that the Sindhī Potential corresponds originally to the Prākrit Present tense. In Sindhī itself there are many reminiscences, that the Potential properly represents the old Present of the Prākrit; for it is very often, chiefly in poëtry, used without the characteristic تھو, in the sense of the Present. After the custom had gained ground, to express the Present by joining the تھو thō to the old Present, the old Present was reserved to denote a Potential mood. The inflexional terminations of the Sindhī Potential correspond very closely to those of the Prākrit Present, as: Prāk. I pers. Sing. āmi (Sansk. āmi), Sindhī ã; II pers. Sing. asi (Sansk. asi), Sindhī ẽ (or ĩ), 'a' being dropped (as a conjunctive vowel) and s being first changed to h and then dropped altogether; III pers. Sing. a-ti or a-di (Sansk. a-ti), and by elision of t or d: a-e, Sindhī ē. In the I pers. Plur. the Prākrit has different terminations, as ā-mō (Sansk. ā-mah), ā-mu, ā-ma, or a-mō, a-mū etc. These latter terminations have given rise to the Sindhī terminations ū̃, m being elided and final 'u' lengthened to ū and nasalized at the same time; II pers. Plur. a-ha (Sansk. a-tha), Sindhī ō, h having been dropped and 'a' lengthened to ō; III pers. Plur. a-nti (Sansk. a-nti), Sindhī ane, t having been elided in this conjunct letter. — The Hindūstānī, Panjābī and Gujarātī coincide in this respect with the Sindhī, forming the Potential in the same way, as the Sindhī, only with modified inflexional terminations. The proper Potential of the Marāṭhī, which is now commonly called by the Grammarians the "Past Habitual" [1]), exhibits likewise the signs of the old Prākrit Present. — The Bangālī alone has preserved the old Present tense, formed by joining the inflexional terminations to the root of the verb; the Present is in Bangālī also used in the sense of a Potential.

2) The Sindhī has a regular Aorist or Praeterite tense denoting, that an action once took place in time past.

a) The Aorist is formed from neuter verbs, by joining to the past participle the terminations of the (now in Sindhī) obsolete substantive verb as, to be. This tense is therefore originally a compound, and the participle must be put, according to the gender referred to, either in the masc. or the feminine. The inflexional terminations are only affixed to the I and II pers. of the Sing. masc. and fem., to the I pers. of the Plur. masc. and fem. and to the II pers. of the Plur. masc., the III person of the Sing. and Plur. masc. and fem. being left without any inflexional terminations, as well as the II pers. of the Plur. fem.

b) From transitive verbs, the participle past of which always has a passive signification, the Aorist is

1) As in the Marāṭhī Grammar, published by the American Mission, Bombay 1854.

formed by joining to the past participle the same inflexional terminations, as to that of neuter verbs, the III pers. of the Sing. and Plur. masc. and fem. and the II person of the Plur. fem. being likewise left without inflexional terminations. If the Agent is to be expressed, this must be put in the Instrumental, the participle past agreeing throughout with its subject (expressed or only hinted at) in gender and number.

The inflexional terminations of the Aorist are:

	Singular.		Plural.	
	Masc.	Fem.	Masc.	Fem.
I pers.	-se	-se	-sī̃, sū̃	-sī̃, sū̃.
II pers.	-ẽ	-ā (ẽ)	-u	—
III pers.	—	—	—	—

The past participle of neuter and active verbs commonly ends, as we have seen, in yō or iō, fem. ī. If therefore the past participle be of the masc. gender, its final ō is shortened before the inflexional termination of the I person to u = u-se, whereas the final ī of the fem. gender is changed, as before the other pronominal suffixes, to ya or ia = ya-se, ia-se; e. g. هَلِئو haliō, m., gone, I pers. masc. هَلِئُسِ haliu-se, I went or have gone, fem. هَلِئَسِ halia-se; in the same way ڏِٺهو ḍiṭhō, past participle of ڏِسَڻُ ḍisaṇu, seen: ڏِٺهُسِ ḍiṭhu-se, masc. J was seen, fem. ڏِٺهِئَسِ ḍiṭhia-se or: ڏِٺهيَسِ ḍiṭhya-se. In poëtry though iō or yō may keep its place before the inflexional termination se, and ia or ya may be lengthened to ia or yā, as: ڇَڏِئوسِ čhaḍiō-se, I was left, fem. ڇَڏِئاسِ čhaḍiā-se.

Before the inflexional termination of the II person masc., ẽ, final ō is dropped altogether, as: هَلِئين hali-ẽ, thou hast gone; ڎِٺهين ḍiṭh-ẽ, thou wast seen; before the inflexional termination of the II person fem. ã, final ī is shortened to 'i' = i-ã (occasionally also as in the masc. to i-ẽ), as: هَلِئَں hali-ã; thou hast gone, ڎِٺهِئَں ḍiṭhi-ã, thou wast seen.

In the first person Plural the inflexional termination sī̃ (sẽ), sũ is affixed to the masc. or fem. Plural of the past participle, as: هَلِئاسِين haliā-sī̃, we have gone, هَلِئُونْسِين haliū̃-sī̃ (fem.); ڎِٺهَاسِين ḍiṭhā-sī̃, we were seen, ڎِٺهِئُونْسِين ḍiṭhiū̃-sī̃ (fem.).

In the II person masc. the final ā of the Plural (هَلِئا) is shortened before the inflexional termination 'u' = a-u, as: هَليَو halya-u, you went; ڎِٺهَو ḍiṭha-u, you were seen; to the II person fem. no inflexional termination is added, the Plural fem. of the past participle alone being used, the subject of which must be indicated either by the absolute personal pronoun or gathered from the context.

It is to be noticed, that in poëtry the inflexional terminations are frequently left out, in which case the subject, if it be not indicated otherwise (by an absolute personal pronoun etc.), must be gleaned from the context.

Annotation. The three praeterite tenses of the Sanskrit, with the exception of a few traces (Varar. VII, 23), have been already discarded in Prākrit, their formation being apparently too intricate for the conception of the vulgar. In their lieu the past participle has been substituted in the sense of an Aorist, either with or without inflexional terminations, the Perfect proper being denoted by a compound tense. The inflexional terminations, which are affixed in Sindhī to the past participle, are derived from the Sanskrit substantive verb 'as', to be, though they be now so much mutilated and differ so considerably from the forms used in Prākrit (Lassen, p. 345), that they are scarcely recognisable. The termination of the I person Sing. -s corresponds to the Sanskrit asmi (Prāk. amhi), 'm' having been thrown out in Sindhī.

In the II pers. (Sansk. and Prāk. asi) s = h, has been dropped and final i (e) lengthened in the masc. to ẽ, whereas in the feminine the initial 'a' of asi has been retained, and the latter half of it dropped altogether. The masculine termination ẽ is however also now and then applied to the feminine.

In the I person Plural the Sanskrit smāh (Prākrit amhō) has been changed to sĩ (sẽ) or sũ; in the II person masc. the Sanskrit stha has been first changed to tha, thence to ha, and with the elision of 'h' to 'u'.

In Hindūstānī, Panjābī and Gujarātī the Aorist is made up by the past participle without the addition of inflexional terminations, but in Marāṭhī inflexional terminations are affixed to the past participle, as in Sindhī. The same is the case in Bangālī, but with this difference, that it can form an Aorist of the active voice not only from neuter verbs, but also from active verbs; in the Passive though it must have recourse to a composition.

3) The Future,

which implies in Sindhī not only the sense of futurity, but also of possibility, uncertainty, is formed

a) In the Active Voice, by affixing to the present participle the same inflexional terminations as to the Aorist.

b) In the Passive Voice, by affixing to the present participle passive the same inflexional terminations, as to the present participle of the Active.

Annotation. The Sindhī has quite left the traces of the Prākrit in forming the Future and fallen back to a composition, in order to make up for the lost future tense. It has approached in this respect again nearer to the Sanskrit, which likewise forms the I Future of the active voice by affixing the inflexional terminations of the substantive verb 'as', to be, to the participial noun ending in tā (tṛ). The modern Arian idioms differ very greatly from each other as to the method, in which they form the Future. The Hindūstānī and Panjābī express the Future by means of a compound verb; they add to the Potential of a verb the past participle gā (instead of the common giā), from the root gam, to go, the gender of which must agree with the subject in question. This is properly a Desiderative, and not a Future; but already in Sanskrit the Desiderative is now and then used in the sense of a Future. Thus we have in Hindūstānī كرونگا karūn-gā, masc., and كرونگي karūn-gī, fem. I shall do, literally: I am gone (گا gā), that I do (كرون karū̃), i. e. I will do or shall do; similarly in Panjābī: karāngā, masc., karāngī, fem.

The Gujarātī on the other hand accedes again more closely to the Prākrit; the conjunctive vowel of the Prākrit (i) has been lengthened in the I person Sing. and Plur., in order to make up for the double ss, which has been reduced to a single one (cf. Introd. §. 19), as: lakh-īs, I shall write, Plur. lakh-īsū̃, we shall write.

In the II and III person Sing. and Plur. the conjunctive vowel has been dropped altogether, as II pers. Sing. lakh-sē, thou wilt write etc.

The Future of the Marāṭhī is quite peculiar, and, as it seems, made up from the different terminations of the Future, used in Prākrit.

The termination of the I person Sing. īn (ēn) seems to have arisen form the Prākrit termination himi (Varar. VII, 12), and that of the I person Plural ū̃, from the Prākrit sisi (= hisi; Lassen, p. 352), the final 'i' of which has been dropped and in compensation thereof medial 'i' lengthened = sīs; final 's' has been hardened to 'r' and thence to 'l'. The II person Plur. ends in āl, which I would refer to the Prākrit termination -ssaha, the latter half of which (aha) seems to have been dropped, and the conjunct ss reduced to 's' by lengthening the preceding (conjunctive) vowel = ās; 's' again seems to be hardened to r = l. A similar process appears in the III pers. Sing., ending in īl (ēl); the Prākrit termination is hidi (= sidi); the initial 'h' has been elided and id(i) lengthened to īd, final 'd' being changed at the same time (as it is usual in the past participle) to 'l'. The III person Plural, ending in tīl is quite perplexing. We would refer to the fact, that in Prākrit hittha is also used instead of hissa (tth = ss; Lassen, p. 353; Varar. VII, 15), though restricted to the I pers. Plural. In Marāṭhī it appears, that tth has also been used in the III pers. Plural, so that the III pers. Plural would properly terminate in hitthinti; of this initial hi has been elided and the aspirate conjunct tth reduced to tt = t; n is in Marāṭhī always dropped in the termination of the III pers. Plural and in consequence the preceding vowel (i) lengthened; thus we get tīt, of which final 't' must have been changed to l = tīl.

The Bangālī forms the Future by affixing to the root of the verb the inflexional termination iba; this is very remarkable and without any analogy in any of the Prākrit dialects. It reminds us very strongly of the Latin termination bo in the formation of the Active Future of the I and II conjugation, which Bopp (Comp. Gramm. II, §§. 526, 663) derives from the Sanskrit bhū. It would be near at hand, to compare this affix with the Sindhī affix bō, employed to form the present participle passive; but its origin will hardy allow of such a comparison.

II. Compound tenses.

1) The compound Potential.

The Potential may be compounded:

a) with the present participle and the Potential of the auxiliary verb هُئَڻُ huaṇu, to be, in order to denote an enduring action or state, as: آئُون پَڙهَندو هُئان I may be reading.

b) with the past participle and the Potential of the auxiliary verb هُئَڻُ huaṇu, to be, as: آئُون رُلِئو هُئان I my have wandered about; مُون ڏِٺو هُئي it may have been seen by me, i. e. I may have seen it.

2) The present tense.

The Sindhī has two forms for the Present tense:

a) The common or indefinite Present tense, which denotes, that an action is commenced or going on at the time being, is formed by putting after the Potential (and occasionally before it) the augment ٿهو thō[1]), which must

---

1) Instead of ٿهو thō: پِئو peō (fem. پِئي peī) is also used, but with this difference, that a more enduring action is thereby denoted. Cf. §. 53, 2.

agree with the gender of the subject, as: آنُون هَلَان تهو I go; fem. آنُون هَلَان تهِي I go.

b) The definite Present, which implies habit, usage or that an action is still going on at the time of speaking, is formed by compounding the present participle with the Present of the auxiliary verb هُوَنُ huaṇu, as: آنُون لِكهَنْدو آنهيَان I am writing, or I am used to write; رُوَندو آهِي he is in the habit of weeping.

In poëtry the auxiliary verb is often left out and the participle used by itself, determined by a noun or pronoun as subject.

Annotation. The Potential, which, as stated already, represents the old Present tense, is no longer considered sufficient, to express the Present by itself; the augment تهو thō is therefore added, to render more prominent the sense of the Present. This augment تهو thō is derived from the Sanskrit adjective स्थ stha (as used at the end of compounds) and signifies 'standing', as: آنُون پَسَان تهو I see, litterally: standing I see, I am in the state of seeing.

In Hindūstānī thā is used as an augment for forming the Imperfect, whereas the common or indefinite Present is expressed by the present participle alone, and the definite Present by the addition of the auxiliary verb hōnā. The same is the case in Panǰābī, with the only difference, that the Sanskrit stha has been assimilated in Panǰābī to sā. In Gujarātī the indefinite Present is formed by adding the auxiliary (defective) verb čhaū etc., I am etc. (derived from the Sansk. substantive verb 'as', to be) to the Potential, as: hū lakhū čhaū, I write, and the definite Present by joining the Present of the auxiliary verb hōvū, to be, to the present participle, as: hū lakhō hōū čhaū, I am writing.

The Marāṭhī forms the common or indefinite Present by affixing the inflexional terminations of the Sansk. substantive verb 'as', to be, to the present participle, ending (originally) in tā, with which the terminations coalesce, as tō̃, tōs etc. Besides this the Marāṭhī uses three other compound forms for the definite Present, the first of which is compounded with the present participle ending in 'at' or 'it', and the irregular form of the auxiliary verb asaṇē̃, viz: āhē̃, as: mī lihīt āhē̃, I am writing; the second adds the auxiliary verb āhē̃ etc. to the indefinite Present ending in tō̃ etc., as: mī lihitō̃ āhē̃, I am writing. Both these forms of the definite Present, wich do not differ from each other as to their signification, denote an action going on or enduring at the time of speaking. The third form adds to the present participle ending in 'at' or 'it', the regular Present of the auxiliary verb asaṇē̃ to be, viz: asatō̃ etc., as: mī lihīt asatō̃, I am in the habit of writing, and implies a habit, custom or natural disposition; it may therefore be termed the Present Habitual. — The Bangālī has, as noticed already, a simple Present, formed by affixing the inflexional terminations to the root of the verb, and a definite Present formed by uniting the auxiliary verb āčhi etc. with the present participle ending in itē, the initial ā of which is dropped in this composition, as: āmi dēkhitēčhi, I am seeing.

3) The Habitual Aorist,

which implies, that an action was repeated in past time or went on at the time indicated, is formed by adding to the Aorist the indeclinable augment تهي thē, which may follow or precede it, as the augment of the Present; e. g.: هُو آيو تهي he came (repeatedly), or: was coming.

This tense is quite peculiar to the Sindhī, no analogy to it being met with in the kindred idioms. The indeclinable augment تهي thē is apparently the Locative of thō, and signifies: 'in standing', which agrees well with the import of this tense.

4) The Imperfect,

which denotes, that an action was progressing or repeated at a particular time past, is formed by adding to the present participle the Aorist of the auxiliary verb هُونُ huaṇu, as: رُلَنْدو هوسِ I was wandering about; لودهِبو هوسِ I was being driven out. The Imperfect may be rendered more emphatic by premising the past participle پِئو piō (having fallen), as: هُو پِئا ڏِسَنْدَا هُئا, they were in the habit of seeing.

Annotation. In Hindūstānī the Imperfect is formed, as already alluded to, by adding thā to the present participle; the same is the case in Panǰabi, which adds sā; the Marāṭhī joins the Aorist of the auxiliary verb asanẽ, viz: hōtõ etc. to the present participle ending in at or it. The same method is kept to in Guǰarātī and Bangāli, in the latter language with the slight difference, that the Aorist of the auxiliary verb (viz: čhilām etc.) is coalescing with the participle present.

5) The Perfect,

which implies an action, that has been completed in time past, is formed by adding the auxiliary verb آنهِيَان ā̃hiyā̃ etc. to the past participle, as: وِئو آنهِيَان, I am gone, جهَلِئو آنهِيَان I have been seized.

Annotation. All the kindred idioms form the Perfect in the same way as the Sindhī, by adding the Present of the auxiliary verb to the past participle.

6) The Pluperfect,

which implies an action, that has been completed in remote past time chiefly in relation to some other time, expressed or only understood, is formed by adding the Aorist of the auxiliary verb هُونُ huaṇu to the past participle, as: هَلِئو هوسِ I had gone; دهُتِي هُيَسِ I had been enticed (fem.).

Annotation. In Hindūstānī and Panǰābī the Pluperfect is formed by adding thā and sā respectively to the past participle. In Marāṭhī the Aorist hōtõ etc. is joined to the past participle and similarly in Guǰarātī hatō etc. In Bangālī (which must not resort to a passive construction in the case of transitive verbs, as the other idioms) the Aorist of the auxiliary verb, viz: čhilām etc. is united with the past participle ending in yā.

7) The compound Future tenses.

There are two compound Future tenses in Sindhī:

a) The one is compounded with the participle present and the Future of the auxiliary verb هُئَڻُ huaṇu, which may be termed the Definite Future, as: ڏِسَنْدو هُونْدسِ I shall be seeing.

b) The other is compounded with the past participle and the Future of the auxiliary verb هُئَڻُ huaṇu, and may be termed the Past Future, as: هَلِئو هُونْدسِ I shall have gone; هو بَدهو هُوندو he will have been bound.

Both these tenses do not only denote futurity in its strict sense, but imply also possibility, uncertainty or doubt.

Chapter XIV.

The auxiliary verbs.

§. 49.

A. The auxiliary verb هُئَڻُ huaṇu, to be.

Before we can fully develope the conjugational process of the Sindhī, we must first describe the inflexion of the auxiliary verb هُئَڻُ huaṇu, to be, by means of which the compound tenses of other verbs are being made up.

Infinitive: هُئَڻُ hu-aṇu, to be.

Imperative.

	SING.		PLUR.
II pers.	هو or هوءُ be thou.		هو or هُئو be ye.
	hō hō-u,		hō hu-ō,

Precative.

	SING.		PLUR.
II pers.	هُئِجِ hu-ije هوئِجِ hō-ije هُجُ hu-ju هوجِ hō-je	mayst thou be.	هُجو hu-jo, may ye be.

Participles.

1) Present participle: هُوندو hūndō, being.

2) Past participle: هو hō, هُئو huō, having been

Verbal noun.

هُئڻو hu-aṇō, being.

I. THE POTENTIAL.

1) THE SIMPLE POTENTIAL.

SINGULAR.

I pers. آنئُون هُئان هُجان ā̃ũ hu-ā̃, huj-ā̃, I may be.

II pers. تُون هُئِين هُجِين tū̃ hu-ẽ, huj-ẽ, thou mayst be.

III pers. هُو هُئِي هُجِي hū hu-ē; huj-ē, he may be.

PLURAL.

I pers. آسِين هُون، هُجُون asī̃ hū̃, huj-ū̃, we may be.

II pers. اَهِين هو، هُئو، هُجو ahī̃ hō, hu-ō, huj-ō, you may be.

III pers. هُو هُئنِ، هُونِ، هُجَنِ hū hu-ane, hūne, huj-ane, they may be.

In the II pers. Sing. هُئِين، هُجِين hu-ī̃, huj-ī̃ is equally in use. In poëtry we meet in the III person Sing. frequently هوء hō-e, instead of هُئِي hu-ē.

2) THE COMPOUND POTENTIAL.

a) The present participle with the Potential هُئَان etc. 'May be being'.

SINGULAR.

	Masc.	*Fem.*
I pers.	هُوندؤ هُئَان، هُجَان[1]	هُونْدِي هُئَان، هُجَان
	hūndō hu-ā̃, hūǰ-ā̃.	hūndī hu-ā̃, huǰ-ā̃.
II pers.	هُوندؤ هُئِين، هُجِين	هُونْدِي هُئِين، هُجِين
	hūndō hu-ē̃, huǰ-ē̃.	hūndī hu-ē̃, huǰ-ē̃.
III pers.	هُوندؤ هُئِي، هُجِي	هُونْدِي هُئِي، هُجِي
	hūndō huē, huǰ-ē.	hūndī hu-ē, huǰ-ē.

PLURAL.

I pers.	هُونْدَا هُون، هُجُون	هُونْدِئُون هُون، هُجُون
	hūndā hū̃, huǰ-ū̃.	hūndiū̃[2]) hū̃, huǰ-ū̃.
II pers.	هُونْدَا هُئو، هُجو	هُونْدِئُون هُئو، هُجو
	hūndā hu-ō, huǰ-ō.	hūndiū̃ hu-ō, huǰ-ō.
III pers.	هُونْدَا هُئنِ، هُجَنِ	هُونْدِئُون هُئنِ، هُجَنِ
	hūndā hu-ane, huǰ-ane.	hūndiū̃ hu-ane, huǰ-ane.

b) The past participle with the Potential هُئَان etc. 'May have been'.

SINGULAR.

I pers.	هُئو هُئَان huō huā̃.	هُئِي هُئَان huī huā̃.
II pers.	هُئِين „ „ huē̃.	هُئِين „ „ huē̃.
III pers.	هُئِي „ „ huē.	هُئِي „ „ huē.

1) The absolute personal pronouns are left out in the following tenses, as they may be easily supplied.

2) The Plural fem. هُونْدِئُون hūndiū̃ may also be pronounced and written هُونديُون hundyū̃ or هُونْدِيُون hūndiyū̃, and so all the present participles in the fem. Plural.

	Masc.		*Fem.*
	PLURAL.		
I pers.	هُئا هون huā hũ.		هُيُون هون huyũ hũ.
II pers.	هُئو „ „ huō.		هُئو „ „ huō.
III pers.	هُئَنِ „ „ huane.		هُئَنِ „ „ huane.

II. THE PRESENT.

1) THE INDEFINITE PRESENT.

The Potential with تهو thō.
'I am'.

	SINGULAR.	
I pers.	هُئان تهو huā̃ thō.	هُئان تهي huā̃ thī.
II pers.	هُئين تهو huẽ thō.	هُئين تهي huẽ thī.
III pers.	هُئي تهو huē thō.	هُئي تهي huē thī.
	PLURAL.	
I pers.	هون تها hũ thā.	هون تهِئون hũ thiũ.
II pers.	هُئو تها huō thā.	هُئو تهِئون huō thiũ.
III pers.	هُئَنِ تها huane thā.	هُئَنِ تهِئون huane thiũ.

Old Present of the Sansk. substantive verb
'as' to be. 'I am'.

	SING.	PLUR.
I pers.	آنهِيان āhiyā̃.	آنهِيُون ā̃hiyũ.
II pers.	آنهين، آنهِين ā̃hẽ, ā̃hī̃.	آهِيو ā̃hiyō.
III pers.	آهِي āhē.	آنهِنِ، آنهِينِ ā̃hine, ā̃hīne.

This form is commonly used in the Present, and always in compound tenses, whereas هُئان تهو huā̃ thō is seldom to be met with, and never in a compound tense.

The initial vowel ā is often found without a nasal sound as: آهِيان āhiyā̃ instead of آنهِيان ā̃hiyā̃. When کو نہ kō na, کا نہ kā na, کِي نہ kī na not any one etc. precedes آهِي, they are contracted to کونهِي kōnhē, کانهِي kānhē, کِينهِي kīnhē; نہ na, not, preceding آنهِيان etc. may coalesce with it, as: ناهِي nāhē or: نہ آهِي na āhē, he is not.

2) THE DEFINITE PRESENT.

The present participle with the auxiliary: آنهِيان 'I am being'.

SINGULAR.

	Masc.	*Fem.*
I pers.	هُوندو آنهِيان hūndō ā̃hiyā̃.	هُوندِي آنهِيان hūndī ā̃hiyā̃.
II pers.	هُوندو آنهين hūndō ā̃hē̃.	هُوندِي آنهين hūndī ā̃hē̃.
III pers.	آهِي „ „ āhē.	آهِي „ „ āhē.

PLURAL.

I pers.	هُوندا آنهِيُون hūndā ā̃hiyū̃.	هُوندِيُون آنهِيُون hūndiū̃ ā̃hiyū̃.
II pers.	هُوندا آهِيو hūndā āhiyō.	هُوندِيُون آهِيو hūndiū̃ āhiyō.
III pers.	هُوندا آنهِن hūndā ā̃hini.	هُوندِيُون آنهِن hūndiū̃ ā̃hine.

III. THE IMPERFECT.

The present participle with the Aorist of the auxiliary: هوسِ. 'I was' or: 'was being'.

SINGULAR.

	Masc.	*Fem.*
I pers.	هُوندو هوسِ hūndō hōse.	هُوندِي هُيَسِ hūndī huyase.

	Masc.	*Fem.*
II pers.	هُوندو هُئِين hūndō huẽ.	هُوندِي هُئِئَن hūndī huiã[1]).
III pers.	هُوندو هو hūndō hō.	هُوندِي هُئِي، هِي hūndī huī, hī.

PLURAL.

I pers.	هُوندا هُئَاسِين hūnda huāsī̃.	هُوندِيُون هُيُونْسِين hūndiū̃ huyū̃sī̃.
II pers.	هُوندَا هُئَوُ، هُئو hūnda hua-u, huō.	هُوندِيُون هُيُون hūndiū̃ huyū̃.
III pers.	هُوندَا هُئَا، هَا hūnda huā, hā.	هُوندِيُون هُيُون hūndiū̃ huyū̃.

IV. THE AORIST.

1) THE SIMPLE AORIST.

The past participle with the inflexional terminations. 'I was', or: 'have been'.

SINGULAR.

	Masc.	*Fem.*
I pers.	هوسِ hōse.	هُيَسِ huy-ase.
II pers.	هُئِين huẽ.	هُئِئَن، هُئِئين hui-ã, hui-ẽ.
III pers.	هو hō.	هُئِي huī.

PLURAL.

I pers.	هُئَاسِين huā-sī̃.	هُيُونْسِين huyū̃-sī.
II pers.	هُئَوُ، هُئو، هو hua-u, hu-ō, hō.	هُيُون huyū̃.
III pers.	هُئَا، هَا huā, hā.	هُيُون huyū̃.

---

1) Or هُئِئين huiẽ.

Instead of هُنَّاسِين huā-sĩ, هُنَّاسُون huā-sũ, the contracted forms هَاسِين hā-sĩ, هَاسُون hāsũ, are also in use. — The inflexional terminations are now and then dropped altogether, but in this case the absolute personal pronoun must always be prefixed, as: آنئُون هو ãũ hō, I was etc.

2) THE HABITUAL AORIST.

The simple Aorist with تهي thē.
'I used to be'.

SINGULAR.

	Masc.		*Fem.*	
I pers.	هوسِ تهي	hōse thē.	هُيَسِ تهي	huyase thē.
	etc.	etc.	etc.	etc.

PLURAL.

I pers.	هُنَّاسِين تهي	huāsĩ thē.	هُيُونْسِين تهي	huyũsĩ thē.
	etc.	etc.	etc.	etc.

V. PERFECT
VI. PLUPERFECT } not in use.

VII. THE FUTURE.

The present participle with the inflexional terminations. 'I shall be'.

SINGULAR.

	Masc.		*Fem.*	
I pers.	هُوندُسِ	hūndu-se.	هوندِئَسِ	hūndia-se [1]).
II pers.	هُوندين	hūnd-ẽ.	هُوندِئَن	hūndi-ã [2]).
III pers.	هُوندو	hūndō.	هُوندِي	hūndī.

1) Instead of هُوندِئَسِ hūndia-se we find also هُوندِيَسِ hūndi-yase or هُونديَسِ hūndyase.

2) Or هُوندِئين hūndi-ẽ.

PLURAL.

	Masc.	*Fem.*
I pers.	هُوندَاسِين hūndā-sī.	هُوندِئُونْسِين hūndiū-sī.
II pers.	هُوندَؤُ، هُوندو hūnda-u, hūndō.	هُوندِئُون hūndiū.
III pers.	هُوندا hūndā.	هُوندِئُون hūndiū.

The compound future tenses are not in use.

As from all neuter verbs, so also from this auxiliary an impersonal or passive form may be derived, as: III pers. Sing. Present هوئِجي تهو hō-ije thō, literally: it is been; III pers. Sing. Future: هوئِبو hō-ibō, literally: it will be been.

Annotation. The root هو hō (Inf. هُوَڻُ hu-aṇu) corresponds to the Sansk. root भू bhū, to become, which is assimilated in Prākrit to hō or huva; the past participle of it is in Prākrit huō or hūō, thence the Sindhī huō. In reference to the Potential hujā̃ etc., it is to be kept in mind, that Prākrit uses already for the Present (and Future) such forms as hojja, hojjā etc., which Lassen derives from the Sansk. Precative भुयात् (Lassen, p. 357).

The root hō is used in all the kindred idioms.

The old Present آنهيَان ā̃hiyā̃, I am, is derived from the Present of the Sansk. substantive verb अस 'as' to be, Prākrit amhi etc. The Marāṭhī form of it approaches very closely to that of the Sindhī, as: āhē̃ etc. In Hindūstānī (hā̃, haĩ, hai etc.) initial 'a', which has been lengthened in Sindhī and Marāṭhī, has been dropped; the same is the case in Panjābī, as hā̃, haĩ, hai etc. In Gujarātī, where initial 'a' has been likewise thrown off, we find the forms čhaũ, čhē, čhē etc., which correspond to the Prākrit form अच्छि ačči etc. (Lassen, p. 266, 346). In Bangālī we meet with the still more primitive form āčhi etc.

§. 50.

B. The auxiliary verb تهِئَڻُ thianu, to become, to be.

The verb تهِئَڻُ thiaṇu, to become, to be, is also partly used as an auxiliary verb. Its compound tenses are made up by means of the auxiliary verb هُئَڻُ huaṇu.

Infinitive.

تهِئَڻُ thi-aṇu, to become, to be.

Imperative.

	SING.	PLUR.
II pers.	تهِيُ thī-u, become thou.	تهِيٿو، تهِئو thī-ō, thi-ō, become ye.

Precative.

	SING.	PLUR.
II pers.	تهِيجِ، تهِجِ thī-je, thi-je. mayst thou become.	تهِيجو، تهِجو thi-jō, thi-jō. may you become.

Participles.

1) Present participle: تهِيندو thī-ndō, becoming.

2) Past participle: تهِئو thi-ō, become.

3) Past conjunctive participles:

تهِي thī
تهِئو thi-ō } having become.
تهِي كَرِي thī karē

4) Verbal noun: تهِئَڻو thi-aṇō, becoming, being.

I. THE POTENTIAL.

1) THE SIMPLE POTENTIAL.

'May become'.

	SING.	PLUR.
I pers.	تهِئان thi-ā̃.	تهِئُون thi-ū̃.
II pers.	تهِئِين، تهِين thi-ē̃, thī̃.	تهِئو thi-ō.
III pers.	تهِئِي thi-ē.	تهِئَنِ، تهِينِ thi-ane, thī-ne.

2) COMPOUND POTENTIAL.

a) The present participle with the Potential of هُونَ huaṇu. 'May be becoming'.

SINGULAR.

	Masc.	*Fem.*
I pers.	تهِيندو هُئان thīndō huā̃.	تهِينِدِي هُئان thīndī huā̃.
II pers.	تهِيندو هُئِين thīndō huẽ.	تهِينِدِي هُئِين thīndī huẽ.
III pers.	تهِيندو هُئِي thīndō huē.	تهِينِدِي هُئِي thīndī huē.

PLURAL.

I pers.	تهِيندا هُون thīndā hū̃.	تهِينِدِئُون هُون thīndiū̃ hū̃.
II pers.	تهِيندا هُئو thīndā huō.	تهِينِدِئُون هُئو thīndiū̃ huō.
III pers.	تهِيندا هُئنِ thīndā huane.	تهِينِدِئُون هُئنِ thīndiū̃ huane.

b) The past participle with the Potential of هُونَ huaṇu. 'May have become'.

SINGULAR.

	Masc.	*Fem.*
I pers.	تهِئو هُئان[1] thiō huā̃.	تهِي هُئان thī huā̃.
II pers.	هُئِين „ „ huẽ.	هُئِين „ „ huẽ.
III pers.	هُئِي „ „ huē.	هُئِي „ „ huē.

PLURAL.

I pers.	تهِئا هُون thiā hū̃.	تهِئُون هُون thiū̃ hū̃.
II pers.	هُئو „ „ huō.	هُئو „ „ huō.
III pers.	هُئنِ „ „ huane.	هُئنِ „ „ huane.

---

1) Or هُجان hujā̃ etc.

II. THE PRESENT.

1) THE PRESENT INDEFINITE.

The Potential with تهو thō.

'I become'.

SINGULAR.

	Masc.	*Fem.*
I pers.	تهِيَّان تهو thiā̃ thō.	تهِيَّان تهِي thiā̃ thī.
II pers.	تهِئِين تهو thiē̃ thō.	تهِئِين تهِي thiē̃ thī.
III pers.	تهِئِي تهو thiē thō.	تهِئِي تهِي thiē thī.

PLURAL.

I pers.	تهِئُون تهَا thiū̃ thā.	تهِئُون تهِئُون thiū̃ thiū̃.
II pers.	تهِئو تهَا thiō thā.	تهِئو تهِئُون thiō thiū̃.
III pers.	تهِئَنِ تهَا thiane thā.	تهِئَنِ تهِئُون thiane thiū̃.

2) THE PRESENT DEFINITE.

The present participle with آنهِيَان ā̃hiyā̃ etc.

'I am becoming'. etc.

SINGULAR.

	Masc.	*Fem.*
I pers.	تهِيندو آنهِيَان thīndō ā̃hiyā̃.	تهِيندِي آنهِيَان thīndī ā̃hiyā̃.
II pers.	تهِيندو آنهِين thīndō ā̃hē̃.	تهِيندِي آنهِين thīndī ā̃hē̃.
III pers.	تهِيندو آهِي thīndō āhē.	تهِيندِي آهِي thīndī āhē.

PLURAL.

	Masc.	*Fem.*
I pers.	تهِينداَ آنهِيُون thīndā ā̃hiyū̃.	تهِيندِئُون آنهِيُون thīndiū̃ ā̃hiyū̃.
II pers.	تهِينداَ آهِيوَ thīndā āhiyō.	تهِيندِئُون آهِيوَ thīndiū̃ āhiyō.
III pers.	تهِينداَ آنهِنِ thīndā ā̃hine.	تهِيندِئُون آنهِنِ thīndiū̃ ā̃hine.

III. THE IMPERFECT.

The present participle with هوِسِ hōse etc.

'I was becoming' etc.

SINGULAR.

	Masc.	*Fem.*
I pers.	تهِيندوَ هوِسِ thīndō hōse.	تهِيندِي هُيَسِ thīndī huyase.
II pers.	تهِيندوَ هُئِين thīndō huẽ.	تهِيندِي هُئِنَّ[1] thīndī huiā.
III pers.	تهِيندوَ هو thīndō hō.	تهِيندِي هُئِي thīndī huī.

PLURAL.

	Masc.	*Fem.*
I pers.	تهِينداَ هُئاَسِين thīndā huāsī.	تهِيندِئُون هُيُونْسِين thīndiū̃ huyū̃sī.
II pers.	تهِينداَ هُئوَ[2] thīndā hua-u.	تهِيندِئُون هُيُون thīndiū̃ huyū̃.
III pers.	تهِينداَ هُئاَ thīndā huā.	تهِيندِئُون هُيُون thīndiū̃ huyū̃.

---

1) Or هُئِئِين huiẽ.

2) Or هُئوَ huō, hō.

IV. THE AORIST.

1) THE SIMPLE AORIST.

The past participle with the inflexional terminations. 'I became' etc.

SINGULAR.

	Masc.	*Fem.*
I pers.	تهِئُسِ thiuse[1]).	تهِئَسِ thiase.
II pers.	تهِئِين thiē̃.	تهِئَن[2]) thiā̃.
III pers.	تهِئو thiō.	تهِي thī.

PLURAL.

I pers.	تهِئاسِين thiāsī̃.	تهِئُونْسِين thiū̃sī̃.
II pers.	تهِئو، تهِئُو thia-u, thiō.	تهِئُون thiū̃.
III pers.	تهِئا thiā.	تهِئُون thiū̃.

2) THE HABITUAL AORIST.

The simple Aorist with تهي thē.

'I was becoming, was in the habit to become' etc.

SINGULAR.

	Masc.	*Fem.*
I pers.	تهِئُسِ تهي thiuse thē.	تهِئَسِ تهي thiase thē.
	etc. etc.	etc. etc.

PLURAL.

I pers.	تهِئاسِين تهي thiāsī̃ thē.	تهِئُونسِين تهي thiū̃sī̃ thē.
	etc. etc.	etc. etc.

---

1) In poëtry often: تهِئوسِ thiōse, fem. تهِئاسِ thiase.

2) Or: تهِئِين thiē̃.

V. THE PERFECT.

The past participle with the auxiliary آنهِيَان ãhiyã.

'I have become' etc.

SINGULAR.

	Masc.		*Fem.*	
I pers.	تهِئو آنهِيَان	thiō ãhiyã.	تهِي آنهِيَان	thī ãhiyã.
II pers.	آنهِين „ „	ãhẽ.	آنهِين „ „	ãhẽ.
III pers.	آهِي „ „	āhē.	آهِي „ „	āhē.

PLURAL.

I pers.	تهِئا آنهِيُون	thiā ãhiyũ.	تهِئُون آنهِيُون	thiũ ãhiyũ.
II pers.	آهِيو „ „	āhiyō.	تهِئُون آهِيو	thiũ āhiyō.
III pers.	آنهِنِ „ „	ãhine.	آنهِنِ „ „	ãhine.

VI. THE PLUPERFECT.

The past participle with the Aorist هوسِ hōse etc.

'I had become' etc.

SINGULAR.

	Masc.		*Fem.*	
I pers.	تهِئو هوسِ	thiō hōse.	تهِي هُئِيسِ	thī huyase.
II pers.	هُئِين „ „	huẽ.	هُئِئَن „ „	huiã.
III pers.	هو „ „	hō.	هُئِي „ „	huī.

PLURAL.

I pers.	تهِئا هُئَاسِين	thiā huāsĩ.	تهِئُون هُئِيُونسِين	thiū huyũsĩ.
II pers.	تهِئا هُئَو	thiā hua-u.	تهِئُون هُئِيُون	thiū huyũ.
III pers.	هُئَا „ „	huā.	هُئِيُون „ „	huyũ.

VII. THE FUTURE.

1) THE SIMPLE OR INDEFINITE FUTURE.

The present participle with the inflexional terminations. 'I shall become' etc.

SINGULAR.

	Masc.		*Fem.*	
I pers.	تهِيندُسِ	thīnduse.	تهِيندِئَسِ	thīndiase[1]).
II pers.	تهِينديِن	thīndẽ.	تهِيندِئَن	thīndiā̃.[2])
III pers.	تهِيندو	thīndō.	تهِيندِي	thīndī.

PLURAL.

I pers.	تهِينداسِين	thīndāsī̃.	تهِيندِئُونْسِين	thīndiū̃sī̃.
II pers.	تهِيندَوُ	thīnda-u.[3])	تهِيندِئُون	thīndiū̃.
III pers.	تهِيندَا	thīndā.	تهِيندِئُون	thīndiū̃.

2) COMPOUND FUTURE TENSES.

a) The definite Future.

The present participle with the Future هُوندُسِ hūnduse etc. 'I shall be becoming' etc.

SINGULAR.

	Masc.	*Fem.*
I pers.	تهِيندو هُوندُسِ thīndō hūnduse.	تهِيندِي هُوندِئَسِ thīndī hūndiase.
II pers.	تهِيندو هُونديِن thīndō hūndẽ.	تهِيندِي هُوندِئَن thindī hūndiā̃.
III pers.	تهِيندو هُوندو thīndō hūndō.	تهِيندِي هُوندِي thīndī hūndī.

---

1) Or تهِيندِيَسِ thīndiyase, تهِيندَيَسِ thīndyase.

2) Or تهِيندِئِين thīndiẽ.

3) Or تهِيندو thīndō.

PLURAL.

	Masc.	*Fem.*
I pers.	تهِيندَا هُوندَانسِين	تهِينڊِئُون هُونڊِئُونْسِين
	thīndā hūndāsī̃.	thīndiū̃ hūndiū̃sī̃.
II pers.	تهِيندَا هُوندَؤ	تهِينڊِئُون هُونڊِئُون
	thīndā hūnda-u.	thīndiū̃ hūndiū̃.
III pers.	تهِيندَا هُوندَا	تهِينڊِئُون هُونڊِئُون
	thīndā hūndā.	thīndiū̃ hūndiū̃.

b) The past Future.

The past participle with the Future هُوندُسِ hūnduse.

'I shall have become' etc.

SINGULAR.

	Masc.	*Fem.*
I pers.	تهِئو هُوندُسِ	تهِي هُونڊِئَسِ
	thiō hūnduse.	thī hūndiase.
	etc. etc.	etc. etc.

PLURAL.

I pers.	تهِئَا هُوندَاسِين	تهِئُون هُونڊِئُونْسِين
	thiā hūndāsī̃.	thiū̃ hūndiū̃sī̃.
	etc. etc.	etc. etc.

Chapter XV.

Inflexion of the regular verb.

§. 51.

A. Inflexion of the neuter or intransitive verb.

All the neuter verbs end in the Imperative in 'u' (§. 43) and in the participle present in andō (§. 44).

But there is also a considerable number of **transitive** verbs ending in the Imperative in 'u' and in the participle present in **andō**, which take in consequence thereof the same inflexional terminations as the neuter verbs, with the only difference, that in the **Past Tenses** they must invariably resort to the **passive construction**.

We exhibit now the inflexion of a regular neuter verb.

Infinitive.

هَلَنُ hal-aṇu, to go.

Imperative.

	SING.	PLUR.
II pers.	هَلُ hal-u, go thou.	هَلو hal-ō, go ye.

Precative.

هَلِجِ hal-ije, هَلِجُ hal-iju,	mayst thou go.	هَلِجو hal-ij-ō, may ye go.

Participles:

1) present participle: هَلَنْدو hal-andō, going.

2) past participle: هَلِئو hal-iō, having gone.

3) past conjunctive participles:

هَلي hal-ī,
هَلِئو hal-iō,
هَلِجي hal-ijī,
هَلي كَري hal-ī kare,
} having gone.

Verbal noun.

هَلَنو hal-aṇō, going.

I. THE POTENTIAL.

1) THE SIMPLE POTENTIAL.

'I may go' etc.

	SING.	PLUR.
I pers.	آنٌون هَلان ãũ hal-ã.	اَسِين هَلُون asĩ hal-ũ.
II pers.	تُون هَلِين tũ hal-ẽ.	اَهِين هَلو ahĩ hal-ō.
III pers.	هُو هَلِي hū hal-ē.	هُو هَلَنِ hū hal-ane.

2) COMPOUND POTENTIAL.

a) The present participle with the Potential هُئان huã etc. 'I may be going'.

SINGULAR.

	Masc.	*Fem.*
I pers.	هَلَنْدو هُئان halandō huã.	هَلَنْدِي هُئان halandī huã.
II pers.	هَلَنْدو هُئِين halandō huẽ.	هُئِين " " huẽ.
III pers.	هَلَنْدو هُئِي halandō huē.	هُئِي " " huē.

PLURAL.

I pers.	هَلَنْدَا هُون halandā hũ.	هَلَنْدِئُون هُون halandiũ hũ.
II pers.	هَلَنْدَا هُئو halandā huō.	هَلَنْدِئُون هُئو halandiũ huō.
III pers.	هَلَنْدَا هُئَنِ halandā huane.	هَلَنْدِئُون هُئَنِ halandiũ huane.

b) The past participle with the Potential هُئان.
'I may have gone'.

SINGULAR.

	Masc.		*Fem.*	
I pers.	هَليٖو هُئان	haliō huā̃.	هَلي هُئان	halī huā̃.
II pers.	هُئين „ „	huẽ.	هُئين „ „	huẽ.
III pers.	هُئي „ „	huē.	هُئي „ „	huē.

PLURAL.

I pers.	هَليا هُون	haliā hū̃.	هَليُون هُون	haliū̃ hū̃.
II pers.	هُئو „ „	huō.	هُئو „ „	huō.
III pers.	هُئن „ „	huane.	هُئن „ „	huane.

II. THE PRESENT.

1) THE PRESENT INDEFINITE.

The Potential with تهو thō.
'I go' etc.

SINGULAR.

	Masc.		*Fem.*	
I pers.	هَلان تهو	halā̃ thō.	هَلان تهِي	halā̃ thī.
II pers.	هَلين تهو	halẽ thō.	هَلين تهِي	halẽ thī.
III pers.	هَلي تهو	halē thō.	هَلي تهِي	halē thī.

PLURAL.

I pers.	هَلُون تها	halū̃ thā.	هَلُون تهِئُون	halū̃ thiū̃.
II pers.	هَلو تها	halō thā.	هَلو تهِئُون	halō thiū̃.
III pers.	هَلن تها	halane thā.	هَلن تهِئُون	halane thiū̃.

2) THE PRESENT DEFINITE.

The present participle with آنهِيَان ãhiyã etc.

'I am going' etc.

SINGULAR.

	Masc.	*Fem.*
I pers.	هَلَنْدو آنهِيَان halandō ãhiyã.	هَلَنْدِي آنهِيَان halandī ãhiyã.
II pers.	هَلَنْدو آنهِين halandō ãhẽ.	هَلَنْدِي آنهِين halandī ãhẽ.
III pers.	هَلَنْدو آهِي halandō āhē.	هَلَنْدِي آهِي halandī āhē.

PLURAL.

I pers.	هَلَنْدا آنهِيُون halandā ãhiyũ.	هَلَنْدِئُون آنهِيُون halandiũ ãhiyũ.
II pers.	هَلَنْدا آهِيو halandā āhiyō.	هَلَنْدِئُون آهِيو halandiũ āhiyō.
III pers.	هَلَنْدا آنهِنِ halandā ãhine.	هَلَنْدِئُون آنهِنِ halandiũ ãhine.

III. THE IMPERFECT.

The present participle with هوسِ hōse etc.

'I was going' etc.

SINGULAR.

	Masc.	*Fem.*
I pers.	هَلَنْدو هوسِ halandō hōse.	هَلَنْدِي هُيَسِ halandī huyase.
II pers.	هَلَنْدو هُئِين halandō huẽ.	هَلَنْدِي هُئِن halandī huiā.
III pers.	هَلَنْدو هو halandō hō.	هَلَنْدِي هُئِي halandī huī.

PLURAL.

	Masc.	*Fem.*
I pers.	هَلَنْدَا هُنَّاسِين	هَلَنْدِنُون هُيُونْسِين
	halandā huāsī̃.	halandiū̃ huyū̃sī̃.
II pers.	هَلَنْدَا هُنَو	هَلَنْدِنُون هُيُون
	halandā hua-u.	halandiū̃ huyū̃.
III pers.	هَلَنْدَا هُنَا	هَلَنْدِنُون هُيُون
	halandā huā.	halandiū̃ huyū̃.

IV. THE AORIST.

1) THE SIMPLE AORIST.

The past participle with the inflexional terminations. 'I went' etc.

SINGULAR.

	Masc.	*Fem.*
I pers.	هَلِنُّسِ haliu-se.	هَلِنَّسِ halia-se.
II pers.	هَلِئِين hali-ẽ.	هَلِنّ hali-ã.[1]
III pers.	هَلِئو haliō.	هَلِي halī.

PLURAL.

I pers.	هَلِنّاسِين haliā-sī̃.	هَلِنُونْسِين haliū̃-sī̃.
II pers.	هَلِيَو halya-u.	هَلِنُون haliū̃.
III pers.	هَلِنَّا haliā.	هَلِنُون haliū̃.

2) THE HABITUAL AORIST.

The simple Aorist with تهي thē.

'I used to go' etc.

SINGULAR.

I pers. هَلِنُّسِ تهي haliuse thē. هَلِنَّسِ تهي haliase thē.

etc. etc. etc. etc.

---

1) Or هَلِئِين hali-ẽ.

PLURAL.

	Masc.	*Fem.*
I pers.	هَلِئَّاسِين تهي haliā̃sī̃ thē. etc. etc.	هَلِئُونْسِين تهي haliū̃sī̃ thē. etc. etc.

V. THE PERFECT.

The past participle with آنهِيَان ā̃hiyā̃ etc.

'I am gone' or 'have gone' etc.

SINGULAR.

	Masc.		*Fem.*	
I pers.	هَلِئو آنهِيَان	haliō ā̃hiyā̃.	هَلِي آنهِيَان	halī ā̃hiyā̃.
II pers.	آنهِين „	„ ā̃hē̃.	آنهِين „	„ ā̃hē̃.
III pers.	آهِي „	„ āhē.	آهِي „	„ āhē.

PLURAL.

I pers.	هَلِئَّا آنهِيُون	haliā̃ ā̃hiyū̃.	هَلِئُون آنهِيُون	haliū̃ ā̃hiyū̃.
II pers.	آهِيو „	„ āhiyō.	آهِيو „	„ āhiyō.
III pers.	آنهِنِ „	„ ā̃hine.	آنهِنِ „	„ ā̃hine.

VI. THE PLUPERFECT.

The past participle with the Aorist هوسِ hōse.

'I was gone' or 'had gone' etc.

SINGULAR.

	Masc.		*Fem.*	
I pers.	هَلِئو هوسِ	haliō hōse.	هَلِي هُيَسِ	halī huyase.
II pers.	هُئِين „	„ huē̃.	هُئِئَّن „	„ huiā̃.
III pers.	هو „	„ hō.	هُئِي „	„ huī.

PLURAL.

	Masc.	*Fem.*
I pers.	هَلِيَا هُئَاسِين haliā huāsī̃.	هَلِيُون هُيُونْسِين haliū̃ huyū̃sī̃.
II pers.	هَلِيَا هُئو haliā hua-u.	هَلِيُون هُيُون haliū̃ huyū̃.
III pers.	هُئَا „ „ huā.	هُيُون „ „ huyū̃.

VII. THE FUTURE.

1) THE SIMPLE or INDEFINITE FUTURE.

The present participle with the inflexional terminations. 'I shall go' etc.

SINGULAR.

	Masc.	*Fem.*
I pers.	هَلَنْدُسِ halandu-se.	هَلَنْدِئَسِ halandia-se.[1])
II pers.	هَلَنْدِين haland-ẽ.	هَلَنْدِئَن halandi-ā̃.[2])
III pers.	هَلَنْدو halandō.	هَلَنْدِي halandī.

PLURAL.

I pers.	هَلَنْدَاسِين halandā-sī̃.	هَلَنْدِئُونْسِين halandiū̃-sī̃.
II pers.	هَلَنْدَئو halanda-u.	هَلَنْدِئُون halandiū̃.
III pers.	هَلَنْدَا halandā.	هَلَنْدِئُون halandiū̃.

2) COMPOUND FUTURE TENSES.

a) The definite Future.

The present participle with هُوندُسِ hūnduse.

'I shall be going' etc.

SINGULAR.

I pers.	هَلَنْدو هُوندُسِ halandō hunduse.	هَلَنْدِي هُوندِئَسِ halandī hundiase.

1) Or هَلَنْدِيَسِ halandiyase, هَلَنْدْيَسِ halandyase.

2) Or هَلَنْدِئِين halandi-ẽ.

SINGULAR.

	Masc.	*Fem.*
II pers.	هَلَنْدوْ هُونْدِين halandō hūndē̃.	هَلَنْدِي هُونْدِئَن halandī hūndiā̃.
III pers.	هَلَنْدوْ هُونْدوْ halandō hūndō.	هَلَنْدِي هُونْدِي halandī hūndī.

PLURAL.

I pers.	هَلَنْدَا هُونْدَاسِين halandā hūndāsī̃.	هَلَنْدِئُون هُونْدِئُونْسِين halandiū̃ hūndiū̃sī̃.
II pers.	هَلَنْدَا هُونْدَءُو halandā hūnda-u.	هَلَنْدِئُون هُونْدِئُون halandiū̃ hūndiū̃.
III pers.	هَلَنْدَا هُونْدَا halandā hūndā.	هَلَنْدِئُون هُونْدِئُون halandiū̃ hūndiū̃.

b) The Past Future.

The past participle with the Future هُونْدُوسِ hūnduse. 'I shall have (be) gone' etc.

SINGULAR.

I pers.	هَلِئوْ هُونْدُسِ haliō hūnduse.	هَلِي هُونْدِئَسِ halī hūndiase.
II pers.	هَلِئوْ هُونْدِين haliō hūndē̃.	هَلِي هُونْدِئَن halī hūndiā̃.
III pers.	هَلِئوْ هُونْدوْ haliō hūndō.	هُونْدِي „ „ hūndī.

PLURAL.

I pers.	هَلِئَا هُونْدَاسِين haliā hūndāsī̃.	هَلِئُون هُونْدِئُونْسِين haliū̃ hūndiū̃sī̃.
II pers.	هَلِئَا هُونْدَءُو haliā hūnda-u.	هَلِئُون هُونْدِئُون haliū̃ hūndiū̃.
III pers.	هَلِئَا هُونْدَا haliā hūndā.	هَلِئُون هُونْدِئُون haliū̃ hūndiū̃.

Neuter verbs very often take in the Potential and in the Present tense the passive form, without altering in any way their signification, and are then inflected like other passive verbs (see the inflexion of the passive verb), as: ڦَرَڻُ pharaṇu, v. n., to be fruitful, or ڦَرْجَڻُ phar-ǰ-aṇu; لُڙهَڻُ v. n., luṛhaṇu, to float, or لُڙهجَڻُ luṛhe-ǰ-aṇu, ڪاوِڙَڻُ kāviṛaṇu, v. n., to be angry or ڪاوِڙجَڻُ kāviṛ-ǰ-aṇu, اَچَڻُ v. n. ačaṇu, to come, اَچِجَڻُ ač-ij-aṇu, پَوَڻُ v. n. pavaṇu, to fall, or پَئِجَڻُ pa-ij-aṇu etc.

The III pers. Sing. of neuter verbs in the passive form is frequently employed impersonally throughout all the tenses with the exception of the Aorist and Perfect, as: هَلِجي halijē, it may be gone, هَلِجي ٿو halijē thō, it is gone, هَلِبو آهي halibō āhē, it is being gone, هَلِبو هو halibō hō, it was being gone; هَلِبو halibō, it will be gone.

Many neuter verbs are in Sindhī considered both active and neuter, and therefore in the Past tenses constructed either as neuter (i. e. personally) or as transitive verbs (i. e. passively, the agent being put in the Instrumental), as: وِڙهيُسِ viṛhiuse, I quarrelled or: مُون وِڙهِئو mū̃ viṛhiō, by me it was quarrelled, from وِڙهَڻُ viṛhaṇu, v. n., to quarrel; کِلِيُسِ khiliuse, I laughed, or: مُون کِلِئو mū̃ khiliō, by me it was laughed, from کِلَڻُ khilaṇu, v. n., to laugh; but رُئَڻُ ruaṇu, v. n., to weep, is always constructed passively in the past tenses, as: رُنائِين runā̃-ī, he wept (it was wept by him).

On the other hand there are also some active verbs

(but ending in the Imperative in 'u'), which are constructed in the Past tenses like neuter verbs, and not passively, as: سِکھِئُسِ sikhiuse, I learnt (not مُون سِکھِئُو) from سِکھَڻُ sikhaṇu, v. a., to learn; سِکِئُس sikiuse, I longed for, from سِکَڻُ sikaṇu, v. a., to long for.

§. 52.

B) Inflexion of the transitive verb.

The inflexion of the transitive and causal verb agrees on the whole with that of the neuter verb in the Potential, the Present, the Imperfect and the Future; but it differs from the inflexion of the neuter verb by being destitute of the Past Tenses of the Active Voice, which must be circumscribed by the past tenses of the Passive Voice, the past participle of transitive verbs having always a passive signification. The agent must therefore in the past tenses be put in the Instrumental, or it may, if that be a pronoun, be affixed to the past participle in the shape of a Suffix. It is understood, that the past participle passive must agree with its substantive in gender and number, as well as the adjective.

From every transitive and causal verb (and partly also, as noted already, from the neuter verb) a passive theme may be derived, which is regularly inflected through all tenses.

We exhibit now the inflexion of a transitive verb, ending in the Imperative in 'e'.

1) ACTIVE VOICE.

Infinitive:

چھَڏَڻُ čhaḍ-aṇu, to give up.

Imperative.

	SING.	PLUR.
II pers.	چهَڊِ čhaḍ-e, give up.	چهَڊِئو čhaḍ-iō [1]), give ye up.

Precative.

SING.	PLUR.
چهَڊِج čhaḍ-ije. چهَڊِجُ chaḍ-iju.	چهَڊِجو čhaḍ-ijō, please to give up.

Participles:

1) Present participle: چهَڊِينْدو čhaḍ-īnḍō, giving up.

2) Past participle: چهَڊِئو čhaḍ-iō, having been given up.

3) Past conjunctive participles:

چهَڊِي čhaḍ-e چهَڊِئو čhaḍ-iō چهَڊِجي čhaḍ-ijē چهَڊِي كَرِي čhaḍ-ē karē	having given up.

I. THE POTENTIAL.

1) THE SIMPLE POTENTIAL.

'I may give up' etc.

	SING.	PLUR.
I pers.	آنُون چهَڊِئان ā̃ū čhaḍ-iā̃.	اَسِين چهَڊِئُون asī̃ čhaḍ-iū̃.
II pers.	تُون چهَڊِئين tū̃ čhaḍ-iē̃. [2])	اَهِين چهَڊِئو ahī̃ čhaḍ-iō.
III pers.	هُو چهَڊِي hū čhaḍ-ē.	هُو چهَڊِينِ chū čhaḍ-īne. [3])

1) Or چهَڊِيو čhaḍ-yō; the form چهَڊِهو čhaḍ-ehō is also in use.

2) Or چهَڊِين čhaḍ-ē̃, چهَڊِين čhaḍ-ī̃.

3) Or چهَڊِنِ čhaḍ-ine.

2) COMPOUND POTENTIAL.

a) The present participle with the Potential هُئاں.
'I may be giving up' etc.

SINGULAR.

	Masc.	*Fem.*
I pers.	چھڈِیندِو هُئاں čhaḍīndō huā̃.	چھڈِیندِي هُئاں čhaḍīndī huā̃.
II pers.	چھڈِیندِو هُئِین čhaḍīndō huē̃.	چھڈِیندِي هُئِین čhaḍīndī huē̃.
III pers.	چھڈِیندِو هُئِي čhaḍīndō huē.	چھڈِیندِي هُئِي čhaḍīndī huē.

PLURAL.

I pers.	چھڈِیندا هُون čhaḍīndā hū̃.	چھڈِیندِیُون هُون čhaḍīndiū̃ hū̃.
II pers.	چھڈِیندا هُئو čhaḍīndā huō.	چھڈِیندِیُون هُئو čhaḍīindiū̃ huō.
III pers.	چھڈِیندا هُئَنِ čhaḍīndā huane.	چھڈِیندِیُون هُئَنِ čhaḍīndiū̃ huane.

b) The past participle, with the III pers. Singular and Plural of the Potential of the auxiliary verb هُئَڻُ, the agent being put in the Instrumental.

'By me etc. may have been given up.'

SINGULAR.

The object being masc.	The object being fem.
مُون چھڈِئو هُئِي mū̃ čhaḍiō huē.	مُون چھڈِي هُئِي mū̃ čhaḍī huē.
تو چھڈِئو هُئِي tō čhaḍiō huē.	تو چھڈِي هُئِي tō čhaḍī huē.
„ „ هُنَ huna „ „	„ „ هُنَ huna „ „

SINGULAR.

The object being fem.	The object being masc.
آسان چهَڏِئو هُئي asā̃ čhaḍiō huē.	آسان چهَڏِي هُئي asā̃ čhaḍī huē.
اَهان چهَڏِئو هُئي ahā̃ čhaḍiō huē.	اَهان چهَڏِي هُئي ahā̃ čhaḍī huē.
هُنِ چهَڏِئو هُئي hune čhaḍiō huē.	هُنِ چهَڏِي هُئي hune čhaḍī huē.

PLURAL.

مُون چهَڏِيا هُئنِ mū̃ čhaḍiā huane. etc. etc.	مُون چهَڏِئون هُئنِ mū̃ čhaḍiū̃ huane. etc. etc.

II. THE PRESENT.

1) THE PRESENT INDEFINITE.

The Potential with تهو thō.

'I give up' etc.

SINGULAR.

	Masc.	*Fem.*
I pers.	چهَڏِيان تهو čhaḍiā̃ thō.	چهَڏِيان تهِي čhaḍiā̃ thī.
II pers.	چهَڏِئين تهو čhaḍiē̃ thō.	چهَڏِئين تهِي čhaḍiē̃ thī.
III pers.	چهَڏِي تهو čhaḍē thō.	چهَڏِي تهِي čhaḍē thī.

PLURAL.

I pers.	چهَڏِئون تهَا čhaḍiū̃ thā.	چهَڏِئون تهِئون čhaḍiū̃ thiū̃.
II pers.	چهَڏِئو تهَا čhaḍiō thā.	چهَڏِئو تهِئون čhaḍiō thiū̃.
III pers.	چهَڏِينِ تهَا čhaḍīne thā.	چهَڏِينِ تهِئون čhaḍīnē thiū̃.

2) THE PRESENT DEFINITE.

The present participle with آنهيَان ā̃hiyā̃ etc.
'I am giving up' etc.

SINGULAR.

	Masc.	*Fem.*
I pers.	چهَڊِيندو آنهيَان čhaḍīndō ā̃hiyā̃.	چهَڊِيندِي آنهيان čhaḍīndī ā̃hiyā̃.
II pers.	چهَڊِيندو آنهين čhaḍīndō ā̃hẽ.	چهَڊِيندِي آنهين čhaḍīndī ā̃hẽ.
III pers.	چهَڊِيندو آهي čhaḍīndō āhē.	چهَڊِيندِي آهي čhaḍīndī āhē.

PLURAL.

I pers.	چهَڊِيندا آنهيُون čhaḍīndā ā̃hiyū̃.	چهَڊِيندِيُون آنهيُون čhaḍīndiū̃ ā̃hiyū̃.
II pers.	چهَڊِيندا آهِيو čhaḍīndā āhiyō.	چهَڊِيندِيُون آهِيو čhaḍīndiū̃ āhiyō.
III pers.	چهَڊِيندا آنهِنِ čhaḍīndā ā̃hine.	چهَڊِيندِيُون آنهِنِ čhaḍīndiū̃ ā̃hine.

III. THE IMPERFECT.

The present participle with the Aorist هوسِ hōse.
'I gave up' or: 'was giving up' etc.

SINGULAR.

	Masc.	*Fem.*
I pers.	چهَڊِيندو هوسِ čhaḍīndō hōse.	چهَڊِيندِي هُيَسِ čhaḍīndī huyase.
II pers.	چهَڊِيندو هُئين čhaḍīndō huẽ.	چهَڊِيندِي هُئَن čhaḍīndī huiā̃.
III pers.	چهَڊِيندو هو čhaḍīndō hō.	چهَڊِيندِي هُئِي čhaḍīndī huī.

PLURAL.

	Masc.	*Fem.*
I pers.	چهَڈِيندَا هُئَاسِين čhaḍīndā huāsī̃.	چهَڈِينڍِئُون هُيُونسِين čhaḍīndiū̃ huyū̃sī̃.
II pers.	چهَڈِيندَا هُئَو، هُئو čhaḍīndā hua-u, huō.	چهَڈِينڍِئُون هُيُون čhaḍīndiū̃ huyū̃.
III pers.	چهَڈِيندَا هُئَا، هَا čhaḍīndā huā, hā.	چهَڈِينڍِئُون هُيُون čhaḍīndiū̃ huyū̃.

IV. THE AORIST.

1) THE SIMPLE AORIST.

The past participle (passive), with the agent in the Instrumental.

'By me etc. was given up'.

SINGULAR.

The object being masc.		The object being fem.	
چهَڈِئو مُون	mũ čhaḍiō.	چهَڈِي مُون	mũ čhaḍī.
„ تو	tō „	„ تو	tō „
„ هُنَ	huna „	„ هُنَ	huna „
„ اَسَان	asā̃ „	„ اَسَان	asā̃ „
„ اَهَان	ahā̃ „	„ اَهَان	ahā̃ „
„ هُنِ	hune „	„ هُنِ	hune „

PLURAL.

چهَڈِئَا مُون	mũ čhaḍiā.	چهَڈِئُون مُون	mũ čhaḍiū̃.
etc.	etc.	etc.	etc.

2) THE HABITUAL AORIST.

The simple Aorist with تهي thē.

'By me etc. used to be given up'.

SINGULAR.

The object being masc.		The object being fem.	
مُون چهَڈِئو تهي	mũ čhaḍiō thē.	مُون چهَڈِي تهي	mũ čhaḍī thē.
etc.	etc.	etc.	etc.

PLURAL.

The object being masc.	The object being fem.
مُون چهَڊِيا تهي	مُون چهَڊِيُون تهي
mū̃ čhaḍiā thē.	mū̃ čhaḍiū̃ thē.
etc. etc.	etc. etc.

V. THE PERFECT.

The past participle (passive) with آهي āhē and آنهِنِ ā̃hine, the agent being put in the Instrumental.

'By me etc. has been given up'.

SINGULAR.

The object being masc.	The object being fem.
مُون چهَڊِئو آهي	مُون چهَڊِي آهي
mū̃ čhaḍiō āhē.	mū̃ čhaḍī āhē.
etc. etc.	etc. etc.

PLURAL.

The object being masc.	The object being fem.
مُون چهَڊِيا آنهِنِ	مُون چهَڊِيُون آنهِنِ
mū̃ čhaḍiā ā̃hine.	mū̃ čhaḍiū̃ ā̃hine.
etc. etc.	etc. etc.

VI. THE PLUPERFECT.

The past participle (passive) with هو hō, هُئا huā etc.

'By me etc. had been given up'.

SINGULAR.

The object being masc.	The object being fem.
مُون چهَڊِئو هو	مُون چهَڊِي هُئِي
mū̃ čhaḍiō hō.	mū̃ čhaḍī huī.
etc. etc.	etc. etc.

PLURAL.

The object being masc.	The object being fem.
مُون چهَڊِيا هُئا	مُون چهَڊِيُون هُيُون
mū̃ čhaḍiā huā.	mū̃ čhaḍiū̃ huyū̃.
etc. etc.	etc. etc.

VII. THE FUTURE.

1) THE SIMPLE or INDEFINITE FUTURE.

The present participle with the inflexional terminations.

'I shall give up' etc.

SINGULAR.

	Masc.		*Fem.*	
I pers.	چهَڎِينْدُسِ	čhaḏ̣īnduse.	چهَڎِينْدِئَسِ	čhaḏ̣īndia-se.
II pers.	چهَڎِينْدِين	čhaḏ̣īnd-ē̃.	چهَڎِينْدِئَن	čhaḏ̣īndi-ā̃.
III pers.	چهَڎِينْدو	čhaḏ̣īndō.	چهَڎِينْدِي	čhaḏ̣īndī.

PLURAL.

I pers.	چهَڎِينْدَاسِين	čhaḏ̣īndā-sī̃.	چهَڎِينْدِئُونْسِين	čhaḏ̣īndiū̃-sī̃.
II pers.	چهَڎِينْدَؤ	čhaḏ̣īnda-u.	چهَڎِينْدِئُون	čhaḏ̣īndiū̃.
III pers.	چهَڎِينْدَا	čhaḏ̣īndā.	چهَڎِينْدِئُون	čhaḏ̣īndiū̃.

2) COMPOUND FUTURE.

a) The definite Future.

The present participle with هُونْدُسِ hūnduse.

'I shall be giving up' etc.

SINGULAR.

	Masc.	*Fem.*
I pers.	چهَڎِينْدو هُونْدُسِ čhaḏ̣īndō hūnduse.	چهَڎِينْدِي هُونْدِئَسِ čhaḏ̣īndī hūndiase.
II pers.	چهَڎِينْدو هُونْدِين čhaḏ̣īndō hūndē̃.	چهَڎِينْدِي هُونْدِئَن čhaḏ̣īndī hūndiā̃.
III pers.	چهَڎِينْدو هُونْدو čhaḏ̣īndō hūndō.	چهَڎِينْدِي هُونْدِي čhaḏ̣īndī hūndī.

PLURAL.

	Masc.	*Fem.*
I pers.	چهَڊِينْدَا هُونْدَاسِين	چهَڊِينْدِئُون هُونْدِئُونْسِين
	čhaḍīndā hūndāsī̃.	čhaḍīndiū̃ hūndiū̃sī̃.
II pers.	چهَڊِينْدَا هُونْدَؤ	چهَڊِينْدِئُون هُونْدِئُون
	čhaḍīndā hūnda-u.	čhaḍīndiū̃ hūndiū̃.
III pers.	چهَڊِينْدَا هُونْدَا	چهَڊِينْدِئُون هُونْدِئُون
	čhaḍīndā hūndā.	čhaḍīndiū̃ hūndiū̃.

b) The Past Future.

The past participle (passive) with هُوندو hūndō etc., the agent being put in the Instrumental.

'By me etc. will have been given up'.

SINGULAR.

The object being masc.	The object being fem.
مُون چهَڊِئو هُونْدو	مُون چهَڊِي هُونْدِي
mū̃ čhaḍiō hūndō.	mū̃ čhaḍī hūndī.
etc. etc.	etc. etc.

PLURAL.

مُون چهَڊِئَا هُونْدَا	مُون چهَڊِئُون هُونْدِئُون
mū̃ čhaḍiā hūndā.	mū̃ čhaḍiū̃ hūndiū̃.
etc. etc.	etc. etc.

2) PASSIVE VOICE.

Infinitive.

چهَڊِجَڻُ čhaḍ-ij-aṇu, to be given up.

Imperative.

	SING.	PLUR.
II pers.	چهَڊِجُ čhaḍ-ij-u,	چهَڊِجو čhaḍ-ij-ō,
	be given up.	be ye given up.

Participles.

1) Present participle: چهَڊِبو čhaḍibō, being given up.
2) Past participle: چهَڊِئو čhaḍiō, having been given up.
3) Future participle or gerundive: چهَڊِنو čhaḍinō, to be given up.
4) Past conjunctive participles:

چهَڊِجي čhaḍ-ij-ī or چهَڊِجو čhaḍij-ō,
چهَڊِجي كَرِي čhaḍijī karē,
} having been given up.

I. THE POTENTIAL.

1) THE SIMPLE POTENTIAL.

'I may be given up'.

	SING.		PLUR.	
I pers.	چهَڊِجان	čhaḍij-ā̃.	چهَڊِجون	čhaḍij-ū̃.
II pers.	چهَڊِجين	čhaḍij-ē̃.[1]	چهَڊِجو	čhaḍij-ō.
III pers.	چهَڊِجي	čhaḍij-ē.	چهَڊِجَنِ	čhaḍij-ane.

2) COMPOUND POTENTIAL.

a) The present participle with the Potential هُئان huā̃.

'I may be being given up' etc.

SINGULAR.

	Masc.	*Fem.*
I pers.	چهَڊِبو هُئان čhaḍibō huā̃.	چهَڊِبِي هُئان čhaḍibī huā̃.
II pers.	چهَڊِبو هُئين čhaḍibō huē̃.	چهَڊِبِي هُئين čhaḍibī huē̃.
III pers.	چهَڊِبو هُئي čhaḍibō huē.	چهَڊِبِي هُئي čhaḍibī huē.

1) Or چهَڊِجين čhaḍijī̃.

PLURAL.

	Masc.	Fem.
I pers.	چھَڏِبا هُون čhaḍibā hū̃.	چھَڏِبِئُون هُون čhaḍibiū̃ hū̃.
II pers.	چھَڏِبا هُئو čhaḍibā huō.	چھَڏِبِئُون هُئو čhaḍibiū̃ huō.
III pers.	چھَڏِبا هُئَنِ čhaḍibā huane.	چھَڏِبِئُون هُئَنِ čhaḍibiū̃ huane.

b) The past participle with the Potential هُئان huā̃.

'I may have been given up' etc.

SINGULAR.

	Masc.			Fem.		
I pers.	چھَڏِئو هُئان	čhaḍiō	huā̃.	چھَڏِي هُئان	čhaḍī	huā̃.
II pers.	هُئِين	„	huẽ.	هُئِين	„	huẽ.
III pers.	هُئِي	„	huē.	هُئِي	„	huē.

PLURAL.

	Masc.			Fem.		
I pers.	چھَڏِئا هُون	čhaḍiā	hū̃.	چھَڏِئُون هُون	čhaḍiū̃	hū̃.
II pers.	هُئو	„	huō.	هُئو	„	huō.
III pers.	هُئَنِ	„	huane.	هُئَنِ	„	huane.

II. THE PRESENT.

1) THE INDEFINITE PRESENT.

The Potential with تھو thō.

'I am given up' etc.

SINGULAR.

	Masc.	Fem.
I pers.	چھَڏِجان تھو čhaḍijā̃ thō.	چھَڏِجان تھِي čhaḍijā̃ thī.

SINGULAR.

	Masc.	*Fem.*
II pers.	چھَڏِجين تھو čhaḍijẽ thō.	چھَڏِجين تھِي čhaḍijẽ thī.
III pers.	چھَڏِجي تھو čhaḍijē thō.	چھَڏِجي تھِي čhaḍijē thī.

PLURAL.

I pers.	چھَڏِجون تھَا čhaḍijũ thā.	چھَڏِجون تھِيُون čhaḍijũ thiũ.
II pers.	چھَڏِجو تھَا čhaḍijō thā.	چھَڏِجو تھِيُون čhaḍijō thiũ.
III pers.	چھَڏِجَنِ تھَا čhaḍijane thā.	چھَڏِجَنِ تھِيُون čhaḍijane thiũ.

2) THE DEFINITE PRESENT.

The present participle with آنھِيَان ãhiyã.

'I am being given up' etc.

SINGULAR.

	Masc.	*Fem.*
I pers.	چھَڏِبو آنھِيَان čhaḍibō ãhiyã.	چھَڏِبِي آنھِيَان čhaḍibī ãhiyã.
II pers.	چھَڏِبو آنھِين čhaḍibō ãhẽ.	چھَڏِبِي آنھِين čhaḍibī ãhẽ.
III pers.	چھَڏِبو آھِي čhaḍibō āhē.	چھَڏِبِي آھِي čhaḍibī āhē.

PLURAL.

I pers.	چھَڏِبَا آنھِيُون čhaḍibā ãhiyũ.	چھَڏِبِيُون آنھِيُون čhaḍibiũ ãhiyũ.
II pers.	چھَڏِبَا آھِيو čhaḍibā āhiyō.	چھَڏِبِيُون آھِيو čhaḍibiũ āhiyō.
III pers.	چھَڏِبَا آنھِنِ čhaḍibā ãhine.	چھَڏِبِيُون آنھِنِ čhaḍibiũ ãhine.

III THE IMPERFECT.

The present participle with هوسِ hōse.

'I was being given up' etc.

SINGULAR.

	Masc.	*Fem.*
I pers.	چهَڈِبو هوسِ čhaḍibō hōse.	چهَڈِبِي هُيَسِ čhaḍibī huyase.
II pers.	چهَڈِبو هُئِين čhaḍibō huẽ.	چهَڈِبِي هُئِںَ čhaḍibī huiã.
III pers.	چهَڈِبو هو čhaḍibō hō.	چهَڈِبِي هُئِي čhaḍibī huī.

PLURAL.

I pers.	چهَڈِبَا هُئَاسِين čhaḍibā huāsī.	چهَڈِبِئُون هُيُونْسِين čhaḍibiū̃ huyū̃sī.
II pers.	چهَڈِبَا هُئَوْ، هُئو čhaḍibā hua-u, huō.	چهَڈِبِئُون هُيُون čhaḍibiū̃ huyū̃.
III pers.	چهَڈِبَا هُئَا čhaḍibā huā.	چهَڈِبِئُون هُيُون čhaḍibiū̃ huyū̃.

IV. THE AORIST.

1) THE SIMPLE AORIST.

The past participle with the inflexional terminations.

'I was given up' etc.

SINGULAR.

	Masc.	*Fem.*
I pers.	جهَڈِئُسِ čhaḍiu-se.[1])	چهَڈِئَسِ čhaḍia-se.
II pers.	چهَڈِئِين čhaḍi-ẽ.	چهَڈِئَں čhaḍi-ã.
III pers.	چهَڈِئو čhaḍiō.	چهَڈِي čhaḍī.

1) Or چهَڏيُسِ čhaḏyuse, چهَڏيَسِ čhaḏyase.

PLURAL.

	Masc.		*Fem.*	
I pers.	چهَڏِئاسِين	čhaḍiā-sī̃.	چهَڏِئُونسِين	čhaḍiū̃-sī̃.
II pers.	چهَڏِيَوُ	čhaḍya-u.	چهَڏِئُون	čhaḍiū̃.
III pers.	چهَڏِئا	čhaḍiā.	چهَڏِئُون	čhaḍiū̃.

2) THE HABITUAL AORIST.

The simple Aorist with تهِي thē.

'I used to be given up' etc.

SINGULAR.

Masc.		*Fem.*	
چهَڏِئُسِ تهِي	čhaḍiuse thē.	چهَڏِئَسِ تهِي	čhaḍiase thē.
etc.	etc.	etc.	etc.

V. THE PERFECT.

The past participle with آنهِيَان ā̃hiyā̃.

'I have been given up' etc.

SINGULAR.

	Masc.	*Fem.*
I pers.	چهَڏِئو آنهِيَان čhaḍiō ā̃hiyā̃.	چهَڏِي آنهِيَان čhaḍī ā̃hiyā̃.
II pers.	چهَڏِئو آنهِين čhaḍiō ā̃hē̃.	چهَڏِي آنهِين čhaḍī ā̃hē̃.
III pers.	چهَڏِئو آهِي čhaḍiō āhē.	چهَڏِي آهِي čhaḍī āhē.

PLURAL.

	Masc.	*Fem.*
I pers.	چهَڏِئا آنهِيُون čhaḍiā ā̃hiyū̃.	چهَڏِئُون آنهِيُون čhaḍiū̃ ā̃hiyū̃.
II pers.	چهَڏِئا آهِيو čhaḍiā āhiyō.	چهَڏِئُون آهِيو čhaḍiū̃ āhiyō.
III pers.	چهَڏِئا آنهِنِ čhaḍiā ā̃hine.	چهَڏِئُون آنهِنِ čhaḍiū̃ ā̃hine.

VI. THE PLUPERFECT.

The past participle with ھوسِ hōse.

'I had been given up' etc.

SINGULAR.

	Masc.	*Fem.*
I pers.	چھَڏِئو ھوسِ čhaḍiō hōse.	ھھَڏِي هُيَسِ čhaḍī huyase.
II pers.	چھَڏِئو ھُئِين čhaḍiō huē̃.	چھَڏِي هُئِئَن čhaḍī huiā̃.
III pers.	چھَڏِئو ھو čhaḍiō hō.	چھَڏِي ھُئِي čhaḍī huī.

PLURAL.

I pers.	چھَڏِئا ھُئاسِين čhaḍiā huāsī̃.	چھَڏِئُون ھُيُونسِين čhaḍiū̃ huyū̃sī̃.
II pers.	چھَڏِئا ھُئو čhaḍiā hua-u.	چھَڏِئُون ھُيُون čhaḍiū̃ huyū̃.
III pers.	چھَڏِئا ھُئا čhaḍiā huā.	چھَڏِئُون ھُيُون čhaḍiū̃ huyū̃.

VII. THE FUTURE.

1) THE SIMPLE or INDEFINITE FUTURE.

The present participle with the inflexional terminations.

'I shall be given up' etc.

SINGULAR.

	Masc.	*Fem.*
I pers.	چھَڏِبُسِ čhaḍibu-se.	چھَڏِبِئَسِ čhaḍibia-se.
II pers.	چھَڏِبِين čhaḍib-ē̃.	چھَڏِبِئَن čhaḍibi-ā̃.
III pers.	چھَڏِبو čhaḍibō.	چھَڏِبِي čhaḍibī.

PLURAL.

	Masc.		Fem.	
I pers.	چھَڈِبَاسِين	čhaḍibā-sī̃.	چھَڈِبِئُونسِين	čhaḍibiū̃-sī̃.
II pers.	چھَڈِبَوُ	čhaḍiba-u.	چھَڈِبِئُون	čhaḍibiū̃.
III pers.	چھَڈِبَا	čhaḍibā.	چھَڈِبِئُون	čhaḍibiū̃.

2) COMPOUND FUTURE.

a) The definite Future.

The present participle with هُونْدُسِ hūnduse.

'I shall be being given up' etc.

SINGULAR.

	Masc.	Fem.
I pers.	چھَڈِبو هُونْدُسِ čhaḍibō hūnduse.	چھَڈِبِي هُونْدِئَسِ čhaḍibī hūndiase.
II pers.	چھَڈِبو هُونْدِين čhaḍibō hūndẽ.	چھَڈِبِي هُونْدِئَن čhaḍibī hūndiã.
III pers.	چھَڈِبو هُونْدو čhaḍibō hūndō.	چھَڈِبِي هُونْدِي čhaḍibī hūndī.

PLURAL.

	Masc.	Fem.
I pers.	چھَڈِبَا هُونْدَاسِين čhaḍibā hūndāsī̃.	چھَڈِبِئُون هُونْدِئُونْسِين čhaḍibiū̃ hūndiū̃sī̃.
II pers.	چھَڈِبَا هُونْدَوُ čhaḍibā hūnda-u.	چھَڈِبِئُون هُونْدِئُون čhaḍibiū̃ hūndiū̃.
III pers.	چھَڈِبَا هُونْدَا čhaḍibā hūndā.	چھَڈِبِئُون هُونْدِئُون čhaḍibiū̃ hūndiū̃.

b) The Past Future.

The past participle with هُونْدُسِ hūnduse.

'I shall have been given up' etc.

SINGULAR.

	Masc.	*Fem.*
I pers.	چھڏِئو هُونْدُسِ čhaḍiō hūnduse.	چھڏِي هُونْدِئَسِ čhaḍī hūndiase.
II pers.	چھڏِئو هُونْدِين čhaḍiō hūndē̃.	چھڏِي هُونْدِئَن čhaḍī hūndiā̃.
III pers.	چھڏِئو هُونْدو čhaḍiō hūndō.	چھڏِي هُونْدِي čhaḍī hūndī.

PLURAL.

I pers.	چھڏِئا هُونْداسِين čhaḍiā hūndāsī̃.	چھڏِيُون هُونْدِيُونسِين čhaḍiū̃ hūndiū̃sī̃.
II pers.	چھڏِئا هُونْدَؤ čhaḍiā hūnda-u.	چھڏِيُون هُونْدِيُون čhaḍiū̃ hūndiū̃.
III pers.	چھڏِئا هُونْدا čhaḍiā hūndā.	چھڏِيُون هُونْدِيُون čhaḍiū̃ hūndiū̃.

Chapter XVI.

Compound verbs.

§. 53.

The Sindhī possesses a great facility in giving different shadows of meaning to a verb by compounding it with another verb.

1) The most common way of compounding a verb with another is to put the past conjunctive par-

ticiple of the active or passive mood, ending in ī or ē[1]), before it.[2]) The construction of a verb thus compounded depends entirely on the definite verb, not in any way on the past conjunctive participle. In this way are formed

a) So-called Intensitives, which impart to the definite verb a peculiar signification, arising out of the sense of the preceding past conjunctive participle, as: وٺهي وڃڻُ vaṭhī vańaṇu, to take off, literally: to go having taken; مَرِي وڃڻُ marī vańaṇu, to be dead, lit.: to go having died; چَڙهِي وڃڻُ čaṛhī vańaṇu, to ascend, lit.: to go having ascended; کُهلِي پَوَڻُ khulī pavaṇu, to be opened, lit.: to fall having been opened; جِي پَوَڻُ jī pavaṇu, to become alive, literally: to fall having lived; وَهِي پَوَڻُ vahī pavaṇu, to pour down (as rain), literally: to fall having flown. — وَڍهي وِجهَڻُ vaḍhē vijhaṇu, to cut down, lit.: to throw having cut; سوري ڪَڍهَڻُ sōrē kaḍhaṇu, to pull out, lit.: to pull having moved; چاڙهي آڻَڻُ čāṛhē āṇaṇu, to hang up, lit.: to bring having caused to ascend; لوڙهي ڇهڏڻُ lōṛhē čhaḍaṇu, to float off (act.), lit.: to give up having floated away; تَاڻِئو ڇهِنَڻُ tāṇiō čhinaṇu, to pluck out, lit.: to pluck out having pulled; موٽائي نِئڻُ mōṭā-ē niaṇu, to bring back, lit.: to take away having caused to return, etc. etc. It is to be noted, that کهڻِي khaṇī, the past conjunctive participle of کهڻڻُ khaṇaṇu, to lift up, is used with all

1) The past conjunctive participle ending in iŏ is also occasionally used to make up a compound verb.

2) In poëtry though the past conjunctive participle may also follow the definite verb.

sorts of verbs, to intensify their signification, implying, that the action is done forthwith, as: كهڻي لِکهَڻُ khaṇī likhaṇu, to set to writing; كهَڻي اُجارَڻُ khaṇī ujāraṇu, to set to polish, كهَڻي وَڄائِڻُ khaṇī vaǰāiṇu, to set to play (an instrument); كهَڻي وَڃَڻُ khaṇī vañaṇu, to be off.

In the same way the past conjunctive participle of پَوَڻُ pavaṇu, to fall, viz.: پَئِي paī or پِئِي pēī, is put before a verb, to intensify its signification, as پَئِي كهِڻُ paī khiaṇu, to eat on or up, literally: to eat having fallen upon it. The augment تهو thō of the Present tense is dropped, when the verb is thus compounded with پَئِي paī or پِئِي pēī.

سو ڄَڏهِن وَڏو تهِئو تَڏهِن مَري وِئو

When he was grown up, he died. Abd-ul-Laṯīf's life, p. 2.

سُونْهَنِ جِي صَلاحَ وَٺهُ تَ وِيرِ لَنگهي وَڃين

Take the advice of the pilots, that thou mayst pass the full tide. Sh. Surāg. V, 7.

لَڙِئو پَوَنِ لَطِيفَ كهي گوڙا مَنهي گَلَ

Tears trickle down to the kind one upon the cheek. Maj. 459.

سانْدارِي سَمُونْدَ جي نِهوڙي نِئا

In crossing the ocean they were forcibly carried off. Sh. Sām. I, 11.

آڻي پَانُ اَڙاءِ كهَڻي كهورِي وِچ مِين

Bring (and) fasten thy own self in the midst of the furnace. Sh. Jam. Kal. III, 13.

جَان کهَنِي وَجَاٸِي تَہ چَئُونَا هَرَنَ مِرُون پکهِي هَلِنَّا اَچَنِ

When he sets to play, then four times as many deer, wild beasts, birds come on. Story of Rāe Diāču, p. 3.

وَکهَرُ سو وِهَاء جو پَٸِي پُرَانو نَہ تهِٸِي

Buy those goods, which do not become old. Sh. Surāḡ. III, 2.

پوءِ هِنَ ڈهَنڈهَ مَنجهَان مِٽِي کَڍهِي حُجِرَا ۽ مَسْجِدِ جوڙِنَّانئُون

Then having taken out earth from this tank they built cells and a mosque. Abd-ul-Latīf's life, p. 22.

کهِينْدو جو خُوشِيَ پَٸِي سوٸِي مُنْهِن جو سِينُ

He who will eat (it) with pleasure, that is my friend. Maj. 319.

b) Compound verbs, implying possibility, and power are formed by putting a past conjunctive participle before the verbs سَگهَڻُ saghaṇu[1]), to be able, and ڄَاڻَڻُ ǰa-ṇaṇu, to know, as: کَرِي، کَريو سَگهَڻُ karē, karyō sa-ghaṇu, to be able to do; ڏِيٸِي ڄَاڻَڻُ ḍēī ǰāṇaṇu, to know to give.

کَنْهِن پَرِ رُنَّان پِرِنَ کهِي روٸِي نَہ ڄَاڻَان

In what manner shall I weep for my friend? I do not know how to weep. Sh. Kōh. VI, 1.

اوڄَاگو اَکهِنِ کهِي ڄَاڻُيِ نَہ ڏِيٸِي

Thou didst not understand to give sleeplessness to (thy) eyes. Sh. Kōh. I, 12.

---

1) With سَگهَڻُ the Infinitive may also be joined.

c) The idea of **completion** is expressed by putting a past conjunctive participle before the verbs: رَهَڻُ rahaṇu, to remain, وَٺهَڻُ vaṭhaṇu, to take, چُكَڻُ čukaṇu, to be at an end; نِبهَڻُ nibhaṇu or نِبَڻُ nibaṇu, to be ended; similarly before بَسِ كَرَڻُ base karaṇu, to leave off, to have done, as: وَٺهِي رَهَڻُ vaṭhī rahaṇu, to have taken; رَمِي رَهَڻُ ramī rahaṇu, to be off; كهَائِي وَٺهَڻُ khāē vaṭhaṇu, to have done eating; كَرِي چُكَڻُ karē čukaṇu, to have done; چَئِي بَسِ كَرَڻُ čaī base karaṇu, to have done speaking.

اُنْهي كهوِنِن جي ڏِسَنَ وَاسطي بِهي رَهِئو

In order to see those lightenings he sat down. Amulu Māṇ. p. 146.

چَارَڻُ چَنگُ كُلهي كَري رَمِي رَهِئو رَاتِ

The Čāraṇ, having slung the harp upon his shoulder, went in the night. Sh. Sōr. III, 5.

جيكو زَال ڏِي حَرَامَ جي دِلِ سَان تهو ڏِسي اُهو اِنْهي

مِينئِي هُنَ سَان مَنَ مِين حَرَامُ كَري چُكو

Who so ever looks upon a woman with a heart of fornication, that one has even therein committed already fornication with her in his mind. Matth. 5, 4.

تَنْهِن سِين كَري پريتڙِي نِبهَائِي نِبي

With him friendship has been already made. Maǰ. 196.

پوءِ جَڏِهين عِيسَي اِهِي ڳَالهِئُون چَئِي بَس كِئُون تَڏِهين

مَاڻهُون هُنَ جو مَتُ ٻُنْدهِي وِسَا تهِئَا

When Jesus had ended these sayings, then the people, having heard his doctrine, became astonished. Matth. 7, 28.

d) Duration or repetition is expressed by putting before the definite verb the past conjunctive participle ending in iō, to which also the emphatic ī may be affixed, als: پَڙهِئُو پَڙهَڻُ paṛhiō paṛhaṇu, to read over again, to keep on reading.

پَڙهِئُو پَڙهِجَاءِ سَبَقُ اِنْهِين سُورَ جو

Read over again the lesson of this very pain. Sh. Jam. Kal. V, 31.

سوڍِي سو حَرْفُ پَڙهِئُوڍِي تهو پَڙهَان

Even that, that letter I read over and over again Sh. Jam. Kal. V, 33.

2) Another kind of Intensitives is formed by putting the past participle of پَوَڻُ pavaṇu, to fall, viz.: پِئُو piō, before the Imperative, Present[1]) or Imperfect of a definite verb, as: پِئُو مَاڻِجَانْسِ piō māṇijãse, enjoy her; پِئَا تهِئَنِ piā thiane, they become پِئَا ڏِسَنْدَا هُئَا they were seeing.

جَڏِهِين کهَٽَ تي اَچِي تَڏِهِين تُون پَرَ پَٽِي کَڏِهجَانْسِ

پوءِ پِئُو مَاڻِجَانْسِ

When she comes to the couch, then pull out her feathers; afterwards enjoy her. Amulu Māṇ. p. 147.

تَنْهِن مِين تَجِلَا کهِوڻِنِ وَانگِي پِئَا تهِئَنِ

In that (palace) sparks are made like lightenings. Ibid. p. 140.

سَنْدَسِ اَچِرْجَ کهَڻَا چهوکَرَ ٻِئَا پِئَا ڏِسَنْدَا هُئَا

Many of his miracles the other boys used to see. Abd-ul-Laṯīf's life, p. 3.

---

1) In this case the augment تهو thō is dropped as unnecessary.

3) The idea of continuation is expressed by putting a present participle before the verbs رَهَنُ rahaṇu, to remain and وَتَنُ vataṇu, to go about, as: وينْدو رَهي vēndō rahī, he continues going; چارِينْدو وَتي čārīndō vatē, he keeps on grazing.

وينْدو رَهَنْدو وِرچِي مَنْجهان مِصر شَامَ

He kept on travelling in fatigue from Egypt (and) Syria. Maǰ. 357.

سَنْدُسِ پِئُ شَاهُ حَبِيبُ كهيسِ گولِينْدو پهولِينْدوئِي رَهِئو

His father Shāh Habib continued searching (and) seeking him. Life of Abd-ul-Laṭīf, p. 9.

بِيجَلُ كهوڙا چَارِينْدو وَتي

Bījalu goes on grazing the horses. Story of Rāe Diāču, p. 2.

4) Two verbs may also be joined by putting the Infinitive of a verb in the Formative case before the verbs: لَگَنُ lagaṇu, v. n. to apply, اَچَنُ ačaṇu, to come, وَڃَنُ vańaṇu, to go. In this way so-called Inceptives are formed, as: رُوَنَ لَگَنُ ruaṇa lagaṇu, to begin to cry; وَسَنَ اَچَنُ vasaṇa ačaṇu, to come to rain; سَڏَنَ وَڃَنُ sadaṇa vańaṇu, to go to call.

وِڄُون وَسَنَ آئِيُون سَارَنْگُ چَڙهِئو سيجَ

The lightenings have come to flash (to rain); the monsoon has ascended (his) couch. Sh. Sōr. IV, 13.

پوءِ جيسِين هو گِنْهَنَ وِيئُون تِيسِين كهوٽُ اَچي سَهڙِيو

Then whilst they went to buy, the bridegroom arrived. Matth. 25, 10.

Chapter XVII.

The Verb with the Pronominal Suffixes.

§. 54.

The Sindhī uses the pronominal suffixes far more extensively with the verbs, than with the nouns (cf. §. 30). The suffixes attached to the verbs express, strictly speaking, only the Dative and Accusative (the object), and, with the past participle passive, also the Instrumental, though we may translate them by any case, save the Nominative.

The pronominal suffixes attached to verbs are identical with those attached to nouns, with this difference, that the suffix of the I person Plural, ū̃, which is not in use with nouns (but with adverbs and postpositions), is used throughout the verb. There is further a peculiar Instrumental affix, attached to the past participle passive, which is never used with nouns or adverbs, viz.: ī̃ for the Singular, and ū̃ for the Plural.

It appears, that the suffix ī̃ is originally the Instrumental Sing. اِنَ ina, by him (from هِي hī, this), and ū̃ the Instrumental Plural اُنِ une, by them (from هُو hū or اُو ū, that).

To the first person Sing. and Plur. the suffix of the same person is never attached, as in this case the reflexive pronoun پاڻَ pāṇa, self, must be employed.

In the compound tenses and in compound verbs the suffix always accedes to the latter part of the compound, though it properly belongs to the first member of the compound. Similarly the suffix is never attached to the augment ٿهو thō or ٿهي thē, but always to the verb itself.

To the past participle passive even two suffixes may accede, the first expressing the Instrumental and the second the Dative or Accusative, as will be shown afterwards.

The way, in which the several suffixes are attached to the inflexional terminations of the verb, will be best seen from the following survey.

§. 55.

I. The pronominal suffixes attached to the auxiliary verbs هُئَڻُ and ٿِئَڻُ

1) The Imperative.

The same as the II pers. Sing. and Plur. of the Potential.

The Precative.

Suffix		SING.	PLUR.
Sing.	I pers.	هُجَانْمِ huj-ā̃-me. be to me.	هُجوِمِ huǰō-me. be to me.
	III pers.	هُجَانْسِ huj-ā̃-se. be to him.	هُجوسِ huǰō-se. be to him.
Plur.	I pers.	هُجَانُون huj-ā-ū̃. be to us.	هُجوُنُون huǰō-ū̃. be to us.
	III pers.	هُجَانِ huj-ā-ne. be to them.	هُجونِ huǰō-ne. be to them.

In the same way the suffixes are attached to تهِجُ thiju, as: تهِجَانْمِ thij-ā̃-me, become to me, تهِجَانْسِ thiǰ-ā̃-se, become to him.

پوءِ هُو تهِينِ اَگُ مِين تَ تُون پُٺهِ مِين تِجَانِ

Then if those are in front, be thou in their back. Amulu Māṇ. p. 144.

2) The Potential هُنَّان huã, I may be.

SINGULAR.

		Suffixes of the I pers.	Suffixes of the II pers.	Suffixes of the III pers.
Sing.	I	. . . .	هُنَّانِءِ huã-e.	هُنَّانْسِ huã-se.
	II	هُئينْمِ huẽ-me.	. . . .	هُئينْسِ huẽ-se.
	III	هُئيمِ huē-me.	هُئيئي huē-ī.	هُئيسِ huē-se.
Plur.	I	. . . .	هُونْءِ hũ-e.	هُونْسِ hũ-se.
	II	هُئوْمِ huō-me.[1]	. . . .	هُئوْسِ huō-se.
	III	هُنَّنِمِ huani-me.	هُنَّنِي huan-ī.[2]	هُنَّنِسِ huani-se.

PLURAL.

		Suffixes of the I pers.	Suffixes of the II pers.	Suffixes of the III pers.
Sing.	I	. . . .	هُنَّانْوَ huã-va.	هُنَّانِ huã-ne.
	II	هُئينْئُون huẽ-ũ.	. . . .	هُئينِ huẽ-ne.[3]
	III	هُئيئُون huē-ũ.	هُئيوَ huē-va.	هُئينِ huē-ne.
Plur.	I	. . . .	هُونْوَ hũ-va.	هُونِ hũ-ne.
	II	هُئوئُون huō-ũ.	. . . .	هُئوْنِ huō-ne.
	III	هُنَّنئُون huane-ũ.	هُنَّنِوَ huani-va.	هُنَّنِنِ huani-ne.

---

1) Or هوْمِ hō-me, هوْسِ hō-se.

2) Or هُنَّنِئي huane-ī.

3) When a nasalized vowel (ẽ) is followed by a dental nasal, the sign of nasalisation (ن in Arabic characters) is generally dropped as superfluous; thus هُئينِ huẽ-ne, instead of هُئينْنِ huẽ-ne, هُونِ hũ-ne, instead of هُونْنِ hũ-ne.

In the same way the suffixes are attached to the Potential تهِيان thiã̄, I may become, and to the Indefinite Present هُئان تهو huã̄ thō and تهِئان تهو thiã̄ thō, as: هُئينم تهو huẽ̄-me thō, thou art to me etc.

آخِرِ اُهِرينْسِ تَہ جوکهو تهِئيئِي نَہ جَهازَ کهي

Finally push it off, lest any damage befall the ship (literally: lest any damage befall thee as regards the ship). Sh. Surāg̱. III, 7.

جي پُورو تهِيئِم پَساهُ تَہ بهِہ نِجو مَڙهُ مَلِيرَ ڏي

If my breath may expire, yet carry (my) corpe to the Malīr. Sh. Um. Mār. V, 14.

جي هُئنِي هوتَنِ لکهَہ تَہ پَاڙِجِ کو مَہ پُنْهُو سان

If there be to thee lakhs of sweethearts, compare none with Punhū̃. Sh. Maɀδ. V, 4.

3) The Present آنهِيان ã̄hiyã̄.

SINGULAR.

		Suffixes of the I pers.	Suffixes of the II pers.	Suffixes of the III pers.
Sing.	I	. . . .	آنهِيانئِ ã̄hiyã̄-e.	آنهِيانْسِ ã̄hiyã̄-se.
	II	آنهِينْمِ ã̄hẽ̄-me.[1]	. . . .	آنهِينْسِ ã̄hẽ̄-se.
	III	آهِيمِ āhē-me.	آهِيئِي āhē-ī.	آهِيسِ āhē-se.
Plur.	I	. . . .	آنهِيونئِ ã̄hiyū̃-e.	آنهِيونْسِ ã̄hiyū̃-se.
	II	آهِيوَمِ āhiyō-me.	. . . .	آهِيوَسِ āhiyō-se.
	III	آنهِنِمِ ã̄hini-me.	آنهِنِي ã̄hin-ī.[2]	آنهِنِسِ ã̄hini-se.

1) Or آنهِينْمِ ã̄hī̃-me.

2) Or آنهِنِئِي ã̄hine-ī.

PLURAL.

		Suffixes of the I pers.	Suffixes of the II pers.	Suffixes of the III pers.
Sing.	I	. . . .	آنهيَانْوَ ā̃hiyā̃-va.	آنهيَانِ ā̃hiyā̃-ne.
	II	آنهينئُون ā̃hē̃-ū̃.	. . . .	آهِينِ āhē̃-ne.
	III	آهِيئُون āhē-ū̃.	آهِيوَ āhē-va.	آهِينِ āhē-ne.
Plur.	I	. . . .	آنهِيُونْوَ ā̃hiyū̃-va.	آنهِيُونِ ā̃hiyū̃-ne.
	II	آهِيؤئُون āhiyō-ū̃.	. . . .	آهِيؤنِ āhiyō-ne.
	III	آنهِنئُون ā̃hine-ū̃.	آنهِنوَ ā̃hini-va.	آنهِنِ ā̃hini-ne.

Instead of آهِي āhē and آنهِنِ ā̃hine the form اَتهَ atha is also in use, but only when joined by suffixes. It corresponds to the old Prākrit form अत्थि athi (the III pers. Sing. of the substantive verb asmi, I am, see Lassen, p. 345), which in Sindhī has also been transferred to the Plural.

The suffixes are attached to it in the following manner:

	Suffixes of the I pers.	Suffixes of the II pers.	Suffixes of the III pers.
Plur. and Sing.	اَتهَمِ atha-me.	اَتهِي ath-ī, اَتهِيئِي athē-ī.	اَتهَسِ atha-se.
	اَتهُون ath-ū̃.	اَتهَوَ atha-va.	اَتهَنِ atha-ne.

In the Present Definite: هُونْدو آنهِيَان the suffixes accede, as noted already, to the latter part of the compound.

سَرْتِنِ سَانُ سَمَنَ آهِيمِ اُتهِي مِينهَڙِي

With girls of my age I have an appointment, after rain has fallen. Sh. Um. Mār. V, 21.

ڱُجهِي اَتهَمِ ڱالهَڙِي آءُ اوڙِي تَان اوڙِيَان

I have a secret matter, come near, then I will tell (it). Sh. Sōr. II, 22.

تَڏِهِن سُنِي سَبَقُ سَرَهو تهِئو نَاهِسِ کو نِيَازُ

Then having heard the lesson he became glad; he has no other want. Maǰ. 189.

جِي اَتهِي سَدهَ پَسَنَ مِين تَ کهَنُ مَ پِيرَ پَرِي

If thou hast a desire in seeing, then lift not thy step far off. Sh. Kal. II, 4.

بِنَا بهَڄَنَ بهَڱوَانَ جِي اَتهِيئِي بِي سَبهِ خُودِي خَامَ

Except the worshipping of the Lord all other things are to thee selfishness, o ignorant one! Mēnghō 4.

مَتهِي نَ آهِئُون مَنَ مِين اُوءِ جُوتهَا مَارِنِ جَکهَ

We have no wickedness in our heart; those liars calumniate. Maǰ. 255.

اَسَان کهِي اُنْهِنِ پَانْهَنَنِ سَان کو کَمُ نَ آهِي مَگرِ پَنْهَن
جِي دهَنِيَ سَان کَمُ اَتهُون

We have nothing to do with those stones, but our concern is with their master. Life of Abd-ul-Laṯīf, p. 20.

سَاءُ نَ اَتهَوَ سُورَ جو هَاڻِي تهِئُون هَسو

You have no taste of the pain; now you laugh. Sh. Sām. III, Epil. 1.

مَنْدِي نَہ آهِينِ مَنَ مِين سُنجَاتَانئُون ثَوَابُ

No wickedness is in their heart; they have known the retribution. Maj. 218.

4) The Aorist.

a) The masc. form هوسِ hōse.

SINGULAR.

		Suffix I pers.	Suffix II pers.	Suffix III pers.
Sing.	I	. . . .	هوسَانئِ hōsã-e.	هوسَانْسِ hōsã-se.
	II	هُئِينْمِ huẽ-me.	. . . .	هُئِينْسِ huẽ-se.
	III	هوم hō-me.	هوء hō-e.	هوسِ hō-se.
Plur.	I	. . . .	هُئَاسُونئِ huāsũ-e.	هُئَاسُونْسِ huāsũ-se.
	II	هُئوم huō-me.	. . . .	هُئوسِ huō-se.
	III	هُئَمِ hua-me.[1])	هُئَئِ hua-e.	هُئَسِ hua-se.

PLURAL.

		Suffix I pers.	Suffix II pers.	Suffix III pers.
Sing.	I	. . . .	هوسَانْوَ hōsã-va.	هوسَانِ hōsã-ne.
	II	هُئِينئُون huẽ-ũ.	. . . .	هُئِينِ huẽ-ne.
	III	هوسُون hō-sũ.	هوَوَ hō-va.	هوَنِ hō-ne.
Plur.	I	. . . .	هُئَاسُونْوَ huāsũ-va.	هُئَاسُونِ huāsũ-ne.
	II	هُئوسُون huō-sũ.	. . . .	هُئونِ huō-ne.
	III	هُئَاسُون huā-sũ.	هُئَوَ hua-va.	هُئَنِ hua-ne.

1) In poëtry long ā is frequently retained, as; هُئَامِ huā-me, هُئَاء huā-e, هُئَاسِ huā-se etc.

b) The fem. form هُيَسِ huyase.

SINGULAR.

		Suffix I pers.	Suffix II pers.	Suffix III pers.
Sing.	I	. . . .	هُئِيسَانئِ huīsā̃-e.	هُئِيسَانْسِ huīsā̃-se.
	II	هُئِيَنْم huiyā-me.[1])	. . . .	هُئِيَنْسِ huiyā-se.
	III	هُيَمِ huya-me.	هُيَئِ huya-e.	هُيَسِ huya-se.
Plur.	I	. . . .	هُيُونْسُونئِ huyū̃sū̃-e.	هُيُونْسُونئِ huyū̃sū̃-e.
	II	هُيُنْمِ huyū-me.	. . . .	هُيُنْسِ huyū-se.
	III	هُيُنْمِ huyū-me.	هُيُنْئِ huyū-e.	هُيُنْسِ huyū-se.

PLURAL.

		Suffix I pers.	Suffix II pers.	Suffix III pers.
Sing.	I	. . . .	هُئِيسَانْوَ huīsā̃-va.	هُئِيسَانِ huīsā̃-ne.
	II	هُيِينْسُون huyẽ-sū̃.	. . . .	هُئِيَنِ huiyā-ne.
	III	هُئِيسُون huī-sū̃.	هُيَوَ huya-va.	هُيَنِ huya-ne.
Plur.	I	. . . .	هُيُونْسُونْوَ huyū̃sū̃-va.	هُيُونْسُونِ huyū̃sū̃-ne.
	II	هُيُونْسُون huyū̃-sū̃.	. . . .	هُيُنِ huyū-ne.
	III	هُيُونْسُون huyū̃-sū̃.	هُيُنْوَ huyū-va.	هُيُنِ huyū-ne.

1) Or هُئِئِينْمِ huiẽ-me, هُيِينْمِ huyẽ-me, هُيَنْمِ huyā̃-me.

That to هو hō, هُئِي huī etc., when forming with the past participle passive the Pluperfect, also a suffix, denoting the Instrumental, may be attached, will be shown in §. 56, 5.

It is to be observed, that the inflexional termination of the I pers. Sing. masc. and fem., se, becomes sā̃ before the accession of the suffixes; the fem. termination هُيَسِ huyase is at the same time reduced to its original form هُئِي huī, as: هُئِيسَانئِ huī-sā̃-e. The suffix of the I pers. Plur. is in the Aorist sū̃ or sī̃, and not ū̃, as in the Imperative, Potential and Present. In the II pers. fem. Sing. the form هُيِين huyē̃ or هُيِين huyī̃ is employed, when followed by the heavy suffix sū̃ or sī̃, the accent being then thrown on the last syllable of the verb, as: huyḗ-sū̃ or huyī́-sū̃.

In the same way as to هوسِ hōse and هُيَسِ huyase the suffixes accede to ٿِيُسِ thiuse and ٿِيَسِ thiase, and to every other neuter verb in the Aorist, for which ٿِيُسِ thiuse may serve as paradigm.

The Aorist ٿِيُسِ thiuse.

a) The masculine form ٿِيُسِ thiuse.

SINGULAR OF THE SUFFIX.

		Suffix I pers.	Suffix II pers.	Suffix III pers.
Sing.	I	. . . .	ٿِئوسَانئِ thiōsā̃-e.	ٿِئوسَانسِ thiōsā̃-se.
	II	ٿِئِينمِ thiē̃-me.	. . . .	ٿِئِينسِ thiē̃-se.
	III	ٿِيُمِ thiu-me.[1])	ٿِيُئِ thiyu-e.	ٿِيُسِ thiu-se.

1) In poëtry the diminutive affix ڙو ṛō is frequently attached to the past participle, to which the suffixes accede according to the common

SINGULAR OF THE SUFFIX.

		Suffix I pers.	Suffix II pers.	Suffix III pers.
Plur.	I	. . . .	تهِنَاسُونْيِ thiā̃sū̃-e.	تهِنَاسُونْسِ thiā̃sū̃-se.
	II	تهِٹوِمِ thiō-me.	. . . .	تهِٹوِسِ thiō-se.
		تهِنَمِ thia-me.	تهِيَيِ thiya-e.	تهِنَسِ thia-se.

PLURAL OF THE SUFFIX.

Sing.	I	. . . .	تهِٹوِسَانْوَ thiōsā̃-va.	تهِٹوِسَانِ thiōsā-ne.
	II	تهِٹيِنْنُون thiē̃-ū̃.	. . . .	تهِٹيِنِ thiē-ne.
	III	تهِٹوِسُون thiō-sū̃.	تهِنُوَ thiu-va.	تهِنُنِ thiu-ne.
Plur.	I	. . . .	تهِنَاسُونْوَ thiā̃sū̃-va.	تهِنَاسُونِ thiā̃sū-ne.
	II	تهِٹوِسُون thiō-sū̃.	. . . .	تهِٹوِنِ thiō-ne.
	III	تهِنَاسُون thiā-sū̃..	تهِنَوَ thia-va.	تهِنَنِ thia-ne.

b) The feminine form تهِنَسِ thiase.

SINGULAR OF THE SUFFIX.

		Suffix I pers.	Suffix II pers.	Suffix III pers.
Sing.	I	. . . .	تهِيسَانْيِ thīsā̃-e.	تهِيسَانْسِ thīsā̃-se.
	II	تهِنَنْمِ thiā̃-me.	. . . .	تهِنَنْسِ thiā̃-se.
	III	تهِنَمِ thia-me.	تهِيَيِ thiya-e.	تهِيَسِ thiya-se.

---

rules, as: تهِنَڑُّمِ thiaṛu-me, تهِنَڑُّسِ thiaṛu-se etc. But in the I. and II pers. the diminutive affix is never added.

SINGULAR OF THE SUFFIX.

		Suffix I pers.	Suffix II pers.	Suffix III pers.
Plur.	I	. . . .	تهِئُونْسُونِئِ thiũsũ-e.	تهِئُونْسِينْسِ thiũsī-se.
	II	تهِئُنْمِ thiũ-me.[1])	. . . .	تهِئُنْسِ thiũ-se.
	III	تهِئُنْمِ thiũ-me.	تهِئُنِئِ thiũ-e.	تهِئُنْسِ thiũ-se.

PLURAL OF THE SUFFIX.

		Suffix I pers.	Suffix II pers.	Suffix III pers.
Sing.	I	. . . .	تهِيسَانْوَ thīsã-va.	تهِيسَانِ thīsā-ne.
	II	تهِئِينْسُون thiẽ-sũ.	. . . .	تهِئَنِ thia-ne.
	III	تهِيسُون thī-sũ.	تهِيَوَ thiya-va.	تهِيَنِ thiya-ne.
Plur.	I	. . . .	تهِئُونْسِينْوَ thiũsī-va.	تهِئُونْسِينِ thiũsī-ne.
	II	تهِئُونْسُون thiũ-sũ.	. . . .	تهِئُنِ thiu-ne.
	III	تهِئُونْسُون thiũ-sũ.	تهِئُنْوَ thiũ-va.	تهِئُنِ thiu-ne.

جَڏِهِن پِئُسِ وَڃِي ڳولِي وَٺِي آنِينْدو هوسِ تَڏِهِن ٻاهَرِ اِينْدو هو

When his father having gone and searched (after him) took and brought him, then he was coming forth. Life of Abd-ul-Laṯīf, p. 3.

جيتِرو گهُرِبو هوسِ تيتِرو اُنَ بَرْتَنَ مَان کهَنَنْدو هو

As much as was necessary to him, he was taking out of that vessel. Ibid. p. 21.

1) Or without the final nasal: تهِئُمِ thiu-me.

اِيءَ سُنِيندَهِي ڳالهڙِي چرِئو تهڻِس چِتُ

Hearing this story her mind became mad. Maǰ. 375.

تَنِي رِي تَنُورَ مِين تهِڻِم سُورَ سَرْس

Without them (i. e. removed from them) abundant pains have befallen me in the furnace. Maǰ. 663.

دهِيڙِيَ کهي اُتهَارِي پَنْهَن جي کهرِ وِهَارِي پَاڙهِينْدَا هُئَسِ

Having removed the little daughter and placed her in their own house, they made her read (i. e. they instructed her). Life of Abd-ul-Laṯīf, p. 46.

جيکي ٹُکُرَ کهَائِنَ کهَان بَچَنْدَا هُئَنَ سي اُنَ لَئِي جي
ڏهَنْڏهَرَ مِين رَکهَنْدَا هُئَا .

Whatever pieces were remaining to them from eating, those they used to put in the hole of that tamarisk tree. Abd-ul-Laṯīf's life, p. 23.

5) The Future.

a) The masculine form هُونْدُسِ hūnduse.

SINGULAR OF THE SUFFIX.

		Suffix I pers.	Suffix II pers.	Suffix III pers.
Sing.	I	. . . .	هُونْدوَسَانئِ hūndōsā̃-e.	هُونْدوَسَانْسِ hūndōsā̃-se.
	II	هُونْدِينْمِ hūndē̃-me.	. . . .	هُونْدِينْسِ hūndē̃-se.
	III	هُونْدُمِ hūndu-me.[1]	هُونْدُء hūndu-e.[2]	هُونْدُسِ hūndu-se.

1) In poëtry frequently هُونْدوَمِ hūndō-me, هُونْدَامِ hūndā-me etc.

2) Or هُونْدِي hūndē.

SINGULAR OF THE SUFFIX.

		Suffix I pers.	Suffix II pers.	Suffix III pers.
Plur.	I	. . . .	هُونْدَاسُونئِ hūndāsū̃-e.	هُونْدَاسُونْسِ hūndāsū̃-se.
	II	هُونْدوِمِ hūndō-me.[1])	. . . .	هُونْدوسِ hūndō-se.
	III	هُونْدَمِ hūnda-me.	هُونْدَء hūnda-e.	هُونْدَسِ hūnda-se.

PLURAL OF THE SUFFIX.

		Suffix I pers.	Suffix II pers.	Suffix III pers.
Sing.	I	. . . .	هُونْدوسَانْوَ hūndōsā̃-va.	هُونْدوسَانِ hūndōsā-ne.
	II	هُونْدِينئُون hūndē̃-ū̃.	. . . .	هُونْدِينِ hūndē-ne.
	III	هُونْدوسُون hūndō-sū̃.	هُونْدُوَ hūndu-va.	هُونْدُنِ hūndu-ne.
Plur.	I	. . . .	هُونْدَاسُونْوَ hūndāsū̃-va.	هُونْدَاسُونِ hūndāsū-ne.
	II	هُونْدوسُون hūndō-sū̃.	. . . .	هُونْدونِ hūndō-ne.
	III	هُونْدَاسُون hūndā-sū̃.	هُونْدَوَ hūnda-va.	هُونْدَنِ hūnda-ne.

b) The feminine form هُونْدِيَسِ hūndiase.

SINGULAR OF THE SUFFIX.

	Suffix I pers.	Suffix II pers.	Suffix III pers.
Sing. I	. . . .	هُونْدِيسَانئِ hūndīsā̃-e.	هُونْدِيسَانْسِ hūndīsā̃-se.

1) Or هُونْدَوُمِ hunda-u-me.

SINGULAR OF THE SUFFIX.

		Suffix I pers.	Suffix II pers.	Suffix III pers.
Sing.	II	هُونْدِئَنمِ hūndiā̃-me.[1])	. . . .	هُونْدِئَنسِ hūndiā̃-se.
	III	هُونْديَمِ hūndya-me.[2])	هُونْديَئِ hūndya-e.	هُونْدِيَسِ hūndya-se.
Plur.	I	. . . .	هُونْدِئُونْسُونئِ hūndiũsũ-e.	هُونْدِئُونْسُونْسِ hūndiũsũ-se.
	II	هُونْديُنْمِ hūndyũ-me.	. . . .	هُونْديُنْسِ hūndyũ-se.
	III	هُونْديُنْمِ hūndyũ-me.	هُونْديُنئِ hūndyũ-e.	هُونْديُنْسِ hūndyũ-se.

PLURAL OF THE SUFFIX.

		Suffix I pers.	Suffix II pers.	Suffix III pers.
Sing.	I	. . . .	هُونْدِيسَانْوَ hūndīsā̃-va.	هُونْدِيسَانِ hūndīsā-ne.
	II	هُونْدِئِينْسُون hūndiẽ-ũ.	. . . .	هُونْدِئَنِ hūndia-ne.
	III	هُونْدِيسُون hūndī-sũ.	هُونْديَوَ hūndya-va.	هُونْديَنِ hūndya-ne.
Plur.	I	. . . .	هُونْدِئُونْسُونْوَ hūndiũsũ-va.	هُونْدِئُونْسُونِ hūndiũsū-ne.
	II	هُونْدِئُونْسُون hūndiũ-sũ.	. . . .	هُونْديُنِ hūndyu-ne.
	III	هُونْدِئُونْسُون hūndiũ-sũ.	هُونْديُنْوَ hūndyũ-va.	هُونْديُنِ hūndyu-ne.

---

1) Or هُونْدِئِينْمِ hūndiẽ-me.

2) The final ı (y) of هُونْدِي hūndī is frequently dropped in poëtry, as, هُونْدَمِ hūnda-me, instead of هُونْديَمِ hūndya-me (hūndia-me).

In the same way as to هُونْدُسِ hūnduse and هُونْدِئَسِ hūndiase the suffixes are also attached to the Future of the active and passive voice, and consequently to the present participle of both voices.

مَتهو ۾ين کهيکَارَ يَارَ ڏَانُ ڏِينْدوسَانئِ مَنگَنَا

The head, o friend, I shall give to thee with salutation as a present, o bard! Sh. Sōr. III, Epil.

سَٻَاجهو ٻَاجهہ کَرِي تَنْهين سين ميڙِينْدوم

The merciful one, having bestowed mercy, will join me with him. Maǰ. 182.

هوتُ گَڏِبئِ حَبَّ ۾ين رَهَبَرُ مَتهي رَاهہ

(Thy) sweetheart will join thee on the Habb, as a guide on the way. Sh. Maǰδ. V, 5.

ٻِئو ٻِہ جيکِي گهُرَنْدو سو ڏِبُسِ

Whatever else he will ask, that shall be given to him. Story of Rāe Diāču, p. 7.

جيکَڏِهِن ليلهِرَائِي ڪِبِي تَان پُڻُ کَالُ کِي نہ ڇهَڏِينْدوسِين

If laziness will be made, then also death will by no means give us up. Sindhī Read. book, p. 63.

اَوْهَان مُون سَان ڇِڙَنْدَوُ ۽ ٻيلِپي مَان ڪَڍهَنْدوم

You will be angry with me and turn me out of the service. Sindhī Read. book, p. 51.

اَدِيُون عَبْدُ اَللَّطِيف چَوِي سينَ لَهَنْدَمِ سَارَ

Sisters, says Abd-ul-Laṯīf, my friends will remember me. Sh. Um. Mār. I, Epil.

تُون جَنْهِن جِي نَکَ تي وِينْڍهو ڏِسِين سَا سُڃَاڻِي کَڍِهجِ

تَہ اُهَا هُوندِيسَانءِ

On whose nose thou seest the nose ring, that one, having recognised, take out, then that one I shall be to thee. Amulu Māṇ. p. 150.

هَکِڻو هُجُ هُشِيَارُ کِهِوَنِ کِهوَنْدَءِ اوچِتِي

Be ready (and) careful, the lightening will flash upon thee suddenly. Sh. Surāg̱. VI, 5.

اِئِين موچَارو تَہ مَيْنِ وَڃِي پَئُون ۞ هِکَ ٻِئِي جِي وَاهَرَ

سَانُ مَارِي مَنجَائِينڊِيُونْسِينِ

So it is good, that we having gone fall amongst them and with the assistence of each other we shall beat and subject them. Sindhī Read. book, p. 64.

تَہ چَوَنْدِيُنْسِ پَاتِشَاهزَادِي رَاتِ تَمَاشِي تي هَلِي هُئِينَّ

Then they will say to her: o princess, last night thou hadst gone to an amusement. Amulu Māṇ. p. 145.

§. 56.

II. The pronominal suffixes attached to the regular verb.

1) The Imperative.

(The same as the Potential.)

اَچِي چَيَائِين مَاءُ کهِي رُخْصَتَ ڏِينْمِ رَضَا

Having come he said to (his) mother: give me leave (and) permission. Maj. 77.

مَاڙهُنِ چَيو مَائُسِ کهِي تَہ تُان پَان پُڇهِينسِ

The people said to his mother: ask thou thyself him. Maj. 42.

سَا ڏيکهَارِئُون جُوءِ جِتّان لَاهُوتِي لَالُ تهِيو

Show us that place, where the devotee has become red. Sh. Mūm. Rāṇō III, 9.

رَبَّ پَسَايُون رُوءِ اُنْهِين جِي اِحْسَانَ سَان

O Lord, show to us their face with (out of) kindness. Sh. Keḍ. IV, 5.

تَازِي ڏِئُوسِ تَکِڙو جَوْهَرَ پَائِي زِينَ

Give him a quick arab horse, having placed jewels on the saddle. Sh. Sōr. I, 18.

The Precative.

	SINGULAR.		PLURAL.	
Suffix I p. Sing.	چهَڏِجَانْمِ	čhaḏijā̃-me. Give me up.	چهَڏِجوْمِ	čhaḏijō-me. Give ye me up.
Suffix III p. Sing.	چهَڏِجَانْسِ	čhaḏijā̃-se. Give him up.	چهَڏِجوْسِ	čhaḏijō-se. Give ye him up.
Suffix I p. Plur.	چهَڏِجَانئُون	čhaḏijā̃-ū̃. Give us up.	چهَڏِجوئُون	čhaḏijō-ū̃. Give ye us up.
Suffix III p. Plur.	چهَڏِجَانِ	čhaḏijā-ne. Give them up.	چهَڏِجوْنِ	čhaḏijō-ne. Give ye them up.

هُو جِي ڏَهَ بَارَهَنْ ڏهَاکُنَّا سِي تُون مَتهوُنئِين کهَائِي وَنِجَانْسِ

Those ten (or) twelve dishes having eaten from above go away from her. Amulu Māṇ. p. 144.

اَسِين جَڏهِين ٻَئِي گَڏِجِي اَچُون تَڏهِين هِي نَاڻو ڏِجَانئُون

When we both come together, then please to give us this money. Stack's Gram. p. 135.

جَڏهِين آن ڪَچهَرِي بَاهَرَايَان تَڏهِين مَارِي وِجهُوسِ

When I dismiss the court, then kill him. Story of Rāe Diāču, p. 4.

2) The Potential.

SINGULAR OF THE SUFFIX.

		Suffix I pers.	Suffix II pers.	Suffix III pers.
Sing.	I	. . . .	چهَڊِيَانءِ čhaḍ̄iā̃-e.	چهَڊِيَانْسِ čhaḍ̄iā̃-se.
	II	چهَڊِينْمِ čhaḍ̄ē̃-me.[1]	. . . .	چهَڊِينْسِ čhaḍ̄ē̃-se.
	III	چهَڊِيمِ čhaḍ̄ē-me.	چهَڊِيئِي čhaḍ̄ē-ī.	چهَڊِيسِ čhaḍ̄ē-se.
Plur.	I	. . . .	چهَڊِئُونءِ čhaḍ̄iū̃-e.	چهَڊِئُونْسِ čhaḍ̄iū̃-se.
	II	چهَڊِئومِ čhaḍ̄iō-me.	. . . .	چهَڊِئوسِ čhaḍ̄iō-se.
	III	چهَڊِنِمِ čhaḍ̄ini-me.	چهَڊِنِي čhaḍ̄in-ī.	چهَڊِنِسِ čhaḍ̄ini-se.

PLURAL OF THE SUFFIX.

		Suffix I pers.	Suffix II pers.	Suffix III pers.
Sing.	I	. . . .	چهَڊِيَانْوَ čhaḍ̄iā̃-va.	چهَڊِيَانِ čhaḍ̄iā-ne.
	II	چهَڊِينْئُون čhaḍ̄ē-ū̃.	. . . .	چهَڊِينِ čhaḍ̄ē̃-ne.
	III	چهَڊِيئُون čhaḍ̄ē-ū̃.	چهَڊِيوَ čhaḍ̄ē-va.	چهَڊِينِ čhaḍ̄ē-ne.

1) Or چهَڊِئِينْمِ čhaḍ̄iē̃-me, چهَڊِينْمِ čhaḍ̄ī̃-me.

PLURAL OF THE SUFFIX.

Plur.	Suffix I pers.	Suffix II pers.	Suffix III pers.
I	. . . .	چهڏِئُونْوَ čhaḍiū̃-va.	چهڏِئُونِ čhaḍiū̃-ne.
II	چهَڏِئوئُون čhaḍiō-ū̃.	. . . .	چهَڏِئوِنِ čhaḍiō-ne.
III	چهَڏِنِئُون čhaḍine-ū̃.	چهَڏِنِوَ čhaḍini-va.	چهَڏِنِنِ čhaḍini-ne.

In the same way the suffixes accede to the Potential of the passive voice. The Potential and Present of the regular passive is however very rarely found with a suffix, more frequently that of intransitive verbs in the passive form, as: گَڏِجائِ تهو gaḍijā-e thō, I meet with thee.

In the Imperfect the suffixes accede, as stated already, to the auxiliary verb هوسِ hōse.

سَائِيِن صَاحِبْزادِي کهي موکَل ڏِي تَہ آنئُون فَقِيرَ جي پيرين وِجهارائِي آچَانْسِ

Lord, give leave of absence to the prince, that I may come having laid him at the feet of the Faqīr. Amulu Māṇ., p. 1.

مَنهو هِيئِ مِهمَانَ هَلِي چَوُ تَہ هُتِ ڏِئانئِ

Having gone speak, o guest, that I may give thee there this head. Sh. Sōr. I, 13.

تُونهِين رَهِينمِ رُوحَ مِين توهِين ڏانهہ نينَ

Even thou remainest me in the heart, even towards thee (are my) eyes. Maj. 211.

تَڏِهِن پَرِ مِين پَنْهَن جِتُون کِٿِوْ مَتِئُون ڏِيسِ مَاءِ

Then the mother in (her) wise gives her her own advices. Maj. 288.

جيکِي کُهرْجِيئِى سوْ هِنَ مَان کهَنِج

Whatever may be necessary to thee, take that out of this (vessel). Life of Abd-ul-Laṯīf, p. 21.

جيکِي کُهرِيوَ سوْ آڻِي ڏِجوْسِ

Whatever he may ask you for, that bring and give him. Amulu Māṇ., p. 148.

بَانْبهَنِ تهِيئُ بُوتِيُون تَ کُتَا کهِئَنِي کيچَ جَا

O Brahmanī woman! become pieces of flesh, in order that the dogs of Kēč may eat thee! Sh. Maꝫδ. I, 1.

رَاڻَا رِهَاڻِنِ جَا تهَا مَارِينُون مَذْکُورَ

O Rāṇō, the record (pl.) of our conversations kills us. Sh. Mūm. Rāṇō V, 10.

توْڙِي چِکَنِنَ چَاکَ تَ بهِي آهَ نَ سَلَنِ عَامَ کهِي

Though their wounds flow, yet do they not their sigh divulge to the people. Sh. Kal. II, 23.

3) The past participle.

(The III pers. of the Aorist.)

The way, in which the pronominal suffixes accede to the Aorist of neuter verbs, may be seen from the paradigm of تهِئُسِ thiuse. In the Aorist of the passive voice the suffixes are only attached to the III pers. Sing. and Plur. or to the past participle passive. The suffixes thus attached imply either a Dative-Accusative (the object in general) or an Instrumental. The suffixes of the I and II pers. of the Sing. and Plur. may at the same time denote the object or the agent, but in the III pers. Sing. and Plur. different suffixes are employed to express the object or the agent, se and ne denoting the object, and ī̃ and ū̃ the agent (see §. 54). Both ī̃ and ū̃ are considered as heavy suffixes, which draw the accent from the first to the last syllable of the verb; final ō of the past participle must therefore be changed to ā before them (and for euphony's sake with an additional nasal to ā), to give a support to the following heavy suffix. In the fem. Sing. an ā must likewise be inserted between the final ī and the suffixes ī̃ and ū̃, to which even the feminine Plural termination ū̃ must give way, so that the Singular and Plural of both genders become alike, if joined by the instrumental suffixes ī̃ and ū̃.

a) The past participle with single suffixes.

The masc. Sing. چھَڏِئو čhaḍ̄iō.

	Suffix I pers.	Suffix II pers.	Suffix III pers.
Sing.	چھَڏِئم čhaḍ̄iu-me.	چھَڏيُئِ čhaḍ̄yu-e.[1])	چھَڏِئائين čhaḍ̄iā̃-ī̃.
Plur.	چھَڏِئوسون čhaḍ̄iō-sū̃.	چھَڏيُوَ čhaḍ̄yu-va.[2])	چھَڏِئائون čhaḍ̄iā̃-ū̃.

The masc. plur. چھَڏِئا čhaḍ̄ia.

	Suffix I pers.	Suffix II pers.	Suffix III pers.
Sing.	چھَڏِئم čhaḍ̄ia-me.	چھَڏيَئِ čhaḍ̄ya-e.[3])	چھَڏِئائين čhaḍ̄iā̃-ī̃.
Plur.	چھَڏِئاسون čhaḍ̄iā-sū̃.	چھَڏيَوَ čhaḍ̄ya-va.	چھَڏِئائون čhaḍ̄iā̃-ū̃.

1) Or چھَڏِئي čhaḍ̄iē (čhaḍ̄yē).

2) Occasionally also: چھَڏيَان čhaḍ̄y-ā̃.

3) Or contracted چھَڏيي čhaḍ̄yē.

The fem. Sing. چهڏِي čhaḏī.

	Suffix I pers.	Suffix II pers.	Suffix III pers.
Sing.	چهَڏِئَمِ čhaḏia-me.	چهڏيَئِ čhaḏya-e.	چهَڏِئَانئِين čhaḏiā̃-ī̃.
Plur.	چهَڏِيسُون čhaḏī-sū̃.	چهَڏيَوَ čhaḏya-va.	چهَڏِئَانئُون čhaḏiā̃-ū̃.

The fem. Plur. چهَڏِئُون čhaḏiū̃.

Sing.	چهَڏِئُنمِ čhaḏiū̃-me.[1])	چهَڏيُنئِ čhaḏyū̃-e.	چهَڏِئَانئِين čhaḏiā̃-ī̃.
Plur.	چهَڏِئُونسُون čhaḏiū̃-sū̃.	چهَڏيُنوَ čhaḏyū̃-va.	چهَڏِئَانئُون čhaḏiā̃-ū̃.

هِنَ مِٺهَائِيَ مِيوو بِئو کَڌِهِن نَہ کَدهومِ

Another fruit of this sweetness was never eaten by me. Maǰ. 129.

اَچِي سو ڏِٺهوءِ جو کَپَرُ سُٺِي کَنَنِ سِين

Having come thou hast seen that high bank, of which thou hast heard with (thy) ears. Sh. Surāḡ. III, 9.

جَانِي کِنئُوءِ جُدَا سورَٺهِ تهِي سَارِي

(My) friend has been separated by thee, calculates Sōraṭhī. Sh. Sōr. I, Epil.

پُٽرُ ڄَنئَانئِين تَنهِن جو نَالو مِيَان غُلَامِ شَاهُ رَکِهئَانئُون

By her a son was born, to whom by them the name Miā̃ Ghulām Shāh was given. Abd-ul-Latīf's life, p. 35.

---

1) Written and pronounced frequently چهَڏِئُمِ čhaḏiu-me, without an intervening nasal.

ڀِي پِيَالو عِشْقَ جو سَبهُڪِي سَمُجهوسُون

Having drunk a cup of love we understood every thing. Sh. Kal. II, Epil.

ڏِٺهُوَ جي ٻَروچُ مُون جَان هوتُ اَکِهِن سِين

If by you the Barōč, the sweetheart, had been seen with the eyes, as by me. Sh. Hus. XI, 1.

ڪو نَہ مُڪَانسُون ڪَڏِهِن تو ڏَهُنْ نِيَاپو سِين نِينْهَ

Was never sent by them to thee any message with love? Maj. 648.

هُونْدَ نَہ سَٺهِيَمِ هيتِرِي ڪوهِيَارِي جِي ڪَانِ

Would that I had not suffered so much anxiety about the mountaineer. Sh. Ābirī V, 17.

وِچَانئِي وَڍهِئوءِ وِکهَ نَہ کهَڻِئِي هيڪِڙِي

Even from the midst he was cut off by thee; thou didst not make one step. Sh. Hus. X, 27.

مُون ڪَرَ نَہ لَدهَئِي ڪَڏِهِين سَاجَنَ تُنْهُن جِي سَارَ

I have never informed me about thee nor remembered thee, o friend! Maj. 757.

اَنِبهَا سَنِبهَا نَہ ڪَرِي سُونْهَ وِنجَايَسِ سُورَ

What wants unction she does not anoint; her beauty has been wasted by grief. Sh. Um. Mār. III, 7.

مَانِي کهَڻِيسِين ڪِي نَہ اِنْهِي وَاسْطِي اِئِين چِئَانئِين

We have not any bread taken with us, therefore he spoke thus. Matth. 16, 7.

هُونْدَ نَہ پَلِيَو مَان گهِرِيُون سَبهِ گهَڙَا کهَڻِي

I likely would not have been stopped by you; you all would have slided down (into the river), having taken jars (to swim upon). Sh. Suh. I, 3.

پَسَنَ خَاطِرِ پِرِنئَ جي پَاتِيمِ جهَاتَڙِيُون

For the sake of seeing my friend I applied little peepings, i. e. I peeped a little through. Sh. Kambh. II, Epil. 1.

مَچِهَنَ چَوَنِمِ کِي تَہ لَڄَايُنِي تهَرَ جَائِيُون

Lest some say to me: by thee the daughters of the Thar have been put to shame. Sh. Um. Mār. II, 17.

تَہ بَانْهُنِ وِجهِي وَاتُ رِيهُون كِيُو رُنجَ مِين

Then having thrown (your) mouth into (your) sleeves, you would have made wailings in the desert. Sh. Hus. XII, 6.

Suffixes of the III pers. Sing. and Plur. denoting the object.

	چهَڍِئو	چهَڍِيَا
Sing.	چهَڍِئُسِ čhaḍiu-se.	چهَڍِيَسِ čhaḍia-se.
Plur.	چهَڍِئُنِ čhaḍiu-ne.	چهَڍِيَنِ čhaḍia-ne.

	چهَڍِي	چهَڍِئُون
Sing.	چهَڍِيَسِ čhaḍia-se.	چهَڍِئُنْسِ čhaḍiū-se.
Plur.	چهَڍِيَنِ čhaḍia-ne.	چهَڍِئُنِ čhaḍiu-ne.

كو چَوِي پِئُسِ جِنُّ جُسِي مِين كو چَئِي عَقْلُ پهِرِئوسِ

One says: a ǰinn has fallen into his body, another says: his understanding has turned round (i. e. he has become mad). Maǰ. 40.

كَالهَہ گَڏِئوسُون كَاپَڙِي بَابُو بِيكهَارِي

Yesterday met with us a Kāpaṛī, a mendicant bābū. Sh. Mūm. Rāṇō III, 4.

سَبهِيئِي وِئَّمِ وِسِرِي جيکِي سَگا سِينَ

All those have been forgotten by me, whoever (be) my relatives and friends. Maj. 212.

تَرِي تُنَ پِٽّاسِ پاسَنِئُون پاڻِي وَهِي

کهُوهُو جهُرُ جهُنو تهِئو لَاجُو سَبهِ لَڙِيّاسِ

In the bottom she has got leaks, from the sides water flows in,

The mast has become old, all her ropes are dangling. Sh. Surāg̃. III, 6.

اُهَا دهِيئَڙِي پُڻَ جَڏِهِن ڳالهَاءِ اُنَ جو ٻُندهَنْدِي هُئِي تَڏِهِن

پَنْهَن جِي سِرِ اُتهِي ٽُکُرُ مَانِيَ جو کهَڻِي آڻِي ڏِينْدِي هُيِسِ

That little daughter also, when she was hearing the talk of him, used to stand up herself, and having taken and brought a piece of bread, was giving it him. Abd-ul-Latīf's life, p. 46.

جِي هُيَوَ هوتَ پُنْهُوَّ سِين مُون کهَا مُلَاقَاتِ

If there had been to you, like as to me, a meeting with the sweetheart Punhũ. Sh. Hus. XII, 6.

هِنَ اَسَان جِي حَالَ جِي خَبَرَ تَان نَ پِئِي[1]

No intelligence of this our state has come to thee. Maj. 229.

تَنْهِين جِي وَائِي هُونْدَ نَ وِييَوَ وِسِرِي

Their speech perhaps would not be forgotten by you. Sh. Hus. XII, 7.

---

1) پِئِي pi-ē instead of پِيَئِي piya-e.

مُون کهي ڇهَڏِي هَلِيَّا ڳَا پِيَيَنَ مَتهي پِئي

They went having given me up; some (word) has fallen upon their gall bag. Sh. Maʒδ. III, Epil.

جِئين آيُنْسِ مَتِئُون وَنِجُو تهِي وَارِيسِ

In that wise, as the advices came to her, she, having gone, answers him. Maǰ. 424.

سَرِي کِي نَہ کِئُونَ وِينَ مؤکِهِيَ جِي مَارِيَّا

By the wine nothing was done to them; by the ill-language of the released one they were killed. Sh. Jam. Kal. IV, 18.

اَوَڳُنِ رُسِي سَبهُکو ڳُڻِين پرِين رُٺهَامِ

At a vice every body takes offence; (my) friends have taken offence at (my) virtues. Sh. Āsa IV, 24.

کَنْهِين کَامِڻَ کِيَاءِ کِينئَ بهَنْبهوُلِئِين کَرَهَا
اَکِهِنِ مَتهي اَکهِيَا پِڙَ مِين پِيرَ گَسْهَاءِ

By whom were enchantments made to thee? how wast thou confused, o camel?
Upon (thy) eyes are hoods; in the plain (thy) feet were grated. Sh. Kambh. II, 39.

سَنْهي لَکِ نَکِ سَنئِين کَجَلَ بهَرِيَنَ نيڻَ

Of slender loin, of straight nose, their eyes filled with lamp-black. Sh. Sam. I, 35.

b) The past participle with two suffixes.

To the past participle passive two suffixes may be attached, the first denoting the agent and the latter the object (Dative-Accusative), as:

مُون تو کهي چهَڍِئو = čhaḍiō-mā̃-e چهَڍِئومَانئِ

thou wast given up by me, literally: by me it was given up in reference to thee.

To suffixes of the II pers. Sing. and Plur. no further suffix is added, joint suffixes of this kind being mostly found in the III pers. Sing and Plur., very seldom in the I pers. Sing. and Plur.

The suffix used for the I person Singular is in this case not me, but mā̃ (the Instrumental of آنئُون ā̃ū̃), as 'me' would not be strong enough to support the following suffix. The Instrumental suffix of the III pers. Singular ī̃ is either contracted with the preceding ā to ā̃, or is retained before a following suffix; the suffix of the III. person Plural keeps its place before another acceding suffix, but is frequently shortened to ū̃ (u).

No change of gender and number can take place in the participle, when joined by the suffix of the III person Singular or Plural; but when the participle is provided with a suffix of the I person Singular or Plural, it must agree with its subject in gender and number.

SINGULAR.

	Masc.		*Fem.*	
	چهَڍِئو		چهَڍِي	
Suffix I pers. Sing.	چهَڍِئومَانئِ	čhaḍiō-mā̃-e.	چهَڍِيمَانئِ	čhaḍī-mā̃-e.
	چهَڍِئومَانْسِ	čhaḍiō-mā̃-se.	چهَڍِيمَانْسِ	čhaḍī-mā̃-se.
	چهَڍِئومَانْوَ	čhaḍiō-mā̃-va.	چهَڍِيمَانْوَ	čhaḍī-mā̃-va.
	چهَڍِئومَانِ	čhaḍiō-mā-ne.	چهَڍِيمَانِ	čhaḍī-mā-ne.

Masc. and Fem. Sing. and Plur.

Suffix III pers. Sing.				
چھَڏِئانئِيِنْمِ	čhaḍ̄iā̃-ī̃-me	or:	چھَڏِئانْمِ	čhaḍ̄iā̃-me.
چھَڏِئانئِيِنئِ	čhaḍ̄iā̃-ī̃-e	or:	چھَڏِئانئِ	čhaḍ̄iā̃-e.
چھَڏِئانئِيِنْسِ	čhaḍ̄iā̃-ī̃-se	or:	چھَڏِئانْسِ	čhaḍ̄iā̃-se.
چھَڏِئانئِيِنْسُون	čhaḍ̄iā̃-ī̃-sū̃	or:	چھَڏِئانْسُون	čhaḍ̄iā̃-su.
چھَڏِئانئِيِنْوَ	čhaḍ̄iā̃-ī-va	or:	چھَڏِئانْوَ	čhaḍ̄iā-va.
چھَڏِئانئِيِنِ	čhaḍ̄iā̃-ī̃-ne	or:	چھَڏِئانِ	čhaḍ̄iā̃-ne.

Suffix I pers. Plur.			
چھَڏِئوسُونئِ	čhaḍ̄iō-sū̃-e.	چھَڏِيسُونئِ	čhaḍ̄ī-sū̃-e.
چھَڏِئوسُونْسِ	čhaḍ̄iō-sū̃-se.	چھَڏِيسُونْسِ	čhaḍ̄ī-sū̃-se.
چھَڏِئوسُونْوَ	čhaḍ̄iō-sū̃-va.	چھَڏِيسُونْوَ	čhaḍ̄ī-sū̃-va.
چھَڏِئوسُونِ	čhaḍ̄iō-sū-ne.	چھَڏِيسُونِ	čhaḍ̄ī-sū-ne.

Masc. and Fem. Sing. and Plur.

Suffix III pers. Plur.		
	چھَڏِئانئُونْمِ	čhaḍ̄iā̃-ū̃-me.[1]
	چھَڏِئانئُونئِ	čhaḍ̄iā̃-ū̃-e.
	چھَڏِئانئُونْسِ	čhaḍ̄iā̃-ū̃-se.
	چھَڏِئانئُونْسُون	čhaḍ̄iā̃-ū̃-sū̃.
	چھَڏِئانئُونْوَ	čhaḍ̄iā̃-ū̃-va.
	چھَڏِئانئُونِ	čhaḍ̄iā̃-ū-ne.

1) Or shortened: چھَڏِئانئُنْمِ čhaḍ̄iā̃-ū̃-me and with elision of the final nasal: چھَڏِئانئُمِ čhaḍ̄iā̃-u-me.

PLURAL.

	Masc.	*Fem.*
	چھڏِيا	چھڏِيون
Suffix I pers. Sing.	چھڏِيامانءِ	چھڏِيونمانءِ
	čhaḏiā-mā̃-e.	čhaḏiū̃-mā̃-e.
	etc.	etc.
Suffix I pers. Plur.	چھڏِياسونءِ	چھڏِيونسونءِ
	čhaḏiā-sū̃-e.	čhaḏiū̃-sū̃-e.
	etc.	etc.

تُنْهِن جي چيلَنِ وَٽِ وَٺِي آندومانْسِ پَرَ هو ڇُٽائِي نَ سَگِهِئَسِ

I brought him to thy disciples, but they could not cure him. Matth. 17, 16.

سِيدها پادها ڏِنائِينْسِ

He gave him provisions (and) victuals. Story of Rāe Diāču, p. 5.

مِيان غُلامِ شاهه کَھٽَ تان ٽَپو ڏيئِي اَچِي هَٿُ صاحِبزادي جو وَٺِي کَھٽَ تي سيراندِهِي کَهون وِهارِيائِينْسِ

Miã Ghulām Shāh, having jumped from the couch, having come (and) seized the hand of the gentleman, seated him upon the couch at its upper part (literally: from its upper part). Abd-ul-Latīf's life, p. 7.

اُٿِي آيو اُسْتادَ ڏانهَن اُڀِي عَرْضُ ڪِيائِينْسِ

Having risen he came to (his) master and addressed to him standing the petition. Maj. 6.

چِيائِينِ اَبو تَهان جو اِنْهِي پُڇهَنَ جو واسْطو ڪِهڙو

She said to them: fathers, what reason have you to ask after this? Amulu Māṇ. p. 140.

اِهو سَبھُہ فَقِيرَ جو نَذَرُ ڏِيئِي هَلَايَانِ

Having given all this as a gift to the Faqīr he started them off. Amulu Māṇ. p. 140.

سِي پَنْهَن جو نَانو هِڪِڙِيَ ٻُڍِهِيَ وَٽِ دهَرَاوَت رَکهِي چِئَانئُونْسِ

They, having placed their money in deposit with an old woman said to her. Stack's Gram. p. 135.

مَانِي جوڙِي آڻِي اَڳِيَان دهَرِيَانئُونْسِ

Having prepared bread and brought (it), they placed it before him. Abd-ul-Latīf's life, p. 48.

4) The past participle with the auxiliary آهِي āhē etc.

(The Perfect.)

The single suffixes, be they referring to the agent or the object, are joined to آهِي āhē and آنهِنِ, but chiefly to the form اَتهَ atha (§. 55), and not to the participle itself.

But to the form اَتهَ atha a double suffix may be joined, the first implying the agent and the latter the object, as: ڏِنو اَتهِيمَانئِ, I have given to thee, literally: it has been given by me in reference to thee. The suffix of the III. person Singular and of the II. person Plural does not admit of a second suffix.

The original i of अत्थि atthi reappears again and is lengthened at the same time, when followed by a double suffix in the II. and III. person Singular, to give a support to the heavy joint-suffix.

Singular and Plural.

Suffix				
I pers. Sing.	اَتهِيمانئِ	چهَڏِئو	čhaḍiō	athī-mā̃-e.
	اَتهِيمانْسِ	چهَڏِيا	čhaḍiā	athī-mā̃-se.
	اَتهِيمانْوَ	چهَڏِي	čhaḍi	athī-mā̃-va.
	اَتهِيمانِ	چهَڏِئُون	čhaḍiū̃	athī-mā-ne.
II pers. Sing.	اَتهِيئِيمِ	„	„	athē-ī-me.
	اَتهِيئِيسِ	„	„	athē-ī-se.
	اَتهِيئِيسُون	„	„	athē-ī-sū̃.
	اَتهِيئِينِ	„	„	athē-ī-ne.
I pers. Plur.	اَتهُونئِ	„	„	ath-ū̃-e.
	اَتهُونْسِ	„	„	ath-ū̃-se.
	اَتهُونْوَ	„	„	ath-ū̃-va.
	اَتهُونِ	„	„	ath-ū-ne.
III pers. Plur.	اَتهَنِمِ	„	„	atha-ni-me.
	اَتهَنِئِي	„	„	atha-ne-ī.
	اَتهَنِسِ	„	„	atha-ni-se.
	اَتهَنِئُون	„	„	atha-ne-ū̃.
	اَتهَنِوَ	„	„	atha-ni-va.
	اَتهَنِنِ	„	„	atha-ni-ne.

سُنْهَنِي مِين هُنَ كَرِي كهَنِيُون گَالهِئُون سَتهِيُون آتهم

In a dream I have suffered many things for his sake. Matth. 27, 19.

حُسِنِ پَرِيَ رَانِىَ جِي گوڏَ تِي كَنْڌهُ رَكهِئو آهِيس

He has placed his neck upon the knee of Husine, the fairy queen. Amulu Māṇ. p. 152.

پوءِ وَارَ سُكَائِي كَپِڙَا كهُرَايَا اَتهِيئِي

Then having dried the hairs thou hast asked for clothes. Ibid. p. 146.

شِينهَنِ جَاگَايِسِ تَه پَرِيُون آيُون اَتهِيئِي

The lions awakened him (saying): the fairies have come to thee. Ibid. p. 150.

5) The past participle with the auxiliary هو etc.

(The Pluperfect.)

The single suffixes are joined to هو hō etc., which see. Thus in the III person Singular and Plural the instrumental suffix ĩ and ũ is also attached to هو etc., as: چهَڏِئو هُئَانئِين čhaḏiō huã-ĩ[1]), by him it had been given up, چهَڏِئو هُئَانئُون čhaḏiō huã-ũ, by them it had been given up.

But to هو hō etc. a double suffix may also be attached, the first denoting the agent and the latter the object, as: چهَڏِئو هومَانءِ čhaḏiō hō-mã-e, thou hadst been given up by me, literally: it had been given up by me in reference to thee. These double suffixes however are of rare occurence; in the II person Singular and Plural they are not in use.

1) Instead of هُئَانئِين huã-ĩ and هُئَانئُون huã-ũ the contracted forms هَانئِين hã-ĩ and هَانئُون hã-ũ (from هو) are also in use.

SINGULAR.

	Masc.	*Fem.*
Suffix I pers. Sing.	چهڊِئو هومَانئِ	چهڊِي هُئِيمَانئِ
	čhaḍiō hō-mā̃-e.	čhaḍī huī-mā̃-e.
	چهڊِئو هومَانْسِ	چهڊِي هُئِيمَانْسِ
	čhaḍiō hō-mā̃-se.	čhaḍi huī-mā̃-se.
	چهڊِئو هومَانْوَ	چهڊِي هُئِيمَانْوَ
	čhaḍiō hō-mā̃-va.	čhaḍī huī-mā̃-va.
	چهڊِئو هومَانِ	چهڊِي هُئِيمَانِ
	čhaḍiō hō-mā̃-ne.	čhaḍī huī-mā-ne.

Masc. and Fem. Sing. and Plur.

Suffix III pers. Sing.	چهڊِئو[1] هُئَانئِينْمِ	čhaḍiō huā̃-ī̃-me.
	چهڊِئَا هُئَانئِينئِ	čhaḍiā huā̃-ī̃-e.
	چهڊِي هُئَانئِينْسِ	čhaḍī huā̃-ī̃-se.
	چهڊِئُون هُئَانئِينْسُون	čhaḍiū̃ huā̃-ī̃-sū̃.
	هُئَانئِينْوَ „	„ huā̃-ī̃-va.
	هُئَانئِينِ „	„ huā̃-ī-ne.

Suffix I pers. Plur.	چهڊِئو هوسُونئِ	چهڊِي هُئِيسُونئِ
	čhaḍiō hō-sū̃-e.	čhaḍī huī-sū̃-e.
	چهڊِئو هوسُونْسِ	چهڊِي هُئِيسُونْسِ
	čhaḍiō hō-sū̃-se.	čhaḍī huī-sū̃-se.
	چهڊِئو هوسُونْوَ	چهڊِي هُئِيسُونْوَ
	čhaḍiō hō-sū̃-va.	čhaḍī huī-sū̃-va.
	چهڊِئو هوسُونِ	چهڊِي هُئِيسُونِ
	čhaḍiō hō-sū̃-ne.	čhaḍī huī-sū̃-nc.

---

1) Or shortened: هُئَانئِنْمِ huā̃-ī-me, and with elision of the final nasal of the first suffix: هُئَانئِمِ huā̃-i-me etc.

Masc. and Fem. Sing. and Plur.

	هُئاسُونَمِ چهَڍِئو (1)	čhaḍiō huā̃-ū̃-me.
	هُئاسُونئِ چهَڍِئا	čhaḍiā huā̃-ū̃-e.
Suffix III pers. Plur.	هُئاسُونسِ چهَڍِي	čhaḍi huā̃-ū̃-se.
	هُئاسُونسُون چهَڍِئُون	čhaḍiū̃ huā̃-ū̃-sū̃.
	هُئاسُونوَ " "	huā̃-ū̃-va.
	هُئاسُونِ " "	huā̃-ū-ne.

PLURAL.

	Masc.	*Fem.*
Suffix I pers. Sing.	چهَڍِئا هُئامانئِ čhaḍiā huā-mā̃-e. etc. etc.	چهَڍِئُون هُيُونمانئِ čhaḍiū̃ huyū̃-mā̃-e. etc. etc.
Suffix I pers. Plur.	چهَڍِئا هُئاسُونئِ čhaḍiā huā-sū̃-e. etc. etc.	چهَڍِئُون هُيُونسُونئِ čhaḍiū̃ huyū̃-ūs-e. etc. etc.

ڙي کُنبهَرَ جا پُٽرَ مُون سان بِين مَهِينين جو کهُنُ ڪِئو هوءِ

O son of the potter! with me thou hadst made a term of two months. Story of Rāe Diāču, p. 5.

اَسان کهي جا چِٺِهي باسِي هُئِئِ سا ڏِي

Give us that letter, which thou hadst promised. Abd-ul-Latīf's life, p. 49.

جَنهِن خِدمَتگارَ کهي اَڳي سيکهارِئو هانئِين تَنهِن ڏِي نِهارِئانئِين

He looked towards that servant, whom he had instructed beforehand. Ibid. p. 9.

---

1) Or shortened هُئانُنمِ huā̃-ū-me, and with elision of the final nasal of the first suffix: هُئانمِ huā̃-u-me, etc.

جَا فَقِيرَ اَوْهَان سَان ڳالهِ كِي هُئَّانئِين تنهِن سَبَبَان پَانَ نَ ايو

By reason of that word, which the Faqīr had spoken to you, he has not come himself. Abd-ul-Latif's life, p. 49.

اُهو وِينْدهو جِنئَ پَرِیَ چِئو هوس تِنئَ بَانهِیَ جي گهڙ ۾ مين وِدهَانئِين

That nose ring, as it had been said to him by the fairy, he threw into the jar of the slave-girl. Amulu Māṇ., p. 150.

جو پَاتِشَاهِي قَوْلُ چِئو هَانئُون

What royal word had been spoken by them. Ibid. p. 143.

6) The Future.

(Active and passive voice.)

See the paradigm of هُونْدُسِ hūnduse.

SECTION IV.

ADVERBS, POSTPOSITIONS, CONJUNCTIONS AND INTERJECTIONS.

Chapter XVIII.

Adverbs.

§. 57.

The Sindhī has only a limited number of original adverbs.[1]) Adverbs are not derived from adjectives by any change of the adjectival termination, but the adjective as such (in the masc. Sing.) is either used in an adverbial sense, or the adjective, agreeing in gender and number with the subject referred to, is employed, where we would use an adverb as a complement to the verb, as: گھڻو رُئي تھو he weeps much: هُو رُکِي مَانِي کھائي تھو he eats only bread.

A number of substantives are at the same time also used adverbially, either in the Nominative, the Instrumental, the Locative or the Ablative case, similarly some adjectives in the Locative and Ablative have received an adverbial signification.

---

1) Adverbs borrowed from the Arabic or Persian are here only so far taken into consideration, as they are commonly used in Sindhī.

I. Original adverbs. [1])

The most common of them are:

اَپاکَ apāka, accidentally.
اَپرِ apare, excessively.
اَتِ ate, very.
اَڄُ aju, to-day.
اَچانکَ ačanaka, } suddenly;
اَچاچيتِ ačāčēte, } unawares.
اَرِهَنْ arehā, } on the fourth day
تَرِهَنْ tarehā, } (from the present).
اَسَهُ asahu, wholly; completely.
اَلْبَتَّه albattah, certainly (arab.).
اُمالَکَ umālaka, in a moment.
اَڃا aṅā, till now.
بَسِ base, enough.
بِلْکُلِ bilkule, wholly; absolutely (arab.).
بِنِهَ bineha, completely.
پَٽِی paṭia, } completely;
پهَٽِ phaṭe, } at all.

پَرِهَنْ parehā, after to-morrow.
تُرتُ turtu, quickly.
توءِ tōe, then.
ٺَهَپَهَ ṭhahapaha, quickly.
جائِي jāī, positively; nenessarily.
ڄَڻُ jaṇu, to say so; as if.
جهَٽپَٽِ jhaṭepaṭe, } instantly.
چَٽپَٽِ čaṭepaṭe, } instantly.
جيکُسِ jēkuse, perhaps.
چهو čhō, why?
سَدا sadā, always.
شايد šāyad, } perhaps.
شائِتَ šāita, } (pers.)
شاتَ šāta,
کالهَ kālha, } yesterday.
کَلهَ kalha,
کَداچِتِ kadāčite, perhaps.
کَرَ kara[2]), as if; to say so; like.

---

1) The numeral adverbs see §. 29.

2) Or کَرُ karu.

گَڏُ gaḏu, together.

لُرَ lura, straightforward; instantly.

مَسَ masa, مَسَان masã, مَسِين masẽ, } with difficulty.

مُفْتُ muftu, gratuitously. (pers.)

نَ na, not.

نِپَٽُ nipaṭu, very; exceedingly.

نِتُ nitu, نِتُ پرَتُ nitu pratu, } always.

نِڄُ niču, with a wellcome.

نِکَنِين nikaṇĩ, thoroughly; wholly.

نِيٺهِ neṭhe, finally; at last.

ويتَرِ vētare, very greatly.

هَاڻي hāṇē, هَاڻيئِي hāṇē-ī, } now; immediately.

هَرُوبهَرُو harūbharū, certainly.

هِنئَرَ hĩara, now.

هُونْدَ hūnda, possibly; perhaps.

هيرَ hēra, now.

هيڪَارِي hēkārī, still more; still further.

اَتِ اُکَنْڍِي آنهِيَان تِنئَ آتَنَ تِنئَ ڏيهَ

I am very longing as well after the spinning place as after the country. Sh. Um. Mār. II, 1.

اَڃا تُون اَنوتُ کهُورِي خبَرَ نَ لَهِين

As yet thou art ignorant, thou takest no notice of the furnace. Sh. Jam. Kal. III, 11.

ٿهَپَهَ جهَپِي اُتهِي اُڏَاڻِي

Having snatched (it) quickly she rose and flew away. Amula Man. p. 147.

جو مُنهِ مُومَلَ جي پوءِ موٽَڻُ تَنْهين مَسَ تهِئِي

The returning of him, who falls into the face of Mūmala, is effected with difficulty. Sh. Mūm. Rāṇō III, 5.

نيٺهِ پَاتِشَاهُ ويهِي ويهِي ڪهَٽو ٿهِئي

At length the king, sitting (and) sitting, becomes dissatisfied. Amulu Māṇ. p. 143.

ڪَنْزُ قُدُورِي ڪَافِيَا جي پَڙهِي پَرُوڙين سَڀهِ

جَنُ مَنْڍِي مَاڪوڙِي کهُوهَ مين پيئِي ڪَتهِي اُڀهُ

If thou having read the Kanz, the Qudūrī, the Kāfiā[1]), understandest them all,

It is as if a lame ant, which has fallen into a well, contemplates the sky. Sh. Jam. Kal. V, 4.

جيڪُسِ وِسُرِ وِسِرِي آنئُون مَنَان مَعْشُوقَنِ

Perhaps I have been forgotten from the mind of the beloved. Maǰ. 507.

پَاڀُوهَنْدِيئِي پَدهِرَا ڪَرَ کهِلَنِ کهَٽَنهَارَ

In smiling they (i. e. the teeth) are apparent, as if the sunflowers would laugh. Maǰ. 55.

بهَلِي[2]) آئِين نِجُ آئِين

Thou art welcome, thou art welcome! Amulu Mān. p. 141.

II. Peculiar use of Adjectives.

The following adjectives may be either used as (indecl.) adverbs or they may agree with their subject in gender and number even in such constructions, where in English an adverb would be used.

---

1) Grammatical treatises in Arabic.

2) بهَلِي is substantive, after which ڪَرِي karē is to be supplied; i. e. having made a favour thou art come = thou art welcome!

آڏو ā̤ḍō[1]), opposite; in front.

اوچتو ōčitōly, unexpected; unexpected; suddenly; by chance.

اوڏو ōḍō, } near.
اوڏِڙو ōḍirō, dim, } near.

اويلو avēlō, out of time; late.

چَوْڌاري čaudhārī, round about.

ڏاڍو ḍaḍhō, hard, intense; very much.

سَاجهُر sājhuru, early.

سَامُهون sāmuhō̃, in front.

سَوَارو savārō, } early; at an early hour.
سَويرو savērō, } early; at an early hour.

سُودهو sūdhō[2]), } accompanied by; along with (with the Instrumental).
سَنئون saō̃, } accompanied by; along with (with the Instrumental).

مَهَنْڊِيون mahandiyō̃, in front; before.

وِجهو vējhō, } near; close to.
وِجهِڙو vējhirō, dim, } near; close to.

In the same way the Adjectives, implying time or place, derived from adverbs by the affixes āhō̃ or ārō are either used adverbially or they may agree with their subject in gender and number, as:

---

1) آڏو، اوڏو، سَامُهون، وِجهو may be constructed with جي or کهي.

2) سُودهو is probably derived from the Sansk. साद्धम्, with; سَنئون from संहित, joined by.

اوراهوں ōrāhō̃, somewhat on this side; from اوري ōre, on this side.

اگاهوں agāhō̃, somewhat in front; from اگي agē, before, in front.

پوئِتاهوں poĕtāhō̃, a little behind; from پوئِتي poĕtē, in the rear.

مَتهاهوں mathāhō̃, somewhat higher up; from مَتهي mathē, on; upon.

مَنجهارو manjhārō, } somewhat inside; from مَنجهِ manjhe, in.
مَنجهاهوں manjhāhō̃, }

When used adverbially (which is commonly the case), they take also the fem. termination, as:

اگاهِين agāhī̃, in front; in advance.

مَتهاهِين mathāhī̃, on the top; above.

The Adjectives, ending in āitō (§. 10, 20) may at the same time be used adverbially, as:

سُنهائِتو sũhāitō, suitable and suitably.

وَسائِتو vasāitō, optional and optionally.

etc. etc. etc.

The Adjectives of one ending, which are not inflected, may all be used as adverbs; as:

بَرابَرِ barābare, right and rightly.

جَارَ jara, } much; very.
جَالَ jala, }

جَلْدُ jaldu, quick and quickly.

سوڏِيتُ sōḍ̤ītu, true and truly.

عَبَثُ ʿabaϑu, vain and vainly.

etc. etc. etc.

اوچتوئي ڪُئي هِڪڙِي اُنَ ڀَهانڊِي جي ڀرِ مين ٻِرُ ڪِئو

By chance one mouse made a hole in the vicinity of that garner. Sindhī Read. Book, p. 54.

سِينَنِ سَاجهُرُ لَڏِئو تُون هَارِي نِهَارِين اَڄُ

(Thy) friends have departed early, look thou, o lost one! to-day. Sh. Sam. II, Epil. 2.

تَڏِهِين جَرُ هَارِي جَالَ گهَڻو روئي مَاء وَرِيَاسِ

Then his mother, having shed tears (and) having wept very much, returned. Maj. 99.

تَڏِهِين آهِي آڳانجهِي گهَڻو ڪَا مِصرِنِ مُرُوَتَ

Then there is some very ancient generosity of the Egyptians. Maj. 135.

لَايو لَامَ اَلِفَ سِين خُوبُ لِکهَنِ خَطَّ

Joining the Lām with the Alif they write nicely letters. Maj. 144.

جي پَنْدِ پَارِيَّانِئُون تَہ سِگهَائِي سَگهَا ٿِيَّا

If they had performed the advice, they would have quickly become whole. Sh. Jam. Kal. II, 2.

لُکهُون لَگَنِ کوسِيُون ڏَاڏَهَا تَپَنِ ڏِينْهَہ

Hot winds blow, the days are excessively hot. Sh. Dēsī III, Epil.

هُنَ سَان رُڳِيُون ڳَالهِيُون آنْهِنِ

With him there are only words. Amulu Māṇ. p. 150.

چوڌَارِي چِڙَا ٿهَا ٻُرَنِ ڀيلَائِنِ جَا

Round about sound the bells of the woodmen. Sh. Suh. IV, 2.

اَکھِڙُون اَکھِنِ سَامُهِيُون ڏِينْهُه سَجھُوئِي رَاتِ

The eyes are opposite to the eyes the whole day (and) night. Maǰ. 219.

سُتِئَسْ سَوَارِي وِيڙهِي مُنْهُه مُئَنِ جَان

Thou hadst fallen asleep early, having wrapt up (thy) face like the dead ones. Sh. Kāh. I, 11.

مُون کهِي نَه موڙَاءِ آنڙُون اَگَاهِين آنهِيَان

Do not turn me back; I am ahead. Sh. Sōr IV, 12.

III. Substantives used adverbially in the uninflected state.

A number of substantives are at the same time also used as adverbs, as:

اَوِيرَ avēra, اَوِيلَ avēla, } out of time, late; subst. f. اَوِيرَ avēra, delay.

ٻُڇھَان bučhā̃, unpleasingly; subst. f. ٻُڇھَان bučhā̃, disgust.

تَارِيخَ tārīχa, daily; subst. f. تَارِيخَ tārīχa, a date.

جوڙُ ǰōru, زوڙُ zōru, } forcibly; very; subst. m. جوڙُ ǰōru, force.

ڏِينْهَاڙِي ḍ̄ihāṛī, daily; subst. f. ڏِينْهَاڙِي ḍ̄ihāṛī, day.

سُبَهَنْ subahā̃, to-morrow; subst. f. سُبَهَنْ subahā̃, the morrow.

سَوِيرَ savēra, early; subst. f. سَوِيرَ savēra, the early hour of day.

تَڏِهِين سُمْهَنْدِيُون جو اَوِيلَ سو اُتِيئِي سِجُ اُبهِرِي وِينْدَنِ

Then, because they will sleep out of time, therefore the sun will even there rise to them. Amulu Māṇ., p. 145.

مُحِبُ مُنْهِن حو مَجنو مُجهان سو بيزار

My lover Majnō is sorely displeased. Maj. 294.

ڏِينْهَانِي جهَجهو بهانگو اُن مَان سَنگتِنِ کانِ خَرْچِنَّانِئِين تهي

Daily it (the mouse) used to spend a great portion from it for the sake of the companions. Sindhī Read. Book, p. 55.

IV. Substantives and Adjectives used adverbially in the inflected state.

1) Substantives.

آگهِين agahī̃ (instead of agehī̃), before, Locat. with emphatic hī, from اَگُ agu, the front.

اَگِي agē, before; Loc. from. اَگو agō, the forepart.

اَنْدَرِ andare, inside; within; Loc. from اَنْدَرُ andaru, the inside.

اَنْدَرَان andarā̃, اَنْدَرون andarō̃, } from within; Abl. from اَنْدَرُ.

اَننْدَ ananda, well; in good health; Instrum. from اَننْدُ anandu, happiness.

اوڙِکِ ōṛake, at last; Loc. from اوڙِکُ ōṛaku, the end.

بَاهَرِ bāhare, outside, Loc. } from بَاهَرُ bāharu, the outside.
بَاهَرَان bāharā̃, from the outside, Abl.

پَارِ pāre, on the opposite side, Loc. } from پَارُ pāru, the opposite side.
پَارَان pārā̃, from the opposite side, Abl.

پَاسِي pāsē, on the side; near; Loc. from پَاسو pāsō, the side.

پُٺهِئَان puṭheā̃, behind; from the back; Abl. from پُٺهِ puṭhe, the back.

پوءِ pōe, after; Loc. }
پُئَان puā̃[1]), } from behind; after; Abl. }
پُئوُن puō̃, } from behind; after; Abl. } from پوءُ pou, the latter part.

حَقّوُن ȟaqqō̃, justly; Abl. from حَقُّ ȟaqqu, justice.

حُڪُمَان ȟukumā̃, } violently; Abl. }
حُڪُمَنِ ȟukumane, } by force; Instr. } from حُڪُمُ ȟukumu, command.

خُوشِئوُن χušeō̃, willingly, Abl. from خُوشِ χuše, pleasure.

دِلِئوُن dileō̃, willingly; Loc. from دِلِ dile, heart.

زوُرِ zōre, forcibly; Loc. from زوُرُ zōru, force.

مَاڳِ māĝe, }
مَاڳهِين māĝahī̃, emph. } at all; completely; Loc. from مَاڳُ māĝu, place.

مَٿهي mathē, on the top; Loc. }
مَٿهَان mathā̃, from upon; Abl. } from مَٿهو mathō, the head.

مُورِ mūre, } at all; completely; Loc. }
مُورَهِين mūrahī̃, emph. } at all; completely; }
مُورَانئِي mūrā̃-ī, emph. } at all; completely; Abl. } from مُورُ mūru, capital.

مَهَنْدِ mahande, in the beginning; before; Loc. }
مَهَنْدَان mahandā̃; from the beginning; before; Abl. } from مَهَنْدُ mahandu, beginning.

---

1) پُئَان puā̃ etc. instead of پوئَان pōā̃.

نِهچي nihičē, certainly; Instrum. from نِهچو nihičō, certainty.

وِچِ viče, in the midst; Loc. from وِچُ viču, the midst.

هَڏِهين haḍehī̃, emph. } at all; Loc. from هَڏُ haḍu,
هَڏِ haḍe[1]), } the core.

هيٺهِ hēṭhe, below; Loc. } from هيٺهُ hēṭhu,
هيٺهان hēṭhā̃, from below; Abl. } the bottom.

اَنْدَرِ آدِيسِنِ کهي دهَرانئي دهَڻي

Inside is to the Ādēsīs (Jōgīs) the Lord personally. Sh. Rāmak. II, 6.

بَاهَرِ بوِلي بِي پهِري کهَٽَ مِين کهَايَلَ کهُورَ

Outside another speech is used; in the heart there is a wounded fierce look. Sh. Rāmak. III, 2.

بِئو ڏَ. مَنگي مُورِ اَمُلُ ڏِئو اِنَ کهي

Nothing else at all he asks; give the invaluable (thing) to this one. Sh. Sōr. I, 8.

مَهَنْدِ تهِينْدو مُصْطَفَى پُٺهِي لوَکُ لَڏِينْدو

In front will be Mustafa; in the rear the world will march. Sh. Barvō Sindhī II, Epil. 2.

2) Adjectives.

اَگِيَان agiyā̃, before; Abl. from اَگِيوُن agiyō̃, first; prior.

اَنَنْتِ anante, exceedingly; Loc. from اَنَنْتُ anantu, endless.

---

1) مُورِ، مَاگِ and هَڏِ signify in a negative sentence, 'by no means'.

اوري ōrē, on this side; near; Loc.
اوريان oriyā̃, from this side; near; Abl.
} from اوريو ōriyō, of this side; near.

آوسِ avase, helplessly; Loc. from آوَسُ avasu, helpless.

بهلي bhalē, well; Loc. from بهلو bhalō, good.

بيڊوهہ beḍōhe, faultlessly; Loc. from بيڊوهہ beḍōhu, faultless.

پَري parē, far off; Loc.
پَرئان pareā̃, from a distance; beyond; Abl. fem.
} from پَرُ paru, remote, distant.

پِهرين peherē̃, at first; Loc.
پِهرائِي peherā-ī̃, from the first; Abl.
} from پِهرون pehērõ, the first.

چنگِئان čaṅiā̃, well; in a good manner; Abl. fem. from چَنگو čaṇō, good.

دهيري dhīrē, gently; Loc. from دهيرو dhīrō, gentle.

ڏاڍهِئان ḍāḍhiā̃, violently; Abl. fem. from ڏاڍهو ḍādhō, violent.

سابهِئان sabheā̃, effectually; Ablat. from سابهِ sābhe, effectual.

سامْهُني sāmhuṇē, in front; Loc. from سامْهُنو sāmhuṇō, of the front.

سويري savērē, early; Loc. from. سويرو savērō, early.

مَٿهِئان maṭhiā̃, disgustingly; Abl. fem. from مَٿهو maṭhō, bad.

هَوْري haure or هوري hōre, gently; Loc.
هَوْرِئان hauriā̃; Abl. fem.
} from هَوْرو haurō, gentle.

پيڙَ پَرِي وِيئِي اَچڻَ سَانُ عَجِيبَ جي

The pain went far off with the coming of (my) friend. Sh. Jan. Kal. II, 10.

اَوْهِين گهڻو مَتهِيَان بهَائِينْدَوُ

You will feel very disgusted. Sindhī Read. Book, p. 51.

وَاٽَ تي بِيهِي ڏاڍِهِيَان ٽِرِي هوَكَا كَرِي چَوُ

Standing on the road give forcibly three cries and say. Ibid. p. 66.

V. Adverbs derived from the Pronominal bases.

From the pronominal bases a number of adverbs is derived by means of certain affixes, which coalesce with the pronominal base. We exhibit them in the following survey.

Pron. base.	Manner.	Place.	Direction.	Time.
i, ī, ē hē.	اِينَ ĩa[1])	اِتِ ite[2])	اِيڏِي ēḍē[3])	اِيسِين ē-sĩ[4])
	هِينَ hĩa	هِتِ hete	هيڏِي hēḍē	هيسِين hē-sĩ
	اِئين iẽ	here.	in this direction.	up to this time (or place).
	in this wise.			

1) Or short: اِنَ ĩa, هِنَ hĩa; اُنَ ũa, جِنَ jĩa etc.

2) Or اِتي itē, هِتي hetē; also اِتهِي ithē; اُتي utē etc.

3) There are many other forms of this adverb, as: اِيڏَهَنْ ēḍahã, اِيڏَهُنْ ēḍahũ, هيڏَهَن hēḍahã etc.; see Stack's Sindhī Dictionary under the different forms.

4) Or اِيسِينَ ēsĩa, اِيسِنَ ē-sĩa etc. This set of adverbs is generally compounded with the postpositions تَائِين tā-ĩ, توَئِين tō-ĩ or توَنِي tōnī, as: اِيسِينْتَائِين ēsĩtāĩ etc., or shortened: اِيسْتَائِين ēs-tāĩ etc.

Pron. base.	Manner.	Place.	Direction.	Time.
u, ū, ō, hō.	اُونءَ ũa هُونءَ hũa اُئين uẽ هُئين huẽ in that wise.	اُتِ u-te هُتِ hu-te there.	اوڏي ō-ḍ̄ē هوڏي hō-ḍ̄ē in that direction.	اوسِين ō-sĩ هوسِين hō-sĩ up to that time.
ǰō	جِينءَ ǰĩa جِئين ǰi-ẽ. in which wise.	جِتِ[1] ǰi-te جَتِ ǰa-te where.	جيڏي ǰē-ḍ̄ē in which direction.	جيسِين[2] ǰe-sĩ جَاسِين ǰa-sĩ as long as.	جَڏِهين ǰaḍ̄e-hĩ جَان ǰa when.
sō	تِينءَ tĩ-a تِئين ti-ẽ in that wise.	تِتِ ti-te تَتِ ta-te there.	تيڏي tē-ḍ̄ē in that direction.	تيسِين tē-sĩ تَاسِين tā-sĩ so long.	تَڏِهين taḍ̄e-hĩ تَان tã then.

---

1) Or جِتي ǰi-tē; جَتي ǰa-tē, جِتهِ ǰi-the, جِتهي ǰi-thē. There is also a lengthened form جَاتي ǰā-tē, جَاتهي ǰā-thē. All these forms may equally be used with the Correlative ti (as ti-tē etc.) and ki.

2) Instead of the postfix سِين sĩ, the postfixes تَائِين tãĩ, توئِين tõĩ, توڻِي tõṇi, may also be joined to جي ǰē and تي tē, as: جيتَائِين ǰē-tãĩ, تيتَائِين tē-tãĩ etc.

kō	كِينئَ kĩ-a	كِتِ ki-te	كيڈي kēḍē	کیسِین kē-sĩ	کَڈِهِين kaḍe-hĩ
	كِئين ki-ẽ	كَتِ ka-te		کاسِين kā-sĩ	
	in what wise?	where?	in what direction?	how long.	when?

Some of these adverbs are again compounded with adverbial postfixes (and partly prefixes): as: جَانكِي ǰã-kī or جَانكِيتَان ǰã-kī-tã, so long as; جَڈِهَاكو ǰaḍeh-ā-kō, جَڈِهوكو ǰaḍeh-ō-kō, جَڈِهَاكُرَ ǰaḍeh-ā-kura (ā-kara), from such a time as, since. تَانْكِي tã-kī or تَانْكِيتَان tã-kī-tã, as long as; تَڈِهَاكو taḍeh-ākō, تَڈِهوكو taḍeh-ō-kō, تَڈِهَاكُرَ taḍeh-ā-kura, from that time; كَڈِهَاكو kaḍeh-ā-kō[1]) etc., from what time? اِيڈْتي ēḍ-tē, اِيڈتَائِين ēḍ-tāĩ or اِيڈتَاهِين ēḍ-tāhĩ, a little in this direction; جيكَڈِهِن ǰē-kaḍehē if (at any time).

The adverbs implying 'place' and 'direction' may also be put in the Ablative, as: اِتَان it-ã, اِتَاݩُون it-āũ, اِتهون it-ahũ, اِتَاهُون it-āhũ, from this place, hence; اُتَان ut-ã, اُتُون ut-ũ, اُتهُون ut-ahũ, from that place,

1) The forms: جَڈِهَاكو ǰaḍeh-ā-kō etc. are properly double compounds viz.: جَڈِهَان ǰaḍeh-ã, the Ablative and كو kō or كُون kũ, a postposition (identical with كهُون khũ) 'from'. In the same way جَڈِهَاكَرَ ǰaḍeh-ā-kara is compounded from جَڈِهَان ǰaḍeh-ã (Abl.) and كَرَ kara (or kura) postposition, up to, literally: from which time up.

thence; تِتَان tit-ã, تِتُون tit-ū̃, تِتَائُون tit-āū̃, from that place; كِتهَان kith-ã, كِتهُون kith-ū̃, كِتهَاهُون kith-āhū̃ etc. from what place, whence? ايڏان ēḍ-ã, ايڏاٿُون ēḍ-āū̃, ايڏهُون ēḍ-ahū̃, ايڏاهُون ēḍ-āhū̃ etc. from this direction.

The emphatic ī (ĩ) or hī (hẽ) very frequently accedes to these adverbs, as: اِئِينئِي iẽ-ī, in this very wise; اِتَئِي ita-ī or اِتَهِي ita-hĩ[1]), even here; اِتَانئِي itã-ī, اِتَانهِي iṭ-ã-hī, even hence; ايڏَئِي ēḍa-ī, ايڏَهِين ēḍa-hĩ, in this very direction; ايڏَانئِي ēḍ-ã-ī, from this very direction etc.

مُون اَکهُنُون تَنَ تِتِ جِتِي جَنَبُ جيڏِئِين

The eyes of my body are there, where the side (country) of my companions is. Sh. Um. Mār. I, 12.

ڪَالهوڪو ڪَاڏِي وِئو سَنْدو جوڳِنِ جوش

Where is gone to the Jōgīs' emotion of yesterday? Sh. Ramak. I, 30.

اُتَان اوٺهِي آئِيو خَبَرَ اِيءَ کهَرِي

Thence a camelman has come; this information is correct. Sh. Um. Mār. II, 6.

جِنءَ تُون کهُرِين تِئِينئِي تهِئِيئِي

As thou wilt, even so it shall be unto thee. Matth. 15, 28.

---

1) The final ĕ o these adverbs is changed to 'a' before the emphatic ī, for the sake of euphony; but ē keeps its place also, as: اُتِيئِي utē-ī, in that very place.

آنئُون تهو پُڇهَان گهوٽهِيَا کِيسِتَّنْ قَصْدُ کِٿوءِ

تَان چي گهارِئَّان مَکّي شَهَرَ مِين هِيسِتَّنْ قَصْدُ هوءِ

I ask, o gallant young man! how far did your purpose go?

Then he says: I dwell in the city of Mekka, my purpose went up to this place. Maj. 168, 169.

جِيسْتَائِين هُو سَنبِهرَنِ تِيسْتَائِين چَڙهي وِيهُ

As long as they get ready, ascend thou and sit down. Amulu Māṇ. p. 144.

جَتَنِ سَان جَانْکُون سَرْتِيُون مُون سَنگُ تهِئو

کَرِي کوهِيَارو وِٿو تَنُ ڇهِنِي تَانکُون

آنئُون پُڻُ تڏَانْکُون اَدهَ ڏُکهوئِي آنهِيَان

Since I entered into connexion with the Jats, o companions!

The mountaineer is gone off, having torn (my) body;

I am also from that time (only) half (and) afflicted. Sh. Dēsī, Čhāṭ. 6.

VI. Compound adverbs.

The Sindhī uses a considerable number of compound adverbs[1]), which are formed either by reduplicating the adverb (or noun), or adding a similar adverb (or noun), or by adding an adverbial affix or postposition.

---

1) Such compound adverbs may be written in one word or separately. When joined by a conjunctive vowel it is usual to join them also in writing.

1) Reduplicated adverbs,

(with or without a conjunctive vowel; cf. §. 12, II, 2).

بهيرِي بهيرِي bhērē bhērē, constantly.

پَلِ پَلِ pale pale, every moment.

ڏِينْهُ ڏِينْهُ ḍēhu ḍēhu, day by day.

رَاتِئُورَاتِ rateōrāte, night by night.

سَرَاسَرِ sarāsare, entirely.

گهَڙِي گهَڙِي gharī gharī, constantly (hour by hour).

نِيٺهَانِيٺهِ nēṭhānēṭhe, at last.

وَرِهوُوَرِهِ varehōvarihe, year by year.

هَرَ هَرَ hara hara, constantly.

هَنْدهوُهَنْدهِ handhōhandhe, place upon place.

etc. etc. etc.

2) Adverbs compounded with a similar adverb or noun.

اَڄُ سُبَهَنْ aju subahā, in a day or two.

جَڏِهِين تَڏِهِين jaḍehī taḍehī, constantly.

جِئِين تِئِين jiē tiē, in any way.

رَاتوڏِينْهُ ratōḍīha, night and day.

كَڏِهين كَڏَانِي kaḍehē kadānē, now and then.

هيٺهِ مَٿهِي hēṭhe mathē, down and up (up and down).

etc. etc. etc.

3) Adverbs compounded with an adverbial postfix or postposition.

اَڳَبهَرو aga-bharō, a little in front; a little ago.

اَڳِتي agē-tē, in front; in future.

پوئِتَاهوں poë-tahō̃, a little in the rear.

پوئِتي poë-tē, behind.

راتَاکَرِ rāt-ā-kara, since night (lit. from night up).

ڪالهَاکون kālhā-kū̃, since yesterday.

Compare also the compound adverbs of §. 58.

ڏُکهَ نَ سَارِينِ ڏِيلَ مِين وِيرَاوِير وِهَسَنِ

They remember no pains in the body, constantly they are happy. Maj. 801.

هِيڪڙي سَبهِيئِي هَڏَ هَنڌهوهَنڌهِ ڳَنڍهِي مَنْڊُ پڙهِي چهَٽو هَنِئو

One, having joined all bones, place upon place, having read an incantation, besprinkled them. Sindhī Read. Book, p. 53.

Chapter XIX.

POSTPOSITIONS.

§. 58.

The Sindhī has no prepositions, but only postpositions, as all adverbs or particles, which influence in any way the noun, are placed after the noun and not before it. Only رِي rē, رِىَ ria may be optionally used as preposition or postposition.[1])

1) In poëtry the postpositions are frequently turned into prepositions, if required by the metre.

There is only a small number of original postpositions in Sindhī, which require the noun in the Formative; far the greatest part of the postpositions now in use are originally adverbs (i. e. substantives and adjectives used adverbially; cf. §. 57, II. III. IV.), which either retain their original adverbial signification and are consequently constructed with جي jē, or which are already treated as postpositions and require the Formative of the noun governed by them; the greater part of them may therefore be constructed with or without جي jē, and be put before or after the noun, they govern.

I. Postpositions proper, requiring the Formative of the noun governed by them.

بهَرَ bhara, } on, with such a part downward; against;
بهَرِ bhare, } supported from. Sansk. भर, adj.[1])

پَرِ pare, on, upon; Sansk. उपरि.

تَائِين tāī̃, } up to, till; Sansk. स्थाने; Hindūst. تَئِين taī̃.
توئِين tōī̃, }

توڙِي tōṛi[2]), } up to; till.
توڻِي tōṇī, }

---

1) بهَرْ bhar has already in Hindūstānī a signification bordering on that of a postposition. In Sindhī the substantive بهَرُ bharu, prop, support, is also in use, of which بهَرِ bhare is the Locative.

2) Apparently derived from توڙُ tōṛu, the end; توڙِي tōṛī, = توڙِئِي tōṛe-ī, emphatic Locative.

تِي tē[1]), on, upon; Sansk. उत्.

تان tã̄, } from-upon; from; upon (for the sake of).
تون tȭ,

جان jã̄, } like, as; Sansk. यथा.
جِنئَ ǰĩa,
جِينئَ ǰĩa,
جِئين ǰiẽ,

ڏان ḍã̄[2]),
ڏانهه ḍã̄ha, } towards; in the direction of.
ڏِي ḍē,

ڏَهان ḍahã̄, } from the direction of; towards[3]); Abl. form.
ڏَهُون ḍahū̃,
ڏانهون ḍã̄hū,

رِي rē, } without; Sansk. ऋते.
رِئَ ria,

سارُو sārū, according to; conformable to; Sanskrit सारतस्, Prāk. सारदो or सारओ.

---

1) Instead of tē, tã̄ etc. the Panǰābi froms utē and utã̄ are also occasionally used in Sindhi.

2) The forms ڏَهَن ḍahã, ڏَهُن ḍahũ are also in use; emphatic: ڏانهِين ḍã̄hī̃.

3) The Ablative forms ḍahã̄ etc. are generally used in the sense of the Locative.

سَان sā̃, }
سَانُ sāṇu, } with; Sansk. सम्.
سين sē̃, }
سينُ sēṇu, }

سُودهَان sūdhā̃, along with; Sansk. सार्द्धम्.

سِينَءِ sī̃a, up to; till; Sansk. सीमा; Panjābī: sī̃.

کَرَ kara, up to.

کَنِ kane[1]), } to; near to; Sansk. कर्ण, edge (of a vessel); Sindhī کَنو, rim, border; Panjābī: kannī.
کَني kanē, }

کَنَان kanā̃[2]), } from; Abl. form.
کَنوَن kanō̃, }

کهي khē, to; as regards; in reference to; Sansk. कृते.

کهَان khā̃, }
کهوَن khō̃, } from; Abl. form.
کهَوْن khaū, }

گَرِ gare, to; with (Lāṛ).

گهَا ghā, } like, as.
گهَاءِ ghāe, }

لَاکُون lākū̃, from-up; Panjabī: lāgō̃ (Sansk. लाग).

مَنْجهِ manjhe, in; to (with verbs implying motion); Sansk. मध्ये.

---

1) Instead of کَني kanē, گَني gane is used in Lāṛ; similarly گَنَان ganā̃, گَنوَن ganō̃, instead of کَنَان kanā̃ and کَنوَن kanō̃.

2) Frequently written without the final nasal, i. e. کَنَا kanā.

مَنْجهان manjhā̃, from—in; out of; Abl. form.

مين mē, in; to (with verbs implying motion); Sansk. मध्ये; Hindūst. مين.

مَان mā̃, } from—in; out of; Abl. form.
مؤن mō̃, }

وَٽِ vaṭe, near to; with; in exchange of; Sansk. root वट्; Sindhī subst. وَٽُ.

وَٽَان vaṭā̃, from—near; from; away from; Abl. form.

شَاھُ صَاحِبُ هِڪِڙِي ڏُونگَرَ مين وَڃِي ڇهَه مَهِينَا هِڪِڙِي پَاسِي بهَرَ سُمْهِيٺو پِيٺو هو

Shah Ṣāhib, having gone to one mountain, was fallen asleep on one side (lying on one side) for six months. Life of Abd-ul-Laṭīf, p. 39.

خُدَاء جَا گهَڻَا شُڪِرَانَا ڪَرِي کهَٽَ تَان هيٺهِ لهِي پَنْهِن جي ڪَچَهِرِيَ مين وَڃِي ويٺهو

Having offered many thanks to God (and) having descended from his couch he went to his court and sat down. Abd-ul-Laṭīf's life, p. 30.

اَبَا گهورِي وَڃَان خُدَاء جي نَانْوَ تون

O father, I sacrifice (myself) upon the name of God, i. e. for God's sake. Amulu Māṇ., p. 41.

کهِڙِيُون کهَٽَنْهَارَ جِينئَ وِڄُون اُتَرَ وَاء

The lightenings glittered in the north like a sunflower. Sh. Sār. II, 1.

ڪَرِيو مُنْهَڙِ مَلِيرَ ڏِي رُنِي اُبهِي چوء

Having directed her face towards the Malīr she weeps; having stood up she says. Sh. Um. Mār. III, 8.

پَانَ پَچَنِ مِيوَا رِيَ وَاهَپَ رِی وَاڙِ

By themselves the fruits ripen without guarding, without a fence. Sh. Um. Mār. III, 14.

وَرُ پُنْهُوَ سِين پَلَکُ کهُوِ بَارَهَنْ مَاهَ ٻِئَنِ سِين

Return with Punhū a moment! away with twelve months with others! Sh. Maꜩδ. VI, 6.

مَاڙِيَ لَڱُمِ مِينْهِنو سَبهَ ڄَمَانْدَرَ سِينئَ

In the upper rooms reproach has been my lot all (my) life long. Sh. Um. Mār. V, 1.

تَڏِهِن ڇهَا ڏِسَنِ تَہ دُنگُ دَارُوَ جو ڀهَرِيَلُ ڪَنَنِ ڪَرَ

ڌهَرْيو آهِي

Then what do they see? that a vessel of wine, filled up to the rims is placed there. Sindhī Read. Book, p. 68.

مِيڙِيَان سَانڍِهِيَان مَالَ ڪهِي ڪَنْهِن ڪَنِ ڪِي نَہ ڏِيَان

I will collect and guard property and not give any thing to any one. Golden Alphab. X, 7.

ڪِنْهِي آيُسِ ڳَالْهَڙِي ڳُجهِي تو ڱرِي

I am come having taken a matter hidden to thee. Sh. Sōr. II, 18.

ڪَنْهِن جِي گهَرَ مَنْجهِ وَڃِي اُنَ جِي کهِڻَ مَان ڪِي

چوَرَائِي کهَادهَائِين

Having gone to the house of somebody (and) having stolen from his food it (i. e. the mouse) ate it. Sindhī Read. Book, p. 62.

مَاءِ وَتَّان كهي مَجنِي كوتهِي تَنهِن چيو

Having called Majnō̃ from the side of his mother he said. Maǰ. 49.

The following postpositions (mostly of foreign origin) may be optionally constructed with جي ǰē.

بَاجهَان bājhā̃, بَاجهُون bājhū̃, بَاجهوُن bājhō̃,	without (Panǰābī).

بِگِرِ bigire, without; except (Panǰābī).

بِنَا binā, without; except (Hindūst.)

سِوَاءِ sivāe, without; except (Arab. Pers.)

کَرِ kare, کَرِي karē,	by means of; by; on account of; Sansk. कृते.

لَاءِ lāe, لَئِ laē,	for the sake of; on account of; Pānǰābī laī; Hindūst. لِيِي liyē.

تَان سُورِهَ بهَانْيَا سِيلهَ ڏِيکهَنَ بَاجهوُن ڏوسَ جي

Then they (i. e. the flowers) were considered by the hero as thorns without the sight of the friend. Aǰāib, V, 20.

سوڍهِي بِگِرِ سَرْتِيُون هَڏِ نَہ سَاهَ سَرِي

Without the Sōḍhō, o companions! there is no getting on with life; i. e. I cannot live. Sh. Mūm. Rāṇō I, 8.

بِنَا بهَجَن بهگوان جي تُنْهِن جو هَارِيَا کو نَہ حَالُ

Except the adoration of the Lord thou hast no business, o lost one. Mēnghō 12.

پَرَ گهَرَان پَاسو کَري پُڇهُ پرِيَان کَرِ پَانُ

سوڏِي تَان توڏِي سَانُ جَنْهِن لَئِ جَفَائُون کَرِين

Having turned the back to other houses ask on account of thy friend thy own self;
He is even with thee, for whose sake thou causest (thyself) troubles. Sh. Ābirī III, 5.

لوچِين چهو نَہ لَطِيفُ چِي هَارِي لَئِ هوتَنِ

Why searchest thou not, says Latif, for (the sake of) thy sweetheart, o lost one! Sh. Kōh. I, 10.

II. Adverbial postpositions (derived from substantives or adjectives), which are optionally constructed with or without جِي jē, or which require another postposition.

اُبَتَڙِ ubatare (mostly with جِي), contrary to.

آڏو āḍō[1]), in front.

اَڳي agē[2]), اَڳِيون agiō̃, } before; in front.

اَنْدَرِ andare, within.

اَنْدَرَان andarā̃, from within.

اوڏو ōḍō, اوڏِڙو ōḍirō, Dim. } near to.

---

1) آڏو āḍō, اوڏو ōḍō وِجهو vējhō may also be constructed with کهي khē.

2) اَڳي, پوءِ and ڏهَارَان are more frequently constructed with the postposition کهَان or the Ablative, than with جِي.

اوري ōrē, on this side.

اورِئان ōriā̃, from this side.

ٻاهرِ bāhare, outside.

ٻاهران baharā̃, from without.

بَدِرِ badire, بَدِران badirā̃, in lieu of; instead of.

پارِ pāre, on the opposite side; across.

پاران pārā̃, پارون pārō̃, from the opposite side; on the part of.

پاسي pāsē, on the side of; near to.

پٽاندرِ paṭāndare, according to (mostly without جي).

پُٺِئان puṭhiā̃, on the back of; after.

پرپُٺھ paraputhe, behind one's back.

پَري parē, beyond; far from.

پُڄاڻو puńāṇō, پُڄاڻان puńāṇā̃, after; subsequent to.

پوء pōe, after (always constructed with ڪھان or the Ablative).

پُئان puā̃, on the back of; behind.

خاطرِ χātire, on account of (Arab.).

چوڌاري čaudhārī, round about.

چوگردِ čaugirde, around (Pers.)

دهَارَان dhārā̃, دهَارِين dhārē̃, } without; apart; round about (also constr. with کهَان or the Abl.).

ڏهَارَ ḍhāra (always with جِي) on, upon (on the prop of).

رُوبَرُو rūbarū, in the presence of (Pers.).

سَامْهوٗن sāmhō̃[1]), سَامْهُڻو sāmhuṇō, سَامْهُڻي sāmhuṇē, } in front; before; over against.

سَانگي sāngē, سَانگَان sāngā̃, } on account of.

سِرِ sire, on, upon; on the top of.

عِوَضِ ʿivaẕe, in lieu of (Arab.).

کَارَڻِ kāraṇe, on account of; for reason of.

کَاڻِ kāṇe, کَاڻي kāṇē, } for the sake of.

لَڳِ lag̱e, لَڳي lag̱ē, } on account of; as concerns (mostly without جِي).

مَٿهي mathē, upon.

مَٿهَان mathā̃, from upon.

مَنْجهَارَان manǰhārā̃, مَنْجهَاروٗن manǰhārō̃, } from — within; out of.

---

1) Or سَامُهوٗن sāmuhō̃, سَامُهوٗن sāmuhū̃.

مُقَابِلِ muqābile; over against; opposite to (Arab.).

مُوجِبِ mūjibe; according to; conformably to (Arab.).

مَهَنْدِ mahande, } in front; before.
مَهَنْدَان mahandā̃, }

وَاسْطِي vastē, on account of (Arab.).

وَانْگُرُ vãnguru, }
وَانْگي vāngē, } like to; as (mostly without جِي).
وَانْگِيَان vāngiā̃, }

وِچِ viče, in the midst of.

وِگهي vighē[1]), by reason of; by.

ويتَرِ vētare, besides (mostly with جِي).

وِيجهو vējhō, } near to.
وِيجهِڙو vējhirō, Dim. }

هيٺهِ hēṭhe, below.

هيٺهَان hēṭhā, from below.

شَاهَ صَاحِبَ جِي اَگِيوْن مُجِرو بهَرِي عَرْضُ كَرِ

Having paid thy respects before Shāh Sāhib beg (of him). Life of Abd-ul Laṭīf, p. 34.

مَرَنَان اَگي جِي مُئَا سِي مَرِي تهِئَنِ نَہ مَاتُ

Those who have died before dying become not extinct when having died. Sh. Ma;δ. IV, 7.

---

1) وِگهي vighē, apparently shortened from وِگهن vighine, Nom. وِگهِنُ obstacle, Sansk. विघ्न, is used only when speaking of some disability or distress.

هِنَ پَهَاڪِي جو ڪُنُ اِهو آهي تہ آوَتِ پَٽاندَرِ جاوَتِ ڪَرَنُ ڪهُرجي

The point of this proverb is this, that it is necessary, to make (one's) expenses according to the income. Sindhī Read. Book, p. 58.

تهوڙي گهڻي ڏِينْهَنِ پُڄاڻو مَخْدُومُ صَاحِبُ وِصَالُ ڪِئو

After few (or) many days Maχdūm Ṣāhib died. Abd-ul-Laṯīf's life, p. 37.

هِنَ مَحَلَّ کهَان پوءِ تُون مُنْهِن جِي مَاءُ ڀيڻُ آنهين

After this time thou art my mother (and) sister. Ibid. p. 42.

وَتِهِي مُنْهُ کِهو وَنجان وَطَنَ سَامُهُون

Whith what face shall I go to the presence of my country? Sh. Um. Mār. V, 5.

اُنَ هَنْدهَ جي مَتهَان چَتِي ڏِني پيئِي آهي

From the top of that place a piece has been cut out. Life of Abd-ul-Laṯīf, p. 45.

مُنْهِن جِي دهِئُ بهُوتَ وِگهي ڏَاڏهِي پِيڙِيَلَ آهي

My daughter is grievously vexed by a demon. Matth. 15, 22.

شَاهُ جَمَالُ گهوڙي تي چَڙهِيَلُ کهَتَ جي وِجهو اَچِي

گهوڙي تَان لَتهو

Shāh Jamāl, being mounted on a horse, having come near to the couch alighted from the horse. Abd-ul-Laṯīf's life, p. 7.

Chapter XX.

CONJUNCTIONS.

§. 59.

The conjunctions serve to express the relation, in which either the single words of a sentence or two or more sentences stand to one another. According to their signification the conjunctions may be divided into:

1) Copulative.

آوْن aũ,
اَيْن aĩ[1]), } and
اين ẽ,

بِ bi,
بهِ bhi,
بهي bhī,
پِ pi, } also.
پِنِ piṇe,
پُنِ puṇe,
پُنُ puṇu,

تِنئَ—تِنئَ tĩa-tĩa, as well-as.

سو بهي جَڏهِن وَڏو تهِئو تَڏهِن مَري وِئو

He also, after he was grown up, died. Abd-ul-Latīf's life, p. 2.

1) Generally written, for the sake of abbreviation ع.

تَنْهِن ڪَانِ گهڻَا ڀهيرَا مَارَ پِنِ کهَائِنِ تهَا

Therefore they are often also beaten. Sindhī Read. Book, p. 50.

. اَتِ اُڪَنْڊِي آنهيَان تِنئَ آتَنَ تِنئَ ڏِيهَ

I am very longing as well for the spinning place as for the country. Sh. Um. Mār. II, 1.

2) Concessive.

تَه ta, } then (as apodosis in a conditional sentence generally not translated).
تَان tā̃, }

تَه بِ ta bi, } nevertheless; then also; even then.
تَڏِهِين بِ taḏehī̃ bi, }

توڙي tōṛē, }
توڻي tōṇē, } although; notwithstanding.
جيتوڙي jētōṛē[1]), }
جيتوڻي jētōṇē, }

جي jē, although; if.

تَنْهِن جي لِنْگَنِ تون جي ڪَپڙو لَهِڻو وَڃي تَه تَجلو وِڄُ
وَانگي تهِئو وَڃي

If from her limbs the cloth is stripped, (then) a brilliancy like lightening is effected. Amulu Mān. p. 141.

تَان چي مَرَان تَان مَانُ لَهَان جي موٽَان تَه ڪَرَ مِيهُ

Then he says: (if) I die, I obtain honor; I if return, it is, to say so, a shame. Maǰ. 408.

1) Very often also written separately: جي توڙي

تۏڙي چِکَنِنَ چاکَ تَہ بهِہ آهَہ نَہ سَلَنِ عامَ کهي

Though their wounds flow, nevertheless they divulge not (their) sighing to the vulgar. Sh. Kal. II, 23.

دِلِ بهِي ڏِجي هِکَ کهي تۏڙي سَوَ سِگَنِ ·

The heart also shall be given to one, though hundreds covet (it). Sh. Barvō Sindhī III, 7.

تُون سَا مَجْلِسَ مَٽِ جي حاصِلُ هُوِيئي هَزارَ جو

Change thou that company, although the profit of a thousand would accrue to thee. Sh. Ram. Kal. VIII, 25.

3) Adversative.

بِگِرِ	bigire,	but.
پَرَ	para,	
پَڻَ	paṇa,	

تۏڙي	tōṛē,	either.
تۏڻي	tōṇē,	

تۏڙي — نَہ تَہ tōṛē — na ta, either — or.

جان jā̃, either; or.

جان — جان jā̃ — jā̃, either — or.

کِہ	ke,	or.
کِي	kī,	

مَگَرِ magare, except; but.

نَہ تَہ na ta, otherwise; else.

هَتهَان hathā̃,	but rather; on the contrary (Panǰābī).
هَتهَانئِين hathā̃-ī̃, emphat.,	
هَتهوْن hathõ,	
هَتهوْنئِين hathõ-ī̃, emphat.,	

توڙِي كَنْدهِىَ كَنِ[1] نَہ تَہ سَاڻُنِ وَنجَنِ سِيرَ مِين

Either they go to the bank or (they go) with them in the stream. Sh. Suh. VIII, 1.

مَاڙهُون كِہ كَنْڍَنِ مؤن ڈَرَاكهَہ تهَا چهِنَنِ جَان كَانڊِيرِىَ مؤن اَنجِيرَ

Do men pluck grapes from thorns or figs from a thistle? Matth. 7, 16.

كوئِي مَاڙهُون بِنِ دهَنِيُن جِي نَوكَرِي كَرِي نَہ تهو سَگهِي جو جَان هِكِڙِي سَان وِيرُ رَكهَنْدو ۽ ٻِئِي سَان پرِيتِ كَنْدو جَان هِكِڙِي جِي دَاوَنِ وَتهَنْدو ۽ ٻِئِي كهِي كِي نَہ لِيكهِينْدو

No man can do the service of two masters; for either he will keep enmity with the one and make friendship with the other; or he will seize the skirt of the one and not at all mind the other. Matth. 6, 24.

جو اَچِڻو هو سو تُونئِي آنهِين كِي ٻِئِي جِي وَاٽَ ڍِسُون

Art thou he, wo was coming, or shall we look out for another? Matth. 11, 3.

---

1) كَنِ kane is postposition and not the III pers. Plur. of the Present (كَرِينِ = كَنِ) as Stack supposed; see Stack's Gramm. p. 101, Note. The verse quoted there does not quite agree with the Risālō.

اَسَان کهي اُنهنِ پَانهَنَنِ سَان کوٓ کَمُ نـَ آهِي مَگرِ پَنهن جي دهَنِيَ سَان کَمُ اَتهُون

We have no concern with those stones, but our concern is with their master. Life of Abd-ul-Latīf, p. 20.

4) Causal and Final.[1])

تـَ ta, that; in order that; also an expletive, in quoting the words of a person.

جَان ǰã,	that; so that; in order that; because; as.
جِنـَءَ ǰīa,	
جِئين ǰiẽ,	
جِئين تـَ ǰiẽ ta,	

جو ǰō, that, in order that; because.

جيلاَن ǰēlã,	because; wherefore.
جيلهَن ǰēlhã,	
جيلاَهِين ǰēlāhĩ,	
جيلَهِن ǰēlahẽ,	

جيلاَن — تيلاَن ǰēlã-tēlã,	correlat. because-therefore.
جيلاَن — تـَ ǰēlã-ta,	

چهَاجو čhaǰō[2]), because.

---

1) We have classed the causal and final conjunctions under one head, because many of them are used in the one or the other sense.

2) These compound conjunctions are commonly written separately, but by some they are also joined in one word.

چهَا جو literally: why? because etc.; of different kind are such expressions as: هِنَ لاَء تـَ for this sake, that = because.

چھَا ڪَانِ تَہ čha kāṇe ta, } because.
چھَا لَاۓ تَہ čhā lāe ta,
چھَا لَاۓ جو čha lāe jō,
چھو تَہ čhō tā,
چھو جو čhō jō,

سو sō, therefore.

جو — سو jō-sō, correl. because — therefore.

سوڪو sōkō, } because.
سوڪوتَہ sōkō-ta,
سوڪوھُہ sōkōhu,
سوڪوھُہ تَہ sōkōhu-ta,

مَہ ma, not, in a prohibitive sense (constructed with the Imperative or Potential).

مَتَان matā̃, } be it not that; lest (constructed with the Potential).
جو مَتَان jō matā̃,

مَڇھَنِ mačhaṇe, } lest (constructed with the Potential).
مَڇھَنُ mačhaṇu,
مَڇھُنِ mačhune,
مَڇھُنُ mačhunu,

هِيءُ جڙُ نَاهِي تَہ چورِي ڪَرِي پوءِ دَارُون پِئُون

This is not becoming, that we, having comitted a theft, drink wine after. Sindhī Read. Book, p. 69.

مِينگھَا مُنْهُہ پَائِي اُٿِي ڏورِ تَہ لَهِين ڏِيهِہ مِين

O Mēnghō, having directed (thy) face and having risen seek, in order that thou mayst find (it) in the body. Mēnghō 23.

اُتهي طَلَبَ تَوْحِيدَ جِي جَان آنئُون كَرِيَان كَاهه

In order that I, having risen, may make some search for the unity. Maǰ. 9.

مَرْكين مُرْكين اِنَ مِين جِنئَ مَاڙهُون چَوَنِي مِيَان

Thou boasted and smilest thereat, that people call the 'Miã'. Golden Alphab. X, 3.

اِيئَ دوسَنِ جو دَسْتُور جِنئَ چهِنَا چهِنَنِ كِي نَ كِي

This is the custom of the friends, that they do by no means pluck the plucked ones. Sh. Barvō Sindhī III, 9.

چِي حَضْرَتَ هِيئِين نَ گهُرجِي جو كهِلِي هَتهَ هَنَنِ

Saying: your honour, it is not becoming thus, that laughing they shake hands. Maǰ. 348.

تِيدَان دهَنِيَ دهُنَّا چِيلاَن وِنَّا وَحْدَتَ گَڏِجِي

Therefore they were chosen by the Lord, because they were mixed up in the Unity. Sh. Kal. I, 8.

چهَا لاَء تَ سُكهِي پَلَكَ ڏُكهِيَ جمَارَ كهَان چَنگِي آهِي

Because a joyful moment is better than a painful life. Sindhī Read. Book, p. 62.

تهَيئو اَسَانهِن جو آهِي چهو تَ نَالو وَڏو تهِينْدو ۽ نَانو نِكَرَنْدو

The advantage is on our side, because (our) name will become great and renown will come out of it. Ibid. p. 64.

تَڏِهِين سُمْهَندِيُون جو اَوِيلَ سو اُتيئِي سِڄُ اُبهِرِي وِينْدِنِ

Then, because they will sleep out of time, therefore the sun will rise to them in that very place. Amulu Māṇ. p. 143.

پَاڻِي وِيهُہ مَہ پَلَنْگَ تِي ڳِچِيَ سِرِ ڳانو

Do not sit upon a bedstead, having placed a string of cowries upon (thy) neck. Sh. Um. Mār. II, 2.

ڏورِيَّان ڏورِيَّان مَہ لَهَان شَالَ مَہ مِلَان هوتَ
مَنَ اَنْدَرِ جَا لوتَ مَچهُنُ سَا مَاتهِي تهِيِّي

I seek, I seek, may I not find, please God, that
I may not meet with (my) sweetheart,
Lest the grief, that is within (my) heart, may be
calmed down! Sh. Hus. VII, 3.

مَتَان هَرَنَ ۽ گَڏَهَہ جَان پوءِ اَرْمَانُ كَرِين

Be it not that thou repent of it after, like the deer and the donkey. Sindhī Read. Book, p. 68.

5) Conditional.

جي jē, } if.
جيكَر jēkara, }

جيكَڏِهِين jēkaḍehī̃, if (at any time).

جي توپِي دهَرِين كَنْدهَہ تِي تَہ صُوفِي سَالِمُ تهِيُّ

If thou puttest a cap on thy neck, then become a sound Sūfī. Sh. Jam. Kal. V, 8.

اِهڙا عَاشِقَ هُئَنِ جيكَرَ تَنِي سِين توهہ

If there be such lovers, show kindness to them. Maj. 776.

جيكَڏِهِين رَاڳُ كَنْدَاسُون تَڏِهِين رَاڳُ جي سُرَ تِي دهَنِيُسِ
جَاڳِي لِيكهو سَارِيَ جَمَارَ جو وَتهَنْدو

If we sing, then upon the melody of the song its master will awake (and) settle (with us) the account of the whole life. Sindhī Read. Book, p. 68.

6) Interrogative.

کِ ke, کِي kī,	interrogative expletive, generally not translated.

پاتِشاهْزادِي آسِين کِي تو کهِي مَنَع تهِيُون کَرْيُون

O princess, do we dissuade you? Amul. Māṇ. p. 145.

Chapter XXI.

INTERJECTIONS.

§. 60.

In treating of the Interjections we abstract form such nouns or phrases, as are or may be used in the sense of Interjections, e. g. مَاٹهِ māṭhe, silence! (s. f.), چَنگو čaṅō, good! سَچُ saču, true! اَللّٰهُ اَعْلَمُ allāhu aɜlamu, God knows! (lit. God is wiser, scil. than I), and only adduce such particles, as have now become strictly interjectional.

Besides the Vocative signs, mentioned already in §. 16, 8, the following are the most common; they imply:

1) Assent.

آنْهه ā̃he, آنءِ ā̃e, آنئِين ā̃ī, هَان hā̃, هَائو hāō, هَوُ ha-u, هَئو haō,	yes.

بَلِي balē, } yes! true; even so!
بَلَى balā, }

بهَلَا bhalā, } well; good!
بهَلِي bhalī, }

جِيئُ ǰīu[1]), yes! (a respectful term of ascent.)

مَرُ maru, } yea! indeed! well!
وَرُ varu, }

ڊيوَ توکهي چَوَنْدَا تَ تُون سُڃَاڻَنْدين تَ چَئِجَانِ هَوُ

The Dēvs will say to thee: wilt thou recognise her? Then say: yes. Amulu Māṇ., p. 150.

بهَلَا اُهي شَيُون مُون کهي ڏيکهَارِ

Well, show me those things. Ibid. p. 147.

تُنْدِي مَتهَاهِين کهُتَّاء ٻوڙُ چَوَنِي جِيئُ چَوُ

Abate too high acrimony; if they say to thee: b̄ōḍu (pooh), say thou: ǰīu (very well). Sh. Jam. Kal. VIII, 22.

جَنِ کهي عِشْقُ اَللّٰهَ جو مَرُ تها سِي مَرْکَنِ

They, who have love to God, they, indeed, boast. Maǰ. 778.

پَلَکَ نَ رَهِي دِلِ توُ رِي وَرُ مِيَان صَاحِبَ ٻروُ چَا

My heart does not remain a moment without thee, truly! o Sir! o Lord! o Barōč! Sh. Ābirī Čhōṭ. Epil. 2.

---

1) جِيئُ ǰīu is apparently the Imperative of جِئَڻُ ǰiaṇu, live!

2) Commendation.

آلو آلو alō alō, bravo! bravo!

چهابَسِ	čhābase,	bravo! (Pers.)
شَابَسِ	šābase,	
عَشْقُ	ʒašqu,	praise to! (Arab.)
عِشْقُ	ʒišqu,	

وَاهُ vāhu, well done!

سَبهِنِي چِئو بِيلِي پَاتِشَاهَ اُهَا سَاگِي هِيتِرِنِ مؤن كَڍهِي
آهِي شَابَسِ اَتهَسِ . آيْن آلو آلو تهِي وِئو

All said: friend, the prince has that very same drawn out from so many! praise be to him! and having got a bravo! bravo! he went away. Amulu Māṇ. p. 151.

عَشْقُ رَاء ڍِئَاچ كهِي جَنْهِن سِرُ ڍِيِئِي ڍِيكهَارِئو

Praise to Rāe Ḏiāču, who has given (and) exhibited (his) head! Story of Rāe Ḏiāču, p. 17.

3) Astonishment.

لو lō, look there! behold!

مَارِ	māre,	wonderful! oh!
مَارِبهِينِي	mārebhīṇi,	
مَارِمَانجهَان!	māremānjhā̃,	

جِيڏِيُون آنئُون تَا نَ چَوَنْدِي لو ڏُكهُ ڏورَاپو سَجّنِين

Companions, I shall not say then: behold the pain and the reproach of (my) friends! Sh. Suh. V, Epil. 1.

4) Desire.

چهَالَ	ċhāla[1]),	would to God! please God! (Arab.)
شَالَ	šāla,	
مَانَ	māna,	would that!
مَنَ	mana,	
اَللّٰهُ تُهَارَ	allāhu tuhāra[2]),	God keep thee! good bye!
تُهَارِ „	„ tuhāre,	
توهَارَ „	„ tōhāra,	

پَرْچَنِ شَالَ پَونْهَارَ ڏهوُلِيَا مَارُو مُون سِين پَرْچَنِ شَالَ پَونْهَارَ

Would to God, that the Paũhārs were reconciled, o darling Mārū! Would to God, that the Paũhārs were reconciled with me! Sh. Um. Mār. I, Epil.

كَنْڌِهِيَ اَچِي سُپِرِين مَانَ بَرِبَرِ كَنِ

Would that (my) sweetheart having come to the shore, would make (= say) alas! alas! Sh. Suh. V, 20.

جَان اِينْدَا تَا اُسَهوَ اِلٰهِي توهَارَ

When (we) shall come, depart! God protect thee! Maj. 437.

5) Uncertainty.

اَللّٰهُ جي	allāhu jē[3]),	God knows! perhaps!
اَلَا جي	alā jē,	

نِنْجَانَا niṅāṇā, God knows!

1) Corrupted from the Arabic phrase:

إِنْ شَاءَ ٱللّٰهُ if it please God.

2) Properly: اَللّٰهُ تو اَهَارَ God be thy protection.

3) This is an eliptic phrase: if God (will or please).

6) Dissent.

خَيْرُ χairu, خَيْرُئِي خَيْرُ χairuī - χairu,	not so exactly (a polite negation; Arab.)

نَہ na, no.

آسَان کَا اَڳِي تُنْھِن جِي چوٗرِي کَئِي چِي ڙِيون نَہ آھَان چوٗرِي کَا نَہ کَئِي

Have we before committed any theft on thee? She says: no, girls; ye have not committed any theft. Amulu Māṇ. p. 145.

7) Disapprobation and reproach.

اوٗھِہ ōhe, ohō!

ٻوڎُ bōḍu, pooh! fy! (a contemptuous reply.)

ڦِٺِھ phiṭhe, hoot!

ٿُھو thū, fy!

ڇِہ čhi, ڇِھِي čhī,	tush!

مَانھِيَان mãhiyã, fy! hoot!

ھُنْ hū, tush! pish!

ھيٺِھ hēṭhe, down with! away with!

8) Grief and complaint.

اَفسوٗسُ afsōsu, alas!

آھَہ āha, alas!

آھَا āhā[1]), alas! what a pity!

---

1) آھَا ahā is at the same time also an interjection denoting pleasure, aha!

ٻَرِٻَرِ b̄areb̄are, alas! ah! woe!

حَيْفُ ḣaifu, woe to! (Arab.)

گھوڙا گھوڙا ghōṛā ghōṛā, alas! alas! o misery!

وَاوِيلَا vāvēlā, alas! lackaday! (Arab. Pers.)

وَاءِ vāe, } also! woe!
وو vō, }
وِي vē, }

هَا hā, } alas!
هَاءِ hāe, }
هَئِي ha-e[1]), }
هَئي haē, }

هُوئي hūē, } ah! alas!
هوئي hōē, }
هُئي huē, }

هَيْهَاتِ haihāte, alas!

حَيْفُ مُنْهِن جِي حَالَ کهي جَان ٻُڇِهي آنُون ٻيکَارِ

Woe to my state, that I am wicked (and) useless! Maj. 756.

گھوڙَا گھوڙَا کَرَنُ اُنهِي کَمَ مِين جَنْهِن جو ٻِلو تهِڻُو

نَاهِي ڏَاهَپَ جِي رِيتِ نَاهِي

To make, alas! alas! in such a business, for which a remedy is impossible, is not the custom of wisdom. Sindhī Read. Book, p. 56.

1) Contracted also هِي hē.

وۋ بھينرُ آنئُون جِنّنْدِيَسِ تَا نَ جَتَنِ رِي

Woe! sisters! I shall not live then without the Jat! (Plur.) Sh. Dēsī VII, Epil. 2.

ھَئِي ھَئِي كِئو ھَتھڙَا كھَامِئو كھَنْيَائِئِين

Having made alas! alas! she lifted up, burning, her hands. Maj. 758.

ھَيْھَاتِ ھَيْھَاتِ لِمَا تُوعَدُونَ سُنجِي تھِي اوْطَاق

Lackaday! lackaday! why were ye terrified? empty has become the men's apartment!

THE SYNTAX.

We divide the Syntax into two parts, the analytical and synthetical. In the analytical part the chief constituent parts of speech, which have been described in the elementary grammar, are to be considered according to their exact signification, their intrinsic value and their special application. In the synthetical part it will be shown, how the different parts of speech are linked together in order to form a sentence and how two or more sentences are joined together.

I. THE ANALYTICAL PART.

SECTION I.

THE NOUN.

Chapter I.

On the absence of the article in Sindhī.

§. 61.

The Sindhī possesses no article definite, as little as the Sanskrit and the modern Ārian tongues of India. The noun may therefore be definite or indefinite, as: زالَ the woman or: a woman.

There are no fixed rules, by which a noun may be known as definite or indefinite, the only safe guide is attention to the context. On the whole it may be remarked:

1) A certain number of nouns have by themselves a definite meaning, as: هِنئُون hĩõ, the mind, سِجُ siju, the sun, اُبهِرَنْدو ubhirando, the east, سُرگُ surgu, the heaven, اُبهُ ubhu, the sky etc. Similarly all proper nouns.

2) If a noun stands in apposition to a proper name, it is thereby rendered definite, as: چِينَ وِلَايَتَ the country of China, حُسِنِ پَرِي the fairy Husine.

If for any reason a noun is to be pointed out as indefinite, the numeral adjective هِڪِڙو one, or the indefinite pronoun ڪو, some one, any one, is used. There is some slight difference in the use of هِڪِڙو and ڪو, the first particularizing the noun by implying that only one person or thing is unterstood, the latter generalizing the same, by implying, that some one out of many, or something, which is not further described, is intended. هِڪِڙو may also be used in the Plural, especially before another numeral, to render the number somewhat doubtful, as: هِڪِڙا ٻَہ مَاڻهُون some two men, or about two men, the number not being fixed as certain. — If some portion or quantity of a thing is to be indicated ڪِي (or ڪِين kĩ) is put before the noun, irrespectively of the gender of the noun (as in Hindūstānī ڪُڇهه).

گَڏهَہ سَرهَائِيَ مين اَچِي هَرَنَ کهي چَوَنَ لَڳو

The donkey, having become jolly, began to say to the stag. (Both the donkey and the stag having been mentioned before.) Sindhī Read. Book, p. 68.

هُنَ دِلو حِكْمَتَ جو اُنَنِ كهَان گهُرِڻو نيٿهِ دِلو ۽ اُنَ جي
حِكْمَتَ اُنَ کهي ڏِنو

He asked from them a vessel of (magic) power; at length they gave him the vessel and its (magic) power. Sindhī Read. Book, p. 67.

کي ڇوڪرَ پَنهِن جي سَبَقَ هِنڌُون لَايو پَڙهَنِ

Some boys read (their) lesson, applying the (their) mind. Ibid. p. 50.

اُوچو تُون آكَاسَ تي آن ڀهوٺو مَٿهي ڀهو

High art thou upon the sky; I am a wanderer upon earth. Sh. Sōr. I, 3.

مُنْهِن جُون شَهَرَ ڀهَنڀهورَ مين پَلِ پَلِ پَونِ پچَارُون

In the city of Bhambhōru evil chats are constantly made about me. Sh. Maȝδ. IV, Epil.

كَنْهِن وِيجَ وَٽِ هِكِڙو ٻيلي هو. هِكِڙي ڏِينهَ وِيجَ اُنَ
کهي ڪا دَوَا كُٽَڻَ لَاءِ ڏِني

With some physician there was a servant; one day the physician gave him some medicine to pound. Sindhī Read. Book, p. 51.

اَسَان مين هِكِڙا سَتَ ڀهائُرَ هَا

Amongst us there were some seven brothers. Matth. 22, 15.

اَهِين کي اَمِيرَ آهِيو کي وَزِيرَ آهِيو

Are ye (some) amīrs, are ye (some) vezīrs? Amulu Māṇ. p. 160.

جيڪِي کِيرُ ۽ آکَهرُ تهِيندو سو آئُون پَرَڏيهِنِ کهي ڏِيندسِ

Whatever milk and scum of butter there will be, that I will give to foreigners. Sindhī Read. Book, p. 60.

ڪَنْهِن ڳوٺهَانِي ڪِين قَدْرُ اَنَّ جو بهَانڍِي مِين رَکهِئو هو

Some villager had put some quantity of grain in (his) garner. Ibid. p. 54.

Chapter II.

On the gender of nouns.

§. 62.

The Sindhī possesses only two genders, the masculine and feminine, the neuter having been lost in the course of time. As to the special use of the genders it is to be remarked:

1) The masculine gender is the next and refers either to male beings, or to things and abstract ideas.

a) The masculine gender denotes living beings in general (the females being included therein) as: مَاڻهُون a man (generally); ٻَچو bačō, a child; جَانْوَرُ jānvaru, an animal; گهوڙو ghōṛō, a horse (generally). But in some nouns, implying inferior animals, the feminine includes both genders, as: بَلَا balā, a snake (generally); مَکهِ makhe, a fly; جُون jū̃; a louse etc. But if the gender of a noun is to be expressly mentioned, نَرُ naru, a male, and مَادِي mādī, a female, must be put before it.

مَاڻهُون مَکّي شَهَرَ جَا مِڙِئو ميڙَا ڪَن

The people of the city of Mekka assembling form crowds. Maj. 38.

خُدَاء چيو تہ دهَرتِي اُپَجائِي جِنرا پَنهَن جي جاتِ سارُو
ڏهور ۽ وِڙهَندڙ جانَور

God said: the earth bring forth living beings after their own kind, cattle and creeping animals. Sindhī Read. Book, p. 14.

نَرُ پَکهِي وِهَنُ نہ تهِنُون چهَڏِينِ

They do not allow a male bird to sit down. Amulu Māṇ. p. 141.

It is an anomaly, that the nouns بَازُ bāzu, بَاشو bāšō, شِکِرو šikirō, چَرگُ čaragu, سِيچانو sīčāṇō, بَينسِرو baĩsirō, لَگڙُ lagaṛu, denoting different kinds of female hawks, are masculine, whereas the nouns بَشِينَ bašīna and چِپکَ čipaka, denoting male hawks, are feminine.

b) If a neuter idea is to be expressed, the masculine must be employed, the masculine generally supplying the place of the neuter, as: چَنگو آهي it is good; مُون چيو it was said by one. But this is only the case in the Singular, the masc. Plural of an adjective (or participle) never being used in a neuter sense. It must not be lost sight of, that the masc. form of an adjective cannot be employed in Sindhī in the sense of an abstract substantive [1]) (as in Latin, Greek or German), but that the corresponding substantive must be used (cf. §. 9, I. 1, 2) or the adjective must be accompanied by a substantive denoting 'thing' or 'matter' [2]); only the masc. Singular

1) In sentences like the following: چَنگو کَرَنُ رِهَندو to do good is allowed, چَنگو آهي is an attribute, belonging to کَرَنُ, literally: well doing is allowed.

2) It is a different case, when adjectives are used without a sub-

of the past participle passive may be used in the sense of a neuter substantive.

خُدَاء جِهَڙَا تهِينْدَوْ چَنگَائِيَ ۽ مَنْدَائِيَ جَا سُدهِوَارَا

Ye will become like God, knowing good and evil. Sindhī Read. Book, p. 19.

تِنِ کهِي هو چَنگِيُون شَيُون نَ ڏِينْدو

Will he not give to them good things? Matth. 7, 12.

ضَحِي لوڙِيو لِکهِئو لِکهِئَان چُٽهِي نَ کوءِ

Surely, what is written (in fate), will be fulfilled; from that, which is written, no one will escape. Maj. 258.

مُنْهِن جو چيو نَ کَرِي هَلِي تُون هَتهِ کَرِينْسِ

She does not, what I said, go thou and subdue her. Maj. 285.

c) In such nouns, in which a distinction between a larger or smaller size is admissible, the masc. termination is used to express the idea of relative largeness, as: مَاکوڙو mākōṛō, a large ant, مکهو makhō, a big fly; بهُنگو bhungō, a house (large hut); کوٺهو kōṭhō, a large room; کَاٺهُ kāṭhu, a beam (a big stick) etc.

2) The feminine gender refers either to female beings, or to things and abstract ideas.

a) The feminine being considered the weaker sex, the idea of relative smallness, littleness or weakness is expressed by the fem. termination in all such nouns, which admit of such a variation of meaning, as: مَاکوڙِي mākōṛī, a small ant, مکهِ makhe, a small fly; بهُنگِي bhungī, a small hut etc.

---

stantive, as: سَڄو کهَبو right (and) left, scil. پَاسو, which is to be supplied.

b) A number of adjectives are only found in the fem. form سَنْڍھِ sanḍhe, barren (said of women); پَڇَھر pačhara, barren (said of cattle; گَرْبھِڻِي garbhiṇī or گَرْبھِڻِ garbhiṇe, pregnant (said of women); سُئَا suā, milch (said of animals); ڳبھورَاڙِي gabhōrāṛī, having a child (said of a mother): وَرِيتِي varētī, having a husband (said of a married woman), وَڍَوَرَ vaḍavara, fit to be married etc. etc.

c) Adjectives or pronouns in the feminine are frequently used eliptically, the noun ڳالھِ gālhe, word, matter, being unṭerstood. The noun تَارِيخَ tārīχa, date, day, is also occasionally omitted.

تَڏھِنِ مَاء پُڇھِي ڪھِي مَجْنِي ڪِھَڙِي لَڳِي ڪِيَنَاء

Then the mother asks Majnō̃: what has happened to thee? Maj. 44.

سُونْھَارَا سوَرَٺھِ وَرَ ڪَا مُنْھِن ڄِي ڪَرِ

O fair husband of Sōraṭhe! do some (word) of mine! Sh. Sōr. I, 11.

چوڏھِنئَ چَنْڊُ اُبھِرِئو اُنَترِيھنئَ پَسِيسِ عَامُ

On the fourteenth (day) the moon rose; on the twenty-ninth the vulgar sees it. Sh. Kambh. II, 10.

Chapter III.

Number.

§. 63.

The Sindhī has only two numbers the Singular and the Plural, the Dual having been dropped already in Prākrit (cf. §. 15). As to their special use it may be remarked:

1) Arabic nouns in the so-called broken Plural are (according to their original signification) treated as collective nouns, and consequently constructed with the Singular of a verb (or adjective). The Arabic fem. Plural in آت is likewise treated as a Singular. But now and then the Arabic Plur. is constructed with the Plural of a verb etc., or it is put in the Sindhī Plural form and treated accordingly.

پُڇھُ تَہ اَوْلَادُ ڪوُ مُون کھِي حَقّ دَرْگَاھَ مؤن لِکھِئو آھِي کِہ نَہ

Ask, if some children are destined for me from the threshold of God. Amulu Māṇ., p. 139.

سَبھَاڳَا سِيئِي جِي پَرْچَاۓِنْوَارَا هِنَ وَاسْطي جؤ خُدَاء جؤ اَوْلَادُ چَئِبَا

Blessed are those, who are peace-makers; for they shall be called children of God. Matth. 5, 9.

تَہ وَالِي ڏِنَّارِئِي وِيئُ جِتِ آھِي جَنَّاتِ عَدَنِ جِي

Then the Lord gives thee a meadow, where the gardens of Eden are. Sh. Sōr. I, 9.

نَہ تھَا ڏِسؤ جؤ سَرْدَارُ عَالَمَ جؤ مِڙِنِي اَصْحَابَنِ سَان ۽ سَبھِيئِي نَبِي آيَا آنھِنِ

Do ye not see, that the Lord of the world with all companions, and all prophets are come. Life of Abd-ul-Latīf, p. 37.

2) With numerals the Singular form of a noun may be used, though the Plural is more common (cf. §. 23).

3) The Plural is frequently used in a honorific sense, when speaking with respect of any person. A noun

in the Singular may therefore be constructed with the Plural of a verb (adjective etc.), or the noun itself may be put in the Plural, though implying only a Singular. This is frequently the case with the nouns دوسُ, هوتُ, پرين, سُپرين etc.

For the same reason the II pers. Plural of a verb is used, when addressing politely a person, but not so frequently as in Hindūstānī, the common people being as yet in the habit of addressing each other by the II pers. Singular.

عَبْدُ ٱلّطِيفُ نَنْڍِهپَڻَ مين کَڍِهِنِ کَڍِهِنِ پَان جيڏَنِ چهوَکرَنِ سَان لِکَ لِکوٽِي رَانڍِ کَنْدَا هُئَا ۔

Abd-ul-Latīf used to play in his youth with boys of his age the play lika likōṭī (hide and seek). Life of Abd-ul-Latīf, p. 9.

وو بهينرَ آئون نَہ جِئَنديَسِ تا نَہ جَتَنِ رِي

Woe, o sisters, I shall then not live without the Jat (i. e. Punhū̃). Sh. Dēsī VI, Epil. 2.

پريَنِ جِیَ ڳَالهَ سِينَنِ جِیَ سَنْبهَارَ جَڏَڙو جِيئُ جِئَارِئو

By the discourse of (= about) my beloved, by the recollection of my friend my crippled life has been revived. Sh. Jam. Kal. III, Epil.

شَاهَ وَٽِ اَچِي عَرْضَ کِئَائِين تَہ سَائِين مُون کهِي بهِي پِئَارِئو

Having come to the Shāh he said: Sir, give me also to drink. Life of Abd-ul-Latīf, p. 32.

4) The following nouns modify their signification in the Plural:

SINGULAR.	PLURAL.
اَمِيرُ Āmīru, s. m., Lord; Amīr.	اَمِيرَ, the تَابُون or coffin of the Imāms Hasan and Husain, carried about in the Muharram.
پيکو pēkō, Adj., belonging or relating to one's father.	پيکا pēkā, the relations of one's wife (her father's family).
چانْوَرُ čãvaru, چوکهو čōkhō, } s. m. a grain of cleansed rice.	چانْوَرَ čãvara, چوکهَا čokhā, } cleansed rice (in general).
ڏانو dāṇō, s. m., a grain.	ڏانَا dāṇā, grain (in general).
زَرْدِي zardī, جَرْدِي jardī, } s. f., yellowness.	زَرْدِيُون zardiyũ, the dark spots in the teeth of an old horse.
سَارِي sārī, s. f., a grain of rice (in husk).	سَارِيُون sāriyũ, rice in husk (in general).
سَاهُرو sāhurō, Adj., belonging or relating to one's father-in-law.	سَاهُرَا sāhurā, the relations (or family) of one's father-in-law.
سِيئِي sēī, s. f., a piece of vermicelli.	سِيئُون sēyũ, vermicelli (in general).
نَانَاڻو nanaṇō, Adj., belonging or relating to a mother's father.	نَانَاڻَا nānāṇā, the relations of one's mother (the mother's father's family).

5) The following nouns are only used in the Plural:

بَابُرِيُون bāburiyũ, s. f., tufts of tangled hair (as worn by faqīrs).

پِتهُون pithũ, s. f., pieces.

ٽرِيئُون ṭreyũ, s. f., certain funeral rites, performed during three days after the decease of a person.

جُنْڈَا junḍā, s. m.,
جُنْڈِڑَا junḍiṛā, s. m., Dim.,
جهِنْڈَا jhinḍā, s. m.,
} the short hair of an infant.

جَوِڑَا javiṛā, s. m., a neck ornament of gold beads.

چِٽْرَا čiṭrā, s. m., the hot days.

دهَانِيُون dhāṇiyū̃, s. f., grain boiled and afterwards parched.

رَتِڙِيَا ratiṛiyā, s. m., A kind of superior rice.

کَتِيُون katiyū̃, the Pleiades.

کُهَرَ kuhara, s. m., boiled dry grain.

گَنْجَا ganjā, s. m., a kind of rice.

موٽِيَا mōtiyā, s. m., a kind of rice.

مُهَڈَرَ muhaḍra,
مُهَڈَهَ muhaḍha,
} s. m., barley separated from the husk.

وَاپَنْبَا vāpambā, s. m., the capsules of the Coreya arborea (a medicinal plant).

هَتهوڙِيُون hathōṛiyū̃, s. f., handcuffs.

Chapter IV.

The cases of the noun.

§. 64.

I. The Nominative.

As to the special use of the Nominative it may be noted:

1) Nouns or proper names standing in apposition to another noun are generally coordinated to the same,

as: كَرَاچِي بَنْدَرُ the harbour Karāčī; لِكَ لِكوٿِي رَاندِ the play lika likōṭī; شَمْسُ پَاتِشَاهُ the king Shamsu etc.; but the noun in apposition may also be subordinated by means of the Genitive; cf. §. 67, 4.

مُرْكِي مَرُ مَاتَا رَاڻِي رَاوَ ڏِيَاچَ جِي

Well! smiles the queen-mother of the king Ḍiāču; i. e. saying: well! she smiles etc. Sh. Sōr. III, 6.

لَيْلَا نَالو نَارِ جو جَا قَاضِيَ قَمَرَ ڌِهِيَ

Lailā is the name of a woman, who (is) the daughter of the Qāẕī Qamar. Maj. 33.

ڏِٺهو مُحَرَمُ مَاهُ سَوْنكو شَاهْزَادَنِ تهٿو

The month (= moon) (of) Muharram was seen; anxiety befell the princes. Sh. Kēḍ. I, 1.

2) Substantives implying a number or quantity may be likewise coordinated to another noun, instead of governing it in the Genitive (cf. §. 23), as: ڏَاتَرَ ڏَلَ lots of liberal persons.

اَصُلِ عَاشِقَنِ تِي چُغُلَ چَارِي لَكهَ

There are throughout lakhs (of) tale-bearers and scouts upon lovers. Maj. 254.

مَارِي مِصِرِنِ سِين ڏهُونْڏهَ كِئَانئُون ڍِيرَ

Having cut with (their) swords they made heaps (of) carcasses. Sh. Kēḍ. III, 4.

ڏَانَ ڏَلو چَا دِلِ وَنِئَا وَٺهِي رَاضِي تهِيُ

Having taken buckets (of) heart-pleasing gifts be content! Sh. Sōr. III, 4.

3) The duration of time is expressed by the Nominative (or by the uninflected case generally).

اَٺهَئِي پَهَر عَظِيمَ جو کُنڍُهُ مَنجهِ کَپارَ

The (whole) eight watches (i. e. day and night) the hook of the Great (= God) is in my skull. Sh. Sōr. I, 20.

رَاتِئُون جاڳَنِ جي سِي آنئُون کَنڊَڙِي سِينَ

Those, who watch during the nights, I shall make (my) friends. Sh. Jam. Kal. V, Epil. 2.

رَهُه اَجوکِي رَاتَڙِي تُون لَالَنَ مُون لَائِي

Stay for my sake this night, o darling! Sh. Sam. I, 20.

4) The Nominative is frequently used absolutely to avoid two or more nouns following each other in the inflected case, which is contrary to the Sindhī idiom; the case, in which the nouns should properly stand, must then be taken up by a pronoun or pronominal adjective. If the stress be laid upon some part of a sentence, it may be put quite absolutely, its relation or subordination being taken up by a pronoun. This is especially the case, when a noun is nearer defined by a relative pronoun in the Nominative, the noun being then attracted by the following relative.

مِيوَا مَنجَرَ مَاکِهِيُون سَبهِنِي چکهَنِ چَسَ

Fruits, clusters of flowers, (kinds of) honey, they try the taste of all. Sh. Um. Mār. VI, 9.

خُدَاء جي پَاتِشَاهَه مِين شَاهُوکَارَ جو کِهڙَنُ تَنهِن کهَان

سُئِيَ جي پَاکهِي مِين اُٺهَه جو لَنگهَنُ سَوکهو آهِي

(As to) the entering of a rich one into the kingdom of God, the passing of a camel through the ear of a needle is easier. Matth. 19, 14.

سَا سَائِنءَ کھي سَارِينْدِي ڏَکَنْدِي پھَرَنْدِي ڏِرجَنْدِي ڳاٽ

مَتھي کَري مَاءُ کِنّانئِين

She remembering the Lord, trembling, shaking, fearing, lifted up (her) neck and made: Māu. Sindhī Read. Book, p. 64.

تَہ اَهِين پَنْهَن جو پِءُ جو آسْمَانَ مِين آهي تَنْهن جا

پُٽرَ ٿِيندَؤْ

Then ye will become children of your father, who is in heaven. Matth. 5, 45.

§. 65.

II. The Vocative.

By the Vocative a person or thing taken personally is addressed; the Vocative stands therefore in no connexion with other nouns or with a verb, and is generally put at the beginning of a sentence.

1) The Vocative is used without any interjectional particle, if no particular stress is laid upon the address; but if the attention of the person spoken to is to be roused, the interjectional particles يَا yā, إي ē, اَيْ ai, او ō, هو are used promiscuously with masc. and fem. nouns, اِي ī and اَئِي aī only with fem. nouns.

In addressing an inferior person, or when speaking very affectionately to a person, the interjectional particles ڙي ṛē (ري rē) and اَڙي aṛē (اَري arē) are used with masc. nouns, and ڙِي ṛī (رِي rī) and اَڙِي aṛī (اَرِي arī), (cf. §. 16, 8, Note) with fem. nouns, be they in the Singular or Plural. ٻَڙِي bāṛī, ڙِي ṛī and ڙِيون ṛiũ are also used independently of a noun, in addressing an inferior female (or intimate friend).

جِيَسِ جِيڏِيُون مُنْهِن جَا آءُ پُنْهُون پيهِي

I have been quickened, companions, come in my Punhū̃! Sh. Dēsī II, Epil.

اَللّٰهَ كَارَنِ اوٺِهيَا كَرَهَا مَ كَاهِيْو

جَانِبَ جَڏِي جِيئَ جو آڳَانڍهو آهِيْو

لَاڳَاپو لَاهِيْو مَتَان مُنْهِن جو سُپِرِين

For God's sake, camelmen, do not drive on the camels!

Friend! thou art the protector of my crippled life!

Do not extinguish (my) affection, o sweetheart! Sh. Dēsī III, 1.

يَا عِلِي عَلِي سِرِ يَتِيمَنِ جِي آئِي

آيو حُكُمُ اَللّٰهَ جو يَا اِمَامَ

O ʒAlī, ʒAlī, misfortune is on the orphans!

The order of God has come, o Imāms. Sh. Kēḍ. V, Epil.

ڙِي مَاڙهُوَ جَا بَچَا تُون اَسَان جِي مَاءُ كهِي مَارِي تهو وَنڃين

Hallo! son of man, doest thou go having beaten our mother? Amulu Māṇ. p. 148.

ڙِي بورِچيَانِي مَانِي آنِ

Hallo! cook, bring bread! Ibid. p. 144.

2) Adjectives preceding or following a noun in the Vocative are likewise put in the Vocative. But if an adjective defines another adjective in the sense of an a d v e r b, it remains uninflected.

دوسَ مِٹھا دِلِدَارَ عَالَمُ سَبھُہ آبَادُ کَرِين

Sweet, charming friend! mayst thou fertilize the whole world! Sh. Sār. IV, 12.

گھڻو سَبَاجھا سُپرِين مُون کھي چھڏِئَانئُون مَس

O very kind friend! they (= she, Sing.) have given me up with difficulty (i. e. unwillingly). Maǰ. 664.

3) The Nominative Plural is occasionally used instead of the Vocative, especially with nouns terminating in 'u' (masc.).

ڪِيرِ آهِيو ڪِيڏهُنْ اَچو پُرْسَ پَرَاهِين پَارَ

Who are ye? whence do ye come from? ye men of foreign appearance? Nānga ǰō Qis̱s̱ō, v. 23.

اَهِين گهيلَ ۽ وَڏِي بَارَ کهَنِيلَ مُون وَٽِ اَچو

Ye, that labour and are heavy laden, come unto me. Matth. 11, 28.

4) A number of nouns are commonly found in the Vocative only, as: اَمڙِ amaṛe (اَمِڻ amaṇe), آئِي āī, اَيَلِ āyale, اَمِي amī, مَائِي māī, o mother! an affectionate term for a female; اَدِي adī, دَادِي dādī, o sister! جِيجَا ǰīǰā or جِيجِي ǰīǰī, o aunt; اَدَا adā or دَادَا dādā (Nom. اَدو and دَادو) o brother! اَبَا abā and بَابَا bābā (from اَبو and بَابو), o father! a term, which may be applied even to a child (male or female); مِيَان miyā̃ (Sing. and Plur.) o friend! a respectful address.

اَيَلِ پُنِي آسَ پُنْهُون پَهُتو ڪِيچَ مِين

O mother! hope is fulfilled, Punhū̃ has arrived at Kēč. Sh. Dēsī, Chōṭ. 4.

بَابَا آنُون تُنْهِن جو سَنگُ تهو كَرِيَان لَاَل پَاتِشَاهَہ جي پُتَر سَان

O child (o father!) I make thy espousals with the son of the king Lālu. Amulu Māṇ. p. 142.

اَبو تَنْهَان جو اِنْهِي پُڇهَنَ جو وَاسطو كِهَڙو

Fathers! what reason have you to ask after this very (thing?) Ibid. p. 140.

اَچِي لَالَنَ لَتِ مِيَان مُٿِى جو لوڙهہ لَكَنِ مِين

Having come, o darling, o friend! cover with dust the tomb of the deceased one in the mountain-passes. Sh. Maꜩδ. VI, Epil.

§. 66.

III. The Instrumental.

1) The Instrumental either denotes the agent, by whom an action is performed, or the instrument, by means of which any thing is done.[1]) The Instrumental in Sindhī is not only used with the past tenses of transitive or causal verbs (which always have a passive meaning), but also with any tense of neuter verbs implying a passive signification.[2])

سَاتهِنِ بَدهَا بَارَ تو كهِي آرِسُ اَكهِڙِينِ مِين

By the people of the caravān the loads have been bound up; in thy eyes there is sloth. Sh. Surāg. III, Epil.

1) The sense is different, if the postposition سَانُ be used with a noun denoting an instrument. In this case it is implied, that some one was accompanied or armed with any thing, but not, that he has performed any thing by a certain instrument.

2) Independently of a verb the Instrumental of نَالو nālō, name, is used quite in an adverbial sense, as: هِكِڙو فَقيرُ مُحَمَّدِ عَالِمُ نَالِي one faqir, by name Muhammad ꜩĀlim.

سُنهِڻِيَ کهِي سَيّدُ چَوِي وِڌهو قُرْبَ کهِي

Sūhiṇī was killed, says the Sayyid, by (her) relationship. Sh. Suh. V, 17.

عَاشِقَنِ وِيروِتَارَ نَہ وِسِرِي

By the lovers (God) is never forgotten. Sh. Jam. Kal. VII, 1.

پيرِين آنڱون نَہ پُڄِنِي ڏيهُہ پرِيَان جو ڏُورِ

By means of (my) feet I cannot arrive (there); the country of (my) friend (Pl.) is far off. Sh. Khambh. I, Epil.

ڦِڪِين کِي نَہ پَرْچَنِ مَٽَ تَکِڱانڱون مَنجهِيَان

By drops they are not reconciled; they have espied the jars of the heroes. Sh. Jam. Kal. IV, 9.

2) The Instrumental expresses causality[1]) (by reason of, by dint of):

سَتِينءَ مَاهِ سُکِيَ وِئو مَنجهان رَتُ رَڱنِ

اَٺِينءَ مَاهِ عَاشِقَ سَندِيُون اَکهِڻون اُنجَ مَرَنِ

On the seventh in the month the blood went out of the veins by reason of dryness;
On the eigth in the month the eyes of the lover die of thirst. Maj. 478, 477.

3) The Instrumental expresses the way and manner, in which any thing is done.

سُنَّتَ قَاضِيَ سَامُهُون چَنگِيَ بهَتِ رکهِيَّائِين

He kept the custom (good breeding) in a good manner before the Qāẕī. Maj. 173.

---

1) In a similar sense the postposition کهَان may also be employed.

لَا مَقْصُودَ فِي دَارَيْنِ اِنَ پَرِ اُتَانئُون

'There is no purpose in both mansions', in this wise they spoke. Sh. Jam. Kal. V, 23.

بِنْهِين كهي ٻَهُون پَرِين وِيچَارِ وِرُوهَ

To both helpless ones (there is) pleasant talk in many ways. Maj. 198.

4) The Instrumental expresses the price, for which any thing is bought or sold.[1])

ٻَ جهِرْكيُون پَيْسي كِي نَ تهِيُون وِكَامَنِ

Are not two sparrow sold for a piece? Matth. 10, 29.

كَارِيُون كهَتهِيُون خَاصِيُون اوچهي اُتِ آچِنِ

Fine black woollen blankets come there to hand for a paltry (sum). Sh. Um. Mār. VI, 8.

§. 67.

IV. The Genitive.

1) It must be remembered, that the Genitive in Sindhī is originally an adjective, formed by the affix جو, which always requires the Formative of the noun, to which it accedes; the Genitive admits therefore of gender, inflection and number, like other adjectives. Instead of جو its diminutive form جَڙو jarō is also found in poëtry, and especially سَندو sandō (cf. §. 16, 6) and its dim. form سَندِڙو sandiṛō. The Genitive case-sign جو etc. may also accede to a noun with suffixes; in poëtry it is frequently dropped altogether, to be supplied from the context. سَندو may also be separated from the noun, to which it belongs.

1) But the postposition سَانُ may also be used in this sense.

فَقِيرِيَ جو فَهَمُ سو آهِي نَہ آسَانُ

The understanding of the duties of a faqīr is not easy. Mēngho 37.

جَانِبَ مُنْهِن جِي جِيئَ مِين تُنْهِن جِي طَمَا پوء

O friend, into my soul falls the desire after thee! Sh. Barvō Sindhī II, 2.

دِلِي جِي حِكْمَتَ سَانُ هُونْدِوَارُو ٿِئو

By means of the magic power of the bucket he became wealthy. Sindhī Read. Book, p. 67.

گهَرَ جَا دهَنِي اُتهِي ڇهَا ڏِسَنِ تَہ چورُ گهَر جِيُون مِڙيئِي

وَٺهُون مِيڙِي هَرَ بَنْدهِي دَارُون پِي كهِيو ٿِهِي ٿهو نَچي

The masters of the house having got up what do they see? that a thief, having collected all things of the house, having bound a bundle, having drunk wine (and) having become intoxicated, dances. Ibid. p. 69.

بهَاتوبهَاتِ جَا كهَاڄَ مَاڙهُنِ جِي گهَرَنِ مَان ڏِينهَاڙِي

چورِي كَرِي اُنَ كهِي آڻِي ڏِينْدَا هَا

Having stolen daily from the houses of men all sorts of food they were bringing it to him. Ibid. p. 62.

اُهو پُٽرُ بَنِ جو بهَائِمِ جو سِرُ وَڍهِي

To the forest with that thy son, who will cut off the head of my brother! Story of Rāe Diāču, p. 1.

سَنْڌِي جَا سَاڙِيهَ كِههَ كهَتهُورِي بهَانِئَّان

The grass of (my) fatherland I consider as musk. Sh. Um. Mār. II, 1.

2) As regards the position of the Genitive, it generally precedes the noun, by which it is governed, like

other adjectives; but if the stress be laid on the governing noun, or if the euphony of the sentence should require it, the Genitive follows the same. In poëtry the Genitive precedes or follows the noun, on which it is dependent, either immediately or separated by one or more intervening nouns, as it may be required by the metre or the rhyme.

جيكو ڏِقّتَ پورهِئي جي کَنا ڀڄَنْدو اُنَ جو حَالُ کُتَنِ

جَان ٿِينْدو

Whoever flees from the trouble of labour, his state will become like that of the dogs. Sindhī Read. B., p. 61.

ڪِشْتِي ڪَمِينِيَ جي اَللّٰهَ لَڳِ اُڪارِ

Escort, for God's sake, the boat of the helpless one! Sh. Barvō Sindhī II, Epil.

3) The Genitive has a double signification in Sindhī; it refers either to the subject or to the object of the sentence. The Genitive is called subjective, if the attribute expressed by the Genitive refers to the governing noun (or subject) as to its owner or author, and it is called objective, if it refers to the object, to which the action of the subject is directed.

سَٺهَمِ سَاهيڙِنِ جَا طَعَنَا توهِي لاءِ

I have borne the taunts of (my) companions for thy sake. Sh. Mūm. Rāṇō I, Epil.

آنهِيَان جَنِ سَنْدَڙِي مُون کهِي سِي نَہ ڇَڏِيِنْدَا

Those, whose I am, will not abandon me. Sh. Kōh. II, Epil.

پيرين هيٺهِ پِرِنِّي جي آنْئُون وِڇهَايَان وَارَ

Beneath the feet of (my) friend I spread (my) hair. Maj. 231.

آهيمِ آرِيَ جَامَ جِي اَنْدَرَ مَنجهِ اُسَاتَ

In my heart there is a thirst after the Jam Ārī. Sh. Hus. VIII, Epil.

فَرْيَادُون فِرَاقَ جُون پُنْهَلَ کهِي چَوَنْدِيَسِ مِيَان

Complaints about the separation I shall utter to dear Punhũ, o friend! Sh. Hus. VIII, Epil.

4) One noun is often made dependant on the other by means of the Genitive, where we should properly expect an apposition.[1]) In this way نَالو nalō, name and similar nouns subordinate the appellation in the Genitive. The same subordination in the Genitive takes place, when the genus is nearer defined by the species, as: a fig-tree, or when a geographical appellation, as: town, mountain, river etc. is followed by a proper name, as: the river Indus. In some instances the English idiom resorts to the same construction, as the Sindhī, e. g. the city of London.

بِرهَ جِي بَانِي کَنْهِن کهَان سِکهِئِين سُپرِين

From whom hast thou learnt the word (of) 'separation', dear friend! Sh. Barvō Sindhī II, 8.

زَالَ نَالو رُوکَڙِ جو هوُرِيَّان وَرْدَانئِين

The woman uttered the word (of) 'money' slowly. Sindhī Read. Book, p. 68.

اُهَا سُکِي تهُونِي سَائو وَنُ لَئِي جو وَڏو ۽ تهُلهو تهِي بِيتهو

That very dry post stood as a green tamarisk tree, having become big and thick. Life of Abd-ul-Latīf, p. 23.

هِکِڙو مَاڙهون وَڏمَنَائِتو رَهَاکو تهَٽي جِي گوٺهَ جو هو

There was a very respectable inhabitant of the town of Ṭhaṭā. Ibid. p. 45.

1) See §. 64, 1.

5) The Genitive describes the material, of which something is made or composed; in this case the Genitive quite supplies the place of an adjective.

يُحَنّا جو وَڳو مِلِسَ جو هو ۽ چيلهہ دهَارِين چَمَ جو پٽِڪو

The garment of John was of camel's hair and round his waist a girdle of leather. Matth. 3, 4.

هُوَّ چوڙَا بِيڙَا ڏهَڪي ڪَرِي موتِنِ ۽ ياقُوتَنِ جو وَڳو آڻائِيندِي

She, having put on bracelets and buttons, will cause to bring (call for) a garment of pearls and rubies. Amulu Māṇ. p. 144.

6) The Genitive describes the nature or quality of the noun, on which it is dependent (Genitivus qualitatis). But in this case the Genitive must always be accompanied by an attribute, be that an adjective, pronoun or another noun in the Genitive; the repetition of a noun may also serve as an attribute. In poëtry, and even in prose, the Genitive case-sign is frequently dropped, so that constructions of this kind can hardly be distinguished from those with the Locative, see §. 70, 4.

اُنِنِ مَان هِڪِڙو نَوَنِ وَرهَنِ جو هو ٻِئو اَٺهَنِ وَرهَنِ جو

One of them was nine years old, the other eight years. Sindhī Read. Book, p. 50.

رِيَ بُدهِ وِديا ڪَنْهِن ڪَمَ جِي نَ آهي

Without understanding science is of no use. Ib. p. 54.

ڪِيچَان آيو قَافِلو طَرَحَ موچَارِيَ تورَّ

From Kēč came a caravan, camels of a fine kind. Sh. Dēsī III, 8.

ڪپِڙَا طَرْحِين طَرْحِين جَا ڏِيئِي هَلَايَانِ

Having given clothes of different kinds he started them off. Amulu Māṇ. p. 140.

7) When the Genitive is dependent on nouns, implying a part, quantity or measure, it expresses the whole of that, of which the governing noun forms a part. But if no such noun precede and a part is to be singled out, a postposition must be used (as: مَان, مَنجهَان etc.).

جَنْهِن کهي زَالَ وَتهِي آتِي جِي ٽرين پَنِين مِين لِکايو

Which a woman took (and) hid in three measures of flour. Matth. 13, 33.

مَٽُ سَرِي جو هَتهِ آيُس

A jar of wine fell into his hands. Sindhī Read. Book, p. 62.

تِنِ موں هِکِڙِي مِين مُنْهُن جِي کهٽَ پِيئِي هُونْدِي ٻِئِي مِين پَاتِشَاهَه جِي

In one of those (houses) my beadstead shall be, in the other that of the king. Amulu Māṇ. p. 142.

جِي اَهَان مَنجهَان ٻَ جَڻَا کَنهِن سُوَالَ لَاءِ هِکَ دِلِ تهِينْدَا

If two persons of you become one-hearted respecting a petition. Matth. 18, 19.

8) A certain number of adjectives and appellatives, which have partly taken the signification of substantives, may subordinate another noun in the Genitive. Of this kind are the nouns formed by the affix āku, āū (see §. 8, 9) and others.

عَاشِقَ زَهَرَ پِيَاکَ وِهُ پَسِئو وِهسَنِ گهڻو
کَڙِي ۽ قَاتِلَ جَا هَمِيشَه هِيرَاکَ

Lovers, drinkers of poison, are verry happy when seeing poison;
They are always used to the chain and the executioner. Sh. Kal. II, 33.

تُون رَهَاشُو سُنجَ ٭ پَٽَ جو آنْهِين

Thou art a resident of the waste and desert. Sindhī Read. Book, p. 69.

ٻيڙُ ٽُڪِرين هِيرِتُون نَہ ڪو لِيڪَرُ لَڵُ

A vagabond, accustomed to bits, no breeding and good behaviour. Maj. 304.

جَا مَٿِهي تو مَنِيَا تَنْهِن سِرَ جو آنهِيَان سِيڪَڙُو

Which lustre is upon thee, for that head I am longing. Sh. Sōr. II, 7.

سَيّدُ شَاهُہ حَبِيبُ ذَالِي مُورِ وِيٿَهَلُ ڳوٺهَہ وَنڱي وِلَاسي جو هو

The Sayyid, by name Shāh Habīb, was originally an inhabitant of the village Vangō Vilāsō. Life of Abdul-Laṭīf, p. 1.

9) The Genitive is used, without being dependent on a governing noun, to express a space of time, as: رَاتِ جو by night, ڏِينْهَہ جو by day etc., the noun, by which the Genitive is governed and which is idiomatically left out, being وِيلو, vēlō, time.

This construction is therefore identical with that mentioned in §. 64, 3. In Hindūstānī كو is used in the same sense.

وِچِنِءَ جو آن وِيهِي جَرِ پَلَوُ پَائِيَان

Sitting at (the time of) evening prayer I spread out my skirt on the water. Sh. Sōr. V, 14.

پَاٽَ پِهرِنِءَ رَاتِ جو ڳَڙهَہ پَاسِي ڳَايو

The bard sang the first night at the side of the castle. Sh. Sōr. II, 1.

ڏِينْهَ جوَ تَنْهِنِ جي ڇهانْوَ مين وِهَنْدا هُئا

By day they used to sit in its shade. Life of Abd-ul-Laṯīf, p. 23.

10) A number of adjectives require idiomatically the inflected case of the Genitive (i. e. جي), when a noun is made dependent on them. The most common of them are: آڏو āḏō, in front; اوڏو ōḏō (Dim. اوڏِڙو ōḏiṛō), near to; سامُهون sāmuhō̃, in front of, opposite; مَهَنْدِيون mahandiyō̃, in front; وِجهو vējhō (Dim. وِجهِڙو vējhiṛō), near etc. These adjectives being mostly used as adverbial postpositions (§. 58, II), the same construction has apparently been preserved, when they are used as regular adjectives.

جَڏِهين هي اَورْشَلِيمَ جي اوڏا آيا

When they came near to Jerusalem. Matth. 21, 1.

اُبهَرُ چَنْدرَ پَسُ پرِين تو اوڏا مون ڏورِ

Look at the rising of the moon; the friend is near to thee, far from me. Sh. Kambh. II, 7.

اَکهِئُون اَکهِنِ سامُهيُون ڏِينْهُ سَجوَئِي راتِ

The eyes are opposite the eyes the whole day and night. Maj. 219.

11) The relative adjectives جِهو jehō, جهَڙو jehaṛō, such as, like as, fit to, سَنْدو sandō, like as, جيتِرو jē-tirō, as much as, and جيڏو jēḏō, as large as, are always constructed with the simple Formative of the noun, that depends upon them.

مَحْمُودَانِي مَجنُون اَچَنَ تا نَ جِهو

Majnō̃, the son of Mahmūd, is then not such as to come, i. e. is not likely to come. Maj. 719.

جَاٿِين پِهُلِين جِهڙَا ڏِنَسِ ڏَنْدَ ڏَاتَارَ

Teeths like Jasinum flowers the Bountiful has given her. Maj. 54.

جو سَگورو سَبهِين پَرِين سَنْدو تو سُجَانَ

Which is blessed in all ways, like thou, o wise one. Maj. 825.

تَنْهِن مِين تُونْهِين تُون بِي لَاتِ نَہ لَحظِي جيترو

In that (there is) even thou, thou; (there is) no other sound (as much as the twinkling of an eye =) for a moment. Sh. Jam. Kal. V, 19.

تَان تِرَ جيڏو تو تَنَ سَرْتِي سَرْتُ نَہ آئِيو

Then no mote, as large as a sesamum seed, came into thy body, o friend? Ajāib v. 21.

12) When a noun is subordinated by means of the Genitive to the Infinitive of a neuter or active verb, the case-sign of the Genitive may be optionally dropped.

ڳوٺهَاڻو اُنَ ٿهوڙِڙِي اَنَّ جي سوڙَنَ مَنجهِہ رُنْبهِڙَلُ ٿهئو

The villager occupied himself in (the) removing of that little grain. Sindhī Read. Book, p. 56.

مُغَلَ تَرَارُون کهَڻِي شَاهَہ جي مارَنَ لَاءِ آيَا

The Mughals, having taken (their) swords came for the killing of the Shāh, i. e. 'in order to kill him'. Life of Abd-ul-Latīf, p. 15.

هِنَ نِعمَتَ ڏِسَنَ کهَان پوءِ جوڳو شُکُرُ مَنجَهائِين

After the seeing of this affluence she offered up dutiful thanks. Sindhī Read. Book, p. 55.

آسْمَانَ ۽ دهَرْتِيَ وَنجَنَ توني شَرَعَ جو هِكِڙو تِرُ كَنْهِن طَرَحَ نـ ويندو

Till the passing away of heaven and earth not one jot of the law shall in any way pass off. Matth. 5, 18.

§. 68.

V. The Dative.

1) The Dative denotes the more distant object, in reference to which the subject is acting. This is already indicated by the postposition کهي khē (§. 16, 4), by means of which the Dative case is made up[1]), and which originally signifies: 'on account of, for the sake of, in reference to'. In prose the postposition کهي is always put after the Formative of a noun, but in poëtry it may precede the noun, or it may be dropped altogether.

When a Genitive, depending on a noun in the Dative, follows the same immediately, the postposition کهي is put after the Genitive case-sign.

آءُ اوراهون سُپرين ڏکهِيَ ڏکهُ مَـ ڏيجِ

Come near, dear friend, do not give pain to the distressed. Sh. Ābirī X, 4.

تَان مَسْتِ نَازِ مَلُوکَ کهي اَچِي هِينئَ اَتو

Then Maste Nāze came and said thus to the elegant. Ajāib, v. 90.

---

1) In poëtry the postpositions کَنِ kane, کَنِ kaṇe and گرِ gare are used in the same sense as کهي.

اُسَ مَہ لَگِي اوٺهِيَن لِيڙَنِ لُکهَہ مَہ لَگِ

اَلا آرِيچَنِ کهي کوسو وَاءُ مَہ وَگِ

May no sunshine apply to the camelmen, may no hot wind apply to the camels!
O God, may no hot wind blow to the sons of Ārī!
Sh. Dēsī I, 25.

بَنْڌِهي ڏِکَيدَارَ ڱوٺهَہ جي کهي ڏِنَانئُونسِ

Having bound (him) they delivered him to the police-officer of the town. Sindhī Read. Book, p. 69.

2) The Dative with the auxiliary verbs هُئَڻُ to be, and ٿِيَڻُ to become, to be, expresses the idea of possesssion.

مُون کهي آهِي اُمِيدَ اَللّٰهَ جِي

I have hope in God. Sh. Sōr. I, Epil.

مُون کهي دُنيَا جِي کَمِي کَاڻِي کَانهِي پَرَ اَوْلَادُ کِي نَہ تهو ٿِيئِمِ

I have no lack whatever of wealth, but children are not at all born to me. Amulu Māṇ. p. 139.

3) The Dative denotes the remote object, in reference to which the action takes place. In this case the postposition کهي must be translated by: for, for the sake of.

کهَامِي دِلِ خُمَارَ مِين هِنئون کهي هوتَنِ

(My) heart (and) mind burns for my sweetheart in intoxication. Maj. 728.

کِيچِ تَنْهِين کهي کوٺهَہ کِي نَہ جَنْهِين جي کَڇهَہ مِين

In Kēč there is a call for those, under whose armpit there is nothing (i. e. who have nothing). Sh. Maɜδ. II, 11.

کَاتھِيَ پَانِيَ گَاھَہ کھِي مَاڙھُون مُکَانئُون

They sent men for food, water (and) grass. Sh. Kēḍ. I, 5.

سُورِھَہ مَرِين سوبھَہ کھِي تہ دِلِ جا وَھَمَ وِسَارِ

O hero! thou diest for the sake of victory, forget then the apprehensions of the heart! Sh. Kēḍ. VI, 9.

4) The Dative expresses the idea of motion to a place.

کَاھِي رَسِيَسِ کيچَ کھِي جِتي پَانَ پُنْھُون

Having driven on I came to Kēč, where Punhū himself (is). Sh. Ābirī V, 1.

مُنْدھَہ مَرَنَان پوءِ پَھُچَنْدِءَنْ پُنْھُوَ کھِي

O fair Lady, after death thou wilt come to Punhū. Sh. Ma3δ. IV, 5.

کَاشِيدَانِي کَارِ کِي نہ رَسَانِي کيچَ کھِي

The work of a messenger (i. e. travelling) does not at all bring to Kēč. Sh. Ābirī IV, 10.

5) The Dative is used to express time, when only an indefinite space of time is spoken of, whereas the postpositon مين or مَنجھِ, in, is employed, if the time, during which any thing is done, is to be noted.

قَيْصَرِ چي کَلَاتَ مِين رَاتِ تَنْھِين کھِي رَسُ

Qaisare says: arrive that very night in Kelāt. Sh. Sār. IV, 3.

پرِيَان ڏِي پِرِبھَاتِ وَوُن ڏِيتھَارِي ڏِينْھَ کھِي

Go to (thy) friend at day-break, in clear day. Sh. Suh. Čhōṭ. 11.

وَهَنْدِوَ تَنْهِين وِير کهي فَرَّاشِين فَرْمَاش تهي

Immediately at that time an order was given to the chamberlains. Ajāib, v. 15.

§. 69.

VI. The Accusative.

The Accusative has two forms in Sindhī, it is either identical with the Nominative or with the Dative, i. e. the idea of the Accusative may be expressed also by means of the postposition کهي.

1) The Accusative is commonly expressed by the form of the Nominative, whenever the verb governs only an Accusative, and not at the same time a Dative.

سو جَڏِهين پَنْهَن جا گهوڙا ٻيڙا سِپاهِي رکهي ۽ پَنْهَن جا آچارَ وِچارَ کري

When he shall keep his own horses, boats, soldiers and make his own judgements and thoughts. Amul. Māṇ. p. 139.

جي پَرْنِينْدُسِ تـ اِها حُسِنِ پَرِي پَرْنِينْدُسِ

If I shall marry, I shall marry this very fairy Husine. Ibid. p. 141.

2) But when the subject of the sentence is an animate noun (in the Nominative) the object (Accusative) must be marked out by means of the postposition کهي, to avoid a possible mistake. If the subject be animate, and the object inanimate, the object (Accusative) generally remains in the uninflected form (i. e. without the Postposition), if there be no danger of misapprehension. If both, subject and object, imply inanimate things, the object may likewise remain uninflected.

شَاھُ صَاحِبُ اُنْهِي فَقِيرَ کهِي پَانَ سَانُ وَٺهِي آيو

Shāh S̱āhib, having taken that very faqīr with him, came. Life of Abd-ul-Laṯīf, p. 40.

وَالِدُ شَاھَ جو شَاھَ صَاحِبَ کهِي ڳوليندو وَيٺو

The father of the Shāh continued seeking the Shāh S̱āhib. Ibid. p. 44.

جَڏِهِن مَخْدُومَ هَاشِمَ ٻُڌو تَہ شَاھُ صَاحِبُ مَسْجِدَ مِين

رَاڳُ تهو ڪاري

When Maχdūm Hāshim heard, that the Shāh S̱āhib causes to make music in the mosque. Ibid. p. 35.

جيڪَڏِهِن اِهَا ڳالِ ڪُنِ جو بَادِشَاھُ ٻُنْدهَنْدو

If ever this word the king of the mice will hear. Sindhī Read. Book, p. 62.

جَڏِهِن تَنْهِن کهِي ڪو مَاڙهُون لَهِي تهو تَڏِهِن لِڪَائِي

تهو رکهِي

If that (treasure) some man finds, he keeps it concealed. Matth. 13, 14.

سَنْدهِڻُون سُورَ ڪَرِينِ هَڏَ پُڻُ ڏُکهَنِ هوتَ لَئِ

The (black) marks (from blows) cause pains; the bones also are aching on account of the (= my) sweetheart. Sh. Ābirī, Čhōṭ. 2.

3) When the object (Accus.) of an active verb is for any reason to be rendered more prominent, the postposition کهِي is used for this purpose. This is especially the case, when the object implies living beings, whose mention has been made already, or when two or more persons or things are in any way compared or set against each other. But much scope is left in this

respect to individual judgement. In poëtry كهي is occasionally dropped, but then the contracted form of the Formative must be used in the Plural.

اُنَ مُرِيدَ دهِنّرِیَ كهي سَڏِي چيو

That disciple, having called (that) girl, said. Life of Abd-ul-Laṯīf, p. 48.

ڊيوَنِ چيو تُون اُنهي كهي سُڃاڻَنْڊين

The dēvs said: wilt thou recognise that very one? Amulu Māṇ. p. 151.

اُئين پَيْسَا مِلَنْدَا تَنهين مَان آڻي مِزْمَانَنِ كهي كهارايُون

In that way money will be got; having brought (something) from that let us feed (our) guests. Life of Abd-ul-Laṯīf, p. 41.

اَدِيُون عَبْدُ ٱلّطِيفُ چَوي سَڄَنَ كهي سَارَاهِيُو

Sisters, says Abd-ŭl-Laṯīf, praise ye the (well-known) friend. Sh. Ābirī Čhōṭ., Epil. 3.

پِهرَاڻِين رَوَ كهي ميڙِي ڳَڙا ٻَندهِي سَاڙَنَ لَاءِ پوءِ كَڻَكَ

كهي ٻهَانڊَ مين ميڙِي رَكهو

Having gathered first the tares, having bound bundles to burn (them), gather (and) put afterwards the wheat in the garner. Matth. 13, 30.

جي كِي سِكَنُ سِكهُ نَا تَ پَسُ سِكَنْدِڙين

Whatever longing there is, learn (it); otherwise look at the longing ones. Sh. Jam. Kal. VII, 7.

4) Whenever an active verb is constructed impersonally in the past tenses (§. 94, 5) the object must be pointed out by the postposition كهي, signifying: as regards.

تَڏِهِن تَنهِين کهي سَاتهَه سُتِيئِي ڇهڏِئو

Then it was abandoned by the caravan as regards her, while being asleep, i. e. she was abandoned by the caravan while being asleep. Sh. Kōh. I, 8.

اُنَ جي گَنڍهِڙِي وَٺهِي اُنَ کهي ڇهڏِي ڏِنائِين

Having taken his bundle he started him off. Sindhī Read. Book, p. 53.

5) When a verb governs a double Accusative, both objects remain in the uninflected state, if they imply things; but if the first object be a person or a living being in general, it is rendered more definite[1]) by the accession of the postposition کهي, whereas the second object, be it a person or thing, remains in the uninflected state of the Singular, though it refer to a Plural. If the stress is on the second object (compare §. 94, 3), it may be placed first.

ڏِينڊُسِ مَاسُ مِرَنِ کهي آنُءُ جرَا جِيءُ کَرِي

I shall give (my) flesh to the wild beasts, having made atoms (my) life. Sh. Ābirī IX, Epil.

سو مِهمَانَنِ کهي مَانِي کهَارَائِينڊو هو

That one was in the habit of causing the guests to eat bread, i. e. he was in the habit of entertaining the guests. Life of Abd-ul-Latīf, p. 40.

هَاڙهو هِينِيَ کهي لَنگهَائِجِ لَطِيفُ چَوِي

Make the weak one pass the Hāṛhō, says Laṯīf. Sh. Dēsī IV, 4.

آنُءُ اَوهَان کهي مَاڙهُنِ جو مِهوُ کَنڊُسِ

I will make you fishers of men. Matth. 4, 19.

1) But both objects may also remain in the uninflected state, though implying persons; see §. 94, 3.

6) When an active verb subordinates at the same time a near and a more distant object (i. e. an Accusative and a Dative), the Accusative (in the uninflected state) generally follows the Dative, except a particular stress be laid on the Accusative, in which case it precedes the Dative.

كامِلِ ڏِينْهَانِي قَيْسَ کهي چَنگا کارِي تهِي چاڳَ

The accomplished one causes daily nice blandishments to be made to Qais. Maj. 223.

هَتهَ اَسان کهي دهِيٽِڙِي دهُئارِي

The hands the little daughter shall wash us. Life of Abd-ul-Laṯīf, p. 48.

هِکِڙو هَتهون نَه ڏِين هَتهَ سَانُ ٻِئِي کهي بهَنگُ وِجهِي بهَائِي

But one (grain) thou doest not give to another with thy hand, having thrown in an obstacle, o brother! Mēnghō 11.

§. 70.

VII. The Locative.

The Locative, as noted already, can only be expressed in the Singular of masculine nouns terminating in 'u'; in all other nouns and throughout the Plural the Locative must be circumscribed by the postpositions مين and مَنجهِ, 'in'. In poëtry these postpositions are commonly dropped and only the Formative of a noun is used to express the idea of the Locative, in the Plural the contracted form of the Formative (ending in ẽ or ã) must in this case always be employed. But also in prose the postpositions مين and مَنجهِ are frequently left out idiomatically, especially after nouns implying time.

When a substantive in the Locative is accompanied

by an adjective ending in 'u', the adjective must be likewise put in the Locative; but adjectives of other terminations, pronouns or numerals are only put in the Formative.

1) The Locative expresses in Sindhī not only the place, in which an action is going on, but also direction and motion to a place. The Locative is therefore used after verbs of motion, such as: وَڃَڻُ vańaṇu, to go, اَچَڻُ ačaṇu, to come etc.

وَنِ نَہ وِيٺِھَا ڪانگ وِچِين تھِي وِيلَا ڪَرِي
کِھرِي گھَڙُو ھَٿِہ ڪَرِي سُڻِي سَانجِھِی بَانگ

No crows were sitting on a tree; evening tide has set in; she seizes the opportunity.

She stepped in, having taken the jar into the hand, having heard the call (to prayer) of the evening. Sh. Suh. I, 14.

ڏِيگِين ڏوُگَ ڪَڙھَنِ جِتِ ڪُنِين ڪَڻِڪوُ نَہ لَھِي

In the caldrons the limbs boil, where not a grain does descend in the eddies. Sh. Kal. II, 27.

اُونھِي نِينْھِہ اَتِ گھَڻِي سَھَا ۽ سِيَارَ

In deep, very great love are hares and jackals. Maǰ. 548.

مَتَان ڪَا ٻَڙِي ٻوُلِ ٻَروُچِي وِسَھِي

May not any one, o friend! trust in a Baluchī promise! Sh. Dēsī, Čhōṭ. 7.

وَڃَان تھِي وَڻِڪَارِ ڏِٺھِمِ پيِرُ پُنْھوُن جوُ

I go to the forest; I have seen the footstep of Punhū̃. Sh. Hus. V, 4.

بِئًا دَرَ ڏيِئِي بِئَنِ کهِي آيُسِ تُنْهِن جِي دَرِ

Having given (left) the other doors to others, I came to thy door. Sh. Sōṛ. I, 11.

2) The Locative is used with nouns implying time, to express the point of time, at which an action takes place.

هِکِڙِي ڏِينهِ سَئِلُ کَنْدَا وَنجِي جيسَرَميرَ کهان نِکِرِيَا

One day, making a journey, they arrived at (lit.: came out of) Jesalmēr. Life of Abd-ul-Latīf, p. 40.

کَنْهِين ٽَاڻي گوٺهِ هِکِڙِي مَنجهِ کُئِي هِکِڙِي پَنْهِن جِي

هِرْدِي مين وِيچَارُ کَرِي چَيَائِين

At some time in a village one mouse, having reflected in its mind, said. Sindhī Read. Book, p. 61.

سَجَنُ سوبهَارو بهِيجِ بهِنِيَ گهَرِ آئِيو

(My) beautiful friend came at day-break to (my) house. Sh. Khambh. I, 9.

جِنُڙو جَنْجِيرَنِ مين رَاتِئَان ڏِينْهَان رُوءِ

(My) body weeps in the nights (and) in the days, in the chains (i. e. in prison). Sh. Um. Mār. V, 7.

3) The Locative is used also in the sense of the Latin Ablative absolute, to express a state or circumstance. In this way either an adjective may be used absolutely (i. e. substantively, so that an attribute may be joined to it) or a substantive with an adjective; in either case the participle present هُونْدِي in being, being, should be supplied, but is idiomatically left out.[1])

---

1) About the Locative of the participle present and past, see §. 81, 2.

سو مون تهورو لاه جينئ جئري مِلان هوت کهي

Grant me that favour, that I may meet, whilst living (lit. in the state of being alive) my sweetheart. Sh. Ābirī I, 1.

اَسان جي جئري تنهن جي وار جو نالو بہ کو نہ گِنهندو

Whilst we live no one shall take even the name of thy hair. Amulu Māṇ. p. 151.

لاهہ مہ لڏو لڏ تہ گاڙهي سِجَ گالهہ مِڙين

Do not take down the load; depart, that thou mayst meet with (thy) object, whilst the sun is (yet) red. Sh. Hus. I, 2.

4) The Locative describes the attributes or qualities, in which the subject is, to say so, immersed. In the English idiom such a Locative must be translated by the postposition 'of' or 'with'.

سَنهي لَکِ نکِ سَنئين ڪَجَلَ بهرِيَن نينَ

Of slender waist, of straight nose, with lamp-black their eyes (are) filled. Sh. Sām. I, 35.

سَر تَنَ جي سِينگارَ مين آهي سُورهہ وڏي سَتِ

In the adornment of the head (and) body he is a hero of great boldness. Ajāib, v. 156.

وڏي اوهہ آئيون پُٺهيَ لائي پهرَ

With great udder they came, having behind their young ones. Sh. Sār. IV, 14.

هِهڙين آرين پارين تو کو شاهہ عَبدُ اللطيف نالي پُٽرُ منهن جو ڪاٿهئين ڏٺهو

Hast thou seen any where one by name Shāh Abd-ul-Laṯīf, of such marks and signs, my son? Life of Abd-ul-Laṯīf, p. 9.

چھورو چھنين کپڙين کر ڏسنديئي ڏلُ

An orphan, of torn clothes, to look upon like a basil leaf. Maj. 303.

هرن اکهڙين هنجڙي کنين کووِل جي کارِ

Of deer-eyes, of ears of a wild goose, of a Kōvil's speech. Ibid. 52.

کبوتر جهڙي ڳچي سيني سنهارِي

Of a neck (and) breast like a pigeon, amiable. Ibid. 60.

5) The Locative is used also in computations, the sum or price, at which something is computed, being put in the Locative (cf. also §. 66, 4).

تنهن جو قدمُ پدمِ نہ پاڙيان جي تون ٿهئين جميعُ

Thy step I do not balance with ten billions, if thou become comforted. Sh. Sōr. II, 4.

جو منُ مُلهہ مورِ نہ سُپجي اچي سو گهريوہ

That heart, which is not at all obtained for a price, thou hast asked. Sh. Sōr. II, 15.

§. 71.

VIII. The Ablative.

The idea of the Ablative is expressed either by the Ablative case (cf. §. 16, 5) or by postpositions, as: کهان, کهون, کنا from, مان, مجهان from-in, تان, متهان from-upon etc.

1) The Ablative denotes in the first instance separation, removal, distance from a place or thing; it is therefore commonly used with such verbs, postpositions and adverbs, as imply a distance or separation from any thing (place, time etc.).

پَرَڏيهَان پَندهُ کَرِي هَلِي آيو هِيءُ

This one came, having made a journey from a foreign country. S. Sōr. I, 5.

بهَنگِيَسِ جَان بهَنْبهورَ کهَان تَان سُورَ مِڙيئِي سُکهَ
لَتهِي مَنتهَان لَکهَ[1] پُنْهُون تهِيَسِ پَانَهِين

When I fled from Bhambhōru, then all pains became delights;
Having descended from the mountain-pass I became in my own person Punhū̃. Sh. Ābirī V, 2.

کُلهَنِئَّان کورِيَان کِي جَاجِڪَ جُسي سِين ڏِئَّانِئِي

I will scoop out of (my) shoulders something, o bard, and give it thee with the body. Sh. Sōr. II, 22.

اَجلَان اَڳي سَسُئِي مُنْدهَ جِئَرَائِي مَرُ
ٽولِيَان تَنْهِن مَ ٽَرُ جَنْهِن رُوحُ وِڃَايو رَاهَ مِين

Before death, o Sasuī, o fair Lady! die whilst living!
Turn not aside from that company, by which the soul has been lost on the road. Sh. Maʒδ. IV, 6.

2) The Ablative is therefore used in comparisons, the object, with which a noun is compared, being put in the Ablative, to state the distance or difference of one noun from another (cf. §. 21).

جي بهَانئين تَه پِرِنءَ مِڙَان تَه ڏوهَنئُون گُنُ بهَانِءِ

If thou desirest to meet thy friend, then esteem virtue more than vices; (literally: esteem virtue before vices.) Sh. Jam. Kal. VIII, 22.

---

1) لَکهَ the same as لَکُ, the latter having been, after a poëtical license, aspirated, for the sake of the rhyme.

اوتارو مِڙنِي پِڻِن فقيرن كهان چنگو جوڙائي بهِٽَ تي وِيٺهو

Having built a dwelling better than all other faqīrs (lit. good from), he lived at Bhiṭa (i. e. on the sandhill). Life of Abd-ul-Laṯīf, p. 21.

3) The Ablative expresses the ground, reason or feeling, out of which or with which an action is done.

مَنِجِ مُحَمَّدُ كارِڻِي نِرْتون مَنجهان نِينْهَ

Respect Muhammad, the intercessor, out of understanding (and) love. Sh. Kal. I, 2.

کُتهاڀِيا كهِنِي وَنجو جان سا خُوشِيان كهاءِ

Go, ye scholars, that she may eat with pleasure. Maǰ. 117.

4) The Ablative denotes also instrumentality and accompaniment; but this use is restricted to inanimate nouns and to poëtry; in prose either the Instrumental or the postposition سانُ would be employed for this purpose.

هوءِ چوِنِي تُون كِي مَ چُوُ واتان وَراڻِي وِينُ

Those say to thee: do thou not return a word with (thy) mouth. Sh. Jam. Kal. VIII, 17.

كَرِ تُون حَمْدُ حَكِيمَ كهِي ظاهِرُ زَبانا[1]

Give thou praise to the wise one publicly with (thy) tongue. Sh. Surāg. I, Epil. 1.

مُتهِڻُون لَهِي مُنْهاءِ جِي تو چانگا چهِنِيُون

The mouthfuls, which thou, o camel! hast obtained (and) plucked with the mouth. Sh. Kambh. II, 29.

---

1) زَبانا instead of زَبانان.

سوَنَان وُون صَرّافَ سِينئَ لَڏو هَڏِ مَ لَاهِ.

Go with the gold to the banker, (but) do not at all take down the load! Sh. Surāg̱. IV, 9.

5) With neuter verbs the Ablative (especially with the postposition کهَان) denotes the agent. The same is the case with passive verbs, if the agent be an inanimate noun.

سَائِيِن مُونْهَان ڏوهُ تهِئو سو تُون توهِينْمِ

Master, I have done wrong, forgive me that! Life of Abd-ul-Laṯīf, p. 20.

شَمَعَ تهِينډِيَسِ شَبِ مِين اِنَ خُوشِئَ کهَان کهَامِي

I shall become a candle in the night, being burnt by that delight. Sh. Khambh. I, Epil. 3.

صُورَتَ سُونْهَ کهَان کِيَسِ چِتَ چرِي

By the beauty of (his) face I was made mad in (my) mind. Sh. Suh. IX, 8.

Chapter V.

Pronouns.

I. Personal pronouns.

§. 72.

1) The personal pronouns are generally not expressed, being implied in the inflexional terminations of the verb. They are therefore only used either for the sake of perspicuity or for the sake of emphasis[1]) or contrast. In poëtry a personal pronoun is often omitted,

---

1) Commonly with the emphatic ī (ī̃) or hī, hī̃.

where we should expect one, and must then be supplied from the context.

On the whole the personal pronouns precede the verb, to which they belong, but they may also follow it, especially in poëtry.

آنئُون هيڪَلِي حَبِ مِين نَہ مُون مِتْرُ نَہ ڪاڪو

I am alone on the Hab, I have no friend nor brother. Sh. Suh. II, Epil. 2.

وَرِيتِيُون بهِہ وَرو آن نَہ وَرَنْدِيَسِ وَرَ رِي

Ye married women also return! I shall not return without (my) husband. Sh. Ābirī IV, 9.

وَنجو سَبهِہ موٽِي اَوِين جِي وَرَنِ وَارِيُون

Go again ye all, who have husbands! Ibid. IV, 9.

مُونْهِين ڪهي مَارِينِ مُونْهِين سَنْدَا ڏُڪهَڙَا

Even me kill my own pains.

2) The Genitives مُنْهِن جو and تُنْهِن جو my, thy, are possessive adjectives in the Nominative and inflected accordingly. In poëtry the case-sign جو is frequently dropped, but then the forms مُون and تو must be employed. Instead of the possessive adjectives the pronominal suffixes attached to nouns (verbs and postpositions) or to سَنْدو (cf. §. 40, 2) may also be used, and in certain cases پَنْهِن جو, see §. 77.

The Genitive of the personal pronoun of the I and II pers. Sing. and Plur. (Lat. mei, tui etc.) is expressed by the Formative مُنْهِن جِي, تُنْهِن جِي etc., which is also used before such postpositions, as require جِي, cf. §. 58, II.

هِنڻُوِن مُنْهِن جو هُتِ تِهِڻو هِتِ مِٽِي ۽ مَانهُ

My heart is fixed there, here is (only) earth and flesh. Sh. Um. Mār. VI, 16.

مُون گهَرِ مُون پرِيَنِ جي آچَنَ جو وَارو

It is my friend's turn to come to my house. Sh. Kambh. I, 9.

تو جيڏَا تو يَارَ لَهَرِنِ لَاوَهَارَا کِيَا

Thy companions, thy friends have been carried down the river by the waves. Sh. Surāg̃. VI, 6.

جيکو پُٽرَ جَان دهِيَ کهي مُون کهَان گهَڻو گهُرَنْدو سو

مُنْهِن جي جوڳ نَہ آهي

Whoever loves son or daughter more than me, is not worthy of me. Matth. 10, 37.

اَچُ مُنْهِن جي پُٺُون هَلُ

Come, walk after me, i. e. follow me. Ibid. 19, 21.

3) مُنْهِن جو and تُنْهِن جو are also used substantively, especially in the Plural, in the sense of: my, thy people or friends.

اُکَنْڊهَہ مُون اَپَارَ شَالَ مُنْهِن جَا موٽِيَا

I have a very great longing; would that my (friends) had returned! Sh. Sām. II, 17.

4) The Accusative of the personal pronouns must always be marked by the postposition کهي, which in poëtry however is frequently dropped. But if in a sentence a Dative and Accusative of a personal pronoun (or pronoun of the III pers.) should occur, the Dative takes the postposition کهي as well as the Accusative;

constructions of this kind are however avoided, whenever possible.[1])

مُون کهِي مُون حَبِيبَ طَعْنوڙِي تُنْهِن جو

(To =) Upon me (is) thy reproach, o my friend! Sh. Mūm. Rāṇō II, 14.

كَاكِّان وَنجُ مَ كِيڏهِين رَانَا تو نَ رِهَاءُ

Go not away from Kāk anywhere, o Rāṇō, it is not right for thee. Sh. Mūm. Raṇō I, Epil.

اَوْهَانْ کهِي بهِٽَ نَ تهِي ڇهڏِي ۽ تُون مَ بهَڄُ

Bhiṭa does not give you up, and thou do not run away! Life of Abd-ul-Laṯīf, p. 21.

3) When the personal pronouns are accompanied by an attribute in the inflected case, they must precede it in the Formative.

كَرِ كو بهِيرو كَانْدهَ مُون نِمَانِيَ جِي ڃِجهِرِي

Make some turn, o husband, to the hut of me, the lowly one! Sh. Ḏāharu III, 1.

وو مُون نِمَانِيَ تَان كِي نَ چَيو

Woe, by me the humble one nothing was then said! Sh. Dēsī IV, Epil.

ڏِينْدَا مُون ڏُکهِيَ کهِي اَللّٰهَ لَڳِ اُهُنجَانُ

They will give to me the afflicted a sign, for God's sake. Sh. Kōh. III, Epil.

---

1) This may be done easily by a passive construction, as:

مُون اَوْهَان کهِي هِنَ جِي هَتهِ بَخشُ كِئو

I have presented you into his hands, i. e. made a present of you to him. Amulu Māṇ. p. 148.

§. 73.

II. Demonstrative pronouns.

1) There is no personal pronoun of the III pers. (Singular and Plural) in Sindhī, its place being generally supplied by the demonstrative هو that, he, she; but if a distinction between a nearer and a more distant object is to be made, the demonstrative pronoun هِي this[1]), is referred to the object near at hand, and هُو to the more distant one. When the subject (or object) of the sentence immediately preceding is to be taken up again by a pronoun, the demonstrative pronoun سو[2]) is used.

جَڏهِن ڪِنڪ اُنَ جِي مَرَن جِي اُنَ جِي ڪَنَ تي رَسِي

When the groan of her dying came upon her ear. Sindhī Read. B. p. 64.

تون مُرس آنهِين هُوَ مِهرِي

Thou art a man, she a woman. Amulu Mān., p. 147.

هُنَ کهي رَاتِ رُوحَ ۾ين هِي تهَا بهَائِنِ هِيَ

That one has in his mind (the word) 'night', these ones think this. Maj. 34.

---

1) هِي is also used idiomatically in the following way:

نَہ تَہ هِي مُلڪ هِي تُون

Otherwise this is the kingdom, this thou, i. e. I will have nothing to do with the kingdom nor with thee. Amulu Māṇ. p. 141.

2) The demonstrative pronoun سو, when joined to a personal pronoun, signifies 'therefore'; as:

عُمَرَ سَا آنئُون ڪِينئَ پَٽُ پَهرِيان سُومِرَا

O Umar of the Sūmirō clan, therefore how shall I put on silk? Sh. Um. Mārui VII, 6.

تو کهي ڏيو نَولکهو هَارُ ڏِنو سو بهِ مُون جهَپي هَتهَ مين ڪِٿو

The Dēv has given thee a necklace of nine lakhs; that also I snatched away and took to hands. Amulu Māṇ. p. 147.

هي مِڙَئِي مينْهُون مَنجهَانئُسِ تهِيُون آنْهِنِ سي پَنْهَن جِيُون وَٽهُ

All these buffaloes have come out of it (= were born); take them as thy own. Sindhī Read. B. p. 61.

2) The demonstrative pronoun اِهو, this very, refers emphatically either to an object near at hand, or just mentioned or immediately following, and اُهو that very to a more remote or afore mentioned one. اِجهو this here, and اُجهو that there, are only used in a local sense.

جيکَڏِهِن اِهَا ڳَالِ ڪُنَّنِ جو بَادِشَاهُ ٻُڌَنْدَو

If ever this very (just mentioned) word the king of the mice shall hear. Sindhī Read. B. p. 63.

اُهَا تَ مُنْهن جِي ڀيڻُ آهي

That very one then is my sister. Amulu Māṇ. p. 149.

3) In the Accusative the demonstrative pronouns commonly take the postposition کهي, if they refer to persons (or animate beings generally) which are to be rendered more prominent; but if there be no stress laid on the demonstrative, the uninflected form of it is used. If the demonstratives refer to things or if they precede adjectively another noun in the uninflected form, they remain uninflected in the Accusative, if the postposition کهي be not required for reasons stated at §. 69, 3.

تَنْهِن هِنَنِ کهِي ڏِسِي کهَنِي دَرُ پَاتو

She, having seen these, locked the door. Amulu Mān. p. 149.

جَڏِهِن هو لَهو تَ مُون کهِي اَچِي خَبَرَ ڏِجو

When you find it, come and give me intelligence. Matth. 2, 8.

پوء اُهو آن ڏِسَنْدِيَسِ تَ تو کهِي ٻَانْهِي ڏِيَارِي موکِلِينْدِيَسِ

Then I shall see that, (and) then send to you a slave-girl. Amulu Māṇ. p. 150.

هِي وَنَ نَ لَهَنْدَاء هُوء وَنَ اوڏَانْهِين کهَنَا

These trees you will not obtain; those trees there (are) many.

§. 74.

III. The relative and correlative pronoun.

1) The relative pronoun[1]) in Sindhī is جو, who, which, and the correlative سو that, which usually takes up the relative. Besides the relative جو, the indefinite pronouns جوکو, جيکو whosoever, جيکِي whatsoever may also correspond to the following correlative سو. The place of the relative pronoun may also be taken up by a relative adverb. Instead of the correlative سو a demonstrative may be used, if the stress be laid upon it.

The sentence headed by the relative pronoun may either precede or follow that commenced by the correlative سو, according to the emphasis laid on either

1) The relative جو, when followed by a personal pronoun in the same sentence, signifies 'as' (Lat. quippe qui)

حَيْفُ مُنْهُن جِي حَالَ کهِي جَا ٻُجهِي آنئُون ٻيکَارِ

Woe to my state, as I am bad and useless! Maj. 756.

pronoun; for the sake of emphasis the correlatives may be repeated.

When the relative (and correlative) refers to a pronoun of the I or II person, the verb of the relative sentence is usually in the III person, and not in the I or II person.

In poëtry either pronoun may be dropped.

جَنْهِن کِيدِي بِلِي هوَکارِئو سو پُنُ بهَڄِي وِئو

That, which shouted: a coward (is) the cat, ran also away. Sindhī Read. B. p. 64.

جِي تُون بَيْتَ بهَائِيِين سِي آيَتُون آنهِينِ

Those, which thou considerest as verses, are signs. Sh. Suh. IX, 6.

سَنگِي تهِينْدُء سو جيکِي جَپِينْدِين جَگَدِيسَ کهِي

That will be a companion to thee, whatever thou prayest to the Lord of the world. Mēnghō 8.

سوئِي سَانيهُ مُنْهِن جو سَاجَنُ جِتِ سَنّدوِم

That is my native country, where my sweetheart (is). Maj. 86.

لَاهِيَان جِي نَہ چِتَان آَلَا اُنِ مَہ وِسِرَان

May I not be forgotten by them, whom I do not drop out of (my) mind. Sh. Sām. II, 4.

جِي جِي وَنَ چَنْگو ڦهَلُ نَہ تهَا ڏِئَنِ سِي سِي وَڍهِي بَاهِہ

مِين تهَا وِجهِجَنِ

Those trees, which give no good fruit, are cut off (and) thrown into the fire. Matth. 7, 19.

آن جَا چهَڏِي جهَبَرِين سَا کِيچِ رَسَنْدِي کِينئَ

I, who is (= am) given up in the mountains, how shall she (= I) arrive at Kēč? Sh. Dēsī, III, Epil.

2) The relative pronoun (and, as the case may be, the correlative) usually precedes the substantive, to which it refers, but the relative may also follow, if the substantive has one or more attributes. The subject of a sentence is frequently first expressed by a demonstrative pronoun, and then taken up by the relative and correlative, to render it more prominent.

جَا بِلِي پَنْهَن جِي ٻَارَ کهِي تهِي کهَائِي سَا کُٺِي کهِي
کَڍِهين چهَڍِينْدِي

Which cat (= a cat that) eats her own young one, will that ever give up a mouse? Sindhī Read. B. p. 53.

سؤ سَوْدوٖئِي چهَڍِ جَنْهِن جَوَاهِرُ نَاهِي کؤ

Give up that traffic, in which there is no jewel. Sh. Surāg̃. IV, 8.

فَقِيرُ جؤ ڀُڄِنَاتِيَ وَارؤ هؤ تَنْهِن کهِي خَبَرَ پَهُچِي وِيئِي

The faqīr, who was powerful (in magic), to him information was brought. Amulu Māṇ. p. 147.

ڊُزْڊُ ڊِيوَانؤ ڊهَارِيؤ جؤ پَرَڊِيهِي پَڙهِي
سؤ تُنْهُن جِي ڌِهِئَ سِين کهِلِئؤ هَتهَ هَنِي

A mad, strange thief, a foreigner, who reads (studies),
Shakes laughing hands with thy daughter. Maj. 240, 241.

هؤ جِي وَڏَا وِيرَ وَرِيَامَ سِی سَکهِنَا وِئَا سَنْسَارَ مؤن

Those, who were great men (and) warriors, went destitute out of the world. Menghō 4.

4) The relative and correlative pronoun may in the same sentence be subject and object, so that the sentence is doubly correlative, the object, if a pronoun of the III person, being likewise expressed by the relative and correlative.

جِي جَنِ جَا سِيکَڙُو سِي مِيڙِين کهي تَنِ

For whom they are longing, with them join them. Maj. 203.

سو وَڙُ سِبِئِي کَنِ جو وَڙُ جُڙِي جَنِ سَان

That kindness they bestow, which is bestowed on them. Sh. Surāḡ. IV, 4.

5) In the first member of a correlative sentence (or, as it may be, in the second) سو جو is occasionally used instead of the simple relative جو, which is then taken up again by a following correlative.

تَنِ جَنْهِين جِي تَانگهَ سِي سَجَڻَ هَلِيَّا سَپهَرِ

Those friends, who are wanted, have gone on a journey. Sh. Sam. I, 24.

سِي قَادِرَ اِينْدَا کَڏِهِين تَنِ جَنِ جِي تَاتِ

O Almighty, will those ever come, of whom the discourse is? Maj. 457.

6) With the correlative adverbs the correlative pronouns and adjectives may be joined in the same sentence.

وَحْدُهُ لَا شَرِيکَ لَهُ جَڏِهِن چَيو جَنِ

تَنِ مَنجو مُحَمَّدُ کَارَنِي هِيجَان سَانُ هِنئَنِ

تَڏِهِن مَنجهَان اُنِ اَوَتَڙِ کَنْهِين نَ اوِلِئو

When those, who said: he is alone (God), he has no partner,

Respect Muhammad, the intercessor, out of love with their hearts,

Then (none) out of them was entangled in a place, where there is no landing. Sh. Kal. I, 3.

جِتِي جيتِرِيُون لِکهِيُون لوهَ قَلَمَ مِين
تِتِي تيتِرِيُون گهڙِيُون کهارِنَ آئِيُون

Where so many hours are written in fate,
There so many have come to pass. Sh. Maȝδ. V, 9.

7) The correlative adjectives and adverbs (cf. §. 38, 2), when placed after each other, imply an **indefinite** sense. The same is the case, if a relative be joined with an interrogative.

بِلِي کُئّنِ مَنجهان جيتِرا کيتِرا سَرَهائِىَ سان کهائِي وِيئِي

The cat, having eaten some (a number) of the mice with delight, went off. Sindhī Read. B. p. 64.

پاتِشاهزادِىَ جِئِين تِئِين چَٺَ بَنْدهِي دِلِ وَٺهِي کَڍهايُسِ

The princess, having enticed him somehow, having gained (his) heart, drew him out (i. e. got the secret from him). Amulu Māṇ. p. 147.

§. 75.

IV. The interrogative pronouns.

1) کيرُ who? is applied to persons and ڇها and کوهَ what? to things only; these three pronouns are used absolutely and not joined adjectively to another noun[1]); in which case the interrogative adjectives کيهرو, کيهڙو which? and کيهڙو of what kind? are to be employed.

---

1) کيرُ is occasionally joined adjectively to a noun in poëtry, as:

کيرُ مُنْجُون کَرهِ تِي بانکو بَلا جِىَ

Which hero shall we send to the combat of the snake? Story of the snake v. 59.

The interrogative pronouns are not only used in direct interrogatory sentences but also in indirect interrogatory ones, when the governing sentence contains a negation; but if the governing sentence be positive, the relative جو is preferred. The same rule applies to the interrogative adjectives and adverbs.

پکي سُدهِ نہ اتهِ تہ کيرُ آهي

I do not know exactly, who it is. Life of Abd-ul-Laṯīf, p. 13.

آن بهِ اوهان کهي نہ تهو چوان کيرهي حُکم سان هي تهو کريان

I also do not tell you, by what order I do this. Matth. 21, 26.

آن بِ چوندو سانوَ جنهِن حُکمَ سان هي تهو کريان

I shall also tell you, by what order I do this. Matth. 21, 24.

2) The interrogative pronouns (adjectives and adverbs) are frequently used, where a negative answer is expected.

قِسمَت قيدِ کياسِ نہ تہ کيرَ اچي هِنَ کوٺ مين

By fate I have been put into prison; otherwise who would come into this fort? Sh. Um. Mār. I, 8.

§. 76.

V. The indefinite pronouns.

1) کو some one, any one, when standing by itself, is applied to animate beings and کِي to things only; but when کو is used adjectively, it may be joined to any noun; similarly کِي also may be put before nouns, when a part or quantity is to be expressed, cf. §. 61, 3.

كَمِ نَہ اِينْدُء كو بِئو پَنْهَن جي پوكِهِئِي رِي

Nothing else will be of use to thee, except what thou hast sown thyself. Mēnghō 10.

2) كو is now and then added to a personal pronoun (expressed or only implied in the inflexional termination of the verb) in an interrogative or negative sentence, for the sake of emphasis, with nearly the same sense as كِي.

ڇهَڏِي تُون كو ڇهَپَرِين وِينْدِين هوتَ نَہ ڀهَانْيُمِ هِيئَ

Wilt thou, having forsaken (me) go at all to the mountains? O lover, I did not think thus. Sh. Dēsī, III, Epil.

3) When كو is repeated in the next sentence, it signifies: one—another.

كو چَوِي ڀِئُسِ جِنُّ جُسِي مِين كو چَئِي عَقُلُ ڦِهِرِئوسِ

One says: a demon has fallen into (his) body; another says: his understanding is upset. Maj. 40.

§. 77.

The reflexive pronoun.

1) The reflexive pronoun پَانَ (Sing. and Plur.) 'self', always refers to the subject of the sentence (expressed or only understood); somewhat intricate is the use of its Genitive, the reflexive pronominal adjective پَنْهَن جو, 'own'. When the subject of the sentence is a pronoun of the I and II person (expressed or only implied in the verb), its application is clear enough; but when the subject is of the III person (or any noun), the question arises, whether the possessive pronouns 'his', 'her' etc. refer to the chief subject of the sentence (Lat. suus), or to

some other subject (Lat. ejus etc.); in the first case the reflexive pronoun must be employed, in the latter a demonstrative.

اُٿِي کھيکارِي وَڍِي آدھَرَ ڀھاوَ سَان گڏِجِي پَانَ مِين وِيٺھا

Having risen (and) greeted (and) having met with great respect (and) politeness they sat amongst themselves. Life of Abd-ul-Laṯīf, p. 36.

نِرْمَلَ نِظَارُو پِيئَ پَسَايُو پَنْھَن جو

O pure friend, show thy face! Sh. Sōr. I, 10.

پَنْھَن جَنِ ٻيلِنِ سُودھو مَنجھِہ خِدْمَتَ شَاھَہ صَاحِبَ جي

اَچِي حَاضُرُ ٿِئُو

Having come with his (own) servants to the service of Shāh Sāhib, he was present. Life of Abd-ul-Laṯīf, p. 31.

اُنَ ڀھاڳِي اُنَ جِي سُڃَاڻَنَ تي اَچْرَجُ کَرِي پُڇھَانْسِ

That wealthy one, marvelling at his (the other's) recognising her, asked him. Sindhī Read. B. p. 61.

2) In addressing a person the reflexive pronominal adjective پَنْھَن جو is now and then used (like the Hindūstānī آپ کا etc.), instead of the peculiar pronoun, that would be required, as: سَائِيْن ھِي پَنْھَن جو مَالُ آھِي, master, this is your property, which under certain circumstances could also be translated: master, this is our property, when the spaker includes himself, as:

کَڍِھِي مُنجو مُوشَ کِي پَنْھَن جِي ڏيھَہ ڏَوَارَ

Send forth some mice of our country and land. Story of the mice and the cat, v. 35.

3) The reflexive pronominal adjective پَنْهَن جو may also refer to the object (noun with postp., or Dat. and Acc.) immediately following.

پُٽرُ پَنْهَن جي پِيُ سَان دِهِيُ پَنْهَن جي مَاءُ سَان وِيڙهَائِنَ آيو آنهِيَان

I am come to make quarrel the son with his father, the daughter with her mother. Matth. 10, 35.

4) When the subject of a sentence is a noun with a possessive pronoun, the peculiar possessive pronoun (if such occur with a noun) must be used and not پَنْهَن جو, because the use of پَنْهَن جو would give quite a different sense. Similarly when the subject of a sentence is a personal pronoun and when in the next sentence, joined to the preceding by a conjunctive particle, a noun with a possessive pronoun occurs, the peculiar pronoun must be used for the reasons stated above.

كو مُنّهن جو مُنْهن جي مُلْکَ مِين هُجِي پَهَلَوَانُ

(If) there would be in my kingdom some hero of mine. Story of Shamsādu, v. 40.

آنئُون حُكُمِي مَاڙهُون آنهِيَان ۽ مُنْهُن جي هَٿهَ هيٺهِ سِپَاهِي آنهِن

I am a man under authority and under my hands are soldiers. Matth. 8, 9.

5) The subject, to which پَنْهَن جو refers, must occasionally be gathered from the context; but when thus used without a clear subject, to which it may be referred, it generally implies the I person (Singular or Plural).

ڏيهَ پَنْهَن جي کهُون ڏُورِ تهِي وَڃِي ڪِتهَئِين ڪِجِي قِسْمَت

Having removed far from our country may our lot be made any where! Story of the cat and mice, v. 20.

6) پَنْهَن جو is also used substantively, signifying my, thy etc. property, friends or people.

پَنْهَن جو وَٺُ ۽ وَڃُ

Take what is thine and go. Matth. 20, 14.

SECTION II.

THE VERB.

Chapter VI.

§. 78.

The Infinitive.

1) The Infinitive as well of neuter as of active (causative) verbs is treated in Sindhī as a regular substantive. The complement (object), which is required by an active verb, is subordinated to the Infinitive either by the Genitive or by the Accusative in its uninflected form, or governed by the postposition کهي.

جِئَنُ جَتَ دهَارَان مَعْذُورِ جو مَس تهِئي

The living (= life) of the disappointed one gets on with difficulty without the Jat. Sh. Ābirī V, 9.

مُغَلَ تَرارِئُون کهَڻِي شاهَ جي مَارِنَ لاءِ آيا

The Mughals, having taken their swords, came to kill the Shāh. Life of Abd-ul-Laṯīf, p. 15.

سُورِیَ چڙهَڻُ سيج پَسَڻُ اِيئُ کَمُ عَاشِقَنِ

To ascent the impaling stake, to see the (nuptial) bed, this is the business of the lovers. Sh. Kal. II, 8.

تَنْهِن کهي مُورَهِين جهُکِي مَنجهِہ رکهَڻُ جوڳُ نَاهي

It is by no means proper to put that into the house. Sindhī Read. B. p. 65.

2) The Infinitive is added as an expletive object to the verbs ڏِيَڻُ to give leave, ڇهَڏَڻُ to let go or allow, گهُرَڻُ to desire, and partly also to سَگهَڻُ to be able. But when the verb, which subordinates an Infinitive, requires an object (Accus.), it puts the same in the Accusative, according to the signification of the finite verb.

لُڙِکَ نَہ لِکهَڻُ ڏِينِ کِرِئُو پُونِ قَلَمَ تي

Tears don't let me write (lit. give no writing); dropping they fall upon the pen. Sh. Um. Mār. II, 9.

مُغَلَ شَاهَہ صَاحِبَ کهي اَچَڻُ نَہ ڏِينْدَا هُئَا

The Mughals did not allow the Shāh Ṣāhib to come (lit. gave him no coming). Life of Abd-ul-Laṯīf, p. 15.

نَرُ پَکهي وِهَڻُ نَہ تهِيُون ڇهَڏِينِ

They do not allow a male bird to sit down. Amulu Māṇ. p. 141.

اِنْهِي کهي گهَڻَنِ نَبِيُنِ ۽ دهَرْمِيُنِ ڏِسَڻُ گهُرِيو هو

Many prophets and pious people had wished to see this very (sight). Matth. 13, 17.

3) The Infinitive may also be turned into an adjective by the accession of the Genitive case-sign جو. In this case the Infinitive itself is strictly treated as a

substantive, as regards its government, and جو is nearly used in the same sense as جِهو or جِهَڙو, cf. §. 67, 11.

پَرَ منگرَ مڇهَنِ جي کهِڻَنَ جو کِي نَہ هو

But he was not of the eating of the crocodiles, i. e. he was not destined to be eaten by the crocodiles. Story of Rāe Diāču p. 1.

هِيَ ڳالهِہ رُڳي چَرچي ۽ نَہ ٿِيڻَنَ جي آهي

This word is mere joke and impossible.

Chapter VII.

§. 79.

The Gerundive.

1) The Sindhī derives from the Infinitive of active verbs a regular Gerundive or participle future passive (cf. §. 8, 12, b; §. 46), which agrees with its subject in gender and number, except the construction be rendered impersonal by the use of the postposition کهي, cf. §. 94, 5. The agent is put in the Dative (like in Latin) or expressed by a pronominal suffix.

تو کهي جي کو فَرْيَادُ کَرِڻو هُئي سو تُون اَچي کَرِ

If by thee some complaint is to be made, come and make it. Amulu Māṇ. p. 150.

مُون کهَان جيکِي تو کهي پَائِڻو آهي سو خَيْرَاتَ آهي

Whatever thou hast to get from me, that is alms (i. e. given in alms). Matth. 15, 5.

هَاڻي جيکِي چَوِڻو هُئِي چَوُ

Now, whatever thou hast to say, say. Amulu Māṇ. p. 143.

2) But when the construction is rendered impersonal by the use of کهي or when a Dative occurs in a sentence, the agent must be expressed by the Instrumental, to avoid the double use of کهي.

هِنَ گهوڙي کهي تو جهلِنو هو

Thou shouldst have seized this horse.

جو تو کهي مُون لَهِنو آهي سو ڏِينمِ

What is to be got by me as regards thee (i. e. from thee), give that to me. Matth. 18, 28.

Chapter VIII.

The Participles.

§. 80.

I. The participle present.

1) The participle present agrees as a regular adjective with the subject of the finite verb (expressed or implied).

Is it used, when an action is to be described as lasting or continuing, for which purpose it may be repeated.

سَڄي شَهَرَ جو سَئِلُ کَرِي گهُمَنْدَا گهُمَنْدَا پَاتِشَاهَ جي

گهِٽِيُنِ مِين آيا

Having made the tour of the whole city they came, wandering, wandering to the lanes of the king. Amulu Māṇ. p. 140.

مَتهِنَ ٽُبِکَ ٽُبِکِڙَا ڇِنْگهَنْدَا اَچَنِ

Upon them (i. e. on their heads) are (large) baskets and (small) baskets; groaning they come. Sh. Um. Mār. VI, 12.

2) The participle present is very frequently used in the Locative Sing., terminating in ē, or with the emphatic ī or hī, in ēī and ēhī[1]), to express an action coinciding with what the finite verb declares.

As regards the subject of the present participle, Loc., it is either the same, as that of the finite verb, or it may refer to another noun in the sentence (Genitive, Dative, Accusative etc., usually expressed by a pronominal suffix), or it may not be expressed at all, to be gathered from the context.

When the subject of the present participle Loc. differs from that of the finite verb, it is added in the Formative; the same is the case, if an attribute be joined to the subject (expressed or only understood) of the present participle. But if the Locative of the present participle requires a complement (an object), it is constructed according to the common rules.

اِينْدِي وِينْدِي هِي حَرْفَ چَوَنْدو هو

In coming and going he used to say these words. Life of Abd-ul-Lāṯīf, p. 47.

بُکھَ مَرَنْدِي بِکھِيَا کَنْھِن کھَان کِي نَ گھُرَنِ

Dying of hunger they ask not from any one alms. Sh. Ramak. VII, 7.

ڏورِينْدِي مَنجھِ ڏُونگَرِين مَاڙھُون کو مِڙِيوسِ

Whilst searching about in the mountains some man met him. Maǰ. 122.

تَان کھينْدِيئِي خُمَارِي چَرِئو تھِئُسِ چِتُ

Then whilst eating her mind became drunk (and) mad. Maǰ. 178.

---

1) Occasionally ēhī is shortened to ahī, as: سُنِيندَهِي instead of سُنِينْدِيهِي.

جُنّائِيَ جِي جوءِ چهوکَرِن کهي گهَرَ مَنجهِ هُونْدِي پُڻ

گهَرَ ميں نہ ڄاڻِنِ

The wife and children of a gambler, (although) being in the house, do not consider as in the house. Sindhī Read. B. p. 52.

پَسَنْدِي پِرَ کهي ڏُکهَ سَبهِ ڏورِ تهِئَنِ

In seeing the friend all (their) pains are removed. Maj. 818.

مَيِوُ تُون موٽاءِ مُون رُوَنْدِي رَاتِ وِهَاءِ

Turn thou back the camel; pass the night, whilst I am weeping. Sh. Mūm. Rāṇō I, Epil.

§. 81.

II. The participle past.

1) The past participle of neuter verbs agrees with its subject in gender, number and case; the form in 'alu' is used, when the participle passes more into an adjective. The past participle of active and causal verbs (implying always a passive sense) agrees likewise with its subject in gender, number and case, except the construction be rendered impersonal by the use of the postposition کهي (cf. §. 94, 5).

2) The past participle of active (and partly also of neuter) verbs with a passive signification, is used also substantively, cf. §. 62, 2, and may therefore be constructed with a postposition.

چَارِيَنِ جو چَيو کَرِي قَاضِي تهِئو قَهَارُ

The Qāẓī, having done the word (= what was said) of the scouts, became a tyrant. Maj. 296.

بهڳي پُنجَانَاءِ پَدَمَانئِي پَرِي تهئو .

After being broken it became beyond (= more) a thousand billions. Sh. Surāg̃. IV, 17.

3) The past participle of neuter and active verbs is frequently used in the Locative Singular (cf. §. 80, 2); if the subject of the past participle do not differ from that of the finite verb, it is not expressed, but if it do differ, it is added in the Formative. But the subject of the past participle may also refer to a more distant object, or it may not be expressed at all, in which case the Locative is used absolutely. The impersonal construction of the past participle by means of the post-position کهي is also retained, though the participle be put in the Locative.

The past participle in the Locative is used substantively, but nouns, depending thereupon, are idiomatically only put in the Formative, and not subordinated by the inflected Genitive case-sign جي.

آچِي عَزْرَائِيلَ سُتي جَاڳَائِي سَسُئِي

By ʿAzrāīl having come, Sasuī was awakened whilst sleeping, i. e. in the state of being asleep. Sh. Ābirī VIII, 5.

اَلا اَچِنِ اُوء جَنِ آئِي مَنُ سَرَهو تهئي

O God, may those come, by whose coming (my) heart becomes glad. Sh. Dēsī III, 5.

مُون اُبِيتهي هَلِيَّا بَنْدَرَ جي تَرِّنِ

Whilst I stood upright, they went to the landing-places of the harbour. Sh. Sām. II, 2.

ويجَنِ ويتهيئي دوسُ پيهي دَرِ آئيو

Whilst the physicians were seated (lit. in the state of the physicians being seated), the friend entering came to (my) door. Sh. Jam. Kal. II, 10.

اَکهَرَ چهُتهِي هيکَڙِي بَهُون جي نَ ٻُجهَنِ

Those, who do not understand much, after one letter has been touched. Sh. Jam. Kal. V, 29.

ڏِٺهِي ڏوٺهِڙَنِ کهِي ٿهِڙَمِ ڏِينْهَ گهَڻَا

Since I have seen the Ḏ̄ōthīs, many days have passed to me (lit. In the being seen the Ḏ̄ōthīs). Golden Alphabet XXVIII, 2.

وِيٺهِي جَنْهِن وَٽِ ڏُکهَنْدو ڏاڍهو ٿهِئِي

Sitting near whom the pain becomes intense. Sh. Jam. Kal. VIII, 25.

کهَادِي جَنْهِين کهَنِ ٿهِئِي آچَنِ اوچهَارَا

Which being eaten coughing arises, vomiting comes on. Golden Alphab. XVIII, 10.

§. 82.

III. The past conjunctive participles.

The past conjunctive participles (cf. §. 47) very greatly facilitate the conjunction of the different members of a compound sentence and are therefore very extensively in use. They are translated according to the tense of the finite verb.

1) The past conjunctive participles commonly refer to the subject of the finite verb, and in a passive construction, to the agent (Instrumental); but when to the past conjunctive participle of ٿهِئَڻُ an attribute is added, it must remain in the Nominative, though the subject (agent) referred to be in the Instrumental.

مَٽَ مِين وِجهِي هَٿهِيکَا کَرِي سَانڍهِي رَکهُ

Having thrown (them) into the jar, having secured (them) take care (of them). Life of Abd-ul-Laṯīf, p. 11.

مَرِي رَهَنْدِين مَجِنا اُسَاتِجِي اُنج

Thou wilt go to die, Majnō̃, being dried up by thirst. Maj. 407.

ڊيسَان ڊيو کهَنِي کَڙي مُون کهي نِئو اَهَرِمَنَ

The Dēv Ahriman having taken me from the country carried me off. Ajāib v. 119.

تَڏِهِن سَڏُ سُنِي سَرَهِي تهِي چِتَ مِين چيَانئِين

Then having heard the call, having become glad in (her) heart, she said. Maj. 702.

2) The past conjunctive participles may refer also to the object (Dative, Accusative) in a sentence, and in a passive construction one past conj. participle may refer to the agent (Instrumental) and another to the subject.

سَجَنَ جِي سَارِين تَن رُوئيو وِهامِي رَاتڙِي

To them, who remember (their) friends, the night passes in weeping. Sh. Jam. Kal. I, 18.

تَرسِي طَبِيبَنِ چيتهِي هُونْدَ چَنگا کِيا

Having tarried they would possibly have been cured by the physicians having applied plaster. Sh. Jam. Kal. II, 5.

3) In an impersonal (neuter) or passive construction the past conjunctive participles may be used absolutely, without any reference to a subject, which must be gathered from the context.

رَاتِ وِهَانِي رُنجَ مِين آچِي مَاڳِ تَنْهِين

The night was passed (by her) in the desert, having come to that very place. Maj. 745.

اَنَّ جي پَاچهِىَ کهي ميڙي ٻِي هَنْڌِ نِئَنُ چَنْگو آهِي

Having collected the remnant of the grain, it is good (for me) to carry it to another place. Sindhī Read. B. p. 56.

هُنَ کهي ٭ سَنْدَسِ جَالَ ٭ ٻَارَنِ کهي ٭ جيکِي اَتهَسِ

تَنْهِن سَبهَ کهي وِکِنِي قَرْضُ پَاڙِجي

Having sold him and his wife and his children and whatever he has, the debt shall be paid (scil. by you). Matth. 18, 24.

کوُهُ کِبوُ کهي تَنِ سَڄِي سُنَائي ڳَالهَڙِي

What shall be done to them, having made them hear the whole matter? Sh. Jam. Kal. V, 29.

4) The past conj. participles are also now and then used in the sense of the Latin Ablative absolute, when the subject of the finite verb differs from that of the past conj. participle. But constructions of this kind are rather exceptions.

اِنِىَ پَرِ مِڙَئِي ٻِلِيُون مَرِي پَاچهِي سَارِي ڳوٺهَ مَنجهِ ٻَ

ٻِلِيُون ٻَچُون

After all cats had died in this very manner, two cats in the whole town were left alive. Sindhī Read. Book p. 63.

5) Some past conj. participles are used quite adverbially, as: موٽَائي، موٽِي; وَرَائي، وَرِي 'again' (lit. having returned or caused to return); وَٺهِي with the postposition کهَان from (lit. taking from); ڄَاڻِي ٻُجهِي intentionally (lit. having known, understood), or ڄَاڻِي وَاڻِي or ڄَاڻِي وِيڻِي, وَاڻِي and وِيڻِي being alliterations.

پرِين وَنجُ مَ پَرَڏيهڙي موٽِي چَيُسِ ماءُ

Friend, do not go to a foreign country, his mother said again to him. Maj. 83.

هُنَ گهڙِيَ کهان وَٺِهي تَنْهِن جِي ڌِيءَ چَنْگِي ڀَلِي ٿِهي

From that hour her daughter was made whole. Matth. 15, 28.

Chapter IX.

The tenses of the verb.

§. 83.

I. The Present.

1) The Sindhī has two forms for the present tense, one identical with the Potential, to which the inflexional increment تهو, تِهي etc. is added, the Present indefinite, and the other being compounded with the present participle and the auxiliary verb آنهِيَان etc., the Present definite.

The present tense of the passive voice is formed in the same way as that of the active voice, but its use is very restricted, neuter verbs being substituted wherever possible.

There is also a simple and compound Potential, as well of the active as of the passive voice, to express the idea of the present tense (cf. §. 90).

2) The first form of the Present tense, the Present indefinite, expresses our common Present, i. e. an action begun and still continuing in the present.

The increment تهو may optionally follow or precede

the verb[1]), but when the verb commences a sentence, it is put after it (poëtry excepted). In poëtry تهو is often separated from the verb by some other words, either preceding or following it.

When the negative adverb نَہ, 'not', accedes to the verb, نَہ immediately precedes تهو, and both the verb[2]); but in an interrogative sentence, or when a particular stress be laid on the verb, they may as well follow it.

In poëtry تهو is very frequently omitted and the Present indefinite then coincides with the Potential, so that only the context can decide, whether the Present indefinite or Potential is intended. In prose also تهو is dropped, when the interrogative pronoun چهَا what? and the adverb جَانِ when, precede the verb.

Instead of the increment تهو the past participle پئو (from پَوَنُ to fall) is also used, but with this difference, that a more enduring action is thereby implied.

سَارِئو سَانبهِتَّرِنِ کهي تهي سَئُون ڈِئي سَهَس

Remembering (her) guardians she gives a thousand blows. Story of the cat and mice v. 11.

تهو حُکَم هَلَائي پَانْهِن جا مَالِکُ مُلکَ دهَنِي

The king, the Lord of the kingdom, executes his own orders. Ajāib v. 5.

بُنْدهَنْدَا نَہ تها بُنْدهَنِ ۞ سَمُجهَنِ بِ نَہ تها

Hearing they do not hear nor do they understand. Matth. 13, 13.

---

1) When an interrogative pronoun or adverb, as چهَا, چهو etc., occurs in a sentence, it generally attracts تهو.

2) But when in a sentence نَہ — نَہ neither — nor, occurs, the adverb نَہ is put before that noun, on which the stress is laid.

تَنِ وَنْهِيَنِ وِيڙهِيچَنِ کهِي رُنَّان رَاتوڏِينْهَ

For those rich inhabitants of the jungle I weep nights and days. Sh. Um. Mār. II, 11.

جَان ڏِسَنِ تَہ هِڪِڙِي وَڏي ڪَارِي بَلَا وِيٺهِي آهِي

When they see, one big black snake is seated (there). Life of Abd-ul-Laṯīf, p. 16.

3) When occurrences are related, as the narrator or person, he speaks of, saw them, the Present is frequently used, in order to transfer the hearer to the scene of action. The same is the case, when the thoughts are given, which somebody had at a time.

جَڏِهِن مُغَلَنِ شَاهَہ صَاحِبَ کهِي ڏِٺهو تَہ گهَرَ مَنجهِہ وِيٺهو آهِي

When the Mughals saw the Shāh S̱āhib, that he is (= was) sitting in the house. Life of Abd-ul-Laṯīf, p. 15.

ڇهَا ڏِسِي جو ٻَارَ ٻَچَا ِجوئِسِ پِنَنَ مَنگَنَ مِين رَاتِ
ڏِينْهَ پهِرَنِ تهَا

What does he see? that his children (and) his wife go night and day about in begging. Sindhī Read. Book, p. 62.

اُنهِي مَاڳِ مَکَانُ شَاهَہ صَاحِبَ جو جوڙِي وِيٺهَا ڇهو تَہ
شَاهُہ صَاحِبُ هِتِ آهِي

Having there built a shrine of the Shāh S̱āhib in that very place they sat down: 'because the Shāh S̱āhib is here'. Life of Abd-ul-Laṯīf, p. 26.

4) The Present is also now and then used for the Future, to signify thereby, that the action will be done forthwith.

تُون هَاݨي آرَامُ کَرِ اَسِين تهَا ڏِسُون

Take thou now rest; we see (i. e. shall see). Amulu Māṇ. p. 149.

5) The second form of the Present, the Present definite, denotes a lasting or habitual action. The auxiliary is occasionally dropped, especially in sentences of general import.

جيکو تَنْهِن جي مَرْضِيَ سَارُو هَلَنْدو سو مُنْهِن جو ڀَاءُ ۽ ڀيڻَ ۽ مَاءُ آهي

Whoever is walking according to his will, that is my brother and sister and mother. Matth. 12, 40.

مَاڻهُون ڏيئي ميهِڻَا مُون کهي کَنْدَا کوهُ

Why are the people giving me reproaches? Sh. Maś. V, 14.

§. 84.

II. The Imperfect.

The Imperfect denotes a past action, which is incomplete in reference to some other past action. It implies therefore duration, habit or frequent occurrence.

جيکَڏِهِن شَاهُ صَاحِبُ اُنْهِي ڳوٺهَ ڏي ويندو هو تَ مُغَلَ سَاڻُسِ وِڙهَنْدَا هَا

Whenever the Shāh Ṣāhib was going to that very village, the Mughals were quarrelling with him. Life of Abd-ul-Laṯīf p. 15.

§. 85.

III. The Aorist.

I. The simple Aorist.

The Aorist implies indefinitely, that an action took place in past time. It is therefore commonly used in narrations, where past events are reported irrespectively of their duration. We may therefore translate the Sindhī Aorist either by the Imperfect or Perfect.

The Aorist of neuter verbs has an active meaning; some neuter verbs though (implying a passive sense) may also be constructed with the agent in the Instrumental.

Active verbs are constructed passively in the Aorist (Perfect and Pluperfect), the agent (subject) being put in the Instrumental and the past participle agreeing with the subject (properly the object) in gender, number and case (cf. §. 92, 2), or being constructed impersonally by the use of the postposition کهي (cf. §. 94, 5). It is understood, that the Aorist (Perfect and Pluperfect) of the passive voice is also used personally, agreeing with its subject (expressed or implied in the inflexional terminations) in gender and number.

آنُون سُتِي هوءِ هَلِيَا كاهِنّانئُون كَنْوَاتَ

I was asleep, those went off, they drove away the young camels. Sh. Hus. VI, Epil.

مَارُئّڙِن آنُون جيكَسِ وِييَسِ وِسِرِي

Perhaps I have been forgotten by the dear Mārūs. Sh. Um. Mār. V, 13.

ٻَاٽَ پِهرِنئَ رَاتِ جو ڳَڙهَ پَاسِي ڳَايو

The bard sang the first night at the side of the castle. Sh. Sōr. II, 1.

رُڃُنِ رَاتِ رَهِي ڏُونگَرَ جَنْهِين ڏوريَا

Who, having remained the night in the deserts, looked out for the mountains. Sh. Khāhōṛī I, 3.

هُوءِ جِي ڪَاڪِ ڪَکوِرِيَا تَنِ لَهِي نَہ لَالِي

Those, who were made tawny by the Kāk (river), the redness does not leave. Sh. Mūm. Rāṇō II, 4.

2) The compound or habitual Aorist.

The compound Aorist with the indeclinable increment تهِي denotes in the first instance, that an action was done repeatedly in past time or for any length of time; it is therefore chiefly used, when an occupation, habit or manner is to be described. In the second instance it implies, that an action had been commenced in past time and was still going on at the time mentioned, and in this respect it nearly coincides with the Imperfect, with the only difference, that generally a simple Aorist corresponds to it.

The increment تهِي is usually put before the verb, but is may also follow it; it may be also separated from the verb by some intervening words, in the same way as تهو. Instead of تهِي, پيِٺِي (the Locative of پِٺو with emphatic ī, instead of پِٺِيِٺِي pieī), is also used, which more strictly points out commencement and continuation.

جِتِي رَاتِ تهِي پيِيَسِ تِتِي سُمْهِي تهِي رَهِٺو

Where the night used to befall him, there he used to sleep. Life of Abd-ul-Laṯīf, p. 21.

ڪَارَڻِ قُوتَ پَنْهِن جِي تهِي لَکهِين ڏِنَانِٺِين لَاهَ

On account of her food she used to make lakhs of jumps. Story of the cat and mice v. 13.

كَكِرا كَرْبَلا جا مَادَرِ تهي ميڙِياسِ
پهَتَنِ تَان رَتَ پهُڙا عَلِيَ تهي اُگهَتهاسِ

The pebbles of Karbalā his mother was gathering,
ʿAlī was wiping him away from the wounds the drops of blood. Sh. Kēḍ. V, 2.

تَنْبُورَ حُجِرَنِ مين پَانَهين پَانَ مُرَادَا پِئي وَڳا ۽ مَنجهانُن هِيَ تَنْوَارَ پِئي آئي

The drums in the cells went on sounding by themselves as they pleased, and from them this tune was coming. Life of Abd-ul-Laṯīf, p. 36.

جَڏِهِن شاهُ جَمالُ پَنْهَن جي ڳوٺهَ ڏي تهي وِئو تَه ٻِئي ڏِينْهَ شاهُ صَاحِبُ وِصَالُ كِئو. پوءِ جَڏِهِن شاهَ جَمالَ شاهَ صَاحِبَ جي لَاڏَاڻي جي ڳالهِ ٻُڌِهي تَڏِهِن موٽي پُٺهِتي تهي آيو

When Shāh Jamāl was (as yet) going to his village, the Shāh Ṣāhib died on the second day. Then when Shāh Jamāl heard the message of the removal of the Shāh Ṣāhib, he was coming again behind (the messenger). Ibid. p. 6.

§. 86.

IV. The Perfect.

1) The Perfect denotes an action, that is completed and finished in the past, so that it extends to the Present.

نَه كِي تهِي جِئّان نَه كِي مُئِي آنهِيَان

I do not live at all, nor am I at all dead. Sh. Hus. IX, 16.

اُتهہ مَہ اوڙي آنِ انٺون ڏاکهن ڏِٺِي آنهيَان

Do not bring near the camels, I have been tormented by the camels. Sh. Dēsī I, 14.

2) The Perfect is occasionally used to represent an action as done already, whereas it is intended or expected, that it will be done forthwith.

پَرِيَ ڏِٺهو تہ هَاڻي هَلاَکُ ٿهٿو آهِي

The fairy saw, that he is (has been) now done for. Amulu Māṇ. p. 151.

§. 87.

IV. The Pluperfect.

1) The Pluperfect denotes remote past action, which has taken place previous to some other past event mentioned or understood. But in this connexion its use is not strict (as in Latin), the Aorist commonly being employed, where we would expect a Pluperfect.

ڪَنهِين شَهَرَ مِين پِٺو هو ڪَکهَنِ جو ڪَالُ
اُهِي مَاڙهُون ڪاهِي مَالُ ڪَنهِن اَوسَرَ سَانُ اُتهِي وِئَا

In some town there had fallen in a dearth of grass;
Those people drove off their cattle and went away at (with) some opportunity. Story of the cat and mice, v. 5. 6.

اُهو وِينڌهو جِنيَ پَرِيَ چِٺو هو تِنيَ بَانهِيَ جي گهَڙِي مِين وِڌهَانئِين

As the fairy had told, so she threw that very nose-ring into the jar of the slave-girl. Amulu Māṇ. p. 150.

آوَان ڪَا ڏِٺهِي ڏوٿهِيَا هوتَنِ وَٽِ هُئِي

Had you seen (when you were there) some one at the side of (her) sweetheart, o Ḍōthīs? Sh. Hus. VI, Epil. 2.

2) The Pluperfect is frequently used in Sindhī, where we would use an Imperfect or Perfect. When an action is represented, from the point of the speaker, as completely past some time hence, so that its results were already clear at the time mentioned, or when it is implied, that since an action has taken place, something else has happened, that could be said about it, the Pluperfect is used and not the Aorist nor the Perfect. The Sindhī idiom is much more accurate in discerning the different shades of meaning, than the English, and the correct use of this tense requires therefore a careful attention.

هِڪِڙِي ڏِينْهَ شَاهُ جَمَالُ شَاهَ صَاحِبَ وَٽِ وِيٺهو ۽ ٻِيَا پُڻْ
گهڻَا فَقِيرَ وِيٺها هُئَا

One day Shāh Jamāl sat with the Shāh S̱āhib, and also many other faqīrs were sitting (i. e. had seated themselves before). Life of Abd-ul-Laṯīf, p. 5.

مَخْدُومْ صَاحِبَ کهي سُڌهِ پِيئِي تَہ مِيَان نُورِ مُحَمَّدِ شَاهَ
صَاحِب جِي دَرْسَنَ کَرَنَ لاءِ وِئو هو.

Maχdūm S̱āhib received the intelligence, that Miā̃ Nūr Muhammad had gone (but was no longer there) to have an interview with the Shāh S̱āhib. Life of Abd-ul-Laṯīf, p. 29.

§. 88.

V. The Future and Future Past.

1) The Sindhī has two forms for the Future, the simple or indefinite Future and the Future definite.

The first form corresponds to our common Future and denotes a future action in general, the latter form implies, that the future action will last or endure for some time.

اُتهَ چَارِينْدِيَسِ اُن جَا مَيَان جهلِي مَهَارَ

I shall graze their camels, having seized the bridle of the camels. Sh. Hus. IX, Epil.

اُنهِي مَحَلَّ سُفِيدَ ڍِيو وَٽِ سَوُ پَرِيُون نَچَنْدِيُون هُونْدِيُون

At that very time an hundred fairies will be dancing near the Dēv Sufēd. Amulu Māṇ. p. 144.

2) The simple or indefinite Future is used also to denote possibility, inclination or doubt.

پَاتِشَاهَ تو کهِي آنُون هِڪِڙِي ڳَالهِ ڪَنْدُسِ

O king, I will speak one word to thee. Amulu Māṇ. p. 143.

اِي ڇهوڪَرَ ڪو ڪهَٽو اَسَان کهِي ڏِينْدِين

O boy, wilt thou give us a ram? Life of Abd-ul-Laṭīf, p. 17.

3) The Future indefinite is also used for the Imperative, when an order is not strictly given, but when it is expected, that it will be done spontaneously; it may therefore alternate with the Imperative.

پَنْهَن جي مَاءُ پِئُ کهِي آدَرُ ڏِي ۔ پَنْهَن جي پَاڙِيسِيَ

کهِي پَانَ جِهَڙو کهُرَنْدِين

Honour thy father and thy mother, and love thy neighbour as thyself. Matth. 19, 19.

4) The past Future is seldom to be met with in the sense of a strict past future action, which should have taken place, before another action will be possible, but it generally implies uncertainty, doubt or possibility in reference to a past action, as: هو آيو هُوندو, he may have come. Instead of the past Future the Aorist is commonly used in Sindhī, especially in conditional sentences; see §. 98, 6.

Chapter X.

The Moods.

§. 89.

I. The Indicative.

The Indicative represents an action or thought as real, and is therefore used, not only when matters of fact are related, but also when suppositions (in conditional sentences) are considered as really taking place (cf. §. 98*b*, 3). The Sindhī uses consequently the Indicative in such sentences, in which the speaker makes a subjective assertion, which he considers as true and real, whereas in the English idiom the Subjunctive would be used in such cases.

اِنْهي كهَان دَرِيَاهَ جي سِيرَ مين ٻوڙِجَڻُ سو چَنْگو آتهَسِ

It would be better for him, that he were drowned in the depth of the sea. Matth. 18, 6.

§. 90.

II. The Potential.

The Potential is, as stated already, the old Present and expresses therefore only present time; but by means of the present and past participle and the Potential of the auxiliary verb هُوَڻُ, a Potential of the Present definite and Perfect may be formed; these compound forms however are of very rare occurrence.

1) The Potential, in its widest sense, denotes indefiniteness, possibility, uncertainty or doubt.

پوءِ ڀانئيان تهو آنئون توُ سان گڏُ ماني کهان

Then, think I, I eat together with thee bread. Amulu Māṇ. p. 146.

جيڏيُون ڪينئَ ڪريان مُون اُنِ سين

Companions, how shall I act with (= towards) them? Sh. Ābirī VIII, Epil.

مُون کهي هِيَ ڪاٺهي نہ ڪڍهِين

Wilt thou not pull me out this wood? Amulu Māṇ. p. 148.

سَزا ڏِيَندڙنِ جي هَتهِ ڏِنائس جيسِين هي مُنهن جو لهنو سَبهُہ پيچائي نہ ڏِئي

He delivered him into the hand of the tormentors, as long as he shall not repay all, what is due unto me. Matth. 18, 34.

2) The Potential serves also to express a usual or habitual action.

پاڻي پِئو پٽُ ڪري سَبهُہ سُڪائي سَرُ

Drinking the water it makes (it, i. e. the river)

bare ground, it dries up the whole world. Nānga jō Quissō, v. 40.

پَاچهَائِي نہ پَاڙِيَان سَرْتِيُون سُئِّيَ سَان

A kingdom I do not compare with (my) needle, o companions! Sh. Um. Mār. VI, 18.

مُون سِين هَلِي سَا جَا جِيئُ مِٺهوڙِي نہ كَرِي

That one shall go with me, who does not make (= consider) her life sweet. Sh. Ābiri VI, 2.

3) The Potential is frequently used in the sense of an Optative or polite Imperative, especially for the I. and III. person Singular and Plural.

مِيَان مُحَبّتِنِ كهِي هَادِي هوٿَ مِلَنِ

O friend, may the lovers obtain (their) sweethearts as guides! Maj. 817.

هُئِي مُبَارَكَ مِڙنِي كهِي حَاصُلَ كَمُ تهِئو سَا حَاجَ

May there be blessing to all! that our business (and) affair has succeeded. Story of the cat and mice v. 52.

اَلاَ اوٺهِي آڻِئين جِي نِيَاپَا نِينِ

O God, mayst thou bring camelmen, who take off messages of love. Sh. Um. Mār. II, 9.

سِكهَا آڻِينِ سِيكهَ مِين اِهَا خَبَرَ چَارَ

Quickly, with speed, they shall bring this information and intelligence. Story of the cat and mice v. 38.

4) The Potential is used with the Interjections مَانَ, شَالَ would that, with the conjunctions مَ[1]), not (prohi-

---

1) With نَ the Potential may also be used, if the injunction be more strict.

bitive), مَتَان, مَجِھِنِ, جِمَ may it not be, that, lest; تَہ that, جو , جَان, جِنئَ, that, so that, in order that; توڙي although; جي , جيکَر, جيکَڏِھِن if (cf. §. 98 *b*, 1); and with the adverbs هُونْدَ, possibly, جِکيسِ, perhaps etc., if the sentence be indefinite.

وِيجَ مَہ ڏِيکِي ڏِي آلا چَنْگِي مَہ ٿِيَان

O physican, do not give a powder! o God, may I not become well! Sh. Jam. Kal. II, 13.

مَنگَنهَارَ شَالَ نَہ اَچِين کَڏِهِين موڙِي

Would to God, that thou, o beggar, wouldst not come any more. Sh. Sōr. II, 9.

ڪَاٽِ تَہ پَوِين قَبُولَ مِين مَڄهَنُ پَوِيٿِي کهَٽِ

Cut off, that thou mayst be approved, lest loss befall thee. Sh. Kal. II, 17.

اِيئِين اُٿهَہ اُٿهَاء جِينئَ هُونڌِیَ رَاتِ هُتِ مِڙَان

Thus, o camel, lift up (thy pace), that I may meet there (the friend) in the coming night. Sh. Khamb. II, 15.

اِهَڙو کو ڇهَالُ ڏِٺو جو وَڃِي اُنْهِي وَڳِي تِي پَٿو

Make some such jump, that ye fall upon that garment. Amulu Māṇ. p. 150.

ڏِيئِي جَانِ جَبَّارَ کهِي هُنْدَ تهِئِين پرِيَان پَارَ

Having given (thy) soul to the omnipotent, thou mayst possibly be put into the track of (thy) friend. Sh. Surāḡ. III, Epil.

§. 91.

III. The Imperative.

1) The Imperative is restricted to the II. person Singular and Plural; for the other persons the Potential must be used.

The Imperative has two forms, the Imperative strictly speaking and the Precative (cf. §. 44). The Imperative expresses a command, whereas the Precative implies an exhortation, request or haste.

When a negation accedes to the Imperative, نَ is used to express a strict negation, whereas مَ is used in a prohibitive sense. With the Precative مَ is commonly joined, but نَ may also be employed, if the injunction be more strict.

شِيهَنِ چَيو تُون الكو نَ كَرِ

The lions said: be thou not anxious. Amulu Mān. p. 151.

سُومَرَا سَاهِي تَنْهِن سَتِيَ وِجهُ مَ سَنْگهَرُون

O Sūmarō, do not throw and tighten chains upon the chaste one! Sh. Um. Mār. III, 9.

آءِ اوَرَاهُون سُپِرِين ڎُكهِيَ ڋِيجِ مَ ڎَاكهُ

Come near, good friend, do not apply a funeral pyre to the afflicted one! Sh. Ābirī X, 5.

جيكِي پَاكُ آهِي سو كُتَنِ كهي نَ ڋِجو

What is pure do not give to the dogs. Matth. 7, 6.

2) When two Imperatives are joined together by the conjunction تَ or تَان, the first Imperative is hypothetical.

سِكهَا موٽو سُپِرِين وَڃو تَان وَرِجَاھُ

Return quickly, o dear friend, if you mean to go, then return. Maj. 439.

II. THE SYNTHETICAL PART.

CONSTRUCTION OF THE SENTENCE AND CONJUNCTION OF SENTENCES.

SECTION III.

THE SIMPLE SENTENCE.

Chapter XI.

Subject and Predicate.

§. 61.

In every sentence there must be a subject and a predicate; subject is called that person or thing, of which something is said and predicate that which is said about it.

1) The subject may be expressed either by a substantive or adjective or pronoun or numeral. It is not expressed, if it be a personal pronoun and its predicate a verb, except a stress be laid upon it, as: ڏسان تهو I see, but آنُون تهو ڏِسَان I see (not you). The subject must always be in the Nominative.

2) The Predicate may be expressed either by a verb, or adjective (participle), or substantive, or numeral with the auxiliary verbs هُئڻُ to be and تهِئڻُ to become, to be.

The predicate may be joined to the subject in a threefold manner:

a) by way of asssertion, as: نِينگَرِ تهي رُئي the girl weeps.

b) by way of interrogation, as: كيرُ آيو who is come?

c) by way of command (or desire), as: وَڃُ go (thou).

3) The subject and predicate, if they be substantives or pronouns, may be nearer defined by an attribute. The attribute is commonly an adjective, but it may also be a substantive in the Genitive (with or without an adjective, pronoun etc.), on which another noun in the Genitive may depend again, as:

a great man came وَڏو مَاڻهُون آيو

or: this is a great man هِيُ وَڏو مَاڻهُون آهي

the Lord of the kingdom died مُلکَ جو ڌهَنِي مَرِي وِيُو

مُلکَ جِي ڌهَنِيَ جو پُٽرُ مَرِي وِيُو

the son of the Lord of the kingdom died.

مَغرِبَ مُلکَ جَا وِينْدَا سَبهِ مَرِي

All the people of the kingdom (of) Maghrib will go to die. Nānga jō Qissō, v. 51.

4) The subject and predicate, if they be proper names, substantives or pronouns, may also be nearer defined by a noun in apposition, as:

چِينَ وِلَايَت ڏُورِ آهي the country (of) China is far off;

هِيُ شَهَرُ کَرَاچِي آهي this is the city (of) Karāčī.

Chapter XII.

Concord of the subject and predicate.

§. 93.

1) If the predicate be a verb, it must agree with its subject in person, gender and number. This rule is strictly adhered to in Sindhī, even in such cases, where the subject in the Singular implies plurality, cf. §. 63, 1. 2. A subject in the Singular however may be constructed with the Plural of the predicate, when spoken of politely or honorifically, cf. §. 63, 3.

مَاءِ پِئُ جو چَوَنُ آنئُون نَ تهِي موٿَايَان

I do not reject the word of mother and father. Amul. Māṇ. p. 142.

اُبهَا پُڇهَنِ پَرَ تَ كِتهِي مُحَمَّدُ كَارَڻِي

Standing the strangers ask: where is Muhammad, the intercessor? Nānga ǰō Qissō, p. 15.

2) If the predicate be an adjective, participle, pronoun or substantive, from which a feminine may be derived (cf. §. 14), it must agree with its subject in gender, number and case. (In the same way every attribute must agree with its substantive in gender, number and case, whenever possible.)

تُنْهِن جِي كِيرْهِي مَرْضِي آهِي

What is thy pleasure? Amulu Māṇ. p. 140.

مَتهوُن هِكِڙِي ٻَانْهِي لَتهِي

From above descended a slave-girl. Ibid. p. 140.

سَبهِنِي صَحَابَنِ سِي ڏِٺهَا جَڏَا اُوءِ جُوَانَ

By all the companions they were seen, those maimed young men. Nānga ǰō Qissō, v. 17.

كَا بِلِي بَارَنِ سَانڈِهِي هُڻِي كَنهن رَنگ وَڏِي سِين رَس

Some cat was tending her young ones with some great love (and) pleasure. Story of the cat and mice v. 8.

Chapter XIII.

Enlargement of the sentence by a near and remote object.

§. 94.

1) The verb, which refers to the subject as its predicate, has a double form; it is either of the active voice, if the subject be active, or of the passive voice, if the subject be passive.

The active voice of a verb has a treble signification; it is either neuter (intransitive), or active (transitive), or causal. The verb is called neuter, if the action be restricted to the subject, as: هو تهو وَڃي he goes; active, if the verb necessarily requires a (near) object or Accusative, as: هُنَ كهي تهو جهَلي he seizes him; and causal, if it requires one or two Accusatives.

2) Neuter verbs commonly subordinate only a remote object or Dative, as: مُون كهي نَ تهو وَڻي it does not please me; but some neuter verbs may also subordinate a near object (Accus.), as:

رِيي هَلِئو سَا رَاهَ

He went that way. Ajāib v. 44.

3) Active verbs subordinate a near object (Accus.), and, as the case may be, a remote one (Dative), as: اُنَ كهي مَانِي ڏِي give him bread. Active verbs may

also subordinate a double Accusative, one implying the near object and the other its attribute. In this case the first object is generally defined by the postposition کهي by means of which the construction is rendered impersonal and the concord between the object and its attribute dissolved, so that the attribute remains in the uninflected form of the Singular, though the object, to which it refers, may be a Plural. But both may also remain in the uninflected state (Singular or Plural). Some verbs govern a double Accusative, one of a person, and one of a thing, as پُڇَڻُ to ask somebody a thing, though it may also be constructed with the postposition کهَان, to ask from a person, or with کهي.

کوڙهِيَنِ کهي سُتهو ڪِجو

Make the lepers clean. Matth. 10, 3.

جَانْسِين تهِي جِنَّان گَاندهُ نَہ کَنْدِيَسِ کو ٻئو

As long, as I live, I shall not make any other (my) husband. Sh. Um. Mar. VII, 6.

رکِهِجِ روزَا رَمَضَانَ جَا زَرِ زَکَاتُون ڏِيجِ

Keep the fasts of Ramaẕān, give (thy) wealth as alms. Golden Alphabet 4, 7.

4) Causals, derived from neuter verbs, subordinate a near, and as the case may be, a remote object (§. 69, 6); and causals, derived from active verbs, may subordinate two near objects (a double Accusative), the first generally being defined by the postposition کهي, and the second remaining in the uninflected state (§. 69, 5).

وَتِي وَاٽَاڙُنِ کهي تُون پِيَارِي پَرکهُ

Having made drink the travellers a bowl try (it). Sh. Jam. Kal. IV, 7.

5) Regular passive verbs can only be derived from active or causal verbs; for the passive form, which neuter verbs occasionally assume, does not essentially alter their signification.

In a passive sentence the near object (Accus.) is made the subject, and the subject of the active sentence is turned into the Instrumental[1]), the remote object (Dative) keeping its place, as usual. But with the passive Present, Imperfect and Future the Instrumental is not used, the agent being expressed by means of the postposition کَھان, if it cannot be possibly avoided.

Of the passive voice only the past tenses (past participle passive) are in common use, the other tenses being expressed, wherever possible, by a neuter verb.

The past participle (passive) agrees either with its subject in gender, number and case (§. 93, 2), or the construction may be rendered impersonal, the past participle containing at the same time subject and predicate, in which case the (proper) subject of the passive sentence must be subordinated as a remote object by means of the postposition کھي, 'as regards', 'in reference to'.

This impersonal construction must always take place in the passive, when an active verb governs a double Accusative, one implying the near object and the other its attribute. The near object must in this case be subordinated by the postposition کھي, whereas the other object, as the predicate, remains in the uninflected form of the Singular, referring to the (neuter) past participle.

---

1) In a longer sentence, when the agent is separated by a series of words from the verb, the agent is frequently repeated for the sake of perspicuity, by adding a pronominal suffix, corresponding to the agent, to the verb.

But when a causal verb governs two near objects, the first (implying a person) must be subordinated as remote object by the postposition کهي, whereas the second is made the subject, with which the past participle agrees in gender and number.

تِنئَ مَاڙهُوءَ جو پُٽرُ بِہ هِنَنِ کهَان ڏُکهوئِبو

Thus also the son of man shall be afflicted by them. Matth. 17, 12.

مَوْتُ قَبُولِئو اُنِ ڏِٺهو جَنِ ڏُکهِيَ کهي

Death was agreed to by those, who saw the afflicted one (lit. by whom it was seen as regards the afflicted one). Sh. Maɀδ. VII, 16.

کِهَڙي سَبَبَ سَقِيمُ کِئو اَوْهَان کهي آزَارَ

By what reason (and) disorder have you been made ill? (lit. by what reason and disorder has it been made ill as regards you.) Nānga jō Quissō, v. 24.

پَاتِشَاهَ اَچي صَيْفَلَ وَزِيرَ کهي اِهَا سَڀِي ڳالهِ ٻُنْدهَائِي

The king, having come, related this whole matter to the Vazīr Saifal. Amulu Māṇ. p. 142.

Chapter XIV.

Enlargement of the sentence by a nearer definition of the verb as predicate.

§. 95.

The simple sentence may be enlarged to a considerable extent by a nearer definition of the verb as predicate.

1) The verb may be nearer defined by one or more cases, on which again another case may depend, viz.: the Instrumental (agent etc.), the Accusative (of time etc.), the Ablative and the Locative, and by nouns with postpositions generally.

كَنْهِين ٿَانِي مَنجهِ کو مَاڙهُون دَرْيَاهَ جي ڪَپَ تي پَنْهَن
جي ڀهاڱَ سَانُ وِيٺهو هو

At some time one man sat on the bank of the river with his wealth (of buffaloes). Sindhī Reading Book p. 59.

اُهو پَنْهَن جي وَڏِي ڀهاءُ کهَان هِڪِڙِي وَرِهَ کهَان پوءِ
کُتهَابَ مِين وَنجَنَ لَڳو

That one began to go to school one year later than (from) his elder brother. Ibid. p. 50.

2) The verb may be nearer defined by adverbs generally, especially by adverbs of time, place and manner, and by postpositions with pronouns.

مُون کهِي هَاڻِي ڪا مَصْلَتَ ڏِي

Give me now some advise. Amulu Māṇ. p. 147.

اِينئَ اوڙِتَّانئُون پَانَ مِين چوکها مَهِينَا چَارِ

Thus they talked amongst each other four goodly months. Maj. 235.

سو ڀِ مُون وَٽِ آهِي

This also is with me. Amulu Māṇ. p. 147.

Chapter XV.

Omission of the verb as predicate.

§. 96.

1) The auxiliary verb آنهيَان etc., forming the predicate with or without an adjective etc., is occasionally omitted, especially in poëtry and in short proverbial sentences.

جَا تُنْهِن جي مَنَ مِين سَا مُون ڳَالِ سُنَاءِ

Let me hear that matter, which (is) in thy heart. Maǰ. 45.

اُونْهو کهُوهُ اُتهِين تَنْهِن جو لَبهِي نَه تَرُ

There (is) a deep well there; no bottom of that is found. Nānga ǰō Qissō, v. 38.

ڪِيڏِي بِلو ڳاتهي ڪِيڏِي بِلو ڳاتهي

Where (is) the cowardly cat? where (is) the cowardly cat? Sindhī Read. B. p. 62.

2) In sentences, which contain an imprecation or curse, the verb as predicate is generally omitted. In such like sentences the Potential of پَوَنُ, to fall, should be supplied, which occasionally is met with.

کهُهِ آتَنُ بَنِ جيڏِيُون ڏِيرَانِيُون ڏُکَارِ

May the courtyard (fall) into the well, the companions into the forest, the sisters-in-law into disease! Sh. Suh. IX, Epil. 1.

کهُهِ سي جِئَّنَ ڏِينْهَڙَا جي پِريَانَئِي ڌهَارَ

(May fall) into the well those days of life, which are apart from the friend! Sh. Dēsī VII, Epil.

SECTION IV.

THE COMPOUND SENTENCE.

Two or more sentences may be so joined together, that a compound sentence arises. This is done either by way of coordination or subordination.

Chapter XVI.

I. Coordination of sentences.

§. 97.

1) Two or more sentences may be so joined, that each one remains independant of the other. This is done without or by the copulative, adversative, disjunctive and conclusive particles (cf. §. 59) and by the negative adverb نَہ — نَہ neither — nor.

سَاجَنُ مِيڙِيسِ سُورَ سُکھَ نَہ مِيڙِيسِ سُپِرِين

The lover was joined to her by pain, the sweetheart was not joined to her by pleasure (= by dint of). Sh. Ābirī VII, 13.

گھوڙَا کھَنِي هيٺهِ بَنْڌهو ۽ اَهِين چَڙهِي هَلو

Fasten the horses below and go ye up. Amulu Māṇ. p. 149.

يَا لَنْگهَائِنِ لَطِيفُ چَئِي يَا دهُرَان کَنِ دَانْهَ

Either they bring them across, says Laṯīf, or they make a cry from that very spot. Sh. Suh. VIII, 2.

سُڌهِ اَتهَمِ پَرَ شَاهَ صَاحِبَ ڳَالهِ کَرِنَ کهَان جهَلِئو آهِي

I know it, but the Shāh Ṣāhib has forbidden (me) to tell it. Life of Abd-ul-Laṯīf, p. 44.

2) Sentences are also coordinated by joining together a disjunctive question. In the first member the interrogation is generally not expressed by a particle, but only by the voice of the speaker; in the second (or third) the interrogation is pointed out by the particle كِي kī or كِ ke.

سؤ تُونئِي آنهِين كِ بِئِي جِي وَاٽَ ڏِسُون

Is it thou or shall we look to the way of another? Matth. 11, 3.

Chapter XVII.

Contraction of coordinate sentences into one; concord of two and more subjects and predicates.

§. 98.

1) When two or more sentences have either the same subject or the same predicate or the same object or any other common member of speech, they are contracted into one sentence, with or without a conjunctive particle.

سَائِيِن سَلَامَت سُپِرِين موٽِي مُحِبَّ مِلَنِ

O Lord, may (our) dear friends (and) lovers meet (us) again! Nānga jō Qissō v. 81.

جِنُّ نَ بهُوتُ پَرِي آنهِيَان آنئُون اِنسَانُ

I am not a jinn, demon, fairy, I am a man. Maj. 639.

كيرهو تَ وَڏو بَلِ كِ ويڍِي

Which then is greater, the sacrifice or the altar? Matth. 23, 19.

پَرَ گوش اِهَا گُفْتَارَ پِيئِي حَسَنَ مِيرَ حُسِينَ جي

But this discourse fell into the ear of Mīr Hasan (and) Husain. Nānga jō Qissō v. 75.

2) When there are two or more subjects in a sentence, denoting animate beings, the verb or adjective (with the auxiliary verbs هُونَ and تهِئَنِ) as predicate is put in the Plural; if the subjects have the same gender, the predicate agrees with them, being put in the Plural, but if they be of various gender, the masculine has the precedence.

When two or more subjects imply things (or ideas), the predicate is either put in the Singular, agreeing commonly with the last subject, or in the Plural. If they be of various gender, the Plural of the masculine or feminine is employed, according as one or the other subject is considered more important.

The same rule holds good, when an attribute (adjective etc.) is referring to nouns of different gender.

نَرُ ۽ مَادِي سِرْجِئَا اَتهَسِ

A male and female was created by him. Sindhī Read. Book, p. 15.

مَاء ۽ بهَائُرہ بَاهَرِ بِيتهَا آنْهِنِ

Thy mother and thy brothers stand outside. Matth. 12, 47.

هِنَ ڏهَنڍهَ مِين پَانِي ۽ مَڇِهي تهِينْدِي

In this pond there will be water and fish. Life of Abd-ul-Latīf, p. 27.

پَرَ لَائِق لَشْكَرَ كهِي نَہ تهو وِيرَ تهِئِي وِيسَاهُ

But for an able army there is no delay (nor) pause. Nānga jō Quissō, v. 154.

هَنْدهَ حَوِيلِيُون حُجِرَا ڏورَان جَان ڏِٺهَامِ

When I saw from afar the places, houses, cells. Ajāib, v. 72.

وِڄُڙِنِ وِيس وَسَنَ جَا كِيتَا سَرَ سَاوَلِ تِهِئَا سَاوَا وِي

By the lightenings dresses of rain (i. e. clouds) have been made; reeds and herbs have become green; oh! Sh. Sār. IV, Epil.

اكهِڻُون مُنْهُ مِهَارَ ڏِي جَنِ رَكهِيُون جوڙِي

By whom eyes (and) face have been turned towards the buffalo-keeper. Sh. Suh. V, 9.

پوکهُون ڳُذِرْگَاهَ عَالَمَ جَا اُنَ آبَ تِي

The farms and ferries of the world (people) are upon that water. Nānga jō Qissō, v. 36.

3) When two or more subjects of different persons occur in a sentence, the first person precedes the second (or third), and the second the third, the verb being put in the Plural.

آسِين ۽ فَرِيسِي كهَڻَا روزَا تهَا رَكهُون

We and the Pharisees keep many fasts. Matth. 9, 14.

Chapter XVIII.

II. Subordination of sentences.

§. 99.

Two or more sentences may be so joined together, that one is not independent of the other, but is only making up for the deficiency of the other. A sentence thus depending on another, is called a subordinate sentence, and the other, that is completed thereby, is called the main sentence.

A subordinate sentence may have another sentence coordinated either with or without conjunctive particles; or it may again subordinate another sentence.

A subordinate sentence may be linked to the main sentence either by subjunctive particles, or by relative pronouns and adverbs or by interrogative pronouns and adverbs.

1) Subordination of a sentence by subjunctive particles.

§. 100.

Particles, by which a sentence is subordinated to the main sentence are the concessive, the consecutive, the causal, the final and the conditional, cf. §. 59.

a) With the three first particles the Indicative is used, if the assertion be positive, and the Potential, if the assertion be more vague or uncertain; with final particles the Potential is always used.

توڙِي ڪُسَنِ ڪَاتِ تَہ بہِ سَاڳِي سَلَنِ ڪِي نَہ ڪِي

Though they be killed by the knife, they do not at all divulge any thing. Sh. Kal. II, 8.

بَاتَاڙَ جو مَتهو اِيتِرو ڀهُونءِ تي هَنْيَانئِين تَہ سَنْڌُسِ مِنجُ مُنْجهِئو

It threw the head of dejection so much on the ground, that its brain was confused. Sindhī Reading Book p. 58.

اَللّٰهَ اوڇَا لَاهِئِين جَان سُڃَاڻُون سَچُ

O God, take away the covers, that we may know the truth. Maǰ. 205.

b) In conditional sentences the subordinate sentence generally precedes the main sentence, but the conditional part of the sentence may also follow that, which is conditioned thereby.

The subordinate sentence is introduced by the particles جي ,جيڪَر if, and جيڪَڏِهِن if (at any time), and the main sentence by the concessive particle تَ, تَان, then, which is generally not translated.

1) If the condition and that, which is conditioned thereby, be indefinite, possible, doubtful or uncertain, the Potential is used in both members of the sentence; in the main sentence the Imperative may also be employed.

وِيٺهي هِتِ مَ هوءِ جي هَلِين تَ هوتُ لَهِين

Be not seated here; if thou go, thou mayst obtain (thy) sweetheart. Sh. Ābirī VII, 6.

تَ تُون مَانِين مُورِ جي پَنْدِ اِهَائِي پَارِئِين

Then thou mayst enjoy it at all, if thou perform this very advise. Sh. Ābirī VII, 14.

آن جي ڏِٺها هُونِ تَ اَللّٰهَ کَارَنِ ڳَالهِ کَرِيو

If they may have been seen by you, then, for God's sake, speak! Sh. Hus. X, 22.

2) If the condition be uncertain, possible or only expected, but if that, which is conditioned thereby, be represented as certain and positive, the Potential is used in the subordinate, and the Indicative (commonly the Future) in the main sentence.

آيَلِ آيَلِ تهي جِيَان لَا جي سَارِينِمِ وو سُپِرِين

O mother, o mother, I live, o God, if my dear friends remember me! Sh. Suh. VII, Epil. 2.

جيكَڏهِن تُون هِتِ اَسَان کهي مَسْجِدِ جوڙي ڏِئين تہ اَسِين

تو کهي ڏِينهَاڙي كَعبَۃُ آللّٰهِ جي زِيَارَتَ كَارِينْدَاسِين

If thou construct us here a mosque, then we shall let thee daily make the pilgrimage of the Kaꞌaba of God. Life of Abd-ul-Laṯīf, p. 4.

3) If the condition and that, which is conditioned thereby, be taken as certain and positive, the Indicative is used in both members of the sentence.

جي تُون اَسَان کهي كَڍهِين تهو تہ سُئَرنِ جي وَلَرَ مِين

وَنجَنَ جِي مؤكَل ڏِي

If thou castest us out, allow us to go into the herd of swine. Matth. 8, 31.

جي تُون ڳَالهِ كَنْدِين تہ كوڙهِيو تهِينْدِين

If thou shalt divulge it, thou wilt become a leper. Life of Abd-ul-Latīf, p. 44.

4) If the condition as well as that, which is conditioned thereby, is represented as such, that could have happened under certain circumstances, but which has not happened, because the condition was not fulfilled, the Imperfect, Aorist or Pluperfect is used in the subordinate, and the Aorist in the main sentence, or, under certain circumstances, the Pluperfect (cf. §. 87, 2).

جي دَارُون پِئَنْدو نہ هو تہ نہ مَرِي وِڃو

If he had not kept on drinking liquor, he would not have died.

لِكهِيُم تو ڏِي خَطُّ پَرَ جي هوسِ پكهِڙو

آيْسِ مَنْهَنْدِ كِتَابَ جي هُونْدَ اُڏَامِي سُتَتُ

تَہ رَارَان رُٺِي رَتُ جي هُجِي قَلَمُ وَاقِفُ قَلْبَ جو

I have written a letter to thee; but if I were a bird
I would likely have come before the letter, having flown quickly.
If the pen would be aware of the heart, it would weep blood out of affection. Sh. Barvō Sindhī, Čhōṭ. 6.

سِي جي هوتَ سُڻا تَہ هُونْدَ نَہ وِيو نِكِرِي

If those (cries) had been heard by (my) sweetheart, he would likely not have gone off. Sh. Hus. III, 2.

چيكَرَ گهَرَوَارِي ڄَاتو هو چورُ فُلَاڻي پَهَرِ اِينْدو تَہ هُونْدَ

چيتِيندو رَهِيو

If the master of the house had known, (that) the thief will come at a certain watch (of the night), he would likely have remained on his guard. Matth. 24, 43.

جي سِي سَدومَ مين تهِيا هَا تَہ هُونْدَ اَڄُ توڻي هَلِيو آيو هو

If those (works) had been done at Sodom, it would have likely remained until this day. Matth. 11, 23.

Instead of the Aorist or Pluperfect the Potential (of the Present) may be used (but very rarely) in both members of a conditional sentence, followed by the particle هَا; but more commonly هَا is added to a past tense, for the sake of emphasis.

جي هُوءَ نَہ هَلِي هَا تَہ سَڄَڻَ كهِي نَہ لَهِي هَا

If she had not gone, she would not have obtained (her) friend.

جي كَڏهِين هِىَ ڳالهِ اَهَان جي سَمُجهَ ۾ آئِي هُجي
هَا تَہ هُونْدَ بي ڏوهَنِ تي ڏوهُ نَہ لَايو هَا

If you had ever understood this word, you would not have condemned the guiltless. Matth. 12, 7.

5) If the condition must have been fulfilled in past future time (Futurum exactum), before that, which is conditioned thereby, shall happen, the Aorist is used in the subordinate, and the Future in the main sentence.

جيكَڏِهِن مَخْدُومُ صَاحِبُ شَاهَ صَاحِبَ كهَان اَڳي وِصَالُ
كِئو تَہ شَاهُ صَاحِبُ اَچي مُخْدُوم صَاحِبَ جي جَنَازي سَان
حَاضِرُ تهِيندو

If ever Maχdūm S̱āhib should have died before Shāh S̱āhib, then Shāh S̱āhib will come and be present with the bier of Maχdūm S̱āhib. Life of Abd-ul-Latīf, p. 37.

جي كَنْهِن اَچي سُنڄَاتُسِ تَہ اُنَ كهي آنُون ڏِينْدُسِ

If one shall have come and recognised her, I will give her to him. Sindhī Read. B. p. 59.

6) The conditional particle جي is often omitted in the subordinate sentence, and جيكَرَ on the other hand is used without a main sentence, it being passed over in silence, so that جيكَرَ assumes quite the sense of the interjectional particle مَانَ would that!

پرِيَمِ تُنْهِن جي گهَاءِ مَرَان تَہ مَانُ لَهَان

O my friend, (if) I die of thy wound, I (may) obtain honour. Sh. Jam. Kal. I, 6.

جيكَرَ گوٺهِ هَلُون

If we would go to (our) village, (it would be well) = We should like to go to (our) village. Amulu Mān. p. 151.

2) Subordination of a sentence by the relative pronoun (also the indefinite pronouns جيڪو, جوڪو) and relative adverbs, corresponding generally to a correlative. (§. 74 sqq.)

§. 101.

The subordinate sentence may either precede or follow the main sentence.

وَرُ لوئِيَ جِي لُون ڏاڏانَنِ ڏِنَم جَا

Come back, o louse of the blanket, which was given to me by the grandfather's family. Sh. Um. Mar. VII, 3.

جيڪو جُنَّا تهو کهيڏِي اُنَ جِي گهرَ مَنجهِ هُونْدِ نَہ تهِي ٽِڪِي

Whoever is given to gambling, in his house property does not remain. Sindhī Read. Book, p. 52.

جِنءَ جِنءَ تَپِي ڏِينهُ تِنءَ تِنءَ تَانِيَان پَنْڌهَ مين

As the day gets hot, so I push on in the journey. Sh. Hus. II, 14.

جِتِ نَہ پَکهِيَ پيرُ تِتِ ٽِمْڪِي بَاهِڙِي

Where there is not a footprint of a bird, there glimmers a small fire. Sh. Khāh. II, 11.

جَان کِي کَنْدهِیَ کَانْھَ تَان تَانِي بَنْدهِجِ تُرهو

When there are some reeds of the shore, pull them out and bind together a raft. Sh. Hus. VIII, 3.

3) Subordination of a sentence by an interrogative pronoun or particle.

§. 102.

The dependant sentence is generally introduced by the particles تَہ, جو, and کِہ, that, which are not translated.

ھَمِيرَنِ جو حِسَابُ کِوھُ جَانَان کِينئَ تھِئو

How do I know, how the calculation of the Amīr has been made? Sh. Um. Mār. II.

مُون شَادِیَ جو جَوَابُ ڏِي تَہ کِينئَ کَرِي اٿِين

Give me an answer about the marriage, how thou hast arranged it? Amulu Māṇ. p. 142.

پَنْھَن جِي جِيئَ جو فِکِرُ نَہ کَرِيو جو چھَا کھَائِينْدَاسِين
چھَا پِئَنْدَاسِين نَہ پَنْھَن جِي سَرِيرَ جو کِہ چھَا پَھَرِينْدَاسِين

Take no thought of your life, (saying) what shall we eat, what shall we drink? nor of your body, what we shall put on? Matth. 6, 24.

Chapter XIX.

Abbreviation of subordinate sentences.

§. 103.

A subordinate sentence may be abbreviated:

1) by using the present and past participle (cf. §. 80, 81), either adjectively, or in the Locative Singular, which is more common. The participle supplies the place of a relative or conjunctional subordinate sentence, into which it may be dissolved, when necessary, as:

رُوَنْدِي رَاتِ وِهَاء چِکَائِينْدِي پِيَتِيُون

Pass the night weeping, distilling glasses of liquor; i. e. whilst weeping, or as one who weeps etc. Sh. Jam. Kal. IV, 25.

وَتِهِتِي ڏَاڍهِي ڏُکهَ کَنْهِن کَنْدهِيَ پَاسِ کِرِي پِيئِي

Having been seized = after or when or as she was seized by a violent pain, she fell down near some bank. Story of the cat and mice, v. 29.

2) By using the past conjunctive participles.

هوُتُ پُنْهُون تهَا نِين بَارُوچِي ٻوُلِي کِٿوُ

They carry off (my) sweetheart Punhū̃, speaking Baluchī, i. e. whilst they speak Baluchī. Sh. Dēsī II, 13.

Chapter XX.

On the indirect oration.

§. 104.

When the words or thoughts of a person are given with the very same expressions, as used originally, the oration is called a direct one; but when they are only represented according to their general contents or purport, the oration is called an indirect one. In Sindhī the indirect oration is never made use of, but the words or thoughts of a person are always represented in the direct oration and generally introduced by the particle تَہ.

بهَانْيَانئِين تهِي تَہ كَنْهِن پَرِ كُسَاٿِي نِكِرِي وَڃَان

He was thinking: 'in some way having sneaked off I will get away'; i. e. that he would sneak off etc. Life of Abd-ul-Laṯīf, p. 20.

جَان ڏِسِي تَہ بهِٽَ وَٽِ بِيٺهو آنهِيَان

When he sees: I am sitting near Bhiṭa. Ibid. p. 21.

جي بهَائِين تَہ پرِينِ مِڙَان تَہ سِكهُ چوَرَانِكِي لَاتِ

If thou likest: I will meet (my) friend = to meet (thy) friend, then learn the mimicking sound of the thieves. Sh. Jam. Kal. II, 8.

APPENDIX I.

ON THE SINDHI CALENDAR.

The Muhammadans of Sindh reckon by lunar months after the common Muhammadan aera, called هِجْرَت, the flight of Muhammad from Mekka to Medīnah, the years of this aera are therefore called هِجْرِي[1]. It dates, according to the best accounts from the 18th of July 622 p. Chr. Their months commence with the appearance of each new moon and consist of 30 and 29 days alternately, amounting to 354 days and about nine hours; in consequence thereof New-year's-day falls every year about eleven days earlier than in the previous year.

To keep pace with the seasons the Sindhīs interpose every third year an intercalary month (لُنڍُ lunḍu), repeating that month, in which the sun enters no new sign of the Zodiac.

In naming the lunar months the learned Muhammadans follow the nomenclature of the Arabs; but among the common people the names of those Arabian months only are known, which are noted by some special religious observance, the other months being called by the names of the Hindū months then being.

---

1) Another aera, which is also in use amongst the Muhammadans of Upper India, is called فَصْلِي, or revenue aera; it dates, according to Prinsep, from the year 592¾ p. Chr.

Lunar months of the Arabians.

1)	مُحَرَّمٌ	muharramu	30 days.
	مَحَرَمٌ	maharamu	
2)	صَفَرٌ	ṣafaru	29 days.
3)	رَبِيعٌ ٱلأَوَّلُ	rabīȝulavvalu . .	30 days.
4)	رَبِيعٌ ٱلثَّانِي	rabīȝu-ϑϑānī . .	29 days.
	رَبِيعٌ ٱلآخِرُ	rabīȝu-lāχiru . .	
5)	جُمَادَى ٱلأَوَّلُ	ǰumāda-lavvula	30 days.
6)	جُمَادَى ٱلثَّانِي	ǰumāda-ϑϑānī	29 days.
	جُمَادَى ٱلآخِرُ	ǰumāda-lāχiru	
7)	رَجَبٌ	raǰabu	30 days.
8)	شَعْبَانُ	šaȝabānu.	29 days.
9)	رَمَضَانُ	ramaẕānu	30 days.
10)	شَوَّالُ	šavvālu.	29 days.
11)	ذِي ٱلقَعْدَه	δī-lqaȝadah. . .	30 days.
	ذِي قَعْدَه	δī qaȝadah . . .	
12)	ذِي ٱلْحِجَّه	δī-lħijjah	29 days.
	ذِي حِجَّه	δī ħijjah.	

The Hindūs reckon by solar years, and luni-solar months. They follow either the Vikramāditya (وِكْرَمَاجِيت) aera, called sambatu (Sansk. संवत् year), dating from the year 57 a. Chr., and commencing with the month of katī, or that of Shālivāhana, called šāku (Sansk. शाक), dating from the year 78 p. Chr., and commencing with the month of Čēṭru.

The Hindū year is divided into 12 equal portions, which nearly correspond to our solar months. Each month is divided again (by Hindūs as well as Muhammadans) into two parts (پَکھُ or پَچھُ lunar fortnight), the first from new to full moon (سُدِي sudī), and the second from full to new moon (بَدِي badī). The dates of these two divisions (تِتھِ lunar date), fifteen each, are reckoned separately.

Solar months of the Hindūs.

چيٽرُ čēṭru, from the middle of March to the middle of April.

ويسَاکھُ vēsākhu, from the middle of April to the middle of May.

جيٺھُ jēṭhu, from the middle of May to the middle of June.

آکهاڙُ ākhāṛu, from the middle of June to the middle of July.

سَاوَڻُ sāvaṇu, } from the middle of July to the middle of August.
سرَاڻُ srāṇu, }

بَڏرو badṛō, from the middle of August to the middle of September.

اَسُو asū, from the middle of September to the middle of October.

كَتِي katī, from the middle of October to the middle of November.

نَاهَرِي nāharī, نَهَرِي naharī, مَنگهِر manghiru,	from the middle of November to the middle of December.

پوهُ pōhu, from the middle of December to the middle of January.

مَاگهُ māghu, from the middle of January to the middle of February.

پهَاگُ phāgu, پهَگُنُ phaguṇu,	from the middle of February to the middle of March.

The Hindūs commence the day at midnight, as we do, but the Muhammadans at the previous evening. In the mouth of a Muhammadan therefore the night of a certain day always signifies the night of the previous day, as: جُمِي جِي رَاتِ Friday night = Thursday night, according to our way of reckoning. There is some difference between the Hindū and Musalmān names of the days of the week, as subjoined.

Days of the week.

Hindū.	Musalmān.	
آرتَرُ ārtaru[1]) . . .	آچَرُ āčaru,	Sunday.
سُومَرُ sūmaru . . .	سُومَرُ sūmaru, سُومَارُ sūmāru,	Monday.

1) Or: آڏِتوَارُ āḍitavāru, آئِتوَارُ āitavāru, آرتوَارُ ārtavāru.

Hindū.	Musalmān.
مَنگَل mangalu . . .	اَنگَارو aṅārō, Tuesday.
بُدهَر budharu . . .	اَرْبَا arbā, Wednesday.
وِسْپَتِ vispate	خَمِيس χamīsa, Thursday.
تهَارُون thārū̃ 1) . . .	جُمو ǰumō, Friday.
شُكر šukru	(ǰumō, Friday)
چهَنچهَر čhančharu . .	چهَنچهَر čhančharu, Saturday.

1) Or: تهَانْوَرُ thā̃varu.

APPENDIX II.

SURVEY OF THE DIFFERENT SINDHI-ARABIC ALPHABETS.

The Alphabet used in this Grammar (Hindūstānī).	The Government Alphabet.	The old Sindhī Alphabet.	Roman Characters.
ا	ا	ا	a
ب	ب	ب	b
ٻ	ٻ	ٻ	b̄
بھ	ڀ	ڀ	bh
ت	ت	ت	t
تھ	ٿ	ٿ	th
ٹ	ٽ	ٺ	ṭ
ٹھ	ٺ	ٿ	ṭh
ث	ث	ث	ꞩ
پ	پ	پ	p
پھ	ڦ	ڦ	ph
ج	ج	ج	ǰ
ڄ	ڄ	ڄ	ǰ̄
جھ	جھ	ڃ	ǰh
نج	ڃ	نج	ń (ny)
چ	چ	چ	č
چھ	ڇ	ڇ	čh
ح	ح	ح	ḣ
خ	خ	خ	χ
د	د	د	d
دھ	ڌ	ڌ	dh
ڎ	ڊ	ڊ	ḍ
ڏ	ڍ	ڋ	ḍ̄

The Alphabet used in this Grammar (Hindūstānī).	The Government Alphabet.	The old Sindhī Alphabet.	Roman Characters.
ڈھ	ي	ي	ḍh
ذ	ذ	ذ	δ
ر	ر	ر	r
ڑ	ڙ	ر	ṛ
ز	ز	ز	z
س	س	س	s
ش	ش	ش	š
ص	ص	ص	ṣ
ض	ض	ض	ẕ
ط	ط	ط	ṯ
ظ	ظ	ظ	δ̱
ع	ع	ع	ʿ
غ	غ	غ	γ
ف	ف	ف	f
ق	ق	ق	q
ڪ، ک	ڪ	ک، ڪ	k
کھ	ک	ک	kh
گ	گ	ک	g
ڳ	ڳ	ک	ḡ
گھ	گھ	ک	gh
نگ	ڱ	نک	(ng) ṅ
ل	ل	ل	l
م	م	م	m
ن	ن	ن	n
ن	ڻ	ن	ṇ
و	و	و	v
ھ	ھ	ھ	h
ي	ي	ي	y

MISPRINTS AND EMENDATIONS.

Introduction.

p. I, l. 23 wheras, read: whereas. p. I, note, l. 2 troughout: throughout. p. V, l. 3 ṛ: r̥. p. VII, l. 18 लवङ्क: लवङ्ग. p. XIV, l. 20 मयुर: मयूर. p. XV, l. 18 सक्कणोमि: सक्कणोमि. p. XV, l. 19 सक्नोमि: शक्नोमि. p. XV, l. 29 स्वांड्गु: खांड्गु. p. XV, l. 30 gā̃ū̃: gā̃ū̃. p. XVI, l. 1 मेध: मेघ. p. XVIII, l. 20 ञ: न. p. XIX, l. 7 rī: ṛī. p. XIX, l. 23 मीञ्जारो: सीञ्जारो. p. XX, l. 18 seams: seems. p. XXIV, l. 6 ज़ड्ड: जड़. p. XXX, l. 23 सहर्स: सहर्ष. p. XXXI, l. 29 क्क: क्क. p. XXXVI, l. 9 ञरिज्: ञारिज्. p. XXXVII, l. 13 मुर्द्धन्: मूर्द्धन्. p. XL, l. 5 सिसो: सिसी. p. XLI, l. 3 म्वश्रु: म्वश्रू. p. XLII, l. 12 निञ्छुञो: विञ्छुञो. p. XLVII, l. 27 सन्ध्य: सन्ध्या.

---

p. 3, l. 21 ٹ: ٿ. p. 3, l. 22 ٹ: ٽ. p. 10, l. 15 سَعْقَص: سَعْفَص. p. 11, l. 21 aṇu: aṅu. p. 12, l. 22 سِيكارِي: سِينگارِي. p. 23, l. 19 زَنَر: زَبَر. p. 23, l. 25 the these: these. p. 29, l. 29 goal: goat. p. 30, l. 1 add before pōe: پوء. p. 33, l. 27 vijū: viju. p. 36, l. 5 čārhō: čāṛhō. p. 36, l. 15 tōbō: ṭōbō. p. 36, l. 21 مَارِيندو: مَارِيندؤ. p. 37, l. 27 add before ū: in. p. 37,

l. 33 bhuē: bhūe. p. 39, l. 11 सज्ञा: सञ्ज्ञा. p. 46, l. 20 ٻهۆلُ: ٻهۆلَ. p. 51, l. 16 ڪهۆرو: ڪهۆرو. p. 51, l. 27 وَڍهُنُ: وَڍهَنُ. p. 52, l. 15 پِنّاڪُ: پِنّاڪُ. p. 59, l. 26 Gujurātī: Gujarātī. p. 60, l. 27 ō: ē. p. 62, l. 4 Gujarāthī: Gujarātī. p. 66, l. 25 چۆتِي: چۆتِّي. p. 66, l. 28 اوتهارُ: اوتهَارُ. p. 66, l. 28 اُتهُ: اُتهُ. p. 67, l. 14 کهانڊهِيرو khāndhīro: کهانڊِيرو khāndīrō. p. 67, l. 14 کهانڊهِ khāndhe: کهانڊِ khānde. p. 68, l. 9 ālū: ātu. p. 68, l. 24 patṛu: puṭru. p. 69, l. 9 وَاتَائِتو: وَاتَائِٿو. p. 69, l. 20 kāčhirō: kāčhīrō. p. 69, l. 29 ڏِتهَلُ and ڏِتهو: ڏِتهَلُ, ڏِتهو. p. 72, l. 3 hāṅōkō: hāṇōkō. p. 72, l. 3 hānē: hāṇē. p. 72, l. 12 āṅikō: āṇikō. p. 72, l. 24 čōrānikō: čōrāṇikō. p. 78, l. 11 menaged: managed. p. 82, l. 7 پَانيو: پَانيو. p. 82, l. 26 Shortened from the Sansk. सह read: Sansk. स, shortened from सह. p. 88, l. 14 Bahūvrīhi: Bahuvrīhi. p. 88, l. 25 recognizable: recognisable. p. 90, l. 21 After तकु add: fem. p. 92, l. 4 सुजन्ध्: सुगन्ध्. p. 92, l. 25 after: Sansk. मज्जा add: masc. (also in Sindhī). p. 94, l. 25 تَرَنُ: ٽَرَنُ. p. 99, l. 24 ni: ṇi. p. 106, l. 24 توبو tōbō: ٽوبو ṭōbō. p. 106, l. 25 توبَا tōbā: ٽوبَا ṭōbā. p. 113, l. 6 Whe: We. p. 120, l. 8 put a Comma after palatal. p. 128, l. 22 jōyu: jōyū. p. 140, l. 18 سَائْنِ: سَائِينِ. p. 144, l. 20 ڪهِرِنّان: ڪيهَرِنّان. p. 144, l. 21 ڪهَرِٿو: ڪيهَرِٿو. p. 157, l. 15 hikirō: hikiṛō. p. 157, l. 16 hēkirō: hēkiṛō. p. 159, l. 4 ḍaha: ḍaha. p. 164, l. 14 جۆرَانوِي: چۆرَانوِي. p. 169, l. 23 saha: sata. p. 170, l. 7 čōḍaha: čōḍahā. p. 170, l. 8 pandraha: pandrahā. p. 171, l. 20

اَتهَني: اَتهَنِي. p. 173, l. 3 جِنّرِي: جِنّرِي. p. 173, l. 16 sweathearts: sweethearts. p. 190, l. 20 mũk hã: mũ khã. p. 201, note: Risāls: Risālō. p. 208, l. 15 whit: with. p. 215, l. 5 جيڪيڪي: جيڪيڪِي. p. 216, l. 28 theyself: thyself. p. 230, l. 5 پِڙَرِن: پِڙَرِنِ. p. 234, l. 8 Rīṇō: Rāṇō. p. 236, l. 4 ē: ī. p. 237, l. 20 وَهه: وَهَه. p. 239, l. 7 پَاگَڙِيَاسِ: پَاگَڙِيَاسِ. p. 241, l. 4 ǰōnhē: ǰōṇhē. p. 245, l. 4 جوٿِيُون: چوٿِيُون. p. 248, l. 13 ڪنَاسِ: ڪينَاسِ. p. 255, l. 19 parhāiṇu: paṛhāiṇu. p. 258, l. 16 āā: āu. p. 261, l. 8 ču-anu: ču-aṇu. p. 264, l. 16 ·khāhaṇn: khanhaṇu. p. 267, l. 29 parh-iju: paṛh-iju. p. 274, l. 21 susaṇu: tusaṇu. p. 277, l. 20 kuhanu: kuhaṇu. p. 283, l. 32 una: ūṇa. p. 286, l. 20 b̄udhāyō: b̄uḍhā-y-ō. p. 287, l. 1 the II and I: the I and II. p. 287, l. 14 āni: ani. p. 289, l. 28 ia: iā. p. 294, l. 8 رُوندڙ: رُوندڙ. p. 299, l. 16 هُنُن: هُنّنِ. p. 301, l. 21 هُوندَا: هُوندَا. p. 310, l. 19 هُيُسِ: هُيَسِ. p. 311, l. 7 تهيندِئُسِ: تهيندِئَسِ. p. 311, l. 8 تهيندِئُن: تهيندِئَن. p. 320, l. 20 هُرنديِن: هُونديِن. p. 323, l. 9 čhaḍ-inḍō: čhaḍ-īndō. p. 325, l. 2 The object being fem.: being masc. The object being masc.: fem. p. 336, l. 6 ههَڏِي: چهَڏِي. p. 341, l. 12 ڳهيندڙ: ڪهيندڙ. p. 342, l. 18 مِين: مِين. p. 348, l. 10 corpe: corpse. p. 361, l. 7 ڏِٺُوشِ: ڏِٺُوسِ. p. 368, l. 18 čhaḍiũ-se: čhaḍiũ-se. p. 372, l. 5 čhaḍiã-su: čhaḍiã-sũ. p. 384, l. 2 ōčitōly: ōčitō. p. 384, l. 2 for the second unexpected read: unexpectedly. p. 384, l. 5 ōḍirō: ōḍiṛō. p. 384, note 2, l. 2 मंहित: संहित. p. 389, l. 12 Loc.: Abl. p. 395, l. 20 ڪهُرين: ڪهُرِين.

p. 395, note, l. 1 ĕ o: ĕ of. p. 396, l. 19 Čhāṭ: Čhōṭ. p. 402, l. 2 mē: mẽ. p. 405, l. 2 جغاٹون : جَغَاٹُون. p. 411 The last two quotations are misplaced there and to be inserted on p. 417, after l. 16. p. 414, l. 15 جيلهن : جِيلهَان. p. 416, l. 6 the 'Miã': thee 'Miã'. p. 418, l. 8 form: from. p. 420, l. 8 کذهي : كَذِهِي. p. 423, l. 6 also!: alas! p. 432, l. 13 after God, add: or not?